From Alpha to Omega

From Alpha to Omega

A Beginning Course in Classical Greek

Third Edition

Anne H. Groton

St. Olaf College

Focus Publishing / R. Pullins Co.
Newburyport MA 01950

TABLE OF CONTENTS

iii

READINGS

PREFACE

When I set out to write *From Alpha to Omega* during my sabbatical in 1990-91, I was motivated by the desire to produce an elementary Greek textbook that would fit the St. Olaf College calendar, the St. Olaf College student, and the vigorously traditional St. Olaf College Classics curriculum. This meant that the book had to be divided into no more than fifty chapters, half of them to be completed each semester; that every grammatical concept had to be explained clearly and carefully, in language neither too simple nor too sophisticated; and that the readings for each lesson had to be selected with a view toward preparing students to read Plato in their third semester of Greek. Because we have only three class meetings per week, I limited the number of exercises in each chapter to ten Greek-to-English translation sentences, five English-to-Greek translation sentences, and (beginning in Lesson 5) one short reading. I also restricted to ten or so the number of vocabulary words to be memorized per lesson.

In a society no longer inclined to value a Classical education, those motivated enough to study ancient Greek need all the encouragement they can get. For this reason I strove to make the textbook as pleasant and accessible as possible without sacrificing its rigor. The sentences to be translated in each chapter are designed to help students learn the vocabulary words and constructions introduced in that lesson, while reviewing familiar ones. The readings give students experience in translating whole paragraphs of more or less "real" Greek, in which new vocabulary and syntax are mixed with old. I drew the readings for Lessons 5-25 from Aesop's most amusing and curious fables. For Lessons 26-50 I chose what I thought were interesting as well as instructive passages, usually spread over two or more lessons, from the New Testament, Demosthenes, Xenophon, Thucydides, Lysias, Arrian, Aristotle, and Plato. Although I was wary of overwhelming the students with too many glosses and explanatory notes, I did try in each reading to retain as much as I could of the original Greek.

At the back of the textbook are chapter-by-chapter word lists, followed by Greek-to-English and English-to-Greek glossaries containing all vocabulary words and all other words found in the readings, along with the number(s) of the lesson(s) in which they appear. The book concludes with an appendix of paradigms (including the dual forms not explicitly taught in the textbook) and an index. It has been a happy surprise to me to discover that the book's format suits other academic schedules as well as St. Olaf's. For example, all fifty lessons have been covered successfully in one and a half semesters by a class that meets four times per week, in two ten-week trimesters by a class that meets five times per week, and in a nine-week summer intensive course. When pressed for time, some teachers have preferred to assign only the sentences, not the reading, in each lesson; others have continued to assign all the readings but only half or so of the sentences. Students are free to use the skipped exercises for additional practice or for review before a quiz or examination.

From Alpha to Omega would never have seen the light of day without the wise counsel and support of my St. Olaf colleagues, particularly Professor James May, and without the talents of the obliging staff at Focus Publishing. I am also grateful to my colleagues at other schools who were daring enough to test a brand-new textbook and with their eagle eyes spotted scores of typos and other errors that I had missed. Let me single out for special thanks Professors John Gibert (University of Colorado), Clara Shaw Hardy (Carleton College), John Lenz (Drew University), Leslie Mechem (Skidmore College), and Richard Wevers (Calvin College). Finally, I wish to thank all the dedicated students who struggled cheerfully and patiently through one of the earlier versions of the book and succeeded in learning Greek even from its flawed pages. I hope that they will be pleased with this final version of a textbook created not only for them but, to a large extent, by them.

ἐκ παίδων σμῑκρῶν ἀρξάμενοι, μέχρι οὗπερ ἂν ζῶσι,
καὶ διδάσκουσι καὶ νουθετοῦσιν.

From early childhood, their whole lives through,
people teach and admonish them.　　　— Plato's *Protagoras* 325c

Preface to the Third Edition.

For the corrections and improvements in this third edition, I am indebted to a whole host of enthusiastic students and colleagues. My sincere thanks to all of you.

LESSON 1

INTRODUCTION
The Greek Alphabet

ἀρχὴ δέ τοι ἥμισυ παντός (Well begun is half done.)
—one of Pythagoras' sayings, quoted by Iamblichus in *Pythagoras* 162

1. Greek belongs to a large and colorful family of "Indo-European" languages, all thought to be descended from a very old (and now lost) language spoken by people who roamed over the Eurasian continent during prehistoric times. Other prominent members of the family are the Italic (including Latin and the Romance languages), Germanic (including English), Celtic, Baltic, Slavic (including Russian), Armenian, Iranian, and Indic languages.

2. The Greek language has been in continuous use for more than three thousand years; its vocabulary, grammar, and pronunciation have been evolving gradually over the centuries. There is a great deal of difference between, say, Greek of the seventh century B.C. and Greek of the first century A.D., even though they are both "ancient" from our point of view. Moreover, each geographical region of Greece had its own **dialect.** Some authors wrote in their native dialect; others, working within an established literary genre, wrote in the dialect(s) that tradition demanded.

The ancient Greek taught in this book is **Classical** in date and **Attic** in dialect. It is the sort of Greek that would have been used by educated people during **Greece's Classical age** (roughly the **fifth and fourth centuries B.C.**). These were glory days for Athens—artistically and intellectually as well as militarily. Much of the literature surviving from the Classical period is written in **Attic, the dialect of the Athenians** (Attica is the name of the district that includes Athens). The philosopher Plato, the orators Lysias and Demosthenes, the historians Thucydides and

Xenophon, the comic playwright Aristophanes—to name just a few of Athens' most famous authors—all wrote in Attic.

Once you are familiar with Attic, you will find it relatively easy to learn Greek's other literary dialects: **Epic** (e.g., Homer's *Iliad* and *Odyssey*), **Ionic** (e.g., Herodotus' *Histories*), **Doric** (e.g., the choral songs in Attic tragedies), **Aeolic** (e.g., Sappho's poetry). Knowledge of Classical Greek also equips you to read Greek of the **Hellenistic age**, the period following the Classical age. The local dialects gradually died out and were replaced by **Koine** (the name means "common"), a dialect derived in large part from Attic and used from the third century B.C. to the sixth century A.D. throughout the Greek-speaking world. The New Testament is written in a literary form of Koine.

3.

In 403 B.C., after years of using their own **alphabet**, the Athenians officially adopted the more precise alphabet used by speakers of the Ionic dialect (a close relative of the Attic dialect). This Ionic alphabet became standard for Greek; in later centuries the Coptic, Gothic, Armenian, and Cyrillic alphabets were derived from it. (Our Roman alphabet goes back to the Greek inhabitants of Chalcis in Euboea, who spoke an Attic-Ionic dialect; when they colonized parts of Italy, they passed on their alphabet to the Etruscans, from whom the Romans acquired it.)

Of the Greek alphabet's **twenty-four letters**, the first nineteen were adapted from letters in the Phoenician alphabet and thus have Semitic names; the last five were invented by the Greeks. Only the large, capital forms of the letters existed in antiquity. It was not until the ninth century A.D. that scribes devised cursive forms that could be written quickly; these evolved into the small letters now in use.

The pronunciations suggested below are those thought by scholars to have been used **during the Classical age**. Pronunciations enclosed in square brackets are less authentic but more commonly used today.

THE ALPHABET OF CLASSICAL GREEK

Greek Letter	Equiva-lent to	Name of Letter		Pronounced like the italicized letter(s) in the English word:
Α α	a	ἄλφα	alpha	*ah*
Β β	b	βῆτα	beta	*better*
Γ γ	g	γάμμα	gamma	*g*amble; before γ, κ, μ, ξ, χ = nasal-ized *n* [or before μ = *g*amble]
Δ δ	d	δέλτα	delta	*d*elete
Ε ε	e	ἒ ψῑλόν	epsilon[1]	*e*tch
Ζ ζ	z	ζῆτα	zeta	wis*d*om [or ga*dz*ooks]
Η η	ē	ἦτα	eta	*e*rror [or *a*ce]
Θ θ	th	θῆτα	theta	swee*th*eart [or au*th*or]
Ι ι	i	ἰῶτα	iota	p*i*zza [or ι = p*i*t; ῑ = p*i*zza]
Κ κ	k, c	κάππα	kappa	*c*andy
Λ λ	l	λάμβδα	lambda	*l*antern
Μ μ	m	μῦ	mu	*m*usic
Ν ν	n	νῦ	nu	*n*uclear
Ξ ξ	x	ξῖ	xi	ta*x*i
Ο ο	o	ὂ μῑκρόν	omicron	*o*ff
Π π	p	πῖ	pi	*p*illow
Ρ ρ	r	ῥῶ	rho	*r*ocky—rolled or trilled -*r*
Σ σ, ς	s	σίγμα	sigma[2]	*s*ignal; before β, γ, δ, μ = z
Τ τ	t	ταῦ	tau	*t*ardy
Υ υ	y, u	ὖ ψῑλόν	upsilon	French *u* [or υ = f*oo*t; ῡ = b*oo*t]
Φ φ	ph	φῖ	phi	u*ph*ill [or tele*ph*one]
Χ χ	kh, ch	χῖ	chi	bac*kh*and [or *c*andy or German -*ch*]
Ψ ψ	ps	ψῖ	psi	ti*ps*y
Ω ω	ō	ὦ μέγα	omega	*aw* [or *oh*]

4.   Of Greek's seven **vowels** (α, ε, η, ι, ο, υ, ω), ε and ο are **always short**; η and ω are the **long** versions of ε and ο; α, ι, and υ are **sometimes short, sometimes long**. "Short" and "long" refer to the vowel's *quantity* (i.e., the duration of its sound); in the Classical age long vowels were held out about twice as long as short ones. Apparently the *quality* (i.e., the sound) of α, ι and υ did not change much when those vowels were held out; η and ω, on the other hand, were not only longer but also more open in pronunciation than their short counterparts, ε and ο.

---

[1] After epsilon used to come **digamma**, ϝ (sounding like *w*), until it fell out of use.
[2] Sigma has the form ς only when it is **the last letter in a word**; otherwise it appears as σ. Some scholars prefer to use c, a "lunate" sigma; it has the same shape regardless of where it comes in the word.

5.   A **diphthong** is **two vowels** combined in pronunciation; the sound of the first either merges with or glides into the sound of the second. The two vowels together form **one long syllable**. Classical Greek has eleven diphthongs. The first eight listed below are called "proper diphthongs" because, in each of them, both vowels continued to be pronounced. The last three in the list are called "improper diphthongs" because the iota in each of them eventually became a silent letter (in the Classical age, however, it was still pronounced).

PROPER DIPHTHONGS			Pronounced like the italicized letter(s) in the English word:
AI	Aι	αι	*ai*sle
AY	Aυ	αυ	*ou*ch
EI	Eι	ει	*eigh*t
EY	Eυ	ευ	*etch* gliding into *-oo*
HY	Hυ	ηυ	*error* gliding into *-oo* [or *ace* gliding into *-oo*]
OI	Oι	οι	*oi*ly
OY	Oυ	ου	*oo*ze
YI	Yι	υι	French *u* gliding into *-ee* [or υι = *wee*]

IMPROPER DIPHTHONGS			
ĀI	Āι	ᾳ	*ah* gliding into *-ee* [or exactly as ᾱ]
HI	Hι	ῃ	*error* gliding into *-ee* [or exactly as η]
ΩI	Ωι	ῳ	*aw* gliding into *-ee* [or exactly as ω]

When written *on the same line* as the other vowel, the iota is called an **iota adscript**; when written *below the line*, it is called an **iota subscript**. The ancient Greeks always wrote the iota as an adscript, but since the eleventh or twelfth century, it has been more customary to use subscripts in improper diphthongs, except when the ᾱ, η, or ω (and/or the ι itself) is capitalized.

NOTE   During the Classical period the letters **epsilon**, **omicron**, **upsilon**, and **omega** had the names εἶ, οὖ, ὖ, and ὦ. The longer names they now have (meaning "plain e," "small o," "plain u," "big o") were created for clarity's sake by grammarians in the Byzantine age; by then ο had come to sound like ω, and the diphthongs αι and οι had come to be pronounced like the "plain" vowels ε and υ, causing confusion.

6.   Many Greek words begin with an *h*-sound followed by a vowel or a diphthong; this *h*-sound (called "aspiration") is indicated not by a letter but by a mark (ʽ) called a **rough breathing**, which is placed above the vowel or above the second letter of a proper diphthong (e.g., ἑ-, αἱ-). If the word does not begin with an h-sound, a **smooth breathing** (ʼ) is used instead (e.g., ἐ-, αἰ-). Every vowel or diphthong that comes at the beginning of a word *must* have a breathing to show whether it is aspirated (rough) or unaspirated (smooth).

A breathing is placed *to the left* of a capital letter (e.g., Ἡ-, Ἐ-) unless the capital letter is part of a proper diphthong (e.g., Εὐ-). In an improper diphthong the breathing goes above the *first* vowel, never above the iota (e.g., ᾀ-, ἀι-, Ἀι-). **A word beginning with upsilon or rho always has rough breathing** (ὑ-, υἱ-, ῥ-). Rho is the only consonant ever written with a breathing.

7.　　Of Greek's seventeen **consonants**, nine are **stops** (also called **mutes**); these are further classified as **labials** (π, β, φ), **dentals** (τ, δ, θ), or **palatals** (κ, γ, χ). Two are **liquids** (λ, ρ); two are **nasals** (μ, ν); one is a **sibilant** (σ); three are **double consonants**: ζ (= σδ, later δσ), ξ (= κσ, γσ, or χσ), ψ (= πσ, βσ, or φσ). A Greek word is not permitted to end in any consonant except ν, ρ, ς, ξ, and ψ. (The words ἐκ and οὐκ, which both end in kappa, are the only exceptions to this rule.)

8.　　If one stop (π, β, φ, τ, δ, θ, κ, γ, χ) is followed by a different stop or by a liquid (λ, ρ) or a nasal (μ, ν), they are usually pronounced **together** (e.g., φθ, βδ, κτ, θλ, χρ, γμ, πν). If one liquid or nasal is followed by a different liquid or nasal or by a stop, they are pronounced **separately** (e.g., ρΙν, λΙθ, μΙπ; μν is an exception). Repeated consonants are always separately pronounced (e.g., λΙλ, πΙπ, ρΙρ, σΙσ, τΙτ), as are the two sounds in a double consonant (ζ, ξ, ψ). When a sigma is followed by another consonant (not σ), they may be pronounced **either separately or together**.

A Greek word has as many **syllables** as it has vowels and diphthongs (e.g., θε-αί = 2 syllables). If a vowel or diphthong is separated from the next vowel or diphthong by **one consonant** or by **two or more consonants pronounced together**, the break between the syllables comes *right after* that vowel or diphthong (e.g., φῦ-λα, ἄ-κρον, οἶ-στρος [σ regarded as part of the consonant cluster]). If there are **two or more intervening consonants**, of which the first two are **separately pronounced**, the syllabic break comes *between* those two consonants (e.g., φύλ-λα, ἄρ-χων, ἄν-θραξ, οἶσ-τρος [σ regarded as a separate sound]). Since it is impossible to show the break in a double consonant, just put a hyphen *before* the double consonant (e.g., τά-ξις).

9.　　Greeks in the Classical age used little, if any, spacing or punctuation. Later, four **punctuation marks** were devised: the **comma** (,) and the **period** (.), exactly like their English counterparts; the **colon** or **high dot** (·), corresponding to a semi-colon or colon in English; and the **question mark** (;), equivalent to an English question mark. There are no special marks to indicate exclamations or quotations; some publishers of ancient Greek texts now use modern quotation and exclamation marks for their readers' convenience.

It is customary to **capitalize** the first letter of **a proper name**, of **a word beginning a quotation**, and of **a word beginning a long section** (e.g., a paragraph or a chapter), but not of a word beginning an ordinary sentence.

NOTE   In this textbook a **macron** ("long mark") is printed above a vowel if there would otherwise be no way to tell that the vowel is long: ᾱ, ῑ, ῡ. You will never see a macron above η or ω since both are always long, nor above ε or ο since both are always short. Macra were not used by the ancient Greeks and are seldom used today except in textbooks and lexica. Greek **accents** will be explained in the next lesson. For now, just stress the syllable over which an accent (´, `, or ^) appears.

10.   **EXERCISES**

A.   Divide into syllables and pronounce each of the following words (famous names from Greek history and mythology). Then transliterate each word, i.e., replace each Greek letter or breathing with its English equivalent (refer to §3). Upsilon is transliterated as *u* if it follows a vowel (and thus is the second letter in a diphthong), as *y* if it follows a consonant. Kappa may be transliterated as either *k* or *c*, chi as either *kh* or *ch*. Rough breathing becomes *h*; ῥ is transliterated as *rh*.

NOTE   Do not be alarmed if some of the famous names seem to be slightly misspelled in your English transliterations. Many Greek words have come to us through Latin, and their Latin spelling, not their original Greek spelling, is often the one that English has preserved.

1. Ποσειδῶν	7. Βαῦκις	13. Σωκράτης	19. Λεύκιππος
2. Ἀφροδίτη	8. Ξέρξης	14. Μοῦσα	20. Ἅιδης
3. Ἥφαιστος	9. Κύκλωψ	15. Ζεύς	21. Οἰδίπους
4. Θουκῡδίδης	10. Ῥέᾱ	16. Ἀγαμέμνων	22. Εἰλείθυια
5. Ἀχιλλεύς	11. Δίρκη	17. Ὠκεανός	23. Γλαύκων
6. Τροίᾱ	12. Ὅμηρος	18. Φειδίᾱς	24. Χάρυβδις

B.   Read aloud the following little story (Aesop's Fable 119) for practice in pronouncing the Greek letters. Pay close attention to the breathings and stress the syllables that have an accent. A translation is provided for your enjoyment.

ZEUS CUTS THE CAMEL DOWN TO SIZE

Κάμηλος θεᾱσαμένη ταῦρον ἐπὶ τοῖς κέρᾱσιν ἀγαλλόμενον φθονήσᾱσα αὐτῷ ἠβουλήθη καὶ αὐτὴ τῶν ἴσων ἐφικέσθαι. διόπερ παραγενομένη πρὸς τὸν Δία τούτου ἐδέετο, ὅπως αὐτῇ κέρατα προσνείμῃ. καὶ ὁ Ζεὺς ἀγανακτήσᾱς κατ᾽ αὐτῆς, εἴγε μὴ ἀρκεῖται τῷ μεγέθει τοῦ σώματος καὶ τῇ ἰσχύι, ἀλλὰ καὶ περισσοτέρων ἐπιθῡμεῖ, οὐ μόνον αὐτῇ κέρᾱτα οὐ προσέθηκεν, ἀλλὰ καὶ μέρος τι τῶν ω῎των ἀφείλετο. οὕτω πολλοὶ διὰ πλεονεξίᾱν τοῖς ἄλλοις ἐποφθαλμιῶντες λανθάνουσι καὶ τῶν ἰδίων στερούμενοι.

TRANSLATION

A camel, observing a bull glorying in his horns, became envious of him and wanted to get an equally fine set of horns for herself. So, going up to Zeus, she begged him to grant her some horns. And Zeus, annoyed at her since she was not content with the size and strength of her body but desired greater dimensions, not only did not give her horns but even took away a portion of her ears. Thus do many people [and animals!], eyeing others jealously out of greed, unwittingly lose what is their own.

LESSON 2

INTRODUCTION
The Greek Accents

δεινὸν δ' ἐστὶν ἡ μὴ 'μπειρίᾱ (Inexperience is a dreadful thing.)
—comment by a woman in Aristophanes' *Ecclesiazusae* 115

11.   In the last lesson we asked you to give extra **stress** to the accented syllables, and that, in fact, is what most people now do when they pronounce ancient Greek. In reality, however, the marks were designed to indicate raising or lowering of the **pitch** of the speaker's voice and have nothing to do with stress.

The Greeks of the Classical period had no need for accent marks because they knew by heart which syllables had a change in pitch. The marks are said to have been invented by Aristophanes of Byzantium in the third century B.C., when non-native speakers of Greek required help in learning the language's pitch accents. Eventually, stress entirely replaced pitch.

The accents of Greek words occasionally make a difference in what the words *mean*, so learning them is helpful for understanding what the text says, as well as for pronouncing the words as accurately as possible.

12.   There are three types of *accent marks* (usually referred to simply as *accents*): **acute** ('), **grave** (`), and **circumflex** (ˆ). The acute denotes a **gliding up** of pitch, the grave a **gliding down**, the circumflex a **gliding up followed by a gliding down**. The place for the accent is above the vowel or the diphthong in the syllable that is to be accented; if a breathing also belongs there, it is written to the left of an acute or grave and beneath a circumflex (῎, ῞, ῍, ῝, ῏, ῟). Like the breathings, the accents go above the second vowel of a proper diphthong (e.g., εὖ), above the first vowel of an improper diphthong (e.g., ῷ, ᾧ), and to the left of a capital letter (e.g., ῎Α, ῎ᾼι) unless it is part of a proper diphthong (e.g., Αἴ).

NOTE   There is much scholarly debate about the grave accent; the mark perhaps shows, not that the pitch should glide *down*, but simply that it should *not* glide *up* (i.e., it could remain steady).

13.   In most Greek words one (and only one) syllable is marked with an accent, and that syllable is always **one of the last three syllables**; an accent mark never appears earlier than that in a word. In φιλόσοφος, for example, the acute is as far left as the rules of accenting allow; it could never appear above φι. Traditionally, the last syllable in a word is called the **ultima** (Latin for "last"); the next-to-last syllable is called the **penult** ("almost last"); the syllable before the penult is called the **antepenult** ("before the almost last"). A word's ultima, penult, and antepenult are the only syllables in it that can ever be accented.

NOTE   A few words in Greek have *no* accent, and under certain circumstances a word may receive a *second* accent. This will all be explained in later lessons.

14.   The **acute** and **grave** accents are found above diphthongs, long vowels, and short vowels; the **circumflex** is found *only* above diphthongs or long vowels. (This is logical since the brief sound of a short vowel would not allow enough time for the pitch to glide both up and down.) Thus, whenever you see a circumflex, you automatically know that the vowel beneath it is long; a macron to indicate the quantity of the vowel would be superfluous.

The **acute** appears on the **antepenult** (e.g., θάλαττα), the **penult** (e.g., χώρᾱ), or the **ultima** (e.g., θεά) of a word. The **circumflex** appears on the **penult** (e.g., μοῖρα) or the **ultima** (καλῶς) of a word, never as far back as the antepenult. The **grave** is peculiar in that its *only* use is as a substitute for an acute accent on the ultima: if there would normally be an acute accent on the last syllable of a word and there happens to be no punctuation mark after the word, the acute automatically switches to a grave (e.g. ἀγαθὴ τύχη); otherwise it remains acute (e.g., ἀγαθή· τύχη). Thus the grave appears **only on the ultima**.

15.   In many Greek words the position of the accent (i.e., whether it is supposed to stand on the antepenult, penult, or ultima) is not predictable and must therefore be memorized when each word is learned. In many other Greek words, however, the position of the accent *is* predictable.

In this lesson there are just two **general principles** for you to learn. These apply to accenting *any* Greek word, **once you find out where the accent in the word wants to be** (for now, don't worry about how you find that out).

To understand the general principles, you must first know how to determine whether a syllable is long by nature, long by position, or short:

A syllable is **long by nature** when it contains a naturally long vowel (e.g., χώ-ρᾱ, κλῑ-νη) or a diphthong (e.g., μοί-ρᾳ). One important exception: **the proper diphthongs αι and οι are usually regarded as short when they are the very last letters in a word** (e.g., οι is short in ἵπποι, but long in οἶκος and ἵπποις).

A syllable is **long by position** when its vowel or diphthong is followed by two consonants separately pronounced or by a double consonant (e.g., ἀρ-χή, ἦτ-τον, λεί-ψω, φύ-λαξ). Notice that the length *of the vowel or diphthong* is not changed by its position; in φύλαξ, for example, the alpha is still naturally short even though the *syllable* is long by position. In λείψω the syllable is both naturally long (because it contains the diphthong ει) and long by position.

A syllable is **always short** when it contains a naturally short vowel followed by no consonant (e.g., θε-ός) or by a single consonant (e.g., θύ-ρᾱ).

A syllable is **usually short** when it contains a naturally short vowel followed by two or more consonants pronounced together (e.g., ἄ-κρον; see §8 in Lesson 1). This is true for Attic prose; in Greek poetry the consonants are often considered to be separately pronounced, and thus the syllable is long by position.

TWO GENERAL PRINCIPLES OF ACCENTING

1. **Accent** wants to be on the **antepenult**: **The acute can stay on the antepenult only if the ultima is short** (i.e., if it has a short vowel not followed by a double consonant, or if it ends in -αι or -οι; e.g., διδάσκαλος, διδάσκαλοι). **If the ultima is long by nature or by position, the acute must move to the penult, i.e., one syllable to the right** (e.g., διδασκάλου, διδασκάλοις).

2. **Accent** wants to be on the **penult**: **If the penult is naturally long** *and* **the ultima has a short vowel or ends in -αι or -οι, the accent on the penult will be a circumflex** (e.g., δῶρον, κῆρυξ, παῦε, ἐκεῖναι). If the penult is *not* naturally long or the ultima does *not* have a short vowel or end in -αι or -οι, **the accent on the penult will be an acute** (e.g., τότε, ἵπποι, παύεις, ἐκείνᾱς).

16.   **EXERCISES**

A.   The following are all genuine Greek words transliterated into English; transliterate them back into Greek with proper breathings and accents.

REMINDER   The English equivalents of the Greek letters are given in §3 of Lesson 1. Upsilon is the equivalent of either *u* or *y*.

1.   harmoniā, acute on penult

2.   ainigma, acute on antepenult, proper diphthong

3.   glōtta, circumflex on penult

4.   mēchanē, acute on ultima

5.   rhapsōidiā, acute on penult, improper diphthong

6.   symptōma, acute on antepenult

7.   ichthȳs, acute on ultima

8.   thlīpsis, circumflex on penult

9.   exangeliā, acute on penult, use gamma for *n*-sound

10.   kīnēsis, acute on antepenult

11.   syllogismos, acute on ultima

12.   zōion, circumflex on penult, improper diphthong

13   autarkeia, acute on antepenult

14.   haima, circumflex on penult, proper diphthong

15.   basileus, acute on ultima

B.   Two of the words in each group are incorrectly accented; pick out the only form that does not violate one of the general principles of accenting.

1. κάμηλῳ	κάμηλον	καμῆλοις
2. ἔπιθῡμει	ἐπιθῡμεῖ	ἐπίθῡμει
3. σῶματος	σώματων	σώματος
4. ἄφειλετο	ἀφεῖλετο	ἀφείλετο
5. ἶδιος	ἴδιοι	ἴδιοις
6. προσνεῖμη	πρόσνειμη	προσνείμη
7. αὐτή	αὗτη	αὗται
8. τούτου	τοῦτοις	τούτων
9. ἐφικέσθαι	ἐφῖκεσθαι	ἔφικεσθαι
10. ταύρος	ταῦρον	ταῦρῳ

LESSON 3

Ω-VERBS
Present Active Indicative, Present Active Infinitive, Present Active Imperative

σπεῦδε βραδέως (Make haste slowly.)
—one of Augustus' sayings, quoted by Suetonius in *Augustus* 25

17. Greek has eight **parts of speech**: **nouns, pronouns, adjectives, verbs, adverbs, conjunctions, prepositions**, and **particles**. In this chapter we focus on verbs. Some of the grammatical terminology may be intimidating at first, but don't let it scare you. Many of the terms are traditional and come from Latin; once explained, they should not cause you any trouble. In fact, you should find them convenient to use. After all, they were designed to be helpful, not horrifying!

18. **Verbs** are words that denote *actions* or *states of being*. Like English verbs, Greek verbs have the properties of **person, number, voice, mood**, and **tense**.

A Greek verb has one of **three possible persons**: first, second, or third. The verb is in **first person** if its subject is *the person speaking* ("I," "we"). The verb is in **second person** if its subject is *the person being spoken to* ("you"). The verb is in **third person** if its subject is *someone or something other than the person speaking or the person being spoken to* ("he," "she," "it," "they").

A Greek verb has one of **three possible numbers**: singular, dual, or plural. The **singular** denotes that the subject is *just one* person or thing. The **dual** denotes that the subject is *a pair* of people or things. The **plural** denotes that the subject is *more than one* person or thing. Because the dual is seldom used in Attic Greek (the plural generally takes its place), we do not teach it in this book, but all of the dual forms are listed for reference in the appendix.

A Greek verb has one of **three possible voices**: active, passive, or middle. A verb has **active voice** if its subject *performs an action* (e.g., "I teach," "I teach the children"). A verb has **passive voice** if its subject is *acted upon by someone or something else* ("the children are taught by me"). A verb has **middle voice** if the subject *performs an action for itself or on someone or something of special interest to it* (e.g., "I teach [for myself]," "I have the children taught [because of my interest in them]"; the words in brackets are *implied* by the verb's middle voice, but do not actually appear in the Greek sentence).

Verbs with active or middle voice may be either **transitive** (i.e., combined with a **direct object** that identifies who or what is being acted upon; e.g., "I teach *the children*," "I have *the children* taught") or **intransitive** (i.e., with *no* direct object appearing in the sentence; e.g., "I teach," "I teach [for myself]"). **A passive sentence is the equivalent of a transitive active sentence**; for example, "The children are taught by me" describes the same situation as "I teach the children." In both sentences it is the children who experience the teaching, but the idea is expressed in two different ways: with *children* as the direct object of an active verb; with *children* as the the subject of a passive verb.

A Greek verb has one of **four possible moods**: indicative, imperative, subjunctive, or optative. The mood reflects the speaker's estimate of how *real* the action is. **Indicative mood** suits statements of **fact** or discussions of **reality** and **actual occurrences** (e.g., a statement—"you are here"; a question—"are you here?"). **Imperative mood** is appropriate for **commands**, i.e., requests to *change* reality (e.g., "be here!"). **Subjunctive and optative moods** are associated with a variety of actions that are all only **contemplated** or **imagined** (e.g., a wish—"would that you were here!"; fear or doubt—"you may be here"; a possibility—"you might be here").

A Greek verb in the **indicative mood** has one of **seven possible tenses**: present, imperfect, future, aorist, perfect, pluperfect, or future perfect. A Greek verb in the **imperative**, **subjunctive**, or **optative** mood has one of only **three possible tenses**: present, aorist, or perfect. There is a logical explanation for this. In the indicative mood each tense denotes *both* the **time** of the action (**present**, **past**, or **future**) and its **aspect**, i.e., the *type* of action that the speaker perceives it to be. The speaker may view the action as a process continuing or repeated over time (**imperfective** ["unfinished"] **aspect**), as a simple occurrence (**aoristic** ["undefined"] **aspect**), or as a completed action with an enduring result (**perfective** ["finished"] **aspect**). Thus, each tense of the indicative represents a different *combination* of time and aspect. In the imperative, subjunctive, and optative moods, the tenses denote *only aspect*, not time, so no more than three are needed: **present tense** for imperfective aspect, **aorist tense** for aoristic aspect, and **perfect tense** for perfective aspect.

For those who like to have the whole picture from the start, here are the various combinations of time and aspect signified by the tenses of the indicative:

present tense:	present time, imperfective or aoristic aspect
imperfect tense:	past time, imperfective aspect
future tense:	future time, imperfective or aoristic aspect
aorist tense:	past time, aoristic aspect
perfect tense:	present time, perfective aspect
pluperfect tense:	past time, perfective aspect
future perfect tense:	future time, perfective aspect

The four tenses of the indicative that show *present* or *future* time (present, future, perfect, future perfect) are **primary** (or principal) tenses; the three that show *past* time (imperfect, aorist, pluperfect) are **secondary** (or historical) tenses.

19.　　　　**Inflection.** Every Greek verb alters or *inflects* ("bends") its form to indicate changes in its person, number, voice, mood, and tense. Inflecting a verb means adding suffixes and (sometimes) prefixes to one of its six stems; this process is known as **conjugating** ("joining together"). All the verbs that are conjugated in the same way are grouped together and said to belong to the same **conjugation**. Greek has two main conjugations, a large one to which all the ω-verbs belong, and a small one to which all the μι-verbs belong. This book does not explain the features of μι-verbs until all the forms of ω-verbs have been introduced.

20.　　　　The **present tense** of the indicative mood denotes an action happening in the **present time**. It may be an action happening *now and only now*, or it may be one that goes on *all the time*, including now. Most often it is viewed as a continuing, repeated, or habitual process; if so, the verb has **imperfective aspect**. Sometimes it is viewed as a simple, one-time occurrence; if so, the verb has **aoristic aspect**. Although there is no difference in appearance between a present-tense Greek verb with imperfective aspect and one with aoristic aspect, the context usually makes clear which aspect the author of the sentence had in mind.

παιδεύω ("I teach") will serve as a model or **paradigm** for the conjugation of ω-verbs in the **present indicative mood**, **active voice**. Each Greek word in the paradigm is followed by two possible translations of it; e.g., παιδεύω = "I teach" or "I am teaching."

NOTE　　　　English has several ways to express the present indicative, each conveying a different nuance (e.g., "I teach," "I am teaching," "I continue teaching," "I do teach"). Since Greek uses just one form, broad enough to cover all of those nuances, there is no simple formula for translating the Greek present indicative into English. You must rely on the context to help you choose a suitable translation.

PRESENT ACTIVE INDICATIVE

Singular:			Endings:
1st person	παιδεύω	("I teach/am teaching")	-ω
2nd person	παιδεύεις	("you [*sg.*] teach/are teaching")	-εις
3rd person	παιδεύει	("he/she/it teaches/is teaching")	-ει

Plural:			
1st person	παιδεύομεν	("we teach/are teaching")	-ομεν
2nd person	παιδεύετε	("you [*pl.*] teach/are teaching")	-ετε
3rd person	παιδεύουσι(ν)	("they teach/are teaching")	-ουσι(ν)

To form the present tense, you must first find the **present stem**. When you look up a Greek verb in a dictionary, you will be confronted with **six principal parts**. The first of these will be the first-person singular present active indicative; if it ends in -ω (e.g., παιδεύω), the verb must belong to the ω-conjugation. Dropping the -ω from the first principal part will give you the present stem.

Each **ending** is actually a combination of a **thematic vowel** (a mark of the present tense; usually ε, but o is used before μ or ν) and a **personal ending**: -ω = o + lengthening, -εις = ε + σι (σ dropped out) + ς, -ει = ε + σι (σ dropped out), -ομεν = o + μεν, -ετε = ε + τε, -ουσι = o + νσι (ν dropped out; o lengthened to ου). It is good to be aware that these phonetic changes have occurred, but you need only memorize the endings in their final form, keeping in mind that the first letter of each is a thematic vowel. The ν in the third-person plural ending is a **movable ν**; it is added to a word ending in -σι whenever the following word begins with a vowel or whenever the -σι word falls at the end of a sentence.

Verb forms that have personal endings are called finite (because the action is confined to a specific person—first, second, or third—and number). They do not need to be supplemented with a pronoun ("I," "you," etc.) to clarify who is doing the action. (Pronouns may be added for emphasis, however.)

The accent of most finite verb forms is recessive, i.e., it wants to move as far *to the left* in the word as possible. Thus, if the word has only two syllables, the accent will recede to the penult (and be either a circumflex or an acute, according to general principle #2 in §15 of Lesson 2); if the word has three or more syllables, the accent will recede to the antepenult and stay there unless it is forced back to the penult by general principle #1 (e.g., the acute recedes to the antepenult in παιδεύομεν, but the long ultima draws it back to the penult in παιδεύω).

21.   The **infinitive** is a **non-finite verb** form that in English always begins with "to." It has tense and voice but no person, number, or mood.

Its tense shows *only aspect*, not time (exceptions will be discussed in later lessons). Like an English infinitive, it may function either as part of the main verb (e.g., "I wish *to write*"; here the infinitive is **complementary**, completing the verbal idea) or as a noun (e.g., "*to write* is difficult"; here the infinitive is the subject of the sentence).

The **PRESENT ACTIVE INFINITIVE** of παιδεύω is παιδεύειν ("to teach"), formed by adding -ειν (= thematic vowel ε + εν [the two epsilons contract into the diphthong ει]) to the **present stem**, with **recessive accent**. Despite its name a present infinitive does not signify an event taking place right now; rather, it implies an on-going or habitual action. Thus its tense is not an indication of present time, but of **imperfective aspect**. You may prefer to translate the present infinitive in a way that emphasizes the on-going nature of the action: e.g., "to be teaching" or "to continue teaching."

22.   The **imperative mood**, used for giving commands, has person (but not first person), number, voice, and tense. Tenses in this mood show *only aspect*, not time. The present imperative has **imperfective aspect** and denotes an action that the speaker wishes to see happening for a while or repeatedly. Here are the forms of παιδεύω in the **present imperative mood**, **active voice**.

PRESENT ACTIVE IMPERATIVE

Singular:			Endings:
2nd person	παίδευε	("teach!")	-ε
3rd person	παιδευέτω	("let him/her/it teach!")	-ετω
Plural:			
2nd person	παιδεύετε	("teach!")	-ετε
3rd person	παιδευόντων	("let them teach!")	-οντων

The present active imperative is built on the **present stem**. Its endings are combinations of the **thematic vowel ε/o** and the **personal endings** —, -τω, -τε, -ντων. As you would expect in finite verb forms, the accent is **recessive**. The second-person plural present *imperative* is identical in appearance to the second-person plural present *indicative*. The context will help you distinguish them.

In English there is no difference in form between a second-person *singular* command, addressed to one person, and a second-person *plural* command, addressed to more than one person. In Greek, however, the singular command has a different ending from the plural (-ε instead of -ετε). The third-person imperative is an order pertaining to one person ("let him/her/it...") or to several persons ("let them...") who are being talked *about*, not addressed directly.

Since the present imperative has imperfective aspect, you may prefer a translation that emphasizes the on-going nature of the action: e.g.,"be teaching!" or "continue teaching!" for παίδευε; "let them be teaching!" or "let them continue teaching!" for παιδευόντων.

23. In the **indicative mood** the normal **negative** is οὐ; it is usually placed in front of the verb (e.g., οὐ παιδεύεις, "you are not teaching" or "you do not teach"). A **prohibition** or negative command is introduced by μή ("not"); it is usually placed in front of the imperative form of the verb (e.g., μὴ παίδευε, "don't teach!").

24. **VOCABULARY**

NOTE Words are grouped according to their part of speech and presented in this order: verbs, nouns, pronouns, adjectives, adverbs, prepositions, conjunctions, particles. Within each category the order is alphabetical. English derivatives are printed in italics and placed in square brackets at the end of each entry.

If a verb can be used with an infinitive, the vocabulary item will begin with (+ *infinitive*), and the meanings that are appropriate when the infinitive is used will have the word *to* following them in parentheses. The parentheses indicate that the verb may be used either with an infinitive or without one.

If a word in the vocabulary list has an acute accent on its ultima, do not assume that that accent can never change. Whenever the word is used in a sentence and another word follows it with no intervening punctuation, the accent will switch to a grave (as explained in §14 of Lesson 2). It is for simplicity's sake that the word is printed with an acute accent whenever it is quoted out of context.

γράφω	write, draw [cf. *autograph*]
ἐθέλω	(+ *infinitive*) be willing (to), wish (to)
θύω	offer sacrifice, sacrifice, slay
κλέπτω	steal [cf. *kleptomania*]
παιδεύω	teach, educate [cf. *propaedeutic*]
σπεύδω	(+ *infinitive*) hasten (to), strive (to), be eager (to)
φυλάττω	stand guard, guard, protect, preserve [cf. *prophylactic*]
μή	(*negative adverb used with imperative mood*) not
οὐ (οὔ, οὐκ, οὐχ)	(*negative adverb used with indicative mood*) not

NOTE   οὐ is a **proclitic**, a type of word that "leans ahead" to the word following it and has no accent of its own; there are ten such words in Greek. οὐ is unique in that it *does* receive an accent (acute) if it comes at the end of a clause (οὔ). Before a word with smooth breathing, οὐ becomes οὐκ; before a word with rough breathing, οὐ becomes οὐχ. οὐκ and οὐχ are exceptions to the rule that a Greek word can end only in a vowel, ν, ρ, ς, ξ, or ψ.

καί	(*conjunction*) and; (*adverb*) also, even
καὶ...καί	(correlative conjunctions) both...and

NOTE   As a conjunction, καί ("and") connects parallel words (e.g., two finite verbs, two infinitives, two nouns). If the sentence seems to have a superfluous καί in it, καί is either an adverb, stressing the word that immediately follows it, or a **correlative conjunction** paired with another καί. In a vocabulary list it is conventional to show the first correlative with its acute accent changed to grave, since another word would most likely follow it with no intervening punctuation.

25.   **EXERCISES**

     A.   **Greek-to-English Sentences**

        1.   παιδεύεις καὶ οὐ κλέπτεις.
        2.   μὴ γράφε· σπεῦδε φυλάττειν.
        3.   καὶ θυόντων καὶ παιδευόντων.
        4.   ἐθέλετε κλέπτειν; οὐκ ἐθέλουσιν.
        5.   σπεύδει παιδεύειν· μὴ κλεπτέτω.
        6.   ἐθέλομεν καὶ θύειν καὶ γράφειν.
        7.   μὴ κλέπτε· φυλάττει.
        8.   σπεύδουσι καὶ γράφειν; γραφόντων.
        9.   παιδεύω· θυέτω.
      10.   φυλάττομεν· μὴ σπεύδετε κλέπτειν.

     B.   **English-to-Greek Sentences**

        1.   Offer sacrifice (*plural*) and do not steal!
        2.   Also hasten (*singular*) to teach!
        3.   Is he willing to stand guard? Let him not continue drawing!
        4.   She is not writing; she is both educating and sacrificing.
        5.   Let them steal! We do not wish to guard.

LESSON 4

FIRST DECLENSION
Feminine Nouns, Part 1

καλὸν ἡσυχίᾱ (Leisure is a fine thing.)
—one of Periander's sayings, quoted by Diogenes Laertius 1.97

26. A **noun** is a word signifying or naming a *person*, *place*, or *thing*. Greek nouns are less formidable than Greek verbs, but still challenging. Like verbs, they too are inflected. Inflecting a verb is called conjugating; inflecting a noun is called **declining**. Verbs are classified by their conjugation; nouns are classified by their **declension**. This chapter introduces the first of Greek's three declensions.

27. Unlike a Greek verb, which has six stems, a Greek noun usually has just one. Endings that are added to the stem indicate **gender**, **number**, and **case**.

The **gender** of a noun may be **masculine**, **feminine**, or **neuter**. The gender of nouns denoting male persons is almost always masculine, and the gender of nouns denoting female persons is almost always feminine, but the gender of sexless objects is *not*, as you might expect, almost always neuter; it is just as often feminine (like the Greek word for "marketplace") or masculine (like the Greek word for "river"). For such nouns the gender has nothing to do with their "sex"; it is simply a grammatical trait (comparable to a blood-type), which has to be memorized along with the stem and the endings. Each Greek noun is "born" with a particular gender, and that **gender never changes**.

The **number** of a noun is similar to the number of a verb; it may be **singular**, **dual**, or **plural**, depending on how many people, places, or things the speaker has in mind. Since the dual (implying a pair) is rarely used in Attic Greek, it is relegated to the appendix of this book.

21

The **case** of a noun is a clue to how the noun is functioning in its sentence. It is often difficult for English-speakers to grasp the idea of cases because English uses the *position* of a noun in a sentence, not the *form* of the noun, to indicate its function; for example, in "The dog chases the cat," we know that "dog" is the subject because it is placed *before* the verb, while "cat" is shown to be the object by its placement *after* the verb. If the positions of "dog" and "cat" in the sentence are reversed, "dog" becomes the object, "cat" becomes the subject, and the sentence means the opposite of what it originally did.

In Greek the position of a noun does *not* dictate how it is functioning in the sentence; this is shown instead by the noun's case. The idea of the dog chasing the cat could be expressed in Greek with *any* of the following arrangements of words: "The dog chases the cat," "The cat chases the dog," "The dog the cat chases," "The cat the dog chases," "Chases the dog the cat," "Chases the cat the dog." In none of the Greek versions would there be any doubt that the dog is doing the chasing; the noun for "dog" would be in the case appropriate for the subject of a sentence, while the noun for "cat" would be in the case appropriate for the object. The speaker would be free to choose whether to put the nouns before, after, or on either side of the verb; the decision would depend on which words the speaker wished to emphasize or which grouping of sounds was most pleasing to the ear.

Greek nouns have five cases: *nominative, genitive, dative, accusative, vocative.* It is traditional to list them in that order, with the last four cases seeming to "decline" or fall from the nominative (*case* comes from the Latin word for "a falling"). The next section gives an overview of the cases and their uses.

28.

The **nominative case** designates **subjects** as well as **predicate nouns**. A predicate noun is connected to the subject by a "linking verb" (e.g., "we *are* friends," "you *have become* a nuisance," "they *will be chosen* as delegates"). Unlike a direct object, which is acted upon by the subject, a predicate noun is equated with the subject and therefore must be "equal" to it in case.

The **genitive case** designates a noun that is modifying another noun in the sentence; this relationship can usually be conveyed in English with *of* (e.g., "the grapes *of* wrath," "love *of* life," "the book *of* the student"; here the phrase shows **possession** and could be expressed alternatively as "the student's book"). The genitive case also has the function of Indo-European's ablative case (which survives only in traces in Greek). In this role it serves as the case for nouns denoting a **source** or **point of origin** ("away from," "out of," etc.).

The **dative case** designates someone or something that is associated with the action or the state described in the sentence, but is not the subject or the direct object. Often the English *to* or *for* will be an appropriate translation (e.g., "give the prize *to* the winner"; "*for* ducks, the weather is perfect"). The dative case also has the functions of Indo-European's instrumental and locative cases (almost completely lost in Greek). Thus it is the case appropriate for nouns denoting **means**, **accompaniment**, **location**, or **time** ("by," "with," "in," "at," etc.).

The **accusative case** designates the sentence's **direct object** (the person, place, or thing that directly experiences or undergoes the action of the verb). It is also used for nouns that denote a **destination** or **goal** or an **extent of time or space** ("into," "to," "toward," "for," etc.).

The **vocative case** designates someone or something who is being addressed (e.g., "farewell, *Socrates!*"; "O *death*, where is thy sting?").

29.　　　**First-declension nouns** can be divided into two groups: feminines and masculines. The feminines are discussed here and in the next lesson, the masculines in Lesson 9. Originally all **first-declension feminines** had stems ending in -ᾱ; this remained so in the Doric and Aeolic dialects; in Attic, however, -ᾱ was replaced by -η (e.g., σκηνή) in all cases of the singular, except when -ᾱ was preceded by ε, ι, or ρ (e.g., θεά, ἡσυχίᾱ, χώρᾱ). This meant that, in Attic, there were two different types of first-declension feminines, ᾱ-stems and η-stems:

Singular:	("goddess")	("leisure")	("place")	("tent")	Endings:	
Nominative	θεά	ἡσυχίᾱ	χώρᾱ	σκηνή	-ᾱ	-η
Genitive	θεᾶς	ἡσυχίᾱς	χώρᾱς	σκηνῆς	-ᾱς	-ης
Dative	θεᾷ	ἡσυχίᾳ	χώρᾳ	σκηνῇ	-ᾳ	-ῃ
Accusative	θεάν	ἡσυχίᾱν	χώρᾱν	σκηνήν	-ᾱν	-ην
Vocative	θεά	ἡσυχίᾱ	χώρᾱ	σκηνή	-ᾱ	-η

Plural:						
Nominative	θεαί	ἡσυχίαι	χῶραι	σκηναί	-αι	-αι
Genitive	θεῶν	ἡσυχιῶν	χωρῶν	σκηνῶν	-ων	-ων
Dative	θεαῖς	ἡσυχίαις	χώραις	σκηναῖς	-αις	-αις
Accusative	θεάς	ἡσυχίᾱς	χώρᾱς	σκηνάς	-ᾱς	-ᾱς
Vocative	θεαί	ἡσυχίαι	χῶραι	σκηναί	-αι	-αι

As you can see, first-declension feminines all have the same endings in the plural: -αι, -ων, -αις, -ᾱς, -αι. The singular endings are -ᾱ, -ᾱς, -ᾳ, -ᾱν, -ᾱ only if the preceding letter is ε, ι, or ρ; otherwise they are -η, -ης, -ῃ, -ην, -η. Notice that **the nominative and the vocative forms are identical**. In fact, you will soon discover that the nominative and vocative are identical in the plural of **every declension** (though not always in the singular).

The accent of these and all other Greek nouns is **persistent**, i.e., the location of the accent in the nominative singular shows where the accent wants to stay or "persist." "Location" refers not to antepenult, penult, etc., but to the actual letters making up the accented syllable; in the nominative singular of χώρᾱ, for example, the accented syllable is χω-, and the acute accent tries to remain *with that particular group of letters*. (Notice that this is different from the accent of finite verbs, which wants simply to recede.) When the case-ending changes, the general principles of accenting (see §15 of Lesson 2) may force the noun's accent to move to another syllable or to change its form (e.g., χώρᾱ becomes χῶραι). **It is vital for you to memorize the location of the accent in the nominative singular.**

There are **two peculiarities** in the accenting of first-declension feminine nouns:

1.   **If the accent falls on the ultima in the genitive and dative singular and plural, it changes from acute to circumflex.** Example: One would expect to find θεά, θεάς, θεά since there is no general principle forcing accents on the ultima to change from acute to circumflex; nevertheless the correct inflection is θεά, θεᾶς, θεᾷ.

2.   **In the genitive plural of first-declension nouns, the ultima is always accented**, even if that seems illogical. Example: One would expect to find χώρων since there is no reason for the accent to move from its preferred spot above χω-; nevertheless the correct genitive plural is χωρῶν. Behind this peculiarity lies the fact that -ῶν is a contracted form of the original ending -άων; to indicate the contraction, a circumflex is used.

30.   Greek, like English, has a **definite article** ("the") that is used to mark individuals or groups as definite and known. Greek's definite article changes its form to match the gender, number, and case of the noun that it modifies. In this lesson only the **feminine forms** of the article are necessary for you to learn. They closely resemble the endings of first-declension feminine nouns:

NOM. FEM. SG.:	ἡ	**NOM. FEM. PL.:**	αἱ
GEN. FEM. SG.:	τῆς	**GEN. FEM. Pl.:**	τῶν
DAT. FEM. SG.:	τῇ	**DAT. FEM. Pl.:**	ταῖς
ACC. FEM. SG.:	τήν	**ACC. FEM. PL.:**	τάς

The nominatives ἡ and αἱ are **proclitics** (like οὐ) with no accent. No vocatives exist because a definite article would be superfluous in a direct address. (This applies to English too; we say, e.g., "O goddess, listen!", not "O *the* goddess, listen!".)

When you see a definite article in a Greek sentence, do not assume that you should translate it with "the." Greek often has an article where English would not have one. In Greek, for instance, it is customary to put an article with an **abstract noun** if the speaker is thinking of the concept *as a whole*: e.g., πέμπε τὴν ἡσυχίᾱν ("send leisure [all of it]!"), as opposed to πέμπε ἡσυχίᾱν ("send [some/any] leisure!"). In a different context, however, πέμπε τὴν ἡσυχίαν might mean "send *the* leisure [i.e., the particular sort of leisure that the speaker has in mind]!"; in that case, it would be accurate to include "the" in your English translation. Greek also uses the definite article with a proper name to mark the person or place as well known (e.g., "the Socrates," "the Zeus," "the Greece") or to indicate that it is the same person or place previously mentioned.

31.   The word *dative* is related to the Latin verb for "give." One of the most common uses of the dative case is to designate the **indirect object** in a sentence whose subject **gives, offers, presents, dedicates, entrusts,** or **promises** someone or something (direct object—accusative case) to someone or something else (indirect object—dative case). Either the direct object or the indirect object or both may be omitted (e.g., θύω τὴν βοῦν τῇ θεᾷ "I sacrifice the cow to the goddess"; θύω τῇ θεᾷ "I sacrifice to the goddess"; θύω "I offer sacrifice").

With verbs of **sending, writing,** or **saying,** the speaker has the choice of using an **indirect object** (dative case, no preposition) **or a prepositional phrase** (i.e., a preposition meaning "to" followed by a noun in the accusative case). The indirect object usually has a more personal flavor; the recipient is viewed as the *beneficiary* of the subject's action. As the object of the preposition, the recipient is viewed as the point toward which the action is directed (its *destination* or *goal*).

32.   **VOCABULARY**

NOTE   Greek lexica always give a noun's **nominative and genitive singular** and the appropriate **definite article** (in the nominative singular). The noun's declension is shown by the first two forms, its gender by the article (e.g., ἡ = feminine). This is the way nouns will be presented in the vocabulary at the end of each lesson. **Reminder:** Words are listed according to their part of speech: verbs, nouns, pronouns, adjectives, adverbs, prepositions, conjunctions, particles.

πέμπω	send [cf. *propempticon*]
ἀγορά, -ᾶς, ἡ	marketplace, market [cf. *agoraphobia*]
ἐπιστολή, -ῆς, ἡ	letter, message [cf. *epistle*]
ἡσυχία, -ᾱς, ἡ	leisure, quiet, tranquillity
θεά, -ᾶς, ἡ	goddess
σκηνή, -ῆς, ἡ	tent [cf. *scene*]
χώρᾱ, -ᾱς, ἡ	land, country, countryside, space, position
εἰς	(*preposition + object in accusative case*) into, to
ἐκ (ἐξ)	(*preposition + object in genitive case*) out of (ἐξ is used before words starting with a vowel) [cf. *eclectic, ecstasy*]

NOTE   Like οὐκ and οὐχ, ἐκ violates the rule that a Greek word can end only in a vowel, ν, ρ, ς, ξ, or ψ. There are no other exceptions to the rule.

    ἐν   *(preposition + object in dative case)* in
                [cf. *entropy, enzyme*]

NOTE   εἰς, ἐκ, and ἐν are **proclitics**; like οὐ, ἡ, and αἱ, they have no accent. A Greek preposition, like an English preposition, is usually placed *in front of* the noun that serves as its object. ἐκ and εἰς imply that someone or something is moving *out of* one environment and *into* another; ἐν implies that someone or something is *in* a certain environment, neither entering it nor moving out of it.

    ὦ   *(interjection used with a noun in the
                vocative)* O!

NOTE   ὦ and the vocative used with it normally come in the **interior** of a sentence, but they may be placed at the start of the sentence for emphasis. When addressing someone, it is more customary to *add* ὦ than to leave it out; since ὦ is far more common and familiar-sounding in Greek than "O!" is in English, it is often best to omit it from your translation. ὦ **is never used alone; it is *not* equivalent to our exclamatory "oh!".**

33.   **EXERCISES**

 A. **Greek-to-English Sentences**

HINT   If you see a noun that can serve as the subject, *substitute* that noun for the "he," "she," "it," or "they" that you would have used if there had been no nominative noun in the sentence and you had had to rely solely on the verb-ending. Your sentence should *not* read, for example, "The goddess she is eager."

1. μὴ πεμπέτω τὰς ἐπιστολὰς ἐκ τῆς σκηνῆς.
2. ἐν τῇ ἀγορᾷ φυλάττειν οὐ σπεύδομεν.
3. πέμπε, ὦ θεά, τῇ χώρᾳ τὴν ἡσυχίαν.
4. ἐκ τῶν σκηνῶν καὶ εἰς τὴν ἀγορὰν σπεύδουσιν.
5. καὶ τῇ θεᾷ γράφεις τὴν ἐπιστολήν;
6. φυλάττετε, ὦ θεαί, ἐν ταῖς σκηναῖς τὰς ἐπιστολάς.
7. ἐκ τῆς ἀγορᾶς κλέπτετε καὶ τὰς σκηνάς;

8. τὰς ἐπιστολὰς τῶν θεῶν πέμπει εἰς τὴν χώρᾱν.
9. ἡ θεὰ καὶ τὴν ἀγορὰν καὶ τὴν χώρᾱν φυλάττει.
10. σπεύδω ταῖς θεαῖς θύειν· τὴν ἡσυχίᾱν πέμπουσιν αἱ θεαί.

B.   English-to-Greek Sentences

1. We are writing, and we wish to send the message into the country.
2. Do you (*sg.*) sacrifice also to the goddess of the marketplace?
3. He is not guarding the tents in the countryside.
4. Let them not steal the letters out of the marketplaces!
5. Tranquillity, hasten into the land of the goddess!

LESSON 5

FIRST DECLENSION
Feminine Nouns, Part 2

ἀλλὰ καὶ ὥρη / εὕδειν (But there is also a time for sleeping.)
—comment by Odysseus in Homer's *Odyssey* 11.330-331

34.   In the Attic dialect a **short alpha** was allowed to creep into the **nominative, accusative**, and **vocative singular** endings of *some* ᾱ-stem and *some* η-stem nouns, thus creating two relatively small (but still important) **subcategories of first-declension feminine nouns**:

Singular:		("fate")	("sea")	Endings:	
	Nominative	μοῖρα	θάλαττα	-α	-α
	Genitive	μοίρᾱς	θαλάττης	-ᾱς	-ης
	Dative	μοίρᾳ	θαλάττῃ	-ᾳ	-ῃ
	Accusative	μοῖραν	θάλατταν	-αν	-αν
	Vocative	μοῖρα	θάλαττα	-α	-α

Plural:					
	Nominative	μοῖραι	θάλατται	-αι	-αι
	Genitive	μοιρῶν	θαλαττῶν	-ων	-ων
	Dative	μοίραις	θαλάτταις	-αις	-αις
	Accusative	μοίρᾱς	θαλάττᾱς	-ᾱς	-ᾱς
	Vocative	μοῖραι	θάλατται	-αι	-αι

The plurals of these nouns are no different from the plurals of the nouns in Lesson 4. The singulars are not difficult if you keep in mind that **a short alpha in the nominative dictates that the accusative and vocative singular will also have a short alpha**. In a noun like μοῖρα the circumflex over the penult confirms that the alpha in the nominative singular ending is **short** (the accent would be acute if the α were long, as it

29

is, for example, in the genitive singular ending: μοίρᾱς). If a noun's genitive singular ending has an eta, but its nominative singular ending has an alpha (e.g., θάλαττα, -ης), you can be sure that the α in the nominative singular ending is **short**.

The accent of these nouns is **persistent** with the two peculiarities characteristic of first declension (i.e., circumflexes on the ultima of genitive and dative singular and plural, if accented; genitive plural always accented on the ultima). Notice how the acute in θάλαττα is "pulled" from the antepenult to the penult when the case-ending is a long syllable (e.g., θαλάττης).

35.　　　　**Reflexive use of the definite article.** The definite article is often used in a **reflexive** sense to indicate someone or something that **belongs to the subject, has some relation to it, or is a physical part of it.** Thus, when the Greek literally says, "Teachers earn *the* salaries," "Do you love *the* father?", "We are washing *the* hands," it may actually mean, "Teachers earn *their* salaries," "Do you love *your* father?", "We are washing *our* hands." The context will make clear when the article has this reflexive sense. Example:

ἡ δέσποινα κελεύει **τὰς** θεραπαίνᾱς.
"The lady commands **her own** servants."

36.　　　　**VOCABULARY**

ἀκούω　　　　　　　(+ *genitive or accusative*) hear, listen, listen to [cf. *acoustics*]

NOTE　　　　The **genitive case** is used if it is a *person* who is being heard, the **accusative case** if it is an actual *sound* that is being heard. This makes sense since a person could be the source of a sound, but never the sound itself.

βλάπτω　　　　　　harm, hurt
κελεύω　　　　　　(*with accusative or dative + infinitive*) order (to), command (to), urge (to)

NOTE　　　　The person who receives the order to do something may appear in either the **accusative** or the **dative** case. If the speaker regards the person as the subject of the infinitive (i.e., as the doer of the commanded action), then the accusative case is appropriate—a grammar point that will be discussed in later lessons. If the speaker thinks of the person as the recipient of the order, then the dative case (designating an indirect object) is preferable. Feel free to use whichever of the two cases you wish; your choice will not affect the basic meaning of the sentence.

δέσποινα, -ης, ἡ	mistress (*of the household*), lady, Lady (*title for a goddess*)
θάλαττα, -ης, ἡ	sea [cf. *thalassocracy*]
θεράπαινα, -ης, ἡ	servant (*female*), maid
κλίνη, -ης, ἡ	couch, bed [cf. *clinic*]
μοῖρα, -ᾱς, ἡ	destiny, fate; Μοῖρα = Destiny or Fate (*personified as a goddess*)
ὥρᾱ, -ᾱς, ἡ	season, hour; (*with accusative or dative + infinitive*) it is time (to) [cf. *horoscope, hour*]

NOTE
When ὥρᾱ is combined with an **infinitive,** you will very often find that the sentence appears to have no main verb. Actually it is just that the speaker has chosen to leave out the word for "is," assuming that you will supply it. The best way to translate the idiom into English is to begin with "it is" ("it is the hour to..." or, more simply, "it is time to..."). The person who is expected to do the action is put into the **accusative** or the **dative** case, depending on the speaker's point of view (see the note above on κελεύω). Example: ὥρᾱ τὴν θεράπαιναν [or τῇ θεραπαίνῃ] θύειν ("it is time for the maid to offer sacrifice").

ἐπεί or ἐπειδή	(*conjunction*) when, after, since, because

NOTE
ἐπεί and ἐπειδή are virtually synonymous: each introduces a subordinate adverbial clause that tells when or why the main action of the sentence occurs. The context will show whether the clause is temporal (indicating the time at which something happens) or causal (indicating the reason for its happening).

37.   **EXERCISES**

A.   **Greek-to-English Sentences**

1. ὥρᾱ κελεύειν τὰς δεσποίνᾱς θύειν ταῖς θεαῖς;
2. ἐκ τῆς θαλάττης σπεύδουσι καὶ κλέπτουσι τὰς σκηνάς.
3. ἡ Μοῖρα μὴ ἐθελέτω κλέπτειν τὴν ἡσυχίᾱν ἐκ τῆς χώρᾱς.
4. ἐπεὶ ἡ δέσποινα παιδεύει, σπεύδομεν ἀκούειν.
5. μὴ βλάπτε, ὦ Μοῖρα δέσποινα, τὰς θεραπαίνᾱς.
6. οὐκ ἐθέλω γράφειν τὴν ἐπιστολὴν τῇ δεσποίνῃ.
7. φύλαττε, ὦ θεὰ τῆς χώρᾱς, τὰς σκηνὰς ἐν τῇ ἡσυχίᾳ.
8. γράφεις, ὦ θεράπαινα, ἐν τῇ κλίνῃ; οὐχ ὥρᾱ πέμπειν ἐπιστολάς.
9. ἄκουε τῆς θεᾶς ἐπειδὴ κελεύει· σπεῦδε ἐκ τῆς κλίνης.
10. καὶ τὰς θεραπαίνᾱς πέμπουσιν εἰς τὴν χώρᾱν.

B. **English-to-Greek Sentences**

1. Also order (*pl.*) the maids to hasten out of their beds.
2. Mistress, do you wish to send a message to the countryside?
3. Since they are guarding the market, we are writing in the tent.
4. It is time to sacrifice to Lady Destiny; I hear the goddess.
5. Let the sea not harm the (*female*) servants!

C. **READING**

A FOWL PLAN BACKFIRES
(Aesop's Fable 55)

NOTE   Unfamiliar words are glossed below.

Ἐπειδὴ ἡ δέσποινα ἀκούει τοῦ ἀλεκτρυόνος, κελεύει τὰς θεραπαίνᾱς
σπεύδειν ἐκ τῶν κλῑνῶν καὶ πονεῖν. αἱ θεράπαιναι τῆς δεσποίνης οὐκ
ἐθέλουσι πονεῖν· θύουσι τὸν ἀλεκτρυόνα. ἡ δέσποινα, ἐπειδὴ οὐκ ἀκούει τοῦ
ἀλεκτρυόνος, ἀγνοεῖ τὴν ὥρᾱν καὶ ἐννυχέστερον κελεύει τὰς
5   θεραπαίνᾱς πονεῖν. τὸ ἴδιον βούλευμα τὰς θεραπαίνᾱς βλάπτει.

VOCABULARY

τοῦ ἀλεκτρυόνος (line 1): the rooster (*genitive singular of* ἀλεκτρυών, *a third-declension masculine noun, preceded by the definite article*)

πονεῖν (line 2): from πονέω: work, labor (*a contract verb—the rationale for its accent will be explained in a later lesson*)

τὸν ἀλεκτρυόνα (line 3): the rooster (*accusative singular*)

ἀγνοεῖ (line 4): from ἀγνοέω: not know, be ignorant of (*another contract verb with an accent to be explained later*)

ἐννυχέστερον (line 4): (*adverb*) earlier in the morning (*literally* "more in the night")

τὸ ἴδιον βούλευμα (line 5): their own plan (*literally* "the personal plan"; *nominative singular of* βούλευμα, *a third-declension neuter noun, preceded by the definite article and an adjective*)

LESSON 6

Ω-VERBS
Future Active Indicative,
Future Active Infinitive

δειπνήσειν μέλλομεν, ἦ τί; (Are we going to have dinner, or what?)
—question asked by Euelpides in Aristophanes' *Birds* 464

38. The **future tense** (active voice) of the indicative mood uses the same endings as the present tense (active voice): -ω, -εις, -ει, -ομεν, -ετε, -ουσι(ν). Remember that each of these is actually a combination of a thematic vowel (ε/ο) and a personal ending. These six endings are added to the **future stem**, which is generally just the **present stem + the tense-marker σ**:

FUTURE ACTIVE INDICATIVE   Endings:
SG.:

παιδεύσω	("I shall teach/shall be teaching")	-σ -ω
παιδεύσεις	("you [*sg.*] will teach/will be teaching")	-σ -εις
παιδεύσει	("he/she/it will teach/will be teaching")	-σ -ει

PL.:

παιδεύσομεν	("we shall teach/shall be teaching")	-σ -ομεν
παιδεύσετε	("you [*pl.*] will teach/will be teaching")	-σ -ετε
παιδεύσουσι(ν)	("they will teach/will be teaching")	-σ -ουσι(ν)

Notice that the accent is **recessive,** as expected in finite verb forms, and that **movable ν** is added to the third-person plural. While the present tense is much more likely to have imperfective than aoristic aspect, the future tense is *just as likely* to have **aoristic aspect** (e.g., "we *shall eat* dinner when we are hungry") as it is to have **imperfective aspect**

33

(e.g., "we *shall be eating* dinner for an hour"). The future tense may be translated with "shall," "will," or "am/are/is going to."

If the present stem ends in a vowel or a diphthong, adding a sigma to form the future stem presents no complications. If the present stem ends in a consonant, however, the collision between the consonant and the sigma produces either a double consonant (ψ, ξ) or a phonetic change of some sort, designed to avoid roughness in sound. (The Greeks always strove for **euphony,** a pleasing blend of sounds.) These are the euphonic changes that normally take place:

Stem ending in a labial:	-π, -β, -φ	+ σ = **ψ**
Stem ending in a dental:	-τ, -δ, -θ	+ σ = σσ; one σ drops out: **σ**
Stem ending in a palatal:	-κ, -γ, -χ	+ σ = **ξ**
Stem ending in ππ:	-ππ	+ σ = πτσ; dental τ drops out; π + σ = **ψ**
Stem ending in ττ[1]:	-ττ	+ σ = **ξ**

NOTE   What happens when a stem ends in a **liquid** (λ, ρ), a **nasal** (μ, ν), or ζ will be explained in a later lesson.

Many Greek verbs are irregular in the future tense; this means that knowing how a verb's future *should* look is no guarantee that it *will* look that way! Fortunately the dictionary will always give you the first-person singular future active indicative as the verb's **second principal part** (e.g., παιδεύσω). Dropping the personal ending -ω will leave you with the future stem.

From now on, you will have to learn **two** principal parts for each verb. Here are the first two principal parts of each of the verbs in Lessons 3-5; being able to recognize euphonic changes should help you memorize the forms:

ἀκούω, ἀκούσομαι[2]   κλέπτω, κλέψω
βλάπτω, βλάψω   παιδεύω, παιδεύσω
γράφω, γράψω   πέμπω, πέμψω
ἐθέλω, ἐθελήσω[3]   σπεύδω, σπεύσω
θύω, θύσω   φυλάττω, φυλάξω
κελεύω, κελεύσω

39.   The **FUTURE ACTIVE INFINITIVE** ("to be going to teach") is made by adding the ending **-ειν** (thematic vowel ε + εν; ε + ε $\rightarrow$ ει) to the

---

[1] The letters ττ in a present stem represent κι, γι, or χι, i.e., a palatal followed by a y-sound (consonantal ι), so they act like a single palatal, not like two dentals.

[2] During the Classical age the future tense of ἀκούω always had the endings for middle voice, even though its meaning was active. The forms with active endings (ἀκούσω, ἀκούσεις, etc.) came into use later in antiquity. You will not be asked to translate or compose sentences with the future tense of ἀκούω until you have learned the middle voice (Lesson 11).

[3] ἐθέλω forms its future stem by adding *both* a lengthened thematic vowel (ε becomes η) and a sigma to its present stem: ἐθελήσω. One of the verbs introduced in this lesson, μέλλω, forms its future stem in the same way: μελλήσω.

future stem: παιδεύσειν. Its accent is **recessive**. It may have *either* **imperfective aspect** (e.g., "to be going to be teaching for a while") or **aoristic aspect** (e.g., "to be going to teach on one occasion"). The context will show which aspect is intended.

From a logical standpoint, it would seem that Greek should not need a future infinitive: its three other infinitives (present, aorist, perfect) should be sufficient to indicate aspect (imperfective, aoristic, or perfective), and, as a rule, Greek infinitives do *not* indicate time. There are, however, important exceptions to this rule. In certain instances (to be discussed in later lessons), infinitives *can* show time relative to that of the main verb; in such cases a future infinitive is needed to denote an action occurring *subsequent* to the time of the main verb.

In the vocabulary list at the end of each lesson, the notation (+ *infinitive*) indicates that a present infinitive, an aorist infinitive, or, rarely, a perfect infinitive—but <u>not</u> a future infinitive—may be used to complete the idea expressed by the verb. The only verb in this textbook that ever takes a future infinitive as its complement is **μέλλω** ("I am about," "I intend"), and even with **μέλλω** the present infinitive is a common substitute for the future infinitive. Saying μέλλω παιδεύσειν or παιδεύειν ("I am about to teach") is equivalent to saying παιδεύσω ("I am going to teach"). By itself or with a present infinitive, **μέλλω** may also mean "I delay" or "I hesitate" (e.g. μὴ μέλλε, "don't delay!"; μέλλω παιδεύειν, "I hesitate to teach"). Thus, **μέλλω + future infinitive** will always mean "I am about/ intend to....," while **μέλλω + present infinitive** will mean either "I delay/ hesistate to...." or "I am about/ intend to....," depending on the context.

40.   **VOCABULARY**

         ἀλλάττω, ἀλλάξω   change, alter [cf. *parallax*]

NOTE   ἀλλάττω does not mean "I change" in the sense of "I become different"; rather, it means "I make something or someone change." Thus, in the active voice, it always has a direct object with it; i.e., it is always **transitive**.

         διώκω, διώξω   pursue, chase, hunt, drive away, banish

         ἔχω, ἕξω/σχήσω   have, hold, possess; (+ *infinitive*) be able (to) [cf. *cathexis*]

NOTE   ἕξω has imperfective aspect ("I shall possess [for a period of time]"), while σχήσω has aoristic aspect ("I shall get hold of [on a particular occasion]").

         μέλλω, μελλήσω   (+ *future infinitive or present infinitive*) be about (to), intend (to); (+ *present infinitive*) delay (to), hesitate (to)

κόρη, -ης, ἡ	maiden, girl, daughter; **Κόρη** = Maiden (*another name for Persephone, daughter of the goddess Demeter*) [cf. *hypocorism*]

NOTE   κόρη is an exception to the rule that, in Attic, ᾱ after ρ never changes to η.

οἰκίᾱ, -ᾱς, ἡ	house, household
ἔτι	(*adverb*) still, yet, longer
μηκέτι	(*adverb*) no longer, no more
οὐκέτι	(*adverb*) no longer, no more

NOTE   μηκέτι is used wherever μή would be appropriate (e.g., with imperative mood), οὐκέτι wherever οὐ would be appropriate (e.g., with indicative mood).

πάλιν	(*adverb*) back, backwards, again, once more [cf. *palimpsest, palindrome*]
ἀλλά (ἀλλ᾽)	(*conjunction*) but (ἀλλ᾽ *is written before a vowel*)

NOTE   A Greek word ending in a short vowel is usually **elided** (i.e., the final vowel is dropped and no longer pronounced) when it comes before a word starting with a vowel. These **elisions** are often taken for granted and left unmarked in manuscripts, but in a few common words that are frequently elided, it is conventional to mark the elision with an apostrophe; ἀλλά is one of those words.

41.   **EXERCISES**

A.   Greek-to-English Sentences

1. μέλλεις πάλιν θύσειν τῇ θεᾷ; φυλάξομεν τὴν σκηνήν.
2. παιδεύσω καὶ κελεύσω, ἀλλ᾽ οὐκ ἐθελήσεις ἀκούειν.
3. μὴ μέλλε τὰς θεραπαίνᾱς εἰς τὴν οἰκίᾱν πάλιν πέμπειν.
4. ἐν τῇ σκηνῇ ἔχω γράφειν τὰς ἐπιστολάς, ἀλλὰ θύειν οὐκ ἔχω.
5. κελευέτω ἡ δέσποινα ταῖς θεραπαίναις ἔτι φυλάττειν τὴν οἰκίᾱν.
6. ἐπεὶ ὥρᾱ γράφειν τὴν ἐπιστολὴν τῇ κόρῃ, οὐ μελλήσω γράφειν.
7. αἱ θεαὶ ἐκ τῆς χώρᾱς καὶ εἰς τὴν θάλατταν σπεύσουσιν.

8. μέλλει διώξειν τὰς κόρᾱς; οὐκέτι ἕξομεν τὴν ἡσυχίᾱν.

9. ἄκουε τῆς θεραπαίνης, ὦ δέσποινα, καὶ μηκέτι βλάπτε.

10. ἐκ τῆς ἀγορᾶς κλέψειν μέλλετε τὰς κλίνᾱς;

B. **English-to-Greek Sentences**

1. Shall we pursue the maids into the market?

2. I intend to educate the girls, mistress, since I still have leisure.

3. They will guard the tents, but they will not write the letters.

4. Will you (*sg.*) be able to change your destiny in the countryside?

5. It is time to sacrifice to the goddess; let them not hesitate to hasten out of the house.

C. **READING**

OLD HABITS NEVER DIE
(Aesop's Fable 50)

Ἡ Ἀφροδίτη γαλῆν εἰς κόρην ἀλλάττει. τὴν κόρην νεᾱνίᾱς γαμεῖ. ἀλλ᾽ ἡ θεὰ μέλλει τῆς κόρης πειρᾶσειν. τοὺς τρόπους τῆς γαλῆς ἔτι ἕξει ἡ κόρη; ἡ Ἀφροδίτη μῦν πέμπει εἰς τὴν οἰκίᾱν τῆς κόρης. τὸν μῦν ἡ κόρη διώξει; μὴ δίωκε, ὦ κόρη· γαλῆ οὐκέτι εἶ. ἀλλ᾽ ἡ κόρη τὸν μῦν διώκει. ἡ θεὰ τὴν κόρην εἰς γαλῆν πάλιν ἀλλάττει. οὐκ ἔχει καὶ ἡ Ἀφροδίτη ἀλλάττειν τοὺς τρόπους.

VOCABULARY

Ἀφροδίτη (line 1): from Ἀφροδίτη, -ης, ἡ: Aphrodite, goddess of love

γαλῆν (line 1): from γαλῆ (*contracted from* γαλέη), -ῆς, ἡ: weasel

νεᾱνίᾱς (line 1): young man (*nominative singular of a first-declension masculine noun*)

γαμεῖ (line 1): from γαμέω, γαμῶ (*a contract verb*): take as a wife, marry

πειρᾶσειν (line 2): from πειράω, πειρᾶσω (*another contract verb*) (+ *genitive*): test, make trial (of)

τοὺς τρόπους (line 2): the habits, character (*accusative plural of* τρόπος, *a second-declension masculine noun, preceded by the definite article*)

μῦν (line 3): mouse (*accusative singular of* μῦς, *a third-declension masculine noun; used with the definite article later in the line*)

εἶ (line 4): you are (*second-person singular present active indicative of the irregular verb meaning "be"*)

LESSON 7

SECOND DECLENSION
Masculine Nouns

ὑπὸ παντὶ λίθῳ σκορπίον, ὦ ἑταῖρε, φυλάσσεο
(Beware, comrade, of a scorpion under every stone.) —Praxilla, fragment 4

42.   We are not quite finished with the first declension (its masculine subgroup remains to be discussed in Lesson 9), but we are going to put it aside temporarily and devote the next two chapters to the **second declension.** Nouns in this declension can be divided into two groups: masculines and neuters. The masculines are covered in this lesson, the neuters in Lesson 8. You will be glad to learn that the second declension has fewer complications than the first!

43.   All **second-declension masculines** have the same set of endings; there are no variations caused by features of the Attic dialect. The endings resemble those of the first declension, but with o, not ᾱ or η, as the stem-vowel. Here are two typical **o-stem** masculine nouns:

Singular:	("human being")	("river")	Endings:
Nominative	ἄνθρωπος	ποταμός	-ος
Genitive	ἀνθρώπου	ποταμοῦ	-ου
Dative	ἀνθρώπῳ	ποταμῷ	-ῳ
Accusative	ἄνθρωπον	ποταμόν	-ον
Vocative	ἄνθρωπε	ποταμέ	-ε
Plural:			
Nominative	ἄνθρωποι	ποταμοί	-οι
Genitive	ἀνθρώπων	ποταμῶν	-ων
Dative	ἀνθρώποις	ποταμοῖς	-οις
Accusative	ἀνθρώπους	ποταμούς	-ους
Vocative	ἄνθρωποι	ποταμοί	-οι

Notice that the accent is **persistent,** remaining above the same letters as in the nominative case unless a long ultima forces it to move (e.g., ἄνθρωπος but ἀνθρώπου). Just as in the first declension, **the genitive and dative singular and plural endings, if accented, have the circumflex,** not the acute. Unlike first-declension nouns, however, second-declension nouns **do** *not* **invariably accent the genitive plural on the ultima;** instead, the accent behaves as you would expect (e.g., in ἀνθρώπων the accent is *not* placed above the ultima, but tries to remain in its preferred position above ἀν-, only to be pulled to the penult by the long ultima).

In second-declension masculines **the vocative singular is** *not* **identical with the nominative singular** (e.g., nominative ἄνθρωπος but vocative ἄνθρωπε). (Reminder: the vocative *plural* is always identical with the nominative *plural*, no matter what the declension.) There are two peculiarities you should be aware of: during the Classical age, θεός ("god") was not used in the vocative singular, but vocatives θεός and θεέ appear in later writings; the vocative singular of ἀδελφός ("brother") is (illogically) accented on the antepenult (ἄδελφε), not on the ultima.

44. The masculine forms of the **definite article** look very much like the endings of second-declension masculine nouns:

NOM. MASC. SG.:	ὁ	**NOM. MASC. PL.:**	οἱ
GEN. MASC. SG.:	τοῦ	**GEN. MASC. PL.:**	τῶν
DAT. MASC. SG.:	τῷ	**DAT. MASC. PL.:**	τοῖς
ACC. MASC. SG.:	τόν	**ACC. MASC. PL.:**	τούς

The nominatives ὁ and οἱ are **proclitics** (like οὐ, εἰς, ἐκ, ἐν, ἡ, and αἱ) and have no accent. As with the feminine forms of the article, there is no vocative case.

45. Occasionally a word will have the endings of an o-stem masculine noun but will actually be **feminine.** Its unusual gender will be shown, not by the form of the noun itself, but by the form of words that modify it (e.g., a definite article or an adjective). In ὁ λόγος and ἡ ὁδός, for example, the articles reveal that λόγος, in conformity with its appearance, is masculine, while ὁδός, contrary to its appearance, is feminine.

Some second-declension nouns may be *either* **masculine or feminine,** often with a major difference in meaning: ὁ ἄνθρωπος ("man"), ἡ ἄνθρωπος ("woman"); ὁ θεός ("god"), ἡ θεός ("goddess"—a synonym for θεά). Such words are called **epicene** and are said to have **common gender**. In a vocabulary list an epicene noun will always be accompanied by two definite articles (ὁ, ἡ).

46. **Dative of Means and Dative of Manner.** A noun in the dative case may indicate the **means** or the instrument by which something is done (e.g., σπεύδομεν τῇ ὁδῷ, "we are hastening by means of the road"; βλάπτεις τὸν ἵππον λίθοις, "you are hurting the horse with stones"). It may also show the manner or the way in which something is done (e.g., παιδεύω χαρᾷ, "I teach with joy" or "I teach joyfully"). The dative of means is usually translated with the preposition *with* or *by*; the dative of manner is usually translated with the preposition *with* or with an adverb formed from the noun and ending in *-ly*. In Greek **no preposition** is required for either the dative of means or the dative of manner.

47.	**VOCABULARY**	

<table>
<tr><td></td><td>χαίρω, χαιρήσω</td><td>be happy; (+ dative) rejoice (in), take delight (in)</td></tr>
</table>

NOTE   Like ἐθέλω and μέλλω, χαίρω forms its future by adding both η and σ to its present stem. The imperatives χαῖρε and χαίρετε are frequently used as greetings ("be happy!"—i.e., "hello!") or as parting words ("be happy!"—i.e., "farewell!").

<table>
<tr><td>ἀδελφή, -ῆς, ἡ</td><td>sister</td></tr>
<tr><td>ἀδελφός, -οῦ, ὁ</td><td>(voc. sg. ἄδελφε) brother [cf. Philadelphia]</td></tr>
<tr><td>ἄνθρωπος, -ου, ὁ, ἡ</td><td>(masc.) human being, person, man, mankind, humankind; (fem.) woman, womankind [cf. anthropology, philanthropic]</td></tr>
</table>

NOTE   ὁ ἄνθρωπος in its generic sense ("mankind" or "humankind") can, and usually does, include *both* men and women; ἡ ἄνθρωπος in its generic sense ("womankind") never includes men. Likewise οἱ ἄνθρωποι means either "men" or "people," whereas αἱ ἄνθρωποι means "women" exclusively. In the vocative the word often has a harsh ring; e.g., ἀκούεις, ἄνθρωπε; ("are you listening, man?").

<table>
<tr><td>θεός, -οῦ, ὁ, ἡ</td><td>(voc. sg. θεός or θεέ) (masc.) god; (fem.) goddess [cf. theology, atheist]</td></tr>
<tr><td>ἵππος, -ου, ὁ, ἡ</td><td>(masc.) horse; (fem.) mare [cf. hippodrome, Philip]</td></tr>
<tr><td>λίθος, -ου, ὁ</td><td>stone [cf. paleolithic, monolith]</td></tr>
<tr><td>λύπη, -ης, ἡ</td><td>pain, grief</td></tr>
<tr><td>ὁδός, -οῦ, ἡ</td><td>way, path, road, journey [cf. exodus, method]</td></tr>
<tr><td>ποταμός, -οῦ, ὁ</td><td>river [cf. hippopotamus, Mesopotamia]</td></tr>
<tr><td>χαρά, -ᾶς, ἡ</td><td>joy, delight</td></tr>
<tr><td>ἀπό (ἀπ', ἀφ')</td><td>(preposition + genitive) away from [cf. apocalypse, apogee, apology]</td></tr>
</table>

NOTE   The omicron of ἀπό is elided before a word beginning with a vowel, and the elision is usually marked with an apostrophe (ἀπ'). If the following word has rough breathing, the pi before the apostrophe is "roughened" into phi (ἀφ').

Unlike ἐκ, which indicates movement *from the interior* of one region into another, ἀπό indicates movement that begins *at the edge* of a place: "The fish are jumping out of (ἐκ) the river." "The horse is galloping away from (ἀπό) the river."

48.   **EXERCISES**

A.   **Greek-to-English Sentences**

1. μὴ μέλλετε πέμπειν τὰς θεραπαίνᾱς ἀπὸ τῆς ὁδοῦ.
2. ἐπεὶ οὐκέτι ἀκούει, μηκέτι γράφε τῇ ἀδελφῇ τὴν ἐπιστολήν.
3. οἱ θεοὶ ἔχουσιν ἀλλάττειν καὶ τὰς ὥρᾱς καὶ τοὺς ἀνθρώπους.
4. τοῖς λίθοις, ὦ ἄδελφε, μέλλεις βλάψειν τὰς οἰκίᾱς;
5. ἀκούετε, ὦ θεοί· φυλάττετε τὰς κόρᾱς καὶ ἐν τῇ ὁδῷ καὶ ἐν τῇ ἀγορᾷ.
6. κελεύσω τὸν ἵππον σπεύδειν ἀπὸ τοῦ ποταμοῦ καὶ εἰς τὴν ἀγορᾱ́ν.
7. χαῖρε, ὦ δέσποινα, τῇ μοίρᾳ· ἡ θεὸς χαρᾱς πέμψει εἰς τὴν οἰκίᾱν.
8. ὥρᾱ τοὺς ἀδελφοὺς τοῖς ἵπποις πάλιν σπεύδειν εἰς τὴν χώρᾱν.
9. θῡόντων χαρᾷ τῷ θεῷ καὶ διωκόντων τὴν λύπην ἀπὸ τῶν οἰκιῶν.
10. κλέπτεις, ὦ ἄνθρωπε, λίθους ἐκ τῆς ἀγορᾶς; ἐθέλεις βλάπτειν τὰς ὁδούς;

B.   **English-to-Greek Sentences**

1. Hello, brothers! Are you still taking delight in your journey?
2. Stones cannot harm a god, but a god can hurt a human being.
3. Listen, man! Send your sisters away from the house!
4. O gods, is grief once more going to chase joy out of the land?
5. When we command, let the horse hasten joyfully into the river.

C.   **READING**

FLEETING JOYS AND FLEEING FISH
(Aesop's Fable 13)

Ἁλιεῖς τὴν σαγήνην ἕλκουσιν ἐν τῷ ποταμῷ. ἐπειδὴ μέλλουσι σχήσειν πολλοὺς ἰχθῦς, χαίρουσι καὶ ὀρχοῦνται. ἀλλ' ἐπεὶ εἰς τὴν σαγήνην βλέπουσιν, οὐχ ὥρᾱ χαίρειν· ἔχουσι λίθους, οὐκ ἰχθῦς. οὐκέτι χαίρουσιν· οὐκέτι ὀρχοῦνται ἐν τῇ ὁδῷ. ἀλλ' ἡ ἐμπειρίᾱ παιδεύσει τοὺς ἁλιεῖς. οἱ θεοὶ τοῖς ἀνθρώποις χαρὰς
5 πέμπουσιν, ἀλλὰ καὶ λύπᾱς. ἡ λύπη ἀδελφὴ τῆς χαρᾶς ἐστιν.

VOCABULARY

ἁλιεῖς (line 1): fishermen (*nominative plural of* ἁλιεύς, *a third-declension masculine noun*)

σαγήνην (line 1): from σαγήνη, -ης, ἡ: net (*for fishing*)

ἕλκουσιν (line 1): from ἕλκω, ἕλξω: drag

πολλοὺς ἰχθῦς (line 2): many fish (*accusative plural of* ἰχθύς, *a third-declension masculine noun, modified by an adjective*)

ὀρχοῦνται (line 2): they dance (*third-person plural present middle indicative of* ὀρχέομαι, *a deponent verb —to be explained later*)

βλέπουσιν (line 2): from βλέπω, βλέψομαι: look

ἐμπειρίᾱ (line 4): from ἐμπειρίᾱ, -ᾱς, ἡ: experience

ἐστιν (line 5): is (*third-person singular present indicative of the verb "be"; it has no accent because it is an enclitic—to be explained later*)

LESSON 8

SECOND DECLENSION: Neuter Nouns; ADJECTIVES: First/Second Declension

κα σύ, τέκνον; (Even you, child?)
—Caesar's dying words to Brutus, quoted by Suetonius in *Julius Caesar* 82

49. Like second-declension masculines, **second-declension neuters** are o-stem nouns. They differ from masculines in the endings of the *nominative and vocative singular* and the *nominative, vocative, and accusative plural*:

Singular:	("gift")	("plant")	Endings:
Nominative	δῶρον	φυτόν	-ον (cf. masc. -ος)
Genitive	δώρου	φυτοῦ	-ου
Dative	δώρῳ	φυτῷ	-ῳ
Accusative	δῶρον	φυτόν	-ον
Vocative	δῶρον	φυτόν	-ον (cf. masc. -ε)
Plural:			
Nominative	δῶρα	φυτά	-α (cf. masc. -οι)
Genitive	δώρων	φυτῶν	-ων
Dative	δώροις	φυτοῖς	-οις
Accusative	δῶρα	φυτά	-α (cf. masc. -ους)
Vocative	δῶρα	φυτά	**-α (cf. masc. -οι)**

Just as in o-stem masculines, the accent of o-stem neuters is **persistent**, the genitive and dative singular and plural endings, if accented, have the **circumflex**, and the **genitive plural is *not* invariably accented on the ultima**.

In second-declension neuters (in fact, in *every* neuter noun in Greek), **the nominative, vocative, and accusative singular are identical, and the nominative, vocative, and accusative plural are identical.** This means that when you see an o-stem neuter ending in -ov or -α, you cannot tell, from its form alone, how it is being used. You must look at the rest of the sentence to find out whether the noun is the subject, the addressee, or the object. Compare the following sentences:

τὸν ἵππον διώκει τέκνον.	"A child is chasing the horse."
τὸν ἵππον δίωκε, τέκνον.	"Chase the horse, child!"
ὁ ἵππος διώκει τέκνον.	"The horse is chasing a child."

It requires logic to determine how the neuter noun τέκνον ("child") functions in each sentence: if "the horse" is accusative, it must be the object, and τέκνον must *not* be; if "the horse" is nominative, it must be the subject, and τέκνον must *not* be.

50.   The neuter forms of the **definite article** resemble the endings of second-declension neuter nouns (as usual, there is no vocative):

NOM. NEUT. SG.:	τό	**NOM. NEUT. PL.:**	τά
GEN. NEUT. SG.:	τοῦ	**GEN. NEUT. PL.:**	τῶν
DAT. NEUT. SG.:	τῷ	**DAT. NEUT. PL.:**	τοῖς
ACC. NEUT. SG.:	τό	**ACC. NEUT. PL.:**	τά

You now know all the forms of the definite article. They are traditionally listed in the order **masculine, feminine, neuter:**

SG.:	ὁ	ἡ	τό	PL.:	οἱ	αἱ	τά
	τοῦ	τῆς	τοῦ		τῶν	τῶν	τῶν
	τῷ	τῇ	τῷ		τοῖς	ταῖς	τοῖς
	τόν	τήν	τό		τούς	τάς	τά

51.   **Plural subject with singular verb.** When a neuter noun (of *any* declension, not just second) is used in the *plural* as the subject of a sentence, Greek does something that seems illogical: it puts the main verb of the sentence into the *singular.* Thus, the Greek version of the sentence "The children have horses" (τὰ τέκνα ἔχει ἵππους) literally means "The children *has* horses." Once in a while, to stress that the subject consists of more than one individual, a plural verb may be used, but most of the time **a neuter plural subject is regarded as a single collective unit, requiring a singular verb.** When translating sentences into Greek, assume that a neuter plural subject and its verb do *not* agree in number.

52.   This is a good time to introduce another of Greek's eight parts of speech. **Adjectives** are words that modify (i.e., describe) nouns. Unlike nouns, they are not "born" with a particular gender; each is merely a genderless stem waiting for an ending that will give it gender as well as number and case.

There are two types of adjectives in Greek, those with the same endings as first- and second-declension nouns and those with the same endings as third-declension nouns. In this lesson we are concerned with the first type only. Here are the paradigms of two **first/second-declension adjectives**:

Stems ending in -ε, -ι, ορ -ρ (ἄξιος, -α, -ον, "worthy"):

SG.:	Masc.	Fem.	Neut.	PL.:	Masc.	Fem.	Neut.
Nom.	ἄξιος	ἀξίᾱ	ἄξιον		ἄξιοι	ἄξιαι	ἄξια
Gen.	ἀξίου	ἀξίᾱς	ἀξίου		ἀξίων	ἀξίων	ἀξίων
Dat.	ἀξίῳ	ἀξίᾳ	ἀξίῳ		ἀξίοις	ἀξίαις	ἀξίοις
Acc.	ἄξιον	ἀξίᾱν	ἄξιον		ἀξίους	ἀξίᾱς	ἄξια
Voc.	ἄξιε	ἀξίᾱ	ἄξιον		ἄξιοι	ἄξιαι	ἄξια

Stems not ending in -ε, -ι, or -ρ (ἀγαθός, -ή, -όν, "good"):

SG.:	Masc.	Fem.	Neut.	PL.:	Masc.	Fem.	Neut.
Nom.	ἀγαθός	ἀγαθή	ἀγαθόν		ἀγαθοί	ἀγαθαί	ἀγαθά
Gen.	ἀγαθοῦ	ἀγαθῆς	ἀγαθοῦ		ἀγαθῶν	ἀγαθῶν	ἀγαθῶν
Dat.	ἀγαθῷ	ἀγαθῇ	ἀγαθῷ		ἀγαθοῖς	ἀγαθαῖς	ἀγαθοῖς
Acc.	ἀγαθόν	ἀγαθήν	ἀγαθόν		ἀγαθούς	ἀγαθάς	ἀγαθά
Voc.	ἀγαθέ	ἀγαθή	ἀγαθόν		ἀγαθοί	ἀγαθαί	ἀγαθά

Endings:	SG.:			PL.:			
	-ος	-ᾱ/-η	-ον		-οι	-αι	-α
	-ου	-ᾱς/-ης	-ου		-ων	-ων	-ων
	-ῳ	-ᾳ/-η	-ῳ		-οις	-αις	-οις
	-ον	-ᾱν/-ην	-ον		-ους	-ᾱς	-α
	-ε	-ᾱ/-η	-ον		-οι	-αι	-α

These adjective endings are a combination of the endings of second-declension masculine nouns, first-declension feminine nouns, and second-declension neuter nouns—all of which you already know. Adjectives with stems ending in ε, ι, or ρ have ᾱ rather than η in the feminine singular, as you would expect on the model of first-declension nouns.

Like nouns, adjectives have **persistent** accent: the preferred location for the accent is shown by the **masculine nominative singular**. In first/second-declension adjectives an accented ultima in the genitive and dative always has a *circumflex*, as in first- and second-declension nouns. The ultima is accented only if it is the preferred location for the accent; thus, in the feminine genitive plural, the accent does *not* always appear on the ultima, as it would in a first-declension noun.

Greek lexica do not tell you explicitly that a word is an adjective; instead they simply list its **nominative singular** forms: e.g., ἀγαθός, -ή, -όν.

53.   **A noun and its adjective must agree with each other.** This does not mean that the two words must have the same ending. It means only that the adjective's ending must indicate the **gender**, **number**, and **case** of the noun. In ἄξιος ἵππος the noun and adjective happen to have identical endings (since the ending that ἄξιος, -α, -ον uses to denote masculine nominative singular is the same as the nominative singular ending of ἵππος), but in ἀγαθὴ ὁδός the two endings are not identical (since the ending that ἀγαθός, -ή, -όν uses to denote feminine nominative singular is *not* the same as the nominative singular ending of ὁδός). Notice that an adjective's ending is a clue to the gender of the noun it modifies.

54.   **Position of adjectives.** If a definite article, an adjective, and a noun form a unit and act (or are acted upon) together in a sentence, the adjective is said to be **attributive** (e.g., *"the good child* lives here"; "they put *the good child* to bed"). If the adjective functions together with the main verb to describe the subject, the adjective is said to be **predicate** (e.g., "the child is *good*"), and the verb is called a **linking verb** because it links or equates the subject with the predicate adjective.

In Greek an adjective's position *in relation to a definite article* determines whether the adjective is attributive or predicate. An adjective has **attributive position** if it is **immediately preceded by a definite article** that agrees with the modified noun. In each of the following phrases the adjective is attributive:

τὸ ἀγαθὸν τέκνον	"the good child"
τὸ τέκνον τὸ ἀγαθόν	" the good child" (literally, "the child —the good one")
τέκνον τὸ ἀγαθόν	" the good child" (literally, "a child—the one that's good")

The most common location for an attributive adjective is *before* the noun that it modifies, as in the first example above; here the article does double duty, making the following adjective attributive and the following noun definite. It is not unusual, however, to find an attributive adjective (with its article) located *after* the noun; in such cases the emphasis is on the noun, and the adjective functions as a clarifying afterthought. Another article—identical to the one preceding the adjective—then precedes the noun and makes it definite, as in the second example. Occasionally the noun is left indefinite, as in the third example.

An adjective has **predicate position** if it is *not* **immediately preceded by a definite article** that agrees with the modified noun. Although a predicate adjective tends to come *after* the noun that it modifies, it may be placed *before* it for emphasis. Here are two examples:

τὸ τέκνον ἀγαθόν.   "The child [is] good."

ἀγαθὸν τὸ τέκνον.   "The child [is] good."

Greek frequently **omits the linking verb** when it is a form of "be," so a complete sentence may consist of just an article, a noun, and a *predicate* adjective. On the other hand, the result of combining an article, an *attributive* adjective, and a noun is always a mere phrase, never a complete sentence.

If the person or thing in the speaker's mind is **indefinite** or **unknown** (e.g., "a good child," not "the good child"; "good children," not "the good children"), *no definite article is used* with either the noun or its adjective (e.g., ἀγαθὸν τέκνον, τέκνον ἀγαθόν, ἀγαθὰ τέκνα, τέκνα ἀγαθά). To make a noun indefinite in the singular, English has to add the indefinite article (*a* or *an*), but Greek does not.

55.   A linking verb may equate the subject with a **predicate noun** rather than with a predicate adjective. A predicate noun always has the same case as the subject (**nominative**) since the two nouns are parallel to each other, but it retains its own gender and number. It is customary *not* to use a definite article with a predicate noun (e.g., οἱ ἵπποι δῶρον, "the horses are a/the gift"). **The absence of the article helps to distinguish the predicate noun from the subject**, but it also leaves ambiguous whether a definite or indefinite person or thing is meant.

56.   VOCABULARY

εὑρίσκω, εὑρήσω   find, find out, discover [cf. *eureka*]

NOTE   The basic stem of this verb is εὑρ-; adding -ισκ- produces the present stem; adding a lengthened thematic vowel + sigma produces the future stem.

λείπω, λείψω   leave, leave behind [cf. *eclipse, ellipsis*]

NOTE   λείπω does *not* mean "leave" in the sense of "go away" (intransitive, requiring no direct object), but in the sense of "leave behind" (transitive, always with a direct object). It is often combined with a prefix; ἀπολείπω, for example, is a stronger form of λείπω, meaning "leave," "leave behind," or "abandon."

βίος, -ου, ὁ   life, lifetime, livelihood [cf. *biology*]

δῶρον, -ου, τό   gift [cf. *Dorothy, Theodore*]

ἔργον, -ου, τό   work, task, occupation, deed [cf. *ergometer*]

θησαυρός, -οῦ, ὁ   treasure, treasury, storehouse [cf. *thesaurus*]

τέκνον, -ου, τό	child, offspring
φυτόν, -οῦ, τό	plant, tree (*something that is grown in a garden or an orchard*) [cf. *neophyte*]
ἀγαθός, -ή, -όν	good (*at doing something*), brave, (*morally*) good, virtuous [cf. *Agatha*]
ἄξιος, -ᾱ, -ον	worthy; (+ *genitive or infinitive*) worthy (of, to), deserving (of, to) [cf. *axiom*]
καλός, -ή, -όν	beautiful, handsome, fair (*of appearance*), (*morally*) good, fine, noble [cf. *calisthenics, kaleidoscope*]

57. **EXERCISES**

A. **Greek-to-English Sentences**

1. μηκέτι πέμπετε λύπᾱς, ὦ θεοί, τοῖς ἀγαθοῖς ἀνθρώποις.

2. τὰ φυτὰ τὰ καλὰ ἐθέλω κλέπτειν ἐκ τῆς χώρᾱς.

3. λειπέτω τὴν οἰκίᾱν τῆς ἀξίᾱς δεσποίνης καὶ σπευδέτω εἰς τὴν ἀγορᾱν.

4. μέλλεις, ὦ Μοῖρα, ἀλλάξειν τὸν βίον τῆς ἀνθρώπου τῆς ἀγαθῆς;

5. τὰ τέκνα ἀπὸ τῆς οἰκίᾱς σπεύδει καὶ οὐκέτι φυλάττει τὸν θησαυρόν.

6. μὴ μέλλε, ὦ ἄνθρωπε, διώκειν τὸν καλὸν ἵππον ἐκ τῆς ὁδοῦ.

7. ὥρᾱ παιδεύειν, ἀλλ᾽ οὐκ ἔχομεν εὑρίσκειν ἐν τῇ σκηνῇ τὰ τέκνα.

8. ἐν τῇ οἰκίᾳ εὑρήσουσιν αἱ κόραι τὰς κλίνᾱς τὰς καλάς.

9. αἱ ἀγαθαὶ θεράπαιναι ἄξιαι καὶ τῶν δώρων καὶ τῶν χαρῶν.

10. χαῖρε, ὦ ἄδελφε· ἡ χώρᾱ καλή· καλὸς ὁ βίος· ἡ ἡσυχίᾱ θησαυρός.

B. **English-to-Greek Sentences**

1. The handsome brothers possess beautiful trees and fine horses.

2. Let him once more send worthy gifts to his noble sister.

3. Leave behind your work, fair maid, and take delight in life.

4. When I shall find the good road, I shall hasten joyfully into the countryside.

5. Are you still intending to abandon your children, man?

C.   READING

THE TREASURE HUNT
(Aesop's Fable 42)

Γεωργὸς ἄξιος μέλλει ἀπολείψειν τὸν βίον καὶ ἐθέλει τῶν τέκνων πειρᾶν. Τὸν βίον ἀπολείψω, ὦ τέκνα, ἀλλ᾽ ἐν τῇ ἀμπέλῳ εὑρήσετε θησαυρόν. χαίρετε. ἐπεὶ ὁ γεωργὸς ὁ ἀγαθὸς τὸν βίον ἀπολείπει, οἱ ἀδελφοὶ σπεύδουσιν ἐν τῇ ἀμπέλῳ σκάπτειν. οὐκ ἔχουσιν εὑρίσκειν τὸν καλὸν θησαυρόν, ἀλλὰ τῷ ἀξίῳ ἔργῳ

5   ποιοῦσι τὰ φυτὰ τῆς ἀμπέλου καλά. τοῖς τέκνοις οὐ δῆλον τὸ ἀγαθὸν δῶρον τοῦ γεωργοῦ· τὸ ἔργον θησαυρὸς τοῖς ἀνθρώποις.

VOCABULARY

γεωργός (line 1): from γεωργός (*a compound of* γῆ "*earth*" + ἔργον), -οῦ, ὁ: farmer (*literally*, "one who works the earth")

πειρᾶν (line 1): pres. act. infin. of the contract verb πειράω, -άσω (+ *gen.*): test, make trial (of)

ἀμπέλῳ (line 2): from ἄμπελος, -ου, ἡ: vineyard, vine

σκάπτειν (line 4): from σκάπτω, σκάψω: dig

ποιοῦσι (line 5): from the contract verb ποιέω, ποιήσω: make

δῆλον (line 5): from δῆλος, -η, -ον: clear, visible, evident

LESSON 9

FIRST DECLENSION
Masculine Nouns;
SUBSTANTIVES

εἷς ἐστι δοῦλος οἰκίᾱς ὁ δεσπότης
(The master is a slave to his household.)
—Menander, fragment 716

58.　　　　We now return to the **first declension**. Besides the feminine ᾱ-stem
and η-stem nouns and their subcategories (Lessons 4 and 5), there exist
masculine ᾱ-stem and η-stem nouns. They are identical to the feminines
except in the nominative, genitive, and vocative singular:

Singular:	("student")	("youth")	Endings:	
Nominative	μαθητής	νεᾱνίᾱς	-ης	-ᾱς
Genitive	μαθητοῦ	νεᾱνίου	-ου	-ου
Dative	μαθητῇ	νεᾱνίᾳ	-ῃ	-ᾳ
Accusative	μαθητήν	νεᾱνίᾱν	-ην	-ᾱν
Vocative	μαθητά	νεᾱνίᾱ	-α/η	-ᾱ
Plural:				
Nominative	μαθηταί	νεᾱνίαι	-αι	-αι
Genitive	μαθητῶν	νεᾱνιῶν	-ων	-ων
Dative	μαθηταῖς	νεᾱνίαις	-αις	-αις
Accusative	μαθητάς	νεᾱνίᾱς	-ᾱς	-ᾱς
Vocative	μαθηταί	νεᾱνίαι	-αι	-αι

Like first-declension feminines in Attic, first-declension masculines
in Attic keep their original ᾱ after ε, ι, or ρ, but otherwise change it to η.
In the **nominative singular** the masculines have -ς added to ᾱ or η; in the
genitive singular they have -ου (borrowed from second declension) substituting for -ᾱς or -ης. The **vocative singular of ᾱ-stems** *always* ends in a
long alpha. The **vocative singular of η-stems** ends in a short alpha if the

53

nominative ends in -της (e.g., μαθητής) or if the word is a compound (e.g., βυρσοδέψης; see the reading for this lesson) or the name of a nationality (e.g., Πέρσης, "Persian"); otherwise the vocative ends in -η.

Like the feminines, the masculines of first declension have **persistent** accent, use a **circumflex** if the accent falls on the ultima in the genitive and dative singular and plural, and **always accent the genitive plural on the ultima**.

NOTE

The η-stem masculines whose nominative singular ends in -της show the agent or doer of an action (e.g., μαθητής = "one who learns," i.e., "student") or a person concerned with or involved in something (e.g., οἰκέτης = "one involved in the household," i.e., "family member").

59.

In the vocabulary for this lesson there are two adjectives of the first/second declension that have no special set of endings to indicate the feminine gender: ἀθάνατος, -ον ("immortal"), ἀνάξιος, -ον ("unworthy"). These and others like them are called **two-ending adjectives** (as opposed to the **three-ending adjectives** presented in Lesson 8). They use masculine endings to modify both masculine and feminine nouns: e.g., ὁ ἀνάξιος νεανίας and ἡ ἀνάξιος κόρη. Many (but not all) such adjectives are compounds of ἀ- (ἀν- before a vowel) and a stem. Like the prefix *un-* in English, the **alpha privative** is roughly equivalent to "not"; it implies the absence or lack of a particular trait (e.g., ἀθάνατος = "without death," "undying").

60.

Substantives. In both English and Greek (but much more frequently in Greek), the noun modified by an adjective may be omitted from the sentence. Speakers omit a noun for various reasons, sometimes because of their desire to avoid unnecessary words, sometimes because of the stylistic effectiveness of leaving the noun up to the reader's (or audience's) imagination. In *The Star-Spangled Banner,* for example, "the land of the **free** and the home of the **brave**" has much more punch (not to mention better rhyme with the preceding line!) than, e.g., "the land of the free voters and the home of the brave citizens."

Since a Greek adjective always has an ending specifying gender, number, and case, it has the ability, *by itself,* to convey the ideas expressed by the nouns meaning "man," "men," "woman," "women," "thing," "things." A speaker will avoid using one of those nouns when the adjective ending is sufficiently explicit: e.g., ἀγαθός = "a good [man]"; ἀξία = "a worthy [woman]," κακά = "evil [things]," i.e., "evils." The adjective thus becomes the equivalent of the noun it would have modified. A word that is made to function as a noun is called a **substantive**.

61.

In the last lesson the difference between **attributive and predicate position** was explained in connection with adjectives. What was said there is equally applicable to **prepositional phrases**. A prepositional phrase is naturally adverbial, but it can also be made to act as an adjective or even as a noun (substantive). Its function depends on its position *in relation to a definite article.* Compare, for example, these four sentences:

οἱ ἄνθρωποι ἐν τῇ σκηνῇ θύουσιν.	" The people are sacrificing in the tent."
οἱ ἐν τῇ σκηνῇ ἄνθρωποι θύουσιν.	" The people in the tent are sacrificing."
οἱ ἄνθρωποι οἱ ἐν τῇ σκηνῇ θύουσιν.	" The people in the tent are sacrificing."
οἱ ἐν τῇ σκηνῇ θύουσιν.	" The people in the tent are sacrificing."

In the first sentence the prepositional phrase is in the predicate position (i.e., *not* immediately after a definite article); this means that it *must* be functioning as an **adverb**, modifying the predicate part of the sentence (i.e., the verb) and answering the question "*Where* are the people sacrificing?".

In the second and third sentences the prepositional phrase is in the attributive position (i.e., immediately after a definite article) and thus forms a unit with the article οἱ and the noun ἄνθρωποι: "the in-the-tent people." The prepositional phrase is being made to function as an **adjective**, modifying a noun and answering the question "*Which* people are sacrificing?".

In the fourth sentence the prepositional phrase is again in the attributive position, but the bland noun that it modified in the two preceding sentences has been omitted; the prepositional phrase and the article together form a **substantive** ("the in-the-tent [people]"), answering the question "*Who* are sacrificing?". The article supplies the gender, number, and case of the substantive.

In the last three sentences a negative adverb (οὐ or μή) could be inserted between the article and the prepositional phrase to make the expression mean "the *not* in-the-tent people." οἱ οὐκ ἐν τῇ σκηνῇ would imply that the speaker has in mind **particular** people who are not in the tent; οἱ μὴ ἐν τῇ σκηνῇ would be a **generic** reference to the people (whoever they are) who are not in the tent.

62.   **Genitive of Possession.** To indicate the possessor of something or someone, English uses an apostrophe ("the master's house") or the preposition *of* ("the house *of* the master"). **Greek never uses an apostrophe to show possession; instead it puts the possessor into the genitive case.** This "possessive genitive" may either follow or precede the noun that it modifies. Here, for example, are two different ways to write "the master's house" in Greek:

ἡ οἰκίᾱ τοῦ δεσπότου

or

τοῦ δεσπότου ἡ οἰκίᾱ

It is also common to find the genitive of possession in the *attributive position*, i.e., after a definite article that agrees with the modified noun. This indicates that the speaker regards the genitive both as a possessive and as an attribute of the modified noun ("the of-the-master house"). Here, then, are two other possible ways to write "the master's house" in Greek:

ἡ τοῦ δεσπότου οἰκίᾱ

or

ἡ οἰκίᾱ ἡ τοῦ δεσπότου

Notice that Greek does not mind having two—or even three—definite articles in a row, as long as they are not identical (e.g., ἡ τοῦ is fine, but τοῦ τοῦ would not be).

63. **VOCABULARY**

δουλεύω, δουλεύσω	(+ *dative*) be a slave (to), serve
δεσπότης, -ου, ὁ	master (*of the household*), lord, despot (*voc. sg. is irregularly accented on the antepenult:* δέσποτα)
μαθητής, -οῦ, ὁ	student, disciple
νεᾱνίᾱς, -ου, ὁ	young man, youth
οἰκέτης, -ου, ὁ	servant (*of the household*), family member

NOTE οἰκέτης may mean a slave owned by a δεσπότης or a δέσποινα and attached to his or her household; it may also mean a member of the immediate family of the δεσπότης or δέσποινα, i.e., the very opposite of a slave. The context will show whether it is one of the "domestics" or one of the family members who is meant.

ἀθάνατος, -ον	immortal, undying [cf. *Athanasius*]
ἀνάξιος, -ον	worthless; (+ *genitive or infinitive*) unworthy (of, to), undeserving (of, to)
δοῦλος, -η, -ον	enslaved; δοῦλος, -ου, ὁ = slave (*male*); δούλη, -ης, ἡ = slave (*female*)

NOTE The nouns δοῦλος and δούλη are in fact just the masculine and feminine forms (respectively) of the adjective δοῦλος, -η, -ον, used substantively.

ἐλεύθερος, -ᾱ, -ον	(+ *genitive*) free (of), free (from)

κακός, -ή, -όν   ugly, bad (*at doing something*), cowardly,
                           (*morally*) bad, evil, wicked [cf. *cacophony*]

πρότερος, -ᾱ, -ον   former, earlier

64.   **EXERCISES**

A.   **Greek-to-English Sentences**

1. κακὴ ἡ τῶν ἀναξίων μαθητῶν μοῖρα. οἱ ἀθάνατοι τὰς λύπᾱς, οὐ τὰς χαρὰς πέμψειν μέλλουσιν.

2. οὐκέτι αἱ δοῦλαι ἀκούουσι τῆς δεσποίνης τῆς ἀγαθῆς.

3. ἐπεὶ ὥρᾱ φυλάττειν τὴν σκηνήν, λείπετε, ὦ καλοὶ νεᾱνίαι, τὴν θάλατταν.

4. πέμπε, ὦ δοῦλε, τὴν ἐπιστολὴν καὶ τὸ δῶρον τῷ προτέρῳ δεσπότῃ.

5. καὶ ἐλευθέρᾱ καὶ οὐκ ἀξίᾱ δουλεύειν ἡ κόρη.

6. οἱ ἐν τῷ ποταμῷ λίθοι βλάψουσι τὰ τέκνα καὶ τὰς θεραπαίνᾱς;

7. σπεῦδε, ὦ ἄξιε μαθητά, εἰς τὴν τοῦ δεσπότου οἰκίᾱν.

8. ἐθέλομεν τῇ ἀγαθῇ καὶ ἀθανάτῳ θεᾷ πάλιν δουλεύειν.

9. ἀπὸ τῶν οἰκετῶν, ὦ νεᾱνίᾱ κακέ, κλέψεις τὸν καλὸν θησαυρόν;

10. οἱ δοῦλοι μὴ λειπόντων τὰ ἔργα· οἱ ἐλεύθεροι μὴ μελλόντων σπεύδειν τοῖς ἵπποις εἰς τὴν ἀγορᾱν.

B.   **English-to-Greek Sentences**

1. Can the women in the marketplace teach the deserving student?

2. I am going to chase the fine horses out of the road. Farewell, master!

3. O former slaves, since we no longer serve the wicked despot, it is time to abandon the house.

4. The lives of those in the country are free from unworthy deeds. Let the children rejoice in the tranquillity.

5. Young man, order the servants to hasten back into the tents and to sacrifice to the immortal goddesses.

C. READING

ASININE BEHAVIOR
(Aesop's Fable 190)

Ὄνος κηπουρῷ δουλεύει. ἐπειδὴ ἐκ τοῦ ἔργου πολλὰς λύπᾱς ἔχει, τοῖς ἀθανάτοις εὔχεται· Ὁ δεσπότης κακός. οὐκέτι ἐθέλω τῷ κηπουρῷ δουλεύειν. τὸν ὄνον οἱ θεοὶ κελεύουσι κεραμεῖ δουλεύειν. ἀλλὰ πάλιν, ἐπειδὴ ἔτι τῶν λῡπῶν οὐκ ἐλεύθερος ὁ ὄνος, τοῖς ἀθανάτοις εὔχεται. τὸν ὄνον οἱ θεοὶ βυρσοδέψῃ 5 πέμπουσιν. ὁ ὄνος, ἐπειδὴ βλέπει τὸ τοῦ δεσπότου ἔργον, τοὺς προτέρους δεσπότᾱς ποθεῖ. μὴ σπεύδετε, ὦ οἰκέται, ἀπολείπειν τοὺς δεσπότᾱς.

VOCABULARY

ὄνος (line 1): from ὄνος, -ου, ὁ: donkey

κηπουρῷ (line 1): from κηπουρός (*a compound of* κῆπος *"garden"* + οὖρος *"watcher"*), -οῦ, ὁ: gardener

πολλὰς (line 1): many (*fem. acc. pl. of the adjective* πολύς)

εὔχεται (line 2): he prays (*third-pers. sg. pres. mid. indic. of the deponent verb* εὔχομαι, εὔξομαι)

κεραμεῖ (line 3): potter (*dat. sg. of* κεραμεύς, *a third-declension masculine noun*)

βυρσοδέψῃ (line 4): from βυρσοδέψης (*a compound of* βύρσᾱ *"hide"* + δέψω *"soften"*), -ου, ὁ: tanner

βλέπει (line 5): from βλέπω, βλέψομαι: see

ποθεῖ (line 6): from a contract verb ποθέω, ποθήσω: long for, miss, regret

LESSON 10

Ω-VERBS
Imperfect Active Indicative; CORRELATIVES

ὅ τι καλὸν φίλον ἀεί (A thing of beauty is a joy forever.)
—sung by the chorus in Euripides' *Bacchae* 881

65. You are already familiar with two tenses of the indicative mood (active voice): **present** and **future**. The present tense is built on the present stem, found in the verb's first principal part; the future tense is built on the future stem, found in the verb's second principal part. Present and future are two of Greek's four **primary** (or principal) tenses. This lesson introduces the **imperfect tense**, one of Greek's three **secondary** (or historical) tenses. (See §18 in Lesson 3.)

66. The **imperfect tense** of the indicative mood shows an action that was occurring at some time in the **past**. As its name suggests, the imperfect tense has imperfective aspect; i.e., the action is perceived as a process that continued or was repeated over time. In English this idea is most clearly expressed by *was/were* and *-ing* (e.g., "we *were* study*ing* for years"), but it may also be represented by English's simple past tense ("we *studied* for years"). Sometimes the context shows that the verb would be better translated as, e.g., "We were *trying to* study," "We were *starting to* study," or "We *used to* study." **While the present and future tenses may have *either* imperfective or aoristic aspect, the imperfect tense *always* has imperfective aspect.**

67. Like the present tense, the imperfect tense is built on the **present stem**. Thus the **first principal part** supplies the stem for both the present tense and the imperfect tense. (Be glad you have no new principal part to learn!)

Unlike the present tense, the imperfect tense has an **augment** (either syllabic or temporal) and **secondary endings**.

An **augment** is a prefix that increases ("augments") the length of the word; **it signals that the verb is in a secondary tense**. If the present stem begins with a consonant, an epsilon with smooth breathing (ἐ-) is prefixed to it (e.g., παιδευ- becomes ἐπαιδευ-). This is called a **syllabic** augment because it adds another syllable to the word. When a verb begins with ῥ, a second rho is always inserted after the syllabic augment; e.g., ῥῑπτ- becomes ἐρρῑπτ-.

If the present stem begins with a vowel or a diphthong, a different sort of augment is used: the vowel or diphthong at the start of the stem is **lengthened**. This is called a **temporal** augment because it increases the time (*tempus* = Latin word for "time") it takes to pronounce the first syllable.

α	becomes η	αι	becomes ῃ
ε	becomes η	ει	becomes ῃ (sometimes stays ει)
ι	becomes ῑ	αυ	becomes ηυ (sometimes stays αυ)
υ	becomes ῡ	ευ	becomes ηυ (sometimes stays ευ)
ο	becomes ω	οι	becomes ῳ

As you can see, the lengthenings result in η, ῑ, ῡ, ω, ῃ, ηυ, and ῳ. No augment is needed if the present stem *already* begins with one of those long vowels or diphthongs. An initial ᾱ is usually changed to η, and ᾳ becomes ῃ. Initial ου is left unchanged. No Greek verb begins with the diphthong υι.

Being one of the secondary tenses, the imperfect tense has **secondary endings**. These differ somewhat from the primary endings you learned earlier:

IMPERFECT ACTIVE INDICATIVE   Endings:
SG.:

ἐπαίδευον	("I was teaching")	-ον	(cf. primary -ω)
ἐπαίδευες	("you [*sg.*] were teaching")	-ες	(cf. primary -εις)
ἐπαίδευε(ν)	("he/she/it was teaching")	-ε(ν)	(cf. primary -ει)

PL.:

ἐπαιδεύομεν	("we were teaching")	-ομεν	(same as primary)
ἐπαιδεύετε	("you [*pl.*] were teaching")	-ετε	(same as primary)
ἐπαίδευον	("they were teaching")	-ον	(cf. primary -ουσι(ν))

Like the primary endings, these secondary endings are combinations of a thematic vowel (ε/ο) and a personal ending: **-ον** = ο + μ (μ changed to ν); **-ες** = ε + ς; **-ε** = ε + —; **-ομεν** = ο + μεν; **-ετε** = ε + τε; **-ον** = ο + ντ (τ dropped out). Notice that the first-person singular and the third-person plural are identical in appearance. The accent in these finite verb forms is, as expected, **recessive**. You now know the other major use of **movable ν**: besides being added to -σι words, it is added to the third-person singular verb-ending -ε, but only when the word comes at the end of a sentence or when the following word begins with a vowel.

All of the verbs in Lessons 3-10 form their imperfects regularly except for ἔχω, (originally σέχω), whose imperfect is εἶχον (from ἔσεχον; σ disappeared, and εε contracted to ει). The imperfect of εὑρίσκω is *either* εὕρισκον or ηὕρισκον. In **compound verbs** the augment usually comes *between* the prefix and the stem, and the last letter of the prefix, if it is a vowel, generally drops out; e.g., the imperfect of ἀπολείπω is **ἀπέλειπον**.

68.   The ancient Greeks were very conscious of **parallelism** in their sentences. Words that "correlate" or draw a connection between parallel words or clauses are called **correlatives**. You already know the correlative conjunctions καί...καί ("both...and").

Among the most popular correlatives in Greek are **μέν...δέ**. Both are **postpositive**, i.e., **they prefer not to be the first word in their clause.** Instead they like to come *right after* the first word in their clause. By itself **μέν is a particle** (a word whose primary function is to add a certain nuance to the sentence) meaning "indeed" or "certainly." By itself **δέ is a conjunction** meaning "and" or "but" (weaker than ἀλλά). It is frequently found after the first word of a sentence, where it helps to smooth the transition from the preceding sentence.

When used as correlatives, μέν and δέ point out the parallelism of two ideas: **"on the one hand...on the other hand."** The presence of μέν in a sentence should alert the reader to the possibility that the speaker may already have in mind a balance or a contrast between this first thought and a second one, which will have δέ with it. You may decide to leave μέν untranslated and to translate δέ simply as "and" or "but" since an English sentence with "on the one hand...on the other hand" lacks the elegance of a Greek sentence with μέν...δέ.

In correlated clauses the words that are parallel tend to be put first so that they can be emphasized by the μέν and δέ following them; e.g., **θύω μὲν** τοῖς θεοῖς, **φεύγω δὲ** τοὺς κινδύνους ("I *sacrifice* to the gods, and I *escape* the dangers"). If the second clause begins with οὐ or μή, make δέ the third word in that clause; e.g., write οὐ φεύγω δέ, not οὐ δὲ φεύγω. Otherwise οὐ δέ and μὴ δέ could be confused with οὐδέ and μηδέ (see the vocabulary for Lesson 22).

When determining whether or not a word is in the **attributive position**, you should **disregard the presence of μέν or δέ**. In the phrase ὁ μὲν ἄξιος μαθητής, for example, ἄξιος is still considered to come immediately after the article and to occupy the attributive position, even though μέν has insinuated itself between the article and the adjective.

Definite articles may be **combined with μέν and δέ** to mean "this one (he, she, it)...that one (he, she, it)," "the one...the other," or "some...others." No noun or adjective is needed: the form of the article suffices to show the gender, number, and case, while the correlatives convey the idea of balance or contrast. Examples:

ὁ μὲν παιδεύει, ἡ δὲ γράφει.	"He is teaching; she is writing."
ἡ μὲν ἐπαίδευεν, ἡ δ' ἔγραφεν.	" One woman taught; the other wrote."
οἱ μὲν παιδεύσουσιν, οἱ δ' οὔ.	" Some will teach; others will not [teach]."

NOTE   The definite article was originally a demonstrative pronoun meaning "this one" or "that one." When joined with μέν and δέ, it has its old significance.

69.   **VOCABULARY**

λέγω, ἐρῶ[1]/λέξω	say, speak, tell [cf. *dialect, dyslexia, prolegomenon*]
πρᾱ́ττω, πρᾱ́ξω	do, act [cf. *practice, praxis*]
φεύγω, φεύξομαι[2]	flee, avoid, escape, be in exile
ἀλήθεια, -ᾱς, ἡ	truth; (τῇ) ἀληθείᾳ = in truth, truly, really
θάνατος, -ου, ὁ	death; Θάνατος = Death (*personified as a god*) [cf. *euthanasia, thanatopsis*]
κίνδῡνος, -ου, ὁ	danger, risk
φίλος, -η, -ον	(+ *dative*) dear (to); φίλος, -ου, ὁ = friend (*male*); φίλη, -ης, ἡ = friend (*female*) [cf. *bibliophile, hemophiliac, philatelist*]
δέ (δ')	(*postpositive conjunction*) and, but (δ' *before a vowel*)
μέν	(*postpositive particle*) indeed
μὲν...δέ	(*correlatives*) on the one hand...on the other hand
ὁ μὲν...ὁ δέ	(*correlatives*) this one...that one; the one...the other; (*pl.*) some...others
οὖν	(*postpositive particle*) therefore, then

---

[1] In the Attic dialect ἐρῶ (the contracted future tense of εἴρω, another verb meaning "say") is much preferred to λέξω, but until you have been introduced to contracted futures (Lesson 15), you should simply use λέξω.

[2] The future φεύξομαι has middle endings even though it is active in meaning. You will not be asked to form the future of φεύγω until you have learned the middle endings (Lesson 11).

70.   **EXERCISES**

A.   **Greek-to-English Sentences**

1. οἱ μὲν τὰ ἔργα ἔπραττον τῇ χαρᾷ, οἱ δ᾽ οὔ.

2. αἱ δ᾽ ὁδοὶ καὶ λίθους καὶ κινδύνους ἔχουσι· φεύγομεν οὖν τῷ ποταμῷ.

3. μὴ λεγέτω ἡ θεράπαινα ἡ ἀξίᾳ τῇ ἀναξίῳ δεσποίνῃ τὴν ἀλήθειαν.

4. τὰ μὲν τέκνα τὰ ἀπὸ τῆς οἰκίας ἐδίωκε τοὺς ἵππους εἰς τὴν ὁδόν, τὰ δ᾽ ἐν τῇ οἰκίᾳ ἔβλαπτε τὰς καλὰς κλίνᾱς.

5. τὰ δὲ κακὰ ἔργα, ὦ νεᾱνίαι, ἐμέλλετε ἀλλάξειν εἰς ἀγαθά;

6. δοῦλος μὲν ὁ ἀδελφός, ἐλευθέρᾱ δ᾽ ἡ φίλη ἀδελφή.

7. ἐπειδὴ οἱ φίλοι κινδύνους ἐν τῇ θαλάττῃ ηὕρισκον, ἔσπευδον θύειν τοῖς ἀθανάτοις καὶ φεύγειν τὸν θάνατον.

8. ἡ μὲν φυλάξει τὸ καλὸν φυτόν, ὁ δὲ κλέψει τὸν θησαυρόν.

9. ἐπεὶ τὰ ἀγαθὰ λέγω, ὦ κακὲ μαθητά, οὐκ ἀκούεις. τῇ οὖν ἀληθείᾳ οὐκ ἔχω παιδεύειν.

10. μὴ σπεῦδε, ὦ Θάνατε, κλέπτειν τὸν βίον ἀπὸ τῶν ἀνθρώπων.

B.   **English-to-Greek Sentences**

1. Some were rejoicing in their fine houses; others were in exile and could not speak to their friends.

2. On the one hand, the student was striving; on the other hand, he was not willing to do his work.

3. When we were serving our dear master, the children used to chase the beautiful mares away from dangers.

4. The gods can escape Death but not Destiny; truly, therefore, even the immortals are not free.

5. Listen, young man! Do you wish to do a good deed? Then tell the truth.

C.   **READING**

THE BEAR TELLS ALL
(Aesop's Fable 66)

Δύο φίλοι τῇ ὁδῷ τῇ εἰς τὴν χώρᾱν ἔσπευδον. ἐπεὶ ἄρκτον βλέπουσιν, ὁ μὲν φεύγει καὶ ἐν φυτῷ τὴν σωτηρίᾱν εὑρίσκει, ὁ δ᾽ οὐκ ἔχει φεύγειν. ἔπραττεν οὖν τὰ τοῦ θανάτου. ὀσφραίνεται μὲν ἡ ἄρκτος τὸ τοῦ ἀνθρώπου οὖς, ἀπολείπει δέ. ὁ μὲν χαίρει καὶ ἐκ τοῦ φυτοῦ σπεύδει, ὁ δ᾽ οὐ χαίρει. τῷ φίλῳ λέγει, Ὁ φίλος,

5   ἐπεὶ ἐν τοῖς κινδύνοις τὸν φίλον λείπει, οὐ τῇ ἀληθείᾳ φίλος. τοῦθ᾽ ἡ ἄρκτος ἔλεγεν, ὦ ἀνάξιε, ἐπεὶ τὸ οὖς ὠσφραίνετο.

VOCABULARY

δύο (line 1): two (*nom. case of the numeral* δύο—*same form for all genders*)

ἄρκτον (line 1): from ἄρκτος, -ου, ἡ: bear

βλέπουσιν (line 1): from βλέπω, βλέψομαι: see

σωτηρίᾱν (line 2): from σωτηρίᾱ, -ᾱς, ἡ: safety

τὰ τοῦ θανάτου (lines 2-3): the things of death, i.e., things associated with death (*in this case, falling onto the ground and not moving*)

ὀσφραίνεται (line 3): sniffs at (*third-pers. sg. pres. mid. indic. of the deponent verb* ὀσφραίνομαι, ὀσφρήσομαι)

οὖς (line 3): ear (*acc. sg. of the third-declension neuter noun* οὖς)

τοῦθ' (line 5) = τοῦτο: this (*refers to the statement in the preceding sentence;* τοῦτο = *neut. sg. acc. of the demonstrative pronoun* οὗτος)

ὠσφραίνετο (line 6): third-pers. sg. imperf. mid. indic. of ὀσφραίνομαι

LESSON 11

Ω-VERBS
MIDDLE/PASSIVE VOICE;
PREPOSITIONS

τὸν καλὸν ἀγῶνα ἠγώνισμαι (I have fought the good fight.)
—2 Timothy 4:7

71.   The verb forms taught thus far have all been in the active voice. This lesson presents the endings that indicate **middle or passive voice**. It may be helpful to reread the brief discussion of voice in §18 of Lesson 3.

Just as there are two sets of endings (primary and secondary) for active verbs in the indicative mood, so there are two sets of endings (primary and secondary) for middle/passive verbs in the indicative mood. The best way to learn them is to study the paradigms of παιδεύω in the **present middle/passive**, the **future middle**, and the **imperfect middle/ passive indicative**. When the verb could have either middle or passive voice, translations for the middle voice are printed first, followed by translations for the passive voice.

PRESENT MIDDLE/PASSIVE INDICATIVE

Singular:		Endings (primary):
παιδεύομαι	("I teach/am teaching for myself," "I am taught/am being taught")	-ομαι (cf. active -ω)
παιδεύῃ(-ει)	("you teach/are teaching for yourself," "you [sg.] are taught/are being taught")	-ῃ(-ει) (cf. active -εις)
παιδεύεται	("he/she/it teaches/is teaching for him/her/itself," "he/she/it is taught/ is being taught")	-εται (cf. active -ει)

Plural:

παιδευόμεθα ("we teach/are teaching for ourselves," **-ομεθα**
 "we are taught/are being taught") (cf. active **-ομεν**)

παιδεύεσθε ("you teach/are teaching for yourselves," **-εσθε**
 "you [*pl.*] are taught/are being taught") (cf. active **-ετε**)

παιδεύονται ("they teach/are teaching for themselves," **-ονται**
 "they are taught/are being taught") (cf. active **-ουσι(ν**))

FUTURE MIDDLE INDICATIVE

Singular: **Endings (primary):**

παιδεύσομαι ("I shall teach/be teaching for myself") **-σ-ομαι**
 (cf. active **-σω**)

παιδεύσῃ(-σει) ("you [*sg.*] will teach/be **-σ-η (-σ-ει)**
 teaching for yourself") (cf. active **-σεις**)

παιδεύσεται ("he/she/it will teach/be **-σ-εται**
 teaching for him/her/itself") (cf. active **-σει**)

Plural:

παιδευσόμεθα ("we shall teach/be teaching **-σ-ομεθα**
 for ourselves") (cf. active **-σομεν**)

παιδεύσεσθε ("you [*pl.*] will teach/be **-σ-εσθε**
 teaching for yourselves") (cf. active **-σετε**)

παιδεύσονται ("they will teach/be **-σ-ονται**
 teaching for themselves") (cf. active **-σουσι(ν**))

IMPERFECT MIDDLE/PASSIVE INDICATIVE

Singular: **Endings (secondary):**

ἐπαιδευόμην ("I was teaching for myself," **-ομην**
 "I was being taught") (cf. active **-ον**)

ἐπαιδεύου ("you were teaching for yourself," **-ου**
 "you [*sg.*] were being taught") (cf. active **-ες**)

ἐπαιδεύετο ("he/she/it was teaching for **-ετο**
 him/her/itself," "he/she/it was (cf. active **-ε(ν**))
 being taught")

Plural:

ἐπαιδευόμεθα ("we were teaching for ourselves," **-ομεθα**
 "we were being taught") (cf. active **-ομεν**)

ἐπαιδεύεσθε ("you were teaching for yourselves," **-εσθε**
 "you [*pl.*] were being taught") (cf. active **-ετε**)

ἐπαιδεύοντο ("they were teaching for themselves," **-οντο**
 "they were being taught") (cf. active **-ον**)

The present middle/passive is built on the **present stem**, the future middle on the **future stem**, and the imperfect middle/passive on the **augmented present stem**. Present and future add **primary** endings; the imperfect adds **secondary** endings. Middle/passive endings show more clearly than active endings that they are combinations of a thematic vowel (ε/ο) and a personal ending:

Primary middle/passive endings: -ομαι = ο + μαι; -η(-ει) = ε + σαι = εαι (σ dropped out), which contracted to η (often spelled ει in Attic); -εται = ε + ται; -ομεθα = ο + μεθα; -εσθε = ε + σθε; -ονται = ο + νται.

Secondary middle/passive endings: -ομην = ο + μην; -ου = ε + σο = εο (σ dropped out), which contracted to ου; -ετο = ε + το; -ομεθα = ο + μεθα; -εσθε = ε + σθε; -οντο = ο + ντο.

The name "middle/passive" is used for these endings because they can signify **either middle voice** (when the subject not only acts but also has a special interest in the action) **or passive voice** (when the subject is acted upon by someone or something else), depending on the context. However, when these endings are added to the **future** stem (i.e., the stem from the second principal part), they indicate **only middle voice, not passive**. (The future *passive* tense is built on the stem from the sixth principal part. Until that principal part is introduced, you will not be asked to compose or translate sentences with the future passive.)

Changing a verb's voice has **no effect on its tense**. The characteristics of each tense remain the same, regardless of whether the voice is active, middle, or passive. Thus a **present middle/passive** verb in the indicative mood denotes an action in present time and may have either imperfective or aoristic aspect, just as a present active verb may. A **future middle** verb in the indicative mood denotes an action in future time and may have either imperfective or aoristic aspect, just as a future active verb may. An **imperfect middle/passive** verb in the indicative mood denotes an action in past time and has imperfective aspect, just as an imperfect active verb does. Since they are all finite, all middle/passive indicative forms have **recessive** accent.

72.　　The **PRESENT MIDDLE/PASSIVE INFINITIVE** of παιδεύω is παιδεύεσθαι (middle voice: "to teach for oneself"; passive voice: "to be taught"). It is a combination of the **present stem** with the thematic vowel ε and the middle/passive personal ending -σθαι (cf. active -ειν). The accent is **recessive**. As with the present active infinitive, the present middle/passive infinitive shows only **imperfective aspect**, not present time. You may prefer a translation that emphasizes the on-going nature of the action: e.g., "to continue teaching for oneself" or "to continue being taught."

The **FUTURE MIDDLE INFINITIVE** of παιδεύω is παιδεύσεσθαι ("to be going to teach for oneself"). It is a combination of the **future stem** with the thematic vowel ε and the middle personal ending -σθαι (cf. active -σειν). The accent is **recessive**. As with the future active infinitive, the future middle infinitive may have either **imperfective** (e.g., "to be going to be teaching for oneself for a while") or **aoristic** aspect ("to be going to teach for oneself on one occasion").

73.   In the **present middle/passive imperative** παιδεύω is conjugated as follows:

PRESENT MIDDLE/PASSIVE IMPERATIVE

Singular:		**Endings:**
παιδεύου	("teach for yourself!" or "be taught!")	**-ου** (cf. active -ε)
παιδευέσθω	("let him/her/it teach for him/her/ itself!" or "let him/her/it be taught!")	**-εσθω** (cf. active -ετω)
Plural:		
παιδεύεσθε	("teach for yourselves!" or "be taught!")	**-εσθε** (cf. active -ετε)
παιδευέσθων	("let them teach for themselves!" or "let them be taught!")	**-εσθων** (cf. active -οντων)

The present middle/passive imperative is built on the **present stem**. Each middle/passive ending is a combination of the thematic vowel ε and a personal ending: **-ου** = ε + σο = εο (σ dropped out), which contracted to ου; **-εσθω** = ε + σθω; **-εσθε** = ε + σθε; **-εσθων** = ε + σθων. Since they are finite, all middle/passive imperative forms have **recessive** accent.

Notice that the second-person plural present middle/passive *imperative* is identical to the second-person plural present middle/passive *indicative*. παιδεύεσθε, for example, could be either a statement ("you are teaching for yourselves"/"you are being taught") or a command ("teach for yourselves!"/"be taught!"). The context will reveal which mood is meant.

Like the present active imperative, the present middle/passive imperative shows only **imperfective aspect**, not present time. You may prefer a translation that emphasizes the ongoing nature of the action: e.g., "continue teaching for yourself!" or "continue being taught!" for παιδεύου; "let them continue teaching for themselves!" or "let them continue being taught!" for παιδευέσθων.

74.   In a passive sentence the person doing the action (i.e., the agent) may or may not be identified; e.g., "I am taught *by my brother*" or simply "I am taught." To identify the agent, Greek often uses the preposition ὑπό ("by") and a noun in the genitive case; e.g., παιδεύομαι ὑπὸ τοῦ ἀδελφοῦ. This construction is called the **genitive of personal agent**. Be sure to distinguish the genitive of personal agent (a human being) from the dative of means (an instrument or tool):

βλάπτομαι ὑπὸ τῶν νεᾱνιῶν.   "I am being hurt by the young men."
βλάπτομαι τοῖς λίθοις.   "I am being hurt by the stones."

To help you determine the voice of a verb with a middle/passive ending, here are **two clues: (1)** The presence of a **genitive of agent** is a sign that the verb's voice must be **passive**, not middle (since, in a sentence with middle voice, *the subject itself*—and not a noun in the genitive—is the agent). **(2)** The presence of a **direct object** is a sign that the verb's voice must be **middle**, not passive (since, in a passive sentence, *the subject*—and not a direct object—receives the action).

75.   In some verbs the middle voice shows a **reflexive** relationship: the action is done directly *to* the subject, not *for* it. τρέπω ("I turn"), for example, is reflexive in the middle voice (τρέπομαι = "I betake myself" or "I move"). In other verbs the middle voice may have a **special meaning** in addition to the one you would expect it to have. This is the case with four of the verbs you already know:

ἀλλάττομαι	"I change for myself"	or	" I take [something] in exchange for [something]"
γράφομαι	"I write for myself"	or	"I indict [someone]"
παιδεύομαι	"I teach for myself"	or	"I have [someone] taught"
φυλάττομαι	"I guard for myself"	or	" I am on guard against [something/someone]"

In its special sense, each of these four verbs may be combined with an **accusative direct object**. ἀλλάττομαι may also have a second object in the **genitive**; e.g., ἀλλάττομαι τὸν ἵππον τῆς ἁμάξης ("I take the horse in exchange for the cart").

76.   You are already familiar with **prepositions** whose object is always in the genitive case (e.g., ἀπό, ἐκ), those whose object is always in the dative case (e.g., ἐν), and those whose object is always in the accusative case (e.g., εἰς). There are other Greek prepositions whose object can be in the genitive, the dative, **or** the accusative case, and whose meaning changes (sometimes only slightly, sometimes considerably) when the case of the object changes.

One such preposition is ὑπό. As you know from §74, ὑπό often means "by," but its basic meaning is "under." When used with the **genitive**, ὑπό implies **motion out of** or **away from** a source or origin (point **A** in the diagram below); when used with the **accusative**, it implies **motion toward** a goal or destination (point **C**). When used with the

dative, it implies that someone or something is **at a particular location** (point **B**) and is neither leaving it nor approaching it.

A		B		C
•	→	•	→	•
GENITIVE		DATIVE		ACCUSATIVE

Compare ὑπὸ τῆς ἀμάξης φεύγω ("I flee *from under* the wagon"), ὑπὸ τῇ ἀμάξῃ εὑρίσκομαι ("I am found *under* the wagon"), and ὑπὸ τὴν ἄμαξαν σπεύδω ("I flee *under* [or *to a place under*] the wagon"). The genitive of personal agent with ὑπό identifies the human source from which the action springs; e.g., φυλάττομαι ὑπὸ τῶν θεῶν = "I am guarded *by* [*under the agency of*] the gods."

77.   **VOCABULARY**

NOTE   From now on, the names of cases, parts of speech, etc. will be abbreviated to save space; (*mid.*) indicates that the following definition is applicable only when the verb is in the middle voice. In addition to the new words in the vocabulary list, you should learn the special middle meanings of ἀλλάττομαι, γράφομαι, παιδεύομαι, and φυλάττομαι (as explained in §75).

πείθω, πείσω   (*with acc. + infin.*) persuade (to); (*mid. + dat.*) obey

NOTE   πείθω, like the comparable verb κελεύω (Lesson 5), often governs an infinitive; the person persuaded is put into the accusative case. πείθομαι (middle voice) has the special sense of "I obey" (from the notion of persuading oneself); the person or thing obeyed is put into the dative case.

τρέπω, τρέψω   turn; (*mid.*) betake oneself, move [cf. *protreptic*]

NOTE   τρέπω does not mean "I turn" in the sense of "I turn myself around" or "I become"; rather, it means "I make something or someone turn" (cf. ἀλλάττω in Lesson 6). Thus, in the active voice, the verb always has a direct object with it; i.e., it is always **transitive**. In the middle voice, the verb is reflexive (the subject puts *itself* into motion); therefore no direct object is needed with τρέπομαι.

ἄμαξα, -ης, ἡ   cart, wagon
λίμνη, -ης, ἡ   marsh, lake, pond [cf. *limnology*]
τόπος, -ου, ὁ   place, passage (*in a book*) [cf. *topic, topography, utopia*]
τρόπος, -ου, ὁ   turn, way, manner, habit; (*pl.*) character [cf. *trope, entropy, heliotropic, trophy*]
μακρός, -ά, -όν   long, long-lasting [cf. *macrocosm, macron*]

μῑκρός, -ά, -όν   small, little [cf. *microphone, microscope*]

πόρρω   (*adv.*) far, far off; (*prep. + gen.*) far away from

ὑπό (ὑπ', ὑφ')   (*prep. + gen.*) from under, by (*under the agency of*); (*prep. + dat.*) under; (*prep. + acc.*) under, to a place under [cf. *hypocrisy, hypodermic, hypotenuse, hypothesis*]

NOTE   The omicron of ὑπό is elided before a word beginning with a vowel, and the elision is usually marked with an apostrophe (ὑπ'). If the following word has rough breathing, the pi before the apostrophe is "roughened" into phi (ὑφ').

78.   **EXERCISES**

A.   **Greek-to-English Sentences**

1. ἐν τῷ τόπῳ τῷ ἐλευθέρῳ κινδύνων παιδευόμεθα τὰς μῑκρὰς κόρᾱς.

2. ἐκ δὲ τῆς σκηνῆς ἐκλέπτοντο ὑπὸ τῶν οἰκετῶν οἱ καλοὶ ἵπποι.

3. ἀλλάξονται οἱ θεοὶ τὰ τῶν ἀνθρώπων δῶρα τῆς ἡσυχίᾱς;

4. μηκέτι πείθεσθε τῇ ἀναξίῳ δεσποίνῃ, ὦ ἄξιαι θεράπαιναι, ἀλλὰ τρέπεσθε τῇ μακρᾷ ὁδῷ εἰς τὴν χώρᾱν.

5. ἐπείθου τῷ προτέρῳ δεσπότῃ ἐπειδὴ ἐκέλευεν; οὐκ ἐπειθόμην.

6. μὴ τρέπου, ὦ τέκνον, ὑπὸ τὴν ἅμαξαν· ἔχε τὸν πρότερον τόπον.

7. γράψῃ (*or* γράψει) τοὺς νεᾱνίᾱς ἐπεὶ τὴν ἵππον βλάπτουσι τοῖς λίθοις;

8. αἱ μακραὶ λῦπαι τοῖς δούλοις μὴ πεμπέσθων ὑπὸ τῆς Μοίρᾱς.

9. ἤθελε πείθειν τοὺς νεᾱνίᾱς ἐκ τῆς λίμνης τρέπεσθαι, ἀλλ' οὐκ ἤκουον.

10. τὰ μῑκρὰ φυτὰ ὑπὸ τῶν θεραπαινῶν φυλάττεται πόρρω τῆς οἰκίᾱς.

B.   **English-to-Greek Sentences**

1. Move out of the house, dear brothers! We shall offer sacrifice for ourselves far away from the servants.

2. To some, small gifts were sent by the noble lady; to others, long letters were written.

3. Will they obey their master? Let them turn the wagon away from the pond and leave (it) under the tree!

4. Are you going to have your daughter taught in the place? Be on guard against dangers, man!

5. Because he was not truly harmed by his former friends, we do not intend to indict the youth.

C. READING

AN ILL-FATED FROG
(Aesop's Fable 70)

Δύο βάτραχοι φίλοι ἦσαν. ὁ μὲν λίμνην πόρρω τῆς ὁδοῦ εἶχεν, ὁ δὲ μῑκρὸν ὕδωρ ἐν τῇ ὁδῷ. ὁ δ' ἐν τῇ ὁδῷ ὑπὸ τοῦ ἐν τῇ λίμνῃ ἐκελεύετο· Ἀπόλειπε τὴν κακὴν ὁδόν, ὦ φίλε, καὶ τρέπου εἰς τὴν καλὴν λίμνην. ἄλλαττε τοὺς τρόπους καὶ φεῦγε τοὺς κινδύνους τοὺς ἐν τῇ ὁδῷ. ἀλλ' ὁ φίλος οὐκ ἐπείθετο· Μηκέτι
5 πεῖθε, ὦ βάτραχε. μακρὰ μὲν ἡ εἰς τὴν λίμνην ὁδός, μῑκρὸς δ' εἰμί. καὶ οὐκ ἐθέλω τρέπεσθαι ἐκ τοῦ φίλου τόπου. τὴν οὖν ὁδὸν οὐ μέλλω ἀπολείψειν.

ἐν δὲ τῇ ὁδῷ εὑρίσκει ὁ βάτραχος τὸν θάνατον ὑφ' ἁμάξῃ. μὴ μέλλετε, ὦ ἄνθρωποι, ἐπεὶ ἔχετε τρέπειν τὰ κακὰ εἰς καλά.

VOCABULARY

δύο (line 1): two (*nom. case of the numeral* δύο—*same form for all genders*)
βάτραχοι (line 1): from βάτραχος, -ου, ὁ: frog
ἦσαν (line 1): they were (*third-pers. pl. imperf. act. indic. of the verb "be"*)
εἶχεν (line 1): here the verb ἔχω means "inhabit"
ὕδωρ (line 2): water (*acc. sg. of the third-decl. neut. noun* ὕδωρ)
εἰμί (line 5): I am (*first-pers. sg. pres. act. indic. of the verb "be"*)

LESSON 12

εἰμί; ENCLITICS

ἐν ἀρχῇ ἦν ὁ Λόγος

(In the beginning was the Word.)—John 1:1

79. The verb εἰμί means "I am" or "I exist." Because it belongs to the μι-verb conjugation, it has endings that differ slightly from the endings of ω-verbs. Moreover, some of its endings are irregular, even for μι-verbs! (Compare the English verb *be*, which appears as *am, are, is, was, were*, etc.) εἰμί is such a useful word that we are having you learn it now, long before you learn the rest of the μι-verbs. εἰμί occurs only in the present, future, and imperfect tenses of the indicative. Thus it has just two principal parts: εἰμί, ἔσομαι.

PRESENT ACTIVE INDICATIVE	FUTURE MIDDLE INDICATIVE	IMPERFECT ACTIVE INDICATIVE
Singular:		
εἰμί	ἔσομαι	ἦ/ἦν
("I am")	("I shall be")	("I was")
εἶ	ἔσῃ/ἔσει	ἦσθα
("you [sg.] are")	("you [sg.] will be")	("you [sg.] were")
ἐστί(ν)	ἔσται	ἦν
("he/she/it is")	("he/she/it will be")	("he/she/it was")
Plural:		
ἐσμέν	ἐσόμεθα	ἦμεν
("we are")	("we shall be")	("we were")
ἐστέ	ἔσεσθε	ἦτε/ἦστε
("you [pl.] are")	("you [pl.] will be")	("you [pl.] were")
εἰσί(ν)	ἔσονται	ἦσαν
("they are")	("they will be")	("they were")

PRES. ACTIVE INFINITIVE: εἶναι ("to be")

| FUT. MIDDLE INFINITIVE: | ἔσεσθαι |
| | ("to be going to be") |

PRES. ACTIVE IMPERATIVE

Singular:	ἴσθι
	("be!")
	ἔστω
	("let him/her/it be!")
Plural:	ἔστε
	("be!")
	ἔστων
	("let them be!")

The basic stem of εἰμί is εσ-, to which are added primary active endings to form the present indicative, primary middle endings to form the future indicative, and secondary active endings (with εσ- augmented to ησ-) to form the imperfect indicative. Thematic vowels (ε/ο) are used in the future forms (except ἔσται) but not in the present and imperfect forms. The σ of the stem usually drops out before μ, ν, or another σ (ἐσμέν is an exception), and ε is lengthened to ει to compensate for the loss of the sigma (a phenomenon called **compensatory lengthening**); e.g., εἰμί (from ἐσ-μι), εἶναι (from ἐσ-ναι). Notice that ἐστί and εἰσί both have **movable ν**.

The present and imperfect tenses of εἰμί **never** have middle/passive endings; the future tense **never** has active endings. When you translate the future forms, pretend that their middle endings are active; e.g., translate ἔσομαι as "I shall be," not as "I shall be for myself." εἰμί is one of a number of Greek verbs that are **deponent** in at least one tense; i.e., in that tense they are **always active in meaning but middle (or passive) in appearance.**

Like εἰμί, the verbs ἀκούω and φεύγω are deponent in the future tense: **ἀκούσομαι** = "I shall hear"; **φεύξομαι** = "I shall flee." There is no way to say "I shall hear for myself" or "I shall flee for myself" because the middle endings in the future tense of these verbs must be translated as if they were active endings.

80. The accent of εἰμί is **recessive** in the future and imperfect indicative, in the two infinitives, and in the four imperatives. The present second-person singular εἶ has a circumflex because it is a contraction of ἐσσί (both sigmas dropped out). The other five forms in the present indicative are **enclitics**, words that "lean upon" the preceding word so closely that they often give up their accent to it and are left with no accent of their own. (Compare **proclitics**, which "lean forward" to the following word and have no accent of their own.) The enclitic forms of "be" all have two syllables each, but there are other enclitics such as γε (a particle meaning "at least"; see the vocabulary for this lesson) that have just one syllable.

To decide whether an enclitic should receive an accent, look at the word *preceding* it:

If that word has **a circumflex or a grave on its ultima, the enclitic will have no accent**, but the accent on the preceding word's ultima, if a grave, will change to an acute; e.g., ὑπὸ σκηνῇ εἰσι and μῑκρός γε. (The change to acute makes sense because a grave is used only on a word's final syllable. Since an enclitic is regarded as an extension of the preceding word, that word is considered not to end until the final syllable of the enclitic.)

If the preceding word has **an acute on its antepenult or a circumflex on its penult, the enclitic will have no accent**, but the preceding word will receive a second accent (acute) on its ultima; e.g., ἄνθρωπός ἐστι and δῶρόν γε.

If the preceding word has **an acute on its penult, a one-syllable enclitic will have no accent, but a two-syllable enclitic will be accented on its ultima** (with a circumflex if the vowel is naturally long, otherwise with an acute); e.g., φίλος γε and φίλος εἰμί. (You may wonder why the preceding word in this case does not receive a second accent on its ultima, as it does when its penult has a circumflex. It is not permissible to have two acute accents—i.e., two rising pitches—in a row, for that would allow no time for the speaker's pitch to descend between the rises.)

If the preceding word is **elided, the enclitic must be accented** (e.g., δ' εἰσί). An acute on the enclitic's ultima will become a grave, as usual, if there is no punctuation between the enclitic and the next word (e.g., δ' εἰσὶν ἀδελφοί).

If the preceding word is a *proclitic* or another *enclitic*, the ultima of that word will receive an acute from the enclitic (e.g., οὔκ ἐσμεν and ἀδελφοί ἐστέ γε).

81. **VOCABULARY**

εἰμί, ἔσομαι   be, exist; (*third-pers. sg. + acc. & infin.*) it is possible (to)

NOTE   The third-person singular of εἰμί (in any tense) may show possibility. If so, the subject is usually an **infinitive**, and the person for whom the action is/was/will be possible appears in the **accusative** case; e.g., οὐκ ἦν τὴν κόρην φεύγειν = "it was not possible for the girl to escape" or "the girl could not escape."

The present third-person singular ἐστί(ν) sometimes stops behaving like an enclitic and, for greater emphasis, takes an acute accent on its penult: ἔστι(ν). This happens when it is the first word in a sentence, when it means "there exists" or "it is possible," and when it is preceded by ἀλλ', καί, μή, or οὐκ.

λύω, λύσω	loosen, release, destroy [cf. *analysis*]
ἀρχή, -ῆς, ἡ	beginning, power, rule, political office [cf. *archetype, monarchy*]
εἰρήνη, -ης, ἡ	peace [cf. *Irene, irenic*]
λόγος, -ου, ὁ	word, speech, story, argument, reasoning [cf. *logic*]
πόλεμος, -ου, ὁ	war [cf. *polemic*]
ἐχθρός, -ά, -όν	(+ *dat.*) hateful (to), hostile (to); (*as a substantive*) enemy (*personal*)
πολέμιος, -α, -ον	(+ dat.) at war (with), hostile (to); (*as a substantive, usually plural*) enemy (*in war*)
διά (δι᾽)	(*prep.* + *gen.*) through, throughout; (*prep.* + *acc.*) on account of (δι᾽ before a vowel) [cf. *diagnosis, diameter*]
γε (γ᾽)	(*enclitic particle*) at least, at any rate (γ᾽ *before a vowel*)

NOTE

γε calls attention to a single word or clause and restricts the applicability of the statement to that word or clause (e.g., τὴν γ᾽ εἰρήνην ἔχομεν = "we have peace at any rate [even if nothing else]"; ὁ βίος καλὸς ἐπεί γε τὴν εἰρήνην ἔχομεν = "life is beautiful, at least when we have peace"). γε is generally put *after* the word that it emphasizes (but *between* an article and its noun). If it affects a whole clause, it is put *after the conjunction* at the start of that clause. It often has an ironic nuance.

82. **EXERCISES**

A. **Greek-to-English Sentences**

1. οἱ μὲν λόγοι τοῦ νεανίου ἄξιοί εἰσιν, οἱ δὲ τρόποι ἀνάξιοι.

2. διὰ τὸν πόλεμον ἐν κινδύνῳ ἐσμὲν καὶ μέλλομεν διὰ τῆς χώρᾱς φεύξεσθαι.

3. ἐν μέν γε τῇ ἀρχῇ τοῦ πολέμου φίλος ἦσθα, οὐκέτι δ᾽ εἶ.

4. μακρὰ ἔσται ἡ ὁδός, ἀλλ᾽ ἐπειδή γε τὴν θάλατταν εὑρήσομεν, ἐλεύθεροι πάλιν ἐσόμεθα καὶ τὴν εἰρήνην ἕξομεν.

5. ὁ δ᾽ ἐχθρὸς ἐτρέπετο εἰς τὴν οἰκίᾱν καὶ ἔλῡε τὰς κλίνᾱς.

6. ἀλλ᾽ ἡ ἵππος καλή ἐστιν. μὴ λῡέσθω ὑπὸ τῶν πολεμίων.

7. οὐκ ἔστι τούς γ᾽ οἰκέτᾱς ἔχειν τὴν ἀρχὴν ["over"] τῆς οἰκίᾱς.

8. ἀκούσεται μὲν ὁ δοῦλος τοὺς λόγους, οὐ πείσεται δὲ τῷ δεσπότῃ.

9. ἐπεὶ ὁ πόλεμος πόρρω ἦν, τῶν κινδύνων ἐλεύθεροι ἦσαν.

10. σπεύδετε φίλοι τῷ δεσπότῃ εἶναι; ἔστε οὖν ἀγαθοὶ καὶ μὴ πράττετε ἔργα ἐχθρά.

B.   English-to-Greek Sentences

HINT   De sure to use the nominative case (not the accusative case) for predicate adjectives and predicate nouns.

1. Farewell, dear country! The war will be long, and I shall flee through the rivers and the marshes.

2. Our friends at least will listen to the gods, but our enemies will not obey the words of the immortals.

3. When the youth was being educated, he used to say, "You are truly noble, master. Am I worthy to be a student?"

4. In the beginning, I wished to destroy my brother, but we are no longer enemies. Therefore, let there be peace.

5. On account of the dangers, it is not possible for the servants to do their tasks far away from the house.

C.   READING

A SHEEPISH MISTAKE
(Aesop's Fable 158)

Λύκοι μὲν πρόβατα κλέπτειν ἤθελον, κύνες δ' ἐφύλαττον. οἱ οὖν λύκοι τοῖς προβάτοις λέγουσιν· Ἔστω ἡ εἰρήνη. τοῖς μέν γε προβάτοις οὔκ ἐσμεν ἐχθροί, τοῖς δὲ κυσίν. ἐπειδὴ τοὺς κύνας ἀποπέμψετε, φίλοι τῶν προβάτων ἐσόμεθα. τὰ δὲ πρόβατα τοῖς τῶν λύκων λόγοις πείθεται καὶ ἀποπέμπει τοὺς

5   κύνας. οἱ δὲ λύκοι οὐ μέλλουσιν εἰς τὸν τόπον τρέπεσθαι καὶ τὰ πρόβατα λύειν.

μὴ ἀποπέμπετε, ὦ ἄνθρωποι, τοὺς φίλους διὰ τοὺς λόγους τῶν πολεμίων.

VOCABULARY

λύκοι (line 1): from λύκος, -ου, ὁ: wolf
πρόβατα (line 1): from πρόβατον, -ου, τό: sheep
κύνες (line 1): dogs (*nom. pl. of the masc./fem. third-decl. noun* κύων)
κυσίν (line 3): dat. pl. of κύων
κύνας (line 3): acc. pl. of κύων
ἀποπέμψετε (line 3): ἀπο- + πέμψετε

LESSON 13

DEMONSTRATIVES

τόδ' ἐκεῖνο (This is what I said before.)
—the nurse in Euripides' *Medea* 98 recalls her earlier words

83. **Demonstratives** are words that point out or call attention to particular persons or things. A demonstrative is by nature an **adjective**, but it becomes a **pronoun** (i.e., a substitute for a noun) when used substantively. In the sentence "I like that book," for example, *that* is a demonstrative adjective modifying the noun *book*; if *book* is omitted from the sentence, *that* becomes a demonstrative pronoun ("I like that"), and the book is identified not as a book, but only as a thing that the speaker singles out for attention. The term **demonstratives** is convenient because it includes both demonstrative adjectives and demonstrative pronouns.

84. As you learn the demonstrative adjectives, you will also be learning the demonstrative pronouns, since they are identical in form:

1. ὅδε, ἥδε, τόδε ("this," "these"): points out someone or something very close to the speaker or points to what will follow in the next sentence.

SG.:	Masc.	Fem.	Neut.	PL.:	Masc.	Fem.	Neut.
Nom.	ὅδε	ἥδε	τόδε		οἵδε	αἵδε	τάδε
Gen.	τοῦδε	τῆσδε	τοῦδε		τῶνδε	τῶνδε	τῶνδε
Dat.	τῷδε	τῇδε	τῷδε		τοῖσδε	ταῖσδε	τοῖσδε
Acc.	τόνδε	τήνδε	τόδε		τούσδε	τάσδε	τάδε

This odd adjective is a combination of the **definite article** (which was originally a demonstrative itself) and the suffix **-δε**, indicating closeness ("this right here"). Each form is accented as if it were two separate words, an article (with its normal accent) and an enclitic (-δε). Thus, in ὅδε, ἥδε, οἵδε, and αἵδε, the proclitics ὁ, ἡ, οἱ, and αἱ receive acute accents from -δε. Since -δε acts like an enclitic, not like a typical ultima, the rule that a naturally long penult followed by a short ultima has a circumflex does not apply: ἥδε, οἵδε, αἵδε, τήνδε, τούσδε, and τάσδε all have acutes, not circumflexes. There is no vocative. The final ε of each form is elided before a word beginning with a vowel.

2.   οὗτος, αὕτη, τοῦτο ("this," "these"; but sometimes a better translation in English will be "that," "those"): points out someone or something *close* to the speaker, **or** points to what was said in the *preceding* sentence, **or** labels someone or something as well-known, **or** means "the latter."

SG.:	Masc.	Fem.	Neut.	PL.:	Masc.	Fem.	Neut.
Nom.	οὗτος	αὕτη	τοῦτο[1]		οὗτοι	αὗται	ταῦτα[1]
Gen.	τούτου	ταύτης	τούτου		τούτων	τούτων	τούτων
Dat.	τούτῳ	ταύτῃ	τούτῳ		τούτοις	ταύταις	τούτοις
Acc.	τοῦτον	ταύτην	τοῦτο[1]		τούτους	ταύτας	ταῦτα[1]

Like the definite article, οὗτος has rough breathing in the nominative masculine and feminine singular and plural, elsewhere an initial τ. The stem has -ου- except when the ending contains an η or an α; then the stem has -αυ-. The accent is **persistent**. There is no vocative, but the nominative οὗτος may be used as a form of address equivalent to "you there": e.g., οὗτος, σπεῦδε ("you there, hurry!"). After τοῦτ', ἐστί is accented on the penult (ἔστι), just as it is after οὐκ, μή, καί, and ἀλλ'. After ταῦτ' and all the other demonstrative pronouns, however, ἐστί behaves like a normal enclitic.

3.   ἐκεῖνος, ἐκείνη, ἐκεῖνο ("that," "those"): points out someone, **or** something far away from the speaker, **or** labels someone or something as well-known, **or** means "the former" (as opposed to "the latter").

SG.:	Masc.	Fem.	Neut.	PL.:	Masc.	Fem.	Neut.
Nom.	ἐκεῖνος	ἐκείνη	ἐκεῖνο		ἐκεῖνοι	ἐκεῖναι	ἐκεῖνα
Gen.	ἐκείνου	ἐκείνης	ἐκείνου		ἐκείνων	ἐκείνων	ἐκείνων
Dat.	ἐκείνῳ	ἐκείνῃ	ἐκείνῳ		ἐκείνοις	ἐκείναις	ἐκείνοις
Acc.	ἐκεῖνον	ἐκείνην	ἐκεῖνο		ἐκείνους	ἐκείνας	ἐκεῖνα

ἐκεῖνος has normal endings *except* in the neuter nominative and accusative singular (-ο, not -ον). The accent is **persistent**. There is no vocative.

A demonstrative adjective may come before or after the noun it modifies, but it must always be in the **predicate position**. The noun it modifies usually has a definite article, which you should *not* include in your translation: e.g., οὗτος ὁ μαθητής = "that [the] student"; ἡ κόρη ἥδε = "this [the] maiden."

85.   **VOCABULARY**

βλέπω, βλέψομαι   see, behold; (with εἰς + *acc.*) look (at)

---

1. τοῦτο and ταῦτα become τοῦτ' and ταῦτ' before an initial vowel with smooth breathing, and τοῦθ' and ταῦθ' before an inital vowel with rough breathing.

NOTE   If it means "see" or "behold," βλέπω may take a direct object (e.g., βλέπω τὴν οἰκίαν, "I see the house"). If it means "look (at)," it will have εἰς + accusative, or a similar prepositional phrase, with it (e.g., βλέπω εἰς τὴν οἰκίαν, "I look at the house"). The future βλέψομαι, like ἀκούσομαι, ἔσομαι, and φεύξομαι, is deponent.

σοφία, -ᾶς, ἡ	wisdom
φιλοσοφία, -ᾶς, ἡ	philosophy
ἐκεῖνος, -η, -ο	(*dem. adj./pron.*) that, those, the well-known, the former (*as opposed to "the latter"*)
ὅδε, ἥδε, τόδε	(*dem. adj./pron.*) this, these, the following
οὗτος, αὕτη, τοῦτο	(*dem. adj./pron.*) this, these, that, those, the aforesaid, the well-known, the latter; οὗτος! = you there!
σοφός, -ή, -όν	wise [cf. *sophist, sophomore*]
φιλόσοφος, -ον	philosophical; (*as a substantive*) philosopher
νῦν	(*adv.*) now, at this time
τότε (τότ', τόθ')	(*adv.*) then, at that time (τότ' before smooth breathing, τόθ' before rough breathing)
γάρ	(*postpositive conjunction introducing an explanation*) for, for indeed

86.   **EXERCISES**

A.   **Greek-to-English Sentences**

1.   ἐσπεύδομεν φεύγειν, τότε γὰρ ἐν τούτῳ τῷ τόπῳ κίνδῡνοι ἦσαν.

2.   οὗτος, τρέπου εἰς τὴν οἰκίᾱν καὶ βλέπε εἰς ταύτᾱς τὰς καλὰς κλίνᾱς.

3.   μέλλουσι φεύξεσθαι τὸν φιλόσοφον, τοὺς γὰρ νεᾱνίᾱς ἐκεῖνος βλάπτει.

4.   οὐ πόρρω τοῦδε τοῦ ποταμοῦ εὑρήσετε ταῦτα τὰ μῑκρὰ φυτά.

5.   τοῖς λίθοις τούτοις τάσδε τὰς κόρᾱς βλάψει τὸ κακὸν τέκνον;

6.   ἐπεὶ τοὺς πολεμίους βλεψόμεθα, φευξόμεθα εἰς τήνδε τὴν λίμνην.

7.   τότ' ἐκείνῳ τῷ δεσπότῃ αὕτη ἐδούλευεν, ἀλλὰ νῦν ἐλευθέρᾱ ἐστίν.

8.   καὶ αἱ κόραι καὶ οἱ νεᾱνίαι ἀγαθοί εἰσιν, ἐκεῖναι μὲν γὰρ τοῖς θεοῖς θύουσιν, οὗτοι δὲ τὴν ἀγορὰν φυλάττουσιν.

9.   ἡ δέσποινα λέγει τάδ'· Οὗτος μὲν ὁ οἰκέτης τὴν σοφίᾱν ἔχει, ὅδε δ' οὔ.

10.   χαῖρε τοῖς δώροις, ὦ φιλόσοφε, τούτων γὰρ ἄξιος εἶ τῇ ἀληθείᾳ.

B. **English-to-Greek Sentences**

1. I shall say to the servant the following (things): "You there, send this letter to the well-known despot!"
2. Philosophy is dear to these students, for they are now being taught by a noble philosopher.
3. Some were wise, others were not. The latter used to harm beautiful horses; the former did not.
4. After we shall look at the wagons of the enemy [*use a plural noun*], we shall destroy those (wagons).
5. At that time at least, the aforesaid youth was striving to be good, for he was doing brave deeds.

C. **READING**

STICKING TOGETHER
(Aesop's Fable 53)

Γεωργοῦ τὰ τέκνα ἐστασίαζεν. ὁ δὲ πατὴρ οὐκ εἶχε λόγοις πείθειν ἐκείνους τοὺς νεᾱνίᾱς πάλιν τρέπεσθαι εἰς φίλους. ῥάβδους οὖν εὑρίσκει καὶ ἐκ τούτων δέσμην ποιεῖ. τοῖς δὲ τέκνοις κελεύει τήνδε τὴν δέσμην θλᾶν. ἐπεὶ οὗτοι οὐκ ἔχουσιν ἐκεῖνο πράττειν, ὁ πατὴρ τὴν δέσμην λύει καὶ τοῖς νεᾱνίαις κελεύει κατὰ
5 μίαν τὰς ῥάβδους θλᾶν. τοῦτο νῦν ῥᾳδίως πράττουσιν. ὁ δὲ φιλόσοφος πατὴρ τότε λέγει τάδ᾽· Οὐκ ἔστι τοὺς φίλους ὑπὸ τῶν ἐχθρῶν βλάπτεσθαι, ἡ γὰρ ὁμόνοια φυλάττει τούτους. ἔστε οὖν σοφοί, ὦ τέκνα, καὶ μηκέτι στασιάζετε.

VOCABULARY

γεωργοῦ (line 1): from γεωργός, -οῦ, ὁ: farmer
ἐστασίαζεν (line 1): from στασιάζω, στασιάσω: quarrel
πατήρ (line 1): father (*nom. sg. of the irreg. third-decl. masc. noun* πατήρ, πατρός)
ῥάβδους (line 2): from ῥάβδος, -ου, ἡ: stick
δέσμην (line 3): from δέσμη, -ης, ἡ: bundle
ποιεῖ (line 3): third-pers. sg. pres. act. indic. of the contract verb ποιέω, ποιήσω: make
θλᾶν (line 3): pres. act. infin. of the contract verb θλάω, θλάσω: crush
κατὰ μίαν (lines 4-5): one by one (κατά "*by*" *is a preposition*; μίαν "*one*" *is a fem. acc. sg. adj. agreeing with an implied* ῥάβδον)
ῥᾳδίως (line 5): easily (*adv.*)
ὁμόνοια (line 6): from ὁμόνοια, -ας, ἡ: concord

LESSON 14

PERSONAL PRONOUNS

ἕτερος γὰρ αὐτὸς ὁ φίλος ἐστί (A friend is another self.)
—Aristotle, *Nicomachean Ethics* 1170b6-7

87.   **Personal pronouns** distinguish the one speaking (first person) from the one spoken to (second person) and the one spoken about (third person). Here are the first- and second-person pronouns in ancient Greek:

	First-Person Singular:		**First-Person Plural:**	
Nom.	ἐγώ	("I")	ἡμεῖς	("we")
Gen.	ἐμοῦ/μου	("of me")	ἡμῶν	("of us")
Dat.	ἐμοί/μοι	("to/for me")	ἡμῖν	("to/for us")
Acc.	ἐμέ/με	("me")	ἡμᾶς	("us")

	Second-Person Singluar:		**Second-Person Plural:**	
Nom.	σύ	("you")	ὑμεῖς	("you")
Gen.	σοῦ/σου	("of you")	ὑμῶν	("of you")
Dat.	σοί/σοι	("to/for you")	ὑμῖν	("to/for you")
Acc.	σέ/σε	("you")	ὑμᾶς	("you")

When two forms are listed, the first (with persistent accent) is emphatic, the second is an enclitic and less emphatic. **For objects of prepositions, the emphatic forms are preferred**. Although nominative personal pronouns are not strictly necessary, they are often added to a sentence to make it more forceful or striking.

Greek originally had a **third-person pronoun**, but it fell out of use in the Attic dialect. As a substitute for it *in the nominative case*, any one of the **demonstrative pronouns** is acceptable (e.g., ὅδε or οὗτος or ἐκεῖνος = "he"; ἥδε or αὕτη or ἐκείνη = "she"). *In cases other than the nominative*, the adjective/pronoun αὐτός, -ή, -ό serves as the usual substitute. αὐτός, -ή, -ό is declined just as ἐκεῖνος, -η, -o is, but with an accent on its ultima:

	Singular:			**Plural:**		
	Masc.	**Fem.**	**Neut.**	**Masc.**	**Fem.**	**Neut.**
Nom.	αὐτός	αὐτή	αὐτό	αὐτοί	αὐταί	αὐτά
Gen.	αὐτοῦ	αὐτῆς	αὐτοῦ	αὐτῶν	αὐτῶν	αὐτῶν
Dat.	αὐτῷ	αὐτῇ	αὐτῷ	αὐτῖς	αὐτῖς	αὐτῖς
Acc.	αὐτόν	αὐτήν	αὐτό	αὐτύς	αὐτάς	αὐτα

αὐτός, -ή, -ό is a remarkably versatile word with three distinct meanings, each of which is associated with a particular use.

1. When modifying any noun (either expressed or implied) and standing in the **attributive position**, it is an **adjective meaning "same"**; e.g., ἡ αὐτὴ κόρη τῷ αὐτῷ φίλῳ τὰ αὐτὰ βιβλία πέμπει ("the same maiden sends the same books to the same friend"); ἡ αὐτὴ τῷ αὐτῷ τὰ αὐτὰ πέμπει ("the same [woman] sends the same [things] to the same [man/person]").

2. When modifying an expressed noun in any case, or an implied noun in the nominative, and standing in the **predicate position**, it is an **intensive adjective meaning "-self"** or **"the very"**; e.g., αὐτὸς ὁ νεανίας τῇ φίλῃ αὐτῇ τὰ βιβλία αὐτὰ πέμπει ("the youth himself sends the books themselves to the friend herself" or "the very youth sends the very books to the very friend"); αὐτὸς τὰ βιβλία πέμπει ("[he] himself sends the books" or "the very [man] sends the books"); αὐτὴ τὰ βιβλία πέμπει ("[she] herself sends the books" or "the very [woman] sends the books").

3. When **acting as a noun** in the **genitive, dative,** or **accusative case**, it is a substitute for the **third-person pronoun,** meaning "him," "her," "it," or "them"; e.g., αὐτοῖς αὐτὸ πέμπω ("I send it to them"); αὐτοῦ καὶ αὐτῆς ἀκούω ("I hear him and her"); ἀπ' αὐτοῦ αὐτοὺς διώκω ("I chase them away from him/it").

NOTE   If you see a form of αὐτός in the **nominative case**, it **cannot** be the third-person pronoun; it must mean either "-self" or (in the attributive position) "same."

88.   **Dative of Possession**. To show possession, Greek often uses a third-person form of εἰμί, a noun in the dative case identifying the possessor(s), and a noun in the nominative case identifying the thing(s) possessed; e.g., ὁ ἵππος ἐμοί ἐστι ("the horse is [i.e., belongs] to me") = ἔχω τὸν ἵππον ("I possess the horse").

89.

VOCABULARY

πλήττω, πλήξω   strike (*with a direct blow*) [cf. *apoplexy*]

NOTE   This verb is often compounded with a prefix. ἐπιπλήττω means "strike at" or "rebuke"; it takes an object in the **dative** case.

φέρω, οἴσω   bear, bring, carry [cf. *metaphor, periphery*]

NOTE   The future οἴσω is borrowed from οἴω, another verb meaning "bear."

βιβλίον, -ου, τό   book [cf. *bibliography*]

NOTE   βιβλίον literally means "little papyrus" or "roll of papyrus." Ancient writing paper was made from fibers of papyrus, a plant common in Egypt.

ἱμάτιον, -ου, τό   cloak; (*plural*) clothes
ἐγώ   (*personal pronoun*) I, me

NOTE   ἐγώ γε and ἐμοί γε are usually written and accented as if they were single words, ἔγωγε and ἔμοιγε, because the enclitic is so closely connected with the pronoun. Neither ἐμοῦ γε nor ἐμέ γε, however, is written or accented that way.

ἡμεῖς   (*personal pronoun*) we, us
σύ   (*personal pronoun*) you (*sg.*)
ὑμεῖς   (*personal pronoun*) you (*pl.*)
αὐτός, -ή, -ό   (*adjective*) same; (*intensive adjective*) -self, the very; (*personal pronoun*) him, her, it, them [cf. *autocratic, autonomy, autopsy*]
ἐπί (ἐπ', ἐφ')   (*prep. + gen.*) upon, on (*the surface of*), in the time of; (*prep. + dat.*) on, at, by (*location*); (*prep. + acc.*) to, against (ἐπ' before smooth breathing, ἐφ' before rough breathing) [cf. *epiglottis, epitaph*]

NOTE   The basic sense of ἐπί is "upon," but it has many possible shades of meaning. What was said in Lesson 11 (§76) about the significance of the cases is still applicable: the dative with ἐπί pinpoints a **location** (e.g., ἐπὶ τῇ θαλάττῃ, "by the sea"); the accusative with ἐπί implies **motion toward** a destination (e.g., ἐπὶ τὴν θάλατταν, "to the sea"). Although the genitive with ἐπί does not imply motion away from a source, it does identify the source from which **support** comes; e.g., if a ship is sailing ἐπὶ τῆς θαλάττης ("on the sea"), it derives physical support from the sea beneath it.

90. **EXERCISES**

A. Greek-to-English Sentences

1. ἐγὼ μέν εἰμι μαθητής, σὺ δ᾽ εἶ οἰκέτης, ἀλλ᾽ ἡμῖν οἱ αὐτοὶ τρόποι εἰσίν.
2. κίνδυνοι καὶ ἐν ταῖς ὁδοῖς ἔσονται, ἀλλ᾽ οἱ θεοὶ αὐτοὶ ὑμᾶς φυλάξουσι καὶ οἴσουσιν ἐπὶ τὸν ποταμόν.
3. ἡμεῖς μὲν μακρὰς ἐπιστολὰς ἐγράφομεν, ἐκεῖνοι δ᾽ οὐκ ἤθελον ὑμῖν αὐτὰς φέρειν.
4. ἐπειδὴ τῇδε τῇ θεραπαίνῃ μῑκρὰ κόρη ἐστί, παιδεύσει αὐτὴ αὐτήν;
5. βιβλία μὲν καλά, ἱμάτια δὲ κακὰ ἦν ἐκείνῳ τῷ φιλοσόφῳ.
6. τοῦτο τὸ βιβλίον οὐκ ἄξιόν ἐστι πλήττεσθαι· μηκέτι βλάπτε αὐτό.
7. μὴ ἐπιπλήττετε τοῖς μαθηταῖς, αὐτοῖς γὰρ ἡ σοφίᾱ ἐστίν.
8. οὐκ ἔστι σε πάλιν πείθειν ἐμέ γε, σοῦ γὰρ οὐκέτι ἀκούσομαι.
9. ἐπὶ μὲν τῆς εἰρήνης φίλοι τοῖς ἐπὶ τῇ θαλάττῃ ἦμεν, ἐπὶ δὲ τοῦ πολέμου αὐτοῖς πολέμιοι ἐσόμεθα.
10. λέγε μοι, οὗτος, τὴν ἀλήθειαν. τόδε τὸ ἱμάτιον κλέψειν μέλλεις; διὰ τοῦτ᾽ ἐχθρὸς ἔμοιγ᾽ ἔσει.

NOTE On #10: διὰ τοῦτο ("on account of this") or διὰ ταῦτα ("on account of these things") is the equivalent of οὖν ("therefore").

B. English-to-Greek Sentences

1. I myself have the cloak, but do you yourselves have the books?
2. It is not possible for the same horse to carry both him and her to that river.
3. Hear us, O gods! Send peace itself to us and do not strike us with grief!
4. In the time of the war these very youths will hasten against the enemy (pl.) and destroy them.
5. You there, will you (sg.) look at me when I speak to you? Do you have a wagon? Bring it to me!

C.   READING

BLAME IT ON MOM
(Aesop's Fable 216)

Τέκνον βιβλίον κλέπτει καὶ τῇ φίλῃ μητρὶ φέρει. ἐπεὶ αὕτη οὐκ ἐπιπλήττει, τὸ τέκνον ἱμάτιον κλέπτει καὶ τῇ αὐτῇ φέρει. ἐπεὶ δ' αὕτη πάλιν οὐκ ἐπιπλήττει, τὸ τέκνον σπεύδει τὰ μείζονα κλέπτειν. ἀλλ' ἐπειδὴ νεανίας γίγνεται καὶ ἔτι κλέπτει, διὰ τὰ κακὰ ἔργα πέμπεται εἰς τὸν θάνατον. ἐν δὲ τῇ ὁδῷ, ἐπεὶ ἐκεῖνος τὴν μητέρα βλέπει, αὐτῇ λέγει· Διὰ σέ
5   γ' αὐτήν, ὦ μῆτερ, ἐμοὶ ἥδ' ἡ μοῖρά ἐστιν. ἐν γὰρ τῇ ἀρχῇ, ἐπεὶ βιβλία καὶ ἱμάτια ἐγὼ ἔκλεπτον, ἔδει σε ἐπιπλήττειν μοι.

μὴ οὖν μέλλετε, ὦ ἄξιαι μητέρες, τοῖς ἀναξίοις τέκνοις ἐπιπλήττειν.

VOCABULARY

μητρί (line 1): dat. sg. of the third-decl. fem. noun μήτηρ: mother

μείζονα (line 3): greater things (*neut. pl. acc. of* μείζων, *comparative degree of the adjective* μέγας)

γίγνεται (line 3): becomes (*pres. deponent indic. of* γίγνομαι, γενήσομαι)

μητέρα (line 5): acc. sg. of μήτηρ

ἔδει (line 6): it was necessary for (*third-pers. sg. imperf. act. indic. of the impersonal contract verb* δεῖ, *with acc. of person + infinitive*)

μητέρες (line 7): voc. pl. of μήτηρ

LESSON 15

CONTRACT VERBS (-άω, -έω, -όω); CONTRACTED FUTURES

> ὃν οἱ θεοὶ φιλοῦσιν ἀποθνῄσκει νέος
> (Whom the gods love dies young.)—Menander, fragment 111

91.   A **contract verb** is a verb whose present stem ends in -α, -ε, or -o. Whenever the regular endings for **present tense** or **imperfect tense** are added to such a stem, its final vowel contracts with each ending's initial vowel.

NOTE   Verbs whose present stem ends in a vowel other than -α, -ε, or -o do not undergo contraction (e.g., λύω, παύω, παιδεύω, ἀκούω; ἐσθίω, παίω, κλείω).

92.   Here is a summary of all the contractions that occur in verbs whose present stem ends in -α, -ε, or -o:

α + ε =	ᾱ	ε + ε =	ει	o + ε =	ου		
α + ει =	ᾳ	ε + ει =	ει	o + ει =	οι		
α + η =	ᾱ	ε + η =	η	o + η =	ω		
α + ῃ =	ᾳ	ε + ῃ =	ῃ	o + ῃ =	οι		
α + o =	ω	ε + o =	ου	o + o =	ου		
o + οι =	ῳ	ε + οι =	οι	o + οι =	οι		
α + ου =	ω	ε + ου =	ου	o + ου =	ου		
α + ω =	ω	ε + ω =	ω	o + ω =	ω		

GENERAL PRINCIPLES

1.   The result of every contraction is either a **long vowel** (ᾱ, η, ω) or a **diphthong** (ᾳ, ῃ, ῳ, ει, οι, ου).

2.   An **o/ω-sound prevails** over an α/ᾱ-sound or an ε/η-sound, regardless of which of the two sounds comes first (e.g., α + o = ω, not ᾱ).

3.   When an **α/ᾱ-sound** combines with an **ε/η-sound**, the **first of the two sounds prevails** (e.g., α + ε = ᾱ, not η).

4.   The iota in a diphthong is never lost through contraction, but it becomes **subscript** if the new diphthong begins with a long vowel (e.g., α + ει = ᾳ).

5.   Two epsilons contract to ει, not η; two omicrons contract to **ου**, not ω; epsilon and omicron (regardless of their order) also contract to **ου**, not ω. Thus, if a contraction involves only epsilons, only omicrons, or only an epsilon and an omicron, a **diphthong** rather than a long vowel will be the result.

6.   The long vowel or diphthong resulting from a contraction takes an **acute** if the **second** of the contracting letters would have had an acute (by the rules for recessive accent) in the uncontracted form (e.g., τῑμάτω from τῑμαέτω). If the **first** of the contracting letters would have had an acute, the long vowel or diphthong takes a **circumflex** (e.g., τῑμᾷ from τῑμάει). If **neither** of the contracting vowels or diphthongs would have had an accent, the word is accented exactly as it would have been in the **uncontracted** form (e.g., ἐτίμᾱ from ἐτίμαε).

    Contract verbs contract only in the tenses built on the present stem, i.e., in the present and the imperfect. In the other tenses, **the final vowel of the stem is lengthened** (α → ᾱ if ε, ι, or ρ precedes, otherwise η; ε → η; ο → **ω**), and then the normal endings are added (e.g., τῑμάω, τῑμήσω; φιλέω, φιλήσω; δηλόω, δηλώσω).

    The **first principal part** of a contract verb is left **uncontracted** to show which vowel ends the stem, but when the first-person singular present active indicative is used in a sentence or in any context other than a list of principal parts, **it should always be contracted** (e.g., τῑμάω should appear as τῑμῶ).

    In the imperfect active indicative of contract verbs, a movable ν is never added to the third-person singular ending. This makes sense since, after the contraction has occurred, the word no longer ends with an epsilon (e.g., ἐτίμαε > ἐτίμᾱ; ἐφίλεε > ἐφίλει; ἐδήλοε > ἐδήλου).

93.   If you understand the principles of contraction, you should have no need to memorize the endings of contract verbs, but, for your convenience, here are the paradigms of **τῑμάω** ("honor"), **φιλέω** ("love"), and **δηλόω** ("show"):

τῑμάω

PRES. ACT. INDIC.	IMPERF. ACT. INDIC.	PRES. ACT. IMPER.
Singular:	Singular:	Singular:
τῑμῶ (-άω)	ἐτίμων (ἐτίμαον)	
τῑμᾷς (-άεις)	ἐτίμᾱς (ἐτίμαες)	τίμᾱ (τίμαε)
τῑμᾷ (-άει)	ἐτίμᾱ (ἐτίμαε)	τῑμάτω (-αέτω)
Plural:	Plural:	Plural:
τῑμῶμεν (-άομεν)	ἐτῑμῶμεν (-άομεν)	
τῑμᾶτε (-άετε)	ἐτῑμᾶτε (-άετε)	τῑμᾶτε (-άετε)
τῑμῶσι(ν) (-άουσι)	ἐτίμων (ἐτίμαον)	τῑμώντων (-αόντων)

PRES. ACT. INFIN.: τῑμᾶν[1] (-άειν)

PRES. M./P. INDIC.	IMPERF. M./P. INDIC.	PRES. M./P. IMPER.
Singular:	Singular:	Singular:
τῑμῶμαι (-άομαι)	ἐτῑμώμην (-αόμην)	
τῑμᾷ (-άῃ/-άει)	ἐτῑμῶ (-άου)	τῑμῶ (-άου)
τῑμᾶται (-άεται)	ἐτῑμᾶτο (-άετο)	τῑμάσθω (-αέσθω)
Plural:	Plural:	Plural:
τῑμώμεθα	ἐτῑμώμεθα (-αόμεθα)	
τῑμᾶσθε	ἐτῑμᾶσθε (-άεσθε)	τῑμᾶσθε (-άεσθε)
τῑμῶνται (-άονται)	ἐτῑμῶντο (-άοντο)	τῑμάσθων (-αέσθων)

PRES. M./P. INFIN.: τῑμᾶσθαι (-άεσθαι)

---

[1]τῑμᾶν and **δηλοῦν** *seem* to be exceptions since one expects τῑμᾷν (α + ει = ᾳ) and δηλοῖν (ο + ει = οι), but the ει in -ειν developed from ε + ε, not ε + ι. It is therefore treated not as a diphthong, but as if it were a single epsilon (α + ε = ᾱ; ο + ε = ου). Thus all -άω verbs have infinitives ending in -ᾶν, all -όω verbs have infinitives ending in -οῦν.

φιλέω

PRES. ACT. INDIC.	**IMPERF. ACT. INDIC.**	**PRES. ACT. IMPER.**
Singular:	Singular:	Singular:
φιλῶ (-έω)	ἐφίλουν (ἐφίλεον)	
φιλεῖς (-έεις)	ἐφίλεις (ἐφίλεες)	φίλει (φίλεε)
φιλεῖ (-έει)	ἐφίλει (ἐφίλεε)	φιλείτω (-εέτω)
Plural:	Plural:	Plural:
φιλοῦμεν (-έομαι)	ἐφιλοῦμεν (-έομεν)	
φιλεῖτε (-έετε)	ἐφιλεῖτε (-έετε)	φιλεῖτε (-έετε)
φιλοῦσι(ν) (-έουσι)	ἐφίλουν (-ἐφίλεον)	φιλούντων (-εόντων)

PRES. ACT. INFIN.:   φιλεῖν (-έειν)

PRES. M./P. INDIC.	**IMPERF. M./P. INDIC.**	**PRES. M./P. IMPER.**
Singular:	Singular:	Singular:
φιλοῦμαι (-έομαι)	ἐφιλούμην (-εόμην)	
φιλῇ (-εῖ) (-έῃ/-έει)	ἐφιλοῦ (-έου)	φιλοῦ (-έου)
φιλεῖται (-έεται)	ἐφιλεῖτο (-έετο)	φιλείσθω (-εέσθω)
Plural:	Plural:	Plural:
φιλούμεθα (-εόμεθα)	ἐφιλούμεθα (-εόμεθα)	
φιλεῖσθε (-έεσθε)	ἐφιλεῖοθε (-έεσθε)	φιλεῖσθε (-έεσθε)
φιλοῦνται (-έονται)	ἐφιλοῦντο (-έοντο)	φιλείσθων (-εέσθων)

PRES. M./P. INFIN.:   φιλεῖσθαι (-έεσθαι)

δηλόω

PRES. ACT. INDIC.	IMPERF. ACT. INDIC.	PRES. ACT. IMPER.
Singular:	**Singular:**	**Singular:**
δηλῶ (-όω)	ἐδήλουν (ἐδήλοον)	
δηλοῖς (-όεις)	ἐδήλους (ἐδήλοες)	δήλου (-δήλοε)
δηλοῖ (-όει)	ἐδήλου (ἐδήλοε)	δηλούτω (-οέτω)
Plural:	**Plural:**	**Plural:**
δηλοῦμεν (-όομεν)	ἐδηλοῦμεν (-όομεν)	
δηλοῦτε (-όετε)	ἐδηλοῦτε (-όετε)	δηλοῦτε (-όετε)
δηλοῦοι(ν) (-όουσι)	ἐδήλουν (ἐδήλοον)	δηλούντων (-οόντων)

PRES. ACT. INFIN.:	δηλοῦν[1] (-όειν)

PRES. M.P. INDIC.	IMPERF. M./P. INDIC.	PRES. M./P. IMPER.
Singular:	**Singular:**	**Singular:**
δηλοῦμαι (-όομαι)	ἐδηλούμην (-οόμην)	
δηλοῖ (-όῃ/ -όει)	ἐδηλοῦ (-όου)	δηλοῦ (-όου)
δηλοῦται (-όεται)	ἐδηλοῦτο (-όετο)	δηλούσθω (-οέσθω)
Plural:	**Plural:**	**Plural:**
δηλούμεθα (-οόμεθα)	ἐδηλούμεθα (-οόμεθα)	
δηλοῦσθε (-όεσθε)	ἐδηλοῦσθε (-όεσθε)	δηλοῦσθε (-όεσθε)
δηλοῦνται (-όονται)	ἐδηλοῦντο (-όοντο)	δηλούσθων (-οέσθων)

PRES. M./P. INFIN.:	δηλοῦσθαι (-όεσθαι)

94.   When we introduced the future tense in Lesson 6, we did not tell you how to form the future of verbs whose stems end in a liquid (λ, ρ), a nasal (μ, ν), or ζ. These often have a future that looks like the present tense of an -έω contract verb. βάλλω, βαλῶ ("throw") is a typical liquid verb with a **contracted future**:

	PR. ACT.	FUTURE ACTIVE	PR. M./P.	FUTURE MIDDLE
SG.	βάλλω	βαλῶ (βαλέω)	βάλλομαι	βαλοῦμαι (βαλέομαι)
	βάλλεις	βαλεῖς (βαλέει)	βάλλῃ/ -ει	βαλῇ (-εῖ) (βαλέῃ/-έει)
	βάλλει	βαλεῖ (βαλέει)	βάλλεται	βαλεῖται (βαλέεται)
PL.	βάλλομεν	βαλοῦμεν (βαλέομεν)	βαλλόμεθα	βαλούμεθα (βαλεόμεθα)
	βάλλετε	βαλεῖτε (βαλέετε)	βάλλεσθε	βαλεῖσθε (βαλέεσθε)
	βάλλουσι(ν)	βαλοῦοι(ν) (βαλέουσι)	βάλλονται	βαλοῦνται (βαλέονται)
Inf.	βάλλειν	βαλεῖν (βαλέειν)	βάλλεσθαι	βαλεῖσθαι (βαλέεσθαι)

[1]τιμᾶν and **δηλοῦν** *seem* to be exceptions since one expects τιμᾷν (α + ει = ᾳ) and δηλοῖν (ο + ει = οι), but the ει in -ειν developed from ε + ε, not ε + ι. It is therefore treated not as a diphthong, but as if it were a single epsilon (α + ε = ᾱ; ο + ε = ου). Thus all -άω verbs have infinitives ending in -ᾶν, all -όω verbs have infinitives ending in -οῦν.

The basic stem of βάλλω is βαλ-; the λ is doubled to make the present stem. (Such stem changes are common in the present tense of liquid and nasal verbs.) The future tense is built on the **basic stem** with -εσ- + primary endings; σ then drops out, and ε **contracts** with the following vowel: βαλ-έ[σ]-ω → **βαλῶ**. Many liquid and nasal verbs have a contracted future of this sort.

Verbs in -ζω all form their futures by adding σ to the present stem; the ζ then acts like a dental and **drops out** before the σ (e:g., ἁρπάζ-σω → ἁρπάσω). But besides that, in some -ζω verbs, an ε is inserted after the σ, the σ itself drops out, and **contraction** occurs (e.g., κομίζ-σω → κομίσω → κομισέω → κομιέω → **κομιῶ**). The second principal part will always reveal which type of future a -ζω verb has.

95.   **VOCABULARY**

NOTE   From now on, use ἐρῶ, the contracted future of λέγω, rather than λέξω.

ἁρπάζω, ἁρπάσω	seize, snatch, plunder [cf. *Harpies*]
βάλλω, βαλῶ	throw, hit (*with a thrown weapon*), shoot [cf. *ballistics, parable*]
γελάω, γελάσομαι	laugh; (*with ἐπί + dat.*) laugh (at), ridicule

NOTE   The future of γελάω is deponent (like the futures of ἀκούω, βλέπω, εἰμί, and φεύγω), so it will always have middle endings but active meanings. It is also an exception to the rule that α in the present stem becomes η in the future stem. When translating "ridicule" into Greek, be sure to include ἐπί in your sentence.

δηλόω, δηλώσω	make clear, show, explain
κομίζω, κομιῶ	care for, carry, escort; (*mid.*) acquire

NOTE   The various meanings of κομίζω are all connected with the notion of caring for someone—by showing hospitality, carrying or escorting the person to another place, carrying the person back to safety, etc. The middle κομίζομαι has the special sense of "I acquire" (literally, "I carry off [something] for myself").

τῑμάω, τῑμήσω	honor, value
φιλέω, φιλήσω	love, kiss; (+ *infin.*) be fond of (doing), be accustomed (to) [cf. *bibliophile, hemophiliac, philologist*]
ὠφελέω, ὠφελήσω	help, aid
τῑμή, -ῆς, ἡ	honor, worth, price [cf. *timocracy, Timothy*]
δῆλος, -η, -ον	clear, visible, evident

96.   **EXERCISES**

A.   **Greek-to-English Sentences**

1. ἁρπάσεις, ὦ ἀγαθὲ φίλε, τὰ ἱμάτια ἐκ τῆς τῶν πολεμίων σκηνῆς αὐτῆς;
2. ὑμῖν ἐρῶ τὴν δήλην ἀλήθειαν· τοὺς μὲν οἱ θεοὶ ὠφελοῦσι, τοὺς δ᾽ οὔ.
3. ἐκεῖνοι οἱ αὐτοὶ δεσπόται ὑφ᾽ ἡμῶν καὶ ἐφιλοῦντο καὶ ἐτīμῶντο.
4. οὐ μέλλομεν ἡμεῖς γε βαλεῖν τόνδε τὸν θησαυρὸν εἰς τὴν θάλατταν.
5. μὴ φίλει βάλλειν λίθοις τοὺς ἵππους, οὐ γὰρ διὰ τοῦτο κομιῇ τῑμήν.
6. ὁ νεᾱνίᾱς ὠφελεῖται ὑπὸ τοῦ ἀδελφοῦ καὶ κομίζεται ἐκ τῶν κινδύνων.
7. ἐπὶ καλὰ φιλοσόφοις ταύτοις οὐ φιλοῦμεν γελᾶν, αὐτοὺς γὰρ τῑμῶμεν.
8. τὰ καλὰ φυτά, ὦ θεράπαινα, δῆλά σοί ἐστιν; δήλου μοι αὐτά.
9. φιλεῖς τὴν ἀδελφήν; ὠφέλει οὖν αὐτὴν καὶ μὴ γέλᾱ ἐπ᾽ αὐτῇ.
10. δηλοῦν τοὺς τόπους τοὺς ἐν τοῖς βιβλίοις, ὦ ἄξιοι μαθηταί ἔχετε;

B.   English-to-Greek Sentences

1. Then the girl used to laugh at her little brother, but now she is fond of helping him.
2. O gods, snatch us out of this long war; let peace be visible to us.
3. Those same young men are hitting the house with stones and showing their bad character.
4. At that time the virtuous philosopher was acquiring honor and being loved by his students.
5. I shall not escort you, O despot, for I at least no longer honor you.

C.   **Reading**

MIGHTY MOUSE

(Aesop's Fable 155)

Λέων μῦν ἁρπάζει καὶ ἐσθίειν αὐτὸν ἐθέλει. Μὴ ἔσθιέ με, λέγει ὁ μῑκρὸς μῦς, ἐπεί γὰρ ἐν κινδύνῳ ἔσει, ἔσται με ὠφελεῖν σε. ὁ δὲ λέων γελᾷ · Οὐκ ἔστι σέ, ὦ μῦ, ὠφελεῖν ἐμέ. ἀλλ᾽ οὐκέτι ἐθέλω ἐσθίειν σε, χαῖρε.

ἀλλ᾽ ἐπειδὴ ὁ λέων ὑπὸ κυηγετῶν ἁρπάζεται, ὁ αὐτὸς μῦς τὸ δίκτυον αὐτὸ
5 τρώγει καὶ τὸν λέοντα λύει. Μηκέτι γέλᾱ ἐπ᾽ ἔμοιγε, λέγει ὁ μῦς, τῑμὴ γὰρ καὶ μυσίν ἐστιν.

οὗτος ὁ λόγος δηλοῖ τάδε · τῑμᾶτε καὶ τοὺς μῑκρούς, ἐν γὰρ κινδύνῳ ἐκεῖνοι ὑμᾶς ἐκ θανάτου κομιοῦσιν.

λέων (line1): nom. sg. of the third-declension noun λέων, -οντος, ὁ: lion

μῦς (line 1): acc. sg. of the third-declension noun μῦς, ουός, ὁ: mouse

ἐσθίειν (line 1): from ἐσθίω, ἔδομαι: eat

μῦ (line 3): voc. sg. of μῦς (*see note above on* μῦς *in line 1*)

κυηγετῶν (line 4): from κυηγέτης, -ουφσα, ὁυ: hunter

δίκτυον (line 4): from δίκτυον, -ου, τὸ: net (*for hunting*)

τρώγει (line 5): from τρώγω, τρώξομαι: gnaw

λέοντα (line 5): acc. sg. of λέων (*see note above on* λέων *in line 1*)

μυσίν (line 6): dat. pl of μῦς (*see note above on* μῦν *in line 1*)

LESSON 16

THIRD DECLENSION
Stop, Liquid, and Nasal Stems

τέκνον, ἢ ταύτᾱν ἢ ἐπὶ ταύτᾱς
(Child, come home either holding that shield or on it.)
—instructions from the mother of a Spartan soldier,
quoted by Plutarch in *Moralia* 241f

97.   The **third declension** is also called the **consonant declension** because it consists of nouns whose stems end in a consonant (or in a vowel that *behaves* like a consonant by not contracting with other vowels). Unlike first- and second-declension nouns, third-declension nouns are not categorized according to their gender. Instead they are grouped according to the *type of consonant* (or vowel) at the end of their stem. This lesson concerns nouns whose stems end in a **stop** (dentals τ, δ, θ; labials π, β, φ; palatals κ, γ, χ), a **liquid** (λ, ρ), or a **nasal** (μ, ν).

The **gender** of a third-declension noun is relatively unpredictable, so be sure to take note of the definite article accompanying each noun in the vocabulary list.

98.   Many third-declension nouns have stems ending in a **stop**: ἀσπίς, -ίδος, ἡ ("shield"), χάρις, -ιτος, ἡ ("grace"), λέων, -οντος, ὁ ("lion"), ὄνομα, -ατος, τό ("name"), κλώψ, κλωπός, ὁ ("thief"), φύλαξ, -ακος, ὁ ("guard"), etc. Others have stems ending in a **liquid** or a **nasal**: ῥήτωρ, -ορος, ὁ ("orator"), ἀγών, -ῶνος, ὁ ("contest"), etc. Since there are no μ-stem nouns and only one λ-stem noun in Greek, "liquid-stem" and "nasal-stem" essentially mean ρ-stem and ν-stem.

Here are the third-declension endings, followed by paradigms of the eight nouns mentioned above:

ENDINGS OF THE THIRD DECLENSION

	MASCULINE AND FEMININE NOUNS		NEUTER NOUNS	
	Singular:	Plural:	Singular:	Plural:
Nom.	— or -ς	-ες	—	-α
Gen.	-ος	-ων	-ος	-ων
Dat.	-ι	-σι(ν)	-ι	-σι(ν)
Acc.	-α or -ν	-ας	—	-α
Voc.	— or -ς	-ες	—	-α

THIRD-DECLENSION NOUNS WITH STEMS ENDING IN A STOP

	("shield") ἀσπίς, -ίδος, ἡ (stem = ἀσπιδ-)	("grace") χάρις, -ιτος, ἡ (stem = χαριτ)	("lion") λέων, -οντος, ὁ (stem = λεοντ-)	("name") ὄνομα, ατος, τό (stem = ὀνοματ-)	("thief") κλώψ, κλωπός, ὁ (stem = κλωπ-)	("guard") φύλαξ, -ακος, ὁ (stem = φυλακ-)
Singular:						
Nom.	ἀσπίς	χάρις	λέων	ὄνομα	κλώψ	φύλαξ
Gen.	ἀσπίδος	χάριτος	λέοντος	ὀνόματος	κλωπός	φύλακος
Dat.	ἀσπίδι	χάριτι	λέοντι	ὀνόματι	κλωπί	φύλακι
Acc.	ἀσπίδα	χάριν	λέοντα	ὄνομα	κλῶπα	φύλακα
Voc.	ἀσπί	χάρι	λέον	ὄνομα	κλώψ	φύλαξ
Plural:						
Nom.	ἀσπίδες	χάριτες	λέοντες	ὀνόματα	κλῶπες	φύλακες
Gen.	ἀσπίδων	χαρίτων	λεόντων	ὀνομάτων	κλωπῶν	φυλάκων
Dat.	ἀσπίσι(ν)	χάρισι(ν)	λέουσι(ν)	ὀνόμασι(ν)	κλωψί(ν)	φύλαξι(ν)
Acc.	ἀσπίδας	χάριτας	λέοντας	ὀνόματα	κλῶπας	φύλακας
Voc.	ἀσπίδες	χάριτες	λέοντες	ὀνόματα	κλῶπες	φύλακες

THIRD-DECLENSION NOUNS WITH STEMS ENDING IN A LIQUID OR A NASAL

	("orator") ῥήτωρ, -ορος, ὁ (stem = ῥητορ-)			("contest") ἀγών, -ῶνος, ὁ (stem = ἀγων-)	
	Singular:	Plural:		Singular:	Plural:
Nom.	ῥήτωρ	ῥήτορες	Nom.	ἀγών	ἀγῶνες
Gen.	ῥήτορος	ῥητόρων	Gen.	ἀγῶνος	ἀγώνων
Dat.	ῥήτορι	ῥήτορσι(ν)	Dat.	ἀγῶνι	ἀγῶσι(ν)
Acc.	ῥήτορα	ῥήτορας	Acc.	ἀγῶνα	ἀγῶνας
Voc.	ῥῆτορ	ῥήτορες	Voc.	ἀγών	ἀγῶνες

99.   SPECIAL FEATURES OF THE THIRD DECLENSION

1.   The **stem** is found by dropping -ος from the **genitive singular**.

2.   The **nominative singular** *looks* irregular, and many Greek students simply memorize each noun's first form without ever trying to learn the logic behind it. Knowing how the nominative singular is formed may help you remember it: **either -ς is added to the stem** (a labial or palatal will then combine with the sigma to form ψ or ξ; a dental will drop out; e.g., ἀσπίδς → ἀσπίς) **or** (if the stem ends in -οντ, -ν, or -ρ) **no ending is added, but the vowel in the stem is lengthened** (e.g., ῥήτορ→ ῥήτωρ; if the stem ends in -οντ, the tau will drop out as well; e.g., λέοντ→ λέων). Neuters whose stems end in a dental may simply **drop the dental** from the stem to form their nominative (e.g., ὀνοματ→ ὄνομα).

3.   The **vocative singular** is usually identical with the **nominative singular**, but there are two exceptions: masculine/feminine nouns with stems ending in a *dental* (e.g., ἀσπίς, -ίδος, ἡ) and masculine/feminine nouns with stems ending in an *unaccented vowel + liquid or nasal* (e.g., ῥήτωρ, -ορος, ὁ; ἀγών, -ῶνος does not fall into this category, because its -ων is accented) use their **pure stem** (i.e., the stem with no ending attached) as the vocative. If the pure stem ends in a consonant that is not allowed at the end of a Greek word (only ν, ρ, ς, ξ, and ψ are allowed), that consonant simply drops out; e.g., the vocative of ἀσπίς is ἀσπί, not ἀσπίδ. The **vocative plural** is always identical with the **nominative plural**.

4.   To form the **accusative singular, masculine/feminine nouns usually add α** (e.g., ἀσπίδα, κλῶπα, φύλακα), but if the stem of the noun ends in an *unaccented dental*, that dental drops out, and **ν is added** instead (e.g., χάριν [stem = χάριτ-]). The ending of the **accusative plural** (-ας) has a *short* alpha (unlike the first declension's -ᾱς). The accusative of all third-declension **neuter** nouns is **identical with the nominative**, in both singular and plural.

5.   The **dative plural** ends in **-σι(ν)**. The σ unites with π, β, or φ to form **ψ**, or with κ, γ, or χ to form **ξ**. Before σ, dentals and ν drop out (e.g., ὀνόματσι → ὀνόμασι; ἀγῶνσι → ἀγῶσι). When the stem ends in -ντ, both letters drop out, and the ο of the stem lengthens to **ου** (e.g., λέοντσι → λέουσι). **Movable ν** is added to the dative-plural ending **-σι** (-ψι, -ξι) just as it is to the verb-ending -σι.

6.   Greek has **no** labial-stem, palatal-stem, or nasal-stem neuter nouns and only a **few** liquid-stem neuter nouns (none of which is regular enough to present as a paradigm), but it has **many** dental-stem neuter nouns.

7.   The **accent** of third-declension nouns is generally **persistent** (i.e., the syllable accented in the **nominative singular** is accented in the other cases too), but nouns with **monosyllabic stems** are always accented on the **ultima** in the genitive and dative, singular and plural (with a circumflex above long vowels or diphthongs, otherwise the acute; e.g., κλώψ, κλωπός, κλωπί; κλωπῶν, κλωψί[ν]).

100.   **VOCABULARY**

ποιέω, ποιήσω	make, create, do [cf. *poem, poet*]
ἀγών, -ῶνος, ὁ	contest, competition; ἀγῶνα ἔχειν = hold a contest [cf. *agony, antagonist, protagonist*]
ἀσπίς, -ίδος, ἡ	shield
κλώψ, κλωπός, ὁ	thief
λέων, -οντος, ὁ	lion
ὄνομα, -ατος, τό	name [cf. *onomatopoeia, anonymous*]
ῥήτωρ, -ορος, ὁ	orator, speaker [cf. *rhetoric*]
φύλαξ, -ακος, ὁ	guard, guardian
χάρις, -ιτος, ἡ	grace, favor, gratitude; χάριν ἔχειν (+ *dat.*) = be grateful (to) [cf. *charisma, Eucharist*]

NOTE   Combining χάριν (direct object) with a form of ἔχω is a way of expressing the idea "be grateful (to)"; the recipient of the gratitude is put into the **dative** case. Example: ὑμῖν εἴχομεν χάριν "we were grateful to you" (literally, "we had gratitude to you"). In idioms like this one, the verb can take virtually *any* form, but in a vocabulary list it will always appear as an infinitive (cf. ἀγῶνα ἔχειν above).

χάριν   (*postpos. prep. + gen.*) for the sake of

NOTE   The accusative singular of χάρις can act as a preposition; it comes *after* the noun that is its object (e.g., ἐμοῦ χάριν = "for the sake of me" or "for my sake").

ἤ   (*conjunction*) or
ἤ...ἤ   (*correlative conjunctions*) either...or

101. **EXERCISES**

A. Greek-to-English Sentences

1. κελεύω σοι, ὦ ἀγαθὲ νεανίᾱ, τὴν ἀσπίδα ἁρπάζειν καὶ διώκειν τὸν λέοντα ἐκ τῆς χώρᾱς.
2. τὰ μὲν τῶν τέκνων ὀνόματα μακρὰ ἦν, τὰ δὲ τέκνα αὐτὰ μῑκρά.
3. τούτοις τοῖς αὐτοῖς λίθοις οἱ οἰκέται ποιούντων ἢ οἰκίᾱς ἢ ὁδούς.
4. ἡμῶν χάριν, ὦ ἄξιε ῥῆτορ, γράψεις τοῖς πολεμίοις ἐπιστολὴν καὶ πείσεις αὐτοὺς ποιεῖν εἰρήνην;
5. ἔμοιγ᾽ οἱ μαθηταὶ εἶχον χάριν, τότε γὰρ ἐπαιδεύοντο ὑπ᾽ ἐμοῦ.
6. τοῖς μὲν κλωψὶ λίθοι, τοῖς δὲ φύλαξιν ἀσπίδες εἰσίν.
7. ἐν τοῖς ἀγῶσιν ἢ κομιεῖ τῑμὴν καὶ καλὸν ὄνομα ἢ εὑρήσεις θάνατον.
8. αἱ δὲ θεράπαιναι γελῶσιν ἐπὶ τοῖς ῥήτορσι καὶ αὐτοὺς οὐ τῑμῶσιν.
9. ὁ δεσπότης ἐγράφετο καὶ τοὺς κλῶπας καὶ τοὺς κακοὺς φύλακας.
10. τῶν μαθητῶν χάριν ὁ ῥήτωρ ἐποίει μακροὺς λόγους ἐν τῇ ἀγορᾷ.

B. English-to-Greek Sentences

1. The same despot used to hold a competition for the orators and honor them with gifts.
2. It is not possible, at least for the students, either to say the long names or to explain the passages.
3. Be grateful to your guardian, young man, for he protected you with his shield.
4. O noble guards, do you intend to throw this worthless thief into the river or the lake?
5. For the sake of the children, we ourselves shall be on guard against those lions.

C.   READING

WHERE TO DRAW THE LION
(Aesop's Fable 279)

Τέκνον φίλον γέρων ἔχει, ἀλλὰ φοβεῖται· Κίνδῦνοι ἐν τῇ χώρᾳ εἰσίν. ἔστι
γάρ σε, ὦ τέκνον, λύεσθαι ὑπὸ λέοντος ἐπεὶ ἐκ τῆς οἰκίᾱς τρέπῃ. ἐν οὖν τῇ οἰκίᾳ κελεύω σε
μένειν διὰ τοῦ βίου. φύλαξ δ' ἐγὼ αὐτὸς ἔσομαι.

ἐν ἀρχῇ μὲν τὸ τέκνον χαρᾶς εἶχεν ἐν τῇ οἰκίᾳ, ἐπεὶ δ' ὁ γέρων λέοντα
5   γράφει εἰς τὸν τοῖχον, τὸ τέκνον λύπην ἔχει· Σοῦ χάριν, ὦ κακὲ λέον, οὐκέτι ἔχω
λείπειν τὴν οἰκίᾱν. διὰ τοῦτο βλάψω σε. τὸ δὲ τέκνον ἐπὶ τὸν λέοντα τὴν χεῖρα βάλλει.
ἀλλὰ σκόλοψ ἐκ τοῦ τοίχου τὴν χεῖρα βλάπτει, καὶ τὸ τέκνον διὰ πυρετὸν ἀπολείπει τὸν
βίον. τούτῳ δὲ τῷ τρόπῳ λύεται ὑπὸ λέοντος.

οὐκ ἔστιν, ὦ ἄνθρωποι, φεύγειν τὴν μοῖραν.

VOCABULARY

γέρων (line 1): from γέρων, -οντος, ὁ: old man
φοβεῖται (line 1): from φοβέω, φοβήσω: frighten
μένειν (line 3): from μένω, μενῶ: remain, stay
εἰς (line 5): here = "on" (*to amuse his son, the father was drawing pictures of animals
        on the wall*)
τοῖχον (line 5): from τοῖχος, -ου, ὁ: wall (*of a house or enclosure*)
χεῖρα (line 6): from χείρ, χειρός, ἡ: hand
σκόλοψ (line 7): from σκόλοψ, -οπος, ὁ: thorn
πυρετόν (line 7): from πυρετός, -οῦ, ὁ: fever

LESSON 17

THIRD DECLENSION: Sigma Stems;
ADJECTIVES: Third Declension

ἄνδρες γὰρ πόλις, καὶ οὐ τείχη οὐδὲ νῆες ἀνδρῶν κεναί

(A city is its men, not its walls or empty ships.)

—Nicias encourages his troops in Thucydides' *Peloponnesian War* 7.77

102. Many **third-declension nouns** have stems ending in a **vowel** (ε, α, or ο) + **sigma**. In the great majority of these nouns, the stem-vowel is an **epsilon**. The few having **alpha** as their stem-vowel all happen to be neuter. The only noun with **omicron** as its stem-vowel is αἰδώς, -οῦς, ἡ ("shame").

Sigma-stem nouns use the same endings as stop-, liquid-, and nasal-stem nouns, but whenever an ending beginning with a vowel is added to a σ-stem, **the sigma drops out** (a common phenomenon when a sigma is "intervocalic," i.e., placed between two vowels); this brings the stem-vowel into contact with the initial vowel of the ending, prompting the two of them to **contract**.

The principles of contraction are identical with those presented in Lesson 15 (Contract Verbs). Some of the vowel combinations will be unfamiliar to you because they are not ones that appear in contract verbs: α + α = ᾱ; α + ι = αι; ε + α = η (since the ε/η sound comes first); ε + ι = ει; ο + α = ω (since the ο/ω sound always dominates); ο + ι = οι. Here is the chart from Lesson 15, supplemented:

103

α + α =	ᾱ	ε + α =	η	ο + α =	ω
α + ε =	ᾱ	ε + ε =	ει	ο + ε =	ου
α + ει =	ᾳ	ε + ει =	ει	ο + ει =	οι
α + η =	ᾱ	ε + η =	η	ο + η =	ω
α + ῃ =	ᾳ	ε + ῃ =	ῃ	ο + ῃ =	οι
α + ι =	αι	ε + ι =	ει	ο + ι =	οι
α + ο =	ω	ε + ο =	ου	ο + ο =	ου
α + οι =	ῳ	ε + οι =	οι	ο + οι =	οι
α + ου =	ω	ε + ου =	ου	ο + ου =	ου
α + ω =	ω	ε + ω =	ω	ο + ω =	ω

103. ENDINGS OF SIGMA-STEM NOUNS

Singular:	εσ-stem (m./f.)	εσ-stem (n.)	ασ-stem (n.)	οσ-stem (f.)
Nom.	-ης (stem, ε → η)	-ος (pure stem)	-ας (pure stem)	-ως (stem, ο → ω)
Gen.	-ους (-ε[σ]ος)	-ους (-ε[σ]ος)	-ως (-α[σ]ος)	-ους (-ο[σ]ος)
Dat.	-ει (-ε[σ]ι)	-ει (-ε[σ]ι)	-αι/-ᾳ (-α[σ]ι)	-οι (-ο[σ]ι)
Acc.	-η (-ε[σ]α)	-ος (pure stem)	-ας (pure stem)	-ω (-ο[σ]α)
Voc.	-ες (pure stem)	-ος (pure stem)	-ας (pure stem)	-ως (stem, ο → ω)

Plural:

Nom.	-εις (-ε[σ]ες)	-η (-ε[σ]α)	-ᾱ (-α[σ]α)	αἰδώς, the only οσ-
Gen.	-ων (-ε[σ]ων)	-ων (-ε[σ]ων)	-ων (-α[σ]ων)	stem noun, is not
Dat.	-εσι(ν) (-ε[σ]σι)	-εσι(ν) (-ε[σ]σι)	-ασι(ν) (-α[σ]σι)	used in
Acc.	-εις (copies nom.)	-η (-ε[σ]α)	-ᾱ (-α[σ]α)	the plural.
Voc.	-εις (-ε[σ]ες)	-η (-ε[σ]α)	-ᾱ (-α[σ]α)	

PARADIGMS OF SIGMA-STEM NOUNS

	("Socrates") Σωκράτης, ους, ὁ (stem = Σωκρατεσ-)	("trireme") τριήρης, -ους, ἡ (stem = τριηρεσ-)	("wall") τεῖχος, -ους, τό (stem = τειχεσ-)	("reward") γέρας, -ως, τό (stem = γερασ-)	("shame") αἰδώς, -οῦς, ἡ (stem = αἰδοσ-)
Singular:					
Nom.	Σωκράτης	τριήρης	τεῖχος	γέρας	αἰδώς
Gen.	Σωκράτους	τριήρους	τείχους	γέρως	αἰδοῦς
Dat.	Σωκράτει	τριήρει	τείχει	γέραι/-ᾳ[1]	αἰδοῖ
Acc.	Σωκράτη	τριήρη	τεῖχος	γέρας	αἰδῶ
Voc.	Σώκρατες	τριῆρες	τεῖχος	γέρας	αἰδώς
Plural:					
Nom.	no plural	τριήρεις	τείχη	γέρᾱ	no plural
Gen.		τριήρων[2]	τειχῶν	γερῶν	
Dat.		τριήρεσι(ν)	τείχεσι(ν)	γέρασι(ν)	
Acc.		τριήρεις	τείχη	γέρᾱ	
Voc.		τριήρεις	τείχη	γέρᾱ	

[1]The ending -ᾳ is illogical (α should be short); nevertheless it is often used.
[2]The accent should be τριηρῶν (from τριηρέων); nevertheless τριήρων is preferred.

104.   SPECIAL FEATURES OF SIGMA STEMS

1.   The **stem** is less obvious in σ-stem nouns than it is in stop-, liquid-, and nasal-stem nouns. An **-ους** ending in the **genitive singular** (where -ος would be expected) shows that there has been a contraction, but it does not tell whether the noun is an εσ-stem (-ους = -ε[σ]ος) or an οσ-stem (-ους = -ο[σ]ος). To be sure of the stem-vowel, you must look at the ending of the nominative singular, too. When the **genitive singular** ends in **-ως** (= -α[σ]ος), you can assume that the noun is an ασ-stem.

2.   For the **nominative singular**, all σ-stems use their **pure stem**, but masculine/feminine εσ-stems and αἰδώς also **lengthen their stem-vowel**, while neuter εσ-stems switch to a variant of their pure stem, in which **o has replaced ε**.

3.   **Masculine εσ-stems are all proper names** and thus are seldom found in the plural. Since their nominative singular ends in -ης, it is easy to confuse these nouns with first-declension masculines like δεσπότης, -ου; be sure to check the genitive singular. τριήρης is the **only feminine εσ-stem**.

4.   In the **accusative singular** -εσα contracts to **-η**, -οσα to **-ω**. You would logically expect the **accusative plural** of masculine/feminine εσ-stems to end in -ης (= -ε[σ]ας), but instead the ending **-εις** (= -ε[σ]ες) is borrowed from the nominative plural. The accusative of all **neuter** σ-stems is **identical with the nominative**, in both singular and plural.

5.   The **vocative singular** of σ-stem nouns is **identical with the nominative singular** except in masculine/feminine εσ-stem nouns, which use their **pure stem** (e.g., vocative of τριήρης, -ους, ἡ = τριῆρες).

6.   As with contract verbs, the accent of σ-stem nouns is determined by where the words would have been accented in their *uncontracted* forms (see §92, General Principle #6, in Lesson 15). Since they are nouns, their original accents would have been **persistent**. The one exception is the **vocative singular of masculine εσ-stems**, which has a recessive accent (e.g., Σώκρατες).

105.   Just as first- and second-declension nouns furnish the endings for -ος, -η, -ον adjectives, so third-declension nouns furnish the endings for **third-declension adjectives**. One common type of third-declension adjective has the endings of **nasal-stem** nouns (e.g., εὐδαίμων, -ον, "happy"; cf. ἀγών); another has the endings of **εσ-stem** nouns (e.g., ἀληθής, -ές, "true"; cf. τριήρης):

	Masc./Fem.	Neuter	Masc./Fem.	Neuter
Singular:				
Nom.	εὐδαίμων	εὔδαιμον	ἀληθής	ἀληθές
Gen.	εὐδαίμονος	εὐδαίμονος	ἀληθοῦς	ἀληθοῦς
Dat.	εὐδαίμονι	εὐδαίμονι	ἀληθεῖ	ἀληθεῖ
Acc.	εὐδαίμονα	εὔδαιμον	ἀληθῆ	ἀληθές
Voc.	εὔδαιμον	εὔδαιμον	ἀληθές	ἀληθές
Plural:				
Nom.	εὐδαίμονες	εὐδαίμονα	ἀληθεῖς	ἀληθῆ
Gen.	εὐδαιμόνων	εὐδαιμόνων	ἀληθῶν	ἀληθῶν
Dat.	εὐδαίμοσι(ν)	εὐδαίμοσι(ν)	ἀληθέσι(ν)	ἀληθέσι(ν)
Acc.	εὐδαίμονας	εὐδαίμονα	ἀληθεῖς	ἀληθῆ
Voc.	εὐδαίμονες	εὐδαίμονα	ἀληθεῖς	ἀληθῆ

These **two-ending adjectives** have no distinct set of endings for the feminine (cf. ἀθάνατος, -ον, ἀνάξιος, -ον, and φιλόσοφος, -ον). The accent in the masc./fem. voc. sg. and the neuter nom./acc./voc. sg. of adjectives like εὐδαίμων is unusual in being **recessive**; all the other forms have the **persistent** accent typical of adjectives, here based on the location of the accent in the masc./fem. nom. sg. All the features of nasal-stem and εσ-stem nouns apply also to nasal-stem and εσ-stem adjectives.

106.   **VOCABULARY**

αἰδώς, -οῦς, ἡ	shame (*either good or bad sense*), modesty, respect
γέρας, -ως, τό	prize, privilege
δαίμων, -ονος, ὁ, ἡ	divine being, guardian spirit [cf. *demon*]
Σωκράτης, -ους, ὁ	Socrates
τεῖχος, -ους, τό	wall (*of a city*)
τριήρης, -ους, ἡ	trireme (*warship with three banks of oars*)
ἀληθής, -ές	true, real, sincere
εὐδαίμων, -ον	happy, fortunate, prosperous [cf. *eudemonics*]
εὖ	(*adv.*) well, kindly; εὖ ἔχειν/πράττειν = fare well
κακῶς	(*adv.*) badly, wickedly; κακῶς ἔχειν/ πράττειν = fare badly
πρός	(*prep. + gen.*) from, by (*in oaths*); (*prep. + dat.*) at, near; (*prep. + acc.*) to, toward, against (*basic meaning of* πρός = in the direction of, facing) [cf. *prosody, prosthesis*]

NOTE   When a person is viewed as the *source* rather than the *agent* of an action, πρός + genitive replaces ὑπό + genitive (e.g., ἐπέμπετο πρὸς ἐμοῦ, "it was sent *from* me"; ἐπέμπετο ὑπ' ἐμοῦ, "it was sent *by* me"). πρός in an oath is best translated as "by"; among the most common oaths in Greek is πρὸς θεῶν ("by the gods!").

Many verbs have προσ- as their prefix: e.g., προσβάλλω, προσβαλῶ (+ *dat*,) "attack", προσποιέω, προσποιήσω "add to"; (*mid.* + *infin.*) "pretend (to)."

107.   **EXERCISES**

A.   **Greek-to-English Sentences**

1. ἐν μὲν τοῖς ἀγῶσι γέρᾱ ἐκομίζου, ἐν δὲ τῇ ἀγορᾷ ἐτῑμῶ ὑπὸ τῶν ῥητόρων. διὰ ταῦτ' εὐδαίμων ἦσθα.

2. προσποιῇ εὖ ἔχειν, ὦ Σώκρατες, ἀλλὰ τῇ ἀληθείᾳ κακῶς ἔχεις. ἴσθι ἀληθὴς καὶ δήλου μοι τὰς λύπᾱς.

3. εὖ φυλάττετε τὰ τείχη, ὦ φύλακες, καὶ μὴ ἀπολείπετε τὰς χώρᾱς.

4. ἥδ' ἡ κόρη ἔχει τὴν αἰδῶ, οὐ γὰρ γελᾷ ἐπὶ τοῖς ἀθανάτοις δαίμοσιν.

5. ἐπεὶ πρὸς τῇ θαλάττῃ ἐσμέν, ἔχομεν βλέπειν εἰς τὰς καλὰς τριήρεις.

6. πρὸς σὲ τὰ αὐτὰ ὀνόματα τὰ κακὰ οὐ βαλῶ, ἡ γὰρ αἰδὼς ἔμοιγ' ἐστίν.

7. μὴ πέμπε, ὦ δαῖμον, εὐδαίμονα βίον ἐκείνοις τοῖς ἀναξίοις κλωψίν.

8. φεύγετε, πρὸς θεῶν, φεύγετε· ὁ γὰρ λέων μέλλει προσβαλεῖν ἡμῖν.

9. οἱ μαθηταὶ φιλοῦσι παιδεύεσθαι ὑπὸ τοῦ Σωκράτους, ἀληθεῖς γὰρ λόγους πρὸς αὐτοῦ ἀκούουσιν.

10. τὴν ἀσπίδα νῦν ἁρπαζέτω ὁ φύλαξ καὶ τρεπέσθω πρὸς τὸ τεῖχος.

B.   **English-to-Greek Sentences**

1. The shields are being sent to us from the despot; we shall carry them against the enemy.

2. Let this trireme hasten through the sea, for it is going to attack that trireme.

3. Some were doing real tasks near the wall; others were pretending to do them.

4. In the contests I shall either fare badly and find death or fare well and acquire prizes.

5. By the gods, Socrates, you have a fortunate life, for you obey your guardian spirit and speak with modesty.

C.   READING

OUTFOXED
(Aesop's Fable 147)

Ἐν γήρᾳ οὐκ εἶχε λέων ζῷα διώκειν καὶ ἁρπάζειν. ἐτρέπετο οὖν εἰς σπήλαιον καὶ προσεποιεῖτο εἶναι ἐν λύπῃ· Οἴμοι, ἔλεγεν ὁ λέων, κακῶς ἔχω. μέλλω ἀπολείψειν τὸν βίον. χαίρετε, φίλοι. ὑμᾶς γὰρ πάλιν οὐ βλέψομαι.

ἐπεὶ τὰ ζῷα τοῦ λέοντος ἀκούει, πόλλ᾽ εἰς τὸ σπήλαιον σπεύδει καὶ ὑπὸ
5   τοῦ λέοντος ἐσθίεται. ἀλλ᾽ ἡ ἀλώπηξ οὐκ ἐθέλει πρὸς τὸν λέοντα τρέπεσθαι. κελεύει ὁ λέων· Σπεῦδε, ὦ ἀγαθὴ ἀλώπηξ, εἰς τὸ σπήλαιον. ἐγὼ γὰρ κακῶς πράττω καὶ σοί γ᾽ οὐ προσβαλῶ. Ἔγωγε πρὸς σέ, ὦ λέον, οὐ τρέψομαι, τὰ μὲν γὰρ τῶν ζῴων ἴχνη βλέπω τὰ εἰς τὸ σπήλαιον, τὰ δ᾽ ἐκ τοῦ σπηλαίου οὔ.

ἐπειδὴ δῆλα τὰ ἴχνη ἐστίν, ὦ ἄνθρωποι, μὴ μέλλετε φεύγειν τοὺς κινδύνους.

VOCABULARY

γήρᾳ (line 1): from γῆρας, -ως, τό: old age
ζῷα (line 1): from ζῷον, -ου, τό: animal
σπήλαιον (line 2): from σπήλαιον, -ου, τό: cave
οἴμοι (line 2): woe is me! (*exclamation of distress*)
πόλλ᾽ (line 4) = πολλά: many (*neut. nom. pl. of the adj.* πολύς; *accent moves to penult when* πολλά *is elided*)
ἐσθίεται (line 5): from ἐσθίω, ἔδομαι: eat
ἀλώπηξ (line 5): from ἀλώπηξ, -εκος, ἡ: fox
ἴχνη (line 8): from ἴχνος, -ους, τό: footstep, track

LESSON 18

Ω-VERBS
First Aorist Active and Middle Indicative,
First Aorist Active and Middle Infinitives,
First Aorist Active and Middle Imperative

νίψον ἀνόμημα μὴ μόναν ὄψιν (Wash off your sin, not only your face.)
—palindrome on a font in the cathedral of Hagia Sophia, Istanbul

108.   Lessons 18 and 19 introduce you to the **third principal part** of Greek verbs. The stem supplied by this principal part is used to form the **aorist** tense in the **active** and **middle** voices. A different stem (supplied by the sixth principal part) is used to form the aorist **passive**. (Compare the similar situation with the *second* principal part, which supplies the stem for future active and middle, but not for future passive.) Until you have learned the sixth principal part (Lesson 27), you will not be asked to put any verbs into the aorist passive.

109.   You have already encountered the term **aoristic** in connection with the aspect of a verb. An aoristic action is one that the speaker perceives not as an activity continuing over time, but as a **mere occurrence or event**. It may happen in the present, past, or future. Since the aoristic aspect does not specify whether the action is/was/will be prolonged, repeated, or finished, the name ἀόριστος, "undefined" (ἀ-privative + ὁρίζω "mark a boundary" or "define"), is appropriate.

Like the imperfect tense, the **aorist tense** shows an action that occurred in the **past**, but the aspect of that action is **aoristic**, not imperfective. (Note: More accurate names for the imperfect tense and the aorist tense would be *past imperfective* and *past aoristic*.) Like the imperfect, the aorist is a **secondary** tense; it therefore has **secondary endings** and an **augment**.

The majority of Greek verbs have what is called a **first aorist** (otherwise known as a *sigmatic aorist* or a *weak aorist*); some Greek verbs have what is called a **second aorist** (otherwise known as an *asigmatic aorist* or a *strong aorist*). A few Greek verbs have **both** a first aorist and a second aorist. The verbs presented in this lesson all have first aorists; the verbs presented in Lesson 19 have second aorists or both first and second aorists.

Here is the conjugation of παιδεύω in the first aorist active and middle:

INDICATIVE MOOD

First Aorist Active
Singular:
ἐπαίδευσα
("I taught")
ἐπαίδευσας
("you [*sg.*] taught")
ἐπαίδευσε(ν)
("he/she/it taught")

First Aorist Middle
ἐπαιδευσάμην
("I taught for myself")
ἐπαιδεύσω
("you taught for yourself")
ἐπαιδεύσατο
("he/she/it taught for him/her/itself")

Plural:
ἐπαιδεύσαμεν
("we taught")
ἐπαιδεύσατε
("you [*pl.*] taught")
ἐπαίδευσαν
("they taught")

ἐπαιδευσάμεθα
("we taught for ourselves")
ἐπαιδεύσασθε
("you taught for yourselves")
ἐπαιδεύσαντο
("they taught for themselves")

INFINITIVES

First Aorist Active
παιδεῦσαι
("to teach")

First Aorist Middle
παιδεύσασθαι
("to teach for oneself")

IMPERATIVE MOOD

First Aorist Active
Singular:
παίδευσον
("teach!")
παιδευσάτω
("let him/her/it teach!")

First Aorist Middle
παίδευσαι
("teach for yourself!")
παιδευσάσθω
("let him/her/it teach for him/her/itself!")

Plural:
παιδεύσατε
("teach!")
παιδευσάντων
("let them teach!")

παιδεύσασθε
("teach for yourselves!")
παιδευσάσθων
("let them teach for themselves!")

SUMMARY OF FIRST AORIST ENDINGS

Indicative

Active		Middle	
	-σα		-σαμην
	-σας		-σω (-σα[σ]ο)
	-σε(ν)		-σατο
	-σαμον		-σαμεθα
	-σατε		-σασθε
	-σαν		-σαντο

Infinitives

Active	-σαι	Middle	-σασθαι

Imperative

Active		Middle	
	-σον		-σαι
	-σατω		-σασθω
	-σατε		-σασθε
	-σαντων		-σασθων

As you can see, most of the first aorist endings are combinations of the letters σα and the secondary personal endings; there is *no intervening thematic vowel* (o/ε). A predictable contraction occurs in the second-person singular middle indicative (-σα[σ]ο → -σω). In the first-person singular active indicative, σα used to be σμ (sigma by itself was the original sign of the aorist tense), but the μ changed to α, producing the σα that then insinuated itself into almost all the other aorist forms. It did *not* insinuate itself into the third-person singular active, where the final ε is an ending borrowed from the perfect tense.

To signify past tense, **augments** are added to all aorist **indicative** forms, but not to aorist **infinitives** or **imperatives**. This is logical since infinitives and imperatives show only aspect (in this case **aoristic**), not time. Augmenting is done exactly as in the imperfect tense: a temporal augment is used if the word begins with a vowel; otherwise a syllabic augment (ἐ-) is used.

The -αι of the active infinitive is an old dative ending (infinitives originated as nouns). Scholars are unsure how the endings of the second-person imperatives came to be -ον and -αι. Notice that the only difference in form between the active infinitive (παιδεῦσαι) and the second-person singular middle imperative (παίδευσαι) is accent: the **first aorist active infinitive is always accented on the penult**, while the first aorist middle imperative has recessive accent (as do all the other finite forms of the first aorist and the first aorist middle infinitive).

Adding σα to a present stem that ends in a consonant causes the same euphonic changes as in the future tense:

labial (-π, -β, -φ) or **-πτ**   + σα   = **ψα**
dental (-τ, -δ, -θ) or **-ζ**   + σα   = **σα**
palatal (-κ, -γ, -χ) or **-ττ**   + σα   = **ξα**

Contract verbs, as you would expect, lengthen their final vowel (α → η or, after ε, ι, or ρ, ᾱ; ε → η; ο → ω) before adding σα. **Liquid and nasal** verbs *either* add η (a lengthened ε) + σα to their present stem *or* add σα, drop σ, and lengthen their stem-vowel (α → η or, after ι or ρ, ᾱ; ε → ει). Examples:

φιλέω   →   ἐφίλησα
μέλλω   →   ἐμέλλησα
ἀγγέλλω [basic stem[1] = ἀγγελ-]   →   ἤγγελ[σ]α   →   ἤγγειλα

110.   Of the verbs you already know, the following thirty have **first aorists**.

ἀκούω	ἀκούσομαι	ἤκουσα
ἀλλάττω	ἀλλάξω	ἤλλαξα
ἁρπάζω	ἁρπάσω	ἥρπασα
βλάπτω	βλάψω	ἔβλαψα
βλέπω	βλέψομαι	ἔβλεψα
γελάω	γελάσομαι	ἐγέλασα
γράφω	γράψω	ἔγραψα
δηλόω	δηλώσω	ἐδήλωσα
διώκω	διώξω	ἐδίωξα
δουλεύω	δουλεύσω	ἐδούλευσα
ἐθέλω	ἐθελήσω	ἠθέλησα
θύω	θύσω	ἔθῡσα
κελεύω	κελεύσω	ἐκέλευσα
κλέπτω	κλέψω	ἔκλεψα
κομίζω	κομιῶ	ἐκόμισα
λύω	λύσω	ἔλῡσα
μέλλω	μελλήσω	ἐμέλλησα
παιδεύω	παιδεύσω	ἐπαίδευσα
πείθω	πείσω	ἔπεισα
πέμπω	πέμψω	ἔπεμψα
πλήττω (ἐπιπλήττω)	πλήξω (ἐπιπλήξω)	ἔπληξα (ἐπέπληξα)
ποιέω (προσποιέω)	ποιήσω (προσποιήσω)	ἐποίησα (προσεποίησα)
πράττω	πράξω	ἔπρᾱξα
σπεύδω	σπεύσω	ἔσπευσα
τῑμάω	τῑμήσω	ἐτίμησα

---

[1] If, as here, the present stem is an expansion of an even simpler stem, use that simpler, basic stem to construct the aorist.

τρέπω	τρέψω	ἔτρεψα
φιλέω	φιλήσω	ἐφίλησα
φυλάττω	φυλάξω	ἐφύλαξα
χαίρω	χαιρήσω	ἐχαίρησα
ὠφελέω	ὠφελήσω	ὠφέλησα

From now on, you must memorize three principal parts for every verb. The **third principal part** is always the first-person singular aorist active indicative.

111. The **genitive of value** (in a context of buying or selling, it is also called **genitive of price**) is a common construction in Greek to indicate what someone or something is worth. The words δραχμή ("drachma") and ὀβολός ("obol") occur often in the genitive to indicate the price of an object; e.g., τὴν ἀσπίδα πωλῶ δραχμῆς ("I am selling the shield for a drachma").

112. **VOCABULARY**

ἀγγέλλω, ἀγγελῶ, ἤγγειλα   announce, report

NOTE   λ is added to the basic stem ἀγγελ- to make the present stem. εσ is added to ἀγγελ- to form the future, but the σ drops out, and contraction occurs. The first aorist's σ also drops out, and the stem-vowel is lengthened (ε→ ει) to compensate.

ἐρωτάω, ἐρωτήσω, ἠρώτησα   (+ *double acc.*) ask, question

NOTE   The question being asked and the person being questioned both go into the accusative case. This is called a **double accusative**.

πωλέω, πωλήσω, ἐπώλησα	sell [cf. *monopoly*]
ἄγγελος, -ου, ὁ, ἡ	messenger [cf. *angel, evangelism*]
δραχμή, -ῆς, ἡ	drachma (*unit of money & weight = 6 obols*)
ὀβολός, -οῦ, ὁ	obol (*small unit of money & weight*)
μόνος, -η, -ον	alone, only [cf. *monograph, monolithic, monotheism, monk*]
ὀλίγος, -η, -ον	little, few [cf. *oligarchy*]
πολύς, πολλή, πολύ	(*irreg. adj.—no voc. sg.*) much, many; οἱ πολλοί = the many, the people [cf. *polygraph, polymer, polyphony, polytheism*]

NOTE   πολύς is irregular in the *masculine* sg. nom. and acc. (πολύς, πολύν) and the *neuter* sg. nom. and acc. (πολύ, πολύ). Otherwise its stem is πολλ-, and it has normal -ος, -η, -ον endings. It is not used in the vocative singular. All forms are accented on the ultima. πολλά is usually elided before a vowel; its accent then shifts to the penult (πόλλ'). See the appendix for a full paradigm.

μόνον	(*neut. sg. acc. of* μόνος *used as adv.*) only
οὐ μόνον...ἀλλὰ καί	(*correlatives*) not only...but also
πολύ or πολλά	(*neuter sg. or pl. acc. of* πολύς *used as adv.*) much
περί	(*prep. + gen.*) about, concerning; (*prep. + dat.*) around; (*prep. + acc.*) around (*basic meaning of* περί = around) (*never elided*) [cf. *period, peripatetic, periphery, periscope*]

NOTE

περί + accusative is much more common than περί + dative. The dative is used mostly in descriptions of clothing "around" a person's body or with verbs that express care or anxiety centered "around" someone or something.

113.   **EXERCISES**

A.   **Greek-to-English Sentences**

1. ἠρώτησάν με τόδε· Πολλῶν ὀβολῶν ἐπώλησας τὰ βιβλία ταῦτα;
2. πρὸς θεῶν, ὦ φύλακες, σπεύσατε ἐπὶ τὸ τεῖχος, ὥρα γὰρ φυλάξαι.
3. τοῖς μὲν ῥήτορσι πολλαὶ δραχμαὶ ἦσαν, τοῖς δ' ἀγγέλοις ὀλίγαι.
4. ἐρωτησάτω ὁ φιλόσοφος αὐτοὺς τόδε· Μόνοι ὑμεῖς ἄξιοι εἶναι μαθηταί;
5. ἐπειδὴ ἠκούσαμεν ταῦτα, πολὺ ἐπεπλήξαμεν τοῖς ἀγγέλοις.
6. ἐπὶ μὲν τοῦ πολέμου τοῖς πολλοῖς πολὺς κίνδυνος, ἐπὶ δὲ τῆς εἰρήνης πολλὴ ἡσυχίᾱ.
7. τρέψαι εἰς τὴν ἀγορὰν καὶ πώλησον τὰς ἀσπίδας, οὐ μόνον τὰς καλὰς ἀλλὰ καὶ τὰς ὀλίγης τῑμῆς.
8. πόλλ' ἡμῖν ἤγγειλεν ὅδ' ὁ αὐτὸς ἄγγελος περὶ ἐκείνου τοῦ πολέμου.
9. τοὺς οὐκ ὀβολοῦ ἀξίους κλῶπας ἐδίωξας περὶ τὰ τείχη καὶ ἥρπασας.
10. οὐ μόνον πολλὰ γέρᾱ ἐκομίσω ἐν τῷ ἀγῶνι, ἀλλὰ καὶ πολλὴν τῑμήν.

B.   **English-to-Greek Sentences**

1. Dear messenger, you alone are accustomed to be sincere; report the truth about the contest.
2. We sold the fine books for many drachmas, the ugly clothes for a few obols.
3. That evil thief not only stole the shield but also destroyed it.

4. The people ridiculed Socrates much and sent him to death.

5. I asked them this: "Did you stand guard in the same position or move around the walls?"

C. READING

HERMES FINDS HIMSELF A BARGAIN
(Aesop's Fable 90)

Ἑρμῆς ὁ τῶν θεῶν ἄγγελος ἔσπευδεν εὑρίσκειν ἐν πόσῃ τῑμῇ ἐστιν. ἐκεῖνος οὖν ἐτρέψατο εἰς τὸ ἀγαλματοποιοῦ ἐργαστήριον. ἔβλεψεν εἰς ἄγαλμα Διὸς καὶ τὸν ἀγαλματοποιὸν ἠρώτησε· Πόσου τόδε τὸ ἄγαλμα πωλῆσαι ἐθέλεις; Ὀβολοῦ. ἐπεὶ ταύτην τὴν ὀλίγην τῑμὴν ἤκουσεν, ὁ Ἑρμῆς ἐγέλασε καὶ
5 ἠρώτησε· Πόσου τόδε τὸ τῆς Ἥρᾱς; Δραχμῆς. ὁ δ᾽ Ἑρμῆς πάλιν ἐγέλασε καὶ ἠρώτησε· Καὶ πόσου τόδε τὸ τοῦ Ἑρμοῦ τοῦ καλοῦ καὶ ἀγαθοῦ ἀγγέλου; πολλοῦ γὰρ ἄξιος ἐκεῖνός γ᾽ ἐστίν. ὁ δ᾽ ἀγαλματοποιὸς ἐγέλασε· Πρὸς θεῶν, ὦ φίλε, οὐ μόνον τὸ τοῦ Διὸς ἀλλὰ καὶ τὸ τῆς Ἥρᾱς σοι πωλήσω καὶ πρὸς αὐτοῖς τόδε τὸ τοῦ Ἑρμοῦ τὸ ἄγαλμα δῶρόν σοι ποιήσω.
10 μὴ ἔστε κενόδοξοι, ὦ ἄνθρωποι, ἡ γὰρ ἀλήθεια ἡ περὶ ὑμῶν δήλη ἔσται.

VOCABULARY

Ἑρμῆς (line 1): from Ἑρμῆς, -οῦ, ὁ: Hermes, one of the Olympian gods; he is often depicted as a trickster and a bit of a rascal

ἐν πόσῃ τῑμῇ ἐστιν (line 1): how much honor he had (*literally,* "in how much honor he is"; *indirect question*)

πόσῃ (line 1): from πόσος, -η, -ον: how much? (*interrogative adj./pronoun*)

ἀγαλματοποιοῦ (line 2): from ἀγαλματοποιός, -οῦ, ὁ: sculptor

ἐργαστήριον (line 2): from ἐργαστήριον, -ου, τό: workshop

ἄγαλμα (line 2): from ἄγαλμα, -ατος, τό: statue

Διός (line 3): from Ζεύς, Διός, ὁ: Zeus, king of the Olympian gods (*this third-decl. noun has an odd nominative singular; you would expect Δίς*)

πόσου (line 3): at what price? (*literally,* "of how much?"; *genitive of value*)

Ἥρᾱς (line 5): from Ἥρᾱ, -ᾱς, ἡ: Hera, queen of the Olympian gods

πρός (line 8): here = "in addition to"

κενόδοξοι (line 10): from κενόδοξος, -ον: conceited

LESSON 19

Ω-VERBS
Second Aorist Active and Middle Indicative, Second Aorist Active and Middle Infinitives, Second Aorist Active and Middle Imperative; REFLEXIVE PRONOUNS

> γνῶθι σαυτόν (Know thyself.) —one of Thales' sayings,
> quoted by Diogenes Laertius 1.40
> and said to have been inscribed on Apollo's temple at Delphi

114.   **Second aorists** (also known as *asigmatic* or *strong* aorists) lack the distinctive σα of first aorists. Of the verbs you have learned so far, only the following five (and their compounds) have second aorists:

βάλλω	βαλῶ	ἔβαλον	(compound: προσέβαλον)
εὑρίσκω	εὑρήσω	εὗρον/ηὗρον	
ἔχω	ἔξω/σχήσω	ἔσχον	
λείπω	λείψω	ἔλιπον	(compound: ἀπέλιπον)
φεύγω	φεύξομαι	ἔφυγον	

NOTE   Either spelling, εὗρον or ηὗρον, can be used. ἔσχον means "I got hold of."

Two verbs from previous lessons have **both** a second aorist and a first aorist:

λέγω	ἐρῶ/λέξω	εἶπον/ἔλεξα
φέρω	οἴσω	ἤνεγκα/ἤνεγκον

There is **no difference in meaning** between first and second aorist in either verb. Attic Greek much prefers εἶπον to ἔλεξα (which is why we have listed εἶπον first). ἤνεγκα is missing its σ, but in all other respects is conjugated like a regular first aorist.

115.   Here is the conjugation of **βάλλω** in the second aorist active and middle:

INDICATIVE MOOD

Second Aorist Active	**Second Aorist Middle**
Singular:	
ἔβαλον	ἐβαλόμην
("I threw")	("I threw for myself")
ἔβαλες	ἐβάλου (-ε[σ]ο)
("you [sg.] threw")	("you [sg.] threw for yourself")
ἔβαλε(ν)	ἐβάλετο
("he/she/it threw")	("he/she/it threw for him/her/itself")
Plural:	
ἐβάλομεν	ἐβαλόμεθα
("we threw")	("we threw for ourselves")
ἐβάλετε	ἐβάλεσθε
("you [pl.] threw")	("you [pl.] threw for yourselves")
ἔβαλον	ἐβάλοντο
("they threw")	("they threw for themselves")

INFINITIVES

Second Aorist Active	**Second Aorist Middle**
βαλεῖν (-εεν)	βαλέσθαι
("to throw")	("to throw for oneself")

IMPERATIVE MOOD

Second Aorist Active	**Second Aorist Middle**
Singular:	
βάλε	βαλοῦ (-ε[σ]ο)
("throw!")	("throw for yourself!")
βαλέτω	βαλέσθω
("let him/her/it throw!")	(" let him/her/it throw for him/her/itself!")
Plural:	
βάλετε	βάλεσθε
("throw!")	("throw for yourselves!")
βαλόντων	βαλέσθων
("let them throw!")	("let them throw for themselves!")

SUMMARY OF SECOND AORIST ENDINGS

Indicative

Active		Middle	
-ον			-ομην
-ες			-ου (-ε[σ]ο)
-ε(ν)			-ετο
-ομεν			-ομεθα
-ετε			-εσθε
-ον			-οντο

Infinitives

Active		Middle	
-εῖν[1] (-εεν)			-έσθαι[1]

Imperative

Active		Middle	
-ε			-οῦ[1] (-ε[σ]ο)
-ετω			-εσθω
-ετε			-εσθε
-οντων			-εσθων

With their **augment, thematic vowel** (ε/ο), and **secondary endings**, second aorists look much like imperfects. What marks them as aorists is their stem, which is built on the **root** or simplest form of the verb. It is often the case that one or more letters have been added to the root to construct the present stem. If so, you can recover the root simply by removing those additional letters from the present stem; e.g., βαλλ- = **βαλ-** + λ; εὑρισκ- = **εὑρ-** + ισκ.

Second aorists like ἔλιπον (from λείπω), ἔφυγον (from φεύγω), and ἔσχον (from ἔχω—originally σέχω) give the impression of having lost the epsilon still visible in their present stem. The real reason for this "loss" is a phenomenon called **vowel gradation**. Just as a strong verb in English may have a different vowel in each of its principal parts (e.g., *sing, sang, sung*), so a Greek verb may have a variable vowel that appears either as an epsilon (ε-grade), as an omicron (o-grade), or—in its most reduced state—not at all (zero-grade). **The ε-grade is characteristic of the present stem; the zero-grade is characteristic of the root and of the second aorist stem.** From this you can infer that whenever a verb's present stem has an epsilon, the second aorist stem of that verb will probably *not* have one.

The second aorists of φέρω and λέγω are peculiar. ἤνεγκον is based on ἐνκ-, a zero-grade stem (ε-grade = ἐνεκ-); the ἐν was doubled to give ἐνενκ-, and ν before κ turned into γ, producing ἐνεγκ-. εἶπον goes back to a root that began with a digamma: ϝεπ-. The first two letters were doubled (ϝεϝεπ-) to make the aorist stem. When ϝ ceased to be pronounced and fell out of use, the two epsilons contracted into the diphthong ει. Augmenting this ει does not change it to η.

---

[1] In the second aorist the accent is always on the **ultima** of the active infinitive and second-person singular middle imperative and on the **penult** of the middle infinitive. In all other second aorist forms, the accent is **recessive**. The aorists εἶπον, εὗρον, and ἔλαβον accent the ultima in the second-person singular active imperative: εἰπέ, εὑρέ, λαβέ.

116. A **reflexive pronoun** is one that "reflects" or directs attention back to the subject of the sentence, but is not the subject itself. It occurs only in the **genitive**, **dative**, and **accusative** cases.

REFLEXIVE PRONOUNS

First-Person Singular:

ἐμαυτοῦ, -ῆς
("of myself")
ἐμαυτῷ, -ῇ
("to/for myself")
ἐμαυτόν, -ήν
("myself")

First-Person Plural:

ἡμῶν αὐτῶν, -ῶν
("of ourselves")
ἡμῖν αὐτοῖς, -αῖς
("to/for ourselves")
ἡμᾶς αὐτούς, -άς
("ourselves")

Second-Person Singular:

σεαυτοῦ, -ῆς   [σαυτοῦ, -ῆς]
("of yourself")
σεαυτῷ, -ῇ   [σαυτῷ, -ῇ]
("to/for yourself")
σεαυτόν, -ήν   [σαυτόν, -ήν]
("yourself")

Second-Person Plural:

ὑμῶν αὐτῶν, -ῶν
("of yourselves")
ὑμῖν αὐτοῖς, -αῖς
("to/for yourselves")
ὑμᾶς αὐτούς, -άς
("yourselves")

Third-Person Singular:

ἑαυτοῦ, -ῆς, -οῦ   [αὑτοῦ, -ῆς, -οῦ]
("of him/her/itself")
ἑαυτῷ, -ῇ, -ῷ   [αὑτῷ, -ῇ, -ῷ]
("to/for him/her/itself")
ἑαυτόν, -ήν, -ό   [αὑτόν, -ήν, -ό]
("him/her/itself")

Third-Person Plural:

ἑαυτῶν, -ῶν, -ῶν
("of themselves")
ἑαυτοῖς, -αῖς, -οῖς
("to/for themselves")
ἑαυτούς, -άς, -ά
("themselves")

Each form combines a personal pronoun or ἑ- with the intensive adjective αὐτός (in the proper case, number, gender). αὐτός is physically attached to the pronoun or ἑ- in all forms except the first- and second-person plural. In the first and second persons, no neuter endings are needed since the subject to which the pronoun refers must be someone either speaking ("I," "we") or spoken to ("you"), who would naturally refer to him- or herself as masculine or feminine. In the second- and third-person singular, **contracted forms** (printed in brackets) are common. Watch out for look-alikes such as αὐτήν ("her," personal pronoun referring to someone other than the subject) and αὑτήν ("herself," reflexive).

Reflexive pronouns can function in whatever ways personal pronouns can, i.e., as direct objects, indirect objects, objects of prepositions— with the exception that a reflexive pronoun is *never* the subject of a sentence. In the **third person** the difference in meaning between personal and reflexive pronouns is great: e.g., αὐτοὺς τιμῶσι means "they honor *them* [i.e., people other than themselves]," while ἑαυτοὺς τιμῶσι means "they honor *themselves*." In the **first and second persons**, however, the **personal pronouns can be used just as if they were reflexives**; e.g., ἐμὲ τῑμῶ ("I honor *me*") means essentially the same thing as ἐμαυτὴν τῑμῶ ("I honor *myself*"). Faced with a choice between ἐμέ and ἐμαυτήν, an author might select ἐμαυτήν because it, unlike ἐμέ, reveals the gender of the subject.

It is important to keep in mind the difference between reflexive pronouns and **intensive adjectives**. In the sentence "I myself honor myself," the first *myself* is an intensive adjective (expressed in Greek by αὐτός or αὐτή) modifying the subject; the second is a reflexive pronoun serving as the sentence's direct object.

117.   Personal pronouns, reflexive pronouns, and demonstratives are often used in the **genitive** case to show **possession**, i.e., to identify the person(s) to whom something belongs. When this occurs, a **personal pronoun** will always have **predicate** position, while a **reflexive pronoun** or a **demonstrative** will always have **attributive** position. Examples:

Personal Pronoun:
  τὸ ὄνομα **αὐτοῦ** λέγει   "he speaks *his* [not his own] name" (literally, "the name of him")

Reflexive Pronoun:
  τὸ **ἑαυτοῦ** ὄνομα λέγει   "he speaks *his own* name" (literally, "the of himself name")

Demonstrative:
  τὸ **τούτου** τοῦ κλωπὸς ὄνομα λέγει   "he speaks *this thief's* name" (literally, "the of this thief name")

  τὸ **τούτου** ὄνομα λέγει   "he speaks *this one's* name" (literally, "the of this [person/thing] name")

118.   **VOCABULARY**

NOTE   Don't forget to learn the second aorists of βάλλω, εὑρίσκω, ἔχω, λέγω, λείπω, φέρω, and φεύγω (see §114).

  λαμβάνω, λήψομαι, ἔλαβον   take, receive, grasp, understand [cf. *epilepsy, syllable*]

NOTE   The root is λαβ-. In the present tense, the nasal -μ- and the suffix -αν are added; in the deponent future tense, the stem-vowel is lengthened. λαμβάνω may be compounded with the prefix συν- ("together"; see the note on σύν below): **συλλαμβάνω, συλλήψομαι, συνέλαβον** "gather together," "collect," "arrest."

μένω, μενῶ, ἔμεινα	remain, stay; (+ *acc.*) wait for

NOTE

This nasal verb has a **contracted future**. In the aorist the sigma drops out, and the stem-vowel (ε) lengthens to ει (cf. ἤγγειλα in Lesson 18 vocabulary).

αἰτίᾱ, -ᾱς, ἡ	blame, guilt, responsibility, accusation, charge, cause [cf. *aetiological*]
ἑαυτοῦ, -ῆς, -οῦ (αὐτοῦ, -ῆς, -οῦ)	(*reflexive pronoun*) himself, herself, itself, themselves
ἐμαυτοῦ, -ῆς	(*reflexive pronoun*) myself
ἡμῶν αὐτῶν, -ῶν	(*reflexive pronoun*) ourselves
σεαυτοῦ, -ῆς (σαυτοῦ, -ῆς)	(*reflexive pronoun*) yourself
ὑμῶν αὐτῶν, -ῶν	(*reflexive pronoun*) yourselves

NOTE

Since reflexives lack the nominative case, it is customary to present them in the genitive. Contractions αὐτοῦ, -ῆς, -οῦ and σαυτοῦ, -ῆς are common.

αἴτιος, -ᾱ, -ον	blameworthy; (+ *gen.*) guilty (of), responsible (for)
μετά (μετ’, μεθ’)	(*prep. + gen.*) among, with, together with; (*prep. + acc.*) after (μετ’ *before smooth breathing*, μεθ’ *before rough breathing*) [cf. *metabolism, metamorphosis, meteor, method*]

NOTE

As a prefix, μετα- means "among" or "after" or indicates a change.

σύν	(*prep. + dat.*) with, together with, with the help of [cf. *syllogism, symbol, symmetry, synchronic, synod, system, syzygy*]

NOTE

Both μετά and σύν may be used to express **accompaniment** ("together with"). σύν may also be added to a **dative of means** or a **dative of manner** to strengthen it (e.g., σὺν ἵπποις). συν- appears often as a prefix meaning "together" or "with": if the letter following the prefix is σ or ζ, συν- becomes **συ-**; if the following letter is a labial, συν- becomes **συμ-**; if the following letter is a palatal, συν- becomes **συγ-** (the γ is nasalized); if the following letter is λ, μ, or ρ, the ν of συν- likens itself to that letter (a phenomenon called **assimilation**). The English derivatives listed above illustrate these changes.

119.   **EXERCISES**

A.   **Greek-to-English Sentences**

1.   διὰ τὴν ἑαυτοῦ αἰτίᾱν ὁ κλὼψ ἔφυγε καὶ ἔβαλεν ἑαυτὸν εἰς τὴν λίμνην.

2.   λάβετε τὰς ἀσπίδας, ὦ ἀγαθοὶ νεᾱνίαι, καὶ μείνατε τοὺς πολεμίους.

3.   ἐπώλησαν μὲν πολλὰ βιβλία, συνέλαβον δὲ πολλὰς δραχμὰς.

4.   ἔχεις αὐτὴ ἐνεγκεῖν τὸ σαυτῆς τέκνον τὸ μῑκρὸν εἰς τὴν οἰκίᾱν ἡμῶν;

5.   ἐπεὶ ἠγγείλαμεν τὸν θάνατον τοῦ δεσπότου τῷ ἐκείνου ἀδελφῷ, εἶπε·
     Μακρὸς αὐτοῦ ὁ βίος ἦν.

6.   τὴν ταύτης τῆς κόρης ἐπιστολὴν λήψεσθε καὶ οἴσετε σὺν ὑμῖν αὐταῖς;

7.   αἴτιοι ἦσαν τοῦδε τοῦ πολέμου, ἀλλὰ νῦν σπεύδουσι σχεῖν εἰρήνην.

8.   σὺν τῷ φίλῳ δαίμονι τῷ ἐμαυτοῦ εὗρον τὸν θησαυρὸν ὑπὸ τῷ λίθῳ.

9.   μετὰ τῶν αὐτῶν μαθητῶν ἔμειναν οἱ φιλόσοφοι αὐτοὶ ἐν τῇ ἀγορᾷ.

10.   μετὰ τοῦθ᾿ οἱ πολλοὶ αἰτίᾱς ἀναξίους ἔβαλον ἐπὶ τὸν Σωκράτη.

B.   **English-to-Greek Sentences**

1.   They threw themselves into his wagon, for they did not wish to re-
     main in their own land.

2.   After that we said to ourselves, "Since the enemies are among us, it
     is time to flee."

3.   I asked myself this: "Did I abandon my own horse in the road?"

4.   The guilt of those servants is clear: they are blameworthy, for they
     took her treasure.

5.   With the gods' help, you found peace and brought joy to yourself.

C. READING

CHAT WITH A CAT
(Aesop's Fable 16)

Αἴλουρος ἀλεκτρυόνα ἔλαβε καὶ ἔμελλεν αὐτὸν ἔδεσθαι. τοῖσδε τοῖς λόγοις εἶπεν· Ἐν αἰτίᾳ σε, ὦ ἀλεκτρυὼν ἀνάξιε, ἔχω, νυκτὸς γὰρ κράζεις καὶ οἱ ἄνθρωποι διὰ τοῦτ' οὐκ ἔχουσιν ὕπνον εὑρεῖν. ἀλλ' ὁ ἀλεκτρυὼν εἶπεν· Οὐ λέγεις σὺν τῇ σοφίᾳ, ὦ αἴλουρε κακέ, τούτῳ γὰρ τῷ τρόπῳ τοὺς ἀνθρώπους

5   ὠφελῶ. ἐπειδὴ ἐμοῦ ἀκούουσιν, ἐπὶ τὰ ἑαυτῶν ἔργα σπεύδουσιν.

ὁ δ' αἴλουρος εἶπεν· Ἀλλά σε ἔτι ἐν αἰτίᾳ ἔχω, τῇ γὰρ μητρὶ καὶ ταῖς σαυτοῦ ἀδελφαῖς προσβάλλειν φιλεῖς. ὁ δ' ἀλεκτρυὼν εἶπεν· Ἐπειδὴ αὐταῖς προσβάλλω, τοὺς ἀνθρώπους πάλιν ὠφελῶ, διὰ γὰρ τὸν φόβον πόλλ' ᾠὰ αἱ ἀδελφαὶ καὶ ἡ μήτηρ μου τίκτουσιν. μετὰ ταῦθ' ὁ αἴλουρος εἶπε· Μηκέτι λέγε,

10   τοῖς γὰρ λόγοις οὐκ ἔστι σε φυγεῖν με. ἄδειπνος οὐ μενῶ. τότε δὲ τὸν ἀλεκτρυόνα ἔφαγεν.

ἐπειδὴ ἐχθρὸς μέλλει λύσειν σε, σοῦ γ' οὐ πολὺ ἀκούσεται.

VOCABULARY

αἴλουρος (line 1): from αἴλουρος (αἴολος "rapid" + οὐρά "tail"), -ου, ὁ: cat
ἀλεκτρυόνα (line 1): from ἀλεκτρυών, -όνος, ὁ: rooster
ἔδεσθαι (line 1): from ἐσθίω, ἔδομαι, ἔφαγον: eat
ἐν αἰτίᾳ σε...ἔχω (line 2): i.e., "I consider you worthy of blame"
νυκτός (line 2): at night (*gen. of time within which*; νύξ, νυκτός, ἡ: night)
κράζεις (line 2): from κράζω, κεκράξομαι, ἔκραξα: crow
ὕπνον (line 3): from ὕπνος, -ου, ὁ: sleep
μητρί (line 6): dat. sg. of irreg. third-decl. noun μήτηρ, μητρός, ἡ: mother
φόβον (line 8): from φόβος, -ου, ὁ: fear
ᾠά (line 8): from ᾠόν, -οῦ, τό: egg
τίκτουσιν (line 9): from τίκτω, τέξω, ἔτεκον: give birth to, lay (*eggs*)
ἄδειπνος (line 10): from ἄδειπνος, -ον: unfed (*literally*, "dinnerless")
ἔφαγεν (line 11): from ἐσθίω, ἔδομαι, ἔφαγον = eat

LESSON 20

Ω-VERBS
Perfect Active Indicative,
Perfect Active Infinitive;
Pluperfect Active Indicative

ἐκβέβληκέ με / ὁ φίλος ὁ χρηστός σου
(That fine friend of yours has thrown me out of the house.)
—Chrysis shocks her neighbor with this news in Menander's *Samia* 407-408

120.   We come now to the **fourth principal part**, which supplies the stem for the **perfect and pluperfect tenses** in the **active voice**. (The fifth principal part supplies the stem for the middle and passive voices of these tenses.) Compared to the other tenses, the pluperfect is not much used, but you still need to be familiar with it. Perfect imperatives, on the other hand, are so rare in Attic Greek that we do not expect you to take time now to learn them; their forms can be found in the appendix, pp. 464 and 468.

121.   The perfect and pluperfect tenses both have **perfective aspect**, i.e., the actions they denote are already completed (perfected). The perfect tense describes a state that exists in the **present** as the result of a completed action (e.g., "*I have won,*" which implies that I am *now* in the state of being a winner); the pluperfect tense describes a state that existed in the **past** as the result of a completed action (e.g., "*I had won,*" which implies that I was *then* in the state of being a winner). As you can see from the examples, English uses the auxiliary verb *have/has* for the perfect tense, *had* for the pluperfect.

The perfect is one of Greek's **primary** (present and future) tenses and thus has primary endings, while the pluperfect is a **secondary** (past) tense with secondary endings. Both, however, use **reduplication**—the doubling of the sound at the start of a word—as a sign of their perfective

125

aspect. To form the perfect stem, you reduplicate the verb's basic stem by adding a prefix to it.

1.   If the stem begins with *just one consonant* (not ῥ) or with a *stop* (π, β, φ, τ, δ, θ, κ, γ, χ) + *a liquid or a nasal* (λ, ρ, μ, ν), the prefix that you add consists of two letters: **a repeat of the stem's initial consonant, followed by an epsilon.**

> Examples: παιδεύω - reduplicated prefix = πε-
> γράφω - reduplicated prefix = γε-

If the stem's initial consonant is an *aspirated* stop (φ, θ, χ), the corresponding *smooth* stop (π, τ, κ) is used for the prefix (to avoid having two consecutive syllables each starting with a rough sound).

> Example: θύω - reduplicated prefix = τε- (to avoid θεθ-)

2.   In all other cases (i.e., if the stem begins with a *vowel* or with ῥ or with a *double consonant* or with *two or more consonants that are not stop + liquid or nasal*), reduplicating the stem is **exactly like augmenting it.**

> Examples: ἐρωτάω - reduplicates by **lengthening** ἐ- to ἠ-
> ῥίπτω - reduplicates by **adding** ἐ- (and
>   doubling the ρ)
> ζητέω - reduplicates by **adding** ἐ-

122.   Here is the conjugation of παιδεύω, παιδεύσω, ἐπαίδευσα, πεπαίδευκα in the perfect and pluperfect active indicative:

PERFECT ACTIVE INDICATIVE	PLUPERFECT ACTIVE INDICATIVE
Singular:	
πεπαίδευκα ("I have taught")	ἐπεπαιδεύκη ("I had taught")
πεπαίδευκας ("you [*sg.*] have taught")	ἐπεπαιδεύκης ("you [*sg.*] had taught")
πεπαίδευκε(ν) ("he/she/it has taught")	ἐπεπαιδεύκει(ν) ("he/she/it had taught")
Plural:	
πεπαιδεύκαμεν ("we have taught")	ἐπεπαιδεύκεμεν ("we had taught")
πεπαιδεύκατε ("you [*pl.*] have taught")	ἐπεπαιδεύκετε ("you [*pl.*] had taught")
πεπαιδεύκᾱσι(ν) ("they have taught")	ἐπεπαιδεύκεσαν ("they had taught")

PERFECT ACTIVE INFINITIVE: πεπαιδευκέναι
("to have taught")

SUMMARY OF PERFECT & PLUPERFECT ACTIVE ENDINGS

Perfect Active Indicative	Pluperfect Active Indicative
-[κ]α	-[κ]η (-εα)
-[κ]ας	-[κ]ης (-εας)
-[κ]ε(ν)	-[κ]ει(ν) (-εε)
-[κ]αμεν	-[κ]εμεν
-[κ]ατε	-[κ]ετε
-[κ]ᾱσι(ν) (-α[ν]σι)	-[κ]εσαν

Perfect Active Infinitive: -[κ]έναι
(accent always on the penult)

As you can see, the letter κ is characteristic of the perfect and plu-perfect tenses in the active voice. We have printed it in brackets, how-ever, because often it is missing: whenever the reduplicated stem ends in a labial or a palatal consonant, **κ is omitted**, and, along with that, there may be a change in the labial/palatal consonant or in the stem-vowel, or in both.[1] Forms with κ are called **first perfects** or **first pluperfects**; forms with no κ are called **second perfects** or **second pluperfects**. Most verbs have either a first perfect or a second perfect; if a verb has *both* types, the two perfects usually differ in meaning.

Perfect endings resemble first aorist endings (without the σ), except in the third-person plural. Pluperfect endings also resemble first aorist endings, but α is contracted with or replaced by ε. (Only the third-person plural endings reveal that perfect endings are primary, pluperfect end-ings secondary.) **The pluperfect uses the same stem as the perfect, but augments it.** If a verb reduplicates by adding ἐ- or by lengthening its ini-tial vowel, its perfect stem will already have augmented form and can serve as the pluperfect stem with no further change.

Movable ν is added to the third-person singular (-ε) and third-per-son plural (-σι) of the perfect and even to the third-person singular of the pluperfect (-ει). (This is peculiar, for ν is normally not added to the -ει endings of contract verbs.)

The **perfect active infinitive** shows aspect (*perfective*), not time. It has no augment, but it does have the reduplication characteristic of per-fective aspect.

123.   Here are the first four principal parts of every verb introduced so far. The **fourth principal part** is always the first-person singular perfect active indicative.

---

[1] A verb that is ε-grade in the present stem often become **o-grade** in the perfect active stem; e.g., λείπω → λέλοιπα.

VERBS WITH FIRST PERFECTS

Verbs with stems ending in a vowel: κ is used for the perfect. Contract verbs lengthen their vowel before the κ.

δηλόω	δηλώσω	ἐδήλωσα	δεδήλωκα
δουλεύω	δουλεύσω	ἐδούλευσα	δεδούλευκα
ἐρωτάω	ἐρωτήσω	ἠρώτησα	ἠρώτηκα
ἔχω	ἕξω/σχήσω	ἔσχον	ἔσχηκα (stem = σχε-)
θύω	θύσω	ἔθῦσα	τέθυκα
κελεύω	κελεύσω	ἐκέλευσα	κεκέλευκα
λύω	λύσω	ἔλῦσα	λέλυκα
παιδεύω	παιδεύσω	ἐπαίδευσα	πεπαίδευκα
ποιέω	ποιήσω	ἐποίησα	πεποίηκα
προσποιέω	προσποιήσω	προσεποίησα	προσπεποίηκα
πωλέω	πωλήσω	ἐπώλησα	πεπώληκα
τῑμάω	τῑμήσω	ἐτίμησα	τετίμηκα
φιλέω	φιλήσω	ἐφίλησα	πεφίληκα
ὠφελέω	ὠφελήσω	ὠφέλησα	ὠφέληκα

Verbs with stems ending in a dental (or ζ): κ is used for the perfect; the dental (or ζ) itself drops out before the κ.

ἁρπάζω	ἁρπάσω	ἥρπασα	ἥρπακα
κομίζω	κομιῶ	ἐκόμισα	κεκόμικα
πείθω	πείσω	ἔπεισα	πέπεικα/πέποιθα[1]

Verbs with stems ending in a liquid or a nasal: κ is used for the perfect; ε may be added to the stem and lengthened before the κ.

ἀγγέλλω	ἀγγελῶ	ἤγγειλα	ἤγγελκα
βάλλω	βαλῶ	ἔβαλον	βέβληκα
προσβάλλω	προσβαλῶ	προσέβαλον	προσβέβληκα
ἐθέλω	ἐθελήσω	ἠθέλησα	ἠθέληκα
εὑρίσκω	εὑρήσω	εὗρον/ηὗρον	εὕρηκα/ηὕρηκα
λέγω	ἐρῶ/λέξω	εἶπον/ἔλεξα	εἴρηκα[2]
μένω	μενῶ	ἔμεινα	μεμένηκα
χαίρω	χαιρήσω	ἐχαίρησα	κεχάρηκα

---

[1] The first perfect and the second perfect of πείθω differ in meaning: πέπεικα "I have persuaded" (+ *acc. &/or infin.*); πέποιθα "I trust" (+ *dat. &/or infin.*).

[2] εἴρηκα = ϝέϝρηκα; the digammas dropped out, and the ε was lengthened to ει to make up for the loss of the consonants (**compensatory lengthening**).

VERBS WITH SECOND PERFECTS

Verbs with stems ending in a labial (or πτ, which loses its τ): no κ is used for the perfect; if the labial is not a φ, it is often "roughened" into one.

βλάπτω	βλάψω	ἔβλαψα	βέβλαφα
βλέπω	βλέψομαι	ἔβλεψα	βέβλεφα
γράφω	γράψω	ἔγραψα	γέγραφα
κλέπτω	κλέψω	ἔκλεψα	κέκλοφα
λαμβάνω	λήψομαι	ἔλαβον	εἴληφα[1]
συλλαμβάνω	συλλήψομαι	συνέλαβον	συνείληφα[1]
λείπω	λείψω	ἔλιπον	λέλοιπα
ἀπολείπω	ἀπολείψω	ἀπέλιπον	ἀπολέλοιπα
πέμπω	πέμψω	ἔπεμψα	πέπομφα
τρέπω	τρέψω	ἔτρεψα	τέτροφα

Verbs with stems ending in a palatal (or ττ [= κι, γι, or χι]): no κ is used for the perfect; if the palatal is not a χ, it is often "roughened" into one.

ἀλλάττω	ἀλλάξω	ἤλλαξα	ἤλλαχα
διώκω	διώξω	ἐδίωξα	δεδίωχα
πλήττω	πλήξω	ἔπληξα	πέπληγα
ἐπιπλήττω	ἐπιπλήξω	ἐπέπληξα	ἐπιπέπληγα
πράττω	πράξω	ἔπρᾱξα	πέπρᾱγα/πέπρᾱχα[2]
φέρω	οἴσω	ἤνεγκα/ἤνεγκον	ἐνήνοχα[3]
φεύγω	φεύξομαι	ἔφυγον	πέφευγα
φυλάττω	φυλάξω	ἐφύλαξα	πεφύλαχα

Verbs with stems ending in a digamma: no κ is used for the perfect; ϝ drops out.

ἀκούω	ἀκούσομαι	ἤκουσα	ἀκήκοα (ἀκήκοϝα)[4]

Verbs that are never used in the perfect active tense:

γελάω	γελάσομαι	ἐγέλασα	—
μέλλω	μελλήσω	ἐμέλλησα	—
σπεύδω	σπεύσω	ἔσπευσα	—

---

[1] εἴληφα = σέσληφα; when the sigmas dropped out, ε was lengthened to ει.

[2] Either spelling may be used, with no change in meaning.

[3] ἐνεκ- repeats its first two letters as a prefix and then lengthens its original initial vowel (ἐνην-). This is called **Attic reduplication.** The pluperfect is ἐνηνόχη.

[4] ἀκοϝ- repeats ἀκ- as a prefix and then lengthens its original initial vowel (ἀκηκ-)—another case of **Attic reduplication.** The pluperfect is ἠκηκόη or ἀκηκόη.

124.   VOCABULARY

ζητέω, ζητήσω, ἐζήτησα, ἐζήτηκα

            seek, search for, investigate; (+ *infin.*) seek (to)

ῥίπτω, ῥίψω, ἔρρῑψα, ἔρρῑφα

            throw, hurl, cast aside

γῆ (*contracted from* γέᾱ), γῆς, γῇ, γῆν, ἡ (*rarely plural*)

            earth, ground, land; Γῆ = Earth (*personified*) [cf. *geodesic, geographic, georgic*]

δένδρον, -ου, τό   tree [cf. *dendrite, philodendron*]

Ἑλλάς, -άδος, ἡ   Hellas, Greece

Ἕλλην, -ηνος, ὁ, ἡ   a Hellene, a Greek

οὐρανός, -οῦ, ὁ   sky, heaven; Οὐρανός = Sky (*personified*) [cf. *uranic, Uranus*]

Ἑλληνικός, -ή, -όν   Hellenic, Greek

κατά (κατ᾽, καθ᾽)   (*prep. + gen.*) down from, against; (*prep. + acc.*) down, down along, in accordance with, according to, by (*in various idioms*) (κατ᾽ *before smooth breathing*, καθ᾽ *before rough breathing*) [cf. *cataclysm, catalyst, catastrophe*]

NOTE   κατά means "by" in phrases like κατὰ γῆν "*by* land" and κατὰ θάλατταν "*by* sea"; it never indicates a personal agent.

ὑπέρ   (*prep. + gen.*) over, above, on behalf of; (*prep. + acc.*) over, to a place over, beyond [cf. *hyperbole, hyperborean, hypermetric*]

125.   EXERCISES

     A.   **Greek-to-English Sentences**

       1. ὑπὲρ τῶν Ἑλλήνων πόλλ᾽ οὐ μόνον εἰρήκᾱσιν ἀλλὰ καὶ πεπρᾱ́γᾱσιν.

       2. αὐτοὶ μὲν ἐσπεύδομεν κατὰ θάλατταν, ὑμεῖς δὲ κατὰ γῆν ἐτρέπεσθε.

       3. ἐπεὶ τοῦτ᾽ ἠκηκόεσαν, τὰς ἑαυτῶν ἀσπίδας ἔρρῑψαν καὶ ἔφυγον.

       4. ἡ μὲν κατὰ τοὺς λόγους σου, ὦ δέσποτα, τὴν ἐπιστολὴν γέγραφεν, ἡ δ᾽ οὔ.

       5. πέποιθας ἐκείνοις τοῖς κλωψὶ τὰ γέρᾱ σου φέρειν; ταῦτα κλέψουσι καὶ ἐπὶ σοὶ γελάσονται.

       6. ἡ Μοῖρα ἠθελήκειν ὠφελῆσαι τὴν Ἑλλάδα καὶ τοῖς Ἕλλησι τὴν εἰρήνην κατ᾽ οὐρανοῦ ἐπεπόμφειν.

7. λέοντα ὑπὸ τῷ δένδρῳ βεβλέφαμεν καὶ λίθους πρὸς αὐτὸν ἐρρίφαμεν.

8. ἐπεὶ τὰ τέκνα εὖ πεπαίδευκας, πολλὰ δῶρα λήψει πρὸς ἡμῶν γε.

9. ζητῶ ἐρωτῆσαι σέ, ὦ Σώκρατες, περὶ τῆς αἰτίας τῆς κατὰ σοῦ. εἰπέ μοι· βέβλαφας τοὺς νεανίας, ἢ οὔ;

10. ὁ φιλόσοφος λέγεται εὑρηκέναι τὴν ἀλήθειαν καὶ εἰρηκέναι, Εὕρηκα.

B. English-to-Greek Sentences

1. O wise Greeks, I have found true words in your books; therefore I shall seek to make my life Hellenic.

2. According to Socrates, he has remained in Greece on our behalf and has honored the guardian spirits of this earth.

3. We have escorted our friends down the long road and have sent them over the river.

4. Many have hurled charges against Socrates, but you at least, O students, have not abandoned him.

5. In the sky above the trees she had seen the handsome messenger of the gods and had rejoiced.

C. READING

ALL CAW, NO CAUTION
(Aesop's Fable 126)

Κόραξ κρέας ἡρπάκει καὶ ἐπὶ δένδρου αὐτὸ ἐφύλαττεν. ἀλώπηξ δ' ὑπὸ τῷ δένδρῳ ἦν. τῷ κόρακι αὕτη εἶπε· Καλὸς μὲν εἶ, ὦ κόραξ, καὶ τὰ πτερά σου μακρά, τὴν δὲ φωνὴν οὐκ ἀκήκοα. εἰπέ μοι· σοὶ καὶ καλὴ φωνή ἐστιν; ἐπειδὴ ὁ κόραξ τούτους τοὺς λόγους ἤκουσε, τὸ κρέας κατὰ τοῦ δένδρου ἔρριψε καὶ
5 πολὺ ἐκεκράγει, τὴν γὰρ ἑαυτοῦ φωνὴν ἐζήτει δηλοῦν. ἐπειδὴ ἡ ἀλώπηξ τὸ κρέας εἰλήφειν, ἐγέλασε· Πρὸς θεῶν, ὦ κόραξ, ἡ μέν γε φωνή σου πολλή, ἡ δὲ σοφία ὀλίγη.

ἐπεὶ πεποίθατε, ὦ ἄνθρωποι, τοῖς τῶν κολάκων λόγοις, κακῶς πράττετε.

VOCABULARY

κόραξ (line 1): from κόραξ, -ακος, ὁ: crow
κρέας (line 1): from κρέας, -ως, τό: flesh, meat
ἀλώπηξ (line 1): from ἀλώπηξ, -εκος, ἡ: fox
πτερά (line 2): from πτερόν, -οῦ, τό: feather, wing
φωνήν (line 3): from φωνή, -ῆς, ἡ: voice
ἐκεκράγει (line 5): from κράζω, κεκράξομαι, ἔκραξα, κέκραγα: caw (*perf. tense is used as if it were pres. tense, pluperf. as if it were imperf.*)
κολάκων (line 8): from κόλαξ, -ακος, ὁ: flatterer

LESSON 21

INTERROGATIVE τίς AND INDEFINITE τις

τίς εἶ; τίν' ὄψιν σήν, γύναι, προσδέρκομαι;
(Who are you, madam? What face do I behold?)
—Menelaus begins to recognize his wife in Euripides' *Helen* 557

126.   τίς is a small but significant word in Greek. When modifying a noun, it is an **interrogative adjective** meaning "what?" or "which?". When used without a noun, i.e., as a substantive, it is an **interrogative pronoun** meaning "who?" or "which person?" or "what?" or "which thing?". τίς has third-declension endings, one set for masculine and feminine, one set for neuter:

	Masc./Fem.			**Neuter**		
Singular:						
Nom.	τίς		("who?")	τί		("what?")
Gen.	τίνος	(τοῦ)	("of whom?")	τίνος	(τοῦ)	("of what?")
Dat.	τίνι	(τῷ)	("to/for whom?")	τίνι	(τῷ)	("to/for what?")
Acc.	τίνα		("whom?")	τί		("what?")
Plural:						
Nom.	τίνες		("who?")	τίνα		("what?")
Gen.	τίνων		("of whom?")	τίνων		("of what?")
Dat.	τίσι(ν)		("to/for whom?")	τίσι(ν)		("to/for what?")
Acc.	τίνας		("whom?")	τίνα		("what?")

The accents on **τίς** and **τί** remain forever **acute** even when they should, according to the general principles of accenting, change to grave (e.g., τίς ἵππος, not τὶς ἵππος; τί δῶρον, not τὶ δῶρον). The **contracted forms** of the genitive and dative singular, **τοῦ** (= τίνος) and **τῷ** (= τίνι), are common in Attic Greek; they look exactly like the genitive and dative masculine/neuter singular forms of the definite article. **τίνα** is written as **τίν'** be-

133

fore a word beginning with a vowel, but τί and τίνι are never elided. **Movable ν** is added to the dative plural (τίσιν).

When used as an adjective, τίς must agree with its noun in **gender, number, and case** (e.g., τίν᾽ ἐπιστολὴν πέμπεις; "*what/which* letter are you sending?"). When used as a pronoun, τίς takes masculine/feminine endings to indicate a **human being**, neuter endings to indicate an **inanimate object** (e.g., τίνα πέμπεις; "*what person/whom* are you sending?" or "*what things/what* are you sending?"; τί πέμπεις; "*what thing/what* are you sending?").

The neuter singular accusative τί is frequently found as an **adverb** meaning **"why?"** (literally, "in respect to what?"). The context will show whether τί has this adverbial sense or means simply "what?".

NOTE　　　Many English-speakers no longer pay attention to the distinction between *who* (in the subjective case, equivalent to Greek's nominative case) and *whom* (in the objective case, equivalent to Greek's genitive, dative, and accusative cases), but you will endear yourself to your Greek teacher if you use *who* and *whom* correctly in your English translations. Examples: "*Who* is coming?" "By *whom* were you invited?" "To *whom* did you send the invitation?" "*Whom* did you invite?"

127.　　　The **indefinite adjective/pronoun** τις has the same forms as interrogative τίς, but they are **enclitics** and thus are accented differently:

	Masc./Fem.		**Neuter**		
Singular:					
Nom.	τις	("someone")	τι		("something")
Gen.	τινός (του)	("of someone")	τινός	(του)	("of something")
Dat.	τινί (τῳ)	("to/for someone")	τινί	(τῳ)	("to/for something")
Acc.	τινά	("someone")	τι		("something")
Plural:					
Nom.	τινές	("some people")	τινά	(ἄττα)	("some things")
Gen.	τινῶν	("of some people")	τινῶν		("of some things")
Dat.	τισί(ν)	("to/for some people")	τισί(ν)		("to/for some things")
Acc.	τινάς	("some people")	τινά	(ἄττα)	("some things")

Being an enclitic, **τις** prefers a position just **after** the word that it qualifies. The only occasion for it to come first in its clause is when its forms are combined with μέν and δέ to mean "some...others" (e.g., **τινὲς μὲν...τινὲς δέ**; cf. οἱ μὲν...οἱ δέ). The genitive plural **τινῶν**, when accented, has a circumflex since the omega is naturally long (see Lesson 12, § 80). The neuter plural **τινά** has an alternative form, **ἄττα**, which is not an enclitic. **τινά** is written as **τιν᾽** before a word beginning with a vowel, but **τι, τινί**, and **ἄττα** are never elided. **Movable ν** is added to the dative plural (**τισίν**).

Greek has no word that precisely corresponds to English's indefinite article *a/an*, but τις, when used as an indefinite adjective, comes close; it may mean "a," "an," "a certain," "some," or "any." As an adjective, τις must agree with its noun in **gender, number, and case**. When used as an indefinite pronoun, τις takes masculine/feminine endings to indicate a **human being** ("someone," "anyone"), neuter endings to indicate an **inanimate object** ("something," "anything"). Examples: κλῶπά τινα βλέπω ("I see *a* thief"); βλέπω τινά ("I see *someone*" or "I see *some things*"); βλέπω τι ("I see *something*").

128.   You already know how to show possession with a **personal pronoun**, a **reflexive pronoun**, or a **demonstrative** in the genitive case. Possession may also be shown with a **possessive adjective**: ἐμός, -ή, -όν ("my," "mine," "my own"); ἡμέτερος, -α, -ον ("our," "ours," "our own"); σός, -ή, -όν ("your," "yours," "your own" [*one person's*]); ὑμέτερος, -α, -ον ("your," "yours," "your own" [*more than one person's*]). Attic Greek has no adjectives meaning "his," "his own," "her," "her own," "its," "its own," or "their." σφέτερος, -α, -ον ("their own") is occasionally used, but not in this textbook. (See further in the appendix.)

A possessive adjective agrees in **gender, number, and case** with the noun that it modifies. As always, the position of the adjective affects the meaning:

Attributive:

τὸ ἐμὸν βιβλίον   "my book"/"my own book"
τὸ βιβλίον τὸ ἐμόν   "my book"/"my own book"

Predicate:

ἐμὸν βιβλίον   "a book of mine"/"a book of my own"
ἐμὸν τὸ βιβλίον.   "The book is mine."/"The book is my own."

129.   In Lesson 19 you learned that the reflexive pronouns ἡμῶν αὐτῶν and ὑμῶν αὐτῶν can be used in the attributive position to show **possession**. This is true, but a much more common (not to mention more elegant) way to express the notion of "our own" or "your [*pl.*] own" is to replace ἡμῶν or ὑμῶν with the possessive adjective ἡμέτερος, -α, -ον or ὑμέτερος, -α, -ον in the **attributive** position, while retaining αὐτῶν in the **predicate** position (as if ἡμῶν or ὑμῶν were still there for αὐτῶν to modify). Examples: τὸ ἡμέτερον βιβλίον αὐτῶν = "our own book"; τὸ ὑμέτερον βιβλίον αὐτῶν = "your own book."

130.   VOCABULARY

ἀποθνῄσκω, ἀποθανοῦμαι, ἀπέθανον, τέθνηκα
                    die, be killed

NOTE   The basic stem of ἀποθνῄσκω is θαν-, altered to θνη- in the first and
                fourth principal parts; the suffix -ισκ- is attached to θνη- in the present
                and imperfect tenses. ἀπο- is normally added as a prefix in all the tenses
                except perfect and pluperfect. Notice that the future is contracted and de-
                ponent. This verb is **always active or** (only in the future tense) **middle in
                form**, but it may be **either active** ("die") **or passive** ("be killed") **in
                meaning**. Clues in the context (e.g., genitive of agent = sign of passive
                voice) will show which sense is intended.

ἀποκτείνω, ἀποκτενῶ, ἀπέκτεινα, ἀπέκτονα
                    kill

NOTE   κτείνω has the prefix ἀπο- in the perfect and pluperfect, and usually
                in the other tenses as well. Notice that the future is contracted and built
                on the basic stem κτεν-. The first aorist ἀπέκτεινα lost its sigma but length-
                ened its stem-vowel in compensation. The second perfect ἀπέκτονα uses
                the o-grade stem. This verb is **invariably active in both form and mean-
                ing**. To say "is/was/will be/has been killed," the Greeks used a differ-
                ent verb, ἀποθνῄσκω.

φοβέω, φοβήσω, ἐφόβησα, πεφόβηκα

	(*act.*) frighten; (*mid./pass.* + *acc.*) be frightened (of), be afraid (of), fear
φόβος, -ου, ὁ	fear, fright [cf. *agoraphobia*]
τίς, τί	(*interrog. adj.*) what? which?; (*interrog. pron.*) who? what?
τις, τι	(*indef. adj., enclitic*) a, an, a certain, some, any; (*indef. pron., enclitic*) someone, something, anyone, anything, some, any
τινὲς μὲν...τινὲς δέ	(*correlatives*) some...others
ἐμός, -ή, -όν	(*poss. adj.*) my, mine, my own
ἡμέτερος, -ᾱ, -ον	(*poss. adj.*) our, ours, our own
σός, -ή, -όν	(*poss. adj.*) your, yours, your own (*one person's*)
ὑμέτερος, -ᾱ, -ον	(*poss. adj.*) your, yours, your own (*more than one person's*)
τί	(*neut. sg. acc. of* τίς *used as adv.*) why?

131. **EXERCISES**

A. **Greek-to-English Sentences**

1. τίς πέπληγε καὶ ἀπέκτονε τὸν ἐμὸν λέοντα τὸν καλὸν καὶ πολλοῦ ἄξιον;
2. τινὲς μὲν τότ' ἀπέθανον κατὰ τὴν μοῖραν, τινὲς δ' ἔφυγον θάνατον.
3. τίς φιλόσοφος δηλώσει ὑμῖν τὴν ἀληθῆ αἰτίᾱν τοῦ ὑμετέρου πολέμου;
4. κλωπί τῳ ἐπεπωλήκεσαν οὐ μόνον τὰ βιβλία ἀλλὰ καὶ τὰ ἱμάτια.
5. τίνων χάριν ἐποίησας ταύτᾱς τὰς ὁδούς; τίνας ἠθέλησας ὠφελῆσαι;
6. τὰ μῑκρὰ τέκνα ἠρώτησέ με τόδε· Τί δῶρα ἄττα ἡμῖν οὐκ ἐνήνοχας;
7. ἐπὶ τοῦ πολέμου ἀπεκτείναμεν τοὺς ἡμετέρους ἀδελφοὺς αὐτῶν.
8. ἐπεὶ σὴ ἵππος καλὴ τέθνηκεν ὑπό τινος, πολλὴν λύπην ἔχεις.
9. Μὴ φοβεῖσθε, ὦ φίλοι, εἶπεν ὁ ἄγγελος, ὑμῖν γὰρ χαρὰν τιν' ἀγγελῶ.
10. ἔμοιγε φόβος πολύς ἐστι, μετὰ γὰρ πολλῶν κινδύνων κακῶς ἔχω.

B. **English-to-Greek Sentences**

1. What dangers are you afraid of, my daughter? Who has frightened you with these stories?
2. Socrates is a friend of ours; therefore we shall not command anyone to kill him.
3. Many Greeks died in the time of the war, but now Greece has peace.
4. Some, on account of fear, have fled to certain places; others have remained in their houses.
5. Why have you cast aside your shields, youths? When the enemies will attack, you will be killed by someone.

C. **READING**

OUT OF THE FRYING PAN, INTO THE NILE
(Aesop's Fable 32)

Ἄνθρωπόν τις ἀπέκτεινε καὶ ὑπὸ τῶν ἐκείνου συγγενῶν ἐδιώκετο κατὰ τὸν Νεῖλον ποταμόν. λέων δ' ἐκ τῆς χώρᾱς ἔσπευσε καὶ ἐκεῖνον ἐφόβησεν. διὰ τὸν πολὺν φόβον τοῦ λέοντος ὁ φονεὺς ἐπεφεύγειν εἰς δένδρον τι καὶ ἐν τούτῳ μένειν ἤθελεν. ἀλλ' ἐπεὶ δράκοντα ἐν τῷ αὐτῷ δένδρῳ ὑπὲρ ἑαυτοῦ ἔβλεψε, πάλιν
5 ἐφοβεῖτο καὶ τὴν σωτηρίᾱν ἐζήτει. ἔρρῑψεν οὖν ἑαυτὸν εἰς τὸν ποταμὸν αὐτόν. ἐν δὲ τούτῳ ὑπὸ κροκοδείλου ἀπέθανεν.

τί δηλοῖ, ὦ μαθηταί, οὗτος ὁ ἐμὸς λόγος; ἐπεὶ ἄνθρωπον ἀπέκτονας, καὶ ἡ γῆ καὶ ὁ οὐρανὸς καὶ τὸ ὕδωρ ζητήσουσιν ἀποκτεῖναί σε.

VOCABULARY

συγγενῶν (line 1): from συγγενής, -ές: related; (*as a substantive*) relative
Νεῖλον (line 2): from Νεῖλος, -ου, ὁ: the Nile, river in Egypt
φονεύς (line 3): from φονεύς, -έως, ὁ: murderer (*an ευ-stem third-decl. noun*)
δράκοντα (line 4): from δράκων, -οντος, ὁ: snake
σωτηρίαν (line 5): from σωτηρία, -ᾱς, ἡ: safety
κροκοδείλου (line 6): from κροκόδειλος, -ου, ὁ: crocodile
ὕδωρ (line 8): from ὕδωρ, ὕδατος, τό: water

LESSON 22

Ω-VERBS
Perfect Middle/Passive Indicative, Perfect Middle/Passive Infinitive; Pluperfect Middle/Passive Indicative

πεφόβημαι / πτηνῆς ὡς ὄμμα πελείᾱς
(I'm as fearful as the eye of a dove on the wing.)
—nervous words from the chorus in Sophocles' *Ajax* 139-140

132. The **fifth principal part** of a Greek verb supplies the stem for the perfect middle/passive tense and the pluperfect middle/passive tense. For verbs whose basic stem ends in a **vowel**, the fifth principal part is easily derivable from the fourth principal part. For verbs whose basic stem ends in a **consonant**, the fifth principal part is less predictable: its stem-vowel may differ from the stem-vowel in the fourth principal part. Moreover, when the middle/passive ending is added, the collision of letters may cause the consonant at the end of the stem to drop out or change into a different letter, according to the principles of euphonics.

133. ### PERFECT AND PLUPERFECT MIDDLE/PASSIVE: VERBS WHOSE BASIC STEM ENDS IN A VOWEL

These verbs all have perfect active stems ending in κ. To form the perfect middle/passive indicative, **drop the κ** from the perfect active stem and add the **primary** middle/passive endings (-μαι, -σαι, -ται, -μεθα, -σθε, -νται) with no intervening thematic vowel. To form the pluperfect middle/passive indicative, **augment** the perfect active stem, **drop the κ**, and add the **secondary** middle/passive endings (-μην, -σο, -το, -μεθα, -σθε, -ντο) with no thematic vowel.

PERFECT MIDDLE/ PASSIVE INDICATIVE	PLUPERFECT MIDDLE/ PASSIVE INDICATIVE

Singular:

πεπαίδευμαι
("I have taught for myself"
or "I have been taught")

ἐπεπαιδεύμην
("I had taught for myself"
or "I had been taught")

πεπαίδευσαι
("you have taught for yourself"
or "you [*sg.*] have been taught")

ἐπεπαίδευσο
("you had taught for yourself"
or "you [*sg.*] had been taught")

πεπαίδευται
("he/she/it has taught for
him/her/itself" or "he/she/it
has been taught")

ἐπεπαίδευτο
("he/she/it had taught for
him/her/itself" or "he/she/it
had been taught")

Plural:

πεπαιδεύμεθα
("we have taught for ourselves"
or "we have been taught")

ἐπεπαιδεύμεθα
("we had taught for ourselves"
or "we had been taught")

πεπαίδευσθε
("you have taught for yourselves"
or "you [*pl.*] have been taught")

ἐπεπαίδευσθε
("you had taught for yourselves"
or "you [*pl.*] had been taught")

πεπαίδευνται
("they have taught for themselves"
or "they have been taught")

ἐπεπαίδευντο
("they had taught for themselves"
or "they had been taught")

To form the perfect middle/passive infinitive, **drop the κ** from the perfect active stem and add the ending **-σθαι** with no thematic vowel. This infinitive is always accented on the **penult**.

PERFECT MIDDLE/PASSIVE INFINITIVE:

πεπαιδεῦσθαι   ("to have taught for oneself"
          or "to have been taught")

134.   Here are the first five principal parts of all the verbs you now know whose **basic stem ends in a vowel**. The fifth principal part is always the first-person singular perfect middle/passive indicative.

γελάω	γελάσομαι	ἐγέλασα	—	—
δηλόω	δηλώσω	ἐδήλωσα	δεδήλωκα	δεδήλωμαι
δουλεύω	δουλεύσω	ἐδούλευσα	δεδούλευκα	δεδούλευμαι
ἐρωτάω	ἐρωτήσω	ἠρώτησα	ἠρώτηκα	ἠρώτημαι
ἔχω	ἕξω/σχήσω	ἔσχον	ἔσχηκα	ἔσχημαι
ζητέω	ζητήσω	ἐζήτησα	ἐζήτηκα	ἐζήτημαι
θύω	θύσω	ἔθυσα	τέθυκα	τέθυμαι
κελεύω	κελεύσω	ἐκέλευσα	κεκέλευκα	κεκέλευσμαι[1]
λύω	λύσω	ἔλῡσα	λέλυκα	λέλυμαι

[1]κελεύω and a few other verbs insert a sigma before the perfect middle/passive endings that begin with μ or τ (i.e., before -μαι, -μεθα, -μην, -ται, -το).

παιδεύω	παιδεύσω	ἐπαίδευσα	πεπαίδευκα	πεπαίδευμαι
ποιέω	ποιήσω	ἐποίησα	πεποίηκα	πεποίημαι
προσποιέω	προσποιήσω	προσεποίησα	προσπεποίηκα	προσπεποίημαι
πωλέω	πωλήσω	ἐπώλησα	πεπώληκα	πεπώλημαι
τῑμάω	τῑμήσω	ἐτίμησα	τετίμηκα	τετίμημαι
φιλέω	φιλήσω	ἐφίλησα	πεφίληκα	πεφίλημαι
φοβέω	φοβήσω	ἐφόβησα	πεφόβηκα	πεφόβημαι
ὠφελέω	ὠφελήσω	ὠφέλησα	ὠφέληκα	ὠφέλημαι

135.

PERFECT AND PLUPERFECT MIDDLE/PASSIVE: VERBS WHOSE BASIC STEM ENDS IN A CONSONANT

As you know from Lesson 20, these verbs often lose their final consonant or change it in the process of forming their perfect active stem. The fifth principal part of consonant-stem verbs is built on the same reduplicated stem as the fourth principal part, but if a consonant has been lost or changed at the end of that stem, **the consonant must be restored or put back into its original form** before the perfect middle/passive endings are added. If a κ has been added to make the fourth principal part, it must be **dropped** to make the fifth. If the stem-vowel has changed from ε to ο in the fourth principal part, it usually **returns to ε** in the fifth.

Examples: δεδίωχα (*basic stem* = διωκ-) → δεδιωκ-
ἥρπακα (*basic stem* = ἁρπαζ-) → ἡρπαζ-
λέλοιπα (*basic stem* = λειπ-) → λελειπ-

When the consonant at the end of the reduplicated stem collides with a middle/passive ending, a **euphonic change** may occur:

1.	Before **μ** (-μαι, -μεθα):	labial (π, β, φ)	+ μ	= μμ
		palatal (κ, γ, χ)	+ μ	= γμ
		dental (τ, δ, θ), ζ, ν	+ μ	= σμ
		λ, ρ	+ μ	= λμ, ρμ
2.	Before **σ** (-σαι, -σο):	labial (π, β, φ)	+ σ	= ψ
		palatal (κ, γ, χ)	+ σ	= ξ
		dental (τ, δ, θ), ζ	+ σ	= σ
		λ, ρ, ν	+ σ	= λσ, ρσ, νσ
3.	Before **σθ** (-σθε, -σθαι):	labial (π, β, φ)	+ σθ	= φθ
		palatal (κ, γ, χ)	+ σθ	= χθ
		dental (τ, δ, θ), ζ	+ σθ	= σθ
		λ, ρ, ν	+ σθ	= λθ, ρθ, νθ

4.   Before τ (-ται, -το):

labial (π, β, φ)	+ τ	= πτ
palatal (κ, γ, χ)	+ τ	= κτ
dental (τ, δ, θ), ζ	+ τ	= στ
λ, ρ, ν	+ τ	= λτ, ρτ, ντ

5.   Before ν (-νται, -ντο):   Verbs with stems ending in a consonant do not use the endings -νται and -ντο.

Rather than trying to beautify the sound of a consonant colliding with -ν, the Greeks expressed third-person plural in a *periphrastic* (round-about) way: they used a **perfect middle/passive participle** with εἰσί (per-fect) or ἦσαν (pluperfect). You will not be asked to construct these forms until you have studied participles.

To illustrate the euphonic changes outlined above, here are the paradigms of four consonant-stem verbs in the **perfect and pluperfect middle/passive**:

Labial Stem:	**Palatal Stem:**	**Dental Stem:**	**Liquid Stem:**
λείπω (λειπ-)	διώκω (διωκ-)	ἁρπάζω (ἁρπαζ-)	ἀγγέλλω (ἀγγελ-)

PERFECT MIDDLE/PASSIVE INDICATIVE

λέλειμμαι	δεδίωγμαι	ἥρπασμαι	ἤγγελμαι
.λέλειψαι	δεδίωξαι	ἥρπασαι	ἤγγελσαι
λέλειπται	δεδίωκται	ἥρπασται	ἤγγελται
λελείμμεθα	δεδιώγμεθα	ἡρπάσμεθα	ἠγγέλμεθα
λέλειφθε	δεδίωχθε	ἥρπασθε	ἤγγελθε
λελειμμένοι εἰσί(ν)	δεδιωγμένοι εἰσί(ν)	ἡρπασμένοι εἰσί(ν)	ἠγγελμένοι εἰσί(ν)

PERFECT MIDDLE/PASSIVE INFINITIVE

λελεῖφθαι	δεδιῶχθαι	ἡρπάσθαι	ἠγγέλθαι

PLUPERFECT MIDDLE/PASSIVE INDICATIVE

ἐλελείμμην	ἐδεδιώγμην	ἡρπάσμην	ἠγγέλμην
ἐλέλειψο	ἐδεδίωξο	ἥρπασο	ἤγγελσο
ἐλέλειπτο	ἐδεδίωκτο	ἥρπαστο	ἤγγελτο
ἐλελείμμεθα	ἐδεδιώγμεθα	ἡρπάσμεθα	ἠγγέλμεθα
ἐλέλειφθε	ἐδεδίωχθε	ἥρπασθε	ἤγγελθε
λελειμμένοι ἦσαν	δεδιωγμένοι ἦσαν	ἡρπασμένοι ἦσαν	ἠγγελμένοι ἦσαν

136.   Here are the first five principal parts of all the verbs you now know whose **basic stem ends in a consonant**[1]:

---

[1] ἐνήνεγμαι, the perfect middle/passive of φέρω, has **Attic reduplication**; see footnote 3 on p. 129. The pluperfect is ἐνηνέγμην.

DENTAL STEMS

ἁρπάζω	ἁρπάσω	ἥρπασα	ἥρπακα	ἥρπασμαι
κομίζω	κομιῶ	ἐκόμισα	κεκόμικα	κεκόμισμαι
πείθω	πείσω	ἔπεισα	πέπεικα/πέποιθα	πέπεισμαι
σπεύδω	σπεύσω	ἔσπευσα	—	—

LIQUID OR NASAL STEMS

ἀγγέλλω	ἀγγελῶ	ἤγγειλα	ἤγγελκα	ἤγγελμαι
ἀποθνῄσκω	ἀποθανοῦμαι	ἀπέθανον	τέθνηκα	—
ἀποκτείνω	ἀποκτενῶ	ἀπέκτεινα	ἀπέκτονα	—
βάλλω	βαλῶ	ἔβαλον	βέβληκα	βέβλημαι
προσβάλλω	προσβαλῶ	προσέβαλον	προσβέβληκα	προσβέβλημαι
ἐθέλω	ἐθελήσω	ἠθέλησα	ἠθέληκα	—
εὑρίσκω	εὑρήσω	εὗρον/ηὗρον	εὕρηκα/ηὕρηκα	εὕρημαι/ηὕρημαι
λέγω	ἐρῶ/λέξω	εἶπον/ἔλεξα	εἴρηκα	εἴρημαι/λέλεγμαι
μέλλω	μελλήσω	ἐμέλλησα	—	—
μένω	μενῶ	ἔμεινα	μεμένηκα	—
χαίρω	χαιρήσω	ἐχαίρησα	κεχάρηκα	κεχάρημαι

LABIAL STEMS

βλάπτω	βλάψω	ἔβλαψα	βέβλαφα	βέβλαμμαι
βλέπω	βλέψομαι	ἔβλεψα	βέβλεφα	βέβλεμμαι
γράφω	γράψω	ἔγραψα	γέγραφα	γέγραμμαι
κλέπτω	κλέψω	ἔκλεψα	κέκλοφα	κέκλεμμαι
λαμβάνω	λήψομαι	ἔλαβον	εἴληφα	εἴλημμαι
συλλαμβάνω	συλλήψομαι	συνέλαβον	συνείληφα	συνείλημμαι
λείπω	λείψω	ἔλιπον	λέλοιπα	λέλειμμαι
ἀπολείπω	ἀπολείψω	ἀπέλιπον	ἀπολέλοιπα	ἀπολέλειμμαι
πέμπω	πέμψω	ἔπεμψα	πέπομφα	πέπεμμαι
ῥίπτω	ῥίψω	ἔρρῑψα	ἔρρῑφα	ἔρρῑμμαι
τρέπω	τρέψω	ἔτρεψα	τέτροφα	τέτραμμαι

PALATAL STEMS

ἀλλάττω	ἀλλάξω	ἤλλαξα	ἤλλαχα	ἤλλαγμαι
διώκω	διώξω	ἐδίωξα	δεδίωχα	δεδίωγμαι
πλήττω	πλήξω	ἔπληξα	πέπληγα	πέπληγμαι
ἐπιπλήττω	ἐπιπλήξω	ἐπέπληξα	ἐπιπέπληγα	ἐπιπέπληγμαι
πράττω	πράξω	ἔπρᾱξα	πέπρᾱγα/-ᾱχα	πέπρᾱγμαι
φέρω	οἴσω	ἤνεγκα/-ον	ἐνήνοχα	ἐνήνεγμαι
φεύγω	φεύξομαι	ἔφυγον	πέφευγα	
φυλάττω	φυλάξω	ἐφύλαξα	πεφύλαχα	πεφύλαγμαι

DIGAMMA STEMS

ἀκούω   ἀκούσομαι   ἤκουσα   ἀκήκοα   —

137. With perfect and pluperfect passive verbs, the **dative of personal agent** (with no preposition) is often used to identify the person responsible for the action. In all other tenses, however, the **genitive of personal agent** with ὑπό is preferred (e.g., ἐμοὶ τοῦτο πέπρᾱκται "this has been done *by me*"; ὑπ' ἐμοῦ τοῦτ' ἐπράττετο "this was being done *by me*").

138. **VOCABULARY**

ἄγω, ἄξω, ἤγαγον, ἦχα, ἦγμαι

    lead; βίον ἄγειν = lead a life
    [cf. *pedagogue*]

NOTE   ἤγαγον is reduplicated (ἀγ-αγ-) and then augmented. This happens in the aorist of a few verbs; cf. ἤνεγκα, from ἐν-ενκ-, the aorist of φέρω.

νόμος, -ου, ὁ   law, custom [cf. *autonomy, metronome*]
ψῡχή, -ῆς, ἡ   spirit, soul, life [cf. *psychedelic, psychology*]
ἄλλος, -η, -ο   other, another; οἱ ἄλλοι = the others, the rest [cf. *allegory, allergy, allomorph*]

NOTE   ἄλλος is declined like αὐτός, οὗτος, ὅδε, and ἐκεῖνος, with -ο (not -ον) as the neuter nominative and accusative singular ending.

ζῷον, -ου, τό   animal [cf. *protozoa, zodiac, zoology*]
παρά (παρ')   (*prep. + gen.*) from, from the side of; (*prep. + dat.*) at, at the side of, beside, at the house of; (*prep. + acc.*) to, to the side of, contrary to (παρ' before a vowel) [cf. *paradigm, paradox, parasite, parish*]

NOTE   Like πρός (Lesson 17), παρά may be used with the genitive to show the person who is the *source* of an action (similar to ὑπό + genitive of personal agent).

τε (τ', θ')   (*enclitic conj.*) and (τ' before smooth breathing, θ' before rough breathing)
τε...καί or τε...τε   (*correlatives*) both...and

NOTE   Unlike καί, τε never functions as an adverb meaning "even" or "also." When it appears by itself, it means simply "and," but its most common use is as a correlative, combined with καί or another τε to mean "both...and." As an enclitic, τε prefers to come right *after* the word it connects (e.g., ἐγώ τε καὶ σύ), but *between* closely related words like an article and its noun (e.g., ὅ θ᾽ ἵππος τά τ᾽ ἄλλα ζῷα).

οὐδέ (μηδέ)	(*conj.*) and not, nor; (*adv.*) not even (οὐδ᾽/μηδ᾽ *before a vowel*)
οὐδέ (μηδέ)...οὐδέ (μηδέ)	(*correlatives*) neither...nor
οὔτε (μήτε)	(*conj.*) and not, nor (οὔτ᾽/μήτ᾽ *before smooth breathing*, οὔθ᾽/μήθ᾽ *before rough breathing*)
οὔτε (μήτε)...οὔτε (μήτε)	(*correlatives*) neither...nor

NOTE   οὐδέ (μηδέ)...οὐδέ (μηδέ) correlate **clauses**, while οὔτε (μήτε)...οὔτε (μήτε) correlate either **clauses** or **single words**. The forms compounded with μη- are used wherever μή rather than οὐ is appropriate, e.g., with imperatives.

139.   **EXERCISES**

A.   **Greek-to-English Sentences**

1. τί ἄλλο Ἑλληνικὸν ζῷον παρὰ τῶν Ἑλλήνων πέπεμπται πρὸς ἐμέ;
2. παρὰ τὸν νόμον τούτους τε τοὺς σοφοὺς ῥήτορας καὶ τούσδε τοὺς ἀγαθοὺς μαθητὰς ἀπέκτονεν ἐκεῖνος ὁ δεσπότης.
3. μήτε κατὰ θάλατταν μήτε κατὰ γῆν σπεῦδε, ἀλλὰ μένε ἐν τῇ Ἑλλάδι.
4. πρὸς θεῶν, τί κακὸν ἔργον πέπρᾱκται σοί, ὦ ἀνάξιε κλώψ, καθ᾽ ἡμῶν;
5. τοῖς μὲν φιλοσόφοις πόλλ᾽ εἴρηται περὶ τῆς ψῡχῆς, ἐμοὶ δ᾽ οὐκ ἔστι δήλη ἡ ἀλήθεια.
6. πεφόβησαι διὰ τοὺς τῶν σεαυτῆς οἰκετῶν λόγους; ῥῖψον τὸν σὸν φόβον.
7. οὐδ᾽ ἐπέπληκτο ὁ νεᾱνίᾱς τοῖς πολεμίοις οὐδ᾽ ἕν τινι τρόπῳ ἐβέβλαπτο.
8. παρὰ μὲν σοὶ πολὺς θησαυρός ἐστι, παρὰ δ᾽ ἐμοὶ οὐδὲ μῑκρὰ κλίνη.
9. ταῖς τριήρεσιν ἐνήνεχθε εἰς ἄλλην τινὰ χώρᾱν καὶ τοῖς θεοῖς ὠφέλησθε.
10. μετὰ τῶν τε τέκνων τῶν τε δούλων μου εὐδαίμονα βίον ἦχα ἐπ᾽ εἰρήνης.

B.   **English-to-Greek Sentences**

1. Concerning the soul, I have been taught well by both Socrates and the rest.
2. Neither had we acted contrary to the laws, nor had we led a bad life in any manner.
3. A messenger has been sent from the enemy; he is both leading animals and bearing other gifts.
4. Fear not, child, for you have been abandoned neither by me nor by your guardian spirit.
5. Guards, by whom have you been ordered to remain at my house? My life is not in danger.

C.   READING

MONKEYING AROUND
(Aesop's Fable 83)

Ἐν συνόδῳ τῶν ζῴων πίθηκος εὖ ὠρχήσατο. διὰ τοῦτο τὰ ἄλλα ζῷα ἤθελε
ποιήσασθαι ἐκεῖνον βασιλέᾱ. ἀλώπηξ δ᾽ αὐτῷ ἐφθόνει· Σοφή τε καὶ καλή εἰμι. τί οὖν
οὔτε τῑμὰς οὔτε γέρᾱ κεκόμισμαι ἐγὼ αὐτή; τῷ γὰρ πιθήκῳ οὐδὲ σοφίᾱ ἐστίν. ἀλλὰ
τὴν ἀληθῆ ψῡχὴν αὐτοῦ δηλώσω.

5   ἔν τινι πάγῃ κρέας ἡ ἀλώπηξ εὑρήκειν. πρὸς τὸ κρέας τὸν πίθηκον αὐτὴ ἤγαγε
καὶ εἶπε τάδ᾽· Ὁ νόμος κελεύει με τὸν βασιλέᾱ τῶν ζῴων τῑμᾶν. τόδ᾽ οὖν τὸ κρέας
εὕρηται καὶ πεφύλακται ἐμοὶ σοῦ χάριν. λαβὲ αὐτό.

ἐπεὶ δὲ τὸ κρέας ἥρπαστο τῷ πιθήκῳ, οὐκ ἦν αὐτὸν φυγεῖν ἐκ τῆς πάγης. ἡ δ᾽
ἀλώπηξ ἐγέλασεν ἐπ᾽ αὐτῷ· Τίνα ψῡχὴν ὁ βασιλεὺς ἡμῶν ἔχει; οὐ σοφήν γε.

10   τί τούτῳ τῷ λόγῳ δεδήλωται; τοῖς σοφοῖς οὐ μόνον τὸ κρέας ἀλλὰ καὶ ἡ
πάγη δήλη ἔσται.

VOCABULARY

συνόδῳ (line 1): from σύνοδος, -ου, ἡ: meeting
πίθηκος (line 1): from πίθηκος, -ου, ὁ: monkey
ὠρχήσατο (line 1): from ὀρχέομαι, ὀρχήσομαι, ὠρχησάμην, —, — (*deponent verb, always
     in the middle voice but with active meaning*): dance
βασιλέᾱ (line 2): acc. sg. of βασιλεύς, -έως, ὁ: king (ευ-*stem third-decl. noun*)
ἀλώπηξ (line 2): from ἀλώπηξ, -εκος, ἡ: fox
ἐφθόνει (line 2): from φθονέω, φθονήσω, ἐφθόνησα, ἐφθόνηκα, ἐφθόνημαι
     (+ *dat.*): envy
πάγῃ (line 5): from πάγη, -ης, ἡ: trap, snare
κρέας (line 5): from κρέας, -ως, τό: flesh, meat

LESSON 23

RELATIVE PRONOUNS; πᾶς; EXPRESSIONS OF TIME

μὴ τοίνυν δι᾽ ἃ πάλαι παρὰ πάντα τὸν
χρόνον ἡ πόλις εὐδοξεῖ, ταῦτ᾽ ἀνέλητε νῦν
(Don't ruin our city's age-old claims to fame.)
—Demosthenes appeals to the Athenian jurors in *Against Leptines* 142

140.   A **relative clause** is a subordinate clause that acts like an **attributive adjective**, modifying a particular noun or pronoun in the sentence. The modified noun or pronoun is known as the *antecedent*. **Relative pronouns** are words that introduce relative clauses and "relate" them to their antecedents; in English the most common relative pronouns are *who/whom* (referring to a person), *which* (referring to a thing), and *that* (referring to a person or a thing).

Here are all the forms of Greek's relative pronoun (there are no vocatives):

	Singular: Masc.	Fem.	Neut.	Plural: Masc.	Fem.	Neut.
Nom.	ὅς	ἥ	ὅ	οἵ	αἵ	ἅ
Gen.	οὗ	ἧς	οὗ	ὧν	ὧν	ὧν
Dat.	ᾧ	ᾗ	ᾧ	οἷς	αἷς	οἷς
Acc.	ὅν	ἥν	ὅ	οὕς	ἅς	ἅ

As you can see, the relative pronoun resembles the definite article, but wherever the article has τ-, the relative pronoun has *rough breathing* instead. While some forms of the definite article (the proclitics ὁ, ἡ, οἱ, αἱ) have no accent, *every* form of the relative pronoun is accented.

A relative pronoun in Greek always has **the same gender and number as its antecedent**; its **case**, however, is determined not by the case of

147

the antecedent, but by **the function of the relative pronoun in the relative clause**. This makes sense since the relative pronoun is taking the place that the antecedent itself would have had if it had been repeated in the relative clause. Example: πέφευγεν ὁ κλὼψ ὃν συνελάβομεν ("the thief whom we arrested has escaped"). This sentence combines two ideas: πέφευγεν ὁ κλώψ ("the thief has escaped"—main idea) and τὸν κλῶπα συνελάβομεν ("we arrested the thief"—subordinate idea). The relative pronoun ὅν ("whom") makes it unnecessary to repeat the noun κλώψ in the relative clause. If κλώψ had been repeated, it would have had to be in the accusative case as the direct object of "we arrested"; the relative pronoun substituting for κλῶπα must therefore be not only masculine and singular but also in the accusative case (= English's objective case—*whom*, not *who*).

In English the antecedent usually comes before the relative clause that modifies it (in fact, the Latin term *antecedent* literally means "going before"). In Greek the relative clause may come **either before or after** its antecedent, depending on whether the speaker wishes to stress the clause or the antecedent. Example: The English sentence "The maiden to whom I sent the gifts is noble" loses much of its sense if it is rearranged as "To whom I sent the gifts the maiden is noble," but either word order would be acceptable in Greek: **either** ἡ κόρη ᾗ τὰ δῶρα ἔπεμψα καλή ἐστι **or** ᾗ τὰ δῶρα ἔπεμψα ἡ κόρη καλή ἐστι could convey that idea.

A **demonstrative pronoun** often serves as an antecedent (e.g., πράττεις ταῦθ᾽ ἃ ἐθέλεις "you do those things that you wish"). It is also not unusual for an antecedent to be **omitted** altogether; the relative pronoun will reveal the gender of the absent antecedent (e.g., πράττεις ἃ ἐθέλεις "you do [the things] that you wish").

141. The common adjective **πᾶς, πᾶσα, πᾶν** ("all," "every," "whole") is declined with *third-declension* endings in the masculine and neuter, but with *first-declension* endings in the feminine gender:

	Singular:			**Plural:**		
	Masc.	**Fem.**	**Neut.**	**Masc.**	**Fem.**	**Neut.**
Nom./Voc.	πᾶς	πᾶσα	πᾶν	πάντες	πᾶσαι	πάντα
Gen.	παντός	πάσης	παντός	πάντων	πασῶν	πάντων
Dat.	παντί	πάσῃ	παντί	πᾶσι(ν)	πάσαις	πᾶσι(ν)
Acc.	πάντα	πᾶσαν	πᾶν	πάντας	πάσᾱς	πάντα

The masculine/neuter stem **παντ-** loses -ντ- in the dative plural and masculine nominative singular; it loses -τ- in the neuter nominative/accusative singular. (To compensate, the α in the stem is lengthened.) Since the stem is monosyllabic, the accent *should* jump to the ultima in the genitive and dative singular and plural, but it does so only in the singular. To the feminine stem **πᾱσ-** are added endings typical of a noun like θάλαττα, -ης; the feminine genitive plural (πᾱσῶν) is accented on the ultima, as if it were a first-declension noun, not an adjective.

The uses of πᾶς correspond to the uses of *all, every,* and *whole* in English:

1.   When **modifying a noun with an article** and standing in the **predicate** position, πᾶς means "all" (e.g., πᾶσα ἡ τριήρης "all the trireme" or "the trireme, all of it"; αἱ τριήρεις πᾶσαι "all the triremes" or "the triremes, all of them").

2.   When **modifying** a noun without an article and standing in the **predicate** position, πᾶς means "every (conceivable)" or "all (conceivable)" (e.g., τριήρης πᾶσα "every trireme"; πᾶσαι τριήρεις "all triremes").

3.   When standing in the **attributive** position, πᾶς means "whole" or "entire" (e.g., ἡ πᾶσα τριήρης or ἡ τριήρης ἡ πᾶσα "the whole trireme").

4.   When used by itself, πᾶς is a **substantive**: e.g., πᾶς "everyone"; πάντες "all people"; πάντα "all things."

142.   In the vocabulary for this lesson are the words for "day" (ἡμέρᾱ, -ᾱς, ἡ), "night" (νύξ, νυκτός, ἡ), "year" (ἔτος, -ους, τό), and "time" (χρόνος, -ου, ὁ). They and other words like them are frequently used in **expressions of time**.

The **genitive of time within which** establishes the time period *during some part of which* an action takes place (e.g., πωλήσω τὸ βιβλίον **ταύτης τῆς ἡμέρᾱς** "I shall sell the book sometime during that day").

The **dative of time when** specifies *the point at which* an action takes place, or gives the date of an event (e.g., πωλήσω τὸ βιβλίον **ταύτῃ τῇ ἡμέρᾳ** "I shall sell the book on that day"—here the speaker views the whole day as a single point or date, not as a 24-hour stretch of time). The preposition ἐν is often added.

The **accusative of extent of time** indicates *how long* an action lasts (e.g., πωλήσω τὸ βιβλίον **πολλὰς ἡμέρᾱς** "I shall be offering the book for sale for many days"). The accusative implies that the action continues or extends over the *entire* time period, while the genitive implies only that the action occurs during *some part* of that period.

143.   **VOCABULARY**

    ὁράω (*imperf.* ἑώρων), ὄψομαι, εἶδον (*imper.* ἰδέ—*irreg. accent in sg.* [*cf.* εἰπέ, εὑρέ, λαβέ]), ἑόρᾱκα or ἑώρᾱκα, ἑόρᾱμαι or ὧμμαι
        see, behold, look (at); (*pass.*) be seen, appear [cf. *idea, optic, panorama*]

NOTE ὁράω has three different basic stems: ϝορ- (first, fourth, fifth principal parts), ϝιδ- (third principal part), and ὀπ- (second and alternative fifth principal part). The original digammas in ϝορ- and ϝιδ- have dropped out, leaving behind unusual-looking forms (ϝορ- → ὁρ-; ϝε-ϝορ- → ἑορ-; ἐϝιδ- → εἰδ-). ἑώρων, ἑώρᾱκα, and ἑώρᾱμαι were augmented or reduplicated with ϝη- rather than ϝε-; then *metathesis* (transference of quantity) occurred, η becoming short, ο becoming long.

ἔτος, -ους, τό	year [cf. *etesian*]
ἡμέρᾱ, -ᾱς, ἡ	day [cf. *ephemeral, hemeralopia*]
νύξ, νυκτός, ἡ	night [cf. *nyctalopia, nyctitropism*]
χρόνος, -ου, ὁ	time [cf. *chronology, diachronic*]
ὅς, ἥ, ὅ	(*relative pronoun*) who, which, that
πᾶς, πᾶσα, πᾶν	all, every, whole, entire [cf. *diapason, pandemonium, pantheon, pantograph*]
τήμερον	(*indeclinable adverb*) today
ἀμφί (ἀμφ᾽)	(*prep. + gen.*) about, concerning; (*prep. + acc.*) around (*basic meaning = on both sides of*) (ἀμφ᾽ *before a vowel*) [cf. *amphibious, amphitheater, amphora*]

NOTE ἀμφί with accusative may indicate the attendants or followers of a person (e.g., οἱ ἀμφὶ τὸν Σωκράτη "those around Socrates").

ἀνά (ἀν᾽)	(*prep. + acc.*) up, up along, by (*in various idioms*) (ἀν᾽ *before a vowel*) [cf. *anachronism, anagram, analogy, anaphora*]

NOTE When they show direction of movement, ἀνά and κατά are opposites, but in other senses they may be synonymous (e.g., ἀνὰ πᾶσαν ἡμέρᾱν and καθ᾽ ἡμέρᾱν both mean "day by day" or "daily"). As a prefix, ἀνα- may have the sense of "up," "back(wards)," "again," or "in accordance with."

ἕως	(*subordinating conjunction*) while, as long as

NOTE ἕως has another meaning and function that you will learn later. When it means "while" or "as long as," it introduces an adverbial clause whose action takes place **at the same time** as the main action of the sentence (e.g., ἕως ἔλεγον, ἠκούομεν "*while they spoke, we listened*"), whereas the action in an adverbial clause introduced by ἐπεί usually occurs **earlier** than the main action (e.g., ἐπεὶ εἶπον, ἐφύγομεν "*after they spoke* [or *had spoken*—Greek prefers the aorist here, even though the pluperfect tense might seem more logical], we fled").

144.   **EXERCISES**

A.   **Greek-to-English Sentences**

1. μηδὲ πείθου τούτῳ τῷ ἀναξίῳ ἀγγέλῳ μηδὲ πρᾶττε πάντα ἃ κελεύει.

2. πάντες οἱ ἀμφὶ σὲ καὶ σὺ αὐτός, ὦ Σώκρατες, ὄψεσθε τὸν ἐμὸν θησαυρὸν ὃς ἄξιός ἐστιν ὁρᾶσθαι.

3. οἳ τὴν ἀληθῆ εἰρήνην εὑρήκᾱσιν οἵδ᾽ οἱ ἄνθρωποι εὐδαίμονές εἰσιν.

4. πολλὰς ἡμέρᾱς ἐζητήκαμεν τὰ ζῷα ἃ ὁ ἡμέτερος δεσπότης ἐθέλει ἔχειν.

5. τί εἶδες ἐπεὶ ἐτρέψω εἰς τὴν ἀγορᾱν; εἰπέ μοι τὸν πάντα λόγον ἕως ἀκούω.

6. ἕως με ἑώρᾱ αὕτη ᾗ δουλεύω, οὐκ εἶχον αὐτὴ κλέψαι ὀβολούς τινας.

7. ὀλίγου χρόνου ἐρρίφεσαν εἰς τὴν ἅμαξαν πάντα τὰ γέρᾱ ἃ τότ᾽ αὐτῷ ἦν.

8. κατ᾽ ἐμοῦ τε καὶ σοῦ αἰτίαι τινὲς τήμερον λέγονται ὑπὸ τούτου τοῦ ῥήτορος ὃς ἡμῖν βέβλαπται.

9. ἀνὰ πᾶν ἔτος λελύκᾱσιν οἱ πολέμιοι τὴν γῆν ὑμῶν, ὦ Ἕλληνες, ἀλλ᾽ οὐ μέλλετε ἀπολείψειν τὴν Ἑλλάδα.

10. τῇ αὐτῇ νυκτὶ παρὰ τοὺς νόμους ἤγαγον τὰ ἑαυτῶν τέκνα ἐκ τῶν οἰκιῶν καὶ τοῖς ἵπποις ἔφυγον κατὰ τὸν ποταμόν.

B.   **English-to-Greek Sentences**

1. For many days she has remained in this house that you (*pl.*) see, for all the roads around it have dangers.

2. While they were stealing the horses, we saw those thieves and chased them up the river.

3. Not even the long years of grief have changed your (*sg.*) good character, which everyone much loves.

4. At night I fear the evil things that I have not feared the whole day.

5. Within the same time he not only killed every enemy in Greece, but also was killed himself.

C.   READING

BAT, BUSH, AND BIRD
(Aesop's Fable 181)

Νυκτερὶς καὶ βάτος καὶ αἴθυια φίλαι ἦσαν καὶ πᾶσαι ἤθελον ἐμπορικὸν βίον ἄγειν. ἡ μὲν νυκτερὶς πολλὰς δραχμὰς παρὰ δανειστῶν τινων συνέλαβεν, ἡ δὲ βάτος ἱμάτια μεθ' ἑαυτῆς ἔλαβεν, ἡ δ' αἴθυια πολὺν χαλκόν. τότε διὰ τῆς θαλάττης ἔσπευσαν. ἀλλὰ τήν τε ναῦν ἐν ᾗ αὐταὶ ἐφέροντο καὶ πάντα τὸν θησαυρὸν αὐτῶν χειμὼν

5   ἔλῡσεν. ἀπ' ἐκείνου τοῦ χρόνου ἡ μὲν νυκτερὶς τοὺς δανειστὰς φοβεῖται καὶ οὖν τῆς ἡμέρᾱς οὐχ ὁρᾶται, ἡ δὲ βάτος τὰ τῶν παριόντων ἱμάτια ἁρπάζει, ἡ δ' αἴθυια παρὰ τῇ θαλάττῃ μένει καὶ ἀνὰ πᾶσαν ἡμέρᾱν τὸν χαλκὸν ζητεῖ.

ὁ λόγος δηλοῖ τόδε· σπεύδομεν ταῦτα πάλιν ἔχειν, ἃ πρότερον εἴχομεν.

VOCABULARY

νυκτερίς (line 1): from νυκτερίς, -ίδος, ἡ: bat
βάτος (line 1): from βάτος, -ου, ἡ: bramble bush
αἴθυια (line 1): from αἴθυια, -ᾱς, ἡ: seagull
ἐμπορικόν (line 1): from ἐμπορικός, -ή, -όν: having to do with trade;
        ἐμπορικὸς βίος = "a merchant's life"
δανειστῶν (line 2): from δανειστής, -οῦ, ὁ: money-lender
χαλκόν (line 3): from χαλκός, -οῦ, ὁ: copper, copper money
ναῦν (line 4): acc. sg. of ναῦς, νεώς, ἡ: ship (*an αυ-stem third-decl. noun*)
χειμών (line 4): from χειμών, -ῶνος, ὁ: storm
ἀπ' ἐκείνου τοῦ χρόνου (line 5): from that time forth
παριόντων (line 6): of the ones passing by (*pres. act. participle of* πάρειμι)
πρότερον (line 8): earlier (*adverb from* πρότερος, -ᾱ, -ον)

LESSON 24

Ω-VERBS
Present Active Participle, Future Active Participle, First and Second Aorist Active Participles, Perfect Active Participle

τὴν δ᾽ ἐθέλων ἐθέλουσαν ἀνήγαγεν ὅνδε δόμονδε
(Willingly he led her willingly back to his house.)
Clytemnestra succumbs to the charms of her lover Aegisthus,
as described by Nestor in Homer's *Odyssey* 3.272

145.   A **participle** is a **verbal adjective**, i.e., an adjective built on the stem of a verb. It is thus a hybrid: part-verb, part-adjective. Like a verb, it has **tense** and **voice**, can take an **object**, and can be modified by **adverbs** and **prepositional phrases**, but by itself it cannot be the main verb in a sentence. Like an adjective, it **modifies a noun** or, when the noun is omitted, functions as a **substantive**.

Both English and Greek use participles, but the system of participles is far more elaborate in Greek. Here, for example, are all of the participles that can possibly be made from the verb *teach* in English: *teaching, being taught, having taught, having been taught, going to teach, going to be taught.* As you can see, **the ending -*ing* is characteristic of English participles**. They change their form to reflect voice (active, passive) and tense (present, past, future), but not to reflect the gender, number, and case of the noun being modified.

Greek participles, on the other hand, change their form not only to reflect voice (**active, middle, passive**) and tense (**present, future, aorist, perfect**), but also to reflect the **gender, number**, and **case** of the noun they are modifying. The ancient Greeks loved the elegant succinctness of participles and filled their sentences with them. Learning how to form and manipulate participles is therefore an essential task for every student of Greek. This lesson introduces you to all the **active participles** and describes two ways in which they are used.

153

146. Here are paradigms of all the active participles of παιδεύω (present, future, first aorist, and perfect tenses). To illustrate participles of the second aorist type, a paradigm of the aorist active participle of βάλλω is given at the end.

NOTE The vocatives are all identical with the nominatives.

PRESENT ACTIVE PARTICIPLE
("teaching")

Singular:	Masc.	Fem.	Neut.
Nom./Voc.	παιδεύων	παιδεύουσα	παιδεῦον
Gen.	παιδεύοντος	παιδευούσης	παιδεύοντος
Dat.	παιδεύοντι	παιδευούσῃ	παιδεύοντι
Acc.	παιδεύοντα	παιδεύουσαν	παιδεῦον

Plural:	Masc.	Fem.	Neut.
Nom./Voc.	παιδεύοντες	παιδεύουσαι	παιδεύοντα
Gen.	παιδευόντων	παιδευουσῶν	παιδευόντων
Dat.	παιδεύουσι(ν)	παιδευούσαις	παιδεύουσι(ν)
Acc.	παιδεύοντας	παιδευούσᾱς	παιδεύοντα

FUTURE ACTIVE PARTICIPLE
("going to teach")

Singular:	Masc.	Fem.	Neut.
Nom./Voc.	παιδεύσων	παιδεύσουσα	παιδεῦσον
Gen.	παιδεύσοντος	παιδευσούσης	παιδεύσοντος
Dat.	παιδεύσοντι	παιδευσούσῃ	παιδεύσοντι
Acc.	παιδεύσοντα	παιδεύσουσαν	παιδεῦσον

Plural:	Masc.	Fem.	Neut.
Nom./Voc.	παιδεύσοντες	παιδεύσουσαι	παιδεύσοντα
Gen.	παιδευσόντων	παιδευσουσῶν	παιδευσόντων
Dat.	παιδεύσουσι(ν)	παιδευσούσαις	παιδεύσουσι(ν)
Acc.	παιδεύσοντας	παιδευσούσᾱς	παιδεύσοντα

FIRST AORIST ACTIVE PARTICIPLE
("teaching" or "having taught")

Singular:	Masc.	Fem.	Neut.
Nom./Voc.	παιδεύσᾱς	παιδεύσᾱσα	παιδεῦσαν
Gen.	παιδεύσαντος	παιδευσάσης	παιδεύσαντος
Dat.	παιδεύσαντι	παιδευσάσῃ	παιδεύσαντι
Acc.	παιδεύσαντα	παιδεύσᾱσαν	παιδεῦσαν

Plural:	Masc.	Fem.	Neut.
Nom./Voc.	παιδεύσαντες	παιδεύσᾱσαι	παιδεύσαντα
Gen.	παιδευσάντων	παιδευσᾱσῶν	παιδευσάντων
Dat.	παιδεύσᾱσι(ν)	παιδευσάσαις	παιδεύσᾱσι(ν)
Acc.	παιδεύσαντας	παιδευσάσᾱς	παιδεύσαντα

PERFECT ACTIVE PARTICIPLE
("having taught")

Singular:	Masc.	Fem.	Neut.
Nom./Voc.	πεπαιδευκώς	πεπαιδευκυῖα	πεπαιδευκός
Gen.	πεπαιδευκότος	πεπαιδευκυίᾱς	πεπαιδευκότος
Dat.	πεπαιδευκότι	πεπαιδευκυίᾳ	πεπαιδευκότι
Acc.	πεπαιδευκότα	πεπαιδευκυῖαν	πεπαιδευκός

Plural:	Masc.	Fem.	Neut.
Nom./Voc.	πεπαιδευκότες	πεπαιδευκυῖαι	πεπαιδευκότα
Gen.	πεπαιδευκότων	πεπαιδευκυιῶν	πεπαιδευκότων
Dat.	πεπαιδευκόσι(ν)	πεπαιδευκυίαις	πεπαιδευκόσι(ν)
Acc.	πεπαιδευκότας	πεπαιδευκυίᾱς	πεπαιδευκότα

NOTE   **Second perfect participles** have exactly the same endings as first perfect participles, but their stems end in a letter other than a kappa (e.g., λελοιπώς, λελοιπυῖα, λελοιπός).

SECOND AORIST ACTIVE PARTICIPLE
("throwing" or "having thrown")

Singular:	Masc.	Fem.	Neut.
Nom./Voc.	βαλών	βαλοῦσα	βαλόν
Gen.	βαλόντος	βαλούσης	βαλόντος
Dat.	βαλόντι	βαλούσῃ	βαλόντι
Acc.	βαλόντα	βαλοῦσαν	βαλόν

Plural:	Masc.	Fem.	Neut.
Nom./Voc.	βαλόντες	βαλοῦσαι	βαλόντα
Gen.	βαλόντων	βαλουσῶν	βαλόντων
Dat.	βαλοῦσι(ν)	βαλούσαις	βαλοῦσι(ν)
Acc.	βαλόντας	βαλούσᾱς	βαλόντα

147.   Like πᾶς, all of these participles have a **mixed declension**: they use **third-declension endings** for their masculine and neuter forms, **first-declension endings** for their feminine forms. The feminines have endings like those of θάλαττα, -ης or, if the letter before the ending is an ι, like those of μοῖρα, -ᾱς.

In the present, future, and second aorist, the participial **suffix** is **-οντ-** (a combination of the thematic vowel ο + ντ); in the feminine forms, this suffix appears as **-ουσ-** (a contraction of οντ + semivocalic ι). In the first aorist, σα replaces the thematic vowel in -οντ-, creating the suffixes **-σαντ-** and **-σᾱσ-**. In the perfect, the participial suffix is **-οτ-** (originally -ϝοτ-) for masculine and neuter forms, **-υι-** (a contraction of υσ + semivocalic ι) for feminine forms.

Adding the ending -σι (**dative plural**) to -οντ- or -σαντ- causes the ντ to drop out and the preceding vowel to lengthen, producing **-ουσι** or

-σᾱσι; in the perfect active participle, the τ of -οτ- drops out before -σι, but the vowel remains an omicron (-οσι). In the **masculine nominative singular**, the participial suffix loses its τ (in the first aorist its ν also) and has a long vowel (**-ων**); the first aorist and the perfect also add ς (**-σᾱς, -ως**). In the **neuter nominative singular**, the τ of the suffix drops out, leaving **-ον** or **-σαν**; the perfect also adds **-ς** (**-ος**).

Like infinitives, participles are never augmented. The only difference between the present active participle and the future active participle is the tense-marker **-σ-** added to the stem to make the future tense. The first aorist active participle is distinguished by its **-σα-**, the second aorist by the same special stem (zero-grade) that it has in its finite forms. The perfect has the **reduplicated stem** characteristic of the perfect tense. First perfects, as usual, attach a κ to the end of that stem; second perfects do not.

Active participles all have the **persistent accent** typical of adjectives. In the present, future, and first aorist, the accent remains on the final syllable of the stem, i.e., **on the syllable just before the participial suffix**, unless a long ultima forces it to move to the right. In the perfect and second aorist, the accent remains **on the participial suffix itself**. This helps to distinguish the second aorist active participle from the present active participle (e.g., βάλλων, βαλών). In the **feminine genitive plural**, the accent always jumps to the **ultima**, as it does in all first-declension nouns and πᾶς. **Movable ν** is added to the masculine and neuter dative plural of all active participles.

148.   The **present participle of εἰμί** ("being") is nothing more than the endings of the present active participle, written with accents and smooth breathings:

Singular:	Masc.	Fem.	Neut.
Nom./Voc.	ὤν	οὖσα	ὄν
Gen.	ὄντος	οὔσης	ὄντος
Dat.	ὄντι	οὔσῃ	ὄντι
Acc.	ὄντα	οὖσαν	ὄν

Plural:	Masc.	Fem.	Neut.
Nom./Voc.	ὄντες	οὖσαι	ὄντα
Gen.	ὄντων	οὐσῶν	ὄντων
Dat.	οὖσι(ν)	οὔσαις	οὖσι(ν)
Acc.	ὄντας	οὔσᾱς	ὄντα

NOTE   The accents of the masculine/neuter genitive and dative singular and plural violate the rule that third-declension nouns/adjectives with monosyllabic stems are accented on the ultima in the genitive and dative singular and plural.

149. The present active participle of a **contract verb** is formed in the same way as the present active participle of a regular verb. Predictable contractions occur when the ε, α, or ο of the stem makes contact with the ω or ο of the participial suffix (εω, αω, οω, αο → **ω**; εο, οο → **ου**). Full paradigms for the three types of contract verbs are presented in the appendix, pp. 478-479.

150. The tense of a participle, like the tense of an infinitive, is associated with a particular **aspect**. Present tense implies **imperfective** aspect; aorist tense implies **aoristic** aspect; perfect tense implies **perfective** aspect. Future tense implies that the action is **intended or expected**.

A participle's tense is also a clue to the **relative time** of the action, i.e., whether it takes place earlier than, at the same time as, or later than the action of the main verb. Here is the significance that each tense **most often** has:

Present Participle: action **contemporaneous** with that of the main verb (e.g., γράφουσα εἶδε [or ἔβλεψε] τὸν λέοντα "while she was writing [literally, 'writing'], she saw the lion")

Aorist Participle: action **prior to** that of the main verb (e.g., ἰδοῦσα [or βλέψασα] τὸν λέοντα, ἔφυγε ("after she saw [literally, 'seeing' or 'having seen'] the lion, she fled")

Perfect Participle: state **contemporaneous** with the action of the main verb, but the result of an earlier action now **completed** (e.g., τῑμῶμέν σε εὖ πεπαιδευκότα τὰ τέκνα "we honor you because you have taught [i.e., are now finished with teaching; literally, 'having taught'] the children well")

Future Participle: action that, at the time represented by the main verb, is still in the future but already **anticipated** (e.g., τῑμήσομέν σε εὖ παιδεύσοντα τὰ τέκνα "we shall honor you if you will teach [literally, 'going to teach'] the children well")

NOTE A future participle may express the **purpose** or motivation behind an action, especially when the participle is combined with a verb of motion (e.g., "go," "come," "send," "summon"). Example: ἔπεμψάν με παιδεύσοντα τὰ τέκνα ("they sent me to teach [i.e., in order that I might teach; literally, 'going to teach'] the children").

These are generalizations, not strict rules. Since the participle's tense is intended primarily to show aspect, not time, you may have to rely on other words in the sentence (e.g., **adverbs** like νῦν and τότε) to determine what the relative time is. Example: δοῦλοι τότ' ὄντες, ἐλεύθεροι νῦν εἰσι ("although then they were slaves, now they are free").

NOTE　　　　There are no imperfect or pluperfect participles in Greek. The present and perfect participles already suffice to show imperfective and perfective aspect; the imperfect and pluperfect participles, if they existed, would be redundant.

151.　　　　Every Greek participle can be categorized as **attributive, circumstantial,** or **supplementary**, according to its use in a particular sentence. Supplementary participles will not be discussed until the next lesson.

An **attributive participle** modifies a noun, agreeing with it in gender, number, and case, and stands in the **attributive position** (i.e., right after an article). Its purpose is the same as that of an attributive adjective or a relative clause: to **characterize the noun** that it modifies. It is often advisable to translate an attributive participle with a relative clause. Example: φίλος ἐστὶν ὁ δοῦλος ὁ ἄγων καθ᾽ ἡμέρᾱν τὰ τέκνα is literally "the slave daily leading the children is dear," but it could also be rendered as "the slave who daily leads the children is dear."

In the example just given, the participle comes immediately after an article (ὁ ἄγων...) and thus is clearly in the attributive position. A participle is also considered to be in the attributive position if the only words between it and the preceding article are **the participle's own modifiers** (adverbs, prepositional phrases) **or objects**; e.g., the words in the example could be rearranged as ὁ τὰ τέκνα καθ᾽ ἡμέρᾱν ἄγων δοῦλος without changing their meaning. (Putting the words in the order ὁ δοῦλος τὰ τέκνα καθ᾽ ἡμέρᾱν ἄγων or ὁ δοῦλος ἄγων καθ᾽ ἡμέρᾱν τὰ τέκνα would shift the participle into the predicate position and change the meaning of the clause; see below.) Like any attributive adjective, an attributive participle may function as a **substantive** if the noun that it modifies is omitted; e.g., ὁ τὰ τέκνα καθ᾽ ἡμέρᾱν ἄγων = "the [man] who daily leads the children"; ἡ τὰ τέκνα καθ᾽ ἡμέρᾱν ἄγουσα = "the [woman] who daily leads the children."

A **circumstantial participle** modifies a noun, agreeing with it in gender, number, and case, and stands in the **predicate position** (i.e., *not* right after an article). Its purpose is not to characterize the noun, but to join with it to **describe the circumstances** under which the sentence's main action takes place.

Just as the attributive participle is an abbreviated version of an adjectival (relative) clause, so the circumstantial participle is an abbreviated version of an **adverbial clause**. Exactly which type of adverbial clause the participle represents must be deduced from the context. Example: ὁ δοῦλος ἄγων τὰ τέκνα ἔλεγε is literally "[under the circumstances of] leading the children, the slave was talking," but, depending on the context, this could mean "while he was leading..." (temporal clause) or "although he was leading..." (concessive clause) or "because he was leading..." (causal clause) or "if he was leading..." (conditional clause), etc.

Conjunctions like ἐπεί ("after," "when," "since," "because") and ἕως ("while") are used only to introduce adverbial clauses with finite verbs; they are **never** used with participles. To help clarify the relationship of a circumstantial participle to the rest of the sentence, a particle such as καίπερ ("although"), ἅτε ("because"), or ὡς ("as if") may be placed at the start of the participial clause; see the vocabulary for this lesson.

152.   **VOCABULARY**

καλέω, καλῶ, ἐκάλεσα, κέκληκα, κέκλημαι
                      call, summon, invite, name [cf. *Paraclete*]

δεῖπνον, -ου, τό	meal, dinner
ἐλπίς, -ίδος, ἡ	hope (+ *gen. or infinitive*)
θύρᾱ, -ᾱς, ἡ	door [cf. *thyroid*]
ξενίᾱ, -ᾱς, ἡ	hospitality, guest-friendship
ξένος, -ου, ὁ	stranger, guest, host [cf. *xenon, xenophobia*]
ἄνευ	(*prep.* + *gen.*) without
ἅτε	(*particle* + *ptcple.*) because
καίπερ	(*particle* + *ptcple.*) although (*enclitic* -περ *makes the accent acute*)
ὡς	(*particle* + *ptcple.*) as if, with the avowed intention of, on the grounds of; (*conj.*) as, since, because, after, when [= ἐπεί]

NOTE
        As a particle, ὡς implies that the participle gives someone's *professed* reason for an action (which may or may not be the real reason). ὡς is used most often with future participles since they show intention or purpose. Like εἰς, ἐκ, ἐν, ὁ, ἡ, οἱ, αἱ, and οὐ, ὡς is a proclitic and thus has no accent. After ὡς (just as after καί, οὐκ, ἀλλ', μή, or τοῦτ'), ἔστι(ν) is accented on its penult.

153.   **EXERCISES**

A.   **Greek-to-English Sentences**

1.   οἱ τῇδε τῇ ἡμέρᾳ λιπόντες τὴν χώρᾱν εἰσὶν οὔτ' ἄνευ ἐλπίδος οὔτ' ἄνευ φόβου.

2.   ταύτῃ τῇ οἰκίᾳ, ἅτε πολλὰς θύρᾱς καὶ κλίνᾱς ἐχούσῃ, πολὺ χαίρομεν.

3.   ἐκεῖνον τὸν φιλόσοφον τὸν πάντα τὰ ἑαυτοῦ ἱμάτια πωλήσαντα εἶδες;

4.   τίνας ξένους, ὦ δέσποινα, ἐπὶ τὸ δεῖπνον κέκληκας ὡς αὐτοὺς τῑμήσουσα;

5.   ὁ ἀγαθὸς δεσπότης ἀποθανὼν πάσᾱς τὰς ἐλπίδας ἡμῶν κέκλοφεν.

6.   ὥρᾱ ἡμᾶς, τέκνα οὐκέτι ὄντας, ἔχειν χάριν τοῖς ἡμᾶς εὖ πεπαιδευκόσιν.

7.   οὐκ ἄνευ τινὸς τῶν ἐν οὐρανῷ θεῶν ἐκομισάμην τάδε τὰ γέρᾱ ἃ νῦν ὁρᾷς.

8. κατὰ τὸν τῶν Ἑλλήνων νόμον τἰμᾱ ξενίᾳ τε δώροις τε τὸν τάδ' ἠγγελκότα.

9. ἡμῖν μέν, ῥήτορσιν οὖσι, πολλαὶ χαραί εἰσι, σοὶ δέ, δούλῃ οὔσῃ, ὀλίγαι.

10. τί οὐκ ἀκήκοάς μου, ὦ ἀνάξιε οἰκέτα, καίπερ σε τῷ ὀνόματι καλοῦντος;

B.   English-to-Greek Sentences

1. O gods, attack those who, contrary to the laws of hospitality, have killed (*use perfect or aorist participle*) a guest upon the couch.

2. With the avowed intention of inviting (*use future participle*) you (*sg.*) to dinner, I have betaken myself to your house today.

3. Because they had been leading (*use present participle*) a happy life for many years, they were not willing to change their ways.

4. The child, being little, fears all the guards although they carry (*use present participle*) only shields.

5. We are not without some hope of seeing (*use infinitive*) the trireme that has remained (*use perfect or aorist participle*) in Greece.

C.   READING

DINNER GOES TO THE DOGS
(Aesop's Fable 283)

Ἄνθρωπός τις ἐκάλει ἐπὶ τὸ δεῖπνον τοὺς ἑαυτοῦ ξένους, ὁ δὲ τούτου κύων ἄλλον κύνα ἐκάλει, λέγων· Εὖ δειπνήσεις, ὦ φίλε, παρ' ἐμοί. ὁ δ' ἄλλος εἰς τὴν οἰκίᾱν σπεύσᾱς καὶ ἰδὼν τὸ καλὸν δεῖπνον, εἶπε· Βαβαί, πολλαὶ χαραί μοι ἔσονται ἐν ταύτῃ τῇ νυκτί. χαίρων οὖν καὶ σείων τὴν κέρκον, χάριν ἐδήλωσε πρὸς τὸν φίλον τὸν
5 κεκληκότα ἐπὶ τὸ δεῖπνον.

ἀλλ' ὁ μάγειρος ἰδὼν τὴν ἐκείνου κέρκον, αὐτὸν ἥρπασε καὶ ἔρρῑψε διὰ τῆς θύρᾱς. οἱ δ' ἄλλοι κύνες αὐτὸν ἰδόντες ἠρώτων· Πῶς ἐδείπνησας; καὶ οὗτος, οὐκ ἐθέλων τὰ ἀληθῆ εἰπεῖν, εἶπε· Τὴν ὁδὸν ἰδεῖν οὐκ εἶχον ἅτε πολὺ πεπωκώς.

ὁ λόγος τόδε δηλοῖ· καίπερ κακῶς πρᾱ́ξαντες, οἱ ἄνθρωποι φιλοῦσι προσποιεῖσθαι
10 εὖ πεπρᾱγέναι.

VOCABULARY

κύων (line 2): from κύων, κυνός, ὁ: dog
δειπνήσεις (line 2): from δειπνέω, δειπνήσω, ἐδείπνησα, δεδείπνηκα, δεδείπνημαι: dine
βαβαί (line 3): wow! (*exclamation of surprise or amazement*)
σείων (line 4): from σείω, σείσω, ἔσεισα, σέσεικα, σέσεισμαι: shake, wag
κέρκον (line 4): from κέρκος, -ου, ἡ: tail
μάγειρος (line 6): from μάγειρος, -ου, ὁ: cook
πῶς (line 7): how? (*interrogative pronoun*)
πεπωκώς (line 8): from πίνω, πίομαι, ἔπιον, πέπωκα, πέπομαι: drink

LESSON 25

Ω-VERBS
Present Middle/Passive Participle, Future Middle Participle, First and Second Aorist Middle Participles, Perfect Middle/Passive Participle

γηράσκω δ' αἰεὶ πολλὰ διδασκόμενος
(The older I grow, the more I learn.)
—one of Solon's sayings, quoted by Plutarch in *Solon* 31

154. This lesson introduces the **middle/passive participles**: the **present** middle/passive, **future** middle, **aorist** middle, and **perfect** middle/passive. As you would expect, participles built on the stems from the first and fifth principal parts have *either middle or passive voice*, while those built on the stems from the second and third principal parts have *only middle voice*. The aorist passive participle and the future passive participle both use the stem from the sixth principal part; you will not be asked to learn them until Lessons 27 and 28.

All the participles presented in this lesson are formed with the same suffix (-μεν-) and have regular -ος, -η, -ον adjectival endings. They differ from one another only in their stems. (The perfect participle is also distinctive in its accent.)

155. Here are the middle and middle/passive participles of παιδεύω. To illustrate participles of the second aorist type, a paradigm of the aorist middle participle of βάλλω is given after all the other paradigms.

PRESENT MIDDLE/PASSIVE PARTICIPLE
("teaching for oneself" / "being taught")

Singular:	Masc.	Fem.	Neut.
Nom.	παιδευόμενος	παιδευομένη	παιδευόμενον
Gen.	παιδευομένου	παιδευομένης	παιδευομένου
Dat.	παιδευομένῳ	παιδευομένῃ	παιδευομένῳ
Acc.	παιδευόμενον	παιδευομένην	παιδευόμενον
Voc.	παιδευόμενε	παιδευομένη	παιδευόμενον

Plural:	Masc.	Fem.	Neut.
Nom./Voc.	παιδευόμενοι	παιδευόμεναι	παιδευόμενα
Gen.	παιδευομένων	παιδευομένων	παιδευομένων
Dat.	παιδευομένοις	παιδευομέναις	παιδευομένοις
Acc.	παιδευομένους	παιδευομένᾱς	παιδευόμενα

FUTURE MIDDLE PARTICIPLE
("going to teach for oneself")

Singular:	Masc.	Fem.	Neut.
Nom.	παιδευσόμενος	παιδευσομένη	παιδευσόμενον
Gen.	παιδευσομένου	παιδευσομένης	παιδευσομένου
Dat.	παιδευσομένῳ	παιδευσομένῃ	παιδευσομένῳ
Acc.	παιδευσόμενον	παιδευσομένην	παιδευσόμενον
Voc.	παιδευσόμενε	παιδευσομένη	παιδευσόμενον

Plural:	Masc.	Fem.	Neut.
Nom./Voc.	παιδευσόμενοι	παιδευσόμεναι	παιδευσόμενα
Gen.	παιδευσομένων	παιδευσομένων	παιδευσομένων
Dat.	παιδευσομένοις	παιδευσομέναις	παιδευσομένοις
Acc.	παιδευσομένους	παιδευσομένᾱς	παιδευσόμενα

FIRST AORIST MIDDLE PARTICIPLE
("teaching for oneself" / "having taught for oneself")

Singular:	Masc.	Fem.	Neut.
Nom.	παιδευσάμενος	παιδευσαμένη	παιδευσάμενον
Gen.	παιδευσαμένου	παιδευσαμένης	παιδευσαμένου
Dat.	παιδευσαμένῳ	παιδευσαμένῃ	παιδευσαμένῳ
Acc.	παιδευσάμενον	παιδευσαμένην	παιδευσάμενον
Voc.	παιδευσάμενε	παιδευσαμένη	παιδευσάμενον

Plural:	Masc.	Fem.	Neut.
Nom./Voc.	παιδευσάμενοι	παιδευσάμεναι	παιδευσάμενα
Gen.	παιδευσαμένων	παιδευσαμένων	παιδευσαμένων
Dat.	παιδευσαμένοις	παιδευσαμέναις	παιδευσαμένοις
Acc.	παιδευσαμένους	παιδευσαμένᾱς	παιδευσάμενα

PERFECT MIDDLE/PASSIVE PARTICIPLE
("having taught for oneself"/"having been taught")

Singular:	Masc.	Fem.	Neut.
Nom.	πεπαιδευμένος	πεπαιδευμένη	πεπαιδευμένον
Gen.	πεπαιδευμένου	πεπαιδευμένης	πεπαιδευμένου
Dat.	πεπαιδευμένῳ	πεπαιδευμένῃ	πεπαιδευμένῳ
Acc.	πεπαιδευμένον	πεπαιδευμένην	πεπαιδευμένον
Voc.	πεπαιδευμένε	πεπαιδευμένη	πεπαιδευμένον

Plural:	Masc.	Fem.	Neut.
Nom./Voc.	πεπαιδευμένοι	πεπαιδευμέναι	πεπαιδευμένα
Gen.	πεπαιδευμένων	πεπαιδευμένων	πεπαιδευμένων
Dat.	πεπαιδευμένοις	πεπαιδευμέναις	πεπαιδευμένοις
Acc.	πεπαιδευμένους	πεπαιδευμένᾱς	πεπαιδευμένα

NOTE: If the perfect middle/passive stem ends in a consonant, a euphonic change may have to be made when the stem and the participial suffix (-μεν-) meet: labial + μ = μμ; palatal + μ = γμ; dental or ν + μ = σμ; λ + μ = λμ; ρ + μ = ρμ.

SECOND AORIST MIDDLE PARTICIPLE
("throwing for oneself"/"having thrown for oneself")

Singular:	Masc.	Fem.	Neut.
Nom.	βαλόμενος	βαλομένη	βαλόμενον
Gen.	βαλομένου	βαλομένης	βαλομένου
Dat.	βαλομένῳ	βαλομένῃ	βαλομένῳ
Acc.	βαλόμενον	βαλομένην	βαλόμενον
Voc.	βαλόμενε	βαλομένη	βαλόμενον

Plural:	Masc.	Fem.	Neut.
Nom./Voc.	βαλόμενοι	βαλόμεναι	βαλόμενα
Gen.	βαλομένων	βαλομένων	βαλομένων
Dat.	βαλομένοις	βαλομέναις	βαλομένοις
Acc.	βαλομένους	βαλομένᾱς	βαλόμενα

156. Like all other participles, these middle and middle/passive participles have **no augments**. The present, future, and second aorist participles add a thematic vowel (o) before the participial suffix (-μεν-). The first aorist participle replaces that thematic vowel with σα. The perfect participle has a **reduplicated** stem with *no thematic vowel*; if the reduplicated stem ends in a consonant, a euphonic change may be required (see the note in the preceding section).

The accent in each of these participles is **persistent**, remaining, if possible, on the syllable **just *before* the participial suffix**. In the perfect participle, however, the accent remains, if possible, **on the suffix itself**. The feminine genitive plural is accented in the way normal for adjectives (i.e., persistently); it is only in active participles that the accent shifts to the ultima.

157. The **future participle** of εἰμί must be a middle participle since ἔσομαι is a middle deponent (i.e., always middle in form, active in meaning). The literal translation of ἐσόμενος, -η, -ον is "going to be."

158. In the present middle/passive participle of a **contract verb**, the stem-vowel contracts in a predictable way with the omicron of -ομεν- (αο → ω; εο, οο → ου). Full paradigms for the three types of contract verbs are presented in the appendix, p. 479.

159. A **supplementary participle** resembles a circumstantial participle in that it modifies a noun, agreeing with it in gender, number, and case, and stands in the **predicate** position. The purpose of a supplementary participle, however, is not to describe the circumstances surrounding the main action in the sentence, but to **complete ("supplement") the idea of the main verb**. While a circumstantial participle is an optional item in a sentence, a supplementary participle is essential: the point of the sentence would be lost if it were removed.

Supplementary participles tend to appear only with certain verbs. They are often combined with forms of εἰμί to express a verbal idea in a *periphrastic* (roundabout) way: εἰσί(ν) and ἦσαν, for example, are used with the **perfect middle/passive participle** (agreeing in gender, number, and case with the subject of the sentence) to make the **third-person plural perfect and pluperfect middle/passive** indicative of consonant-stem verbs (e.g., πεπεμμένοι ἦσαν "they had been sent"—literally, "they were having been sent").

The vocabulary for this lesson includes **παύω**, which means "stop" in the active voice, "cease" in the middle voice. This verb is well suited for use with a supplementary participle (e.g., παύω αὐτοὺς γράφοντας "I stop them from writing"—γράφοντας modifies the object; παύομαι γράφων "I cease to write"—γράφων modifies the subject). Verbs of emotion may also be supplemented with a participle (e.g., χαίρω γράφουσα "I take delight in writing" or "I am happy to write"—γράφουσα modifies the subject). A literal translation is often *not* the best way to convey the sense of a supplementary participle.

NOTE The participle and the finite verb that it supplements need not be next to each other in the sentence.

160. You have now been introduced to most of the major **prepositions** in Greek. Those you have learned can be conveniently summarized as follows:

+ **gen.:** ἄνευ, ἀπό, ἐκ, πόρρω, χάριν   + **dat.:** ἐν, σύν   + **acc.:** ἀνά, εἰς
+ **gen. or acc.:** ἀμφί, διά, κατά, μετά, ὑπέρ
+ **gen. or dat. or acc.:** ἐπί, παρά, περί, πρός, ὑπό

161. VOCABULARY

διδάσκω, διδάξω, ἐδίδαξα, δεδίδαχα, δεδίδαγμαι
  teach (*often with double acc. of person &*
  thing) [cf. *didactic*]

παύω, παύσω, ἔπαυσα, πέπαυκα, πέπαυμαι
  (*act.*) stop, bring to a stop; (*mid.*) stop,
  come to a stop, cease [cf. *pause*]

διδάσκαλος, -ου, ὁ, ἡ   teacher, dramatist

δόξα, -ης, ἡ   opinion, reputation, fame, glory
  [cf. *doxology, orthodox, paradox*]

παιδίον, -ου, τό   young child, little child

παῖς, παιδός, ὁ, ἡ   child, son, daughter [cf. *pediatrics*]

NOTE   Although παῖς is a third-declension noun with a monosyllabic stem, its genitive plural is **not** accented on the ultima (παίδων). Its genitive singular (παιδός) and dative singular and plural (παιδί, παισί), however, are.

σῶμα, -ατος, τό   body (*opposite of* ψυχή) [cf. *chromosome, psychosomatic*]

μέγας, μεγάλη, μέγα   big, large, great, tall [cf. *megalomania, megalopolis, megaphone*]

NOTE   μέγας is like πολύς: its declension is normal except in the masculine nominative and accusative singular (μέγας, μέγαν) and the neuter nominative/accusative singular (μέγα). All the other forms have regular -ος, -η, -ον endings attached to the stem μεγάλ- (but the masculine vocative singular may be either μεγάλε or μέγας). The irregular forms are accented on με- instead of -γα-.

ἀεί   (*adv.*) always, ever

μέγα or μεγάλα   (*neut. acc. sg./pl. of* μέγας *used as adv.*)
  greatly, much

πολλάκις   (*adv.*) many times, often

162. EXERCISES

A. **Greek-to-English Sentences**

1. μεγάλα μὲν βιβλία ἀεὶ φιλοῦσιν οἱ διδάσκαλοι, μῑκρὰ δ᾽ οἱ μαθηταί.

2. τῷ τῆς νυκτὸς πολλάκις φοβουμένῳ εἶπον ἐγὼ τάδε· Τίνας φοβῇ;

3. παῦσαι ῥίπτων ἐκείνους τοὺς μεγάλους λίθους, ὦ παῖ, ἡμᾶς γὰρ βλάψεις.

4. ἡ παῖς καίπερ ἐπὶ τὸ δεῖπνον κεκλημένη ἀπὸ ταύτης τῆς θύρᾱς ἔσπευσεν.

5. εἰς τὴν ὁδὸν ἦγεν ὁ κλὼψ τὸν μέγαν ἵππον, ὡς κατὰ γῆν φευξόμενος.

6. περὶ τοῦ τε σώματος καὶ τῆς ψῡχῆς πολλὰ τοὺς παῖδάς μου δεδίδαχεν ἥδ᾽ ἡ διδάσκαλος ἡ πάντα τὰ γέρᾱ κομισαμένη.

7. ἐπεὶ παύσονται ἀποκτείνοντες ἄλλους δόξης χάριν, ἡ εἰρήνη ἔσται.

8. μέγα βεβλαμμέναι εἰσὶν οὐ μόνον τοῖς λόγοις ὑμῶν ἀλλὰ καὶ τοῖς ἔργοις.

9. κατὰ τὴν σὴν δόξαν ἐστὶ τὸ παιδίον, ἅτε καλὸν ὄν, ἄξιον δώρου τινός;

10. οἷς μεγάλη ἐλπὶς ἦν σοφίαν ἀληθῆ εὑρεῖν, οὗτοι ἔχαιρον διδασκόμενοι.

B. **English-to-Greek Sentences**

1. In the marketplace I often saw the young child who had been taught (*use perfect participle*) by me.
2. Did the teacher laugh at you (*sg.*) because you feared (*use present participle*) the big children?
3. Having betaken themselves (*use aorist participle*) to Socrates, they asked him this: "What is your opinion about the fate of the body?"
4. Neither have we ourselves ceased to seek glory, nor have we stopped others from seeking it.
5. The despot has always been honored greatly, as if he were going to be (*use future participle*) a god after his death.

C. **READING**

A HARE-RAISING EXPERIENCE
(Aesop's Fable 143)

Οἱ λαγωοὶ ἑαυτοῖς εἶπον· Κακὸς παντὶ τρόπῳ ἐστὶν ἡμῶν ὁ βίος, τὰ γὰρ ἄλλα ζῷα ἢ διώκει ἡμᾶς ἢ ἐφ' ἡμῖν γελᾷ. τοῖς ἀεὶ φοβουμένοις καὶ καθ' ἡμέραν φεύγουσι τίς ἐλπίς ἐστιν; ἡμᾶς οὖν αὐτοὺς ῥίψομεν εἰς τὴν λίμνην καὶ ἀποθανούμεθα.

ταῦτ' εἰπόντες, ἐπί τινα κρημνὸν ἔσπευσαν ὡς ἀποθανούμενοι. πάντες δ'
5 οἱ βάτραχοι, τοὺς λαγωοὺς ἰδόντες καὶ τὸν μέγαν κτύπον αὐτῶν ἀκούσαντες, κατὰ τοῦ κρημνοῦ ἑαυτοὺς ἔρριψαν διὰ τὸν φόβον. τότε τις τῶν λαγωῶν εἶπε· Παύεσθε, ὦ φίλοι, ἐθέλοντες ἀποθνήσκειν· νῦν γάρ, ὡς ὁρᾶτε, εὑρήκαμεν ζῷα ἡμῶν δειλότερα.

τί οὗτος ὁ λόγος ὑμᾶς, ὦ μαθηταί, διδάσκει; καίπερ κακῶς πράττοντες,
10 εὐδαίμονές ἐστε πρὸς ἄλλους τινάς γε.

VOCABULARY

λαγωοί (line 1): from λαγωός, -οῦ, ὁ: rabbit
κρημνόν (line 4): from κρημνός, -οῦ, ὁ: overhanging bank
βάτραχοι (line 5): from βάτραχος, -ου, ὁ: frog
κτύπον (line 5): from κτύπος, -ου, ὁ: loud noise
ἡμῶν δειλότερα (line 8): more cowardly than we are (*gen. of comparison + comparative degree of* δειλός, -ή, -όν: cowardly, miserable)
πρός (line 10): here = "in comparison with"

LESSON 26

DIRECT AND INDIRECT QUESTIONS; ALTERNATIVE QUESTIONS

ὦ τάλᾱς ἐγώ, / ἆρ' εἰμὶ μάντις;
(O wretched me, am I a soothsayer?)
—Creon divines his son's death in Sophocles' *Antigone* 1211-1212

163. You already know the simplest way of forming a **direct question** in Greek: by placing a question mark (;) at the end of a sentence that would otherwise be a declarative statement. No change in word order is required. Example: ἔχεις ἵππον. "You have a horse." ἔχεις ἵππον; "Do you have a horse?"

In both English and Greek, a direct question is often signaled not just by a question mark at its end but also by an interrogative word at or near its start. Besides the interrogative adjective/pronoun τίς, which you learned in an earlier lesson, there are the following **interrogative adverbs** in Greek:

πόθεν	"from where?" "whence?"
ποῖ	"to where?" "whither?"
πότε (πότ', πόθ')	"when?"
ποῦ	"where?"
πῶς	"how?"

Just as τίς changes from an interrogative adjective/pronoun to an indefinite one when accented as an enclitic, so these five adverbs become **indefinite** in meaning (and therefore no longer introduce questions) when accented as enclitics:

ποθέν	"from somewhere"
ποι	"to somewhere"
ποτέ (ποτ', ποθ')	"sometime," "sometimes," "ever," "once"
που	"somewhere"
πως	"somehow"

167

164.   Greek, unlike English, may use an **interrogative particle** to introduce a direct question that would otherwise be signaled only by a question mark at its end. The particle has no grammatical function except to indicate emphatically that the sentence is a question. It can either be omitted in your English translation or represented by an adverb like "really" or "surely." The most common interrogative particle in Attic Greek is ἆρα (ἆρ'); it is actually a contraction of ἦ (another interrogative particle) + ἄρα (an inferential particle meaning "therefore"). Example: ἆρ' ἔχεις ἵππον; "Do you have a horse?"

When a direct question begins with ἆρ' οὐ or ἆρα μή, with οὐκοῦν (a combination of οὐκ + οὖν) or μῶν (a contraction of μή + οὖν), or with simple οὐ or μή, **a particular answer to the question is expected**:

ἆρ' οὐ	or	οὐκοῦν	or οὐ	expects the answer **"yes"**
ἆρα μή	or	μῶν	or μή	expects the answer **"no"**

Examples:

ἆρ' οὐκ ἔχεις ἵππον;	" Don't you have a horse?" (expects "yes")
μῶν ἔχεις ἵππον;	" Then you don't have a horse, do you?" (expects "no")

Notice that, in English, it is the structure of the sentence, not the presence of any special word in it, that indicates the speaker's expectation of a certain answer.

165.   In both English and Greek, a question may be incorporated into another sentence, most often as its direct object. Example: ἠρώτησα, Ἔχεις ἵππον; ("I asked, 'Do you have a horse?'.") The speaker may choose to quote the question in its **direct** form, as in the example just given. As an alternative to quotation marks (which the ancient Greeks did not use), this textbook capitalizes the first word of every directly quoted question.

The speaker's other option is to use an **indirect question**, i.e., to present the question in an indirect form: "I asked *whether you had a horse*." To create this indirect question, the English speaker had to add the conjunction *whether* and change the tense of the verb in the question to match the tense of the main verb. The process is simpler in Greek: a word for *whether* is added, but the tense of the verb is left unchanged: ἠρώτησα εἰ ἔχεις ἵππον.

Here are general guidelines for forming indirect questions in Greek:

1.   **Both the mood and the tense used in the direct question are retained in the indirect question.** (Under certain circumstances the speaker has the option to change the mood, but you need not worry about that now.)

2. If the direct question had **no introductory word**, the conjunction εἰ ("whether") is added at the beginning of the indirect question.

3. If the direct question began with ἆρα, the indirect question also does.

4. If the direct question had οὐ, the indirect question also has οὐ; if the direct question had μή, the indirect question also has μή.

5. If the direct question began with a form of τίς or one of the **interrogative adverbs**, that word may be retained *or*—more often—an indirect equivalent may be substituted for it. Here are the **indirect equivalents** of τίς, πόθεν, ποῖ, πότε, ποῦ, and πῶς. (The words in parentheses are alternative forms.)

INDIRECT INTERROGATIVE ADJECTIVE/PRONOUN

ὅστις, ἥτις, ὅ τι (*adj.*) "what?" "which?"; (*pron.*) "who?" "what?"

Singular:	Masc.		Fem.	Neut.	
Nom.	ὅστις		ἥτις	ὅ τι	
Gen.	οὗτινος	(ὅτου)	ἧστινος	οὗτινος	(ὅτου)
Dat.	ᾧτινι	(ὅτῳ)	ᾗτινι	ᾧτινι	(ὅτῳ)
Acc.	ὅντινα		ἥντινα	ὅ τι	
Plural:	Masc.		Fem.	Neut.	
Nom.	οἵτινες		αἵτινες	ἅτινα	(ἅττα)
Gen.	ὧντινων	(ὅτων)	ὧντινων	ὧντινων	(ὅτων)
Dat.	οἷστισι(ν)	(ὅτοις)	αἷστισι(ν)	οἷστισι(ν)	(ὅτοις)
Acc.	οὕστινας		ἅστινας	ἅτινα	(ἅττα)

The indirect interrogative adjective/pronoun is made by combining the relative pronoun (ὅς, ἥ, ὅ, etc.) and the indefinite adjective/pronoun (τις, τι, etc.) into one compound word and **declining each part**; the relative-pronoun part is accented as if it and the enclitic τις were still separate words. Each of the alternative forms has an acute accent on its penult. ὅντινα, ἥντινα, and ἅτινα become ὅντιν᾽, ἥντιν᾽, and ἅτιν᾽ before a vowel. ὅ τι is written as two words to distinguish it from the conjunction ὅτι, which you will learn later. The dative plural has a **movable ν**.

INDIRECT INTERROGATIVE ADVERBS

ὁπόθεν	"from where?" "whence?"
ὅποι	"to where?" "whither?"
ὁπότε (ὁπότ᾽, ὁπόθ᾽)	"when?"
ὅπου	"where?"
ὅπως	"how?"

The indirect interrogative adverbs are simply the direct interrogative adverbs with a prefixed ὁ-; each form has an acute accent on its penult.

6. The verb in the direct question may have to be put into a different **person** in the indirect question. This happens in English as well as Greek, whenever a first (*I/we*) or second (*you*) person in a quoted question is no longer appropriate in the question's reported form. Examples: **Direct:** "We asked them, 'What are *you* [i.e., the people we are speaking *to*] doing?'"; **Indirect:** "We asked them what *they* [i.e., the people we are now speaking *about*] were doing."

7. The main verb in a sentence containing an indirect question is most often a verb of asking, but it may also be a verb of saying, thinking, or perceiving.

Examples of Direct and Indirect Questions:

Direct: ἐρώτα αὐτούς, Ἆρ' εἴχετε ἵππον;
"Ask them, 'Did you really have a horse?'."

Indirect: ἐρώτα αὐτοὺς ἆρ' εἶχον ἵππον.
"Ask them whether they really had a horse."

Direct: ἐρωτήσω αὐτήν, Οὐκ ἔχεις ἵππον;
"I shall ask her, 'Do you not have a horse?'."

Indirect: ἐρωτήσω αὐτὴν εἰ οὐκ ἔχει ἵππον.
"I shall ask her whether she does not have a horse."

Direct: ἠρωτήσαμέν σε, Τίν' ἵππον ἔχεις;
"We asked you, 'What horse do you have?'."

Indirect: ἠρωτήσαμέν σε ὅντιν' ἵππον ἔχεις.
or ἠρωτήσαμέν σε τίν' ἵππον ἔχεις.
"We asked you what horse you had."

Direct: ἐρωτᾷ με, Ποῦ ἐστιν ὁ ἵππος;
"He asks me, 'Where is the horse?'."

Indirect: ἐρωτᾷ με ὅπου ἐστὶν ὁ ἵππος.
or ἐρωτᾷ με ποῦ ἐστιν ὁ ἵππος.
"He asks me where the horse is."

166. A question that includes alternatives is called an **alternative question** (or a **double question**). In *direct* alternative questions, Greek uses the correlatives πότερον (or πότερα)...ἤ ("either...or").

Example:
[πότερον] φεύξει ἢ μενεῖς;   " [Either] will you flee, or will you remain?"

The brackets show that Greek, like English, often omits the word for "either" in direct alternative questions. In *indirect* alternative questions, Greek uses either the correlatives πότερον (or πότερα)...ἤ or the correlatives εἴτε (εἴτ', εἴθ')...εἴτε (εἴτ', εἴθ') ("whether...or").

Example:

εἰπέ μοι εἴτε φεύξει εἴτε μενεῖς.   " Tell me whether you will flee or
                                        remain."

167.   VOCABULARY

ὀφθαλμός, -οῦ, ὁ   eye [cf. *ophthalmology*]
ὅστις, ἥτις, ὅ τι   (*indirect interrogative adjective/pronoun*)
                               (*adj.*) what? which?; (*pron.*) who?
                               what?¡
πόθεν   (*direct interrog. adverb*) from where?
                               whence?
ποῖ   (*direct interrog. adverb*) to where?
                               whither?
πότε (πότ', πόθ')   (*direct interrog. adverb*) when? (πότ' *before*
                               smooth breathing, πόθ' *before rough*
                               breathing)
ποῦ   (*direct interrog. adverb*) where?
πῶς   (*direct interrog. adverb*) how?
ὁπόθεν   (*indirect interrog. adverb*) from where?
                               whence?
ὅποι   (*indirect interrog. adverb*) to where?
                               whither?
ὁπότε (ὁπότ', ὁπόθ')   (*indirect interrog. adverb*) when? (ὁπότ'
                               before smooth breathing, ὁπόθ' *before*
                               rough breathing)
ὅπου   (*indirect interrog. adverb*) where?
ὅπως   (*indirect interrog. adverb*) how?
ποθέν   (*enclitic adverb*) from somewhere
ποι   (*enclitic adverb*) to somewhere
ποτέ (ποτ', ποθ')   (*enclitic adverb*) sometime, sometimes,
                               ever, once (ποτ' *before smooth breathing,*
                               ποθ' *before rough breathing*)
που   (*enclitic adverb*) somewhere
πως   (*enclitic adverb*) somehow
εἰ   (*conj. introducing an indirect question*)
                               whether

NOTE   εἰ is a proclitic like εἰς, ἐκ, ἐν, ὁ, ἡ, οἱ, αἱ, οὐ, and ὡς; it has no accent.
Like ἀλλ', καί, μή, οὐκ, ὡς, and τοῦτ', it causes a following ἔστι to be accented on its penult.

εἴτε (εἴτ᾽, εἴθ᾽)...εἴτε (εἴτ᾽, εἴθ᾽)

> (*correlatives introducing alternative indirect questions*) whether...or (εἴτ᾽ *before smooth breathing*, εἴθ᾽ *before rough breathing*)

πότερον (or πότερα)...ἤ   (*correlatives introducing alternative questions, direct or indirect*) either...or; whether...or

ἆρα (ἆρ᾽)   (*contraction of interrogative particle* ἦ + *inferential particle* ἄρα) introduces a question not expecting a particular answer (ἆρ᾽ *before a vowel*)

ἆρ᾽ οὐ or οὐκοῦν [= οὐκ + οὖν] or οὐ

> introduces a question expecting the answer "yes"

ἆρα μή or μῶν [= μή + οὖν] or μή

> introduces a question expecting the answer "no"

168.   **EXERCISES**

A.   **Greek-to-English Sentences**

1. πότερα τὸν μέγαν θησαυρὸν φυλάξει τὰ παιδία ἢ ἐκ τῆς οἰκίας κλέψει;
2. ὁ φιλόσοφος ἠρώτησεν εἴ ποτ᾽ ἔχομεν τοῖς ὀφθαλμοῖς τοὺς θεοὺς ἰδεῖν.
3. ποῖ ἔσπευδες, ὦ παῖ; οὐχ ἑώρᾱς οἵτινες κίνδῡνοι ἐν τῇ ὁδῷ εἰσιν;
4. μῶν μέλλετε ἐρωτήσειν ἡμᾶς ὅ τι πράττομεν; πᾶσι γὰρ δῆλόν ἐστι τὸ ἔργον ὃ πράττομεν.
5. ἐρώτησον τούτους τοὺς ξένους τοὺς οὐκ ὄντας Ἕλληνας ὁπόθεν πεπεμμένοι εἰσίν.
6. ἆρα μή τι κακὸν ὡς ἀγγελοῦσα, ὦ δέσποινα, εἰς τὴν ἀγορὰν τέτραψαι;
7. ἕως τὴν ἀσπίδα ἐπώλουν ἐγώ, ὁ αὐτὸς κλὼψ πολλὰς δραχμὰς ἐκ τοῦ ἱματίου ἐμοῦ πως ἥρπαζεν.
8. οἱ μὲν ἠρώτων με, Ἆρ᾽ ἐστί τις ἐλπίς σοι; οἱ δέ, Πῶς τὸν θάνατον φεύξει;
9. ἆρ᾽ οὐ παύσονται ἐρωτῶντές με ὅτῳ τὰ δῶρα πέμψαι ἐθέλω; αὐτοῖς εἴρηκα πολλάκις τὸ ἐκείνου ὄνομα.
10. καίπερ ἀεὶ τετῑμηκότες τοὺς δεσπότᾱς, αὐτοὺς νῦν φοβούμεθα καὶ ἐρωτῶμεν εἴτε πόλεμον ποιήσουσιν εἴτ᾽ εἰρήνην.

B.   English-to-Greek Sentences

1. Some asked, "Where is that trireme?"; others (asked), "How can we pursue the enemy without it?".

2. This long book will not somehow harm the eyes of the students who often take delight in it, will it?

3. Having summoned the teacher, the despot ordered her to say which opinions she was teaching and whether they were true.

4. Won't you (*sg.*) ever find out whither the servant has led the horse that you (*sg.*) greatly love?

5. (Either) have I now made clear who the stranger is, or shall I also announce what name he has?

C.   READING

HEALING OF THE MAN BORN BLIND—Part 1
(adapted from John 9:11-17)

The passage below is the first part of a three-part story about an incident in the life of Jesus. You should find the Greek fairly easy to translate because Koine, the dialect of the New Testament, is similar to Attic; moreover, its sentences tend to be short and syntactically simple.

Background to the Story: *On the Jewish sabbath-day (during which no work was supposed to be done), Jesus performs a miracle by giving sight to a man who has been blind since birth. Those who knew the man earlier are amazed to find that he can now see. They ask him what has happened; he answers them as follows.*

Ὁ ἄνθρωπος ὁ λεγόμενος Ἰησοῦς πηλὸν ἐποίησε καὶ ἔχρῑσέ μου τοὺς ὀφθαλμοὺς καὶ εἶπέ μοι, Νίψαι· καὶ νιψάμενος ἔβλεψα. καὶ οἱ ἄλλοι εἶπον αὐτῷ, Ποῦ ἐστιν ἐκεῖνος; λέγει, Οὐκ οἶδα. ἄγουσιν αὐτὸν πρὸς τοὺς Φαρισαίους. πάλιν οὖν ἠρώτων αὐτὸν καὶ οἱ Φαρισαῖοι ὅπως ἔβλεψεν. ὁ δ' εἶπεν αὐτοῖς,
5   Ἐκεῖνος πηλῷ ἔχρῑσέ μου τοὺς ὀφθαλμούς, καὶ ἐνιψάμην, καὶ βλέπω. ἔλεγον οὖν ἐκ τῶν Φαρισαίων τινές, Οὐκ ἔστιν οὗτος ὁ ἄνθρωπος παρὰ Θεοῦ, τὸ γὰρ σάββατον οὐ τηρεῖ. ἄλλοι ἔλεγον, Πῶς ἔχει ἄνθρωπος ἁμαρτωλὸς τάδε τὰ σημεῖα ποιεῖν; καὶ σχίσμα ἦν ἐν αὐτοῖς. λέγουσιν οὖν τῷ ποτε τυφλῷ πάλιν, Τί λέγεις περὶ τούτου ὃς ἀνέῳξέ σου τοὺς ὀφθαλμούς; ὁ δ' εἶπε, Προφήτης ἐστίν.

VOCABULARY

ὁ λεγόμενος (line 1): the one called

Ἰησοῦς (line 1): from Ἰησοῦς, -οῦ, -οῦ, -οῦν, -οῦ, ὁ: Jesus (*Hebrew name*)

πηλόν (line 1): from πηλός, -οῦ, ὁ: mud

ἔχρῑσε (line 1): from χρίω, χρίσω, ἔχρῑσα, —, κέχρῑμαι: anoint

νίψαι (line 2): from νίζω, νίψομαι, ἔνιψα, —, νένιμμαι: wash

οἶδα (line 3): I know (*literally*, "I have seen"—*perf. act. indic. of* οἶδα, *an irregular verb that occurs only in the perf., pluperf., and fut. perf.*)

Φαρισαίους (line 3): from Φαρισαῖοι, -ων, οἱ: Pharisees, a sect of Jews who believed in strict obedience to the law of Moses

ὁ δ' (line 4): = οὗτος δέ

πηλῷ (line 5): see note on πηλόν (line 1)

ἐνιψάμην (line 5): see note on νίψαι (line 2)

σάββατον (line 7): from σάββατον, -ου, τό: sabbath, sabbath-day

τηρεῖ (line 7): from τηρέω, τηρήσω, ἐτήρησα, τετήρηκα, τετήρημαι: pay attention to, observe

ἁμαρτωλός (line 7): from ἁμαρτωλός, -όν: sinful

σημεῖα (line 8): from σημεῖον, -ου, τό: sign, miracle

σχίσμα (line 8): from σχίσμα, -ατος, τό: schism, division of opinion

τυφλῷ (line 8): from τυφλός, -ή, -όν: blind

ἀνέῳξε (line 9): from ἀνοίγω, ἀνοίξω, ἀνέῳξα, ἀνέῳχα, ἀνέῳγμαι: open up

ὁ δ' (line 9): = οὗτος δέ

προφήτης (line 9): from προφήτης, -ου, ὁ: prophet

LESSON 27

Ω-VERBS
Aorist Passive Tense

ἀπεκρίθη...τοῦ βαρβάρου ἔθνεος τὸ Ἑλληνικόν
(The Greek nation was set apart from the barbarian.)
—Herodotus in *The Histories* 1.60 praises the Greeks as a special breed

169.   We come now to the **sixth principal part** of the Greek verb, which supplies the stem for both the **aorist passive** tense and the **future passive** tense. This lesson deals exclusively with the aorist passive; the future passive is not discussed until Lesson 28.

170.   Every Greek verb has *either* a first aorist passive *or* a second aorist passive (occasionally both). All verbs whose basic stem ends in a vowel, as well as many verbs whose basic stem ends in a consonant, have a **first aorist passive**.

FIRST AORIST PASSIVE INDICATIVE		Endings:
Singular: ἐπαιδεύθην	("I was taught")	**-θην**
ἐπαιδεύθης	("you [sg.] were taught")	**-θης**
ἐπαιδεύθη	("he/she/it was taught")	**-θη**
Plural: ἐπαιδεύθημεν	("we were taught")	**-θημεν**
ἐπαιδεύθητε	("you [pl.] were taught")	**-θητε**
ἐπαιδεύθησαν	("they were taught")	**-θησαν**

FIRST AORIST PASSIVE INFINITIVE		Ending:
παιδευθῆναι	("to be taught" or "to have been taught")	**-θηναι**

FIRST AORIST PASSIVE IMPERATIVE		Endings:
Singular: παιδεύθητι	("be taught!")	**-θητι**
παιδευθήτω	("let him/her/it be taught!")	**-θητω**
Plural: παιδεύθητε	("be taught!")	**-θητε**
παιδευθέντων	("let them be taught!")	**-θεντων**

175

FIRST AORIST PASSIVE PARTICIPLE
("being taught" or "having been taught")

Singular:	Masc.	Fem.	Neut.
Nom./Voc.	παιδευθείς	παιδευθεῖσα	παιδευθέν
Gen.	παιδευθέντος	παιδευθείσης	παιδευθέντος
Dat.	παιδευθέντι	παιδευθείσῃ	παιδευθέντι
Acc.	παιδευθέντα	παιδευθεῖσανῇ	παιδευθέν

Plural:	Masc.	Fem.	Neut.
Nom./Voc.	παιδευθέντες	παιδευθεῖσαι	παιδευθέντα
Gen.	παιδευθέντων	παιδευθεισῶν	παιδευθέντων
Dat.	παιδευθεῖσι(ν)	παιδευθείσαις	παιδευθεῖσι(ν)
Acc.	παιδευθέντας	παιδευθείσᾱς	παιδευθέντα

The first aorist passive is formed by appending the suffix -θη- or -θε- to the verb's basic stem and then adding a personal ending; no thematic vowel is used. Contract verbs lengthen their vowel (α, ε → η; ο → ω) before the suffix (e.g., δηλόω → ἐδηλώθην). Verbs whose stem ends in a dental (δ, ζ, θ) drop the dental and add a sigma (e.g., πείθω →ἐπείσθην). Verbs whose stem ends in β or π "roughen" the labial to φ (e.g., πέμπω → ἐπέμφθην), and verbs whose stem ends in γ or κ "roughen" the palatal to χ (διώκω → ἐδιώχθην) to match the "roughness," i.e., the aspirated sound, of the θ that follows. If the syllable before -θη-/-θε- begins with θ, the first theta must be changed to τ to avoid having two consecutive syllables each beginning with a theta (e.g., θύω → ἐτύθην, not ἐθύθην).

You would expect the first aorist passive to use secondary middle/passive endings (-μην, -σο, -το, -μεθα, -σθε, -ντο, etc.), but instead, defying logic, it uses secondary **active** endings: -ν, -ς, —, -μεν, -τε, -σαν, etc. (Passive endings are not strictly needed since the suffix -θη-/-θε- is sufficient to show that the form is passive.) Since the first aorist passive is a secondary tense, each of the six indicative forms also has an **augment**. (Remember that infinitives, imperatives, and participles are never augmented.) All the indicative and imperative forms have recessive accent; **the infinitive and the participle are accented persistently**, with the accent remaining, if possible, on the syllable that begins with θ.

The first aorist passive participle is of **mixed declension**: its feminine forms have first-declension endings (with the genitive plural always accented on the ultima); its masculine and neuter forms have third-declension endings. The participial stem is composed of -θε- + -ντ-; in the nominative singular, -θεντς becomes -θεις; -θεντ + semivocalic ι + α become -θεισα; -θεντ becomes -θεν. In the masculine and neuter dative plural, θεντσι becomes θεισι (with movable ν).

171. **Second Aorist Passive.** Certain verbs whose basic stem ends in a consonant form their aorist passive **without a θ**; the suffix they add is simply -η- or -ε- (e.g., indic. ἐγράφην, infin. γραφῆναι, imper. γράφηθι, ptcple.

γραφείς). Some also change their stem-vowel (e.g., κλέπτω → ἐκλάπην). Although πλήττω has a second aorist passive (ἐπλήγην), its compound ἐπιπλήττω has a first aorist passive (ἐπεπλήχθην); a second aorist passive with alpha instead of eta is typical of other compounds of πλήττω (e.g., κατεπλάγην from καταπλήττω, "strike down").

NOTE   The ending for the second-person singular aorist passive imperative is actually -θι, but in every first aorist passive, -θι becomes -τι to avoid having two consecutive syllables each beginning with a theta (e.g., παιδεύθητι, not παιδεύθηθι). In all second aorist passives, -θι remains unchanged (e.g., κλάπηθι).

Except for the lack of θ and, in some verbs, a change in stem-vowel, second aorist passives are **identical** to first aorist passives. Whether a verb has a first or a second aorist passive must be learned from the sixth principal part. Interestingly, a verb with a second aorist *active* will **never** have a second aorist *passive* (e.g., λείπω → second aor. act. ἔλιπον, but first aor. pass. ἐλείφθην).

Some verbs (e.g., ἀλλάττω, βλάπτω, λέγω, τρέπω) have **both** a first and a second aorist passive. Either form may be used, with no difference in meaning.

In certain verbs the aorist passive has a special **reflexive or middle sense** in addition to its regular passive sense; e.g., depending on the context, ἐτρέφθην (or ἐτράπην) may mean "I was turned," "I betook myself," or "I moved."

172.   The **sixth** (and final) **principal part** of a verb is its first-person singular aorist passive indicative. For your convenience, we have listed below all the principal parts of all the verbs you now know. The verbs are grouped in categories according to the type of letter that comes at the end of the basic stem used to form the aorist passive. Second aorist passives are printed in **boldface**.

Principal Parts of All Verbs from Previous Lessons

Basic stem ending in a vowel (-αυ, -ευ, -ου, -υ; contract verbs; verbs with a consonant-stem in some tenses, but a vowel-stem in the aorist passive):

παύω	παύσω	ἔπαυσα	πέπαυκα	πέπαυμαι	ἐπαύθην
ουλεύω	δουλεύσω	ἐδούλευσα	δεδούλευκα	δεδούλευμαι	ἐδουλεύθην
κελεύω	κελεύσω	ἐκέλευσα	κεκέλευκα	κεκέλευσμαι	ἐκελεύσθην[1]
παιδεύω	παιδεύσω	ἐπαίδευσα	πεπαίδευκα	πεπαίδευμαι	ἐπαιδεύθην
ἀκούω	ἀκούσομαι	ἤκουσα	ἀκήκοα	—	ἠκούσθην[1]
θύω	θύσω	ἔθυσα	τέθυκα	τέθυμαι	ἐτύθην
λύω	λύσω	ἔλυσα	λέλυκα	λέλυμαι	ἐλύθην

---
[1] κελεύω and ἀκούω insert a sigma before -θη-.

γελάω	γελάσομαι	ἐγέλασα	—	—	ἐγελάσθην[1]
ἐρωτάω	ἐρωτήσω	ἠρώτησα	ἠρώτηκα	ἠρώτημαι	ἠρωτήθην
τιμάω	τιμήσω	ἐτίμησα	τετίμηκα	τετίμημαι	ἐτιμήθην
ζητέω	ζητήσω	ἐζήτησα	ἐζήτηκα	ἐζήτημαι	ἐζητήθην
καλέω	καλῶ	ἐκάλεσα	κέκληκα	κέκλημαι	ἐκλήθην
ποιέω	ποιήσω	ἐποίησα	πεποίηκα	πεποίημαι	ἐποιήθην
προσποιέω (same as ποιέω)					
πωλέω	πωλήσω	ἐπώλησα	πεπώληκα	πεπώλημαι	ἐπωλήθην
φιλέω	φιλήσω	ἐφίλησα	πεφίληκα	πεφίλημαι	ἐφιλήθην
φοβέω	φοβήσω	ἐφόβησα	πεφόβηκα	πεφόβημαι	ἐφοβήθην
ὠφελέω	ὠφελήσω	ὠφέλησα	ὠφέληκα	ὠφέλημαι	ὠφελήθην
δηλόω	δηλώσω	ἐδήλωσα	δεδήλωκα	δεδήλωμαι	ἐδηλώθην
εὑρίσκω	εὑρήσω	εὗρον/ ηὗρον	εὕρηκα/ ηὕρηκα	εὕρημαι/ ηὕρημαι	εὑρέθην/ ηὑρέθην (εὑρε-)
ἔχω	ἕξω/σχήσω	ἔσχον	ἔσχηκα	ἔσχημαι	ἐσχέθην (-σχε-)
βάλλω	βαλῶ	ἔβαλον	βέβληκα	βέβλημαι	ἐβλήθην (-βλη-)
προσβάλλω (same as βάλλω)					

Basic stem ending in a liquid or a nasal (-λ, -ρ, -ν):

ἀγγέλλω	ἀγγελῶ	ἤγγειλα	ἤγγελκα	ἤγγελμαι	ἠγγέλθην
ἐθέλω	ἐθελήσω	ἠθέλησα	ἠθέληκα	—	—
μέλλω	μελλήσω	ἐμέλλησα	—	—	—
χαίρω	χαιρήσω	ἐχαίρησα	κεχάρηκα	κεχάρημαι	**ἐχάρην**
ἀποθνῄσκω	ἀποθανοῦμαι	ἀπέθανον	τέθνηκα	—	—
ἀποκτείνω	ἀποκτενῶ	ἀπέκτεινα	ἀπέκτονα	—	—
μένω	μενῶ	ἔμεινα	μεμένηκα	—	—

Basic stem ending in a dental (-δ, -ζ, -θ):

σπεύδω	σπεύσω	ἔσπευσα	—	—	—
ἁρπάζω	ἁρπάσω	ἥρπασα	ἥρπακα	ἥρπασμαι	ἡρπάσθην
κομίζω	κομιῶ	ἐκόμισα	κεκόμικα	κεκόμισμαι	ἐκομίσθην
πείθω	πείσω	ἔπεισα	πέπεικα/ πέποιθα	πέπεισμαι	ἐπείσθην

---

[1]γελάω inserts a sigma before -θη-; it is also an exception to the rule that contract verbs lengthen their vowel in the aorist passive.

Basic stem ending in a labial (-π, -β, -φ):

ἀπολείπω (same as λείπω)

βλέπω	βλέψομαι	ἔβλεψα	βέβλεφα	βέβλεμμαι	ἐβλέφθην
κλέπτω	κλέψω	ἔκλεψα	κέκλοφα	κέκλεμμαι	**ἐκλάπην**
λείπω	λείψω	ἔλιπον	λέλοιπα	λέλειμμαι	ἐλείφθην
ὁράω	ὄψομαι	εἶδον	ἑόρᾱκα/	ἑώρᾱμαι/	ὤφθην (ὀπ-)
			ἑώρᾱκα	ὦμμαι	
πέμπω	πέμψω	ἔπεμψα	πέπομφα	πέπεμμαι	ἐπέμφθην
ῥίπτω	ῥίψω	ἔρρῑψα	ἔρρῑφα	ἔρρῑμμαι	ἐρρίφθην
τρέπω	τρέψω	ἔτρεψα	τέτροφα	τέτραμμαι	ἐτρέφθην/
					ἐτράπην
βλάπτω	βλάψω	ἔβλαψα	βέβλαφα	βέβλαμμαι	ἐβλάφθην/
					ἐβλάβην
λαμβάνω	λήψομαι	ἔλαβον	εἴληφα	εἴλημμαι	ἐλήφθην
					(-ληβ-)

συλλαμβάνω (same as λαμβάνω)

γράφω	γράψω	ἔγραψα	γέγραφα	γέγραμμαι	**ἐγράφην**

Basic stem ending in a palatal (-κ, -γ, -χ):

διώκω	διώξω	ἐδίωξα	δεδίωχα	δεδίωγμαι	ἐδιώχθην
φέρω	οἴσω	ἤνεγκα/	ἐνήνοχα	ἐνήνεγμαι	ἠνέχθην
		ἤνεγκον			(ἐνεκ-)
ἄγω	ἄξω	ἤγαγον	ἦχα	ἦγμαι	ἤχθην
ἀλλάττω	ἀλλάξω	ἤλλαξα	ἤλλαχα	ἤλλαγμαι	ἠλλάχθην/
					ἠλλάγην
λέγω	ἐρῶ/λέξω	εἶπον/	εἴρηκα	εἴρημαι/	ἐρρήθην/
		ἔλεξα		λέλεγμαι	ἐλέχθην
πλήττω	πλήξω	ἔπληξα	πέπληγα	πέπληγμαι	ἐπεπλήχθην
ἐπιπλήττω	ἐπιπλήξω	ἐπέπληξα	ἐπιπέπληγα	ἐπιπέπληγμαι	ἐπεπλήχθην
πράττω	πράξω	ἔπρᾱξα	πέπρᾱγα/	πέπρᾱγμαι	ἐπράχθην
			πέπρᾱχα		
φεύγω	φεύξομαι	ἔφυγον	πέφευγα	—	—
φυλάττω	φυλάξω	ἐφύλαξα	πεφύλαχα	πεφύλαγμαι	ἐφυλάχθην
διδάσκω	διδάξω	ἐδίδαξα	δεδίδαχα	δεδίδαγμαι	ἐδιδάχθην

173. **VOCABULARY**

ἀνοίγω or ἀνοίγνῡμι (*imperf.* ἀνέῳγον), ἀνοίξω, ἀνέῳξα, ἀνέῳχα, νέῳγμαι, ἀνεῴχθην

open, open up

NOTE This compound verb with the prefix ἀνα- is much more common than the simple verb οἴγω "open." ἀνοίγνῡμι, an alternative form of the present tense, belongs to the μι-conjugation and will not be used until later in the textbook. Like ὁράω, οἴγω originally began with a digamma and was augmented and reduplicated with an eta: ἠ- + ϝοιγον, ϝοιξα, ϝοιχα, ϝοιγμαι, ϝοιχθην. When the digamma was lost, ἠ became short, and οι became long (by the principle of *quantitative metathesis*), producing the bizarre-looking forms ἔῳγον, ἔῳξα, ἔῳχα, ἔῳγμαι, ἐῴχθην.

κρίνω, κρινῶ, ἔκρῑνα, κέκρικα, κέκριμαι, ἐκρίθην

> separate, choose, judge, decide (*a contest or dispute*) [cf. *crisis, critic*]

NOTE   κρίνω often takes ἀπο- as a prefix. The compound **ἀποκρίνω, ἀποκρινῶ, ἀπέκρῑνα, ἀποκέκρικα, ἀποκέκριμαι, ἀπεκρίθην** may also mean "separate" or "choose," but in the **middle voice** it has the special meaning of "answer" or "reply." The person to whom the answer is given goes into the **dative** case.

ἡλικίᾱ, -ᾱς, ἡ	age, prime of life; **ἡλικίᾱν ἔχειν** or **ἐν ἡλικίᾳ εἶναι** = be of age, be grown up
υἱός, -οῦ, ὁ	son
νέος, -ᾱ, -ον	young, new [cf. *neon, neophyte*]
παλαιός, -ά, -όν	old, ancient [cf. *paleography, Paleozoic*]
τυφλός, -ή, -όν	blind
ἄρτι	(*adverb*) just now
ἤδη	(*adverb*) already
πάλαι	(*adverb*) long ago

174.   EXERCISES

A.   Greek-to-English Sentences

1. πᾶσαι αἱ δραχμαὶ αἱ ὑπὸ τοῦ ῥήτορος πάλαι συλληφθεῖσαι ἐκλάπησαν τήμερον ὑπὸ τοῦ υἱοῦ τοῦ δεσπότου.

2. ἀνοίξατε τοὺς ὀφθαλμούς, ὦ μαθηταί, καὶ ἀποκρίνασθε τῷ διδασκάλῳ.

3. οὐ μόνον τοῖς νέοις ἀλλὰ καὶ τοῖς παλαιοῖς ἤδη ἐστὶ πολὺς φόβος περὶ τούτου τοῦ πολέμου.

4. ἐπεὶ ἡ μεγάλη θύρᾱ ἀνεῴχθη, ὁ τυφλὸς ξένος ὤφθη καὶ ἐκομίσθη εἰς τὴν οἰκίᾱν ὑπὸ τῶν θεραπαινῶν.

5. τραπέντες εἰς ἐκείνην τὴν τριήρη, ἠνέχθημεν διὰ τῆς καλῆς θαλάττης.

6. τινὲς μὲν τῶν ἐμῶν υἱῶν ἐθέλουσιν ὑπ' ἐμοῦ ὠφεληθῆναι, τινὲς δ' οὔ.

7. ἐκελεύσθης τούς τ' ἀγαθοὺς καὶ τοὺς κακοὺς κρῖναι κατὰ τοὺς νόμους.

8. τί ἐρωτᾷς, ὦ υἱέ μου, ὑπὸ τίνος κρίνεται ὁ ἀγών; ἆρ' οὐκ ἐδηλώθη ἄρτι σοι ὁ κρίνων; μῶν σὺ τυφλὸς εἶ;

9. ἅτε ἐν τῇ ἡλικίᾳ ἤδη οὖσα, οὐκέτι ἐθέλω μετὰ τῶν νέων κορῶν μένειν.

10. εἴπετε ἡμῖν ὅποι ἄρτι ἐπέμφθητε ἢ ὅ τι πράξοντες ἀφ' ἡμῶν ἐσπεύσατε.

B. **English-to-Greek Sentences**

1. She asked me whether my sons were already grown up, and I replied, "They are still young."

2. Because the contest was judged badly, we, although being worthy, did not acquire any prizes.

3. Let the blind stranger be honored; I order him to be invited to dinner by all.

4. Just now the doors were opened, and the children were led out of the house by the slaves.

5. Which animals were sacrificed to the immortal gods long ago in this ancient place?

C. **READING**

HEALING OF THE MAN BORN BLIND — Part 2
(adapted from John 9:19-21, 24-27)

Suspecting that the man is lying to them about the healing of his eyes, the Pharisees summon his parents and interrogate them.

καὶ οἱ Φαρισαῖοι ἠρώτησαν αὐτοὺς λέγοντες, Οὗτός ἐστιν ὁ υἱὸς ὑμῶν ὃς τυφλὸς ἐγεννήθη; πῶς οὖν βλέπει ἄρτι; ἀπεκρίθησαν οὖν οἱ γονεῖς αὐτοῦ καὶ εἶπον, Οὗτός ἐστιν ὁ υἱὸς ἡμῶν ὃς τυφλὸς ἐγεννήθη· ὅπως δὲ νῦν βλέπει οὐκ ἴσμεν, ἢ ὅστις ἀνέῳξεν αὐτοῦ τοὺς ὀφθαλμοὺς ἡμεῖς οὐκ ἴσμεν. αὐτὸν
5 ἐρωτήσατε, ἡλικίαν γὰρ ἔχει· αὐτὸς περὶ ἑαυτοῦ ἀποκρινεῖται.

ἐκάλεσαν οὖν οἱ Φαρισαῖοι τὸν ἄνθρωπον πάλιν, καὶ εἶπον αὐτῷ, Δόξα τῷ Θεῷ. ἡμεῖς ἴσμεν τὴν ἀλήθειαν· ὁ Ἰησοῦς ἁμαρτωλός ἐστιν. ἀπεκρίθη οὖν ἐκεῖνος αὐτοῖς, Οὐκ οἶδα εἰ ἁμαρτωλός ἐστιν, ἀλλὰ τόδ' οἶδα· τυφλὸς πόλλ' ἔτη ὢν ἄρτι βλέπω. ἠρώτησαν οὖν αὐτόν, Πῶς ἀνεῴχθησάν σου οἱ ὀφθαλμοί; ἀπεκρίθη
10 αὐτοῖς, Εἶπον ὑμῖν ἤδη καὶ οὐκ ἠκούσατε· τί πάλιν ἐθέλετε ἀκούειν; μὴ καὶ ὑμεῖς ἐθέλετε αὐτοῦ μαθηταὶ γενέσθαι;

VOCABULARY

Φαρισαῖοι (line 1): from Φαρισαῖοι, -ων, οἱ: Pharisees, a sect of Jews who believed in strict obedience to the law of Moses

ἐγεννήθη (line 2): from γεννάω, γεννήσω, ἐγέννησα, γεγέννηκα, γεγέννημαι, ἐγεννήθην: give birth to, bear

ἀπεκρίθησαν (line 2): they answered (*Classical Greek would use the aorist middle,* ἀπεκρίναντο, *but Koine Greek uses the aorist passive*)

γονεῖς (line 2): nom. pl. of γονεύς, -έως, ὁ: parent (*ευ-stem third-decl. noun*) ἴσμεν (line 4): we know (*literally, "we have seen"—perf. act. indic. of* οἶδα, *which occurs only in the perf., pluperf., and fut. perf.*)

Ἰησοῦς (line 7): from Ἰησοῦς, -οῦ, -οῦ, -οῦν, -οῦ, ὁ: Jesus (*Hebrew name*)

ἁμαρτωλός (line 7): from ἁμαρτωλός, -όν: sinful

οἶδα (line 8): I know (*perf. act. indic.; see note on* ἴσμεν *in line 4*)

γενέσθαι (line 11): from γίγνομαι, γενήσομαι, ἐγενόμην, γέγονα, γεγένημαι, —: become (*translate middle deponent* γενέσθαι *actively*)

LESSON 28

Ω-VERBS
Future Passive Tense; Future Perfect Active and Middle/Passive Tenses; οἶδα

ἃ μὴ οἶδα οὐδ᾽ οἴομαι εἰδέναι
(I don't assume that I know whatever I don't know.)
Socrates demonstrates his wisdom in Plato's *Apology* 21d

175.   The **future passive tense** uses the same stem as the aorist passive, but without the augment. To this stem it adds a **sigma**, a **thematic vowel** (ε/ο), and **primary passive endings**. The future passive participle has the same suffix (**-μεν-**) and endings (**-ος, -η, -ον**) as the present and perfect middle/passive participles and the future and aorist middle participles. The accent is recessive in the indicative; the accent of the infinitive is always on -θη-; the accent of the participle persists, if possible, on the syllable before the suffix -μεν-.

FUTURE PASSIVE INDICATIVE   Endings:
Singular:
    παιδευ**θή**σομαι   ("I shall be taught")   **-θη**σομαι
    παιδευ**θή**σει (-η)   ("you [*sg.*] will be taught")   **-θη**σει (-η)
    παιδευ**θή**σεται   ("he/she/it will be taught")   **-θη**σεται
Plural:
    παιδευ**θη**σόμεθα   ("we shall be taught")   **-θη**σομεθα
    παιδευ**θή**σεσθε   ("you [*pl.*] will be taught")   **-θη**σεσθε
    παιδευ**θή**σονται   ("they will be taught")   **-θη**σονται

FUTURE PASSIVE INFINITIVE
    παιδευ**θή**σεσθαι   ("to be going to be taught")   **-θη**σεσθαι

FUTURE PASSIVE PARTICIPLE
    παιδευ**θη**σόμενος, -η, -ον   ("going to be taught")

NOTE   If the verb has a second aorist passive (e.g., ἐγράφην), the stem of the future passive will not have a theta (γραφήσομαι, γραφήσεσθαι, γραφησόμενος).

176.   You now know how to form the active, middle, and passive voices of six tenses: **present, imperfect, future, aorist, perfect,** and **pluperfect.** There is still one more tense in Greek, the **future perfect**; this indicates an action that *will have been completed* by some point in the future. Since the future perfect is relatively rare, we do not expect you to spend time learning it or working with it in the exercises, but you should be able to recognize it if it occurs in a reading.

The idea of the future perfect is usually expressed periphrastically, i.e., with two words instead of one. The **future tense of εἰμί** is simply combined with either the **perfect active participle** or the **perfect middle/ passive participle**, and the participle is made to agree with the subject. Examples:

Future Perfect Active:
        πεπαιδευκυῖα ἔσται   ("she will have taught")

Future Perfect Middle/Passive:
        πεπαιδευμένοι ἐσόμεθα   ("we shall have taught for ourselves" or
                                "we shall have been taught")

An alternative method is to add a **sigma** + a **thematic vowel** (ε/ο) + **primary endings** to the **perfect active stem** (e.g., τεθνήξω, -εις, -ει, -ομεν, -ετε, -ουσι) or the **perfect middle/passive stem** (e.g., λελύσομαι, -η/-ει, -εται, -ομεθα, -εσθε, -ονται). If the letter before the sigma is a consonant, it combines with the sigma (e.g., τεθνήξω); if it is a short vowel, it becomes long (e.g., λελύσομαι).

For the future perfect active, the periphrastic method is nearly always used; ἀποθνήσκω is one of only two verbs in Greek whose future perfect active is not periphrastic (τεθνήξω "I shall have died"). **Either method is used for the future perfect middle/passive.** The future perfect middle/passive infinitive (perfect middle/passive stem + -σεσθαι) and the future perfect middle/passive participle (perfect middle/passive stem + -σόμενος, -η, -ον) occasionally appear.

177.   The irregular verb οἶδα "I know" (literally, "I have seen") is always active in meaning and occurs only in the perfect (translated like a present), pluperfect (translated like an imperfect), and future perfect (translated like a future) tense. It looks odd because it belongs to the μι-conjugation and because its stem (which is also the stem of εἶδον "I saw") may be either Ϝοιδ-, Ϝειδ(ε)-, or Ϝιδ-.

The forms of οἶδα are presented below. Notice that many of them are similar to forms of εἰμί; in fact, the perfect second-person singular imperative of οἶδα and the present second-person singular imperative of εἰμί are **identical**. Moreover, the perfect participle of οἶδα is easy to confuse with the aorist participle of εἶδον. Because οἶδα is a very common verb, it is important for you to memorize all the forms, no matter how vexing they may be!

PERFECT ACT. INDICATIVE	**PLUPERFECT ACT. INDICATIVE**	
Singular:	**Singular:**	
οἶδα ("I know")	ἤδη ("I knew")	[cf. ἤδη (*adv.*)]
οἶσθα ("you [*sg.*] know")	ἤδησθα ("you [*sg.*] knew")	
οἶδε(ν) ("he/she/it knows")	ἤδει(ν) ("he/she/it knew")	

		Similar forms of εἰμί:
Plural:	**Plural:**	
ἴσμεν ("we know")	ἦσμεν ("we knew")	[cf. ἦμεν]
ἴστε ("you [*pl.*] know")	ἦστε ("you [*pl.*] knew")	[cf. ἦστε]
ἴσᾱσι(ν) ("they know")	ἦσαν ("they knew")	[cf. ἦσαν]

FUTURE PERFECT DEPONENT INDICATIVE

Similar forms of εἰμί:

Singular:

εἴσομαι	("I shall know")	[cf. ἔσομαι]
εἴσῃ (-ει)	("you [*sg.*] will know")	[cf. ἔσῃ/ἔσει]
εἴσεται	("he/she/it will know")	[cf. ἔσται]

Plural:

εἰσόμεθα	("we shall know")	[cf. ἐσόμεθα]
εἴσεσθε	("you [*pl.*] will know")	[cf. ἔσεσθε]
εἴσονται	("they will know")	[cf. ἔσονται]

PERFECT ACTIVE IMPERATIVE

Singular:

ἴσθι	("know!")	[cf. ἴσθι]
ἴστω	("let him/her/it know!")	[cf. ἔστω]

Plural:

ἴστε	("know!")	[cf. ἔστε]
ἴστων	("let them know!")	[cf. ἔστων]

PERFECT ACTIVE INFINITIVE

εἰδέναι	("to know")	[cf. εἶναι]

PERFECT ACTIVE PARTICIPLE

εἰδώς, εἰδυῖα, εἰδός[1]   ("knowing")
[cf. aor. act. ptcple. of εἶδον: ἰδών, ἰδοῦσα, ἰδόν ("seeing")]

---

[1] εἰδώς, εἰδυῖα, εἰδός is declined like a regular perfect active participle, but **without the kappa** (e.g., gen. sg. = εἰδότος, εἰδυίας, εἰδότος; dat. pl. = εἰδόσι, εἰδυίαις, εἰδόσι).

178.   VOCABULARY

ἁμαρτάνω, ἁμαρτήσομαι, ἥμαρτον, ἡμάρτηκα, ἡμάρτημαι,
    ἡμαρτήθην

                  make a mistake, fail, err, sin; (+ *gen.*)
                  miss (a *target*), miss out on

γεννάω, γεννήσω, ἐγέννησα, γεγέννηκα, γεγέννημαι,
    ἐγεννήθην

                  beget, give birth to, bear

οἶδα (*pluperf.* ᾔδη), εἴσομαι, —, —, —, —

                  know; (+ *infin.*) know how (to)

πιστεύω, πιστεύσω, ἐπίστευσα, πεπίστευκα, πεπίστευμαι,
    ἐπιστεύθην

                  (+ *dat. or with prepositions such as* εἰς +
                      acc.) believe (in), trust (in), have faith
                      (in)

ἁμαρτίᾱ, -ᾱς, ἡ   mistake, failure, error, sin

κόσμος, -ου, ὁ   order, adornment, world, universe
                  [cf. *cosmetic, cosmic*]

κύριος, -ᾱ, -ον   having authority; (*as a substantive*)
                  (*masc.*) lord, master, (*fem.*) lady, mis-
                  tress

οὔποτε (οὔποτ', οὔποθ')/μήποτε (μήποτ', μήποθ')

                  (*adverb*) never (οὔποτ'/μήποτ' *before smooth*
                  breathing; οὔποθ'/μήποθ' *before rough*
                  breathing)

οὔπω/μήπω   (*adverb*) not yet

ὅτι (*never elided*)   (*subordinating conj.*) because, since

NOTE   As a conjunction introducing a causal (adverbial) clause, ὅτι is
equivalent to ἐπεί, ἐπειδή, or ὡς. A clause beginning with ὅτι may be anticipated by an expression like **διὰ τοῦτο** (e.g., διὰ τοῦτ' ἐσμὲν εὐδαίμονες,
ὅτι ἔχομεν δαίμονα "on account of this we are happy, [namely,] because
we have a guardian spirit").

179.   EXERCISES

A.   Greek-to-English Sentences

1.   ὁ δ' οἰκέτης ἀπεκρίνατο, Οὔπω οἶδα εἴθ' ὁ κύριος γέραι τινὶ τῑμηθήσεται
    εἴτε ταύτης τῆς τῑμῆς ἁμαρτήσεται.

2.   διὰ τοῦτο πιστευθήσῃ ὑφ' ἡμῶν, ὅτι οὔποθ' ἡμᾶς σὺ βέβλαφας ἐθέλων.

3.   ποῦ ἐν τῷ κόσμῳ ἐγεννήθης, ὦ ἀνάξιε κλώψ, καὶ τί κακὸν ζῷόν σε
    ἐγέννησεν;

4.   ἆρ' οὔποθ' ἕξομεν ἄγειν εὐδαίμονα βίον ἄνευ ἁμαρτιῶν, ὦ Σώκρατες;

5. καίπερ τὰ ἀληθῆ εὖ εἰδότες, οὔπω αὐτὰ πάντα ἀγγελοῦμεν τοῖς πολλοῖς ἅτε μέγα φοβηθησομένοις.

6. ἴσθι σοφός, ὦ υἱέ μου, καὶ ἀεὶ ζήτει εἰδέναι οὐ πόλλ', ἀλλὰ πολύ.

7. οὐχ ἡμάρτομεν τῆς ὁδοῦ ὅτι ἡ εὖ δεδιδαγμένη κῡρίᾱ ᾔδειν ὅπου ἐστίν.

8. μὴ πιστεύετε τῷδε τῷ φύλακι, μέλλει γὰρ τραπήσεσθαι (*reflexive sense*) ἀπὸ τῆς χώρᾱς.

9. τί σύ, ἰδών με, οὐκ ἀνέῳξας τὴν θύρᾱν; πρὸς θεῶν, ὦ δοῦλε, ἡμάρτηκας.

10. ὁ ἐκ τοῦ θεοῦ γεγεννημένος ἔσπευσε διὰ τοῦ κόσμου καὶ ἠρώτησε τὰς τυφλὰς ἀδελφὰς εἰ ἴσᾱσιν εὑρεῖν ἐκεῖνον τὸν τόπον.

B. **English-to-Greek Sentences**

1. I asked my son, "You won't be frightened by your new teacher, will you?" He replied, "I don't know yet."

2. On account of this we shall never be chosen, because we were born neither handsome nor wise.

3. The little girl fled, not trusting the people whom she did not know.

4. O lord of the universe, will our words be heard by you, although you know our sins (*use participle*)?

5. Even the ancient orators sometimes erred and often did not know how to stop the great wars.

C. **READING**

HEALING OF THE MAN BORN BLIND—Part 3
(adapted from John 9:28-39)

The Pharisees are both baffled and offended by the man's answers.

καὶ ἐλοιδόρησαν αὐτὸν λέγοντες, Σὺ μαθητὴς εἶ ἐκείνου, ἡμεῖς δὲ τοῦ Μωϋσέως ἐσμὲν μαθηταί. τὸν Ἰησοῦν οὐκ ἴσμεν ὁπόθεν ἐστίν. ἀπεκρίθη ὁ ἄνθρωπος, Θαυμάζω ὅτι οὐκ ἴστε ὁπόθεν ἐστίν. ἴσμεν γὰρ τόδ'· οἱ ἁμαρτωλοὶ οὔποτ' ἀκουσθήσονται ὑπὸ τοῦ Θεοῦ, ἀλλ' ὁ θεοσεβὴς ἀκουσθήσεται. τίς ἐκ
5 τοῦ αἰῶνος ἀνέῳξε τοὺς ὀφθαλμοὺς τυφλοῦ γεγεννημένου; ὃς ἔχει τοῦτο ποιεῖν, οὗτος οὐκοῦν ἐστι παρὰ τοῦ Θεοῦ; ἀπεκρίθησαν αὐτῷ, Ἐν ἁμαρτίαις σὺ ἐγεννήθης. διδαχθησόμεθα ὑπὸ σοῦ; καὶ ἐξέβαλον αὐτόν.

ὁ δ' Ἰησοῦς εὑρὼν αὐτὸν εἶπε, Σὺ πιστεύεις εἰς τὸν Υἱὸν τοῦ ἀνθρώπου; ἀπεκρίθη ἐκεῖνος, Τίς ἐστι, Κύριε; εἶπεν ὁ Ἰησοῦς, Καὶ ἑώρακας αὐτόν, καὶ ὁ
10 λέγων μετὰ σοῦ ἐκεῖνός ἐστιν. ὁ δ' εἶπε, Πιστεύω, Κύριε· καὶ προσεκύνησεν αὐτῷ. καὶ εἶπεν ὁ Ἰησοῦς, Εἰς κρίμα ἐγὼ εἰς τὸν κόσμον τοῦτον ἦλθον· οἱ μὲν οὐ βλέποντες βλέψονται, οἱ δὲ βλέποντες τυφλοὶ γενήσονται.

VOCABULARY

ἐλοιδόρησαν (line 1): from λοιδορέω, λοιδορήσω, ἐλοιδόρησα, λελοιδόρηκα,
    λελοιδόρημαι, ἐλοιδορήθην: reproach

Μωϋσέως (line 2): from Μωϋσῆς, -έως, -εῖ, -ῆν, ὁ: Moses (*Hebrew name*)

Ἰησοῦν (line 2): from Ἰησοῦς, -οῦ, -οῦ, -οῦν, -οῦ, ὁ: Jesus (*Hebrew name*)

θαυμάζω (line 3): from θαυμάζω, θαυμάσομαι, ἐθαύμασα, τεθαύμακα, τεθαύμασμαι,
    ἐθαυμάσθην: be surprised (ὅτι *after* θαυμάζω = "that")

ἁμαρτωλοί (line 3): from ἁμαρτωλός, -όν: sinful

θεοσεβής (line 4): from θεοσεβής, -ές: worshipping God, pious

ἐκ τοῦ αἰῶνος (lines 4-5): from the dawn of the age, i.e., since human history began
    (αἰών, -ῶνος, ὁ: span of time, age)

ἐξέβαλον (line 7): from ἐκβάλλω: throw out

ὁ δ᾽ (line 10): = οὗτος δέ

προσεκύνησεν (line 10): from προσκυνέω, προσκυνήσω, προσεκύνησα,
    προσκεκύνηκα, προσκεκύνημαι, προσεκυνήθην (+ *dat.*): worship

εἰς κρῖμα (line 11): for judgment (κρῖμα, -ατος, τό: judgment)

ἦλθον (line 11): from ἔρχομαι, ἐλεύσομαι, ἦλθον, ἐλήλυθα, —, —: come

γενήσονται (line 12): from γίγνομαι, γενήσομαι, ἐγενόμην, γέγονα, γεγένημαι, —: be-
    come (*translate the middle deponent form actively*)

LESSON 29

THIRD DECLENSION
Vowel Stems and Syncopated Stems

ἔγημα Μεγακλέους... / ἀδελφιδῆν ἄγροικος ὢν ἐξ ἄστεως
(I, a country boy, married Megacles' niece, a city girl.)
—Strepsiades reminisces in Aristophanes' *Clouds* 46-47

180.   Some nouns of the **third declension** have stems ending in a **vowel**
(-ι, -υ) or a **diphthong** (-ευ, -αυ, -ου). Since these nouns use regular third-
declension endings, you may wonder why they deserve special attention. The reason is that, in many of them, the stem-vowel or diphthong
is changeable and varies as the noun is declined. Here are the paradigms
of **πόλις, -εως, ἡ** "city-state," **ἄστυ, -εως, τό** "city," and **βασιλεύς, -έως, ὁ**
"king." (Nouns in -αυ and -ου are rarer than those in -ευ and need not
concern you now.)

	πόλις, -εως, ἡ	ἄστυ, -εως, τό	βασιλεύς, -έως, ὁ
	(stem = πολι/ε/η-)	(stem = ἀστυ/ε/η-)	(stem = βασιλευ/ηυ/ηϝ-)
	"city-state"	"city"	"king"
Singular:			
Nom.	πόλις	ἄστυ	βασιλεύς (-ηυς)
Gen.	πόλεως (-ηος)	ἄστεως (-ηος)	βασιλέως (-ηϝος)
Dat.	πόλει	ἄστει	βασιλεῖ (-ηϝι)
Acc.	πόλιν	ἄστυ	βασιλέᾱ (-ηϝα)
Voc.	πόλι	ἄστυ	βασιλεῦ
Plural:			
Nom./Voc.	πόλεις (-εες)	ἄστη (-εα)	βασιλῆς (-ηϝες) or -εῖς
Gen.	πόλεων	ἄστεων	βασιλέων (-ηϝων)
Dat.	πόλεσι(ν)	ἄστεσι(ν)	βασιλεῦσι(ν) (-ηυσι)
Acc.	πόλεις (= nom.)	ἄστη (-εα)	βασιλέᾱς (-ηϝας)

SPECIAL FEATURES OF THIRD-DECLENSION VOWEL STEMS

1.   In all third-declension nouns whose stems end in a vowel or a diphthong, the accent is **persistent**, remaining (if possible) above the same letter as in the nominative singular. The **vocative singular** is nothing more than the **pure stem** (i.e., the stem with no ending attached). If the pure stem ends in an accented diphthong, the accent will always be a circumflex (e.g., βασιλεῦ).

2.   In nouns like πόλις and ἄστυ, **epsilon** takes the place of the iota or upsilon in every form except the nominative, vocative, and accusative singular. Contraction also occurs in πόλε-ες (→ πόλεις) and ἄστε-α (→ ἄστη). One would expect to find πόλε-ας → πόλης in the accusative plural, but the ending -εις, borrowed from the nominative, is used instead.

3.   In nouns like πόλις and ἄστυ, **eta** takes the place of the iota or upsilon before -ος of the **genitive singular** (πόλη-ος, ἄστη-ος); then η becomes short, while ο becomes long (by the principle of **quantitative metathesis**), producing πόλεως and ἄστεως, which keep the accent they *originally* had (even though an acute on the antepenult of a word with a long ultima is a violation of the rules). The **genitive plural** is accented in this same illegal way, by analogy with the genitive singular.

4.   In nouns like βασιλεύς, **ηυ replaces ευ** in every form except the vocative singular, and the **υ changes to a digamma** whenever the following letter is a vowel (βασιλήϝ-ος, βασιλήϝ-ι, βασιλήϝ-α, βασιλήϝ-ες, βασιλήϝ-ων, βασιλήϝ-ας). Then the **digamma drops out**, and **quantitative metathesis** occurs, producing βασιλέως, βασιλέϊ (→ βασιλεῖ), βασιλέα, βασιλέης (→ βασιλῆς), βασιλέᾱς. βασιλήϝων becomes βασιλέων to avoid having two long vowels in a row. Before a consonant, **υ does not change to ϝ**, but **η is shortened to ε** (βασιλήυ-ς → βασιλεύς; βασιλήυ-σι → βασιλεῦσι). After the Classical age, -εις becomes a common ending for the nominative plural (as if the contracting letters were -εσες, not -ηϝες).

181.   You already know how to decline third-declension nouns whose stems end in a **liquid** (e.g., ῥήτωρ, -ορος, ὁ). There is a small but important subcategory of these nouns with stems ending in **-ερ**. What complicates the picture is that the stem-vowel is sometimes lengthened (**-ηρ**) and sometimes entirely lost (**-ρ**); when the vowel is omitted, the stem is said to be **syncopated**.

Here are the paradigms of πατήρ, -τρός, ὁ "father," μήτηρ, -τρός, ἡ "mother," and θυγάτηρ, -τρός, ἡ "daughter."

	πατήρ, -τρός, ὁ (stem = πατερ-) "father"	μήτηρ, -τρός, ἡ (stem = μητερ-) "mother"	θυγάτηρ, -τρός, ἡ (stem = θυγατερ-) "daughter"
Singular:			
Nom.	πατήρ	μήτηρ	θυγάτηρ
Gen.	πατρός	μητρός	θυγατρός
Dat.	πατρί	μητρί	θυγατρί
Acc.	πατέρα	μητέρα	θυγατέρα
Voc.	πάτερ	μῆτερ	θύγατερ
Plural:			
Nom./Voc.	πατέρες	μητέρες	θυγατέρες
Gen.	πατέρων	μητέρων	θυγατέρων
Dat.	πατράσι(ν)	μητράσι(ν)	θυγατράσι(ν)
Acc.	πατέρας	μητέρας	θυγατέρας

SPECIAL FEATURES OF SYNCOPATED-STEM NOUNS

1. The **vocative singular** is simply the pure stem (-ερ with no ending attached). The **nominative singular** has a lengthened stem-vowel and no ending.

2. The syncopated stem is used in the **genitive and dative singular and the dative plural**. For easier pronunciation -τρσ- in the dative plural became -τρασ-.

3. Because of their syncopated stems, these nouns are **irregularly accented**. It may help if you imagine the accent as wishing to remain above the stem-vowel; if that vowel disappears (i.e., in a syncopated stem), the accent goes instead above the vowel that *follows* the ρ of the stem. There are still, however, two exceptions: in the nominative singular of μήτηρ and θυγάτηρ (but not of πατήρ), the penult is accented; in the vocative singular of all three nouns, the accent is recessive.

182.
VOCABULARY

ἄστυ, -εως, τό	city [cf. *Astyanax*]
βασιλεύς, -έως, ὁ	king [cf. *basil, basilica*]
ἑσπέρᾱ, -ᾱς, ἡ	evening [cf. *Hesperia*]
θόρυβος, -ου, ὁ	uproar, confusion (*opposite of* ἡσυχίᾱ)
θυγάτηρ, -τρός, ἡ	daughter
μήτηρ, -τρός, ἡ	mother
πατήρ, -τρός, ὁ	father
πόλις, -εως, ἡ	city-state, city, state [cf. *acropolis, metropolis*]

NOTE   πόλις is a broader term than ἄστυ, which usually means "city" in the material sense (buildings). πόλις often signifies a community of citizens. It is the word applied to each independent state that grew up around a city in Classical Greece. Both πόλις and ἄστυ may be used as opposites of χώρα ("countryside").

πρύτανις, -εως, ὁ   prytanis (*one of the 50 members of a tribe chosen by lot to run the administration of Athens for a month*)

στρατηγός, -οῦ, ὁ   general (*one of the 10 officials elected annually to run Athens' army and navy*) [cf. *strategy*]

183.   EXERCISES

A.   **Greek-to-English Sentences**

1. εἰπέ μοι, ὦ μῆτερ, ὅπως ἡμάρτηκα, ἡ γὰρ ἁμαρτίᾱ οὐ δήλη ἐμοί ἐστιν.

2. οὐ πιστεύεις τοῖς τε στρατηγοῖς καὶ τοῖς πρυτάνεσι τῆς σεαυτοῦ πόλεως;

3. διὰ τί ἦν ὁ μέγας θόρυβος ἐν τῷ ἄστει; μῶν ἐφοβοῦντο οἱ πολλοὶ ἐκεῖνον τὸν νέον βασιλέᾱ;

4. διὰ τοῦτ᾽ εὐδαίμων εἰμί, ὅτι τῇδε τῇ ἑσπέρᾳ ἐμοὶ γεγέννηται ἄρτι θυγάτηρ, ἣν ἰδοῦσα ἤδη φιλῶ.

5. οὐ μόνον τοὺς πατέρας ἀλλὰ καὶ τὰς μητέρας τῑμᾶτε, ὦ παῖδες, ὑμᾶς γὰρ ἐγέννησαν καὶ οὔποτε πέπαυνται ὠφελοῦντες.

6. μηκέτι πεμπέτω τὰ δῶρα τῷ ἀναξίῳ βασιλεῖ τῷ οὐκ εἰδότι βίον εὖ ἄγειν.

7. ἐπειδὴ ἀνέῳξεν ὁ ἄγγελος τὰς θύρᾱς, εἶδε τοὺς πρυτάνεις ἐπὶ τῶν κλῑνῶν.

8. ὁ δὲ σοφὸς στρατηγὸς ἐκεκελεύκει τοὺς νεᾱνίᾱς φυλάττειν τὰ τείχη.

9. ποῦ καὶ πότε ποιηθήσονται οἱ ἀγῶνες οὓς ὁ πατὴρ αὐτοῦ μέλλει κρινεῖν;

10. τῆς αὐτῆς ἑσπέρᾱς ὁ ἵππος ὁ τῆς θυγατρός μου ἐκλάπη ὑπό τινος.

B.   **English-to-Greek Sentences**

1. I have already received letters from my mother; therefore I urge you also, father, to write to me.

2. Let the philosophers speak to the king, for, although being wise, he himself is not able to know all (things).

3. O prytanis, was not a great uproar heard in the marketplace of the city on the same evening?

4. We asked our young daughter whether she had been taught well or badly by that teacher.

5. When they were unwilling to make peace, these generals whom you just now saw destroyed the entire state.

C. READING

ATHENS REACTS TO BAD NEWS — Part 1
(adapted from Demosthenes' *De Corona* 168-169)

The passage below is the first half of an excerpt from **On the Crown**, *a famous speech made by Demosthenes, the great Athenian orator and statesman, in c. 330 B.C. In the speech Demosthenes vigorously defends himself against charges brought by his rival, Aeschines, who opposed the bestowal of an honorary crown on Demosthenes.*

As he reviews and compares the services rendered to Athens by Aeschines and by himself, Demosthenes recalls the fateful evening in 339 when the Athenians learned that Philip II, the king of Macedonia, along with his formidable army, had occupied Elatea, a town strategically located at the intersection of several trade routes 70 miles northwest of Athens.

ὁ δὲ Φίλιππος ἔχων τὴν δύναμιν τὴν Ἐλάτειαν κατέλαβεν. ἀλλὰ τὸν τότε συμβάντα ἐν τῇ πόλει θόρυβον ἴστε μὲν πάντες, μῑκρὰ δ' ἀκούσατε ὅμως αὐτὰ τὰ ἀναγκαιότατα.

Ἑσπέρᾱ μὲν γὰρ ἦν, ἦλθε δ' ἀγγέλλων τις πρὸς τοὺς πρυτάνεις, Ἐλάτεια
5 κατείληπται. καὶ μετὰ ταῦθ' οἱ μέν, εὐθὺς τὸ δεῖπνον λείποντες, τοὺς ἐκ τῶν σκηνῶν τῶν κατὰ τὴν ἀγορὰν ἐξεῖργον, οἱ δὲ τοὺς στρατηγοὺς μετεπέμποντο καὶ τὸν σαλπιγκτὴν ἐκάλουν, καὶ θορύβου πλήρης ἦν ἡ πόλις.

τῇ δ' ὑστεραίᾳ ἡμέρᾳ οἱ μὲν πρυτάνεις τὴν βουλὴν ἐκάλουν εἰς τὸ βουλευτήριον, ὑμεῖς δ' εἰς τὴν ἐκκλησίᾱν ἐτρέπεσθε.

VOCABULARY

Φίλιππος (line 1): from Φίλιππος, -ου, ὁ: Philip II, king of Macedonia
δύναμιν (line 1): from δύναμις, -εως, ἡ: military force, troops
Ἐλάτειαν (line 1): from Ἐλάτεια, -ᾱς, ἡ: Elatea, town in central Greece
κατέλαβεν (line 1): seized (*the prefix* κατα- *strengthens the verb*)
συμβάντα (line 2): masc. acc. sg. aor. act. ptcple. from συμβαίνω, συμβήσομαι,
    συνέβην, συμβέβηκα, συμβέβαμαι, συνεβάθην: happen
μῑκρά (line 2): for a little while (*neut. acc. pl. of adj. used as adverb*)
ὅμως (line 2): nevertheless (*particle*)
αὐτά (line 2): here = "just"
ἀναγκαιότατα (line 3): from ἀναγκαιότατος, -η, -ον: most necessary (*i.e., the bare es-
    sentials of the story, not all the details*)
ἦλθε (line 4): from ἔρχομαι, ἐλεύσομαι, ἦλθον, ἐλήλυθα, —, —: come
εὐθύς (line 5): immediately (*adv.*)
τοὺς ἐκ τῶν σκηνῶν (lines 5-6): i.e., vendors operating out of stalls ("tents")
κατά (line 6): here = "throughout"
ἐξεῖργον (line 6): from ἐξείργω, ἐξείρξω, —, —, —, —: drive out

μετεπέμποντο (line 6): sent after, summoned (*verb is usually in mid. voice*)

σαλπιγκτήν (line 7): from σαλπιγκτής, -οῦ, ὁ: trumpeter

πλήρης (line 7): from πλήρης, -ες: full (of) (+ *gen.*)

ὑστεραίᾳ (line 8): from ὑστεραῖος, -ᾱ, -ον: following, next

βουλήν (line 8): from βουλή, -ῆς, ἡ: council

βουλευτήριον (line 9): from βουλευτήριον, -ου, τό: council-chamber

ἐκκλησίᾱν (line 9): from ἐκκλησίᾱ, -ᾱς, ἡ: assembly (*of citizens*)

LESSON 30

DEPONENT VERBS; GENITIVE ABSOLUTE; εἷς, οὐδείς/μηδείς

εἷς ἀνὴρ οὐδεὶς ἀνήρ (One man is no man.)
—proverb quoted by the sophist Dio Chrysostom in *In Contione* 11

184. You have already encountered ten verbs (ἀκούω, ἁμαρτάνω, ἀποθνῄσκω, βλέπω, γελάω, εἰμί, λαμβάνω, οἶδα, ὁράω, φεύγω) that use future middle endings to express a future active meaning. These verbs are said to be **partially deponent** (from the Latin participle *dēpōnēns* "putting aside"); they cast off their active endings, but **only in the future tense**.

There are other verbs in Greek that are deponent not just in one principal part, but **in all of their principal parts**. Although their form is always middle or passive, their sense is always active. It is easy to spot a verb that is **completely deponent**: any principal part that normally has an active ending will either have a middle/passive ending or be missing altogether. Here are two examples:

> ἀφικνέομαι, ἀφίξομαι, ἀφῑκόμην, —, ἀφῖγμαι, —   "arrive (at)"
> βούλομαι, βουλήσομαι, —, —, βεβούλημαι, ἐβουλήθην   "wish"

The first verb, ἀφικνέομαι, is called a **middle deponent** because it has an aorist middle; the second, βούλομαι, is called a **passive deponent** because it has an aorist passive. Whether a deponent verb has an aorist middle or an aorist passive must be learned from the principal parts.

NOTE   Since a passive deponent has a sixth principal part, it is capable of forming a future passive as well as a future middle. Usually the future middle is preferrred, but if both forms are in use, they differ only in aspect; e.g., βουλήσομαι = "I shall be wishing" (imperfective); βουληθήσομαι = "I shall wish" (aoristic).

185.   In the preceding lessons you were introduced to the various Greek

195

participles and shown how they could be used in attributive, circumstantial, and supplementary ways. There is one species of circumstantial participle that we have not yet discussed; it is known as the **genitive absolute**. Compare the following sentences:

ἀνοίγων τὴν θύρᾱν, τὸν θησαυρὸν εἶδον.
"As I opened the door, I saw the treasure."
(*literally*, "Opening the door, I...")

τοῦ οἰκέτου ἀνοίγοντος τὴν θύρᾱν, τὸν θησαυρὸν ὄψομαι.
"When the servant opens the door, I shall see the treasure."
(*literally*, "With the servant opening the door, I...")

σοῦ ἀνοίξοντος τὴν θύρᾱν, τὸν θησαυρὸν ὄψομαι.
"Since you intend to open the door, I shall see the treasure."
(*literally*, "With you going to open the door, I...")

τῆς θύρᾱς ὑπὸ σοῦ ἀνοιχθείσης, τὸν θησαυρὸν εἶδον.
"After the door was opened by you, I saw the treasure."
(*literally*, "With the door having been opened by you, I...")

καίπερ τῆς θύρᾱς ἀνεῳγμένης, τὸν θησαυρὸν οὐχ ὁρῶ.
"Although the door has been opened, I do not see the treasure."
(*literally*, "Although with the door having been opened, I...")

In all five examples, the participle describes the **circumstances** under which the main action (i.e., seeing the treasure) occurs. The participle in the first sentence modifies the subject ("I") of the main clause, so it naturally agrees with it in gender, number, and case. In the other four sentences, the noun modified by the participle is **not** part of the main clause; it is therefore put into the **genitive case** and floats there, grammatically separate ("absolute") from the main clause, but parallel to it; the participle agrees with it in gender, number, and case. The participle may also have its own objects and modifiers in whatever cases are appropriate (e.g., τὴν θύρᾱν is the direct object of the participles in the second and third sentences; ὑπὸ σοῦ modifies ἀνοιχθείσης in the fourth sentence).

Clarifying **particles** like καίπερ, ἅτε, and ὡς may be used with genitive absolutes, as with any circumstantial participle; in the absence of a particle, you must rely on the context to help you decide whether the participial clause denotes time, cause, concession, or some other relationship to the main clause. **Present participles** have imperfective aspect and (usually) show action contemporaneous with that of the main verb; **future participles** have either imperfective or aoristic aspect and show intention; **aorist participles** have aoristic aspect and (usually) show action prior to that of the main verb; **perfect participles** have perfective aspect and (usually) show a state contemporaneous with that of the main verb.

186. The Greek word for "one" is εἷς, μία, ἕν, an adjective of mixed declension, inflected as follows (it has no vocatives and no plurals):

Singular:	Masc.	Fem.	Neut.
Nom.	εἷς	μία	ἕν
Gen.	ἑνός	μιᾶς	ἑνός
Dat.	ἑνί	μιᾷ	ἑνί
Acc.	ἕνα (*elided as* ἕν')	μίαν	ἕν

The stem ἑν- was originally σεμ-; in the feminine forms it was syncopated to σμ-, and the initial sigma dropped out. The nominative εἷς is derived from ἑνς. Because the stem is monosyllabic, the otherwise persistent accent jumps to the ultima in the genitive and dative of the masculine and neuter (by the rule for words with third-declension endings) and feminine too (by analogy with the masculine and neuter).

εἷς, μία, ἕν may be combined with the adverb οὐδέ to make **οὐδείς, οὐδεμία, οὐδέν,** or with μηδέ to make **μηδείς, μηδεμία, μηδέν,** meaning "none," "no," "no one," or "nothing." Except for an acute instead of a circumflex in the masculine nominative, the compounds have the same accents as the simple forms. Although there is a subtle difference in meaning between οὐδείς ("[actually] no one") and μηδείς ("[thought of as] no one"), in general you will be correct if you simply use οὐδείς wherever οὐ is appropriate, μηδείς wherever μή is appropriate.

Singular:	Masc.		Fem.		Neut.	
Nom.	οὐδείς	(μηδείς)	οὐδεμία	(μηδεμία)	οὐδέν	(μηδέν)
Gen.	οὐδενός	(μηδενός)	οὐδεμιᾶς	(μηδεμιᾶς)	οὐδενός	(μηδενός)
Dat.	οὐδενί	(μηδενί)	οὐδεμιᾷ	(μηδεμιᾷ)	οὐδενί	(μηδενί)
Acc.	οὐδένα	(μηδένα)	οὐδεμίαν	(μηδεμίαν)	οὐδέν	(μηδέν)

NOTE οὐδείς and μηδείς are sometimes found in the plural (e.g., οὐδένες, μηδένες), meaning "no people" or "nobodies."

187. **VOCABULARY**

ἀφικνέομαι, ἀφίξομαι, ἀφικόμην, —, ἀφῖγμαι, —
  (*with* ἐπί *or* εἰς + *acc.*) arrive (at), come
  (to)

βούλομαι, βουλήσομαι, —, —, βεβούλημαι, ἐβουλήθην
  (+ *infin.*) wish (to), desire (to), prefer (to)

NOTE ἐθέλω and βούλομαι can both mean "wish," but ἐθέλω implies consent or willingness, while βούλομαι implies desire or preference.

ἀνήρ, ἀνδρός, ὁ   man, husband [cf. *android, philander*]

NOTE ἀνήρ is declined like πατήρ, but its stem (ἀνερ-) is syncopated in every form except the nominative and vocative singular; in the syncopated forms, δ is added between ν and ρ, for euphonic reasons: SG.: ἀνήρ, ἀνδρός, ἀνδρί, ἄνδρα, ἄνερ; PL.: ἄνδρες, ἀνδρῶν, ἀνδράσι(ν), ἄνδρας. Notice the irregular position of the accent (on the ultima of the nominative, genitive, and dative singular and of the genitive plural, otherwise on the penult).

βουλή, -ῆς, ἡ	plan, counsel, council (*a group of 500 citizens, 50 from each of the 10 tribes, chosen by lot to serve as Athens' senate for a year*)
ἐκκλησία, -ᾱς, ἡ	assembly (*from ἐκκαλέω because the citizens were "called forth" to assemble*) [cf. *ecclesiastic*]
κῆρυξ, -ῦκος, ὁ	herald
πατρίς, -ίδος, ἡ	fatherland, native country
φωνή, -ῆς, ἡ	voice, sound [cf. *phonetics, phonograph, symphony, telephone*]
εἷς, μία, ἕν	one; καθ' ἕνα, κατὰ μίαν, or καθ' ἕν = one by one, singly [cf. *henotheism*]
κοινός, -ή, -όν	(+ *dat. or gen.*) common (to) [cf. *cenobite*]
οὐδείς, οὐδεμία, οὐδέν/μηδείς, μηδεμία, μηδέν	
	none, no; (*as a substantive*) no one, nothing

NOTE

Two negatives often appear in the same sentence. If the first negative is a compound (e.g., οὐδείς/μηδείς) and the second is a simple οὐ or μή, the two cancel each other out, making a **positive statement**. Example:

οὐδὲν οὐκ οἶδα.   " I know something."
          Literally: "I do not know nothing."

If the οὐ or μή comes *before* the compound, or if *both* negatives in the sentence are compounds, the second simply **emphasizes the negativity** of the first. Examples:

οὐκ οἶδα οὐδέν.   " I don't know anything."
          Literally: "I don't know not even one thing."

οὐδεὶς οὐδὲν οἶδεν.   " No one knows anything."
          Literally: "No one knows not even one thing."

188.   EXERCISES

A.   **Greek-to-English Sentences**

1.   τοῦ βασιλέως κελεύσαντος ὑμᾶς εὑρεῖν τὴν κόρην, ἵπποι ἐζητήθησαν.

2.   καίπερ ἑνὸς υἱοῦ ἀγαθοῦ ὄντος, οἱ ἄλλοι οὔτε τοῦ πατρὸς οὔτε τῆς πατρίδος ἄξιοί εἰσιν.

3.   οἱ πολέμιοι μὴ ἀποκτεινόντων μηδέ’ ἄνδρα ἐν ταύτῃ τῇ παλαιᾷ πόλει.

4.   οὐκοῦν σὺ βούλῃ εἰπεῖν τῇ βουλῇ, ὦ πρύτανι, περὶ τοῦ κινδύνου τοῦ κοινοῦ πᾶσιν ἡμῖν;

5.   οὐδεὶς οὐκ οἶδεν ὅπου εἰσὶν οἱ κήρῡκες οἳ ἄρτι ἀφίκοντο εἰς τόδε τὸ ἄστυ.

6.   πάντων τῶν ἀνδρῶν βουλομένων τότε θῦσαι, μέγας ἦν ὁ θόρυβος.

7.   εἰς τὴν ἐκκλησίᾱν κληθήσονται καθ’ ἕν’ οἱ ῥήτορες ὑπὸ τοῦ κήρῡκος.

8.   ἆρ’ ἀκούεις τὴν φωνὴν τὴν ἐκείνου τοῦ βεβλαμμένου λέοντος;

9.   ἅτε τῶν στρατηγῶν ἤδη ἀφῑγμένων, ὥρᾱ σπεύδειν εἰς τὴν τριήρη.

10. ἐγὼ μὲν ἐβουλήθην ἔχειν εἰρήνην, οἱ δ’ ἄλλοι μιᾷ φωνῇ ἔκρῑναν πόλεμον.

B.   **English-to-Greek Sentences**

1.   No one does not love the herald, for he has a fine voice and always speaks true words in the assembly.

2.   When my husband was not yet born (*use genitive absolute*), war came to Greece and brought much grief.

3.   Although the council preferred to trust that king (*use genitive absolute*), one of the generals greatly feared him.

4.   Because the immortal gods are not far off (*use genitive absolute*), our native country is fortunate.

5.   You yourselves don't know anything about the common laws of this state, do you?

C. READING

ATHENS REACTS TO BAD NEWS — Part 2
(adapted from Demosthenes' *De Corona* 170-173)

After the council-members had prepared the agenda for the special meeting, they left the council-chamber and joined the rest of the Athenian citizens sitting on the Pnyx, a small hill west of the Acropolis.

καὶ ἀπήγγειλαν οἱ πρυτάνεις τὰ προσηγγελμένα ἑαυτοῖς. ἠρώτα μὲν ὁ κῆρυξ, Τίς ἀγορεύειν βούλεται; ἀνίστατο δ' οὐδείς. πολλάκις δὲ τοῦ κήρῡκος ἐρωτῶντος, ἀνίστατο οὐδείς, πάντων μὲν τῶν στρατηγῶν παρόντων, πάντων δὲ τῶν ῥητόρων, καλούσης δὲ τῆς κοινῆς τῆς πατρίδος φωνῆς τὸν ἐροῦντα
5 ὑπὲρ σωτηρίας· ἡ γὰρ φωνὴ τοῦ κήρῡκος νομίζεται εἶναι φωνὴ κοινὴ τῆς πατρίδος.

ἀλλ' ἐκεῖνος ὁ καιρὸς καὶ ἡ ἡμέρᾱ ἐκείνη οὐ μόνον εὔνουν καὶ πλούσιον ἄνδρα ἐκάλει, ἀλλὰ καὶ παρηκολουθηκότα τοῖς πράγμασιν ἐξ ἀρχῆς, καὶ συλλελογισμένον ὀρθῶς τίνος χάριν ταῦτ' ἔπρᾱττεν ὁ Φίλιππος καὶ τί
10 βουλόμενος.

ἐφάνην οὖν οὗτος ἐν ἐκείνῃ τῇ ἡμέρᾳ ἐγώ, καὶ παρελθὼν εἶπον εἰς ὑμᾶς.

Conclusion: Demosthenes made a speech urging the Athenians to send an embassy to Thebes, a rival city-state in Boeotia (the region adjoining Attica), to secure an alliance with the Thebans. His proposal was accepted, and Demosthenes himself went along as one of the ambassadors. The following year (338 B.C.), the Athenians and the Thebans fought together against Philip at the battle of Chaeronea, but were badly defeated.

VOCABULARY

ἀπήγγειλαν...προσηγγελμένα (line 1): the prefixes ἀπο- and προσ- specify the direction (ἀπαγγέλλω "report *back*"; προσαγγέλλω "announce *to*")

ἀγορεύειν (line 2): from ἀγορεύω, ἀγορεύσω, ἠγόρευσα, ἠγόρευκα, ἠγόρευμαι, ἠγορεύθην: speak in the assembly

ἀνίστατο (line 2): stood up (*imperf. mid. of* ἀνίστημι, ἀναστήσω, ἀνέστησα or ἀνέστην, ἀνέστηκα, ἀνέσταμαι, ἀνεστάθην: make stand up)

παρόντων (line 3): from πάρειμι (*imperf.* παρῆν), παρέσομαι, —, —, —, —: be present (*concessive ptcple.*—"although")

ῥητόρων (line 4): supply παρόντων

καλούσης δὲ τῆς...φωνῆς τὸν ἐροῦντα (line 4): and although the voice...kept summoning the man who would speak

σωτηρίᾱς (line 5): from σωτηρίᾱ, -ᾱς, ἡ: safety

νομίζεται (line 5): from νομίζω, νομιῶ, ἐνόμισα, νενόμικα, νενόμισμαι, ἐνομίσθην: think, consider (νομίζεται εἶναι = "is considered to be")

καιρός (line 7): from καιρός, -οῦ, ὁ: critical moment

εὔνουν (line 7): masc. acc. sg. of εὔνους, -ουν (*contracted adj.*): well-intentioned

πλούσιον (line 7): from πλούσιος, -ᾱ, -ον: wealthy

παρηκολουθηκότα (line 8): from παρακολουθέω, παρακολουθήσω, παρηκολούθησα, παρηκολούθηκα, —, —: follow closely

πράγμασιν (line 8): from πρᾶγμα, -ατος, τό: thing, affair; (*pl.*) matters of state

συλλελογισμένον (line 9): from συλλογίζομαι, συλλογίσομαι, συνελογισάμην, —, συλλελόγισμαι, —: reckon together, infer

ὀρθῶς (line 9): rightly (*adv.*)

Φίλιππος (line 9): from Φίλιππος, -ου, ὁ: Philip II, king of Macedonia

ἐφάνην (line 11): I appeared (*aor. pass. of* φαίνω, φανῶ, ἔφηνα, πέφαγκα or πέφηνα, πέφασμαι, ἐφάνθην or ἐφάνην: make appear)

οὗτος (line 11): predicate noun ("as that man" or "as such a one")

παρελθών (line 11): coming forward to speak (*aor. act. participle of* παρέρχομαι, πάρειμι, παρῆλθον, παρελήλυθα, —, —: pass by)

LESSON 31

ADVERBS: Positive Degree; RESULT CLAUSES

οὐκ ἀνδριαντοποιός εἰμ᾽, ὥστ᾽ ἐλῑνύσοντα ἐργάζεσθαι ἀγάλματα
(I'm not a sculptor, cut out to make immobile statues.)
—Pindar in *Nemea* 5.1 prefers to be a poet

189. This chapter is a formal introduction to Greek **adverbs**, some of which you already know from previous lessons. While adjectives modify nouns, adverbs modify **verbs** (e.g., "this is a book that I understand *well*"), **adjectives/participles** (e.g., "this is a *well* understood book"), or other **adverbs** ("this is a *fairly* well understood book"). Only the positive degree of adverbs is presented here; the comparative and superlative degrees are covered in the next lesson.

190. In English, an adverb showing the **manner** in which something is done may be created by adding a suffix, usually -*ly*, to an adjective: e.g., *fair* → *fairly*. A Greek adverb of manner may be **derived from an adjective** in a similar way: the final ν of the **masculine genitive plural** is simply changed to ς, and the accent of the genitive plural is retained in the adverb (e.g., masc. gen. pl. = ἐλευθέρων; adverb = ἐλευθέρως; masc. gen. pl. = κακῶν; adverb = κακῶς).

With some adjectives, Greek prefers to use the **neuter accusative singular or plural** as if it were an adverb of manner. This corresponds to the flexibility of certain English adjectives that may function as adverbs with no change of form (e.g., "a *fast* horse"; "the horse runs *fast*"). In the following list, those adjectives whose neuter accusative (or a different word altogether) usually acts as a substitute for the expected adverb are grouped together at the end:

ἀθάνατος, -ον	→ ἀθανάτως	"immortally"
αἴτιος, -ᾱ, -ον	→ αἰτίως	"responsibly," "guiltily"
ἀληθής, -ές	→ ἀληθῶς	"truly"

ἀνάξιος, -ον	→ ἀναξίως	"undeservedly," "worthlessly"
ἄξιος, -ᾱ, -ον	→ ἀξίως	"deservedly"
αὐτός, -ή, -όν	→ αὕτως	"in this very way" [*irregular accent*]
δοῦλος, -η, -ον	→ δούλως	"in a slavish way"
ἐκεῖνος, -η, -ο	→ ἐκείνως	"in that way"
ἐλεύθερος, -ᾱ, -ον	→ ἐλευθέρως	"freely"
Ἑλληνικός, -ή, -όν	→ Ἑλληνικῶς	"in a Greek way"
εὐδαίμων, -ον	→ εὐδαιμόνως	"fortunately," "prosperously"
ἐχθρός, -ά, -όν	→ ἐχθρῶς	"hatefully"
κακός, -ή, -όν	→ κακῶς	"badly," "wickedly"
καλός, -ή, -όν	→ καλῶς	"well," "beautifully"
κοινός, -ή, -όν	→ κοινῶς	"commonly," "in common"
οὗτος, αὕτη, τοῦτο	→ οὕτω(ς)	"in this way," "so," "thus" [*no initial τ*]
παλαιός, -ά, -όν	→ παλαιῶς	"in an old way"
πᾶς, πᾶσα, πᾶν	→ πάντως	"entirely," "in all respects"
πολέμιος, -ᾱ, -ον	→ πολεμίως	"in a hostile way"
σοφός, -ή, -όν	→ σοφῶς	"wisely"
τυφλός, -ή, -όν	→ τυφλῶς	"blindly"
φίλος, -η, -ον	→ φίλως	"in a friendly way"
φιλόσοφος, -ον	→ φιλοσόφως	"in a philosophic way"

[Forms in brackets are rarely or less commonly used.]

ἀγαθός, -ή, -όν	→ εὖ[1]	[or ἀγαθῶς]	"well," "kindly"
δῆλος, -η, -ον	→ δῆλον or δῆλα	[or δήλως]	"clearly"
μακρός, -ά, -όν	→ μακρόν or μακρά	[or μακρῶς]	"at length"
μέγας, μεγάλη, μέγα	→ μέγα or μεγάλα	[or μεγάλως]	"greatly"
μῑκρός, -ά, -όν	→ μῑκρόν or μῑκρά	[or μῑκρῶς]	"a little," "for a little while"
μόνος, -η, -ον	→ μόνον	[or μόνως]	"only"
νέος, -ᾱ, -ον	→ νέον	[or νέως]	"recently"
ὅδε, ἥδε, τόδε	→ ὧδε		"in this way, " "so," "thus"
ὀλίγος, -η, -ον	→ ὀλίγον or ὀλίγα	[or ὀλίγως]	"a little," "for a little while"
πολύς, πολλά, πολύ	→ πολύ or πολλά		"much"
πρότερος, -ᾱ, -ον	→ πρότερον		"formerly," "earlier"

---

[1] εὖ is the adverbial form of ἐΰς, ἠΰ, "good," an adjective found only in epic poetry.

NOTE   The adverb πολλάκις ("often") is formed from the adjective stem πολλ- ("many") + the adverbial suffix -ακις ("times").

191.   Like English, Greek also has many adverbs that are **not derived from adjectives** and whose form is relatively unpredictable. Of these, you already know ἀεί, ἄρτι, ἔτι, ἤδη, καί ("even"), μή and its compounds, νῦν, ὁπόθεν, ὅποι, ὁπότε, ὅπου, ὅπως, οὐ and its compounds, πάλαι, πάλιν, πόθεν, ποῖ, πόρρω, πότε, ποῦ, πῶς, and τότε. The adverb τήμερον is derived from the noun ἡμέρα.

192.   **Result clauses** (also called **consecutive clauses**) are adverbial clauses introduced by the conjunction **ὥστε** ("so as," "so that"). Often the main clause will have a demonstrative like **οὕτω(ς)** ("so," "thus"), **τοιοῦτος** ("of such a sort," "such"), or **τοσοῦτος** ("so great," "so much") that anticipates the result clause and functions as a correlative with ὥστε. Result clauses come in two varieties:

1.   The result described by a **natural result clause** is one that would *naturally* follow from, or be *likely* to follow from, the action of the main verb, but whether that result ever actually occurs is left unspecified. The verb in a natural result clause is always an **infinitive**, whose subject is left understood if it is identical with the subject of the main verb; otherwise it appears as a noun or pronoun in the **accusative** (see the second example below). In a natural result clause, only distinctions of **aspect**, not of time, are made. The negative is **μή**; the best translation for ὥστε is often "**so as**." If the infinitive has an accusative subject, a literal translation may sound awkward; in such cases try using "might," "could," or "would." Examples:

   εἶχον ἐγὼ τριήρεις ὥστε προσβαλεῖν τοῖς πολεμίοις.
   ("I had triremes so as to attack the enemy.")

   ὁ θόρυβος τοσοῦτος ἦν ὥστε τοὺς ἐν τῇ οἰκίᾳ ἀκούειν.
   ("The uproar was so great as those in the house might hear.")

   οὕτω κακῶς διδάσκουσιν ὥστε μὴ τιμᾶσθαι ὑπὸ μηδενός.
   ("So badly do they teach as not to be honored by anyone.")

2.   The result described by an **actual result clause** is one that actually was produced, is being produced, or will be produced by the action of the main verb. The verb in an actual result clause is **finite** and in the **indicative mood** (because the result is one that does or did or will *in fact* occur). In an actual result clause, distinctions of **both time and aspect** are made. The negative is **οὐ**; the best translation for ὥστε is often "**so that**." Examples:

   εἶχον ἐγὼ τριήρεις ὥστε προσέβαλον τοῖς πολεμίοις.
   ("I had triremes so that I attacked the enemy.")

ὁ θόρυβος τοσοῦτος ἦν ὥστε οἱ ἐν τῇ οἰκίᾳ ἤκουον.
("The uproar was so great that those in the house heard.")

οὕτω κακῶς διδάσκουσιν ὥστε τῑμῶνται ὑπ᾽ οὐδενός.
("So badly do they teach that they are honored by no one.")

193.   **VOCABULARY**

ζάω, ζήσω, —, —, —, —   live

NOTE   ζάω occurs only in the active voice. In its contracted forms, it has an
η everywhere you would expect an ᾱ: pres. act. indic. ζῶ, ζῇς, ζῇ, ζῶμεν,
ζῆτε, ζῶσι(ν); pres. act. imper. ζῆ, ζήτω, ζῆτε, ζώντων; pres. act. infin. ζῆν;
ptcple. ζῶν, ζῶσα, ζῶν; imperf. act. indic. ἔζων, ἔζης, ἔζη, ἐζῶμεν, ἐζῆτε, ἔζων.

αἰσχρός, -ά, -όν   shameful, disgraceful
ῥᾴδιος, -ᾱ, -ον   easy
τοιόσδε, τοιάδε, τοιόνδε   (= τοῖος, -ᾱ, -ον + -δε) of such a sort, such
τοιοῦτος, τοιαύτη, τοιοῦτο(ν)   (= τοῖος, -ᾱ, -ον + οὗτος, αὕτη, τοῦτο; *Attic*
                                   often adds -ν *to* τοιοῦτο) of such a sort,
                                   such
τοσόσδε, τοσήδε, τοσόνδε   (= τόσος, -η, -ον + -δε) so great, so much;
                                   (*pl.*) so many
τοσοῦτος, τοσαύτη, τοσοῦτο(ν)
                                   (= τόσος, -η, -ον + οὗτος, αὕτη, τοῦτο; *Attic*
                                   often adds -ν *to* τοσοῦτο) so great, so
                                   much; (*pl.*) so many

NOTE   In Attic these four compounds are more common than their simple
equivalents, τοῖος, -ᾱ, -ον and τόσος, -η, -ον. τοιόσδε and τοσόσδε, like ὅδε,
point to something very close or to what follows; τοιοῦτος and τοσοῦτος,
like οὗτος, point to something close or to what has preceded or to a result
clause. τοιοῦτος, τοσόσδε, and τοσοῦτος use the **neut. acc. sg. or pl. as an
adverb**; τοιόσδε uses **τοιῶσδε**. The penult is always accented; -δε affects
the accent as if it were a separate enclitic.

οὕτω(ς)   (*adv.*) in this way, so, thus (οὕτως *before a
                 vowel*; οὕτω *and* ἐκ *are the only two
                 Greek words with a* **movable sigma**)
ὧδε   (*adv.*) in this way, so, thus
ὡς   (*adv.; modifies an adv. or an adj. in an ex-
             clamation*) how!
ὥστε   (*conj.* + *infin.*) so as; (*conj.* + *finite verb in
             indic. mood*) so that (*accented as if* -τε
             were a separate enclitic)

194.   EXERCISES

A.   **Greek-to-English Sentences**

1. μῑκρὸς ὁ κίνδῡνος ἔσται καὶ τοιοῦτος ὥστε φοβῆσαι μηδένα τῶν παίδων.

2. ὡς ῥᾳδίως, ὦ ξένε, ἔρρῑψας ἐκεῖνον τὸν λίθον, καίπερ ὄντα τοσόνδε, ὑπὲρ τὸ τοῦ ἄστεως τεῖχος.

3. πολλῶν υἱῶν ἤδη γεννηθέντων, οὐκοῦν βούλῃ ἔχειν καὶ μίαν θυγατέρα;

4. νῦν κελεύομεν ὑμῖν, ἅτε αἰσχρῶς ἀποκτείνᾱσι τὸν ἀγαθὸν ἄγγελον, φυγεῖν ἐκ τῆσδε τῆς πόλεως.

5. τοιαύτη ἦν ἡ προτέρᾱ δέσποινα ἐμοῦ ὥστε ὑπὸ πᾱσῶν τῶν ἄλλων θεραπαινῶν μέγα ἐφιλεῖτο.

6. οὐδενὸς ἀληθῶς εἰπόντος, οἱ πρυτάνεις οὐκ ἦσαν ὅστις ἐστὶν αἴτιος τοῦ τῆς καλῆς ἵππου θανάτου.

7. ἐγὼ δ' οὕτως εὐδαιμόνως ἔζων ὥστε καθ' ἡμέρᾱν ἔθῡον αὐτὸς τῷ δαίμονι ᾧ μεγάλην χάριν εἶχον.

8. τοσοῦτός ἐστιν ὁ ἐν τῇ ἀγορᾷ θόρυβος, ὦ κυρίᾱ, ὥστε σέ γε μηδ' ἔχειν τὴν σεαυτῆς φωνὴν ἀκούειν.

9. πόλλ' ἔτη ζήτω ὁ βασιλεὺς ὁ ποιήσᾱς τε τούσδε τοὺς σοφοὺς νόμους καὶ ὧδε τῑμήσᾱς πάντας τοὺς θεούς.

10. καίπερ τῆς μητρὸς πολλάκις ἐρωτώσης εἰ ὁ πατὴρ ἀφῖκται εἰς τὴν οἰκίᾱν, οὐδείς ποτ' ἀπεκρίνετο.

B.   **English-to-Greek Sentences**

1. How disgracefully every contest was judged by that wicked king, whom no one trusts!

2. So beautiful was the evening that they all desired to remain in the marketplace, looking at the sky.

3. Your words, dear husband, are such as to send hope into the very souls of the (people) listening.

4. Because the gods have so commanded, we live blindly, not knowing when Death shall arrive.

5. Thus spoke my daughter: "So great is your honor, worthy mother, as nothing easily could destroy it."

C. READING

*The passage below is the first third of an excerpt from the **Memorabilia**, Xenophon's reminiscences of his friend and teacher, Socrates, who had been condemned to death by the Athenians in 399 B.C. Written about twenty years after Socrates' trial, the **Memorabilia** include a number of dialogues (as remembered and reconstructed by Xenophon) between Socrates and various people.*

In the following paragraph Socrates launches into a conversation with Epigenes on the benefits of keeping fit.

WHY EPIGENES SHOULD SHAPE UP — Part 1
(adapted from Xenophon's *Memorabilia* 3.12)

Ἐπιγένην δέ τινα, νέον τ' ὄντα καὶ τὸ σῶμα κακῶς ἔχοντα, ἰδών, ὁ
Σωκράτης εἶπεν, Ὡς ἰδιωτικῶς τὸ σῶμα ἔχεις, ὦ Ἐπίγενες. καὶ ἐκεῖνος ἀπεκρίνατο,
Ἰδιώτης γάρ εἰμι, ὦ Σώκρατες. Οὐδέν γε μᾶλλον, εἶπεν ὁ Σωκράτης, τῶν ἐν Ὀλυμπίᾳ
μελλόντων ἀγωνιεῖσθαι· ἢ δοκεῖ σοι μῑκρὸς εἶναι ὁ περὶ τῆς ψῡχῆς πρὸς τοὺς πολεμίους
5 ἀγών, ὃν οἱ Ἀθηναῖοι φιλοῦσι ποιεῖν; καὶ οὐκ ὀλίγοι μὲν διὰ τὴν τοῦ σώματος καχεξίᾱν
ἀποθνήσκουσιν ἐν τοῖς πολεμίοις κινδόνοις, πολλοὶ δὲ δι' αὐτὸ τοῦτο ζῶντές θ'
ἁλίσκονται καὶ ἁλόντες ἢ δουλεύουσι διὰ τοῦ βίου ἢ ἐκτίνουσι τοσαύτᾱς δραχμὰς ὥστε
ἐνδεεῖς τῶν ἀναγκαίων ὄντες καὶ κακῶς πράττοντες ζῶσι· πολλοὶ δὲ δόξαν αἰσχρὰν
κομίζονται διὰ τὴν τοῦ σώματος καχεξίᾱν δοκοῦντες ἀποδειλιᾶν. ἢ καταφρονεῖς τῶν
10 ἐπιτῑμίων τῆς καχεξίᾱς τούτων, καὶ ῥᾳδίως φέρεις τὰ τοιαῦτα;

VOCABULARY

Ἐπιγένην (line 1): from Ἐπιγένης, -ους, ὁ: Epigenes, a young Athenian (Ἐπιγένην,
    borrowed from 1st decl., is used as acc. sg. in place of the expected Ἐπιγένη)
ἔχοντα (line 1): here = "maintaining"
ἰδιωτικῶς (line 2): in the manner of a private citizen (*from* ἰδιωτικός, -ή, -όν: private),
    i.e., unprofessionally, not like a trained athlete
ἔχεις (line 2): here = "you are maintaining"
ἰδιώτης (line 3): from ἰδιώτης, -ου, ὁ: private citizen, a non-professional
οὐδέν...μᾶλλον (line 3): [you are] not at all more [non-professional], i.e., as an
    Athenian citizen, who may be called upon to fight in time of war, you are
    no less professional an athlete than (+ *gen.*) (οὐδέν = *acc. neut. sg. used as
    adv.;* μᾶλλον = *comparative degree of the adv.* μάλα)
Ὀλυμπίᾳ (line 4): from Ὀλυμπίᾱ, -ᾱς, ἡ: Olympia, sanctuary of Zeus in southern
    Greece, site of the ancient Olympic Games
ἀγωνιεῖσθαι (line 4): from ἀγωνίζομαι, ἀγωνιοῦμαι, ἠγωνισάμην, —, ἠγώνισμαι,
    ἠγωνίσθην: compete

δοκεῖ (line 4): from δοκέω, δόξω, ἔδοξα, —, δέδογμαι, ἐδόχθην: seem (*the subject of*
    δοκεῖ *is* ἀγών *in line* 5)
εἶναι (line 4): complementary infinitive with δοκεῖ
Ἀθηναῖοι (line 5): from Ἀθηναῖος, -ᾱ, -ον: Athenian
καχεξίᾱν (line 6): καχεξίᾱ, -ᾱς, ἡ: bad condition
ἁλίσκονται (line 7): from ἁλίσκομαι, ἁλώσομαι, ἑάλων, ἑάλωκα, —, —: be captured
ἁλόντες (line 7): aorist participle of ἁλίσκομαι (*active in form, passive in meaning*)
ἐκτίνουσι (line 8): from ἐκτίνω, ἐκτείσω, ἐξέτεισα, ἐκτέτεικα, ἐκτέτεισμαι, ἐξετείσθην:
    pay out (*for their ransom*)
ἐνδεεῖς (line 8): from ἐνδεής, -ές (+ *gen.*): lacking, in want (of)
ἀναγκαίων (line 8): from ἀναγκαῖος, -ᾱ, -ον: necessary; (*as a plural substantive*) neces-
    sities
δοκοῦντες (line 10): see note on δοκεῖ (line 4)
ἀποδειλιᾶν (line 10): from ἀποδειλιάω, ἀποδειλιάσω, —, —, —, —: be a
    coward
καταφρονεῖς (line 10): from καταφρονέω, καταφρονήσω, κατεφρόνησα,
    καταπεφρόνηκα, καταπεφρόνημαι, κατεφρονήθην (+ *gen.*): think little (of)
ἐπιτῑμίων (line 10): from ἐπιτῑμιον, -ου, τό: penalty
τούτων (line 11): goes with τῶν ἐπιτῑμίων (line 10)

LESSON 32

COMPARATIVE AND SUPERLATIVE DEGREES OF ADJECTIVES AND ADVERBS; GENITIVE OF COMPARISON; PARTITIVE GENITIVE

αἱ δεύτεραί πως φροντίδες σοφώτεραι
(The second thoughts are somehow wiser.)
—Phaedra's nurse reconsiders in Euripides' *Hippolytus* 436

195.   Up to now, all of the Greek adjectives and adverbs presented to you have been in the **positive degree**, i.e., in their basic form (e.g., *wise, wisely*). The **comparative degree** is a form of the adjective or adverb indicating a higher **or** a rather high degree of what is denoted by the basic form (e.g., *wiser, more wise, rather wise; more wisely, rather wisely*). The **superlative degree** is a form of the adjective or adverb indicating the highest **or** a very high degree of what is denoted by the basic form (e.g., *wisest, most wise, very wise; most wisely, very wisely*). In English the comparative and superlative degrees are used only in contexts of **comparison** (*-er, -est, more, most*), but in Greek they are also used to show **intensity** (*rather, very*), without regard to any comparison.

196.   Like English, Greek may form the comparative degree with an **adverb** meaning "more" (μᾶλλον), the superlative degree with an adverb meaning "most" (μάλιστα). The modified adjective or adverb remains in the positive degree. Examples: μᾶλλον σοφός, -ή, -όν "more wise"; μᾶλλον σοφῶς "more wisely"; μάλιστα σοφός, -ή, -όν "most wise"; μάλιστα σοφῶς "most wisely." The comparative and superlative degrees of **participles** are always created in this way (e.g., μᾶλλον βεβλαμμένοι "more harmed"; μάλιστα βεβλαμμένοι "most harmed").

With an adjective that is *not* a participle, the normal method is to add a special **suffix** to the adjective's basic stem. The **comparative** degree uses the suffix **-τερος, -τερᾱ, -τερον** (with regular -ος, -ᾱ, -ον endings); the **superlative** degree uses **-τατος, -τατη, -τατον** (with regular -ος, -η, -ον endings). The accent persists, if possible, on the syllable before the suffix.

In **first/second-declension adjectives** a vowel must be inserted between the basic stem (i.e., the part of the word left over after removing -ος, -ᾱ/-η, -ον) and the special suffix. That vowel is an **omicron** if the preceding syllable has a diphthong, a naturally long vowel, or a short vowel followed by two consonants (e.g., κοινότερος, κοινότατος; δηλότερος, δηλότατος; μακρότερος, μακρότατος); it is an **omega** if the preceding syllable has a short vowel not followed by two consonants (e.g., σοφώτερος, σοφώτατος).

In **third-declension adjectives** whose stems end in a **sigma**, that σ and the τ of the suffix directly meet (e.g., ἀληθέστερος, ἀληθέστατος). **Third-declension adjectives** whose stems end in a **nasal** add -εστερος, -εστερᾱ, -εστερον as if they were σ-stems (e.g., εὐδαιμονέστερος, εὐδαιμονέστατος).

The **comparative** degree of an **adverb** is simply the **neuter accusative singular** of the corresponding comparative adjective (e.g., κοινότερον, δηλότερον, μακρότερον, σοφώτερον). The **superlative** degree of an **adverb** is simply the **neuter accusative plural** of the corresponding superlative adjective (e.g., κοινότατα, δηλότατα, μακρότατα, σοφώτατα).

197.   Listed below are all the previously introduced adjectives that form their comparative and superlative predictably. You can assume that the adverb derived from each adjective also has regular comparative and superlative degrees.

ἀθάνατος, -ον	ἀθανατώτερος, -ᾱ, -ον	ἀθανατώτατος, -η, -ον
αἴτιος, -ᾱ, -ον	αἰτιώτερος, -ᾱ, -ον	αἰτιώτατος, -η, -ον
ἀληθής, -ές	ἀληθέστερος, -ᾱ, -ον	ἀληθέστατος, -η, -ον
ἀνάξιος, -ον	ἀναξιώτερος, -ᾱ, -ον	ἀναξιώτατος, -η, -ον
ἄξιος, -ᾱ, -ον	ἀξιώτερος, -ᾱ, -ον	ἀξιώτατος, -η, -ον
δῆλος, -η, -ον	δηλότερος, -ᾱ, -ον	δηλότατος, -η, -ον
δοῦλος, -η, -ον	δουλότερος, -ᾱ, -ον	δουλότατος, -η, -ον
ἐλεύθερος, -ᾱ, -ον	ἐλευθερώτερος, -ᾱ, -ον	ἐλευθερώτατος, -η, -ον
Ἑλληνικός, -ή, -όν	Ἑλληνικώτερος, -ᾱ, -ον	Ἑλληνικώτατος, -η, -ον
εὐδαίμων, -ον	εὐδαιμονέστερος, -ᾱ, -ον	εὐδαιμονέστατος, -η, -ον
κοινός, -ή, -όν	κοινότερος, -ᾱ, -ον	κοινότατος, -η, -ον
μακρός, -ᾱ́, -όν	μακρότερος, -ᾱ, -ον	μακρότατος, -η, -ον
μῑκρός, -ᾱ́, -όν	μῑκρότερος, -ᾱ, -ον	μῑκρότατος, -η, -ον
μόνος, -η, -ον	μονώτερος, -ᾱ, -ον	μονώτατος, -η, -ον
νέος, -ᾱ, -ον	νεώτερος, -ᾱ, -ον	νεώτατος, -η, -ον

πολέμιος, -ᾱ, -ον	πολεμιώτερος, -ᾱ, -ον	πολεμιώτατος, -η, -ον
σοφός, -ή, -όν	σοφώτερος, -ᾱ, -ον	σοφώτατος, -η, -ον
τυφλός, -ή, -όν	τυφλότερος, -ᾱ, -ον	τυφλότατος, -η, -ον
φιλόσοφος, -ον	φιλοσοφώτερος, -ᾱ, -ον	φιλοσοφώτατος, -η, -ον

The following adjectives form their comparative and superlative degrees with the regular suffixes -τερος, -ᾱ, -ον and -τατος, -η, -ον, but **drop the preceding o**:

παλαιός, -ά, -όν	παλαίτερος, -ᾱ, -ον	παλαίτατος, -η, -ον
φίλος, -η, -ον	φίλτερος, -ᾱ, -ον **or**	φίλτατος, -η, -ον **or**
	φιλαίτερος, -ᾱ, -ον	φιλαίτατος, -η, -ον

The adjective **πρότερος, -ᾱ, -ον** is actually a comparative, derived from the adverb πρό ("before"); its superlative is **πρῶτος, -η, -ον**:

[πρό (*adv.*) "before"]
πρότερος, -ᾱ, -ον "former," "earlier"
πρῶτος, -η, -ον "first," "earliest"

NOTE   Adjective/pronouns such as αὐτός, εἷς, ἐκεῖνος, ὅδε, οὗτος, πᾶς, τοιόσδε, τοιοῦτος, τοσόσδε, and τοσοῦτος and adverbs not derived from adjectives (μή, νῦν, οὐ, πότε, τότε, etc.) rarely, if ever, occur in the comparative or superlative degree.

198.   A comparative adjective or adverb may be followed by the conjunction **ἤ**, meaning "**than**"; if so, the nouns or pronouns denoting the people or objects being compared will all be in the **same case**. Alternatively, a comparative adjective or adverb may simply be placed near a noun or pronoun in the **genitive case** (with no ἤ); the reader must infer from the presence of a comparative word that the noun or pronoun in the genitive denotes the people or objects to which others are being compared. This construction is called the **genitive of comparison**. Example:

" I wish to know whether anyone is wiser than Socrates"
can be expressed in either of the following ways:

βούλομαι εἰδέναι εἴ τίς ἐστι σοφώτερος **ἢ ὁ Σωκράτης**.
or   βούλομαι εἰδέναι εἴ τίς ἐστι σοφώτερος **τοῦ Σωκράτους**.

199.   With a **comparative or a superlative** adjective or adverb, a **partitive genitive** is often used to identify the whole group from which a part is being singled out: e.g., ὑμῶν ἡ σοφωτέρᾱ ("the wiser of you [two]"); οἱ σοφώτατοι τῶν Ἑλλήνων ("the wisest of the Greeks"). A partitive genitive may also be used with pronouns, substantives, and numerals (e.g., τίς ἡμῶν "which of us?"; ὀλίγοι τῶν ῥητόρων "few of the orators"; ἓν τούτων τῶν δώρων "one of these gifts"). Notice that a partitive genitive may come either before or after the word it modifies, but is normally **not** in the attributive position.

200.   Placing the particle ὡς or ὅτι in front of a **superlative** adjective or adverb makes it express the highest degree possible: e.g., ὡς σοφωτάτη ἡ βουλὴ ἦν ("the plan was the wisest possible"); ζῆ ὅτι σοφώτατα ("live as wisely as possible!").

201.   **VOCABULARY**

γίγνομαι, γενήσομαι, ἐγενόμην, γέγονα, γεγένημαι, —
                    be born, become, happen

NOTE   You would not expect a middle deponent verb to have any active forms, but γίγνομαι does have one: the perfect active γέγονα, which is virtually synonymous with the perfect middle γεγένημαι ("I have been born" or "I am"). Both τὰ γεγονότα and τὰ γεγενημένα can mean "the past" (literally, "the things having happened"). Forms of γίγνομαι are often combined with a predicate noun/adjective (e.g., γίγνεται βασιλεύς "he is [born] a king"; γενοῦ εὐδαίμων "be[come] happy!"). Notice that the translation "be" may be preferable to the literal rendering "be born" or "become."

σῴζω, σώσω, ἔσωσα, σέσωκα, σέσωσμαι or σέσωμαι, ἐσώθην
                    save, bring safely (to) [cf. *creosote*]

δεινός, -ή, -όν   terrible, dreadful, marvelous, clever
                    [cf. *dinosaur, dinothere*]

λοιπός, -ή, -όν   remaining, rest; τοῦ λοιποῦ (χρόνου) = in
                    the future; καὶ τὰ λοιπά (*abbreviated*
                    κτλ.) = etc.; (*no comp. or superl.*) (*adv.*
                    λοιπόν "as for the rest")

πρῶτος, -η, -ον   (*superl. adj.*) first, earliest (*adv.* πρῶτον/
                    πρῶτα) [cf. *protocol, proton,*
                    protoplasm]

μάλιστα   (*superl. adv.*) most

μᾶλλον   (*comp. adv.*) more, rather

ἤ   (*conj. following a comparative*) than

μήν   (*postpositive particle*) surely, yet,
                    however

NOTE   The combinations ἀλλὰ μήν ("but yet") and καὶ μήν ("and surely" or "and yet," depending on the context) are used to introduce a new point or topic.

ὡς or ὅτι   (*particle preceding and strengthening a*
                    superlative) as...as possible

202.   EXERCISES

A.   Greek-to-English Sentences

1. πῶς σωθήσεται τὰ λοιπὰ δένδρα, ὦ ἄνδρες, τὰ ἤδη γεγονότα παλαίτερα;

2. ἐπεὶ ἐγένου εἷς τῶν πρυτάνεων, ὦ φίλτατε ἄδελφέ μου, μῶν ἤλλαξας καὶ τοὺς σεαυτοῦ τρόπους τοὺς ἀγαθούς;

3. τῆσδε τῆς ἑσπέρᾱς τοσοῦτος θόρυβος ἐγένετο ἐν τῷ ἄστει ὥστε αἰσχρῶς ἐφύγομεν, οὐκ ἀκούοντες οὐδενός.

4. εὖ διδαχθείς, ἠρώτησέ τις τῶν νέων μαθητῶν τοιάδε· Τοῦ λοιποῦ ἕξομεν διδασκάλους σοφωτέρους ἢ τοὺς πρώτους;

5. ἀλλὰ μὴν οἶδα τόδ’· ἐκείνου τοῦ λέοντος οὐδὲν ζῷον δεινότερόν ἐστιν.

6. καίπερ ζῶντες ὅτι Ἑλληνικώτατα, οὔποτ’ ἀληθῶς ἐσόμεθα Ἕλληνες.

7. καὶ μὴν τίνες ἐλευθερώτερον ζῶσιν ἢ ὑμεῖς, ὑπὸ τῶν θεῶν ἀεὶ φιλούμενοι μᾶλλον τῶν ἄλλων ἀνθρώπων;

8. ὡς ῥᾳδίως, ὦ ῥῆτορ, σέσωκας τούτοις τοῖς σοφοῖς λόγοις τὴν πόλιν τήν τε παλαιτάτην καὶ μάλιστα πεφιλημένην ἡμῖν.

9. τῶν λοιπῶν εἰς πατρίδα σωθέντων, ὁ μακρότερος πόλεμος ἐπαύσατο.

10. τίς ἀξιωτέρᾱ σου, ὦ μῆτερ, γίγνεται; οὐδεμία ἔμοιγε φιλαιτέρᾱ ποτ’ ἔσται.

B.   English-to-Greek Sentences

1. No one of the earliest philosophers is dearer than Socrates, for he knew how to live as sincerely as possible.

2. And yet, although very dreadful things are happening in the city (*use genitive absolute*), hope of a happier day remains.

3. Bring our daughter safely back to Greece, O most honored gods, and in the future do not send her away from us!

4. They asked the wisest (*pl.*) of the heralds whether the rather old roads were longer than the new (roads).

5. Have you become blinder than a stone, my husband? So clear is your mistake that I myself see it.

C. READING

WHY EPIGENES SHOULD SHAPE UP — Part 2
(adapted from Xenophon's *Memorabilia* 3.12)

Socrates' dialogue with Epigenes turns into a full-blown lecture on the advantages of staying in shape and the disadvantages of not.

καὶ μὴν ὑγιεινοτέρᾱ τε καὶ εἰς τὰ ἄλλα χρησιμωτέρᾱ ἐστὶν ἡ εὐεξίᾱ τῆς κακεξίᾱς. ἢ τῶν διὰ τὴν εὐεξίᾱν γιγνομένων καταφρονεῖς; καὶ γὰρ ὑγιαίνουσιν οἱ τὰ σώματα εὖ ἔχοντες καὶ ἰσχύουσι· καὶ πολλοὶ μὲν διὰ τοῦτ’ ἐκ τῶν πολεμίων ἀγώνων σῴζονταί τ’ εὐσχημόνως καὶ τὰ δεινὰ πάντα φεύγουσι, πολλοὶ δὲ τούς

5   τε φίλους καὶ τὴν πατρίδα ὠφελοῦσι καὶ δόξαν μεγάλην κομίζονται καὶ τόν τε λοιπὸν βίον ὅτι εὐδαιμονέστατα ζῶσι καὶ τοῖς ἑαυτῶν παισὶ καλὰς ἀφορμὰς εἰς τὸν βίον καταλείπουσιν. πρὸς πάντα γὰρ ἃ πράττουσιν ἄνθρωποι χρήσιμον τὸ σῶμά ἐστιν· ἐν πάσαις δὲ ταῖς τοῦ σώματος χρείαις πολὺ διαφέρει ἡ εὐεξίᾱ τοῦ σώματος. καὶ γὰρ ἐν τῷ διανοεῖσθαι, ἐν ᾧ μῑκροτάτη σώματος χρείᾱ εἶναι

10   φαίνεται, πολλοὶ μεγάλα σφάλλονται διότι τὰ σώματα κακῶς ἔχουσιν.

VOCABULARY

ὑγιεινοτέρᾱ (line 1): from ὑγιεινός, -ή, -όν: healthy
εἰς (line 1): here = "for"
χρησιμωτέρᾱ (line 1): from χρήσιμος, -η, -ον: useful
εὐεξίᾱ (line 1): from εὐεξίᾱ, -ᾱς, ἡ: good condition
κακεξίᾱς (line 2): from κακεξίᾱ, -ᾱς, ἡ: bad condition
καταφρονεῖς (line 2): from καταφρονέω, καταφρονήσω, κατεφρόνησα,
    καταπεφρόνηκα, καταπεφρόνημαι, κατεφρονήθην (+ *gen.*): think little (of)
ὑγιαίνουσιν (line 2): from ὑγιαίνω, ὑγιανῶ, ὑγίᾱνα, —, —, —: be healthy
ἔχοντες (line 3): here = "maintaining"
ἰσχύουσι (line 3): from ἰσχύω, ἰσχύσω, ἴσχῡσα, ἴσχῡκα, —, —: be strong
εὐσχημόνως (line 4): from εὐσχήμων, -ον: dignified, respectable
ζῶσι (line 6): here = "live out" (direct object = τόν...λοιπὸν βίον)
ἀφορμάς (line 6): from ἀφορμή, -ῆς, ἡ: starting-point, resource
εἰς (line 6): here = "for"
καταλείπουσιν (line 7): leave behind, bequeath
πρός (line 7): here = "in regard to"
χρήσιμον (line 7): see note on χρησιμωτέρᾱ (line 1)
χρείαις (line 8): from χρείᾱ, -ᾱς, ἡ: use, function
διαφέρει (line 8): from διαφέρω (= δια- + φέρω): differ, make a difference
τῷ διανοεῖσθαι (line 9): the process of thinking (*verbal noun made by combining the
    definite article with the infinitive of* διανοέομαι, διανοήσομαι, —, —, διανενόημαι,
    διενοήθην: think)

χρείᾱ (line 9): see note on χρείαις (line 8)

φαίνεται (line 10): from φαίνω, φανῶ, ἔφηνα, πέφηνα or πέφαγκα, πέφασμαι, ἐφάνην or ἐφάνθην: show; (*mid.*) appear

σφάλλονται (line 10): from σφάλλω, σφαλῶ, ἔσφηλα, ἔσφαλκα, ἔσφαλμαι, ἐσφάλην: trip up (*in wrestling*), overthrow

διότι (line 10): contraction of διὰ τοῦθ' ὅτι

ἔχουσιν (line 10): here = "they maintain"

LESSON 33

IRREGULAR COMPARATIVE AND SUPERLATIVE DEGREES OF ADJECTIVES AND ADVERBS; -υς, -εια, -υ ADJECTIVES; DATIVE OF DEGREE OF DIFFERENCE

ὡς οὐδὲν γλύκιον ἧς πατρίδος οὐδὲ τοκήων / γίγνεται
(Nothing is sweeter than one's own country or parents.)
—Odysseus speaks from experience in Homer's *Odyssey* 9.34-35

203.   Certain Greek adjectives form their comparative and superlative degrees irregularly. Not only do they use a **different stem** from that of the positive degree, but they also add **different suffixes**: **-ἳων, -ῑον** (or **-ων, -ον**) for the **comparative** (with the endings of a third-declension nasal-stem adjective), **-ιστος, -η, -ον** for the **superlative** (with the endings of a first/second-declension adjective).

ἀγαθός, -ή, -όν "good"	βελτίων, -ῑον "better (*morally*)"	βέλτιστος, -η, -ον "best (*morally*)"
or	ἀμείνων, -ον "better (*in ability/worth*)"	ἄριστος, -η, -ον "best (*in ability/worth*)"
or	κρείττων, -ον "better (*in might*)," "stronger"	κράτιστος, -η, -ον "best (*in might*)," "strongest"
κακός, -ή, -όν "bad"	κακῑων, -ῑον "worse (*morally*)"	κάκιστος, -η, -ον "worst (*morally*)"
or	χείρων, -ον "worse (*in ability/worth*)"	χείριστος, -η, -ον "worst (*in ability/worth*)"
or	ἥττων, -ον "worse (*in might*)," "weaker," "less"	ἥκιστος, -η, -ον[1] "worst (*in might*)," "weakest," "least"

---

[1] ἥκιστος, -η, -ον is rare, but its adverb ἥκιστα ("least of all") is common.

καλός, -ή, -όν "beautiful," "fine"	καλλίων, -ῑον "more beautiful," "finer"	κάλλιστος, -η, -ον "most beautiful," "finest"
μέγας, μεγάλη, μέγα "great," "large"	μείζων, -ον "greater," "larger"	μέγιστος, -η, -ον "greatest," "largest"
πολύς, πολλή, πολύ "much," "many"	πλείων (or πλέων), -ον "more"	πλεῖστος, -η, -ον "most"
μῑκρός, -ά, -όν "small"	**or** μῑκρότερος, -α, -ον ἐλάττων, -ον "smaller"	μῑκρότατος, -η, -ον ἐλάχιστος, -η, -ον "smallest"
ὀλίγος, -η, -ον "little," "few"	ἐλάττων, -ον "less," "fewer"	ὀλίγιστος, -η, -ον "least," "fewest"
ῥᾴδιος, -ᾱ, -ον "easy"	ῥᾴων, -ον "easier"	ῥᾷστος, -η, -ον "easiest"

NOTE   Some of the irregular comparatives that now lack an iota originally had one: e.g., ἀμεν-ῑων → ἀμείνων; κρετ-ῑων → κρείττων; ἡκ-ῑων → ἥττων; χερ-ῑων → χείρων; μεγ-ῑων → μείζων; ἐλαχ-ῑων → ἐλάττων.

Adjectives ending in -ρος, -ρᾱ, -ρον **drop the ρ** (which was actually *added* to their basic stem to form the positive degree) before adding -ῑων, -ῑον and -ιστος, -η, -ον to form the comparative and superlative degrees:

αἰσχρός, -ά, -όν	αἰσχίων, -ῑον	αἴσχιστος, -η, -ον
ἐχθρός, -ά, -όν	ἐχθίων, -ῑον	ἔχθιστος, -η, -ον

The **adverbs** corresponding to irregular comparative and superlative adjectives are derived in predictable ways: the **neuter accusative singular** of the comparative adjective serves as the comparative adverb (e.g., κάλλῑον "more beautifully"); the **neuter accusative plural** of the superlative adjective serves as the superlative adverb (e.g., κάλλιστα "most beautifully"). **μᾶλλον** and **μάλιστα** are the comparative and superlative of **μάλα**, an adverb meaning "very" or "much."

204.   All of the irregular comparative adjectives listed above are declined like εὐδαίμων, -ον, but **contractions** are common. In the following paradigm of βελτῑων, -ῑον, the contracted forms are given in parentheses:

Singular:	Masc./Fem.		Neut.
Nom.	βελτῑων		βέλτῑον
Gen.	βελτῑονος		βελτῑονος
Dat.	βελτῑονι		βελτῑονι
Acc.	βελτῑονα	(βελτῑω)	βέλτῑον
Voc.	βέλτῑον		βέλτῑον

Plural:	Masc./Fem.		Neut.	
Nom./Voc.	βελτίονες	(βελτίους)	βελτίονα	(βελτίω)
Gen.	βελτιόνων		βελτιόνων	
Dat.	βελτίοσι(ν)		βελτίοσι(ν)	
Acc.	βελτίονας	(βελτίους)	βελτίονα	(βελτίω)

As you can see, there are just two contracted endings to remember: -ω (= -ονα) and -ους (= -ονες; the masc./fem. acc. pl. borrows the contracted ending -ους from the masc./fem. nom./voc. pl. rather than contracting -ονας to -ως). The accent in the masc./fem. voc. sg. and the neuter nom./acc./voc. sg. is unusual in being **recessive**; all the other forms have the **persistent** accent typical of adjectives, here based on the location of the accent in the masc./fem. nom. sg. When contraction occurs, the accent stays where it was in the uncontracted form.

205.   You have already met adjectives of **mixed declension** (e.g., πᾶς, πᾶσα, πᾶν, the aorist passive participle, all active participles). Adjectives in -υς, -εια, -υ are also of this type. Here is the paradigm of ἡδύς, -εῖα, -ύ ("sweet"):

	Singular:			Plural:		
	Masc.	**Fem.**	**Neut.**	**Masc.**	**Fem.**	**Neut.**
Nom.	ἡδύς	ἡδεῖα	ἡδύ	ἡδεῖς (= ἡδέες)	ἡδεῖαι	ἡδέα
Gen.	ἡδέος	ἡδείᾱς	ἡδέος	ἡδέων	ἡδειῶν	ἡδέων
Dat.	ἡδεῖ	ἡδείᾳ	ἡδεῖ	ἡδέσι(ν)	ἡδείαις	ἡδέσι(ν)
Acc.	ἡδύν	ἡδεῖαν	ἡδύ	ἡδεῖς (= nom.)	ἡδείᾱς	ἡδέα
Voc.	ἡδύ	ἡδεῖα	ἡδύ	ἡδεῖς (= nom.)	ἡδεῖαι	ἡδέα

In the masculine and neuter forms, the stem ends in υ or ε. In the feminine forms, ἡδευ- became ἡδεϝ-, to which -ια was added; later the digamma disappeared. The masc. acc. pl. borrows the form of the masc. nom./voc. pl. Adjectives like ἡδύς often have comparatives in -ῑων, -ῑον and superlatives in -ιστος, -η, -ον: **ἡδίων, -ῑον; ἥδιστος, -η, -ον.**

206.   When a comparison is being drawn, there are two possible ways to show the degree of difference between the items being compared: with an **adverb** modifying the comparative word (e.g., πολὺ ἡδίων σοῦ εἰμι "I am much sweeter than you") or with a **dative of degree of difference**, i.e., a noun (or a neuter singular adjective) in the dative case, added to the sentence to make the comparison more precise (e.g., πολλῷ ἡδίων σοῦ εἰμι "I am [by] much sweeter than you"; πολλαῖς ἡμέραις πρότερον ἀφῑκόμην "I arrived [by] many days earlier").

207.   VOCABULARY

ἀγαθός, -ή, -όν; *comp.* **βελτίων, -ῑον**; *superl.* **βέλτιστος, -η, -ον**
                    good (*morally*), virtuous

ἀγαθός, -ή, -όν; *comp.* **ἀμείνων, -ον**; *superl.* **ἄριστος, -η, -ον**
                    good (*in ability/worth*)

ἀγαθός, -ή, -όν; *comp.* **κρείττων, -ον**; *superl.* **κράτιστος, -η, -ον**
                    good (*in might*), strong

αἰσχρός, -ά, -όν; *comp.* **αἰσχίων, -ῑον**; *superl.* **αἴσχιστος, -η, -ον**
                    shameful, disgraceful

ἐχθρός, -ά, -όν; *comp.* **ἐχθίων, -ῑον**; *superl.* **ἔχθιστος, -η, -ον**
                    hateful, hostile

ἡδύς, -εῖα, -ύ; *comp.* **ἡδίων, -ῑον**; *superl.* **ἥδιστος, -η, -ον**
                    sweet, pleasant

κακός, -ή, -όν; *comp.* **κακίων, -ῑον**; *superl.* **κάκιστος, -η, -ον**
                    bad (*morally*), wicked

κακός, -ή, -όν; *comp.* **χείρων, -ον**; *superl.* **χείριστος, -η, -ον**
                    bad (*in ability/worth*)

κακός, -ή, -όν; *comp.* **ἥττων, -ον**; *superl.* **ἥκιστος, -η, -ον** (*superl. adv.*
        ἥκιστα = least of all)
                    bad (*in might*), weak

καλός, -ή, -όν; *comp.* **καλλίων, -ῑον**; *superl.* **κάλλιστος, -η, -ον**
                    beautiful, fine

μέγας, μεγάλη, μέγα; *comp.* **μείζων, -ον**; *superl.* **μέγιστος, -η, -ον**
                    great, large

μῑκρός, -ά, -όν; *comp.* **ἐλάττων, -ον**; *superl.* **ἐλάχιστος, -η, -ον**
                    small, little

ὀλίγος, -η, -ον; *comp.* **ἐλάττων, -ον**; *superl.* **ὀλίγιστος, -η, -ον**
                    little; (*pl.*) few

πολύς, πολλή, πολύ; *comp.* **πλείων** (or **πλέων**), **-ον**; *superl.* **πλεῖστος, -η, -ον**
                    much; (*pl.*) many

ῥᾴδιος, -ᾱ, -ον; *comp.* **ῥᾴων, -ον**; *superl.* **ῥᾷστος, -η, -ον**
                    easy

μάλα (*adv.*); *comp.* **μᾶλλον**; *superl.* **μάλιστα**
                    very, much

208.   **EXERCISES**

A.   Greek-to-English Sentences

1. τοῦ μακροῦ πολέμου παυθέντος, ὅτι μάλιστα χαίρομεν τῇ ἡδείᾳ εἰρήνῃ.

2. ἐν τῇ ἄλλῃ χώρᾳ, ὦ φίλτατε υἱέ, ὄψῃ κάλλιστά τε φυτὰ καὶ μέγιστα ζῷα.

3. δι' ἐκεῖνο τὸ αἴσχιστον ἔργον οἱ μάλα κακοὶ δεσπόται γεγένηνται ἡμῖν ἐχθίονες (or ἐχθίους).

4. ἆρ' οὔκ εἰμι εὐδαιμονεστέρᾱ τοῦ ἀδελφοῦ μου ᾧ ὀλίγιστοι φίλοι εἰσίν;

5. οὕτως ἡδέως λέγουσιν οἱ ῥήτορες ὥστε μηδέν' ἔχειν παύεσθαι ἀκούοντα.

6. καίπερ σοῦ πολλῷ ἀμείνονος ὄντος, παρὰ δόξαν στρατηγὸς ἐκρίθην.

7. οὐδείς ἐστιν ἀξιώτερος θανάτου ἢ ὁ ἀποκτείνᾱς τοὺς ἀρίστους ἄνδρας.

8. ἡμεῖς ἐπὶ τὴν μείζονα (or μείζω) πόλιν ἀφῑκόμεθα ὀλίγαις ἡμέραις πρότερον τῶν λοιπῶν.

9. πολὺ ῥᾷον διδάσκω τοὺς ὑπ' ἐμοῦ διδάσκεσθαι βουλομένους μαθητάς.

10. ὅδ' ὁ θησαυρός, ἅτε ὀλίγῳ μῑκρότερος τῶν ἄλλων ὤ'ν, ἔλαττον τῑμᾶται.

B.   English-to-Greek Sentences

1. The gods have sent to us no sweeter gift than a very good friend.

2. Do not fear that most evil thief, for the guard pursuing him is (*use a form of* γίγνομαι) much stronger than he.

3. I said to the assembly, "No one is worse than this general, and the deeds of no one are more shameful."

4. Was the orator who had more drachmas and a better house a little worthier or greater than the rest?

5. They asked the best philosopher, "How shall we live so as to be hurt least of all and by as few enemies as possible?".

C.   READING

WHY EPIGENES SHOULD SHAPE UP — Part 3;
WHY A WALK TO OLYMPIA IS NO SWEAT
(adapted from Xenophon's *Memorabilia* 3.12-13)

*Below is the conclusion to Socrates' chat with Epigenes, followed by another bit of
Socratic wisdom from the next section in the **Memorabilia**.*

μὴ δ᾽ αἰσχρῶς γήρασκε, ὦ Ἐπίγενες, διὰ τὴν ἀμέλειαν. ἆρ᾽ οὐ βούλῃ
κάλλιστον καὶ κράτιστον τὸ σαυτοῦ σῶμα ἰδεῖν; τοῦτο δ᾽ οὐκ ἔχεις ἰδεῖν ἀμελῶν·
οὐδὲν γὰρ τοιοῦτον γίγνεται αὐτόματον. [**end of conversation**]

Φοβουμένου δέ τινος τὴν εἰς Ὀλυμπίαν ὁδόν, Τί, ἀπεκρίνατο ὁ Σωκράτης,
5   φοβῇ τὴν μακρὰν πορείᾱν; οὐ γὰρ σχεδὸν πᾶσαν τὴν ἡμέρᾱν περιπατεῖς καὶ
οἴκοι καὶ ἐκεῖσε πορευόμενος; περιπατήσᾱς ἀριστᾷς, περιπατήσᾱς δειπνεῖς καὶ
ἀναπαύῃ. ἐκτείνων οὖν πάντας τοὺς περιπάτους οὓς Ἀθήνησιν ἐν πέντε ἢ ἓξ
ἡμέραις περιπατεῖς, ῥᾳδίως Ἀθήνηθεν εἰς Ὀλυμπίαν ἀφίξῃ. καὶ μὴν ἥδῑον ἔσται
ἐξορμᾶν πρότερον ἡμέρᾳ μιᾷ ἢ ὑστερίζειν. μὴ μὲν οὖν μήκῡνε μακρότερον τοῦ
10   μετρίου τὰς ὁδούς, πορεύου δὲ μιᾷ ἡμέρᾳ πλείονας ὁδούς. κρεῖττον γὰρ ἔσται ἐν
τῇ ὁρμῇ σπεύδειν ἢ ἐν τῇ ὁδῷ.

VOCABULARY

γήρασκε (line 1): from γηράσκω, γηράσομαι, ἐγήρᾱσα, γεγήρᾱκα, —, —: grow old
Ἐπίγενες (line 1): from Ἐπιγένης, -ους, ὁ: Epigenes
ἀμέλειαν (line 1): from ἀμέλεια, -ᾱς, ἡ: negligence
ἀμελῶν (line 2): from ἀμελέω, ἀμελήσω, ἠμέλησα, ἠμέληκα, ἠμέλημαι,
ἠμελήθην: be negligent (*participle with conditional force—"if"*)
αὐτόματον (line 3): from αὐτόματος, -η, -ον: self-acting, automatic (*predicate adjective
that may be translated as if it were an adverb*)
Ὀλυμπίᾱν (line 4): from Ὀλυμπίᾱ, -ᾱς, ἡ: Olympia
πορείᾱν (line 5): from πορείᾱ, -ᾱς, ἡ: journey
σχεδόν (line 5): nearly (*adv.*)
περιπατεῖς (line 5): from περιπατέω, περιπατήσω, περιεπάτησα, περιπεπάτηκα,
περιπεπάτημαι, περιεπατήθην: walk around
οἴκοι (line 6): at home (*adv.*)
ἐκεῖσε (line 6): to there (*adv.*)
πορευόμενος (line 6): from πορεύω, πορεύσω, ἐπόρευσα, πεπόρευκα, πεπόρευμαι,
ἐπορεύθην: make go, carry; (*mid./pass.*) go, journey
περιπατήσᾱς (line 6): see note on περιπατεῖς (line 5)
ἀριστᾷς (line 6): from ἀριστάω, ἀριστήσω, ἠρίστησα, ἠρίστηκα, ἠρίστημαι, ἠριστήθην:
eat lunch

δειπνεῖς (line 6): from δειπνέω, δειπνήσω, ἐδείπνησα, δεδείπνηκα, δεδείπνημαι,
     ἐδειπνήθην: eat dinner

ἀναπαύῃ (line 7): from ἀναπαύω: stop, bring to a stop; (*mid.*) take a rest

ἐκτείνων (line 7): from ἐκτείνω, ἐκτενῶ, ἐξέτεινα, ἐκτέτακα, ἐκτέταμαι, ἐξετάθην: stretch
     out, i.e., string together (*conditional ptcple.*—"if")

περιπάτους (line 7): from περίπατος, -ου, ὁ: a walking around, a walk

οὕς (line 7): cognate accusative with περιπατεῖς in line 8 ("the walks which you
     walk [i.e., which you take]")

Ἀθήνησιν (line 7): at Athens (*adv.*)

πέντε (line 7): five (*indeclinable numeral*)

ἕξ (line 7): six (*indeclinable numeral*)

Ἀθήνηθεν (line 8): from Athens (*adv.*)

ἥδῑον (line 8): agrees with the subject, ἐξορμᾶν, a (neuter) infinitive

ἐξορμᾶν (line 9): from ἐξορμάω, ἐξορμήσω, ἐξώρμησα, ἐξώρμηκα, ἐξώρμημαι,
     ἐξωρμήθην: start out

ὑστερίζειν (line 9): from ὑστερίζω, ὑστεριῶ, ὑστέρισα, —, —, —: be late, i.e., have to
     rush

μηκῡνε (line 9): from μηκῡνω, μηκυνῶ, ἐμήκῡνα, —, μεμήκυσμαι, ἐμηκύνθην: lengthen

μετρίου (line 10): from μέτριος, -ᾱ, -ον: moderate, tolerable (*here = a neut. sg. sub-
     stantive,* "what is tolerable")

ὁδούς (line 10, twice): here ὁδός = "a single day's journey"

πορεύου (line 10): see note on πορευόμενος (line 6); direct object = ὁδούς (*cognate ac-
     cusative,* "journey [i.e., make] one-day journeys")

κρεῖττον (line 10): agrees with the subject, σπεύδειν, a (neuter) infinitive

ὁρμῇ (line 11): from ὁρμή, -ῆς, ἡ: a starting out

LESSON 34

NUMERALS

καὶ δὶς γάρ τοι καὶ τρίς φᾱσι καλὸν εἶναι τὰ καλὰ λέγειν
(It's a fine thing, they say, to say fine things over and over again.)
—Socrates repeats himself in Plato's *Gorgias* 498e

209. **Numerals** are a special breed of adjectives. **Cardinal numerals** are those used for counting (*one, two,* etc.). **Ordinal numerals** are those used for putting items in order (*first, second,* etc.). Every cardinal numeral has a corresponding **numerical adverb** (*once, twice, thrice, four times,* etc.).

210. In English, numerals are generally indeclinable, although they may add *-s* to become plural (*hundreds, thousands,* etc.). In Greek, the **ordinals** are all regular adjectives with **first/second-declension endings** (e.g., πρῶτος, -η, -ον), as are the cardinals denoting 1000 (χίλιοι, -αι, -α), 10,000 (μύριοι, -αι, -α), and multiples of 100, 1000, and 10,000. Each of the **cardinals from 1 to 4** is an adjective with **mixed-declension** (εἷς, μία, ἕν) **or third-declension endings** (see paradigms below). The **rest of the cardinals** are either **indeclinable adjectives** or **combinations of adjectives**, which may include one of the inflected cardinals from 1 to 4 (e.g., τρεῖς/τρία καὶ δέκα "thirteen"; εἴκοσιν εἷς/μία/ἕν "twenty-one").

You already know the declension of εἷς, μία, ἕν ("one"). Here are the paradigms for "two," "three," and "four":

| | "two" (stem = δυ-) | "three" (stem = τρι-/τρε-) | |
	Masc./Fem./Neut.	**Masc./Fem.**	**Neut.**
Nom.	δύο	τρεῖς (= τρέες)	τρία
Gen.	δυοῖν	τριῶν	τριῶν
Dat.	δυοῖν	τρισί(ν)	τρισί(ν)
Acc.	δύο	τρεῖς (= nom.)	τρία

227

"four" (stem = τετταρ-)

	Masc./Fem.	Neut.
Nom.	τέτταρες	τέτταρα
Gen.	τεττάρων	τεττάρων
Dat.	τέτταρσι(ν)	τέτταρσι(ν)
Acc.	τέτταρας	τέτταρα

NOTE The endings of δύο ("two") look odd because they are dual in number. In the declension of δύο and τρεῖς, the accent shifts to the ultima in the genitive and dative, following the rule for third-declension words with monosyllabic stems.

From the following lists, you need to memorize only the **numerical adverbs** ἅπαξ, δίς, and τρίς, the **cardinal numerals** for **1, 2, 3, 4, 5, 6, 7, 8, 9, 10, 11, 12, 20, 100, 1000,** and **10,000,** and the corresponding **ordinals.** All other Greek numerals can be derived from these. Deciphering unfamiliar numerals is a simple process if you know what to look for: a stem denoting a multiple of 10 (-κοντα/-κοστ-), 100 (-κοσι-/-κοσιοστ-), 1000 (-χῑλι-/-χῑλιοστ-), or 10,000 (-μῡρι-/-μῡριοστ-) and/or the adverbial suffix -κις ("times"). In compound forms, the smaller numeral may come either before or after the larger; if it comes *after*, καί may be omitted (cf. τέτταρες καὶ εἴκοσι "four & twenty," εἴκοσι καὶ τέτταρες "twenty & four," εἴκοσι τέτταρες "twenty-four"—but **not** τέτταρες εἴκοσι "four-twenty").

	Cardinals	Ordinals	Numerical Adverbs
1.	εἷς, μία, ἕν	πρῶτος, -η, -ον	ἅπαξ
2.	δύο	δεύτερος, -ᾱ, -ον	δίς
3.	τρεῖς, τρία	τρίτος, -η, -ον	τρίς
4.	τέτταρες, τέτταρα	τέταρτος, -η, -ον	τετράκις
5.	πέντε	πέμπτος, -η, -ον	πεντάκις
6.	ἕξ	ἕκτος, -η, -ον	ἑξάκις
7.	ἑπτά	ἕβδομος, -η, -ον	ἑπτάκις
8.	ὀκτώ	ὄγδοος, -η, -ον	ὀκτάκις
9.	ἐννέα	ἔνατος, -η, -ον	ἐνάκις
10.	δέκα	δέκατος, -η, -ον	δεκάκις
11.	ἕνδεκα	ἑνδέκατος, -η, -ον	ἑνδεκάκις
12.	δώδεκα	δωδέκατος, -η, -ον	δωδεκάκις
13.	τρεῖς/τρία καὶ δέκα	τρίτος καὶ δέκατος	τρεισκαιδεκάκις
14.	τέτταρες/-α καὶ δέκα	τέταρτος καὶ δέκατος	τετταρεσκαιδεκάκις
15.	πεντεκαίδεκα	πέμπτος καὶ δέκατος	πεντεκαιδεκάκις
16.	ἑκκαίδεκα	ἕκτος καὶ δέκατος	ἑκκαιδεκάκις
17.	ἑπτακαίδεκα	ἕβδομος καὶ δέκατος	ἑπτακαιδεκάκις
18.	ὀκτωκαίδεκα	ὄγδοος καὶ δέκατος	ὀκτωκαιδεκάκις
19.	ἐννεακαίδεκα	ἔνατος καὶ δέκατος	ἐννεακαιδεκάκις
20.	εἴκοσι(ν)	εἰκοστός, -ή, -όν	εἰκοσάκις

21.	εἷς/μία/ἕν καὶ εἴκοσι(ν) or εἴκοσι (καὶ) εἷς/μία/ἕν	πρῶτος καὶ εἰκοστός	εἰκοσάκις ἅπαξ
30.	τριάκοντα	τριᾱκοστός, -ή, -όν	τριᾱκοντάκις
40.	τετταράκοντα	τετταρακοστός, -ή, -όν	τετταρακοντάκις
50.	πεντήκοντα	πεντηκοστός, -ή, -όν	πεντηκοντάκις
60.	ἑξήκοντα	ἑξηκοστός, -ή, -όν	ἑξηκοντάκις
70.	ἑβδομήκοντα	ἑβδομηκοστός, -ή, -όν	ἑβδομηκοντάκις
80.	ὀγδοήκοντα	ὀγδοηκοστός, -ή, -όν	ὀγδοηκοντάκις
90.	ἐνενήκοντα	ἐνενηκοστός, -ή, -όν	ἐνενηκοντάκις
100.	ἑκατόν	ἑκατοστός, -ή, -όν	ἑκατοντάκις
200.	διᾱκόσιοι, -αι, -α	διᾱκοσιοστός, -ή, -όν	διᾱκοσιάκις
300.	τριᾱκόσιοι, -αι, -α	τριᾱκοσιοστός, -ή, -όν	τριᾱκοσιάκις
400.	τετρακόσιοι, -αι, -α	τετρακοσιοστός, -ή, -όν	τετρακοσιάκις
500.	πεντακόσιοι, -αι, -α	πεντακοσιοστός, -ή, -όν	πεντακοσιάκις
600.	ἑξακόσιοι, -αι, -α	ἑξακοσιοστός, -ή, -όν	ἑξακοσιάκις
700.	ἑπτακόσιοι, -αι, -α	ἑπτακοσιοστός, -ή, -όν	ἑπτακοσιάκις
800.	ὀκτακόσιοι, -αι, -α	ὀκτακοσιοστός, -ή, -όν	ὀκτακοσιάκις
900.	ἐνακόσιοι, -αι, -α	ἐνακοσιοστός, -ή, -όν	ἐνακοσιάκις
1000.	χῑλιοι, -αι, -α	χῑλιοστός, -ή, -όν	χῑλιάκις
2000.	δισχῑλιοι, -αι, -α	δισχῑλιοστός, -ή, -όν	δισχῑλιάκις
3000.	τρισχῑλιοι, -αι, -α	τρισχῑλιοστός, -ή, -όν	τρισχῑλιάκις
10,000.	μῡριοι, -αι, -α	μῡριοστός, -ή, -όν	μῡριάκις
11,000.	μῡριοι καὶ χῑλιοι	μῡριοστὸς καὶ χῑλιοστός	μῡριάκις καὶ χῑλιάκις
20,000.	δισμῡριοι, -αι, -α	δισμῡριοστός, -ή, -όν	δισμῡριάκις
100,000.	δεκακισμῡριοι, -αι, -α	δεκακισμῡριοστός, -ή, -όν	δεκακισμῡριάκις

211. The **partitive genitive** (see Lesson 32, §199) is often used with numerals. Occasionally the preposition ἀπό or ἐκ is added (e.g., πέντε ἐκ τῶν παίδων "five [out] of the children").

NOTE Instead of Roman or Arabic numerals, the ancient Greeks used letters. They had both an **alphabetic** system, in which a number was symbolized by a particular letter of the Greek alphabet (e.g., δ′ = 4), and an **acrophonic** system, in which a number was represented by the first letter of the word standing for that number (e.g., Δ [from δέκα] = 10). Doing computations with either system would have been a major challenge; it is easy to see why people generally relied on the abacus and finger-counting!

212.   VOCABULARY

ἀριθμός, -οῦ, ὁ	number [cf. *arithmetic*]
δύο	two [cf. *duopsony, dyad*]
τρεῖς, τρία	three [cf. *triglyph, triptych*]
τέτταρες, τέτταρα	four [cf. *tetragram, tetralogy*]
πέντε	five [cf. *Pentateuch, pentathlon*]
ἕξ	six [cf. *hexamerous, hexameter*]
ἑπτά	seven [cf. *heptarchy, Heptateuch*]
ὀκτώ	eight [cf. *octagon, octopus*]
ἐννέα	nine [cf. *ennead*]
δέκα	ten [cf. *decade, decalogue*]
ἕνδεκα	eleven [cf. *hendecasyllabic*]
δώδεκα	twelve [cf. *Dodecanese, dodecaphonic*]
εἴκοσι(ν)	twenty [cf. *icosahedron*]
ἑκατόν	one hundred [cf. *hecatomb, hectare*]
χίλιοι, -αι, -α	one thousand [cf. *chiliast*]
μύριοι, -αι, -α	ten thousand [cf. *myriad*]
δεύτερος, -ᾱ, -ον	second [cf. *Deuteronomy, deutoplasm*]
τρίτος, -η, -ον	third [cf. *tritanopia, tritium*]
τέταρτος, -η, -ον	fourth
πέμπτος, -η, -ον	fifth
ἕκτος, -η, -ον	sixth
ἕβδομος, -η, -ον	seventh [cf. *hebdomad*]
ὄγδοος, -η, -ον	eighth
ἔνατος, -η, -ον	ninth
δέκατος, -η, -ον	tenth
ἑνδέκατος, -η, -ον	eleventh
δωδέκατος, -η, -ον	twelfth
ἅπαξ	(*adv.*) once [cf. *hapax legomenon*]
δίς	(*adv.*) twice [cf. *dicotyledon*]
τρίς	(*adv.*) thrice [cf. *trisoctahedron*]

213.　　　　　EXERCISES

A.　　**Greek-to-English Sentences**

1.　τὰ τρία παιδία δεινῶς ἐφοβήθη διὰ τὸν τοσοῦτον ἀριθμὸν τῶν τριήρων.

2.　ἅπαξ ἁμαρτών, ὦ πρύτανι, μὴ ἁμάρτανε δὶς τὴν αὐτὴν ἁμαρτίαν.

3.　ἐγὼ μὲν ἤγαγον δύο τῶν πέντε ἵππων, ὁ δ' ἀδελφὸς τοὺς ἄλλους τρεῖς.

4.　τρὶς εὐδαίμων ἡ μήτηρ τούτων τῶν τριῶν κορῶν ἃς οὐδεὶς οὐ τῑμᾷ.

5.　ὡς ῥᾳδίως τὰς μεγάλᾱς θύρᾱς ἀνέῳξεν ὁ ξένος, ὢν κρείττων ἢ ἓξ ἄνδρες.

6.　τὸ μὲν ἔνατον ἐκ τῶν δέκα δώρων ὀλίγῳ κάλλῑον τοῦ ὀγδόου, τὸ δὲ δέκατον κάλλιστον πάντων ἦν.

7.　τῶν κινδύνων μεγίστων γενομένων, οἱ εἴκοσι φύλακες τοῖς θεοῖς οὐκ ἐπαύοντο θύοντες ἑπτὰ ἢ ὀκτὼ ἡμέρᾱς.

8.　καίπερ ἤδη ἰδοῦσα χῑλίους λέοντας, οὕτω φιλῶ αὐτοὺς ὥστε βούλομαι ὁρᾶν μῡρίους πλείονας.

9.　ταῖς δυοῖν θυγατράσι καὶ τέτταρσιν υἱοῖς μου πλείστᾱς ἐπιστολὰς πέπομφα, ἀλλ' οὔποτε παρ' οὐδενὸς ἐκείνων εἴληφα πλείους ἢ μίαν.

10.　καὶ μὴν πολλῷ ἀμείνω βουλὴν ἔχει ὁ ἕκτος στρατηγὸς ἢ ὁ πέμπτος.

B.　　**English-to-Greek Sentences**

1.　Although three books have been destroyed (*use genitive absolute*), we shall teach the students with the remaining two.

2.　Four of the nine orators spoke so disgracefully that they were thrown out of the assembly by the guards.

3.　The fifth horse is much smaller than the sixth; the seventh is a little older than the eighth.

4.　I asked my mistress thrice whether she wished to invite twelve or twenty guests to dinner.

5.　With many thousands of stones, a hundred men were making a second wall and a large number of houses.

C. READING

THE ATHENIANS GO TOO FAR — Part 1
(adapted from Thucydides' *Peloponnesian War* 6.31)

Below is the first part of a selection from Book 6 of Thucydides' **Peloponnesian War**. *Athens and Sparta had already been fighting each other for sixteen years when, in 415 B.C., the Athenians decided to send an expedition to Sicily, responding to a plea for help from the people of Egesta (allies of Athens), who felt threatened by the pro-Spartan cities of Sicily, especially Syracuse. But the Athenians' real purpose, according to Thucydides, was to conquer Sicily and add that rich island to their empire.*

In the following passage Thucydides describes the size and splendor of the expedition as it prepared to depart from Athens' harbor, the Piraeus.

αὕτη γὰρ ἡ παρασκευὴ ἦν πολυτελεστάτη τε καὶ εὐπρεπεστάτη τῶν εἰς
ἐκεῖνον τὸν χρόνον ἐκπλευσᾱσῶν μιᾶς Ἑλληνικῆς πόλεως. ἀριθμῷ δὲ τριήρων
καὶ ὁπλῑτῶν ἡ μετὰ Περικλέους παρασκευὴ οὐκ ἐλάττων ἦν· τετράκις γὰρ
χίλιοι ὁπλῖται τῶν Ἀθηναίων καὶ τριᾱκόσιοι ἱππῆς καὶ τριήρεις ἑκατόν, καὶ
5   τῶν συμμάχων πεντήκοντα τριήρεις συνέπλευσαν. ἀλλ' οὗτος ὁ στόλος, ὡς
μακρὸς ἐσόμενος, μεγάλαις δαπάναις τῶν τε τριηράρχων καὶ τῆς πόλεως
ἐξηρτύθη. ἡ μὲν πόλις δραχμὴν τῆς ἡμέρᾱς παντὶ ναύτῃ ἔδωκε καὶ
παρεσκεύασε κενᾱς τριήρεις μὲν ἑξήκοντα, ὁπλῑταγωγοὺς δὲ ναῦς τετταράκοντα,
καὶ ὑπηρεσίᾱς ταύταις τᾱς κρατίστᾱς· οἱ δὲ τριήραρχοι ἐπιφορᾱς τ' ἔδοσαν
10   τοῖς θρᾱνίταις καὶ ἔσπευσαν ποιῆσαι τᾱς ἑαυτῶν τριήρεις εὐπρεπεστέρᾱς τῶν
ἄλλων. οὕτως ἡ ἐπὶ πολεμίους παρασκευὴ ἐγένετο ἐπίδειξις εἰς τοὺς ἄλλους
Ἕλληνας.

VOCABULARY

παρασκευή (line 1): from παρασκευή, -ῆς, ἡ: military force
πολυτελεστάτη (line 1): from πολυτελής, -ές: expensive, extravagant
εὐπρεπεστάτη (line 1): from εὐπρεπής, -ές: impressive-looking
εἰς (line 1): here = "up to"
τῶν...ἐκπλευσᾱσῶν (lines 1-2): supply the noun παρασκευῶν ("military forces")
ἐκπλευσᾱσῶν (line 2): from ἐκπλέω, ἐκπλεύσομαι or ἐκπλευσοῦμαι, ἐξέπλευσα,
    ἐκπέπλευκα, ἐκπέπλευσμαι, — (+ *gen*.): sail out (from)
ἀριθμῷ (line 2): in respect to the number (*dative of respect*)
ὁπλῑτῶν (line 3): from ὁπλίτης, -ου, ὁ: hoplite, heavy-armed foot-soldier
Περικλέους (line 3): from Περικλῆς, -έους, ὁ: Pericles, Athenian general who had in-
    vaded southern Greece during the first year of the war
Ἀθηναίων (line 4): from Ἀθηναῖος, -ᾱ, -ον: Athenian
ἱππῆς (line 4): from ἱππεύς, -έως, ὁ: cavalryman

συμμάχων (line 5): from σύμμαχος, -ου, ὁ: ally

συνέπλευσαν (line 5): from συμπλέω: sail together (*like* ἐκπλέω, *line 2*)

στόλος (line 5): from στόλος, -ου, ὁ: expedition

δαπάναις (line 6): from δαπάνη, -ης, ἡ: expense

τριηράρχων (line 6): from τριήραρχος, -ου, ὁ: trierarch, rich Athenian citizen who
  paid for the outfitting of a trireme as his public service

ἐξηρτύθη (line 7): from ἐξαρτύω, ἐξαρτύσω, ἐξήρτῦσα, ἐξήρτῦκα, ἐξήρτῦμαι, ἐξηρτύθην:
  fit out, equip

τῆς ἡμέρᾱς (line 7): here = "per day"

ναύτῃ (line 7): from ναύτης, -ου, ὁ: sailor

ἔδωκε (line 7): aorist of δίδωμι, δώσω, ἔδωκα, δέδωκα, δέδομαι, ἐδόθην: give

παρεσκεύασε (line 8): from παρασκευάζω, παρασκευάσω, παρεσκεύασα, παρεσκεύακα,
  παρεσκεύασμαι, παρεσκευάσθην: provide, furnish

κενᾱς (line 8): from κενός, -ή, -όν: empty, i.e., just the hulls

ὁπλῑταγωγοὺς...ναῦς (line 8): transport ships (ὁπλῑταγωγός, -όν: carrying hoplites;
  ναῦς, νεώς [*acc. pl.* = ναῦς], ἡ: ship)

ὑπηρεσίᾱς (line 9): from ὑπηρεσία, -ᾱς, ἡ: crew of rowers

ἐπιφορᾱς (line 9): ἐπιφορά, -ᾶς, ἡ: addition, bonus

ἔδοσαν (line 9): 3rd pers. pl. aorist of δίδωμι (*see* ἔδωκε, *line 7*)

θρᾱνίταις (line 10): from θρᾱνίτης, -ου, ὁ: thranite, rower who sat in the top level of
  benches and guided the strokes of the two rowers beneath him

εὐπρεπεστέρᾱς (line 10): see note on εὐπρεπεστάτη (line 1)

ἐπί (line 11): here = "against"

ἐπίδειξις (line 11): from ἐπίδειξις, -εως, ἡ: display

εἰς (line 11): here = "for"

LESSON 35

SUBJUNCTIVE MOOD
Present, Aorist, Perfect Tenses; Active, Middle, Passive Voices; Independent Uses of the Subjunctive (Hortatory, Prohibitive, Deliberative)

καὶ μὴ εἰσενέγκῃς ἡμᾶς εἰς πειρασμόν,
ἀλλὰ ῥῦσαι ἡμᾶς ἀπὸ τοῦ πονηροῦ
(And lead us not into temptation, but deliver us from evil.)
—Matthew 6:13

214. In general, Greek verbs are put into the **subjunctive mood** to indicate that the action is a conceivable one (in the mind of the speaker), but not an actual occurrence. A subjunctive verb may be in the **present**, **aorist**, or **perfect** tense; the tenses show **aspect**, not time. The present and aorist subjunctive are much more common than the perfect subjunctive; although you should learn how to recognize perfect subjunctives, you will not be drilled on them in the exercises.

215. The subjunctive mood uses regular **primary** endings, but **lengthens the thematic vowel** wherever possible. Aorist subjunctives have **no augments** (since these appear only in the indicative mood). No infinitives or participles exist in the subjunctive mood. All subjunctives have **recessive accent**; those that seem to have persistent accent are **contractions**, formed according to the principles listed in §92 of Lesson 15. Subjunctives may often be translated with auxiliary verbs like *may*, *might*, and *would*, but it is best not to try to equate each form with a particular translation. The precise meaning always has to be determined from the context.

235

SUBJUNCTIVE MOOD

PRESENT ACTIVE (indic. παιδεύω)			PRESENT MIDDLE/PASSIVE (indic. παιδεύομαι)		
Singular:			**Singular:**		
παιδεύω	-ω		παιδεύωμαι	-ωμαι	
παιδεύῃς	-ῃς		παιδεύῃ	-ῃ	
παιδεύῃ	-ῃ		παιδεύηται	-ηται	
Plural:			**Plural:**		
παιδεύωμεν	-ωμεν		παιδευώμεθα	-ωμεθα	
παιδεύητε	-ητε		παιδεύησθε	-ησθε	
παιδεύωσι(ν)	-ωσι(ν)		παιδεύωνται	-ωνται	

FIRST AORIST ACTIVE (indic. ἐπαίδευσα)			FIRST AORIST MIDDLE (indic. ἐπαιδευσάμην)		
Singular:			**Singular:**		
παιδεύσω	-σ-ω		παιδεύσωμαι	-σ-ωμαι	
παιδεύσῃς	-σ-ῃς		παιδεύσῃ	-σ-ῃ	
παιδεύσῃ	-σ-ῃ		παιδεύσηται	-σ-ηται	
Plural:			**Plural:**		
παιδεύσωμεν	-σ-ωμεν		παιδευσώμεθα	-σ-ωμεθα	
παιδεύσητε	-σ-ητε		παιδεύσησθε	-σ-ησθε	
παιδεύσωσι(ν)	-σ-ωσι(ν)		παιδεύσωνται	-σ-ωνται	

FIRST AORIST PASSIVE
(indic. ἐπαιδεύθην)

Singular:	
παιδευθῶ	-θέ-ω
παιδευθῇς	-θέ-ῃς
παιδευθῇ	-θέ-ῃ
Plural:	
παιδευθῶμεν	-θέ-ωμεν
παιδευθῆτε	-θέ-ητε
παιδευθῶσι(ν)	-θέ-ωσι(ν)

SECOND AORIST ACTIVE (indic. ἔβαλον)			SECOND AORIST MIDDLE (indic. ἐβαλόμην)		
Singular:			**Singular:**		
βάλω	-ω		βάλωμαι	-ωμαι	
βάλῃς	-ῃς		βάλῃ	-ῃ	
βάλῃ	-ῃ		βάληται	-ηται	
Plural:			**Plural:**		
βάλωμεν	-ωμεν		βαλώμεθα	-ωμεθα	
βάλητε	-ητε		βάλησθε	-ησθε	
βάλωσι(ν)	-ωσι(ν)		βάλωνται	-ωνται	

SECOND AORIST PASSIVE
(indic. ἐγράφην)

Singular:

γραφῶ	-έ-ω
γραφῇς	-έ-ης
γραφῇ	-έ-η

Plural:

γραφῶμεν	-έ-ωμεν
γραφῆτε	-έ-ητε
γραφῶσι(ν)	-έ-ωσι(ν)

-άω PRESENT ACTIVE
(indic. τῑμῶ)

Singular:

τῑμῶ	-ά-ω
τῑμᾷς	-ά-ης
τῑμᾷ	-ά-η

Plural:

τῑμῶμεν	-ά-ωμεν
τῑμᾶτε	-ά-ητε
τῑμῶσι(ν)	-ά-ωσι(ν)

-άω PRESENT MIDDLE/PASSIVE
(indic. τῑμῶμαι)

Singular:

τῑμῶμαι	-ά-ωμαι
τῑμᾷ	-ά-η
τῑμᾶται	-ά-ηται

Plural:

τῑμώμεθα	-α-ώμεθα
τῑμᾶσθε	-ά-ησθε
τῑμῶνται	-ά-ωνται

-έω PRESENT ACTIVE
(indic. φιλῶ)

Singular:

φιλῶ	-έ-ω
φιλῇς	-έ-ης
φιλῇ	-έ-η

Plural:

φιλῶμεν	-έ-ωμεν
φιλῆτε	-έ-ητε
φιλῶσι(ν)	-έ-ωσι(ν)

-έω PRESENT MIDDLE/PASSIVE
(indic. φιλοῦμαι)

Singular:

φιλῶμαι	-έ-ωμαι
φιλῇ	-έ-η
φιλῆται	-έ-ηται

Plural:

φιλώμεθα	-ε-ώμεθα
φιλῆσθε	-έ-ησθε
φιλῶνται	-έ-ωνται

-όω PRESENT ACTIVE
(indic. δηλῶ)

Singular:

δηλῶ	-ό-ω
δηλοῖς	-ό-ης
δηλοῖ	-ό-η

Plural:

δηλῶμεν	-ό-ωμεν
δηλῶτε	-ό-ητε
δηλῶσι(ν)	-ό-ωσι(ν)

-όω PRESENT MIDDLE/PASSIVE
(indic. δηλοῦμαι)

Singular:

δηλῶμαι	-ό-ωμαι
δηλοῖ	-ό-η
δηλῶται	-ό-ηται

Plural:

δηλώμεθα	-ο-ώμεθα
δηλῶσθε	-ό-ησθε
δηλῶνται	-ό-ωνται

The subjunctive forms of εἰμί resemble the active subjunctive endings: ὦ, ᾖς, ᾖ, ὦμεν, ἦτε, ὦσι(ν). These are occasionally combined with perfect active participles and perfect middle/passive participles to create periphrastic **perfect subjunctives** (e.g., perf. act. subj. πεπαιδευκὼς ὦ, perf. mid./pass. subj. πεπαιδευμένος ὦ). Once in a great while, subjunctive endings are added directly to the perfect active stem (e.g., πεπαιδεύκω). The subjunctive of οἶδα is εἰδῶ.

216. The subjunctive mood may be used for the main verb in the sentence (i.e., the verb of the independent clause) or for the verb in one or more of the sentence's subordinate (dependent) clauses. Only the **independent uses** are of concern in this chapter; the dependent uses will be described in later lessons.

NOTE The name *subjunctive* comes from the Latin word for "subordinate" since ancient grammarians associated the subjunctive mood with dependent clauses.

1. **Hortatory**—A **subjunctive** in the **first person** (usually plural) may have the sense of an **imperative**: the speakers urge themselves to do something. μή makes the exhortation negative. The difference between present and aorist is one of aspect; e.g., φιλῶμεν τὴν μητέρα ("let us [continue to] love our mother!"); μὴ ἀκούσωμεν τῆς μητρός ("let us not listen [on this occasion] to our mother!").

2. **Prohibitive**—An **aorist subjunctive** in the **second or third person**, preceded by μή, is the equivalent of a **negative imperative**. The Greeks preferred to use the **present imperative** rather than the present subjunctive for a prohibition with imperfective aspect; on the other hand, they preferred the **aorist subjunctive** to the aorist imperative for a prohibition with aoristic aspect; e.g., μὴ βλάπτε τὸν ἵππον ("do not [continue to] harm the horse!"); μὴ βλάψῃς τὸν ἵππον ("do not [start to] harm the horse!"); μὴ βλαφθῇ ὁ ἵππος ("let the horse not be harmed [on this occasion]!").

3. **Deliberative**—A **subjunctive**, in the **first person**, in a **question** may indicate the perplexity of the speaker(s) about what to do or say; the negative form of the question has μή. The difference between present and aorist is one of aspect; e.g, τί διδάσκωμεν; ("what are we to teach [habitually]?"); πῶς ὠφελήσω σε; ("how am I to help you [on this occasion]?"); μὴ εἴπω; ("should I not [start to] speak?").

NOTE Certain subjunctive and indicative forms are identical (e.g., ὠφελήσω = aor. act. subj. & fut. act. indic.). The context will reveal which mood is meant.

217.   VOCABULARY

μάχομαι, μαχοῦμαι, ἐμαχεσάμην, —, μεμάχημαι, —
          (+ *dat.*) fight (against)
παρασκευάζω, παρασκευάσω, παρεσκεύασα,
     παρεσκεύακα, παρεσκεύασμαι, παρεσκευάσθην
          prepare, provide, furnish
φαίνω, φανῶ, ἔφηνα, πέφαγκα or (*intr.*) πέφηνα, πέφασμαι, ἐφάνθην or
     (*intr.*) ἐφάνην   make appear, show; (*mid. & intransitive
                         forms*) appear [cf. *diaphanous, phenomenon*]

NOTE   In the perfect and pluperfect middle/passive of φαίνω, nu changes
to sigma whenever the ending begins with mu (see §135); e.g., πεφάν-
μεθα becomes πεφάσμεθα, and ἐπεφάν-μην becomes ἐπεφάσμην.

ἄργυρος, -ου, ὁ   silver [cf. *argyric*]
μάχη, -ης, ἡ   battle, fight [cf. *logomachy*]
παρασκευή, -ῆς, ἡ   preparation
χρῆμα, -ατος, τό   thing; (*pl.*) goods, property, money
χρῡσός, -οῦ, ὁ   gold [cf. *chrysalis, chrysanthemum*]

NOTE   The diminutives χρῡσίον, -ου, τό "piece of gold" and ἀργύριον, -ου, τό
("piece of silver") in the plural often mean "money" or "cash."

σύμμαχος, -ον   (+ *dat.*) allied (to); (*as a substantive*) ally
φανερός, -ά, -όν   visible, evident, open [cf. *phanerogam*]

218.   EXERCISES

A.   Greek-to-English Sentences

  1. καίπερ βουλόμενοι ἔχειν τὴν εἰρήνην, καλῶμεν πάντας τοὺς συμμάχους καὶ
     παρασκευάζωμεν τὰς τριήρεις.
  2. ὀλίγῳ μὲν φανερωτέρᾱ ἡ ἐνάτη οἰκίᾱ τῆς ὀγδόης ἐστί, φανερωτάτη δὲ
     πᾱσῶν ἡ δεκάτη φαίνεται εἶναι.
  3. μὴ λύσητε τοὺς λέοντας τοὺς οὔποτε μεμαχημένους οὐδενὶ ἀνθρώπῳ.
  4. τρεψώμεθα εἰς τὴν σκηνὴν καὶ ἴδωμεν τὸν χρῡσὸν καὶ τὸν ἄργυρον καὶ τὰ
     ἄλλα χρήματα τοῦ τεθνηκότος βασιλέως.
  5. μὴ παύωμαι λέγουσα; οὐδεὶς γὰρ τῶν ἐν τῇ ἐκκλησίᾳ ἔτι ἀκούει ἐμοῦ.
  6. μετὰ δύο δεινὰς μάχᾱς ἐγενόμεθα σύμμαχοι τοῖς προτέροις πολεμίοις.
  7. τί ποιήσω; ποῖ φύγω; σώσατε τὴν ψῡχήν μου, ὦ θεοί· μὴ ἀποκτείνητέ με.
  8. τῶν χρημάτων κλαπέντων, ὦ ἄδελφε, μὴ αἰσχρῶς λίπῃς τὴν παλαιὰν
     μητέρα ἡμῶν· μὴ ἐκείνη δὶς βλαφθῇ.
  9. ἡμῖν ἐφάνη αὕτη ἡ μάχη οὕτω μακρὰ εἶναι ὥστε μήποτε παύσασθαι.
 10. πότερον ἐρωτῶ τὴν δέσποιναν περὶ τῆς παρασκευῆς τοῦ δείπνου, ἢ μή;

B.   **English-to-Greek Sentences**

1. Do not fight (*aorist*) a third battle, my sons, for your first was dreadful, and your second was much worse!
2. Let us openly ask the ten generals this: "Why was the preparation of our allies so bad?"
3. How am I to provide as fine a dinner as possible without both money and servants?
4. The three thieves snatched so much gold and silver that they appeared to have left nothing in the storehouse.
5. Let him not fight (*aorist*) against his friend for the sake of property.

C.   **READING**

THE ATHENIANS GO TOO FAR — Part 2
(adapted from Thucydides' *Peloponnesian War* 6.34)

When unconfirmed reports of the Athenian expedition reach Syracuse, an assembly is convened to discuss the situation. Hermocrates, one of the speakers at the assembly, insists that the threat from the Athenians is real and gives the following advice to his fellow Syracusans.

Θαρροῦντες οὖν τά τ' αὐτοῦ παρασκευαζώμεθα καὶ εἰς τοὺς Σικελοὺς πέμποντες πρέσβεις φιλίᾱν καὶ συμμαχίᾱν πειρώμεθα ποιεῖσθαι, εἴς τε τὴν ἄλλην Σικελίᾱν πέμπωμεν πρέσβεις, δηλοῦντες ὡς κοινὸς ὁ κίνδῡνός ἐστιν. ἐρωτῶμεν δὲ καὶ τοὺς Ἰταλιώτᾱς εἴτε συμμαχίᾱν ποιήσονται ἡμῖν εἴτε γε

5   σύμμαχοι τῶν Ἀθηναίων οὐ γενήσονται. καὶ μὴν οἱ Καρχηδόνιοι, ἀεὶ φοβούμενοι τοὺς Ἀθηναίους, ἐθελήσουσιν ἢ κρύφα ἢ φανερῶς ἢ ἐξ ἑνός γέ τινος τρόπου ἡμᾶς ὠφελῆσαι. δυνατοὶ δ' εἰσὶ μάλιστα, χρῡσὸν γὰρ καὶ ἄργυρον πλεῖστον ἔχουσιν. πέμπωμεν δὲ πρέσβεις καὶ εἰς τὴν Λακεδαίμονα καὶ εἰς Κόρινθον, ἐρωτῶντες εἰ ἡμᾶς ὠφελήσουσι καὶ τὸν ἐν τῇ Ἑλλάδι πόλεμον

10 κῑνήσουσιν.

Πείθεσθε οὖν καὶ ὅτι τάχιστα εἰς τὸν πόλεμον παρασκευάζεσθε· τῶν γὰρ μετὰ φόβου παρασκευῶν ἀσφαλεστάτων οὐσῶν, χρησιμώτατον ἔσται ὡς ἐπὶ κινδῡνου πράττειν. οἱ δ' Ἀθηναῖοι ἐν πλῷ ἤδη εἰσί· τοῦτ' εὖ οἶδα.

VOCABULARY

θαρροῦντες (line 1): from θαρρέω, θαρρήσω, ἐθάρρησα, τεθάρρηκα, τεθάρρημαι, ἐθαρρήθην: take heart, be encouraged

τά...αὐτοῦ (line 1): with regard to the things here in Syracuse (αὐτοῦ: "at the very place")

παρασκεναζώμεθα (line 1): here = "make preparations"

Σικελούς (line 1): from Σικελός, -ή, -όν: Sicilian (*refers to the native people of Sicily, as opposed to the Greeks who had settled there later*)

πρέσβεις (line 2): from πρέσβυς, -εως, ὁ: ambassador (*declined like πόλις but with υ instead of ι in the nom., acc., and voc. sg.*)

φιλίᾱν (line 2): from φιλίᾱ, -ᾱς, ἡ: friendship (*dir. obj. of* ποιεῖσθαι)

συμμαχίᾱν (line 2): from συμμαχίᾱ, -ᾱς, ἡ: alliance (*dir. obj. of* ποιεῖσθαι)

πειρώμεθα (line 2): from πειράω, πειράσω, ἐπείρᾱσα, πεπείρᾱκα, πεπείρᾱμαι, ἐπειράθην: try (*often in middle voice*)

ἄλλην (line 3): here = "the rest of"

Σικελίᾱν (line 3): from Σικελίᾱ, -ᾱς, ἡ: Sicily, large island just south of the Italian peninsula

ὡς (line 3): here = "that"

Ἰταλιώτᾱς (line 4): from Ἰταλιώτης, -ου, ὁ: Greek inhabitant of Italy (*as opposed to a native Italian*)

Ἀθηναίων (line 5): from Ἀθηναῖος, -ᾱ, -ον: Athenian

Καρχηδόνιοι (line 5): from Καρχηδόνιος, -ᾱ, -ον: Carthaginian, inhabitant of Carthage, a city on the North African coast opposite Sicily

κρύφα (line 6): secretly (*adv.*)

ἐξ ἑνός γέ τινος τρόπου (lines 6-7): in some one way at least

δυνατοί (line 7): from δυνατός, -ή, -όν: able (*here = "able to help us"*)

Λακεδαίμονα (line 8): from Λακεδαίμων, -ονος, ἡ: Sparta, city in Greece

Κόρινθον (line 9): from Κόρινθος, -ου, ἡ: Corinth, city in Greece

κῑνήσουσιν (line 10): from κῑνέω, κῑνήσω, ἐκῑνησα, κεκῑνηκα, κεκῑνημαι, ἐκῑνήθην: set in motion, stir up

τάχιστα (line 11): from ταχύς, -εῖα, -ύ: fast, quick, swift

εἰς (line 11): here = "for"

παρασκευάζεσθε (line 11): here = "make preparations"

ἀσφαλεστάτων (line 12): from ἀσφαλής, -ές: safe

χρησιμώτατον (line 12): from χρήσιμος, -η, -ον: useful, advantageous (*pred. adj. agreeing with* πράττειν, *the subject of* ἔσται)

ὡς (line 12): here = "as if"

ἐν πλῷ (line 13): under sail (πλοῦς [= -όος], -οῦ, ὁ: sailing-voyage)

LESSON 36

OPTATIVE MOOD
Present, Future, Aorist, Perfect Tenses; Active, Middle, Passive Voices; Independent Uses of the Optative (Wishes, Potential Optative)

εἴ μοι γένοιτο φθόγγος ἐν βραχίοσι /
καὶ χερσὶ καὶ κόμαισι καὶ ποδῶν βάσει
(Would that my arms, hands, hair, and feet could speak!)
—Hecuba pleads for Agamemnon's help in Euripides' *Hecuba* 836

219.   The **optative mood** is used when the speaker conceives of a future event as something that *may* or *can* or *should* happen, not as something that *will* happen. An optative verb may have **present**, **future**, **aorist**, or **perfect** tense; the tenses show **aspect**, not time. (The future optative is exceptional and will be explained later.) The perfect optative is rare; you need only be able to recognize it.

220.   The optative mood uses **secondary** endings (except for the primary active ending -μι in first-person sg., borrowed from μι-verbs). Between the stem and the ending comes a thematic vowel (usually ο, sometimes α or ε), followed by the vowel(s) characteristic of the optative: usually ῑ, sometimes ιε or ιη. The aorist optative has **no augment**. There are no optative infinitives or participles.

All optatives have **recessive accent**; those seeming to have persistent accent are **contractions**. The diphthongs -αι and -οι are considered **long** if they come at the end of a word in the optative mood (thus παιδεύοι, not παίδευοι). Like subjunctives, optatives may often be translated with auxiliary verbs (*may, might, can, should, would*), but the exact meaning will depend on the context.

OPTATIVE MOOD

PRESENT ACTIVE
(indic. παιδεύω)

Singular:

παιδεύοιμι	-ο-ῑ-μι
παιδεύοις	-ο-ῑ-ς
παιδεύοι	-ο-ῑ

Plural:

παιδεύοιμεν	-ο-ῑ-μεν
παιδεύοιτε	-ο-ῑ-τε
παιδεύοιεν	-ο-ιε-ν

PRESENT MIDDLE/PASSIVE
(indic. παιδεύομαι)

Singular:

παιδευοίμην	-ο-ῑ-μην
παιδεύοιο	-ο-ῑ-ο (-οῑ[σ]ο)
παιδεύοιτο	-ο-ῑ-το

Plural:

παιδευοίμεθα	-ο-ῑ-μεθα
παιδεύοισθε	-ο-ῑ-σθε
παιδεύοιντο	-ο-ῑ-ντο

FUTURE ACTIVE
(indic. παιδεύσω)

Singular:

παιδεύσοιμι	-σ-ο-ῑ-μι
παιδεύσοις	-σ-ο-ῑ-ς
παιδεύσοι	-σ-ο-ῑ

Plural:

παιδεύσοιμεν	-σ-ο-ῑ-μεν
παιδεύσοιτε	-σ-ο-ῑ-τε
παιδεύσοιεν	-σ-ο-ιε-ν

FUTURE MIDDLE
(indic. παιδεύσομαι)

Singular:

παιδευσοίμην	-σ-ο-ῑ-μην
παιδεύσοιο	-σ-ο-ῑ-ο (-σοῑ[σ]ο)
παιδεύσοιτο	-σ-ο-ῑ-το

Plural:

παιδευσοίμεθα	-σ-ο-ῑ-μεθα
παιδεύσοισθε	-σ-ο-ῑ-σθε
παιδεύσοιντο	-σ-ο-ῑ-ντο

FUTURE PASSIVE
(indic. παιδευθήσομαι)

Singular:

παιδευθησοίμην	-θη-σ-ο-ῑ-μην
παιδευθήσοιο	-θη-σ-ο-ῑ-ο (-θησοῑ[σ]ο)
παιδευθήσοιτο	-θη-σ-ο-ῑ-το

Plural:

παιδευθησοίμεθα	-θη-σ-ο-ῑ-μεθα
παιδευθήσοισθε	-θη-σ-ο-ῑ-σθε
παιδευθήσοιντο	-θη-σ-ο-ῑ-ντο

FIRST AORIST ACTIVE
(indic. ἐπαίδευσα)

Singular:

παιδεύσαιμι	-σα-ῑ-μι
παιδεύσειας/-σαις	-σειας/-σα-ῑ-ς
παιδεύσειε(ν)/-σαι	-σειε(ν)/-σα-ῑ

Plural:

παιδεύσαιμεν	-σα-ῑ-μεν
παιδεύσαιτε	-σα-ῑ-τε
παιδεύσειαν/-σαιεν	-σειαν/-σα-ιε-ν

NOTE

The forms with the odd endings -σειας, -σειε(ν), and -σειαν are used more often than those with the predictable endings -σαις, -σαι, and -σαιεν.

FIRST AORIST MIDDLE
(indic. ἐπαιδευσάμην)

Singular:

παιδευσαίμην	-σα-ῑ-μην
παιδεύσαιο	-σα-ῑ-ο (-ῑ[σ]ο)
παιδεύσαιτο	-σα-ῑ-το

Plural:

παιδευσαίμεθα	-σα-ῑ-μεθα
παιδεύσαισθε	-σα-ῑ-σθε
παιδεύσαιντο	-σα-ῑ-ντο

FIRST AORIST PASSIVE
(indic. ἐπαιδεύθην)

Singular:

παιδευθείην	-θε-ιη-ν
παιδευθείης	-θε-ιη-ς
παιδευθείη	-θε-ιη

Plural:

παιδευθείημεν	-θε-ιη-μεν
παιδευθείητε	-θε-ιη-τε
παιδευθείησαν	-θε-ιη-σαν

SECOND AORIST ACTIVE   SECOND AORIST MIDDLE
(indic. ἔβαλον)   (indic. ἐβαλόμην)

Singular: **Singular:**

βάλοιμι	-ο-ῑ-μι	βαλοίμην	-ο-ῑ-μην
βάλοις	-ο-ῑ-ς	βάλοιο	-ο-ῑ-ο (-οῑ[σ]ο)
βάλοι	-ο-ῑ	βάλοιτο	-ο-ῑ-το

Plural: **Plural:**

βάλοιμεν	-ο-ῑ-μεν	βαλοίμεθα	-ο-ῑ-μεθα
βάλοιτε	-ο-ῑ-τε	βάλοισθε	-ο-ῑ-σθε
βάλοιεν	-ο-ιε-ν	βάλοιντο	-ο-ῑ-ντο

SECOND AORIST PASSIVE
(indic. ἐγράφην)

Singular:

γραφείην	-ε-ιη-ν
γραφείης	-ε-ιη-ς
γραφείη	-ε-ιη

Plural:

γραφείημεν	-ε-ιη-μεν
γραφείητε	-ε-ιη-τε
γραφείησαν	-ε-ιη-σαν

A **contract verb** may form its **present active optative** in either of two ways. Using -ιη- is preferred in the singular; using -ι- is preferred in the plural. The stem-vowel contracts with the following diphthong.

-άω PRESENT ACTIVE OPTATIVE
(indicative τῑμῶ)

Preferred:		*Rare:*	
Singular:			
τῑμῴην	(-α-ο-ίη-ν)	[τῑμῷμι	(-ά-ο-ῑ-μι)]
τῑμῴης	(-α-ο-ίη-ς)	[τῑμῷς	(-ά-ο-ῑ-ς)]
τῑμῴη	(-α-ο-ίη)	[τῑμῷ	(-ά-ο-ῑ)]
Plural:			
τῑμῷμεν	(-ά-ο-ῑ-μεν)	[τῑμῴημεν	(-α-ο-ίη-μεν)]
τῑμῷτε	(-ά-ο-ῑ-τε)	[τῑμῴητε	(-α-ο-ίη-τε)]
τῑμῷεν	(-ά-ο-ιε-ν)	[τῑμῴησαν	(-α-ο-ίη-σαν)]

-άω PRESENT M./P. OPTATIVE
(indicative τῑμῶμαι)

Singular:	
τῑμῴμην	(-α-ο-ί-μην)
τῑμῷο	(-ά-ο-ῑ-[σ]ο)
τῑμῷτο	(-ά-ο-ῑ-το)
Plural:	
τῑμῴμεθα	(-α-ο-ί-μεθα)
τῑμῷσθε	(-ά-ο-ῑ-σθε)
τῑμῷντο	(-ά-ο-ῑ-ντο)

-έω PRESENT ACTIVE OPTATIVE
(indicative φιλῶ)

Preferred:		*Rare:*	
Singular:			
φιλοίην	(-ε-ο-ίη-ν)	[φιλοῖμι	(-έ-ο-ῑ-μι)]
φιλοίης	(-ε-ο-ίη-ς)	[φιλοῖς	(-έ-ο-ῑ-ς)]
φιλοίη	(-ε-ο-ίη)	[φιλοῖ	(-έ-ο-ῑ)]
Plural:			
φιλοῖμεν	(-έ-ο-ῑ-μεν)	[φιλοίημεν	(-ε-ο-ίη-μεν)]
φιλοῖτε	(-έ-ο-ῑ-τε)	[φιλοίητε	(-ε-ο-ίη-τε)]
φιλοῖεν	(-έ-ο-ιε-ν)	[φιλοίησαν	(-ε-ο-ίη-σαν)]

-έω PRESENT M./P. OPTATIVE
(indicative φιλοῦμαι)

Singular:	
φιλοίμην	(-ε-ο-ί-μην)
φιλοῖο	(-έ-ο-ῑ-[σ]ο)
φιλοῖτο	(-έ-ο-ῑ-το)
Plural:	
φιλοίμεθα	(-ε-ο-ί-μεθα)
φιλοῖσθε	(-έ-ο-ῑ-σθε)
φιλοῖντο	(-έ-ο-ῑ-ντο)

NOTE Verbs with contracted futures have a future optative identical with the present optative of φιλέω, see the appendix, p. 472.

-όω PRESENT ACTIVE OPTATIVE
(indicative δηλῶ)

Preferred:		*Rare:*	
Singular:			
δηλοίην	(-ο-ο-ίη-ν)	[δηλοῖμι	(-ό-ο-ῑ-μι)]
δηλοίης	(-ο-ο-ίη-ς)	[δηλοῖς	(-ό-ο-ῑ-ς)]
δηλοίη	(-ο-ο-ίη)	[δηλοῖ	(-ό-ο-ῑ)]
Plural:			
δηλοῖμεν	(-ό-ο-ῑ-μεν)	[δηλοίημεν	(-ο-ο-ίη-μεν)]
δηλοῖτε	(-ό-ο-ῑ-τε)	[δηλοίητε	(-ο-ο-ίη-τε)]
δηλοῖεν	(-ό-ο-ιε-ν)	[δηλοίησαν	(-ο-ο-ίη-σαν)]

-όω PRESENT M./P. OPTATIVE
(indicative δηλοῦμαι)

Singular:	
δηλοίμην	(-ο-ο-ί-μην)
δηλοῖο	(-ό-ο-ῑ-[σ]ο)
δηλοῖτο	(-ό-ο-ῑ-το)
Plural:	
δηλοίμεθα	(-ο-ο-ί-μεθα)
δηλοῖσθε	(-ό-ο-ῑ-σθε)
δηλοῖντο	(-ό-ο-ῑ-ντο)

NOTE

As you can see from the paradigms, **third-person plural active optatives** end in -ν if the optative suffix is -ῑ- or -ιε-, in -σαν if the suffix is -ιη-.

The present optative of εἰμί is εἴην, built on the stem ἐσ-, which loses its sigma. The future optative is ἐσοίμην, deponent like the future indicative ἔσομαι.

PRESENT OPTATIVE				FUTURE OPTATIVE
Singular:				
εἴην	(ἐ[σ]-ίη-ν)			ἐσοίμην
εἴης	(ἐ[σ]-ίη-ς)			ἔσοιο
εἴη	(ἐ[σ]-ίη)			ἔσοιτο
Plural:				
εἶμεν	(ἔ[σ]-ῑ-μεν)	**or** εἴημεν	(ἐ[σ]-ίη-μεν)	ἐσοίμεθα
εἶτε	(ἔ[σ]-ῑ-τε)	**or** εἴητε	(ἐ[σ]-ίη-τε)	ἔσοισθε
εἶεν	(ἔ[σ]-ιε-ν)	**or** εἴησαν	(ἐ[σ]-ίη-σαν)	ἔσοιντο

The present optative of εἰμί may be combined with a perfect active participle or a perfect middle/passive participle to create a periphrastic **perfect optative** (e.g., perf. act. opt. πεπαιδευκὼς εἴην, perf. mid./pass. opt. πεπαιδευμένος εἴην). Occasionally, optative endings are added directly to the perfect active stem (e.g., πεπαιδεύκοιμι). There is also a very rare **future perfect optative** (= perf. ptcple. + ἐσοίμην). The optative of οἶδα is εἰδείην (inflected like εἴην).

221.

Like the subjunctive mood, the optative mood has both dependent and independent uses. Only the **independent uses** are of concern in this chapter; the dependent uses will be described in later lessons.

1.

Wishes—An **optative** may express a **wish (or a curse) directed toward the future**. The wish may or may not be one that is capable of being fulfilled. It is often introduced by the words εἴθε or εἰ γάρ ("if only," "would that"). μή makes the wish negative. The difference between present and aorist is one of aspect: e.g., εἰ γὰρ ἴδοιμί σε ("would that I might see you!"); μὴ ζῷεν ("may they not go on living!"); εἴθε φίλος γένοιο ("if only you would become a friend!").

NOTE

The term *optative* comes from the Latin word meaning "having to do with wishing."

2.

Potential optative—An **optative** with the particle ἄν indicates something that **has the potential to happen**, i.e., something that may, might, can, should, or would happen. οὐ makes the statement negative. ἄν generally comes right after the verb, but it may also (and often does) follow an emphatic word like a negative or an interrogative. The difference between present and aorist is one of aspect: e.g., λέγοιμι ἂν τάδε ("I may say the following"); ὑπ' οὐδενὸς ἂν τῑμῷο ("you would be honored by no one"); οὔποτ' ἂν βλάψειάν με ("they can never harm me").

222.   **VOCABULARY**

χράομαι, χρήσομαι, ἐχρησάμην, —, κέχρημαι, ἐχρήσθην
                         (+ *dat.*) use, be subject to, experience
                         [cf. *chrestomathy*]

NOTE   Sometimes, as here, a verb that is otherwise a middle *deponent* (active in meaning) will also have a *regular* aorist passive (passive in meaning). Like ζάω, χράομαι contracts to an η instead of an ᾱ: pres. indic./subj. χρῶμαι, χρῇ, χρῆται, χρώμεθα, χρῆσθε, χρῶνται; pres. opt. χρῴμην, etc.; pres. imper. χρῶ, χρήσθω, χρῆσθε, χρήσθων; pres. infin. χρῆσθαι; pres. ptcple. χρώμενος, -η, -ον; imperf. indic. ἐχρώμην, ἐχρῶ, ἐχρῆτο, ἐχρώμεθα, ἐχρῆσθε, ἐχρῶντο.

νίκη, -ης, ἡ   victory [cf. *Eunice, Nike*]
στρατιά, -ᾶς, ἡ   army
στρατιώτης, -ου, ὁ   soldier
στρατόπεδον, -ου, τό   camp
στρατός, -οῦ, ὁ   army [cf. *stratocracy*]

NOTE   Although στρατός is the basic word for "army" (or any large group), its synonym στρατιά is often used instead.

ἕτοιμος, -η, -ον   (+ *infin.*) ready (to)
ἱκανός, -ή, -όν   (+ *infin. or dat.*) sufficient (to, for),
                               enough (to, for)
χρήσιμος, -η, -ον   useful, advantageous
ἄν   *particle used with potential optative*
εἴθε (εἴθ') or εἰ γάρ   (*particles*) if only, would that (*introducing
                               a wish*); εἴθ' *before a vowel*

223.   **EXERCISES**

A.   **Greek-to-English Sentences**

1.   εἰ γὰρ ἡ νίκη γένοιτο τοῖς ὑπὲρ τῆς πόλεως εὖ μαχομένοις στρατιώταις.

2.   ἀλλ' οὐδεὶς ἂν γελῴη ἐπὶ σοὶ καίπερ ἔχοντι ὀλίγον ἀριθμὸν χρημάτων.

3.   ἑτοίμη εἴη ἡ θυγάτηρ μου φέρειν τε τὰ κάλλιστα ἱμάτια εἰς τὴν ἀγορὰν καὶ διὰ τῆς ἡμέρᾱς πωλεῖν αὐτά.

4.   εἴθ' ἐγώ, ζητοῦσα ἐν τῇ χώρᾳ χρήσιμα φυτά, μηδὲ βλαβείην μηδ' ὑπὸ μηδενὸς ζῴου ἀποθάνοιμι.

5. ἆρ' ἔχεις ἱκανὰ δῶρα ὥστε πέμψαι ἓν ἢ δύο ἢ τρία παντὶ ἀγαθῷ μαθητῇ;

6. σπεύσωμεν ἐπὶ τὰ τείχη, ἴδοιμεν γὰρ ἂν τὸν μέγαν στρατόν.

7. εἶθ' αἵ τε μητέρες οἵ τε πατέρες σοφίᾳ χρῷντο τοὺς παῖδας διδάσκοντες.

8. τὸ μὲν δεύτερον στρατόπεδον πολλῷ μεῖζον ἦν τοῦ πρώτου, τῷ δὲ τρίτῳ ἦν ὁ χρησιμώτατος τόπος.

9. οἱ παλαίτεροι πρυτάνεις παρασκευάσειαν ἂν μῑκρῷ ἥδῑον δεῖπνον.

10. μὴ παύσῃς τοὺς ῥήτορας λέγοντας, ἀληθῶς γὰρ δηλοῦσι τὰς ἁμαρτίᾱς.

B. English-to-Greek Sentences

1. May our army experience sweet victory, and may the gods preserve the lives of our soldiers!

2. Let us provide enough gold and silver to persuade our allies to remain in the camp!

3. If only you would open those books once or twice and thus be ready to answer the teacher, my son!

4. Three couches appear to be sufficient for the dinner, mistress, but a fourth may be very useful.

5. Because the journey is rather long (*use genitive absolute*), I would not wish to delay one day longer.

C. READING

THE ATHENIANS GO TOO FAR — Part 3
(adapted from Thucydides' *Peloponnesian War* 6.68)

The Syracusans, still unsure about whether to believe the reports of an Athenian attack, nevertheless readied themselves for war. Meanwhile the Athenians sailed to Sicily, landed, and prepared to fight near Syracuse. Before the battle, Nicias, the Athenian general, gave a pep talk to his army.

Ἄλλοτε μέν, ὦ ἄνδρες, χρῴμην ἂν μακρᾷ παραινέσει, τήνδε δὲ τὴν μάχην οὐδεὶς ὑμῶν οὐχ ἕτοιμός ἐστι μάχεσθαι· αὐτὴ γὰρ ἡ παρασκευὴ ἱκανωτέρᾱ ἐστὶ παρέχειν θάρρος ἢ καλῶς λεχθέντες λόγοι μετ' ἀσθενοῦς στρατοῦ. μετὰ γὰρ τοιῶνδε καὶ τοσῶνδε συμμάχων, πῶς τις μεγάλην ἐλπίδα τῆς νίκης οὐκ ἂν ἔχοι;

5 καὶ μὴν μαχόμεθα στρατιώταις πανδημεί τ' ἀμῡνομένοις καὶ οὐ κριθεῖσιν. ὑπερφρονοῦσι μὲν οἱ Σικελιῶται ἡμᾶς, τραπήσονται δέ, διότι ἡ ἐπιστήμη ἐκείνων ἐστὶν ἥττων τῆς τόλμης. πολύ τ' ἀπὸ τῆς ἡμετέρᾱς γῆς αὐτῶν ἐσμεν καὶ πρὸς γῇ οὐδεμιᾷ φιλίᾳ. οἱ μὲν πολέμιοι λέγοιεν ἂν τάδε· Περὶ πατρίδος ἔσται ὁ ἀγών. ἐγὼ δ' ὑμῖν λέγω· Οὐκ ἐν πατρίδι ἔσται ὁ ἀγών· διὰ τοῦτ' ἢ εὑρήσομεν νίκην ἢ οὐ

10 ῥᾳδίως σωθείημεν ἄν. τῆς τ' οὖν ὑμετέρᾱς αὐτῶν δόξης μνησθέντες προσβάλετε προθύμως, ἡ γὰρ ἀπορίᾱ πολλῷ δεινοτέρᾱ τῶν πολεμίων.

VOCABULARY

ἄλλοτε (line 1): at another time (*adv.*)

παραινέσει (line 1): from παραίνεσις, -εως, ἡ: exhortation

παρασκευή (line 2): here = "military force," i.e., the impressive-looking army that has been assembled by the Athenians

ἱκανωτέρᾱ (line 2): here = "more capable (*of doing something*)"

παρέχειν (line 3): from παρέχω: offer, produce

θάρρος (line 3): from θάρρος, -ους, τό: boldness, courage

ἀσθενοῦς (line 3): from ἀσθενής, -ές: weak

πανδημεί (line 5): in a mob, en masse (*adv.*)

ἀμῡνομένοις (line 5): from ἀμῡνω, ἀμυνῶ, ἤμῡνα, —, —, —: ward off; (*mid.*) defend oneself

κριθεῖσιν (line 5): here = "elite"

ὑπερφρονοῦσι (line 6): from ὑπερφρονέω, ὑπερφρονήσω, ὑπερεφρόνησα, ὑπερπεφρόνηκα, ὑπερπεφρόνημαι, ὑπερεφρονήθην: look down at, scorn

Σικελιῶται (line 6): Σικελιώτης, -ου, ὁ: Greek inhabitant of Sicily

τραπήσονται (line 6): here = "will be put to flight"

διότι (line 6): contraction of διὰ τοῦθ' ὅτι

ἐπιστήμη (line 6): from ἐπιστήμη, -ης, ἡ: knowledge, skill (*in fighting*)

τόλμης (line 7): from τόλμη, -ης, ἡ: daring

φιλίᾳ (line 8): from φίλιος, -ᾱ, -ον: friendly

μνησθέντες (line 10): from μιμνήσκω, μνήσω, ἔμνησα, —, μέμνημαι, ἐμνήσθην: remind; (*aor. pass. with mid. sense*) (+ *gen.*) recall

προθΰμως (line 11): from πρόθῡμος, -ον: eager

ἀπορίᾱ (line 11): from ἀπορίᾱ, -ᾱς, ἡ: difficulty, desperate situation

LESSON 37

CONDITIONS

εἰ μὴ τότ' ἐπόνουν, νῦν ἂν οὐκ εὐφραινόμην
(If I had not suffered then, I would not be enjoying myself now.)
—Philemon, fragment 140

224.   A **condition** is an "if-then" statement composed of a premise or **protasis** (πρότασις, -εως, ἡ "that which is put forward") and a conclusion or **apodosis** (ἀπόδοσις, -εως, ἡ "that which is given back"). Logically, the action of the protasis ("if" clause) comes *before* that of the apodosis ("then" clause), but the speaker is free to put the clauses in whatever order is stylistically pleasing. The ancient Greeks were very fond of expressing their ideas in conditional form.

225.   There are four basic types of conditions in Greek: **simple particular** (present and past), **contrary to fact** (present and past), **general** (present and past), and **future** (most, more, and less vivid). They are distinguished by the moods and tenses of their verbs and by the presence or absence of the particle ἄν.

A.   **Simple Particular**

This condition refers to a definite, particular event in present or past time; it does not imply anything about whether or not the event is real or probable.

	Protasis	Apodosis
1. Present:	εἰ + pres. (or perf.) indicative	present (or perf.) indicative
	εἰ ὁ Σωκράτης τόδε λέγει,	τοὺς νεανίας βλάπτει.
	"If Socrates is saying this, he is harming the youth."	
2. Past:	εἰ + past indicative[1]	past indicative[1]
	εἰ ὁ Σωκράτης τόδ' ἔλεγε,	τοὺς νεανίας ἔβλαπτεν.
	"If Socrates was saying this, he was harming the youth."	

---

[1]past indicative = imperfect, aorist, or pluperfect indicative.

251

B.   Contrary to Fact

This condition refers to an event that could be happening now but is not, or to one that could have happened but did not. The apodosis has the particle ἄν.

	Protasis	Apodosis
1. Present:	εἰ + imperfect indicative	imperfect indicative + ἄν
	εἰ ὁ Σωκράτης τόδ’ ἔλεγε,	τοὺς νεανίας ἔβλαπτεν ἄν.
	"If Socrates were saying this, he would be harming the youth."	
2. Past:	εἰ + aorist indicative	aorist indicative + ἄν
	εἰ ὁ Σωκράτης τόδ’ εἶπε,	τοὺς νεανίας ἔβλαψεν ἄν.
	"If Socrates had said this, he would have harmed the youth."	

NOTE   In proper English, a contrary-to-fact apodosis always has the auxiliary verb *would* or *would have*, while a contrary-to-fact protasis has *were* or *had*.

C.   General

This condition refers to a general, customary, or repeated event in present or past time. The protasis of the **present** general condition has εἰ ἄν, which is normally contracted to ἐάν, ἤν, or ἄν. The protasis of the **past** general condition has εἰ without ἄν. A subjunctive/optative verb in a general condition may be either present (= imperfective aspect) or aorist (= aoristic aspect) in tense.

	Protasis	Apodosis
1. Present:	ἐάν (ἤν, ἄν) + subjunctive	present indicative
	ἐὰν ὁ Σωκράτης τόδε λέγῃ,	τοὺς νεανίας βλάπτει.
	"If Socrates (ever) says this, he harms the youth."	
2. Past:	εἰ + optative	imperfect indicative
	εἰ ὁ Σωκράτης τόδε λέγοι,	τοὺς νεανίας ἔβλαπτεν.
	"If Socrates (ever) said this, he harmed the youth."	

D.   Future

This condition refers to an event that has not yet happened but will or might. The form of the condition depends on how vividly the speaker imagines the event or foresees its likelihood of happening. For threats and warnings the **future most vivid** is appropriate. The **future more vivid** is less emotional than the most vivid and has either ἐάν, ἤν, or ἄν in its protasis. English often uses the present tense (instead of the more logical future) to translate the verb in the protasis of a future most vivid or a future more vivid condition. The **future less vivid** is suitable for hypothetical cases or suppositions and is translated with "should...would" or "would...would"; its apodosis always has ἄν. A subjunctive/optative verb in a future condition may be either present (= imperfective aspect) or aorist (= aoristic aspect) in tense.

Protasis	Apodosis
1. Most Vivid: εἰ + future indicative	future indicative
εἰ ὁ Σωκράτης τόδ' ἐρεῖ,	τοὺς νεανίας βλάψει.

"If Socrates says (will say) this, he will harm the youth."

2. More Vivid: ἐάν (ἤν, ἄν) + subjunctive	future indicative
ἐὰν ὁ Σωκράτης τόδε λέγῃ,	τοὺς νεανίας βλάψει.

"If Socrates says (will say) this, he will harm the youth."

3. Less Vivid: εἰ + optative	optative + ἄν
εἰ ὁ Σωκράτης τόδε λέγοι,	τοὺς νεανίας βλάπτοι ἄν.

"If Socrates should say this, he would harm the youth."

NOTE   The optative used in the apodosis of a future less vivid condition always has ἄν with it because it is a type of **potential optative**.

226.   Regardless of the type of condition, a **negative protasis** will always have μή. A **negative apodosis** will have οὐ unless the expected verb form in it has been replaced by an imperative or by another expression that requires μή.

In the apodosis of a condition, substitutes for the indicative are common. A present **imperative**, for instance, may replace a present indicative in the apodosis of a simple condition; e.g., εἰ ὁ Σωκράτης τόδε λέγει, ὦ νεανίαι, μὴ ἀκούετε ("if Socrates is saying this, young men, *do not listen!*").

A **circumstantial participle** may replace the protasis in any type of condition; εἰ and ἄν are then omitted (e.g., ὁ Σωκράτης, **τόδε λέγων** [= ἐὰν τόδε λέγῃ], τοὺς νεανίας βλάψει—future more vivid). Just as a negative protasis always has μή, a participle replacing a negative protasis always has **μή**. The use of μή with a circumstantial participle is proof that the participle is **conditional** since **all other negative circumstantial participles** (temporal, causal, concessive, etc.) **have οὐ**.

227.   **VOCABULARY**

ἀδικέω, ἀδικήσω, ἠδίκησα, ἠδίκηκα, ἠδίκημαι, ἠδικήθην
be unjust, do wrong, injure

NOTE   An accusative direct object may be used with ἀδικέω to identify the injured person(s) or the injury itself. The noun ἀδικία (see below) often serves as direct object; e.g., ἀδικίαν ἠδίκηκα "I have done a wrong." This is a good example of a **cognate accusative**, a noun closely related to the main verb in both form and meaning, or just in meaning; for other examples see the reading for Lesson 33.

διαφθείρω, διαφθερῶ, διέφθειρα, διέφθαρκα or διέφθορα (*no diff. in meaning*), διέφθαρμαι, διεφθάρην
    corrupt, ruin

νῑκάω, νῑκήσω, ἐνίκησα, νενίκηκα, νενίκημαι, ἐνῑκήθην
    conquer, win

ἀδικίᾱ, -ᾱς, ἡ   injustice, wrong, injury

δίκη, -ης, ἡ   justice, right, penalty, punishment, law-suit; δίκην λαμβάνειν παρά τινος = to punish someone [cf. *Eurydice, syndicate, theodicy*]

φύσις, -εως, ἡ   nature [cf. *Monophysite, physiognomy*]

ἄδικος, -ον   unjust, wrong

'Αθηναῖος, -ᾱ, -ον   Athenian

δίκαιος, -ᾱ, -ον   just, right

ἴσος, -η, -ον   (+ *dat.*) equal (to); fair, impartial [cf. *isobar, isosceles, isotope*]

ἴσως   (*adv. of* ἴσος, -η, -ον) fairly, perhaps, probably

εἰ   (*conj. introducing protasis of a condition*) if

εἰ μή   (*conj. + neg. introducing protasis of a condition*) if not, unless

ἄν   *particle used with subjunctive in protasis of pres. gen. or fut. more vivid condition, with indic. in apodosis of contrary-to-fact condition, or with optative in apodosis of fut. less vivid condition*

ἐάν, ἤν, or ἄν   *contractions of* εἰ ἄν

228.   **EXERCISES**

A. **Greek-to-English Sentences**

1. εἰ οἱ πολέμιοι ἡμᾶς νῑκῷεν ἐν μάχῃ, οὐκέτι ἂν ἐλεύθεροι εἶμεν οὐδ' ἴσοις νόμοις χρῴμεθα.

2. παρὰ τούτων τῶν ἀναξίων οἰκετῶν, ἢν τοὺς ἵππους μὴ παύσωνται ἀδικοῦντες, οὐ λήψῃ δίκην;

3. εἰ ἡ ἐκείνου τοῦ στρατηγοῦ φύσις ἀμείνων ἦν, ὑπὸ πάντων τῶν στρατιωτῶν ἴσως ἐφιλεῖτο ἄν.

4. τοῦτον τὸν ξένον, ἀφικόμενόν ποτ' εἰς τὴν πόλιν, ὁ δεσπότης μου σπεύδει καλεῖν ἐπὶ δεῖπνον.

5. ἀλλ' εἰ ἐλάττους ἢ εἴκοσιν ἀσπίδας ἐπώλησας, οὐκ ἂν ἔσχες ἱκανὸν ἀριθμὸν δραχμῶν.

6. ἀλλὰ μὴν τοὺς νεανίας διαφθερεῖς, ὦ διδάσκαλε, μὴ δηλῶν αὐτοῖς τό τε δίκαιον καὶ τὸ ἄδικον.

7. εἰ οἱ θεοὶ ἐβουλήθησαν ἔχειν δίκην ἐν τῷ κόσμῳ, ἐποίησαν ἂν ἄνδρας πολλῷ δικαιοτέρους.

8. μὴ ἀδικήσητε μηδέν', ὦ Ἀθηναῖοι, ἡ γὰρ ἀδικίᾱ αἰσχίστη ἐστίν.

9. εἴ ποτ' ἴδοιεν λέοντα ἢ ἄλλο τι δεινὸν ζῷον, οἱ παῖδες ἐφοβοῦντο.

10. ἐὰν ἐν τοῖς ἀγῶσι δικαίως νῑκήσῃς, πολὺν ἄργυρον καὶ χρῡσὸν κομιεῖ.

B.   **English-to-Greek Sentences**

1.   O Athenians, if you arrive at the wall earlier than the others, you will win and will be greatly honored.

2.   We would be very happy if we had fair laws, but that dreadful despot never ceases to injure us.

3.   If the gods should leave heaven and move to earth, would life become more just?

4.   If you are willing, Socrates, let us now investigate the nature of both justice and injustice.

5.   If I had not been taught well by my mother and my father, perhaps I would have been corrupted by the philosophers.

C.   **READING**

THE ATHENIANS GO TOO FAR — Part 4
(adapted from Thucydides' *Peloponnesian War* 6.79-80)

After Nicias' speech, the Athenians defeated the Syracusans in battle, but, lacking cavalry, were unable to pursue them into Syracuse and capture the city. They spent the rest of the winter collecting more troops, horses, money, and provisions in preparation for a spring campaign.

Meanwhile both the Athenians and the Syracusans sent embassies to the Sicilian city of Camarina to try to win the Camarinaeans as allies. Hermocrates, one of the Syracusan ambassadors, spoke first. Below is an excerpt from his speech to the people of Camarina.

Δειλίᾳ δ' ἴσως τὸ δίκαιον θεραπεύσετε, λέγοντες· Συμμαχίᾱ ἐστὶν ἡμῖν πρὸς Ἀθηναίους. ἀλλὰ ταύτην γε τὴν συμμαχίᾱν ἐποιήσασθε μέλλοντες ὠφελήσειν τοὺς Ἀθηναίους ἤν τις τῶν ἐχθρῶν προσβάλλῃ. νῦν δ' αὐτοὶ ἀδικοῦσιν. ὡς ἄδικον εἴη ἂν εἰ ὑμεῖς εὐλόγῳ προφάσει τοὺς μὲν φύσει πολεμίους βούλοισθε ὠφελεῖν, τοὺς δ' ἔτι μᾶλλον φύσει συγγενεῖς μετὰ τῶν ἐχθίστων

5   διαφθεῖραι. καὶ μὴν μὴ φοβεῖσθε τὴν παρασκευὴν Ἀθηναίων· οὐ γάρ, ἢν ἡμεῖς συμμαχώμεθα πάντες, δεινή ἐστιν.

καὶ εἰ νῑκήσουσιν ἡμᾶς Ἀθηναῖοι, ταῖς μὲν ὑμετέραις γνώμαις νῑκήσουσι, τῷ δ' αὐτῶν ὀνόματι τῑμηθήσονται, καὶ τῆς νίκης οὐκ ἄλλο τι ἆθλον ἢ τοὺς τὴν νίκην παρασχόντας λήψονται· καὶ εἰ αὖ ἡμεῖς νῑκήσομεν, παρ' ὑμῶν, ἅτε τῆς

10   αἰτίᾱς τῶν κινδύνων ὄντων, τὴν δίκην ληψόμεθα. κρίνεσθε οὖν ἢ τὴν ὑπ' Ἀθηναίων δεσποτῶν δουλείᾱν ἢ τὴν πρὸς ἡμᾶς συμμαχίᾱν.

VOCABULARY

δειλίᾳ (line 1): from δειλίᾱ, -ᾱς, ἡ: cowardice; here = "through cowardice" (*dative of cause*)

θεραπεύσετε (line 1): from θεραπεύω, θεραπεύσω, ἐθεράπευσα, τεθεράπευκα, τε-θεράπευμαι, ἐθεραπεύθην: serve; here = "give lip service to the just thing," i.e., claim that you are acting out of concern for what is just

συμμαχίᾱ (line 1): from συμμαχίᾱ, -ᾱς, ἡ: alliance

πρός (line 2): here = "with" (*literally*, "toward [in a friendly sense]")

ὡς ἄδικον εἴη ἄν (line 4): impersonal usage: "how unjust it would be...!"

εὐλόγῳ (line 4): from εὔλογος, -ον: well-reasoned (*the Camarinaeans are trying to create the impression that they are motivated by reason when in fact, says Hermocrates, they are motivated by timidity*)

προφάσει (line 4): from πρόφασις, -εως, ἡ: excuse

τοὺς...φύσει πολεμίους (line 4): i.e., the Athenians

τοὺς...ἔτι μᾶλλον φύσει συγγενεῖς (line 5): i.e., the other Sicilians

συγγενεῖς (line 5): from συγγενής, -ές: related, kin

μετά (line 5): here = "with the help of"

ἐχθίστων (line 5): i.e., the Athenians

παρασκευήν (line 6): here = "military force"

συμμαχώμεθα (line 7): from συμμάχομαι: fight together

ταῖς...ὑμετέραις γνώμαις (line 8): i.e., thanks to what you made up your minds to do (*dative of cause*)

γνώμαις (line 8): from γνώμη, -ης, ἡ: judgment, opinion

τῷ...ὀνόματι (lines 8-9): in the name (*dative of respect*)

ἆθλον (line 9): from ἆθλον, -ου, τό: prize

τοὺς τὴν νίκην παρασχόντας (lines 9-10): i.e., the Camarinaeans (*whom the victorious Athenians will subjugate, regarding them as a prize*)

παρασχόντας (line 10): from παρέχω: furnish

αὖ (line 10): again, on the other hand (*adv.*)

ὄντων (line 11): connects ὑμῶν with τῆς αἰτίας (*which is in the genitive because it is being equated with* ὑμῶν)

δουλείᾱν (line 12): from δουλείᾱ, -ᾱς, ἡ: slavery

πρός (line 12): here = "with" (*literally*, "toward [in a friendly sense]")

LESSON 38

CONDITIONAL RELATIVE CLAUSES; RELATIVE ADVERBS

ὅταν γὰρ εὐτυχήσωμεν, τότε /
χαίρειν παρέσται καὶ γελᾶν ἐλευθέρως
(Once we succeed, you can laugh and rejoice all you want.)
—in Sophocles' *Electra* 1299-1300, Orestes warns his sister not to celebrate yet

229. Any relative clause that refers to an **indefinite** person or thing is considered to have conditional force, i.e., it is regarded as the equivalent of a **protasis** (e.g., "whoever does this" = "if anyone does this"; "whatever/whichever happens" = "if anything happens"). The mood and tense appropriate for the verb in the protasis are also appropriate for the verb in the **conditional relative clause**; if ἄν is needed in the protasis, it is needed also in the conditional relative clause.

A conditional relative clause may begin either with an **indefinite relative pronoun** ("whoever," "whatever," "whichever") or with an ordinary relative pronoun ("[anyone] who" = "whoever"; "[anything] that" = "whatever" or "whichever"). Indefinite relatives are combinations of the ordinary relative pronouns (ὅς, ἥ, ὅ, etc.) + τις, τι; thus they are identical with the indirect interrogatives that you learned in Lesson 26 (ὅστις, ἥτις, ὅ τι, etc.). If a clause begins with an indefinite relative, you can be sure that the clause is conditional. If a clause begins with an ordinary relative pronoun, the clause will be conditional only if the antecedent is an indefinite "anyone" or "anything" (usually just implied); otherwise it will be an ordinary relative clause, whose function is to describe some definite person or thing, not to express a condition.

Like a negative protasis, a negative conditional relative clause always has **μή**, not οὐ. The use of μή is therefore a clue that the relative clause is conditional.

CONDITIONAL RELATIVE CLAUSES
(with equivalent conditions)

Simple Particular

Present:

εἰ ὁ Σωκράτης τόδε λέγει, τοὺς νεανίᾱς βλάπτει.

"If Socrates is saying this, he is harming the youth."

ὅστις/ὃς τόδε λέγει τοὺς νεανίᾱς βλάπτει.

"Whoever is saying this is harming the youth."

Past:

εἰ ὁ Σωκράτης τόδ' ἔλεγε, τοὺς νεανίᾱς ἔβλαπτεν.

"If Socrates was saying this, he was harming the youth."

ὅστις/ὃς τόδ' ἔλεγε τοὺς νεανίᾱς ἔβλαπτεν.

"Whoever was saying this was harming the youth."

Contrary to Fact

Present:

εἰ ὁ Σωκράτης τόδ' ἔλεγε, τοὺς νεανίᾱς ἔβλαπτεν ἄν.

"If Socrates were saying this, he would be harming the youth."

ὅστις/ὃς τόδ' ἔλεγε τοὺς νεανίᾱς ἔβλαπτεν ἄν.

"Whoever were saying this would be harming the youth."

Past:

εἰ ὁ Σωκράτης τόδ' εἶπε, τοὺς νεανίᾱς ἔβλαψεν ἄν.

"If Socrates had said this, he would have harmed the youth."

ὅστις/ὃς τόδ' εἶπε τοὺς νεανίᾱς ἔβλαψεν ἄν.

"Whoever had said this would have harmed the youth."

General

Present:

ἐὰν ὁ Σωκράτης τόδε λέγῃ, τοὺς νεανίᾱς βλάπτει.

"If Socrates (ever) says this, he harms the youth."

ὅστις/ὃς ἂν τόδε λέγῃ τοὺς νεανίᾱς βλάπτει.

"Whoever (ever) says this harms the youth."

Past:

εἰ ὁ Σωκράτης τόδε λέγοι, τοὺς νεανίᾱς ἔβλαπτεν.

"If Socrates (ever) said this, he harmed the youth."

ὅστις/ὃς τόδε λέγοι τοὺς νεανίᾱς ἔβλαπτεν.

"Whoever (ever) said this harmed the youth."

Future

Most Vivid:

εἰ ὁ Σωκράτης τόδ' ἐρεῖ, τοὺς νεανίᾱς βλάψει.

"If Socrates says (will say) this, he will harm the youth."

ὅστις/ὃς τόδ' ἐρεῖ τοὺς νεανίᾱς βλάψει.

"Whoever says (will say) this will harm the youth."

More Vivid:

ἐὰν ὁ Σωκράτης τόδε λέγῃ, τοὺς νεανίας βλάψει.

"If Socrates says (will say) this, he will harm the youth."

ὅστις/ὃς ἂν τόδε λέγῃ τοὺς νεανίας βλάψει.

"Whoever says (will say) this will harm the youth."

Less Vivid:

εἰ ὁ Σωκράτης τόδε λέγοι, τοὺς νεανίας βλάπτοι ἄν.

"If Socrates should say this, he would harm the youth."

ὅστις/ὃς τόδε λέγοι τοὺς νεανίας βλάπτοι ἄν.

"Whoever should say this would harm the youth."

230.   Not all relative clauses begin with relative pronouns; many begin with **relative adverbs** ("from where," "to where," "where," "when," "how," etc.) or with **indefinite relative adverbs** ("from wherever," "to wherever," "wherever," "whenever," "howsoever," etc.). The antecedent of a relative adverb is often just implied (e.g., "I visited [the place] *where* you live"; "will you be ready [at the time] *whenever* I come?"; "[the way] *how* they will survive is unclear").

You already know five indefinite relative adverbs because they are identical with the indirect interrogative adverbs (ὁπόθεν, ὅποι, ὅπου, ὁπότε, ὅπως) presented in Lesson 26. The ordinary relative adverbs to which they correspond are **ὅθεν, οἷ, οὗ, ὅτε**, and **ὡς**. The following chart illustrates these correspondences:

Relative Adverb:		Indir. Interrog. Adv.:		or	Indef. Rel. Adv.:
ὅθεν	"from where"	ὁπόθεν	"from where?"	or	"from wherever"
οἷ	"to where"	ὅποι	"to where?"	or	"to wherever"
οὗ	"where"	ὅπου	"where?"	or	"wherever"
ὅτε	"when"	ὁπότε	"when?"	or	"whenever"
ὡς	"how," "as"	ὅπως	"how?"	or	"howsoever," "as ever"

Conditional relative clauses introduced by relative adverbs function the same way as those introduced by relative pronouns. ὅτε + ἄν = **ὅταν**; ὁπότε + ἄν = **ὁπόταν**.

231.   Just as a relative clause may function as the protasis of a condition, so may a **temporal clause** (an adverbial clause of time, telling *when* something happened). This is particularly common when a temporal clause is introduced by ἐπεί or ἐπειδή. ἐπεί + ἄν = **ἐπάν** or **ἐπήν**; ἐπειδή + ἄν = **ἐπειδάν**.

Examples:

Past General:

ἐπεὶ ὁ Σωκράτης τόδε λέγοι, τοὺς νεανίας ἔβλαπτεν.

"When [= if (ever)] Socrates said this, he harmed the youth."

Future More Vivid:

ἐπειδὰν ὁ Σωκράτης τόδε λέγῃ, τοὺς νεανίας βλάψει.

"When [= if] Socrates says this, he will harm the youth."

232.   VOCABULARY

ἄρχω, ἄρξω, ἦρξα, ἦρχα, ἦργμαι, ἤρχθην

(+ *gen.*) rule; (+ *gen.*) make begin; (*mid. + gen., infin., or ptcple.*) begin
[cf. *archangel*]

NOTE   The basic meaning of this verb is "be first" (in power or time). A partitive genitive may be added to show the group that someone is in charge of or the event that someone is making start (*active voice*) or is at the start of (*middle voice*).

ἄρχων, -οντος, ὁ   archon (*one of the nine chief magistrates chosen each year in Athens*)

θῡμός, -οῦ, ὁ   spirit, soul, heart, passion (*usually courage or anger*)

NOTE   ψῡχή ("spirit") is the breath or life in a person, while θῡμός ("spirit") is the inner force that drives a person to feel emotion or take action.

προθῡμίᾱ, -ᾱς, ἡ   eagerness, goodwill

ὅστις, ἥτις, ὅ τι   (*indef. rel. pron.*) whoever, whatever, whichever

πρόθῡμος, -ον   (+ *gen. or infin.*) eager (for, to); (+ *dat. or* εἰς + *acc.*) well-disposed (toward)

ὅθεν   (*rel. adv.*) from where, whence

οἷ   (*rel. adv.*) to where, whither

ὅτε   (*rel. adv.*) when (ὅτ' *before smooth breathing;* ὅθ' *before rough breathing*); ὅτε + ἄν = ὅταν

οὗ   (*rel. adv.*) where

ὡς   (*rel. adv.*) how, as

NOTE   You now know several uses of ὡς: as a relative adverb ("how," "as"), as an exclamatory adverb ("how...!"), as a particle combined with participles ("as if," "with the avowed intention of," "on the grounds of"), as a particle combined with superlatives ("as...as possible"), and as a conjunction ("as," "since," "because," "after," "when").

ὁπόθεν   (*indef. rel. adv.*) from wherever, whencesoever

ὅποι   (*indef. rel. adv.*) to wherever, whithersoever

ὁπότε	(*indef. rel. adv.*) whenever (ὁπότ' *before smooth breathing;* ὁπόθ' *before rough breathing*); ὁπότε + ἄν = ὁπόταν
ὅπου	(*indef. rel. adv.*) wherever
ὅπως	(*indef. rel. adv.*) howsoever, as ever
ἐπάν or ἐπήν	contraction of ἐπεί + ἄν
ἐπειδάν	contraction of ἐπειδή + ἄν

233.   **EXERCISES**

A.   **Greek-to-English Sentences**

1. ὅθ' ἡ θυγάτηρ σου ἑτοίμη ἐστίν, ἄγαγε αὐτὴν εἰς τὴν οἰκίαν οὗ αἱ ἄλλαι κόραι προθύμως μένουσιν.

2. ὅστις ἂν δικαίως ἄρχῃ καὶ τὸν νόμον τῑμᾷ, ἀεὶ φιλεῖται ὑπὸ τῶν πολλῶν.

3. οὕστινας διδάσκοιεν οἱ φιλόσοφοι, βέλτιστα ζῷεν ἂν καὶ ζητοῖεν ἂν τὴν δίκην.

4. ὁπόταν ἴδωσιν ἐκεῖνοι οἱ παῖδες τὰ κάλλιστα δένδρα, πρόθῡμοί εἰσι λίθοις βάλλειν ταῦτα.

5. ὃς ἂν μὴ κριθῇ ("chosen as") ἄρχων μὴ ἄρξηται εἰπεῖν αἰσχροὺς λόγους ἐπὶ τὸν κριθέντα.

6. ἐπειδὰν ὁ δεινότατος πόλεμος παύηται, οἱ βίοι ἡμῶν πολλῷ ἡδῑόνές τε καὶ εὐδαιμονέστεροι γενήσονται.

7. εἴθε πάντες οἱ νέοι στρατιῶται θῡμῷ φυλάττοιεν τὰ τείχη καὶ τρέποιεν τοὺς πολεμίους ἀπὸ τῆς πόλεως.

8. τί εἴπω ἢ τίσι λόγοις χρῶμαι; οὐ γὰρ οἶδα, ὦ θεοί, ἱκανῶς τῑμᾶν ὑμᾶς.

9. καίπερ οὐδενὸς προθύμου τῆς μάχης ὄντος, ἡ Μοῖρα κελεύει ἡμᾶς οὐκ ἐθέλοντας μάχεσθαι τοῖς Ἀθηναίοις.

10. ὅποι ἂν πέμψῃς ἐμέ, προθῡμίᾳ σπεύσω, ἀλλὰ βουλοίμην ἂν φέρειν τήνδε τὴν ἐπιστολὴν πρὸς τὸν βασιλέᾱ αὐτόν.

B.   **English-to-Greek Sentences**

1. Let whoever is willing to help our city-state begin to seek soldiers and to prepare a very large army.

2. Wherever the archon saw injustice, he was eager both to help those being injured and to punish those injuring.

3. If only you might know how to rule your spirit, child, and (if only you might) live so wisely as never to sin!

4. Whenever a better teacher than I speaks about the nature of the universe, many students eagerly listen.

5. Take (*sg.*) whichever shields will be useful to you; we shall sell whichever you do not wish to take.

C. READING

THE ATHENIANS GO TOO FAR — Part 5
(adapted from Thucydides' *Peloponnesian War* 6.82-86)

When Hermocrates finished his speech, Euphemus, the Athenians' representative, responded. Selections from his speech follow.

Ἀφῑκόμεθα μὲν ἐπὶ τῆς πρότερον οὔσης συμμαχίᾱς ἀνανεώσει, τοῦ δὲ Συρᾱκοσίου ἄρτι προσβαλόντος, ἐροῦμεν καὶ περὶ τῆς ἀρχῆς ἣν δικαίως ἔχομεν. ἄξιοι γὰρ ὄντες ἄρχομεν, ὅτι ναυτικῷ πλείστῳ καὶ προθῡμίᾳ ὠφελοῦμεν τοὺς ἄλλους Ἕλληνας ἐπειδὰν ἐν κινδῡνοις ὦσιν.

5 καὶ μὴν ἡμῖν χρήσιμον ἂν εἴη ὠφελεῖν ὑμᾶς. σῳζομένων γὰρ ὑμῶν καὶ οὕτως ἐχόντων ἀντέχειν τοῖς Συρᾱκοσίοις, ἧττον ἂν ὑπὸ τούτων τινὰ στρατιὰν ἐφ᾽ ἡμᾶς πεμψάντων βλαπτοίμεθα. ἀνδρὶ δὲ τυράννῳ ὄντι ἢ πόλει ἀρχὴν ἐχούσῃ οὐκ ἄλογόν ἐστιν ὅ τι χρήσιμόν ἐστιν.

καὶ οἱ Συρᾱκόσιοι οὐ στρατοπέδῳ, πόλει δὲ μείζονι τῆς ἡμετέρᾱς
10 στρατιᾶς ὑμῖν ἀεί τ᾽ ἐπιβουλεύουσι καί, ὅταν καιρὸν λάβωσιν, οὐκ ἀνιᾶσιν. εἰ οὖν τῷ ὑπόπτῳ τὴν ἡμετέρᾱν στρατιὰν ἐκβαλεῖτε, τοῦ λοιποῦ βουλήσεσθε, κακῶς πράττοντες, καὶ ὀλίγιστον μόριον αὐτῆς ἰδεῖν.

Conclusion: *After the speeches of Hermocrates and Euphemus, the Camarinaeans decided that it would be safest for them to remain neutral. They later changed their minds and sent troops (as did the Spartans) to help the Syracusans. In a momentous naval battle against the combined forces of Sicily (413 B.C.), the Athenians were disastrously defeated. Only a tiny remnant of the huge fleet ever returned to Athens.*

VOCABULARY

ἐπί (line 1): here = "on the matter of," "in regard to" (+ *dat.*)
πρότερον οὔσης (line 1): here = "existing earlier," i.e., previous
συμμαχίᾱς (line 1): from συμμαχίᾱ, -ᾱς, ἡ: alliance
ἀνανεώσει (line 1): from ἀνανέωσις, -εως, ἡ: renewal
Συρᾱκοσίου (line 2): from Συρᾱκόσιος, -ᾱ, -ον: Syracusan (*here Euphemus is referring to Hermocrates*)
ἀρχῆς (line 2): here = "empire"
ναυτικῷ (line 3): from ναυτικός, -ή, -όν: naval; (*as a neut. substantive*) navy
χρήσιμον (line 5): predicate adjective modifying the subject, ὠφελεῖν
ἀντέχειν (line 6): from ἀντέχω (+ *dat.*): hold out (against), resist
ἐφ᾽ (line 7):-here = "against"
τυράννῳ (line 7): τύραννος, -ου, ὁ: tyrant (*one who seizes power rather than inheriting it—not necessarily a cruel or wicked ruler*)

ἀρχήν (line 7): here = "empire"

ἄλογον (line 8): from ἄλογος, -ον: illogical (*here* = "an illogical thing to do")

στρατοπέδῳ, πόλει (line 9): dative of means (*i.e., the Syracusans are more of a threat since they are a whole city, not just a campful of soldiers*)

ὑμῖν (line 10): dative with ἐπιβουλεύουσι

ἐπιβουλεύουσι (line 10): from ἐπιβουλεύω, ἐπιβουλεύσω, ἐπεβούλευσα, ἐπιβεβούλευκα, ἐπιβεβούλευμαι, ἐπεβουλεύθην (+ *dat.*): plot (against)

καιρόν (line 10): from καιρός, -οῦ, ὁ: right time, opportunity

ἀντᾶσιν (line 11): 3rd pl. pres. act. indic. of ἀνίημι, ἀνήσω, ἀνῆκα, ἀνεῖκα, ἀνεῖμαι, ἀνείθην: let go, pass up

ὑπόπτῳ (line 11): from ὕποπτος, -ον: suspicious; (*as a neut. substantive*) suspicion (*here* = *dative of cause*)

ἐκβαλεῖτε (line 11): from ἐκβάλλω: throw out, reject

μόριον (line 12): from μόριον, -ου, τό: small portion (*i.e., so desperate will you be that you'll be glad for any help, no matter how small, from us*)

LESSON 39
PURPOSE CLAUSES

καὶ γὰρ βασιλεὺς αἱρεῖται, οὐχ ἵνα ἑαυτοῦ καλῶς
ἐπιμελῆται, ἀλλ᾽ ἵνα καὶ οἱ ἑλόμενοι δι᾽ αὐτὸν εὖ πράττωσι
(A king is chosen to benefit his choosers, not to help himself.)
—Socrates advises a newly elected general in Xenophon's *Memorabilia* 3.2.3

234.
You already know that a **future participle** (especially when combined with a verb of motion) may show the purpose behind an action (e.g., ὀψόμενος τὴν τριήρη, σπεύδω ἐπὶ τὴν θάλατταν "going to see [i.e., with the aim of seeing] the trireme, I am hastening to the sea"). Another way to express purpose is with an adverbial **purpose clause** (also called a **final clause**) introduced by the subordinating conjunction ἵνα, ὅπως, or ὡς ("in order that"). Negative purpose clauses (used when the intention is not to accomplish something, but to keep something from happening) are introduced by ἵνα μή, ὅπως μή, ὡς μή, or just μή ("in order that…not," "lest").

The **subjunctive** is the normal mood for the verb in a purpose clause, provided that the main verb in the sentence is in a **primary** tense (present, future, perfect, or future perfect indicative; if the main verb is subjunctive, optative, or imperative in mood, it is regarded as primary, no matter what its tense happens to be); e.g., σπεύδω ἐπὶ τὴν θάλατταν ἵνα ἴδω τὴν τριήρη ("I am hastening to the sea to see [literally, 'in order that I may see'] the trireme"). If the main verb is in a **secondary** tense (imperfect, aorist, or pluperfect indicative), the **optative** is the normal mood, but the speaker may choose to use the subjunctive for greater vividness; e.g., ἔσπευδον ἐπὶ τὴν θάλατταν ἵνα ἴδοιμι [or, more vividly, ἴδω] τὴν τριήρη ("I was hastening to the sea to see [literally, 'in order that I might see'] the trireme"). The tense of the verb in the purpose clause shows **aspect**, not time.

When translating a purpose clause, you should feel free to use an **infinitive** ("to…") since, in English, an infinitive is a concise, normal

265

way to express purpose. When translating such an infinitive into Greek, however, you should ordinarily use a purpose clause or a future participle, not an infinitive.

A purpose clause implies that **a person has a goal in mind** and is undertaking a specific action to achieve it, while a result clause implies only that a result actually occurs, or naturally would occur, because of what someone or something is or does, not necessarily because anyone wants it to occur.

Examples:

Actual Result Clause:

ἦν μεγάλη φωνὴ τῷ ἀγγέλῳ ὥστε πάντες ἤκουον.
"The messenger had a loud voice so that all heard."
[*The messenger did not necessarily intend to be heard, but was.*]

Natural Result Clause:

ἦν μεγάλη φωνὴ τῷ ἀγγέλῳ ὥστε ὑπὸ πάντων ἀκούεσθαι.
"The messenger had a loud voice so as to be heard by all."
[*The messenger did not necessarily intend to be heard, but that would have resulted naturally from his loud voice.*]

Purpose Clause:

μεγάλη φωνῇ ἔλεγεν ὁ ἄγγελος ἵνα ὑπὸ πάντων ἀκούοιτο (ἀκούηται).
"The messenger was speaking loudly in order to be heard by all."
[*The messenger wanted to be heard; the sentence does not reveal whether he actually was.*]

235.   The **indirect questions** in preceding chapters all had verbs in the indicative mood because that would have been the mood used in the direct form of the questions. Here is a further complication: when the sentence's main verb is in a **secondary tense**, the speaker has the option of either retaining the mood from the direct question in the indirect question or changing it to the **optative**. Switching to the optative is, in fact, more usual than retaining the original mood (but only in sentences whose main verbs are in a secondary tense). Remember that the *tense* of the verb in the indirect question is always the same as it would have been in the direct question, even if the *mood* is different. Examples:

ἠρώτησά σε ὅ τι εἴποις (*or, more vividly,* εἶπες).
"I asked you what you (had) said."

ἠρώτων σε ὅ τι λέγοις (*or, more vividly,* λέγεις).
"I kept asking you what you were saying."

236.   **VOCABULARY**

βοάω, βοήσομαι, ἐβόησα, —, —, —
        cry, cry out, shout

γαμέω, γαμῶ, ἔγημα, γεγάμηκα, γεγάμημαι, —
> take (*a woman*) as a wife, marry (*a woman*); (*mid. + dat.*) give oneself in marriage (*to a man*), marry (*a man*)

ἕπομαι (*imperf.* εἱπόμην), ἔψομαι, ἑσπόμην, —, —, —
> (*+ dat.*) follow

NOTE   ἑπ- was originally σεπ-. Aorist ἑσπ- = zero-grade stem (-σπ-) augmented with σε- (→ἑ-). Aor. subj. = σπῶμαι; aor. opt. = σποίμην; aor. imper. = σποῦ; aor. infin. = σπέσθαι; aor. ptcple. = σπόμενος, -η, -ον.

βοή, -ῆς, ἡ   shout

γάμος, -ου, ὁ   marriage, wedding; γάμον ποιεῖν = hold a wedding [cf. *monogamous, polygamy*]

γυνή, γυναικός, ἡ   woman, wife [cf. *androgynous, gynecology*]

NOTE   The nominative and vocative singular should both be γύναιξ (stem = γυναικ-), but instead γυνή is used for the nominative, γύναι for the vocative. The accent shifts to the ultima in the genitive and dative, singular and plural, as if the word had a monosyllabic stem: SG.: γυνή, γυναικός, γυναικί, γυναῖκα, γύναι; PL.: γυναῖκες, γυναικῶν, γυναιξί(ν), γυναῖκας.

κλῖμαξ, -ακος, ἡ   ladder, staircase [cf. *climax*]

ὕστατος, -η, -ον   (*superl. of* ὕστερος, -ᾱ, -ον) latest, last

ὕστερος, -ᾱ, -ον   (*comparative; no positive degree exists*) later, next; (*adv.*) ὕστερον = later

ἄνω   (*adv.*) up, upwards

κάτω   (*adv.*) down, downwards

ἵνα or ὅπως or ὡς   (*conj. introducing purp. cl.*) in order that

ἵνα μή or ὅπως μή or ὡς μή or μή
> (*introducing neg. purp. cl.*) in order that...not, lest

237.   **EXERCISES**

A.   **Greek-to-English Sentences**

1. μεγίστῳ οὖν θῡμῷ μαχώμεθα, ὦ στρατιῶται, ἵνα ἡδεῖα νίκη ἡμῖν ἔπηται.

2. ὁπόταν γυναῖκα καλὴν καλὸς ἀνὴρ γαμῇ, τῷ γάμῳ πάντες χαίρουσιν.

3. οὐ μὲν ἤδη ὅπου βούλοιο ποιεῖν τὸν γάμον, ἑτοίμη δ᾽ ἦ ἕπεσθαι ὅποι βούλοιο ἄγειν ἐμέ.

4. βοῇ ἔσπευσεν ὁ υἱὸς κατὰ τῆς κλίμακος ὅπως εἴποι τῷ ἑαυτοῦ πατρὶ ἄρτι σωθέντι ἐκ τοῦ μακροῦ πολέμου.

5. τῇ ὑστάτῃ ἡμέρᾳ ἔθῡσα τοῖς ἀθανάτοις θεοῖς ἵνα μὴ λάβοιεν δίκην παρ᾽ ἐμοῦ, οὐ γὰρ ἐθέλων ἥμαρτον ἔγωγε.

6. κάλεσον τὴν ἐμὴν γυναῖκα, ὦ θεράπαινα, ὅπως παύσῃ τὸ παιδίον βοῶν.

7. διὰ τί ἄνω βλέπεις, ὦ μαθητά; εἰ τρέψειας κάτω τοὺς ὀφθαλμούς, ἴδοις ἂν τὰ βιβλία ἃ ἔλιπες ὑπὸ τῇ κλίμακι.

8. οὕτως ἀδίκως ἄρχεις τῆς πόλεως ὥστε μηδέν᾽ ἐθέλειν σοι εἰς τὴν μάχην ἕπεσθαι μήτε νῦν μήθ᾽ ὕστερον.

9. εἰ γὰρ γημαίμην ἀνδρὶ ἀξιωτάτῳ ἵνα πᾶσαι αἱ ἄλλαι γυναῖκές με τῑμῶσιν.

10. ταῖς τρισὶ γυναιξὶν εἵπετο ὁ κλὼψ ὅπως εὕροι θ᾽ ὅπου ἡ οἰκίᾱ εἴη καὶ ὕστερον κλέψειε πάντα τὰ ἀργύρια ἐξ αὐτῆς.

B.   **English-to-Greek Sentences**

1. Whenever they attack, the soldiers fight with great shouts in order to frighten the enemy and win.

2. We held the wedding later in order that all the guests might have enough time to arrive.

3. Your fame, O king, is such as to be shouted up and down by all who know you.

4. Why are you crying, daughter? Are you not eager to marry the last young man whom we saw?

5. Do not follow me down (from) the staircase, my wife, lest you, who are dearest of all (women) to me, be hurt.

C.   READING

JUSTIFIABLE HOMICIDE? — Part 1
(adapted from Lysias' *On the Murder of Eratosthenes* 6-11)

Lysias (c. 459-380 B.C.) was a renowned λογογράφος, *or speech-writer, in Athens. Litigants who had to speak on their own behalf in court would hire Lysias to write speeches for them. It was up to Lysias to make the style of each speech suit the person who would be delivering it.*

The excerpt that follows is from a speech written by Lysias for a defendant named Euphiletus, who was on trial for having killed a man whom he found in bed with his wife. When the passage begins, Euphiletus is describing the chain of events that led to the murder.

Ἐγὼ γάρ, ὦ Ἀθηναῖοι, ἐπειδὴ ἔδοξέ μοι γῆμαι, γυναῖκα ἠγαγόμην εἰς τὴν οἰκίαν. ἐπίστευον δὲ πάντα τὰ ἐμαυτοῦ ἐκείνῃ, ἐν γὰρ τῷ πρώτῳ χρόνῳ, ὦ Ἀθηναῖοι, πασῶν ἦν βελτίστη, οὖσα οἰκονόμος δεινὴ καὶ φειδωλή. ἐπειδὴ δ᾽ ἡ μήτηρ μου ἀπέθανεν, ἡ ἐμὴ γυνή, ἐπ᾽ ἐκφορὰν ἐμοὶ σπομένη, ὑπὸ τούτου τοῦ
5   ἀνθρώπου ὤφθη καὶ χρόνῳ διαφθείρεται.

ἔστι μοι οἰκίδιον διπλοῦν, ἴσα ἔχον τὰ ἄνω τοῖς κάτω. ἐπειδὴ δὲ τὸ παιδίον ἐγένετο ἡμῖν, ἡ μήτηρ αὐτὸ ἐθήλαζεν· ἵνα δὲ μὴ κινδυνεύῃ κατὰ τῆς κλίμακος καταβαίνουσα, ἐγὼ μὲν ἄνω διῃτώμην, αἱ δὲ γυναῖκες κάτω. καὶ πολλάκις νυκτὸς ἡ γυνὴ κατέβαινεν ἵνα θηλάζοι τὸ παιδίον καὶ μὴ βοῴη, καὶ ταῦτα πολὺν
10   χρόνον οὕτως ἐγίγνετο, καὶ ἐγὼ οὔποθ᾽ ὑπώπτευσα. χρόνῳ δ᾽ ὑστέρῳ ἀφικόμην ἀπροσδοκήτως ἐξ ἀγροῦ, μετὰ δὲ τὸ δεῖπνον τὸ παιδίον ἐβόα, ὑπὸ τῆς θεραπαίνης πληττόμενον, ἵνα ταῦτα ποιῇ· ὁ γὰρ ἄνθρωπος ἔνδον ἦν.

VOCABULARY

ἔδοξέ μοι (line 1): (*impersonal usage*) it seemed good to me, i.e., I decided (*from* δοκέω, δόξω, ἔδοξα, —, δέδογμαι, ἐδόχθην: seem, seem good)

γυναῖκα ἠγαγόμην (line 1): I led for myself (i.e., introduced) a wife

ἐπίστευον (line 2): here = "entrusted"

οἰκονόμος (line 3): from οἰκονόμος, -ου, ἡ: manager (*of the household*)

φειδωλή (line 3): φειδωλός, -ή, -όν: thrifty

ἐκφορὰν (line 4): ἐκφορά, -ᾶς, ἡ: funeral

τούτου τοῦ ἀνθρώπου (lines 4-5): i.e., Eratosthenes

χρόνῳ (line 5): in time, i.e., eventually

οἰκίδιον (line 6): from οἰκίδιον, -ου, τό: little house (*diminutive of* οἰκία)

διπλοῦν (line 6): from διπλοῦς (= -όος), -ῆ, -οῦν: double (*here* = "two-story")

τὰ ἄνω (line 6): the upstairs (*as opposed to* τὰ κάτω, "the downstairs")

ἐθήλαζεν (line 7): from θηλάζω, θηλάσω, ἐθήλασα, τεθήλακα, τεθήλασμαι, ἐθηλάσθην: nurse (*a baby*)

κινδῡνεύῃ (line 7): from κινδῡνεύω, κινδῡνεύσω, ἐκινδῡνευσα, κεκινδῡνευκα, κεκινδῡνευμαι, ἐκινδῡνεύθην: run a risk, be in danger

καταβαίνουσα (line 8): from καταβαίνω, καταβήσομαι, κατέβην, καταβέβηκα, καταβέβαμαι, κατεβάθην: go down

διῃτώμην (line 8): from διαιτάω (*imperf.* διῄτων), διαιτήσω, διῄτησα, δεδιῄτηκα, δεδιῄτημαι, διῃτήθην: (*act.*) support; (*mid./pass.*) lead a life, live

κάτω (line 8): the women's quarters would normally have been upstairs

νυκτός (line 9): even though the women and baby were living downstairs, Euphiletus' wife still spent each night upstairs with her husband

βοῷη (line 9): subject = τὸ παιδίον

ὑπώπτευσα (line 10): from ὑποπτεύω, ὑποπτεύσω, ὑπώπτευσα, ὑπώπτευκα, ὑπώπτευμαι, ὑπωπτεύθην: be suspicious, suspect

ἀπροσδοκήτως (line 11): unexpectedly (*adv. from* ἀπροσδόκητος, -ον)

ἀγροῦ (line 11): from ἀγρός, -οῦ, ὁ: countryside (*Euphiletus owned a farm*)

ἵνα ταῦτα ποιῇ (line 12): subject = τὸ παιδίον (*the baby was deliberately made to cry so that Euphiletus' wife would have an excuse to leave her husband's bed and could spend the night with her lover downstairs*)

ἔνδον (line 12): inside (*adv.*) (*Eratosthenes, thinking that Euphiletus would not be home, had come for a rendezvous and was hiding in the house*)

LESSON 40

εἶμι; INDIRECT DISCOURSE (ὅτι/ὡς)

δείξομεν…ὡς μετερχόμεθα τοὺς τὰ
τοιαῦτα καθ' ἡμῶν διεξιόντας
(We'll show how we pay back the backbiters.)
—in Lucian's *Zeus the Tragedian* 24, Poseidon recommends killing Damis,
an Epicurean philosopher, for denying that the gods exist

238. The basic word for "go" or "come" in ancient Greek is the semi-deponent verb ἔρχομαι (*stem* = ἐρχ-), ἐλεύσομαι (*stem* = ἐλευθ-), ἦλθον (*stem* = ἐλθ-), ἐλήλυθα (*stem* = ἐλυθ- with Attic reduplication; cf. ἐνήνοχα, the fourth principal part of φέρω), —, —. However, for the future and imperfect indicative, present imperative, present subjunctive, present and future optative, present and future infinitives, and present and future participles, writers of Attic prose preferred not to use forms of ἔρχομαι. Instead they borrowed forms from a synonym, εἶμι ("I shall go").

Like εἰμί and οἶδα, εἶμι is an irregular verb belonging to the μι-conjugation; its stem may be ἰ- or εἰ-. Since it has just one principal part, only forms built on that principal part exist. Moreover, the verb occurs only in the active voice. Its present indicative (εἶμι) usually has a **future sense** and replaces ἐλεύσομαι ("I shall go"). Its imperfect (ᾖα/ᾔειν) replaces ἠρχόμην ("I was going"). Its present imperative (ἴθι) replaces ἔρχου. Its present subjunctive (ἴω) replaces ἔρχωμαι; its present optative (ἴοιμι/ἰοίην) replaces either the present ἐρχοίμην or the future ἐλευσοίμην. Its present infinitive (ἰέναι) replaces either ἔρχεσθαι ("to go") or ἐλεύσεσθαι ("to be going to go"); its present participle (ἰών) replaces either ἐρχόμενος ("going") or ἐλευσόμενος ("going to go").

εἶμι resembles εἰμί and οἶδα in many of its forms; in fact, its second-person singular present indicative (εἶ) is identical to that of εἰμί, and its third-person plural imperfect (ᾖσαν) is identical to the third-person plural pluperfect of οἶδα. εἶμι has no forms that are enclitic; that helps to distinguish the otherwise identical εἶμι/εἰμί and εἶσι/εἰσί.

271

Present Active Indicative

Singular:

εἶμι	("I shall go")
εἶ	("you [*sg.*] will go")
εἶσι(ν)	("he/she/it will go")

Plural:

ἴμεν	("we shall go")
ἴτε	("you [*pl.*] will go")
ἴᾱσι(ν)	("they will go")

Imperfect Active Indicative

Singular:

ᾖα/ᾔειν	("I was going")
ᾔεισθα/ᾔεις	("you [*sg.*] were going")
ᾔειν/ᾔει	("he/she/it was going")

Plural:

ᾖμεν	("we were going")
ᾖτε	("you [*pl.*] were going")
ᾖσαν/ᾔεσαν	("they were going")

Present Active Subjunctive

Singular:

ἴω
ἴῃς
ἴῃ

Plural:

ἴωμεν
ἴητε
ἴωσι(ν)

Present Active Optative

Singular:

ἴοιμι/ἰοίην
ἴοις
ἴοι

Plural:

ἴοιμεν
ἴοιτε
ἴοιεν

Present Active Imperative

Singular:

ἴθι	("go!")
ἴτω	("let him/her/it go!")

Plural:

ἴτε	("go!")
ἰόντων	("let them go!")

Present Active Infinitive:

ἰέναι ("to go" or "to be going to go")

Present Active Participle:

ἰών, ἰοῦσα, ἰόν ("going" or "going to go")

Singular:	Masc.	Fem.	Neut.
Nom./Voc.	ἰών	ἰοῦσα	ἰόν
Gen.	ἰόντος	ἰούσης	ἰόντος
Dat.	ἰόντι	ἰούσῃ	ἰόντι
Acc.	ἰόντα	ἰοῦσαν	ἰόν

Plural:	Masc.	Fem.	Neut.
Nom./Voc.	ἰόντες	ἰοῦσαι	ἰόντα
Gen.	ἰόντων	ἰουσῶν	ἰόντων
Dat.	ἰοῦσι(ν)	ἰούσαις	ἰοῦσι(ν)
Acc.	ἰόντας	ἰούσᾱς	ἰόντα

239.   You already know what is involved in transforming a direct question into an indirect question in Greek. Transforming a direct statement, thought, belief, or perception into **indirect discourse** is more complicated because **three different methods** are available. The method to be followed in any given sentence depends on the nature of its **main verb**. Some verbs call for a particular method; others offer the speaker a choice between two of the methods; still others allow the speaker to choose any one of the three possible methods.

For now, you need learn only the first method, which closely resembles the method used to create indirect questions. The reported discourse is placed in a clause containing a **finite verb** and introduced by the subordinating conjunction ὅτι ("that") or ὡς ("that" or "how"). The **tense** and **mood** of the verb in the clause are **the same as they would have been in the direct form** of the discourse.

In a sentence whose main verb is in a secondary tense, the mood of the verb in the indirect discourse **may be changed to the optative** (just as in an indirect question). The tense of the optative reflects what the tense in the direct discourse would have been: present/imperfect (→ present optative), aorist (→ aorist optative), future (→ future optative), perfect/pluperfect (→ perfect optative), future perfect (→ future perfect optative).

NOTE   These are nearly the only circumstances under which the future optative or the very rare future perfect optative (= perfect participle + ἐσοίμην) is ever used.

When the main verb is a verb of **saying**, the preferred type of indirect discourse is the ὅτι/ὡς type. Thus the ὅτι/ὡς type is regularly found with ἀγγέλλω, ἀποκρίνομαι, γράφω (writing being the equivalent of speaking), and above all with λέγω, provided that the "saying" has no special connotation. For the optional use of ὅτι/ὡς with verbs of showing, knowing, and perceiving, see Lesson 42.

Examples of Indirect Discourse with a ὅτι/ὡς Clause

Direct Discourse:

Ὁ Σωκράτης τοὺς νεᾱνίᾱς βλάπτει.   (Present)
"Socrates is harming the youth."

Indirect Discourse:

λέγουσιν ὅτι/ὡς ὁ Σωκράτης τοὺς νεᾱνίᾱς βλάπτει.
"They say that Socrates is harming the youth."

ἔλεγον ὅτι/ὡς ὁ Σωκράτης τοὺς νεᾱνίᾱς βλάπτει.

or   ἔλεγον ὅτι/ὡς ὁ Σωκράτης τοὺς νεᾱνίᾱς βλάπτοι.
"They said that Socrates was harming the youth."

Direct Discourse:

Ὁ Σωκράτης τοὺς νεᾱνίᾱς ἔβλαπτεν.   (Imperfect)
"Socrates was harming the youth."

Indirect Discourse:

λέγουσιν ὅτι/ὡς ὁ Σωκράτης τοὺς νεᾱνίᾱς ἔβλαπτεν.
"They say that Socrates was harming the youth."

ἔλεγον ὅτι/ὡς ὁ Σωκράτης τοὺς νεᾱνίᾱς ἔβλαπτεν.
or   ἔλεγον ὅτι/ὡς ὁ Σωκράτης τοὺς νεᾱνίᾱς βλάπτοι.
"They said that Socrates had been harming the youth."

Direct Discourse:

Ὁ Σωκράτης τοὺς νεᾱνίᾱς ἔβλαψεν.   (Aorist)
"Socrates harmed the youth."

Indirect Discourse:

λέγουσιν ὅτι/ὡς ὁ Σωκράτης τοὺς νεᾱνίᾱς ἔβλαψεν.
"They say that Socrates harmed the youth."

ἔλεγον ὅτι/ὡς ὁ Σωκράτης τοὺς νεᾱνίᾱς ἔβλαψεν.
or   ἔλεγον ὅτι/ὡς ὁ Σωκράτης τοὺς νεᾱνίᾱς βλάψειεν.
"They said that Socrates had harmed the youth."

Direct Discourse:

Ὁ Σωκράτης τοὺς νεᾱνίᾱς βλάψει.   (Future)
"Socrates will harm the youth."

Indirect Discourse:

λέγουσιν ὅτι/ὡς ὁ Σωκράτης τοὺς νεᾱνίᾱς βλάψει.
"They say that Socrates will harm the youth."

ἔλεγον ὅτι/ὡς ὁ Σωκράτης τοὺς νεᾱνίᾱς βλάψει.
or   ἔλεγον ὅτι/ὡς ὁ Σωκράτης τοὺς νεᾱνίᾱς βλάψοι.
"They said that Socrates would harm the youth."

Direct Discourse:

Ὁ Σωκράτης τοὺς νεᾱνίᾱς βέβλαφεν.   (Perfect)
"Socrates has harmed the youth."

Indirect Discourse:

λέγουσιν ὅτι/ὡς ὁ Σωκράτης τοὺς νεᾱνίᾱς βέβλαφεν.
"They say that Socrates has harmed the youth."

ἔλεγον ὅτι/ὡς ὁ Σωκράτης τοὺς νεᾱνίᾱς βέβλαφεν.
or   ἔλεγον ὅτι/ὡς ὁ Σωκράτης τοὺς νεᾱνίᾱς βεβλαφὼς εἴη
        (or βεβλάφοι).
"They said that Socrates had harmed the youth."

240.   It is common for indirect discourse to involve one or more **dependent clauses** as well as an independent clause; e.g., the reported statement might be a condition with both a protasis (dependent clause) and an apodosis (independent clause). After a secondary main verb the

speaker has the option to change the mood of each dependent verb (in addition to the mood of the independent verb) in the indirect discourse to the **optative** (if a subjunctive + ἄν becomes optative, the ἄν is dropped). To avoid ambiguity, however, switching the mood of a **dependent** verb to the optative is **forbidden** if that verb is in a **secondary tense of the indicative**. Otherwise it would be impossible to tell, for example, whether an aorist optative in a protasis represented an aorist indicative (changed to optative) in a past contrary-to-fact condition or an aorist optative (unchanged) in a future less vivid condition.

241.	**VOCABULARY**

αἱρέω, αἱρήσω, εἷλον (*stem* = ἑλ-), ᾕρηκα, ᾕρημαι, ᾑρέθην
    take; (*mid.*) choose [cf. *heresy*]

NOTE ᾑρέθη βασιλεύς = "he was chosen [as] king"; αὐτὸν βασιλέα εἵλοντο = "they chose him [as] king." In **factitive** sentences like these, no word for *as* is needed.

εἶμι, —, —, —, —, —   go, come, travel

NOTE The imperative ἴθι usually just strengthens a following imperative (e.g., ἴθι ἐλθέ "come on now, go!"). ἄγε and φέρε often function in this way, too.

ἔρχομαι, ἐλεύσομαι, ἦλθον (*imper.* ἐλθέ—*irreg. accent in sg.* [*cf.* εἰπέ, εὑρέ, ἰδέ, λαβέ]), ἐλήλυθα, —, —
    go, come

πάσχω, πείσομαι, ἔπαθον, πέπονθα, —, —
    suffer, experience; κακῶς/εὖ πάσχειν = be treated badly/well, fare badly/well

NOTE Stems = πενθ-, πονθ-, or παθ-. πασχ- is derived from παθ-σκ- (θ drops out, κ is roughened). The deponent future of πάσχω (= πείσομαι "I shall suffer") and the middle future of πείθω (= πείσομαι "I shall obey") are identical in form.

φράζω, φράσω, ἔφρασα, πέφρακα, πέφρασμαι, ἐφράσθην
    tell, declare, explain [cf. *phrase*]

ἐπιτήδειος, -ᾱ, -ον   necessary; (*as a masc./fem. substantive*) friend; (*as a neut. pl. substantive*) necessities, provisions

ἔνδον   (*adv.*) inside [cf. *endocrine, endomorph*]

ἔξω   (*adv.*) outside [cf. *exosphere, exotic*]

εὐθύς   (*adv.*) immediately

ὅτι   (*conj. introducing indir. discourse*) that

ὡς   (*conj. introducing indir. discourse*) that, how; (*prep. + acc.; only with persons as its object*) to

242.   **EXERCISES**

A.   **Greek-to-English Sentences**

1. ἔφρασεν ἡ γυνὴ ὅτι ὁ ἀνὴρ ἔνδον εἴη καὶ παρασκευάζοι τὸ δεῖπνον.

2. ἐγεγράφη ὅτι αἱρησοίμην ἓν τῶν δώρων καὶ αὐτὸ φέρων ὡς σὲ ἴοιμι.

3. εἶπεν ὅτι εἰ Σωκράτης βασιλεὺς αἱρεθείη, οἱ φιλόσοφοι ἄρξοιεν.

4. ὡς τὴν γυναῖκα ἐλθών, ἠρώτησα αὐτὴν ὑφ᾽ οὗτινος οὕτω κακῶς πάσχει.

5. ἴθι ἐλθὲ ἔξω, ὦ οἰκέτα, καὶ εὐθὺς εἰπέ μοι πάντα τὰ ἔνδον γενόμενα.

6. ἀπεκρῑνάμην ὅτι αὐτοὺς στρατιώτᾱς ἑλοίμην ἄν, εἰ αὐτοὶ ἔσχον ἵππους.

7. τί λέγεις ὡς ἄνευ ἐπιτηδείων εἶ; ἰδοῦσα γὰρ πολλὰ χρήματα, οὐ πείθομαι.

8. βούλονται ἰέναι κατὰ τὸν ποταμὸν ἵνα ἴδωσι τὰ αὐτὰ δένδρα ἃ ὀψόμενοι ἦσαν πρότερον ὀλίγαις ἡμέραις.

9. εἶμι καὶ εὐθὺς ἀγγελῶ τοῖς ἐπιτηδείοις ὅτι πάλιν τ᾽ ἐλήλυθεν ἡ εἰρήνη τῇ πόλει καὶ οὐκέτι οἱ πολλοὶ κακὰ πείσονται.

10. ἦλθομεν ὡς τὸν ἄρχοντα φράσοντες ὅτι οὐκ ἐθέλομεν μάχεσθαι οὐδενί.

B.   **English-to-Greek Sentences**

1. The soldiers announced that they had been treated badly and did not have sufficient provisions.

2. Choose either to come down from that ladder immediately, son, or to suffer a very bad fate.

3. I replied that my wife was inside but that she would neither appear at the door nor come outside.

4. You (*sg.*) said that you would not have gone to the king if the gods had not commanded you to go.

5. Going to her father, I declared that I wished to marry his daughter and to hold the wedding immediately.

C. READING

JUSTIFIABLE HOMICIDE? — Part 2
(adapted from Lysias' *On the Murder of Eratosthenes* 18-26)

Even after the incident with the crying baby (which Euphiletus had not understood at the time), he did not suspect that anything was wrong in his house. Later, however, he received a secret message from a woman who had been one of Eratosthenes' earlier conquests and now wanted to see him punished; she mentioned Eratosthenes by name and accused him of having seduced both herself and Euphiletus' wife. Flabbergasted, Euphiletus hurried home to interrogate his wife's maid and find out whether there was any truth to the woman's allegations.

ἐλθὼν δ᾽ οἴκαδε ἐκέλευον ἕπεσθαί μοι τὴν θεράπαιναν εἰς τὴν ἀγοράν, ἀγαγὼν δ᾽ αὐτὴν ὥς τινα τῶν ἐμαυτοῦ ἐπιτηδείων ἔλεγον ὅτι ἐγὼ πάντα εἰδείην τὰ γιγνόμενα ἐν τῇ οἰκίᾳ. Ἑλοῦ, εἶπον ἐγώ, ὁπότερον τῶνδε δυοῖν βούλει· ἢ μαστῑγωθεῖσαν μήποτε παύσασθαι κακῶς πάσχουσαν ἢ εἰποῦσαν πάντα τὰ
5 ἀληθῆ μηδὲν παθεῖν κακόν, ἀλλὰ συγγνώμης παρ᾽ ἐμοῦ τυχεῖν τῶν ἁμαρτιῶν.

The maid chose the latter alternative. She confessed all and agreed to inform Euphiletus the next time Eratosthenes came to the house. This happened four or five days later, at night:

ὁ δ᾽ Ἐρατοσθένης, ὦ ἄνδρες, εἰσέρχεται, καὶ ἡ θεράπαινα ἐπεγείρασά με εὐθὺς φράζει ὅτι ἔνδον ἐστίν. καὶ ἐγὼ σῑγῇ ἐξέρχομαι, καὶ ἀφικνοῦμαι ὡς τὸν καὶ τόν, καὶ τοὺς μὲν ἔνδον ηὗρον, τοὺς δ᾽ οὐκ ἐπιδημοῦντας. καὶ δᾷδας λαβόντες εἰσερχόμεθα, ἀνεῳγμένης τῆς θύρας καὶ παρεσκευασμένης ὑπὸ τῆς
10 θεραπαίνης. εἰσιόντες δ᾽ εἴδομεν αὐτὸν γυμνὸν κατακείμενον παρὰ τῇ γυναικί. ἐγὼ δ᾽ εἶπον ὅτι, Οὐκ ἐγώ σε ἀποκτενῶ, ἀλλ᾽ ὁ τῆς πόλεως νόμος, μᾶλλον γὰρ εἵλου τοιαύτην ἁμαρτίᾱν ἁμαρτάνειν εἰς τὴν γυναῖκα τὴν ἐμὴν ἢ τοῖς νόμοις πείθεσθαι.

Conclusion: *Claiming that he was acting in the name of the law, Euphiletus then killed Eratosthenes on the spot! Although Athenian law did permit a husband to kill a man whom he discovered in bed with his wife, the murder was legal only if it was spontaneous and unplanned. Thus Euphiletus had to prove that he had not premeditated Eratosthenes' murder. We do not know whether his defense was successful.*

VOCABULARY

οἴκαδε (line 1): home(wards) (*adv.*)
τινα (line 2): Euphiletus wants this person to be a witness
ὁπότερον (line 3): from ὁπότερος, -ᾱ, -ον: which(ever) (*of two*)
μαστῑγωθεῖσαν (line 4): from μαστῑγόω, μαστῑγώσω, ἐμαστῑγωσα, μεμαστῑγωκα,
    μεμαστῑγωμαι, ἐμαστῑγώθην: whip (*modifies implied* σέ)

παύσασθαι…παθεῖν (lines 4-5): each infinitive phrase describes one of the possible fates for the maid (*subject of both infinitives = implied* σέ)

συγγνώμης (line 5): from συγγνώμη, -ης, ἡ (+ *gen.*): pardon (for), forgiveness (of)

τυχεῖν (line 5): from τυγχάνω, τεύξομαι, ἔτυχον, τετύχηκα, —, — (+ *gen.*): chance upon, obtain

Ἐρατοσθένης (line 6): from Ἐρατοσθένης, -ους, ὁ: Eratosthenes

ἄνδρες (line 6): gentlemen (*referring to the jurors*)

εἰσέρχεται (line 6): εἰσ- + ἔρχεται

ἐπεγείρᾱσα (line 6): from ἐπεγείρω, ἐπεγερῶ, ἐπήγειρα, ἐπεγήγερκα, ἐπεγήγερμαι, ἐπηγέρθην: awaken

στγῇ (line 7): from στγή, -ῆς, ἡ: silence

ἐξέρχομαι (line 7): ἐξ- + ἔρχομαι

τὸν καὶ τόν (lines 7-8): this man and that man

ἐπιδημοῦντας (line 8): from ἐπιδημέω, ἐπιδημήσω, ἐπεδήμησα, ἐπιδεδήμηκα, —, —: be at home

δᾷδας (line 8): from δᾷς (*contracted from* δαίς), δᾷδος, ἡ: torch

εἰσιόντες (line 10): εἰσ- + ἰόντες

γυμνόν (line 10): from γυμνός, -ή, -όν: naked

κατακείμενον (line 10): from κατάκειμαι, κατακείσομαι, —, —, —, —: lie down, be lying down

ὅτι (line 11): ὅτι can act like a quotation mark; in such cases it is left untranslated in English

εἰς (line 12): here = "against"

LESSON 41

φημί;
INDIRECT DISCOURSE
(WITH INFINITIVE)

οὔ φημ' Ὀρέστην σ' ἐνδίκως ἀνδρηλατεῖν
(I assert that you are banishing Orestes unjustly.)
—Apollo tries reasoning with the Furies in Aeschylus' *Eumenides* 221

243.   φημί, φήσω, ἔφησα, —, —, — ("say") is yet another irregular μι-verb similar to εἰμί, εἶμι, and οἶδα. It usually implies that the speaker is **asserting an opinion** or **claiming that something is true**. The combination οὔ φημι often means "I deny." The stem of the verb is either φα- or φη-. In the present active indicative, all six forms are **enclitics** except the second-person singular φής (just as with the present active indicative of εἰμί). Rare or poetic forms are enclosed in square brackets.

Present Active Indicative		Imperfect Active Indicative	
Singular:		**Singular:**	
φημί	("I say")	ἔφην	("I was saying")
φής	("you [*sg.*] say")	ἔφησθα/ἔφης	("you [*sg.*] were saying")
φησί(ν)	("he/she/it says")	ἔφη	("he/she/it was saying")
Plural:		**Plural:**	
φαμέν	("we say")	ἔφαμεν	("we were saying")
φατέ	("you [*pl.*] say")	ἔφατε	("you [*pl.*] were saying")
φᾱσί(ν)	("they say")	ἔφασαν	("they were saying")

Present Active Subjunctive	Present Active Optative
Singular:	**Singular:**
φῶ	φαίην
φῇς	φαίης
φῇ	φαίη

Plural:	Plural:	
φῶμεν	φαῖμεν	[φαίημεν]
φῆτε	φαῖτε	[φαίητε]
φῶσι(ν)	φαῖεν	[φαίησαν]

Present Active Imperative

Singular:

φαθί or φάθι	("say!")
φάτω	("let him/her/it say!")

Plural:

φάτε	("say!")
φάντων	("let them say!")

Present Active Infinitive:

φάναι	("to say")

Present Active Participle:

φάσκων, -ουσα, -ον	[φάς, φᾶσα, φάν] ("saying")

NOTE   φάσκων is borrowed from the verb φάσκω, —, —, —, —, — "say often."

244.   When a sentence's main verb is a verb of **thinking** or **believing**, the second method of **indirect discourse** is preferred. What would have been the finite verb in the direct discourse is changed into an **infinitive**. What would have been a present or imperfect indicative or a present subjunctive or optative becomes a **present infinitive**. What would have been an aorist indicative, subjunctive, or optative becomes an **aorist infinitive**. What would have been a future indicative becomes a **future infinitive**. What would have been a perfect or pluperfect indicative or a perfect subjunctive or optative becomes a **perfect infinitive**. What would have been a future perfect indicative becomes a **future perfect infinitive**.

If the infinitive in indirect discourse replaces a verb in the indicative mood, its tense is no longer just a mark of aspect; it also indicates **time** relative to that of the main verb. A present infinitive corresponding to a present indicative shows **contemporaneous** action; an aorist infinitive corresponding to an aorist indicative shows **prior** action; a future infinitive corresponding to a future indicative shows **subsequent** action; a perfect infinitive corresponding to a perfect indicative shows an action **already complete** at the time of the main verb. When a present infinitive corresponds to an imperfect indicative, or a perfect infinitive corresponds to a pluperfect indicative, an adverb like τότε or πρότερον is usually added to clarify that the action was happening or was complete **prior to** the time of the main verb.

The noun or pronoun that would have been the subject of the finite verb in the direct discourse becomes the **subject of the infinitive** and is put into the **accusative case**; any words agreeing with it, including what would have been predicate nouns or adjectives in the direct discourse, are also put into the accusative. **Important Exception:** The subject of the infinitive is **omitted** if it is identical with the subject of the main sentence; any words agreeing with that omitted subject are put into the **nominative case** (since they are essentially modifying the sentence's subject as well as the omitted subject of the infinitive).

If there are **dependent clauses** in the indirect discourse, their verbs are *not* changed to infinitives, even when the verb in the main clause of the indirect discourse is. When the sentence's main verb is in a secondary tense, the speaker has, as usual, the option to change the mood of any dependent verbs in the indirect discourse (except those in a secondary tense of the indicative) to the optative. There is, of course, no way to change the mood of an infinitive, so the optative option does not apply to an infinitive in indirect discourse.

In both this and the first type of indirect discourse, the same **negatives** and **particles**, including ἄν, that would have been used in the direct discourse are retained. **Exception:** ἄν is dropped whenever, after a secondary main verb, subjunctive + ἄν is changed to optative in a dependent clause of the indirect discourse.

Of the verbs you already know, κρίνω, πιστεύω, and, above all, φημί call for indirect discourse with the infinitive. For stylistic reasons, the speaker may choose to use an infinitive rather than a ὅτι/ὡς clause, even with a verb of saying (especially with ἀγγέλλω and ἀποκρίνομαι and with λέγω when it refers to what "is said" to be true), or a ὅτι/ὡς clause rather than an infinitive, even with a verb of thinking or believing (especially with νομίζω; see the vocabulary).

Since an infinitive phrase in indirect discourse is the equivalent of a ὅτι/ὡς clause, it is generally better **not to translate it literally**, but to expand it into a clause with a finite verb. Study the following examples.

Examples of Indirect Discourse with an Infinitive

Direct Discourse:

> Ὁ Σωκράτης τοὺς νεᾱνίᾱς βλάπτει. (Present)
> "Socrates is harming the youth."

Indirect Discourse:

> τὸν Σωκράτη φᾱσὶ τοὺς νεᾱνίᾱς βλάπτειν.
> "They say that Socrates is harming the youth."

> τὸν Σωκράτη ἔφασαν τοὺς νεᾱνίᾱς βλάπτειν.
> "They said that Socrates was harming the youth."

Direct Discourse:

> Ὁ Σωκράτης τοὺς νεᾱνίᾱς ἔβλαπτεν. (Imperfect)
> "Socrates was harming the youth."

Indirect Discourse:

τὸν Σωκράτη φᾶσὶ τοὺς νεᾱνίᾱς τότε βλάπτειν.
"They say that Socrates was harming the youth."

τὸν Σωκράτη ἔφασαν τοὺς νεᾱνίᾱς πρότερον βλάπτειν.
"They said that Socrates had been harming the youth."

Direct Discourse:

Ὁ Σωκράτης τοὺς νεᾱνίᾱς ἔβλαψεν.   (Aorist)
"Socrates harmed the youth."

Indirect Discourse:

τὸν Σωκράτη φᾶσὶ τοὺς νεᾱνίᾱς βλάψαι.
"They say that Socrates harmed the youth."

τὸν Σωκράτη ἔφασαν τοὺς νεᾱνίᾱς βλάψαι.
"They said that Socrates had harmed the youth."

Direct Discourse:

Ὁ Σωκράτης τοὺς νεᾱνίᾱς βλάψει.   (Future)
"Socrates will harm the youth."

Indirect Discourse:

τὸν Σωκράτη φᾶσὶ τοὺς νεᾱνίᾱς βλάψειν.
"They say that Socrates will harm the youth."

τὸν Σωκράτη ἔφασαν τοὺς νεᾱνίᾱς βλάψειν.
"They said that Socrates would harm the youth."

Direct Discourse:

Ὁ Σωκράτης τοὺς νεᾱνίᾱς βέβλαφεν.   (Perfect)
"Socrates has harmed the youth."

Indirect Discourse:

τὸν Σωκράτη φᾶσὶ τοὺς νεᾱνίᾱς βεβλαφέναι.
"They say that Socrates has harmed the youth."

τὸν Σωκράτη ἔφασαν τοὺς νεᾱνίᾱς βεβλαφέναι.
"They said that Socrates had harmed the youth."

245.   **VOCABULARY**

ἀγαπάω, ἀγαπήσω, ἠγάπησα, ἠγάπηκα, ἠγάπημαι, ἠγαπήθην
　　　　　　　love; (+ *infin. or suppl. ptcple.*) be fond of
　　　　　　　(*doing*), be content (to)

νομίζω, νομιῶ, ἐνόμισα, νενόμικα, νενόμισμαι, ἐνομίσθην
　　　　　　　think, consider, believe

φημί, φήσω, ἔφησα, —, —, —
　　　　　　　say, assert; οὔ φημι = deny [cf. *prophet*]

ἀγάπη, -ης, ἡ   love

ἑταίρᾱ, -ᾱς, ἡ   comrade (*female*), companion (*female*), courtesan

ἑταῖρος, -ου, ὁ   comrade (*male*), companion (*male*)

μνᾶ (*contracted from* μνέᾱ), -ᾶς, -ᾷ, -ᾶν; *pl.* -αῖ, -ῶν, -αῖς, -ᾶς, ἡ
           mina, a weight or a sum of money equal to 100 drachmas

τάλαντον, -ου, τό   talent, a weight or a sum of money equal to 60 minas

φιλίᾱ, -ᾱς, ἡ   friendship

βραδύς, -εῖα, -ύ   slow (*comp.* βραδύτερος, -ᾱ, -ον; *superl.* βραδύτατος, -η, -ον) [cf. *bradycardia*]

ταχύς, -εῖα, -ύ   fast, quick, swift (*comp.* θάττων, -ον; *superl.* τάχιστος, -η, -ον) [cf. *tachygraphy, tachymeter*]

246.   **EXERCISES**

A.   **Greek-to-English Sentences**

1. μὴ πιστεύσητε, ὦ ἑταῖροι, τοῖς φάσκουσιν εἰδέναι πάντα, πολλάκις γὰρ ἁμαρτάνουσιν.

2. ἐκεῖνοι οἱ φιλόσοφοι ἀεὶ ἐνόμιζον εἶναι ἀμείνονες τῶν ἄλλων ἀνθρώπων.

3. τί ἀγαπᾷς, ὦ ἄδικε ἄδελφε, φάναι πάσᾱς ἑταίρᾱς κακὰς γενέσθαι;

4. οἱ στρατιῶται ἔφησαν, εἰ μὴ τῷ στρατηγῷ ἐπείσαντο, κακῶς παθεῖν ἄν.

5. ἴθι φαθί, ὦ μαθητά, ἥντινα νομίζεις εἶναι τὴν ἀληθῆ αἰτίᾱν τῆς φιλίᾱς.

6. θᾶττον μὲν ἵππων λέοντας ἱέναι λέγουσι, βραδύτερον δὲ τριήρων.

7. Οὐκ ἐγὼ μέν, ἔφη ὁ Σωκράτης, ὑμᾶς διαφθείρω, ἡ δ' αἰσχίστη ἀγάπη μνῶν καὶ ταλάντων.

8. ἀπεκρῑνάμην ὅτι ἠγάπων ἂν τὴν ἐμαυτοῦ γυναῖκα εἰ αὐτὴ ἠγάπᾱ με.

9. τί φῄς, ὦ υἱέ; ἐλθὲ ταχέως κατὰ τῆς κλίμακος. διὰ τί οὕτω βραδὺς εἶ;

10. τήνδε τὴν παῖδά φημι ἀγαπᾶσθαι ὑπ' ἐμοῦ πλέον ἢ τοὺς ἐμοὺς ὀφθαλμοὺς αὐτούς.

B.   **English-to-Greek Sentences**

1. Although my husband asserts that he loves me (*use genitive absolute*), I believe that he loves that courtesan more.

2. You deny that you are slow, comrade, but I consider all the others to be much faster than you.

3. Do they say that the trireme was sold for one hundred minas or for one talent of silver?

4. I thought that our wives would remain in the house while we went to the marketplace (*use genitive absolute*).

5. We judged that they had a marvelous friendship, for whithersoever this one went, that one also went.

C. READING

NOT WHAT DARIUS EXPECTED — Part 1
(adapted from Arrian's *Anabasis* 2.25)

Our most reliable extant source on the exploits of Alexander the Great is the history of his campaigns written by Arrian in the second century A.D. In the **Anabasis** *("expedition up from the coast"), Arrian describes Alexander's amazing march from Greece to India and his conquest of that entire region, including all of the Persian Empire.*

The following incident happened while Alexander was besieging the city of Tyre in Lebanon (332 B.C.). In the preceding year, the mother, wife, and children of Darius, king of the Persians, had been captured by Alexander during the battle of Issus in Assyria. Darius himself had fled when his troops were badly defeated.

ἀφίκοντο δὲ παρὰ Δαρείου πρέσβεις ὡς Ἀλέξανδρον, ἀπαγγέλλοντες μύρια μὲν τάλαντα ὑπὲρ τῆς μητρός τε καὶ τῆς γυναικὸς καὶ τῶν παίδων πέμψαι ἐθέλειν Ἀλεξάνδρῳ Δαρεῖον· τὴν δὲ χώρᾱν πᾶσαν τὴν ἐντὸς Εὐφράτου ποταμοῦ ἐπὶ θάλατταν τὴν Ἑλληνικὴν Ἀλεξάνδρου εἶναι· γήμαντα δὲ τὴν Δαρείου
5 παῖδα Ἀλέξανδρον φίλον τ᾽ εἶναι Δαρείῳ καὶ σύμμαχον. καὶ τούτων ἐν τῷ συλλόγῳ τῶν ἑταίρων ἀπαγγελθέντων, Παρμενίωνα μὲν λέγουσιν Ἀλεξάνδρῳ εἰπεῖν ὅτι αὐτὸς ἄν, Ἀλέξανδρος ὢν, ἐπὶ τούτοις ἠγάπησε παύσᾱς τὸν πόλεμον· Ἀλέξανδρον δὲ Παρμενίωνι ἀποκρίνασθαι ὅτι καὶ αὐτὸς ἄν, εἰ Παρμενίων ἦν, οὕτως ἔπρᾱξεν, ἐπεὶ δ᾽ Ἀλέξανδρός ἐστιν, ἀποκρινεῖται Δαρείῳ ἃ ἀπεκρίνατο.
10 ἔφη οὔτε χρημάτων δεῖσθαι παρὰ Δαρείου οὔτε τῆς χώρᾱς, εἶναι γὰρ αὐτοῦ τά τε χρήματα καὶ τὴν χώρᾱν πᾶσαν· γῆμαί τ᾽ εἰ ἐθέλοι τὴν Δαρείου παῖδα, γῆμαι ἄν, καὶ οὐκ ἐθέλοντος Δαρείου. ταῦθ᾽ ὁπότ᾽ ἤκουσε Δαρεῖος, ἐν παρασκευῇ τοῦ πολέμου αὖθις ἦν.

VOCABULARY

Δαρείου (line 1): from Δαρεῖος, -ου, ὁ: Darius, king of Persia
πρέσβεις (line 1): from πρέσβυς, -εως, ὁ: ambassador (*declined like* πόλις *but with* υ *instead of* ι *in the nom., acc., and voc. sg.*)
Ἀλέξανδρον (line 1): from Ἀλέξανδρος, -ου, ὁ: Alexander (the Great), king of Macedonia, son of Philip II
ἀπαγγέλλοντες (line 1): ἀπό + ἀγγέλλω (*prefix just strengthens the verb*)
ὑπέρ (line 2): he will pay a ransom "on behalf of" them, i.e., for them
πέμψαι ἐθέλειν...Δαρεῖον (lines 2-3): Δαρεῖον is the subject of ἐθέλειν in indirect discourse; πέμψαι is a complementary infinitive with ἐθέλειν

τὴν...χώραν...Ἀλεξάνδρου εἶναι (lines 3-4): that the land...be Alexander's (*this infinitive phrase is a direct object of* ἐθέλειν...Δαρεῖον *in line 3*)

ἐντός (line 3): within, on this side (of) (*prep. + gen.*); here = "west (of)"

Εὐφράτου (line 3): from Εὐφράτης, -ου, ὁ: the Euphrates River

θάλατταν τὴν Ἑλληνικήν (line 4): i.e., the Aegean Sea

γήμαντα...Ἀλέξανδρον φίλον ... εἶναι (lines 4-5): that Alexander...be a friend; γήμαντα modifies Ἀλέξανδρον (*this infinitive phrase is another direct object of* ἐθέλειν...Δαρεῖον *in line 3*)

τούτων (line 5): i.e., the offers from Darius

συλλόγῳ (line 6): from σύλλογος, -ου, ὁ: gathering, meeting

ἑταίρων (line 6): the "companions" here are Alexander's elite cavalry

Παρμενίωνα (line 6): from Παρμενίων, -ωνος, ὁ: Parmenion, a Macedonian noble and general, Alexander's second-in-command

λέγουσιν (line 6): subject = people in general, an indefinite "they"

Ἀλέξανδρος ὢ᾽ν (line 7): represents the protasis of a condition

ἐπὶ τούτοις (line 7): on these terms

Ἀλέξανδρον...Παρμενίωνι ἀποκρίνασθαι (line 8): indirect discourse continues (*still depends on the main verb* λέγουσιν *in line 6*)

ἀποκρινεῖται...ἃ ἀπεκρίνατο (line 9): he would give the answer that in fact he did give (*that answer follows in lines 10-12*)

δεῖσθαι (line 10): δέομαι, δεήσομαι, —, —, δεδέημαι, ἐδεήθην: need, have need (of) (+ *gen.*)

αὑτοῦ (line 10): his own (*i.e., they now belonged to him*)

αὖθις (line 13): again (*adv.*) (*i.e., Darius gave up this attempt to negotiate*)

LESSON 42

INDIRECT DISCOURSE (WITH PARTICIPLE); CRASIS

ἐπιλελήσμεσθ' ἡδέως / γέροντες ὄντες
(We have gladly forgotten that we are old.)
—Cadmus and Tiresias kick up their aged heels
to worship the god Dionysus in Euripides' *Bacchae* 188-189

247.   When a sentence's main verb is a verb of **knowing, showing,** or **perceiving,** the third method of **indirect discourse** is preferred. What would have been the finite verb in the direct discourse is changed into a **supplementary participle.** What would have been a present or imperfect indicative or a present subjunctive or optative becomes a **present participle.** What would have been an aorist indicative, subjunctive, or optative becomes an **aorist participle.** What would have been a future indicative becomes a **future participle.** What would have been a perfect or pluperfect indicative or a perfect subjunctive or optative becomes a **perfect participle.** What would have been a future perfect indicative becomes a **future perfect participle.**

The tense of a participle in indirect discourse indicates **relative time** as well as aspect. A present participle corresponding to a present indicative shows **contemporaneous** action; an aorist participle corresponding to an aorist indicative shows **prior** action; a future participle corresponding to a future indicative shows **subsequent** action; a perfect participle corresponding to a perfect indicative shows an action **already complete** at the time of the main verb. When a present participle corresponds to an imperfect indicative, or a perfect participle corresponds to a pluperfect indicative, an adverb like τότε or πρότερον is usually added to clarify that the action was happening or was complete **prior to** the time of the main verb.

287

The noun or pronoun that would have been the subject of the finite verb in the direct discourse becomes the **antecedent of the participle** and is put into the **accusative case**; any words agreeing with it, including what would have been predicate nouns or adjectives in the direct discourse, are also put into the accusative. **Important Exception:** The antecedent of the participle is **omitted** if it is identical with the subject of the main sentence; any words agreeing with that omitted antecedent are put into the **nominative case** (since they essentially modify the sentence's subject as well as the omitted antecedent of the participle).

If there are **dependent clauses** in the indirect discourse, their verbs are *not* changed to participles, even when the verb in the main clause of the indirect discourse is. When the sentence's main verb is in a secondary tense, the speaker has, as usual, the option to change the mood of any dependent verbs in the indirect discourse (except those in a secondary tense of the indicative) to the optative. Since there is no way to change the mood of a participle, the optative option does not apply to a participle in indirect discourse.

In this type of indirect discourse, as in the other two that you have learned, the same **negatives** and **particles**, including ἄν, that would have been used in the direct discourse are retained. Exception: ἄν is dropped whenever, after a secondary main verb, subjunctive + ἄν is changed to optative in a dependent clause of the indirect discourse.

Because a participial phrase in indirect discourse is the equivalent of a ὅτι/ὡς clause, it is generally better **not to translate it literally**, but to expand it into a clause with a finite verb.

Of the verbs you already know, ἀκούω, βλέπω, δηλόω, εὑρίσκω, οἶδα, ὁράω, and φαίνω are ones that, by their nature, call for indirect discourse with a participle. It frequently happens, however, that the speaker chooses, for the sake of clarity or style, to use a ὅτι/ὡς clause rather than a participle, even with a verb of knowing, showing, or perceiving. The next paragraph describes certain circumstances under which a ὅτι/ὡς clause might be preferable to a participle.

If you see a participle combined with a verb of **perceiving**, it may or may not be in indirect discourse. If the perception is **physical**, there is no indirect discourse involved, only a supplementary participle collaborating with the main verb to make a statement (e.g., εὗρον τὸ παιδίον βοῶν "I found the child crying"). If the perception is **intellectual**, the supplementary participle not only collaborates with the main verb but is also in indirect discourse, for it represents the *thought* that went through the perceiver's mind (e.g., εὗρον τὸ παιδίον βοῶν "I found that the child was crying"). To avoid ambiguity, a speaker may opt for a ὅτι/ὡς clause instead of a participle, when intellectual perception (indirect discourse) is meant (e.g., εὗρον ὅτι τὸ παιδίον βοᾷ [or βοῴη] "I found that the child was crying").

Preferences for the three types of indirect discourse can be summarized as follows:

Main Verb	Preferred Method	
of saying:	ὅτι/ὡς clause	[or infinitive]
of thinking/believing:	infinitive	[or ὅτι/ὡς clause]
of knowing/showing/perceiving:	participle	[or ὅτι/ὡς clause]

NOTE

With ἀγγέλλω and ἀκούω, *any* of the three methods of indirect discourse may be used, with virtually no difference in meaning. If the participial type of indirect discourse is used with ἀκούω, the participle and the noun or pronoun it modifies should be in the **accusative** case, not the genitive (e.g., ἀκούω τὸ παιδίον βοῶν "I hear that the child is crying"—indirect discourse, intellectual perception of a fact; cf. ἀκούω τοῦ παιδίου βοῶντος "I hear the child crying"—physical perception).

Examples of Indirect Discourse with a Participle

Direct Discourse:

Ὁ Σωκράτης τοὺς νεανίας βλάπτει.   (Present)
"Socrates is harming the youth."

Indirect Discourse:

τὸν Σωκράτη οἶδα τοὺς νεανίας βλάπτοντα.
"I know that Socrates is harming the youth."

τὸν Σωκράτη ᾔδη τοὺς νεανίας βλάπτοντα.
"I knew that Socrates was harming the youth."

Direct Discourse:

Ὁ Σωκράτης τοὺς νεανίας ἔβλαπτεν.   (Imperfect)
"Socrates was harming the youth."

Indirect Discourse:

τὸν Σωκράτη οἶδα τοὺς νεανίας τότε βλάπτοντα.
"I know that Socrates was harming the youth."

τὸν Σωκράτη ᾔδη τοὺς νεανίας πρότερον βλάπτοντα.
"I knew that Socrates had been harming the youth."

Direct Discourse:

Ὁ Σωκράτης τοὺς νεανίας ἔβλαψεν.   (Aorist)
"Socrates harmed the youth."

Indirect Discourse:

τὸν Σωκράτη οἶδα τοὺς νεανίας βλάψαντα.
"I know that Socrates harmed the youth."

τὸν Σωκράτη ᾔδη τοὺς νεανίας βλάψαντα.
"I knew that Socrates had harmed the youth."

Direct Discourse:

Ὁ Σωκράτης τοὺς νεανίας βλάψει.   (Future)

"Socrates will harm the youth."

Indirect Discourse:

τὸν Σωκράτη οἶδα τοὺς νεανίας βλάψοντα.

"I know that Socrates will harm the youth."

τὸν Σωκράτη ᾔδη τοὺς νεανίας βλάψοντα.

"I knew that Socrates would harm the youth."

Direct Discourse:

Ὁ Σωκράτης τοὺς νεανίας βέβλαφεν.   (Perfect)

"Socrates has harmed the youth."

Indirect Discourse:

τὸν Σωκράτη οἶδα τοὺς νεανίας βεβλαφότα.

"I know that Socrates has harmed the youth."

τὸν Σωκράτη ᾔδη τοὺς νεανίας βεβλαφότα.

"I knew that Socrates had harmed the youth."

248.   When a word ending in a short vowel is followed by a word beginning with a vowel, **elision** generally takes place. The elided letter may be deleted and an apostrophe written in its place—the conventional practice with common words like δέ (δ᾽)—, or the elided letter may be left in the text, with the elision only implied.

When a word ends in a vowel or a diphthong that is normally not elided, the whole word may merge itself with a following word that begins with a vowel or a diphthong; this phenomenon is called **CRASIS** (κρᾶσις, -εως, ἡ "mixing"). The words must be two that naturally belong together (e.g., an article + its noun). The vowel/diphthong ending the first word either *contracts* with the vowel/diphthong starting the second or (if contracting would cause confusion by obscuring the identity of the second, more important word) simply *drops out*. The syllable formed from the contraction is usually marked with a **coronis** (κορωνίς, -ίδος, ἡ "hook"), which looks just like a smooth breathing. Here are a few examples:

τὰ ἄλλα	→ τἄλλα	
τὸ ὄνομα	→ τοὔνομα	
τὸ ἱμάτιον	→ θοἰμάτιον	(τ becomes θ before the rough breathing)
ἐγὼ οἶδα	→ ἐγᾦδα	
καὶ ἐγώ	→ κἀγώ	(weak ι drops out; α and ε then contract)
τοῦ αὐτοῦ	→ ταὐτοῦ	(ου of τοῦ drops out so that αυ-sound prevails)
ὁ ἀνήρ	→ ἁνήρ	(ο drops out so that α-sound prevails; no coronis is used since there would seem to be two different breathings on one vowel)

All you need to be able to do is to **recognize** crasis when you see it. Do not worry about using it when you are translating sentences from English to Greek.

249.   VOCABULARY

αἰσθάνομαι, αἰσθήσομαι, ἠσθόμην, —, ᾔσθημαι, —
        (+ *acc. or gen.*) perceive, sense
        [cf. *anesthesia, aesthetic*]

πυνθάνομαι, πεύσομαι, ἐπυθόμην, —, πέπυσμαι, —
        (+ *gen.*) inquire (*of someone*); (+ *gen. or acc.*) learn (*by inquiry*), learn (*by inquiry*) about, hear, hear about

NOTE   αἰσθάνομαι and πυνθάνομαι (when it means "learn" or "hear" rather than "inquire") are verbs of perception and may take an object in either the genitive or the accusative case. αἰσθάνομαι tends to favor the **accusative**, πυνθάνομαι the **genitive**. Both verbs may be followed by indirect discourse if the perception is regarded as intellectual; *any* of the three types of indirect discourse—ὅτι/ὡς clause, infinitive, accusative participle—may be used, with no difference in meaning (this applies also to ἀγγέλλω and ἀκούω; see note in §247).

μανθάνω, μαθήσομαι, ἔμαθον, μεμάθηκα, —, —
        learn (*by study*), understand; (+ *infin.*) learn how (to) [cf. *mathematics, polymath*]

NOTE   Indirect discourse with μανθάνω may be of the participial or the ὅτι/ὡς variety, as you would expect with a verb of perceiving/knowing. When an infinitive is used, there is no indirect discourse involved, and the verb's meaning changes from "learn" to "learn how (to)." Compare the similar change in meaning of οἶδα from "know (that)" (+ indirect discourse with participle or ὅτι/ὡς) to "know how (to)" (+ an infinitive not in indirect discourse).

γέρων, -οντος, ὁ   old man [cf. *gerontocracy, gerontology*]
γραῦς, γρᾱός, ἡ   old woman

NOTE   The stem is γραυ-, but υ drops out when the ending begins with a vowel (cf. the declension of βασιλεύς in Lesson 29). Because of the monosyllabic stem, the accent shifts to the ultima in the genitive and dative singular and plural. SG.: γραῦς, γρᾱός, γρᾱΐ, γραῦν, γραῦ; PL.: γρᾶες, γραῶν, γραυσί(ν), γραῦς.

πρᾶγμα, -ατος, τό	deed, affair, thing; (*pl.*) circumstances, matters of state, trouble [cf. *pragmatic*]
σωφροσύνη, -ης, ἡ	prudence, discretion, temperance, self-control
χείρ, χειρός, ἡ	hand [cf. *chirography, chiromancy, chiropodist, chiropractic, surgery*]

NOTE   Since the stem χειρ- is monosyllabic, the accent shifts to the ultima in the genitive and dative singular and plural; in the dative plural ι drops out: χερσί(ν).

σώφρων, -ον	prudent, discreet, temperate, self-controlled
αὖ or αὖθις	(*adv.*) again, further, on the other hand, in turn

250.   **EXERCISES**

A.   **Greek-to-English Sentences**

1. ᾔσθοντο οἱ διδάσκαλοι τοὺς μαθητὰς οὐκέτι ἀγαπῶντας μανθάνειν.
2. ἐγᾦδα σέ, εἰ σώφρων ἦσθα, οὐκ ἂν ἀδικοῦντα ταύτᾱς τὰς ἀγαθὰς γραῦς.
3. ἆρ’ ἐπύθου τοὺς σαυτοῦ ἑταίρους ταῖς χερσὶ κλέψαντας τὰ χρήματα;
4. ὁρῶ ὑμᾶς βουλομένους πολλὰς μνᾶς ἔχειν, ἀλλ’ οὐ τὴν σωφροσύνην.
5. κἀγὼ μανθάνω ἑλέσθαι τὰ ἄριστα τῶν ἐν τῇ ἀγορᾷ πωλουμένων.
6. αἰσθάνομαι τοὺς ἀνθρώπους ἐθέλοντας πολλὰ πάσχειν φιλίᾱς χάριν.
7. πεύσεται ὁ βασιλεὺς τῆς γρᾱὸς κακῶς πασχούσης ὑπὸ τῶν χειρῶν σου.
8. ἔμαθον οἱ γέροντες τὴν δίκην κρείττω τε καὶ βελτίω τῆς ἀδικίᾱς ἀεὶ οὖσαν.
9. αὖθις ἀκούω τὸν Σωκράτη οὐ φάσκοντα τοὺς νεᾱνίᾱς διαφθείρειν.
10. εὑρὼν οὐδεμίαν γυναῖκα σώφρονα οὖσαν, ἔγωγ’ οὐκ ἤθελον αὖ γαμεῖν.

B.   **English-to-Greek Sentences**

1. They sense that the old woman is more discreet than the old man, but they do not know the true circumstances.
2. Having learned that there was a thief inside, she slowly opened the door and saw two hands stealing money.
3. Having learned how to speak to the philosophers, he was no longer afraid to inquire of them further.
4. You all understood that self-control was best, but you were led by your passion into a sea of trouble.
5. Announce quickly whatever you (*sg.*) intend to say, for we hear that our comrades have already gone outside.

C.   READING

NOT WHAT DARIUS EXPECTED — Part 2
(adapted from Arrian's *Anabasis* 4.20)

*Another story recorded by Arrian illustrates the respect Alexander gave to Darius'
mother, wife, and daughters while they were his prisoners.*

Καὶ λέγουσι φυγόντα ἐλθεῖν παρὰ Δαρεῖον τὸν εὐνοῦχον τὸν φύλακα αὐτῷ τῆς
γυναικός. καὶ τοῦτον ὡς εἶδε Δαρεῖος, πρῶτα μὲν ἐπύθετο εἰ ζῶσιν αὐτῷ αἱ παῖδες καὶ ἡ
γυνή τε καὶ ἡ μήτηρ. ὡς δ' ἐπύθετο αὐτὰς ζώσᾱς τε καὶ ὅτι ἡ θεραπείᾱ ἀμφ' αὐτάς ἐστιν
ἥτις καὶ παρὰ Δαρείῳ ἦν ἀμφ' αὐτάς, αὖ ἐπύθετο εἰ σωφρονεῖ αὐτῷ ἡ γυνὴ ἔτι. ὡς δ'

5   ἐπύθετο αὐτὴν σωφρονοῦσαν, αὖθις ἠρώτησεν εἰ Ἀλέξανδρος εἰς αὐτὴν ὑβρίζει· καὶ ὁ
εὐνοῦχος ἔφη ὅτι, Ὦ βασιλεῦ, οὕτως ἔχει ἡ σὴ γυνὴ ὡς ἔλιπες, καὶ Ἀλέξανδρος ἀνδρῶν
ἄριστός τ' ἐστὶ καὶ σωφρονέστατος.

ἐπὶ τοῖσδε λέγεται Δαρεῖος ἀνατεῖναι εἰς τὸν οὐρανὸν τὰς χεῖρας καὶ εὔξασθαι ὧδε·
Ὦ Ζεῦ βασιλεῦ, ὃς νέμεις τὰ βασιλέων πράγματα ἐν ἀνθρώποις, σὺ μὲν ἐμοὶ φύλαξον

10   Περσῶν τε καὶ Μήδων τὴν ἀρχήν· εἰ δὲ νῦν βούλει ἐμὲ παύσασθαι ὄντα βασιλέᾱ τῆς
Ἀσίᾱς, σὺ μηδενὶ ἄλλῳ ἢ Ἀλεξάνδρῳ παράδος τοὐμὸν κράτος.

οὕτως οὐδ' ὑπὸ τῶν πολεμίων ἀμελεῖται σώφρονα ἔργα.

VOCABULARY

Δαρεῖον (line 1): from Δαρεῖος, -ου, ὁ: Darius, king of Persia
εὐνοῦχον (line 1): from εὐνοῦχος, -ου, ὁ: eunuch (*one of Darius' servants whose job it
had been to protect the king's wife; the eunuch had been captured by Alexander, but
escaped*); εὐνοῦχον = subj. of ἐλθεῖν
αὐτῷ (lines 1, 2): dative of possession ("belonging to him," "his")
ὡς (lines 2, 3): here = "as" or "when"
θεραπείᾱ (line 3): from θεραπείᾱ, -ᾱς, ἡ: service, treatment
σωφρονεῖ (line 5): from σωφρονέω, σωφρονήσω, ἐσωφρόνησα, σεσωφρόνηκα,
σεσωφρόνημαι, ἐσωφρονήθην: be self-controlled (*here* = "be chaste")
αὐτῷ (line 5): dative of possession ("belonging to him," "his")
ὡς (line 5): here = "as" or "when"
Ἀλέξανδρος (line 6): from Ἀλέξανδρος, -ου, ὁ: Alexander the Great
ὑβρίζει (line 6): from ὑβρίζω, ὑβριῶ, ὕβρισα, ὕβρικα, ὕβρισμαι, ὑβρίσθην (*with* εἰς +
acc.): commit an outrage (against)
ὅτι (line 6): the equivalent of a quotation mark (*do not translate*)
ἔχει (line 6): here = "is"
οὕτως...ὡς ἔλιπες (line 6-7): thus...as you left, i.e., just the way you left [her]
ἐπὶ τοῖσδε (line 8): upon these things, i.e., thereupon, then
ἀνατεῖναι (line 8): from ἀνατείνω, ἀνατενῶ, ἀνέτεινα, ἀνατέτακα, ἀνατέταμαι,
ἀνετάθην: lift up

εὔξασθαι (line 9): from εὔχομαι, εὔξομαι, ηὐξάμην, —, ηὖγμαι, —: pray

Ζεῦ (line 9): from Ζεύς, Διός, ὁ: Zeus, king of the Olympian gods

νέμεις (line 9): from νέμω, νεμῶ, ἔνειμα, νενέμηκα, νενέμημαι, ἐνεμήθην: put in order, manage

ἐν (line 9): here = "among"

Περσῶν (line 10): from Πέρσης, -ου, ὁ: a Persian

Μήδων (line 10): from Μῆδος, -ου, ὁ: a Mede (*the Median empire had been incorporated into the Persian empire back in the sixth century B.C.*)

Ἀσίας (line 11): from Ἀσία, -ᾱς, ἡ: Asia

παράδος (line 11): 2nd sg. aor. act. imper. of παραδίδωμι, παραδώσω, παρέδωκα, παραδέδωκα, παραδέδομαι, παρεδόθην: hand over, transfer

κράτος (line 12): from κράτος, -ους, τό: power

ἀμελεῖται (line 13): from ἀμελέω, ἀμελήσω, ἠμέλησα, ἠμέληκα, ἠμέλημαι, ἠμελήθην: neglect, overlook

LESSON 43

MORE USES OF THE INFINITIVE; πρίν

τί οὖν ἐστι...τοῦ τοῖς φίλοις ἀρήγειν κάλλῑον;
(What is nobler than to help one's friends?)
—Cyrus addresses his army in Xenophon's *Cyropaedia* 1.5.13

251. You have already encountered the following uses of the **infinitive**:

1. **Infinitive + adjective:** defines the meaning of a particular adjective such as ἀνάξιος, -ον ("unworthy"), ἄξιος, -ᾱ, -ον ("worthy"), ἕτοιμος, -η, -ον ("ready"), ἱκανός, -ή, -όν ("sufficient"), and πρόθῡμος, -ον ("eager").

2. **Infinitive in natural result clause:** introduced by ὥστε.

3. **Complementary infinitive:** completes the sense of verbs like ἀγαπάω ("be fond of"), αἱρέομαι ("choose"), ἄρχομαι ("begin"), βούλομαι ("wish"), ἐθέλω ("be willing"), ἔχω ("be able"), ζητέω ("seek"), μανθάνω ("learn how"), μέλλω ("intend," "hesitate"), οἶδα ("know how"), προσποιέομαι ("pretend"), σπεύδω ("be eager"), φιλέω ("be fond of"), φοβέομαι ("be afraid"). The subject of a complementary infinitive is always **identical with the subject of the sentence** and thus is never expressed. (This is true in English, too; we would never say, "They begin *them* to speak" or "They begin *them* to be frightened.")

4. **Infinitive in indirect discourse:** most often after verbs of thinking and believing, sometimes after verbs of saying.

5. **Infinitive + κελεύω** ("order") or **πείθω** ("persuade"): this is an example of an **object infinitive**. An object infinitive serves as the direct object of a verb of willing or wishing; it represents the action that the speaker wants to have done. When a verb of saying (e.g., **λέγω, φράζω**) has the sense of a verb of commanding, it too may be followed by an object infinitive.

Unlike a complementary infinitive, an object infinitive has a **subject different from the subject of the main verb** (cf. βούλομαι ἰέναι "I wish to go" and βούλομαί σε ἰέναι "I wish that you would go"). When the subject of the infinitive is in the accusative case, the infinitive phrase represents an indirect command and may be translated with a "that" clause and a finite verb (e.g., λέγω σε ἰέναι "I say that you should go"). Sometimes the subject of the infinitive appears in the dative or genitive; this implies that the subject of the infinitive is also the person to whom the command is being addressed (e.g., λέγω σοι ἰέναι "I say to you that you should go" or "I tell you to go"; writing λέγω σοί σε ἰέναι would be redundant).

6.   **Infinitive + ἔστι** ("it is possible"): this is an example of a **subject infinitive**, an infinitive acting as the subject of an **impersonal** verb. (In English the impersonal verb may *appear* to have "it" as its subject, but the infinitive later in the sentence is its real subject.) The vocabulary for this lesson includes two impersonal verbs (δεῖ "it is necessary," ἔξεστι "it is possible") that occur only in the third-person singular and typically have subject infinitives.

A **predicate adjective** is often joined to a subject infinitive by a linking verb (e.g., ῥᾴδιόν ἐστι φιλεῖν "to love is easy" or "it is easy to love"). The adjective agrees with the infinitive, which is regarded as a **neuter singular nominative** noun. A linking verb may also connect a **predicate noun** with a subject infinitive; this is common with ἐλπίς, ὥρα, ἀνάγκη, and χρή (for the last two, see the vocabulary in this lesson).

252.   Knowing that a subject infinitive is regarded as a noun (more precisely, a verbal noun or a **gerund**) in the neuter singular *nominative*, you may wonder whether an infinitive is ever used as a noun in the *genitive, dative,* or *accusative case*. The answer is yes. However, the form of the infinitive itself never changes; its case is shown by a definite article placed in front of the infinitive.

An infinitive modified by a definite article is called an **articular infinitive**; in all other respects, it behaves exactly like a normal infinitive. Its tense denotes aspect, not time, and its negative is formed with μή, not οὐ. It may have its own subject (in the accusative case) and its own objects and be modified by adverbs and prepositional phrases. (All of those subjects, objects, and modifiers may be placed *between* the article and the infinitive.) No matter how long and involved the infinitive phrase happens to be, it is considered to be a single verbal noun (gerund) and to have the case shown by the definite article introducing it.

Here are the articular infinitives of παιδεύω in the active voice. (Forms with middle and/or passive voice are omitted to save space.) Because English does not change the form of a gerund to reflect aspect, no translation is really adequate. Each meaning given below applies roughly to all four verbal nouns in that case.

	Present	Future	Aorist	Perfect
Nom.	τὸ παιδεύειν	τὸ παιδεύσειν	τὸ παιδεῦσαι	τὸ πεπαιδευκέναι
	"teaching" or "to teach"			
Gen.	τοῦ παιδεύειν	τοῦ παιδεύσειν	τοῦ παιδεῦσαι	τοῦ πεπαιδευκέναι
	"of teaching"			
Dat.	τῷ παιδεύειν	τῷ παιδεύσειν	τῷ παιδεῦσαι	τῷ πεπαιδευκέναι
	"to/for teaching"			
Acc.	τὸ παιδεύειν	τὸ παιδεύσειν	τὸ παιδεῦσαι	τὸ πεπαιδευκέναι
	"teaching" or "to teach"			

In the nominative and accusative cases, the definite article is often not needed since it may already be obvious that the sentence has a subject infinitive or an object infinitive. The article is useful when the speaker wishes to mark the infinitive clearly as the subject or the object or to show that the whole infinitive phrase is functioning as a single verbal noun (e.g., τὸ Ἀθηναίους μὴ τοῖς νόμοις πείσασθαι ἀγγέλλω "I announce the fact that the Athenians did not obey the laws"). Notice how remarkably concise and elegant the articular infinitive can be.

253.   One final use of the infinitive is with the subordinating conjunction πρίν. In a positive sentence, πρίν means **"before"** and is followed by an **infinitive** that may have its own subject, objects, and modifiers. Example: ἔθυσα πρὶν τὸν Σωκράτη εἰς τὴν οἰκίαν ἀφικέσθαι ("I sacrificed before Socrates came to the house").

In a negative sentence, πρίν means **"until"** and is followed by **subjunctive + ἄν** (which may be changed to the optative, without ἄν, after a secondary main verb) if the sentence anticipates an event (e.g., οὐ θύσω πρὶν ὁ Σωκράτης εἰς τὴν οἰκίαν ἀφίκηται ἄν "I'll not sacrifice until Socrates comes to the house"—resembles a future more vivid condition), or by a **past indicative** if the sentence looks back at an event (e.g., οὐκ ἔθυσα πρὶν ὁ Σωκράτης εἰς τὴν οἰκίαν ἀφίκετο "I did not sacrifice until Socrates came to the house"—resembles a past simple particular condition).

254.   **General Observations about Infinitives**

The tense of an infinitive always shows aspect, not time, except when the infinitive is in indirect discourse and represents a verb in the indicative mood; then it shows relative time as well.

The negative used with an infinitive is always μή or one of its compounds, except in indirect discourse; there, whatever negative would have been used in the equivalent direct discourse is retained.

255.   VOCABULARY

δεῖ, δεήσει, ἐδέησε(ν), —, —, —

(*+ gen.*) there is need (of); (*+ acc. & infin.*)
it is necessary (to), one must

δοκέω, δόξω, ἔδοξα, —, δέδογμαι, ἐδόχθην

think; (*+ complem. infin.*) seem (to); (*third-pers. sg. impersonal + subject inf.*) it
seems (to), it seems good (to)

NOTE   When it means "think," δοκέω takes indirect discourse with the infinitive. When it means "seem," the personal usage (e.g., δοκῶ νῑκῆσαι "I
seem to have won") is preferred to the impersonal (δοκεῖ με νῑκῆσαι "it
seems me to have won," i.e., "it seems that I won").

ἔξεστι(ν), ἐξέσται, —, —, —, —

(*+ dat. & infin.*) it is possible (to)

NOTE   Besides ἔξεστι and ἐξέσται, this impersonal verb occurs only in the
third-person sg. imperfect (ἐξῆν), present subjunctive (ἐξῇ), future
optative (ἐξέσοιτο), pres. infin. (ἐξεῖναι), pres. ptcple. (ἐξόν), fut. ptcple.
(ἐξεσόμενον), and pres. imper. (ἐξέστω).

χρή   (*indecl. noun*) necessity; (*+ understood
                           ἐστί & acc. + inf.*) [there is] need (to),
                           [it is] necessary (to), one ought (to)

NOTE   Although it is actually a noun, χρή is virtually a verb because it
never appears without a form of the verb "be" either implied or expressed. In fact, χρή physically unites with the third-person forms of εἰμί
to produce composite words: imperfect (χρῆν or ἐχρῆν), future indicative
(χρῆσται), present subjunctive (χρῇ), present optative (χρείη), present infinitive (χρῆναι), and an indeclinable participle (χρεών). In the present indicative χρή is used by itself, with ἐστί merely understood. χρή implies a
moral obligation, while δεῖ and ἀνάγκη usually do not.

ἀνάγκη, -ης, ἡ   necessity; (*+ ἐστί & dat. or acc. + inf.*)
                          there is need (to), it is necessary (to),
                          one must

ἀρετή, -ῆς, ἡ   virtue, excellence

πολίτης, -ου, ὁ   citizen [cf. *political, politics*]

σχολή, -ῆς, ἡ   leisure, discussion, school; σχολὴν ἄγειν
                          = have leisure; σχολῇ = in a leisurely
                          way, at one's leisure [cf. *scholastic,
                          school*]

ἀναγκαῖος, -ᾱ, -ον   necessary

πρίν   (*conj. + infin.*) before; (*conj. + subjunctive
                          + ἄν or past tense of indicative*) until

256.   EXERCISES

A.   Greek-to-English Sentences

1. πῶς ἐξέσται σοὶ εὑρεῖν χρόνον ἱκανὸν αἰσθάνεσθαι τὰς τῶν πολῑτῶν ἀρετάς;

2. δεῖ με μαθεῖν πολλὰ περὶ τοῦ εὖ λέγειν πρὶν γενέσθαι ἀγαθὸν ῥήτορα.

3. ἀναγκαῖόν ἐστι κελεύειν τοῖς πολίταις μὴ χρήματα προθῡμότερον ἢ φιλίᾱν ζητεῖν.

4. δοκοῦσι μὲν οἱ πολῖται ἄξειν σχολήν, οὔπω δὲ πεπυσμένοι εἰσὶ τῶν ἐν τῇ πόλει πρᾱγμάτων.

5. μὴ καλέσῃς με εἰς τὴν ἐκκλησίᾱν, ὦ πολῖτα βέλτιστε, πρὶν ἂν ἕτοιμος ὦ.

6. διὰ τὸ πολλοὺς ἀνθρώπους πολλάκις ἁμαρτάνειν, δεῖ δικαίων θεῶν.

7. δοκεῖ μοι χρῆναι τὸν Σωκράτη τῑμᾶσθαι τῷ τὴν πόλιν δεῖπνα αὐτῷ παρασκευάζειν.

8. κἀγὼ ἤθελον φράσαι τοῖς μαθηταῖς μὴ σχολῇ τὰ ἑαυτῶν ἔργα πράττειν.

9. οὐκ ἀνάγκη ἦν αὐτοὺς ἰέναι εἰς τὰς τριήρεις πρὶν ὁ στρατηγὸς ἐκέλευσεν.

10. ἀρ' ᾔσθου σύ γε τοὺς ἐπιτηδείους κακῶς πάσχοντας ὑπὸ τοῦ δεσπότου;

B.   English-to-Greek Sentences

1. For the sake of winning (*use articular infinitive as the object of a preposition*), it is necessary to make clear your virtue.

2. We ought to command the prudent citizens to come back into the city before the night arrives.

3. I shall not write any letters to my mother or my father until I have sufficient leisure for (of) writing.

4. Is it necessary to send the soldiers into such great danger that they will either be harmed or die?

5. It is possible for you to honor your old teacher, students, but you do not seem to be willing.

C.   READING

ARISTOTLE CONTEMPLATES CONTEMPLATION
(adapted from Book 10 of Aristotle's *Nicomachean Ethics* 1177b)

Aristotle, after studying and working with Plato for twenty years, went on to found his own Peripatetic school of philosophy. Hired as tutor for the teenaged Alexander the Great, he exerted a lasting influence on the future king of Macedonia.

In **Nicomachean Ethics** *(a moral treatise named after his own son Nicomachus), Aristotle investigates the human pursuit of happiness. True happiness, he concludes, must be the contemplation of truth because that is the activity in which we exercise our highest virtue, wisdom.*

The passage below comes from near the end of the work. Aristotle is summing up what makes contemplation the best of all activities.

Δόξαι τ' ἂν θεωρίᾱ μόνη δι' αὐτὴν ἀγαπᾶσθαι· οὐδὲν γὰρ ἀπ' αὐτῆς γίγνεται παρὰ τὸ θεωρῆσαι, ἀπὸ δὲ τῶν πρᾱκτικῶν ἢ πλεῖον ἢ ἔλᾱττον περιποιούμεθα παρὰ τὴν πρᾶξιν. δοκεῖ θ' ἡ εὐδαιμονίᾱ ἐν τῇ σχολῇ εἶναι· ἀσχολούμεθα γὰρ ἵνα σχολὴν ἄγωμεν, καὶ πολεμοῦμεν ἵνα εἰρήνην ἄγωμεν. τῶν
5 μὲν πρᾱκτικῶν ἀρετῶν ἐν τοῖς πολῑτικοῖς ἢ ἐν τοῖς πολεμικοῖς πρᾶγμασιν ἡ ἐνέργεια· αἱ δὲ περὶ ταῦτα πράξεις δοκοῦσιν ἄσχολοι εἶναι· αἱ μὲν πολεμικαὶ πράξεις ἄσχολοί εἰσιν. ἔστι δὲ καὶ ἡ τοῦ πολῑτικοῦ πρᾶξις ἄσχολος, καὶ παρὰ τὸ πολῑτεύεσθαι περιποιεῖται τῑμὰς ἢ τήν γ' εὐδαιμονίᾱν αὐτῷ καὶ τοῖς πολίταις. ἀλλ' εἰ τῶν μὲν κατὰ τὰς ἀρετὰς πράξεων αἱ πολῑτικαὶ καὶ πολεμικαὶ κάλλει καὶ μεγέθει προέχουσιν,
10 αὗται δ' ἄσχολοί εἰσι καὶ οὐ δι' αὐτὰς αἱροῦνται, ἡ δὲ τοῦ νοῦ ἐνέργεια σχολῇ προέχειν δοκεῖ καὶ παρ' αὐτὴν οὐδὲν περιποιεῖσθαι, αὕτη οὖν ἡ τελείᾱ εὐδαιμονίᾱ ἂν εἴη ἀνθρώπου.

VOCABULARY

δόξαι (line 1): aorist optative of δοκέω
θεωρίᾱ (line 1): from θεωρίᾱ, -ᾱς, ἡ: contemplation
δι' αὐτήν (line 1): on account of itself, i.e., for its own sake
παρά (line 2): here = "beyond" or "in addition to"
θεωρῆσαι (line 2): from θεωρέω, θεωρήσω, ἐθεώρησα, τεθεώρηκα, τεθεώρημαι, ἐθεωρήθην: contemplate
πρᾱκτικῶν (line 2): from πρᾱκτικός, -ή, -όν: practical (*here = a substantive*, "practical pursuits")
περιποιούμεθα (line 3): from περιποιέω: aim at getting
παρά (line 3): here = "beyond" or "in addition to"
πρᾶξιν (line 3): from πρᾶξις, -εως, ἡ: action, pursuit
εὐδαιμονίᾱ (line 3): from εὐδαιμονίᾱ, -ᾱς, ἡ: happiness
ἀσχολούμεθα (line 4): from ἀσχολέομαι, ἀσχολήσομαι, ἠσχολησάμην, —, ἠσχόλημαι, ἠσχολήθην: engage in business
πολεμοῦμεν (line 4): from πολεμέω, πολεμήσω, ἐπολέμησα, πεπολέμηκα, πεπολέμημαι, ἐπολεμήθην: make war
εἰρήνην ἄγωμεν (line 4): = εἰρήνην ἔχωμεν
τῶν...ἀρετῶν...ἡ ἐνέργεια (lines 4-6): these words go together; supply ἐστί
πολῑτικοῖς (line 5): from πολῑτικός, -ή, -όν: political
πολεμικοῖς (line 5): from πολεμικός, -ή, -όν: military
ἐνέργεια (line 6): from ἐνέργεια, -ᾱς, ἡ: activity, exercise
ἄσχολοι (line 6): from ἄσχολος, -ον: unleisured
τοῦ πολῑτικοῦ (line 7): here = masculine, i.e., the politician
παρά (line 7): here = "beyond" or "in addition to"

πολῑτεύεσθαι (line 8): from πολῑτεύω, πολῑτεύσω, ἐπολῑτευσα, πεπολῑτευκα,
    πεπολῑτευμαι, ἐπολῑτεύθην: be a citizen; (*mid.*) participate in politics

τῶν...κατὰ τὰς ἀρετὰς πράξεων (line 9): of those pursuits in conformity with the vir-
    tues, i.e., among the pursuits that display people's virtues

κάλλει (line 9): from κάλλος, -ους, τό: beauty, nobility

μεγέθει (line 9): from μέγεθος, -ους, τό: size, grandeur

προέχουσιν (line 10): from προέχω: stand out

νοῦ (line 11): from νοῦς (= νόος), νοῦ, ὁ: mind

παρά (line 11): here = "beyond" or "in addition to"

τελείᾱ (line 12): from τέλειος, -ᾱ, -ον: complete, perfect

LESSON 44

VERBAL ADJECTIVES IN -τέος AND -τός

τὸν βουλόμενον...εὐδαίμονα εἶναι σωφροσύνην...
διωκτέον καὶ ἀσκητέον
(Whoever wishes to be happy must pursue and practice self-control.)
—Socrates advocates a disciplined life in Plato's *Gorgias* 507c

257. In Lesson 43 you learned that the idea of **necessity** or **obligation** can be expressed by combining ἀναγκαῖον, ἀνάγκη, δεῖ, or χρή with an infinitive. Another way is with a type of **verbal adjective** formed by adding **-τέος, -τέᾱ, -τέον** to the verb's **aorist passive stem without the augment and -θη-**, or sometimes to its present or future stem instead. The accent is always on the **penult** (-τέ-).

The verbal adjective in -τέος will be listed along with a verb's principal parts **only if** it is unpredictable, i.e., if it uses the present or future stem rather than the aorist passive stem without the augment and -θη-. Here are examples of both predictable (aorist stem) and unpredictable (present or future stem) verbal adjectives in -τέος. Each can be translated as if it were a passive infinitive: "[needing] to be_____'d."

Aorist Stem:

ἐπαιδεύθην	→	παιδευτέος	"to be taught"
ἐφιλήθην	→	φιλητέος	"to be loved"
ἐγράφην	→	γραπτέος	"to be written"—φ becomes π to match the smooth τ following it
ἐλέχθην	→	λεκτέος	"to be said"—γ had become χ to
or ἐρρήθην	→	ῥητέος	match the rough θ; it now becomes κ to match the smooth τ following it
ἐπέμφθην	→	πεμπτέος	"to be sent"—π had become φ to match the rough θ; it returns to its original form
ἐτύθην	→	θυτέος	"to be sacrificed"—θ had become τ to avoid -θυθη; it returns to its original form

303

Present Stem:

φάναι	→	φατέος	"to be said"
ἰέναι	→	ἰτέος	"to be traveled"
(οἶδα) ἴσμεν→		ἰστέος	"to be known"

Future Stem:

ἔχ-σω	→	ἑκτέος	"to be held"—χ becomes κ to match
or σχήσω	→	σχετέος	the smooth τ after it
κλέπ-σω	→	κλεπτέος	"to be stolen"
φεύγ-σομαι	→	φευκτέος	"to be escaped"—γ becomes κ to match
			the smooth τ after it
μαθήσομαι	→	μαθητέος	"to be understood"
μαχέομαι	→	μαχετέος	"to be fought"
μενέω	→	μενετέος	"to be awaited"
οἴσω	→	οἰστέος	"to be carried"
παύσω	→	παυστέος	"to be stopped"
πεύσομαι	→	πευστέος	"to be learned"
σώσω	→	σωστέος	"to be saved"

When it has attributive position, a verbal adjective in -τέος functions as a **substantive**; e.g., τὰ πρᾱκτέα = "the things that have to be done."

When it has predicate position, a verbal adjective in -τέος works in conjunction with a form of the verb εἰμί, either expressed or implied, to convey the idea that something must, or ought to, be done to someone or something. That someone or something may be the sentence's **subject**, with which **the verbal adjective agrees in gender, number, and case**. The person(s) who must, or ought to, do the action may be designated by a noun or pronoun in the **dative case** (dative of personal agent; see Lesson 22, §137), never by ὑπό + genitive. Examples:

οἱ παῖδες παιδευτέοι εἰσὶν ἡμῖν.	" The children are to be taught by us," i.e., "We have to (must, ought to) teach the children."
τῷ βασιλεῖ ἦν αἱρετέᾱ ἡ ὁδός.	" The road was to be chosen by the king," i.e., "The king had to (was obligated to) choose the road."

A sentence with a verbal adjective may also be designed so that its subject is the **impersonal** notion of something's being necessary. **The verbal adjective is put into the neuter singular** or **plural**; the recipients of the action are treated as if they were the **direct object** (even though the verbal adjective is passive and logically should not be able to have a direct object!). The agents are designated by the **dative case** (occasionally by the accusative instead). Examples:

τοὺς παῖδας παιδευτέον (or παιδευτέα) ἐστὶν ἡμῖν.

> " Teaching the children has to be done by us," i.e., "We have to (must, ought to) teach the children."

τῷ βασιλεῖ ἦν αἱρετέον (or αἱρετέα) τὴν ὁδόν.

> " Choosing the road had to be done by the king," i.e., "The king had to (was obligated to) choose the road."

Notice that the neuter verbal adjectives in these sentences may be translated as if they were **gerunds (verbal nouns) in the active voice** ("teaching," "choosing").

The impersonal usage seems odd to us, but the Greeks liked its flexibility. If the -τέος verbal adjective agrees with the subject, the passive sentence must be capable of being rephrased as a **transitive active** sentence with a direct object in the **accusative** case. This is not required for the impersonal usage. Examples: "You will have to hear the orator" could be expressed impersonally as τοῦ ῥήτορος ἀκουστέον (or ἀκουστέα) ἔσται σοί (= "hearing the orator will have to be done by you"), but **not** as ὁ ῥήτωρ ἀκουστέος ἔσται σοί, because ὁ ῥήτωρ would have to be put into the genitive case (genitive of person being heard)—not the accusative—in the active equivalent of the sentence. "She must go into the city" could be expressed impersonally as αὐτῇ ἰτέον (or ἰτέα) ἐστὶν εἰς τὴν πόλιν (= "going into the city has to be done by her"), but **not** with a verbal adjective modifying "she," because the verb in the active equivalent is intransitive with no direct object that could serve as subject of the corresponding passive sentence. Neither Greek nor English permits you to say, "She must be gone'd into the city."

258.   Greek has one other type of verbal adjective. It is built on the same stem as the verbal adjective in -τέος, but it ends in **-τός, -τή, -τόν** (accent generally on the ultima) rather than -τέος, -τέᾱ, -τέον. Verbal adjectives in -τός either show **capability** or **possibility** (e.g., ὁρᾱτός "able to be seen," i.e., "visible") or have the sense of **perfect passive participles** (e.g., παιδευτός "[having been] educated"). Look for clues in the context to help you translate them accurately. A **dative of agent** is normal with verbal adjectives in -τός, just as with those in -τέος.

Example:

> οἶδα ὅτι τὰ ζῷα φιλητά σοί ἐστιν.

Two possible translations:

> "I know that the animals are beloved by you."
>
> " I know that the animals are capable of being loved (have the possibility to be loved) by you."

NOTE   A verbal adjective in -τός may be made comparative with μᾶλλον or with -o/ω- + -τερος, -ᾱ, -ον, superlative with μάλιστα or with -o/ω- + -τατος,-η, -ον.

259.   **VOCABULARY**

αἰσχΰνω, αἰσχυνῶ, ᾔσχῡνα, —, —, ᾐσχΰνθην
                disgrace; (*mid.*) feel ashamed, be
                ashamed

NOTE   The future middle αἰσχυνοῦμαι means "I'll feel ashamed [for a while]"; the future passive αἰσχυνθήσομαι means "I'll be ashamed [on one occasion]."

ἐλαύνω, ἐλῶ (= ἐλάω), ἤλασα, ἐλήλακα, ἐλήλαμαι, ἠλάθην
                drive, ride, march, row, beat out (*metal*),
                forge [cf. *elastic*]

θαυμάζω, θαυμάσομαι, ἐθαύμασα, τεθαύμακα, τεθαύμασμαι,
    ἐθαυμάσθην
                wonder (at), marvel (at), be amazed (at),
                admire [cf. *thaumatology, thaumaturge*]

NOTE   αἰσχΰνομαι, θαυμάζω, and other verbs of emotion may be followed by a clause giving the cause of the emotion and beginning with ὅτι ("that") or, more often, with εἰ or ἐάν ("if"); in the latter case, the clause has the form of a protasis, suggesting that the cause is merely *supposed*, not actually known, by the speaker.

στάδιον, -ου, τό   (*the pl. may be either neut.* στάδια *or masc.*
                στάδιοι) stade (= *600 Greek feet*), race-
                course, stadium

NOTE   στάδιον and other words that measure distance are frequently used in a construction called **accusative of extent of space**, analogous to the accusative of extent of time (see §142). Example: ἑκατὸν στάδια ἤλασαν οἱ στρατιῶται. "The soldiers marched (for) a hundred stades."

χορός, -οῦ, ὁ   dance, chorus (*of a Greek play*)
                [cf. *choreography*]

κενός, -ή, -όν   (+ *gen.*) empty (of), devoid (of)
                [cf. *cenotaph*]

δή   (*postpositive particle*) certainly, quite, in-
                deed (*emphasizes preceding word—can
                be ironic*)

τοι   (*enclitic postpositive particle*) you know,
                you see

NOTE   τοι was originally a dative of σύ ("[let me tell] you"). Conveying a tone of familiarity, confidentiality, or conviction, it corresponds roughly to the "you know" or "you see" that English speakers love to inject in their conversational sentences. It is often combined with other particles (e.g., τοι + ἄν → τἄν, through crasis).

μέντοι   (*postpositive particle*) surely, however
τοίνυν   (*postpositive particle*) therefore, then

NOTE   μέντοι and τοίνυν are accented as if their suffixes, -τοι and -νυν, were detached enclitics.

260.   **EXERCISES**

A.   **Greek-to-English Sentences**

1.   μακραὶ ἐπιστολαὶ γραπτέαι ἔσονται τῷ υἱῷ παρ' ἐμέ, βουλήσομαι γὰρ πυνθάνεσθαι τῶν πρᾱγμάτων αὐτοῦ.

2.   πᾶσι μέντοι ἡμῖν θαυμαστέον τὴν ἀρετὴν τούτων τῶν νέων στρατιωτῶν.

3.   τὸ τοίνυν τοὺς ἑταίρους αἰσχύνειν φευκτέον μᾶλλον καὶ τοῦ ἀποθανεῖν.

4.   ἑκατὸν στάδια ἰτέον τῷ στρατηγῷ πρὶν αὖθις τὴν φιλητὴν γυναῖκα ἰδεῖν.

5.   οὔ τοι θαυμάζω ἐὰν πάσχῃ κακῶς, ὁ γὰρ βίος αὐτοῦ κενὸς τῑμῆς ἐστιν.

6.   καθ' ἡμέρᾱν θυτέον ἦν ὑμῖν ἵνα οἱ θεοὶ ἐλάσαιεν τὸ κακὸν ἐκ τῆς πόλεως.

7.   θαυμάζω ὅτι οὐ δοκεῖς τὸ τῑμᾶν τόν τε πατέρα καὶ τὴν μητέρα χρῆναι.

8.   οὐκ ᾐσχύνου ὅτι οἱ χοροὶ τοσαύτᾱς ἁμαρτίᾱς ἁμάρτοιεν (*optative option*);

9.   ὡς τάχιστα ἐλατέον τὴν τριήρη τοῖς σώφροσι πολίταις διὰ τῆς θαλάττης.

10. σοφὸς δὴ δοκεῖ ὁ φιλόσοφος εἶναι ὃς τοὺς νεᾱνίᾱς οὔποτε διαφθείρει.

B.   **English-to-Greek Sentences**

1.   The racecourse is quite empty now; later, however, many honored (*use verbal adj.*) youth riding horses will be visible.

2.   The chorus must be chosen, you see, by the archon and taught well in order that the citizens not be ashamed.

3.   We tell our students to pursue self-control; therefore we ought to lead a prudent life ourselves.

4.   It was necessary, then, for the children to remain in the house, for the road was not devoid of dangers.

5.   The army will have to march for fifty stades before it arrives at the desired (*use verbal adj.*) camp.

C. READING

THE COST OF COWARDICE IN SPARTA
(adapted from Xenophon's *Constitution of the Lacedaemonians* 9)

Besides the **Memorabilia** *(see the readings for Lessons 31-33), Xenophon wrote several shorter works on various topics. In his influential* **Constitution of the Lacedaemonians***, he attributes the Lacedaemonians' (Spartans') prestige to the unique system of laws bestowed upon them by their legendary leader Lycurgus in the eighth century B.C.*

The following excerpt is from a section in which Xenophon praises Lycurgus for having made life in Sparta full of glory for those who are brave, but full of shame for those who are not. Throughout the passage ἀγαθός *may be translated as "brave,"* κακός *as "cowardly."*

Ἄξιον δὲ καὶ τόδε τοῦ Λυκούργου θαυμασθῆναι, τὸ κατεργάσασθαι ἐν τῇ πόλει αἱρετώτερον εἶναι τὸν καλὸν θάνατον ἀντὶ τοῦ αἰσχροῦ βίου.

ᾗ μέντοι ἐμηχανήσατο ὥστε ταῦτα γίγνεσθαι, καὶ τοῦτο μὴ παραλίπωμεν. ἐκεῖνος τοίνυν παρεσκεύασε τοῖς μὲν ἀγαθοῖς εὐδαιμονίαν, τοῖς δὲ κακοῖς
5 κακοδαιμονίαν. ἐν μὲν γὰρ ταῖς ἄλλαις πόλεσιν ὁπόταν τις κακὸς γένηται, ἐπίκλησιν μόνον ἔχει κακὸς εἶναι, ἀγοράζει δ᾽ ἐν τῷ αὐτῷ τόπῳ ὁ κακὸς τἀγαθῷ καὶ κάθηται καὶ γυμνάζεται, ἐὰν βούληται· ἐν δὲ τῇ Λακεδαίμονι πᾶς μὲν ἄν τις αἰσχυνθείη τὸν κακὸν σύσκηνον παραλαβεῖν, πᾶς δ᾽ ἄν ἐν παλαίσματι συγγυμναστήν. πολλάκις δ᾽ ὁ τοιοῦτος ἐν χοροῖς εἰς τὰς ἐπονειδίστους χώρᾱς
10 ἀπελαύνεται, καὶ μὴν ἐν ὁδοῖς παραχωρητέον αὐτῷ, καὶ οἰκίαν κενὴν γυναικὸς περιοπτέον, καὶ οὐ μῑμητέον τοὺς ἀγαθούς, ἢ πληγὰς ὑπὸ τῶν ἀμεινόνων ληπτέον. ἐγὼ μὲν δή, τοιαύτης τοῖς κακοῖς ἀτῑμίᾱς οὔσης, οὐ θαυμάζω τὸ αἱρεῖσθαι θάνατον ἀντὶ τοῦ οὕτως ἐπονειδίστου βίου.

VOCABULARY

τόδε (line 1): i.e., this deed (*anticipates the artic. infin.* τὸ κατεργάσασθαι)
Λυκούργου (line 1): from Λυκοῦργος, -ου, ὁ: Lycurgus
κατεργάσασθαι (line 1): from κατεργάζομαι, κατεργάσομαι, —, —, κατείργασμαι,
    κατειργάσθην (+ *obj. infin.*): accomplish, bring about
ἀντί (line 2): in place of (*prep. + gen.*); + αἱρετώτερον = "preferable to"
ᾗ (line 3): how, in which way (*rel. adv.*)
ἐμηχανήσατο (line 3): from μηχανάομαι, μηχανήσομαι, ἐμηχανησάμην, —,
    μεμηχάνημαι, —: contrive, devise
τοῦτο (line 3): refers to the thought expressed by the words ᾗ...γίγνεσθαι
παραλίπωμεν (line 3): from παραλείπω: pass over, neglect to mention
εὐδαιμονίᾱν (line 4): from εὐδαιμονίᾱ, -ᾱς, ἡ: prosperity

κακοδαιμονίᾱν (line 5): from κακοδαιμονίᾱ, -ᾱς, ἡ: misfortune

ἐπίκλησιν (line 6): from ἐπίκλησις, -εως, ἡ: bad name, reproach

κακὸς εἶναι (line 6): appositive to ἐπίκλησιν, specifying what the reproach is

ἀγοράζει (line 6): from ἀγοράζω, ἀγοράσω, ἠγόρασα, ἠγόρακα, ἠγόρασμαι, ἠγοράσθην: be in the marketplace, shop

τἀγαθῷ (line 6): dative of resemblance; construe with ἐν τῷ αὐτῷ τόπῳ ("in the same place *as*")

κάθηται (line 7): from κάθημαι (*occurs in perf. tense only*): sit

γυμνάζεται (line 7): from γυμνάζω, γυμνάσω, ἐγύμνασα, γεγύμνακα, γεγύμνασμαι, ἐγυμνάσθην: train; (*mid.*) exercise

Λακεδαίμονι (line 7): from Λακεδαίμων, -ονος, ἡ: Lacedaemon, Sparta

σύσκηνον (line 8): from σύσκηνος, -ου, ὁ: tentmate, messmate

παραλαβεῖν (line 8): from παραλαμβάνω: associate with (someone as a)

παλαίσματι (line 8): from πάλαισμα, -ατος, τό: wrestling-bout

συγγυμναστήν (line 9): from συγγυμναστής, -οῦ, ὁ: exercise partner

ἐπονειδίστους (line 9): ἐπονείδιστος, -ον: ignominious

ἀπελαύνεται (line 10): from ἀπελαύνω: drive back

παραχωρητέον (line 10): from παραχωρέω, παραχωρήσομαι, παρεχώρησα, παρακεχώρηκα, παρακεχώρημαι, παρεχωρήθην: yield, step aside

περιοπτέον (line 11): from περιοράω: overlook, put up with, endure

μῑμητέον (line 11): from μῑμέομαι, μῑμήσομαι, ἐμῑμησάμην, —, μεμίμημαι, ἐμῑμήθην: imitate

πληγάς (line 11): from πληγή, -ῆς, ἡ: blow, stroke

ἀτῑμίᾱς (line 12): from ἀτῑμίᾱ, -ᾱς, ἡ: dishonor

ἀντί (line 13): in place of (*prep. + gen.*)

LESSON 45

CLAUSES OF EFFORT AND FEAR

δείδω μὴ θήρεσσιν ἕλωρ καὶ κύρμα γένωμαι
(I'm afraid that I may turn into booty for the beasts.)
—Odysseus, washed up on the cold and lonely coast of Phaeacia,
fears the worst in Homer's *Odyssey* 5.473

261. As you know, every subordinate clause (including every infinitive or participle that is the equivalent of a subordinate clause) can be classified by its function: **adjectival** (e.g., relative clause, attributive participle), **adverbial** (e.g., temporal, causal, concessive, conditional, purpose, result clause, circumstantial participle), **substantival** (**noun**) (e.g., indirect discourse with infinitive, participle, or ὅτι/ὡς clause, indirect question, subject infinitive, object infinitive, articular infinitive). **Clauses of effort** and **clauses of fear** are **substantival** (noun) clauses; they may serve as **subjects** or as **direct objects** of the main verb.

NOTE Clauses of effort and clauses of fear have traditionally been called "object clauses." We have chosen not to call them that, lest you be misled by the name into thinking that they must always be direct objects. They can, in fact, be subjects, if the main verb is passive or impersonal.

262. A **clause of effort** describes a result that someone strives to accomplish or avert. It is used with verbs that signify an expenditure of effort or care (e.g., βουλεύω "take counsel"; ἐπιμελέομαι "take care"; μηχανάομαι "contrive"; ποιέω/πράττω "take action"). Positive clauses of effort are introduced by the conjunction **ὅπως** (sometimes by ὡς), meaning "how" or "that." Negative clauses of effort begin with **ὅπως μή** (sometimes with ὡς μή), meaning "how...not" or "that...not."

The verb in a clause of effort stands in the **future indicative**. After a secondary main verb, the **future optative** may be used (but tends not to be).

Examples:

μηχανῶμαι ὅπως φανοῦμαι σοφός.
"I am devising how I shall appear wise."

or "I am devising how to appear wise."

ἐπεμελοῦντο ὅπως μὴ ἀποθανοῦνται (ἀποθανοῖντο).
"They took care that they should not be killed."

or "They took care not to be killed."

The difference between effort clauses and purpose clauses is worth noting. **Purpose clauses** occur in sentences that describe a **specific action** undertaken to achieve a desired goal (e.g., "we went to school to become educated"). **Effort clauses** occur in sentences that describe the **putting of effort or care** into achieving a desired goal (e.g., "we contrived to become educated"). A purpose clause, being adverbial, answers the question "why?" and could be deleted from the sentence without changing its main idea. An effort clause, being substantival, answers the question "what?" and is needed to express the sentence's main idea.

To make an effort clause more like a purpose clause, the speaker may replace the future indicative with the present or aorist **subjunctive** or (after a secondary main verb) the present or aorist **optative**. The clause then falls midway between an effort and a purpose clause: it is introduced by a verb of effort or caution and by ὅπως (or ὡς), but the verb in the clause has the form expected in a purpose clause.

263.   **δέδοικα/δέδια** (*pluperf.* **ἐδεδοίκη/ἐδεδίη**), —, **ἔδεισα**, —, —, — ("fear") is obviously a defective verb! It occurs only in the active voice. Its aorist is built on the stem δϝει-. Its perfect has the sense of a **present** tense (and thus is written as the verb's first principal part), while its pluperfect has the sense of an **imperfect** tense. Forms built on the first perfect stem (δε-δϝοι-κ-) are more common in the singular; forms built on the second perfect stem (δε-δϝι-) are more common in the plural. In the paradigms below, the less popular forms are bracketed.

Perfect Active Indicative		**Pluperfect Active Indicative**	
Singular:		**Singular:**	
δέδοικα	[or δέδια]	ἐδεδοίκη	[or ἐδεδίη]
δέδοικας	[or δέδιας]	ἐδεδοίκης	[or ἐδεδίης]
δέδοικε(ν)	[or δέδιε(ν)]	ἐδεδοίκει(ν)	[or ἐδεδίει(ν)]
Plural:		**Plural:**	
δέδιμεν	[or δεδοίκαμεν]	ἐδέδιμεν	[or ἐδεδοίκεμεν]
δέδιτε	[or δεδοίκατε]	ἐδέδιτε	[or ἐδεδοίκετε]
δεδίᾱσι(ν)	[or δεδοίκᾱσι(ν)]	ἐδέδισαν	[or ἐδεδοίκεσαν]
Perfect Active Infinitive:			
δεδιέναι		[or δεδοικέναι]	

Perfect Active Participle:

δεδιώς, -υῖα, -ός   [or δεδοικώς, -υῖα, -ός]

NOTE   The perf. act. subjunctive δεδίω, perf. act. optative δεδιείην, and perf. act. second-pers. sg. imperative δέδιθι are used only rarely. A different form of the perfect indicative, δείδω (derived from δέδϝοα), occurs in Homeric Greek; like δέδοικα, it has the sense of a present tense (see quotation at the start of this lesson).

264.   A **clause of fear** describes an *undesired* result that someone fears may happen, or a *desired* result that someone fears may *not* happen. It is used with **verbs of fear or caution** or equivalent expressions (e.g., φοβέομαι, δέδοικα, φόβος ἐστί μοι, κίνδυνός ἐστί μοι). Fear clauses are usually introduced by **μή**, meaning "that" or "lest"; negative fear clauses usually begin with **μὴ οὐ**, meaning "that...not" or "lest...not."

The verb in a fear clause stands in the **subjunctive mood**. After a secondary main verb, the **optative mood** may be used instead.

Examples:
φοβοῦμαι μὴ οὐ φαίνωμαι σοφός.
"I am afraid that I may not seem wise."
or   "I am afraid lest I not seem wise."

κίνδυνος ἦν μὴ ἀποθάνωσιν (ἀποθάνοιεν).
"There was danger that they might be killed."
or   "There was danger lest they be killed."

NOTE   The reason that μή, a negative, can introduce a positive-sounding clause is that fear clauses are similar to prohibitions (e.g., "I am afraid; may this not happen!" → "I am afraid that this may happen").

265.   The following verbs, because they are midway in meaning between verbs of effort/care and verbs of fear/caution, may be used **either** with a **negative clause of effort** (ὅπως μή + future indicative) **or** with a positive or negative **clause of fear** (μή or μὴ οὐ + subjunctive or optative): **ὁράω** ("see to it lest..."); **σκοπέω** ("look into it lest..."); **φυλάττομαι** ("be on guard lest...").

NOTE   A verb that calls for an effort or fear clause is frequently capable of taking a complementary or object infinitive as an alternative to the clause.

266.   **VOCABULARY**

βουλεύω, βουλεύσω, ἐβούλευσα, βεβούλευκα, βεβούλευμαι, ἐβουλεύθην
(+ *infin. or effort clause—often in mid. voice*) take counsel (to), plan (to), decide (to), deliberate

δέδοικα/δέδια (*pluperf.* ἐδεδοίκη/ἐδεδίη), —, ἔδεισα, —, —, —
        (+ *acc.*) fear, be afraid (of); (+ *infin. or fear
        cl.*) fear, be afraid

ἐπιμελέομαι, ἐπιμελήσομαι, —, —, ἐπιμεμέλημαι, ἐπεμελήθην
        (+ *gen.*) take care (of); (+ *infin. or effort
        cl.*) take care (to)

ἐσθίω, ἔδομαι, ἔφαγον, ἐδήδοκα, ἐδήδεσμαι, ἠδέσθην
        eat [cf. *dysphagia, phyllophagous*]

καθεύδω (*imperf.* ἐκάθευδον or καθηῦδον), καθευδήσω, —, —, —, —
        (*verbal adj.* καθευδητέος) sleep, be asleep

μηχανάομαι, μηχανήσομαι, ἐμηχανησάμην, —, μεμηχάνημαι, —
        (+ *infin. or effort cl.*) contrive (to), devise
        (to)

σκοπέω (*or* σκέπτομαι—*not used in Attic*), σκέψομαι, ἐσκεψάμην, —,
ἔσκεμμαι, —
        (*verbal adj.* σκεπτέος) (+ *fear or neg. effort
        cl.*) look into, examine [cf. *episcopal,
        skeptic, telescope*]

μηχανή, -ῆς, ἡ   machine, device, contrivance
        [cf. *mechanism*]

σῖτος, -ου, ὁ   (*pl. = neut.* σῖτα) grain, food [cf. *parasite*]

ὕπνος, -ου, ὁ   sleep [cf. *hypnosis, hypnotic*]

μή   (*conj. introducing positive fear cl.*) that,
        lest; (*introducing neg. fear cl.*) μὴ οὐ

ὅπως or ὡς   (*conj. introducing positive effort cl.*) how,
        that; (*introducing neg. effort cl.*) ὅπως μή
        or ὡς μή

267.   **EXERCISES**

A.   **Greek-to-English Sentences**

1. οἱ πολέμιοι ἐμηχανήσαντο ὅπως αἰσχυνοῦσι τὸν ἡμέτερον στρατόν.

2. ἐπιμελώμεθα ὅπως ὠφελήσομεν τὰς γραῦς τὰς κακῶς δὴ πασχούσᾱς.

3. πῶς ἔξεστί σοι καθεύδειν ὕπνον καλὸν μετὰ τὸ οὕτως ἡδέα σῖτα φαγεῖν;

4. δεδιὼς τὰς μηχανὰς τοῦ δεσπότου, βεβούλευμαι ὅπως φεύξομαι αὐτάς.

5. χρὴ ὑμᾶς, ἄρχοντας ὄντας, σκέψασθαι μὴ ἡ ἀγορὰ κενὴ σίτου γένηται.

6. ἐδέδιμεν μὴ οἱ ἐλάσαντες θάττους ἵππους βλαφθεῖησαν ἐν τῷ σταδίῳ.

7. παῦσαι, ὦ παῖ, βοῶσα. ὥρᾱ γάρ σε καθεύδειν καίπερ οὐκ ἐθέλουσαν.

8. δέδοικα μὴ σὺ βίον ἄνευ ἱκανοῦ ὕπνου καὶ σίτου ἄγων ἀποθάνῃς.

9. σκεπτέα τοίνυν ἔσται τοὺς νόμους τοῖς μαθηταῖς καὶ τῷ Σωκράτει.

10. οὐ θαυμάσῃ εἰ θεός τις φανεῖται ἀπὸ τῆς μηχανῆς (= *crane used in Greek
    theaters to swing gods or other lofty characters into view*);

B. **English-to-Greek Sentences**

1. Examining the number of horses, I was amazed and feared lest the grain not be sufficient.
2. They say that women love to contrive terrible contrivances, but such unjust words ought not to be said.
3. Sleep a sweet sleep, my little daughter; you need not fear that a lion may eat you during the night.
4. Take care, soldiers, to eat and sleep before marching many stades.
5. There is great danger that the students may harm themselves by not taking care of themselves. Let us decide how to help them.

C. **READING**

FRIGHTENED BUT ENLIGHTENED
(adapted from Xenophon's *Cyropaedia* 3.1.24-30)

Among Xenophon's miscellaneous works is a romanticized life history of Cyrus, the great Persian king who defeated Croesus, king of Lydia, and then went on to conquer Babylon (539 B.C.) and liberate the Jews held captive there. Cyrus belonged to the Achaemenid family, which ruled Persia for several centuries; the dynasty came to an end in 330 B.C. when Darius, the unsuccessful opponent of Alexander the Great (see readings for Lessons 41 & 42), was assassinated. Xenophon himself had served as a Greek mercenary in the army of another Achaemenid named Cyrus, who was killed while trying to depose his older brother, Artaxerxes (401 B.C.).

*In the **Cyropaedia** ("Education of Cyrus"), Xenophon depicts the sixth-century Cyrus as a magnanimous and philosophical ruler. Given Xenophon's admiration for Sparta (see reading for Lesson 44), it should not be surprising that his idealized Cyrus resembles a Spartan more than a Persian! In the passage below, Cyrus is conversing with Tigranes, son of the king of Armenia; Tigranes' father has been captured by Cyrus and is on trial for having neglected to send the tribute and troops he had promised. Tigranes pleads with Cyrus to spare his father on the grounds that he has now learned his lesson: he will be obedient because his fear of what Cyrus might do is an even stronger deterrent than actual force would be. Cyrus does not immediately buy this argument, so Tigranes argues further.*

Καὶ σύ γ', ἔφη, οἶσθα ὅτι ἀληθῆ λέγω· οἶσθα γὰρ ὅτι οἱ μὲν φοβούμενοι μὴ φύγωσι πατρίδα καὶ οἱ μέλλοντες μάχεσθαι, δεδιότες μὴ νῑκηθῶσι, καὶ οἱ δουλείᾱν φοβούμενοι, οὗτοι μὲν ἢ σίτῳ ἢ ὕπνῳ χαίρειν πολλάκις οὐκ ἔχουσι διὰ τὸν φόβον· οἱ δ᾽ ἤδη μὲν φυγάδες ὄντες, ἤδη δὲ νενῑκημένοι, ἤδη δὲ δουλεύοντες, πολλάκις
5 ἔχουσιν ἄμεινον τῶν εὐδαιμόνων ἐσθίειν τε καὶ καθεύδειν.

ἔτι δὲ φανερώτερον ἔσται ἐν τοῖσδ᾽ οἷον φόρημα ὁ φόβος ἐστίν· ἔνιοι γάρ, φοβούμενοι μὴ ληφθέντες ἀποθάνωσι, προαποθνήσκουσιν ὑπὸ τοῦ φόβου· οὕτω πάντων τῶν δεινῶν ὁ φόβος μάλιστα καταπλήττει τὰς ψῡχάς.

At this point Cyrus objects that the Armenian king, having formerly been insolent, is likely to cause trouble again if he is allowed to continue ruling. Tigranes predicts that Cyrus is more likely to have trouble if he takes the government of Armenia away from Tigranes' father and gives it to other people than if he leaves things as they are.

εἰ δέ τινι τῶν ἀναμαρτήτων παραδοὺς τὴν ἀρχήν, ἀπιστῶν αὐτοῖς φανεῖ,
10 ὅρα ὅπως μὴ ἅμα τ' εὖ ποιήσεις καὶ ἅμα οὐ φίλον νομιοῦσί σε· εἰ δ' αὖ, φυλαττόμενος τὸ ἀπεχθάνεσθαι, μὴ ἐπιθήσεις αὐτοῖς ζυγὰ τοῦ μὴ ὑβρίσαι, ὅρα ὅπως μὴ ἐκείνους αὖ δεήσει σε σωφρονίζειν ἔτι μᾶλλον ἢ ἡμᾶς νῦν ἐδέησεν. ὠγαθὲ Κῦρε, φύλαξαι μὴ ἡμᾶς ἀποβαλών, σαυτὸν ζημιώσῃς πλείω ἢ ὁ πατὴρ ἐμοῦ σε ἔβλαψεν.

Conclusion: *Cyrus graciously permits the Armenian king to keep his throne and invites both Tigranes and his father to dinner.*

VOCABULARY

οἱ μὲν φοβούμενοι...καὶ οἱ μέλλοντες...καὶ οἱ...φοβούμενοι (lines 1-3): these three groups of people are the subjects of the verb ἔχουσι (line 3)
φύγωσι (line 1): here = "be exiled from"
δουλείᾱν (line 3): from δουλείᾱ, -ᾱς, ἡ: slavery
φυγάδες (line 4): φυγάς, -άδος, ὁ: exiled person, an exile
ἐν τοῖσδε (line 6): i.e., in what I am about to say
οἷον φόρημα ὁ φόβος ἐστίν (line 6): this relative clause acts as the subject of the sentence and is linked with the predicate adjective φανερώτερον
οἷον (line 6): from οἷος, -ᾱ, -ον: of which sort; here = "what sort of"
φόρημα (line 6): from φόρημα, -ατος, τό: burden
ἔνιοι (line 6): from ἔνιοι, -αι, -α: some
ληφθέντες (line 7): i.e., captured in war
προαποθνήσκουσιν (line 7): from προαποθνήσκω: die early, commit suicide
ὑπό (line 7): here = "under the influence of"
δεινῶν (line 8): here = "dreadful things," "terrors"
καταπλήττει (line 8): from καταπλήττω: strike down (*with terror*), terrify
ἀναμαρτήτων (line 9): from ἀναμάρτητος, -ον: having done no wrong (*i.e., people who, unlike the Armenians, have never offended Cyrus and thus have not had the opportunity to learn from the experience!*)
παραδούς (line 9): aor. act. ptcple. from παραδίδωμι, παραδώσω, παρέδωκα, παραδέδωκα, παραδέδομαι, παρεδόθην hand over, transfer
ἀπιστῶν (line 9): from ἀπιστέω, ἀπιστήσω, ἠπίστησα, ἠπίστηκα, ἠπίστημαι, ἠπιστήθην (+ *dat.*): distrust (ἀπιστῶν αὐτοῖς φανεῖ = "you will give the impression that you have no faith in them")
ὅπως μὴ ἅμα τ' εὖ ποιήσεις καὶ ἅμα οὐ φίλον νομιοῦσί σε (line 10): i.e., lest you, paradoxically, wind up being regarded by them as an enemy, at the same time as you are actually being generous to them

ἅμα (line 10): at the same time (*adv.*)

ἀπεχθάνεσθαι (line 11): from ἀπεχθάνομαι, ἀπεχθήσομαι, ἀπηχθόμην, —, ἀπήχθημαι, — (+ *dat.*): become hateful (to) (φυλαττόμενος τὸ ἀπεχθάνεσθαι = "guarding against your becoming hateful [to them]," *i.e., striving to ingratiate yourself with them*)

ἐπιθήσεις (line 11): from ἐπιτίθημι, ἐπιθήσω, ἐπέθηκα, ἐπιτέθηκα, ἐπιτέθειμαι, ἐπετέθην: place upon

ζυγά (line 11): from ζυγόν, -οῦ, τό: yoke (*i.e., a curb against their rebelling*)

ὑβρίσαι (line 11): from ὑβρίζω, ὑβριῶ, ὕβρισα, ὕβρικα, ὕβρισμαι, ὑβρίσθην: act insolently, rebel (*a redundant μή, not needed in English, is used with the articular infinitive because of the idea of prohibiting*)

ἐκείνους (line 12): direct object of σωφρονίζειν (*subject* = σε)

σωφρονίζειν (line 12): from σωφρονίζω, σωφρονιῶ, —, —, —, —: teach discretion to, chastise

ἡμᾶς (line 12): direct object of implied σωφρονίζειν (*subject = implied* σε)

Κῦρε (line 13): from Κῦρος, -ου, ὁ: Cyrus, 6th-century B.C. king of Persia

ἀποβαλών (line 13): from ἀποβάλλω: cast aside, reject

ζημιώσῃς (line 13): from ζημιόω, ζημιώσω, ἐζημίωσα, ἐζημίωκα, ἐζημίωμαι, ἐζημιώθην: penalize, damage

LESSON 46
MI-VERBS (δίδωμι, ἵστημι)

οὐκέτι ἐδύνατο ἐν τῷ καθεστῶτι τρόπῳ βιοτεύειν
(No longer could he bear to live in the ordinary fashion.)
—Thucydides in *The Peloponnesian War* 1.130 explains what
led to the downfall of Pausanias, a Spartan general

268. Verbs of the **μι-conjugation**, often called **athematic** verbs, differ from ω-conjugation verbs in the **present and imperfect**, sometimes also in the **second aorist active and middle**, and once in a while in the **second perfect and pluperfect active**. The differences are caused by the variability of the basic stem and by the absence of a thematic vowel (ε or ο) in many of the forms. Although relatively few Greek verbs belong to the μι-conjugation, those that do are among the most frequently used in the language.

269. Two common μι-verbs are **δίδωμι** ("give"; basic stem = δο-/δω-) and **ἵστημι** ("make stand"; basic stem = στα-/στη-). In the present and imperfect, the basic stem is **reduplicated** (with δι- or ἱ- in the present, with augmented ἐδι- or ἱ- in the imperfect). In the present active indicative, the **long** stem-vowel (ω or η) appears in the **singular**, the **short** stem-vowel (ο or α) in the **plural**. There is usually **no thematic vowel** between the stem and the ending, but a few exceptions occur. In the paradigms below, less used alternative forms are given in parentheses.

319

δίδωμι, δώσω, ἔδωκα, δέδωκα, δέδομαι, ἐδόθην "give"

INDICATIVE

Present Active[1]	Imperfect Active[2]	Aorist Active[3]
Singular:		
δίδωμι	ἐδίδουν	ἔδωκα
δίδως	ἐδίδους	ἔδωκας
δίδωσι(ν)	ἐδίδου	ἔδωκε(ν)
Plural:		
δίδομεν	ἐδίδομεν	ἔδομεν
δίδοτε	ἐδίδοτε	ἔδοτε
διδόᾱσι(ν)	ἐδίδοσαν	ἔδοσαν

INDICATIVE

Present Mid./Pass.	Imperfect Mid./Pass.	Aorist Middle
Singular:		
δίδομαι	ἐδιδόμην	ἐδόμην
δίδοσαι	ἐδίδοσο	ἔδου
δίδοται	ἐδίδοτο	ἔδοτο
Plural:		
διδόμεθα	ἐδιδόμεθα	ἐδόμεθα
δίδοσθε	ἐδίδοσθε	ἔδοσθε
δίδονται	ἐδίδοντο	ἔδοντο

SUBJUNCTIVE

Present Active[4]	Aorist Active[4]	Present M./P.[4]	Aorist Mid.[4]
Singular:			
διδῶ	δῶ	διδῶμαι	δῶμαι
διδῷς	δῷς	διδῷ	δῷ
διδῷ	δῷ	διδῶται	δῶται
Plural:			
διδῶμεν	δῶμεν	διδώμεθα	δώμεθα
διδῶτε	δῶτε	διδῶσθε	δῶσθε
διδῶσι(ν)	δῶσι(ν)	διδῶνται	δῶνται

---

[1] The first-person ending -μι is an alternative to -ω (which is actually just a lengthened thematic vowel, not an ending). The second-person ending -ς was originally -σι. The third-person ending -σι was originally -τι (cf. ἐστί). The third-person plural ending -ᾱσι was originally -αντι.

[2] In the imperfect active singular, the stem-vowel contracts with a thematic vowel (-οον → -ουν, -οες → -ους, -οε → -ου). For its third-person plural, the imperfect active borrows the first aorist ending -σαν.

[3] The aorist active has two different stems: ἐδωκ- in the singular, ἐδο- in the plural. Endings are a mixture of first aorist (-α, -ας, -ε, -σαν) and second aorist (-μεν, -τε) endings.

[4] In the subjunctive μι-verbs contract their stem-vowel with a lengthened thematic vowel (η/ω).

OPTATIVE[1]

	Present Active		Aorist Active		Present M./P.	Aorist Mid.
Singular:						
	διδοίην		δοίην		διδοίμην	δοίμην
	διδοίης		δοίης		διδοῖο	δοῖο
	διδοίη		δοίη		διδοῖτο	δοῖτο
Plural:						
	διδοῖμεν	(διδοίημεν)	δοῖμεν	(δοίημεν)	διδοίμεθα	δοίμεθα
	διδοῖτε	(διδοίητε)	δοῖτε	(δοίητε)	διδοῖσθε	δοῖσθε
	διδοῖεν	(διδοίησαν)	δοῖεν	(δοίησαν)	διδοῖντο	δοῖντο

IMPERATIVE

	Present Active	Aorist Active	Present M./P.	Aorist Mid.
Singular:				
	δίδου	δός	δίδοσο	δοῦ
	διδότω	δότω	διδόσθω	δόσθω
Plural:				
	δίδοτε	δότε	δίδοσθε	δόσθε
	διδόντων	δόντων	διδόσθων	δόσθων

Present Active Infinitive:
διδόναι

Aorist Active Infinitive:
δοῦναι

Present Middle/Passive Infinitive:
δίδοσθαι

Aorist Middle Infinitive:
δόσθαι

Present Active Participle:
διδούς, διδοῦσα, διδόν (declined like an -ων, -ουσα, -ον participle, but has -ους, not -ων, in nom. masc. sg.)

Present Middle/Passive Participle:
διδόμενος, -η, -ον

Aorist Active Participle:
δούς, δοῦσα, δόν (declined like an -ων, -ουσα, -ον participle, but has -ους, not -ων, in nom. masc. sg.)

Aorist Middle Participle:
δόμενος, -η, -ον

---

[1] In the optative, the accent of μι-verbs is not allowed to recede beyond the syllable with the optative ι in it.

ἵστημι, στήσω, ἔστησα or ἔστην, ἕστηκα
(*pluperf.* εἱστήκη), ἕσταμαι, ἐστάθην "make stand"

INDICATIVE

Present Active	Imperfect Active	Second Aorist Active[1]
Singular:		
ἵστημι	ἵστην	ἔστην
ἵστης	ἵστης	ἔστης
ἵστησι(ν)	ἵστη	ἔστη
Plural:		
ἵσταμεν	ἵσταμεν	ἔστημεν
ἵστατε	ἵστατε	ἔστητε
ἱστᾶσι(ν)	ἵστασαν	ἔστησαν

Present M./P.	Imperfect M./P.	Second Aorist Middle
Singular:		
ἵσταμαι	ἱστάμην	none
ἵστασαι	ἵστασο	
ἵσταται	ἵστατο	
Plural:		
ἱστάμεθα	ἱστάμεθα	
ἵστασθε	ἵστασθε	
ἵστανται	ἵσταντο	

Perfect Active[2]:	Pluperfect Active[2]
Singular:	
ἕστηκα	εἱστήκη
ἕστηκας	εἱστήκης
ἕστηκε(ν)	εἱστήκει(ν)
Plural:	
ἕσταμεν	ἕσταμεν
ἕστατε	ἕστατε
ἑστᾶσι(ν)	ἕστασαν

[1] The first and second aorist differ in meaning: ἔστησα is **transitive** ("I made [something] stand up," "I set up"); ἔστην is **intransitive** ("I stood [myself] up").

[2] First perfect forms are used in the singular, second perfect in the plural. ἕστηκα = "I have stood up," "I am standing"; εἱστήκη = "I had stood up," "I was standing."

SUBJUNCTIVE[1]

Present Active	Second Aorist Act.	Present Mid./Pass.	Perf. Active
Singular:			
ἱστῶ	στῶ	ἱστῶμαι	ἑστῶ
ἱστῇς	στῇς	ἱστῇ	ἑστῇ
ἱστῇ	στῇ	ἱστῆται	ἑστῇ
Plural:			
ἱστῶμεν	στῶμεν	ἱστώμεθα	ἑστῶμεν
ἱστῆτε	στῆτε	ἱστῆσθε	ἑστῆτε
ἱστῶσι(ν)	στῶσι(ν)	ἱστῶνται	ἑστῶσι(ν)

OPTATIVE[2]

Present Active	Second Aorist Act.	Present Mid./Pass.	Perf. Active
Singular:			
ἱσταίην	σταίην	ἱσταίμην	ἑσταίην
ἱσταίης	σταίης	ἱσταῖο	ἑσταίης
ἱσταίη	σταίη	ἱσταῖτο	ἑσταίη
Plural:			
ἱσταῖμεν (ἱσταίημεν)	σταῖμεν (σταίημεν)	ἱσταίμεθα	ἑσταῖμεν
ἱσταῖτε (ἱσταίητε)	σταῖτε (σταίητε)	ἱσταῖσθε	ἑσταῖτε
ἱσταῖεν (ἱσταίησαν)	σταῖεν (σταίησαν)	ἱσταῖντο	ἑσταῖεν

IMPERATIVE[3]

Present Active	Second Aorist Act.	Present Mid./Pass.	Perf. Active
Singular:			
ἵστη	στῆθι	ἵστασο	ἕσταθι
ἱστάτω	στήτω	ἱστάσθω	ἑστάτω
Plural:			
ἵστατε	στῆτε	ἵστασθε	ἕστατε
ἱστάντων	στάντων	ἱστάσθων	ἑστάντων

Present Active Infinitive:
ἱστάναι

Second Aorist Active Infinitive:
στῆναι

Present Mid./Pass. Infinitive:
ἵστασθαι

Second Aorist Mid. Infinitive:
none

Perfect Active Infinitive:
ἑστάναι

Present Active Participle:
ἱστάς, ἱστᾶσα, ἱστάν

Second Aorist Act. Participle:
στάς, στᾶσα, στάν

Present Mid./Pass. Participle:
ἱστάμενος, -η, -ον

Second Aorist Mid. Participle:
none

Perfect Active Participle:
ἑστώς, ἑστῶσα, ἑστός (ἑστῶτος, -ώσης, -ῶτος, etc.)

---

[1]No second aorist middle subjunctive of ἵστημι exists.
[2]No second aorist middle optative of ἵστημι exists.
[3]No second aorist middle imperative of ἵστημι exists.

Since ἵστημι has no second aorist middle, we have to find another μι-verb with a stem ending in -α to use as a paradigm for those forms. Here is the conjugation of ἐπριάμην, a μι-verb that occurs *only* in the second aorist middle (deponent) and means "bought." It serves as the third principal part for the verb ὠνέομαι ("buy"—see the vocabulary).

Second Aorist Middle

	Indicative	Subjunctive	Optative	Imperative
Singular:	ἐπριάμην	πρίωμαι	πριαίμην	
	ἐπρίω	πρίῃ	πρίαιο	πρίω
	ἐπρίατο	πρίηται	πρίαιτο	πριάσθω
Plural:	ἐπριάμεθα	πριώμεθα	πριαίμεθα	
	ἐπρίασθε	πρίησθε	πρίαισθε	πρίασθε
	ἐπρίαντο	πρίωνται	πρίαιντο	πριάσθων

Infinitive: πρίασθαι

Participle: πριάμενος, -η, -ον

270.   You met the demonstrative adjectives τοσόσδε, τοσοῦτος, τόσος, "so much/many," and τοιόσδε, τοιοῦτος, τοῖος, "of such a sort," in Lesson 31. There also exist interrogative, indefinite, and relative adjectives corresponding to these:

Direct Interrogative:	Indefinite (enclitic):	Relative:	Indir. Interrogative/ Indef. Relative:
πόσος, -η, -ον "how much/ many?"	ποσός, -ή, -όν "of some size/ quantity"	ὅσος, -η, -ον "of which size" or "as much/ many as"	ὁπόσος, -η, -ον "how much/many?" or "of whichever size/ quantity"
ποῖος, -ᾱ, -ον "of what sort?"	ποιός, -ά, -όν "of some sort"	οἷος, -ᾱ, -ον "of which sort" or "such as"	ὁποῖος, -ᾱ, -ον "of what sort?" or "of whichever sort"

When οἷος, -ᾱ, -ον is followed by the enclitic τε, the combination means **"able"** (if describing a person) or **"possible"** (if describing a thing).

271.   **VOCABULARY**

δίδωμι, δώσω, ἔδωκα, δέδωκα, δέδομαι, ἐδόθην
    give; δίκην διδόναι = be punished [cf.
    anecdote, antidote, dose]

ἐπίσταμαι, ἐπιστήσομαι, —, —, —, ἠπιστήθην
    (+ *ptcple. in indir. disc.*) understand,
    know; (+ *infin.*) know how (to)

NOTE   In the present tense this compound deponent verb has the same endings as the present middle/passive of ἵστημι, but its subjunctives are accented as if they were not contracted (e.g., ἱστῶμαι but ἐπίστωμαι), and its optatives have regular recessive accent (e.g., ἱσταῖτο but ἐπίσταιτο).

ἵστημι, στήσω, ἔστησα or ἔστην, ἕστηκα (*pluperf.* εἱστήκη),
ἕσταμαι, ἐστάθην (*fut. perf.* ἑστήξω)

        make stand, set (up); (*perf. act.*) have stood (up), am standing; (*pluperf.*) had stood (up), was standing; (*second aor. act.*) stood (up); (*fut. perf. act.*) will be standing [ἵστημι *is the only* μι-*verb with a fut. perf.*] [cf. *apostate, ecstasy, metastasis, system*]

ὠνέομαι (*imperf.* ἐωνούμην), ὠνήσομαι, ἐπριάμην, —, ἐώνημαι, ἐωνήθην
buy

NOTE   The first three principal parts of this verb are deponent and should be translated actively (ὠνέομαι = "I buy"; ὠνήσομαι = "I shall buy"; ἐπριάμην = "I bought"); ἐώνημαι is treated sometimes as a middle deponent ("I have bought"), sometimes as a regular perfect passive ("I have been bought"); ἐωνήθην is a regular aorist passive ("I was bought").

ἐπιστήμη, -ης, ἡ	understanding, knowledge, science [cf. *epistemology*]
τέχνη, -ης, ἡ	art, skill, craft, trade [cf. *technical*]
οἷος, -ᾱ, -ον	(*rel. adj.*) of which sort, such as; (*exclam. adj.*) such a!
οἷός, -ᾱ, -όν τε	(+ *infin.*) able (to), possible (to)
ὁποῖος, -ᾱ, -ον	(*indir. interrog. adj.*) of what sort?; (*indef. rel. adj.*) of whichever sort
ὁπόσος, -η, -ον	(*indir. interrog. adj.*) how much? how many?; (*indef. rel. adj.*) of whichever size/quantity
ὅσος, -η, -ον	(*rel. adj.*) of which size/quantity, as much as, as many as; (*exclam. adj.*) how great a! how many!
ποῖος, -ᾱ, -ον	(*direct interrog. adj.*) of what sort?
ποιός, -ά, -όν	(*indef. enclitic adj.*) of some sort
πόσος, -η, -ον	(*direct interrog. adj.*) how much? how many?
ποσός, -ή, -όν	(*indef. enclitic adj.*) of some size/quantity

272.   EXERCISES

A.   **Greek-to-English Sentences**

1.   πόσον σῖτον ἔδωκας τῷ οἰκέτῃ ἄγοντι τοὺς ἵππους εἰς τὴν ἀγοράν;

2.   πότερον τέχνη ἢ ἐπιστήμη οἷοί τ᾽ ἐσόμεθα τοὺς πολεμίους νῑκᾶν;

3.   ἐπὶ τὸν τόπον οὗ νῦν ἕστηκα μηδεὶς ἀφίκηται πρὶν ἂν κελεύσω αὐτῷ πρὸς ἐμὲ ἰέναι.

4.   διὰ τὸ ἡμᾶς πολλὰ παθεῖν ἠπιστήθημεν λαβεῖν τε καὶ δοῦναι δίκην.

5.   εἰ οἷά τ᾽ εἰμί, ἐπιμελήσομαι ὅπως δώσω δῶρά ποια τῷ σώφρονι δεσπότῃ.

6.   ἐπιστάμενοι τὴν παῖδα φοβουμένην, σκεψόμεθα ὅπως μὴ βλαβήσεται.

7.   ποῖα καὶ πόσα σῖτα τήμερον ἐπρίω παρὰ τῶν πωλούντων ἐν τῇ ἀγορᾷ;

8.   στῆθι ὑπὸ τῷ δένδρῳ, ὦ Σώκρατες, καὶ μὴ ἔλθῃς ἀπὸ τοῦδε τοῦ τόπου.

9.   ἐδεδοίκη μὴ οὐ δοῖέν μοι οἱ θεοὶ ἀρετὴν ἱκανὴν μάχεσθαι τῷ ἐχθρῷ.

10. μὴ δῷς, ὦ βασιλεῦ, πάσᾱς τὰς τῑμὰς ἑνὶ ἀνδρί, πολλοὶ γὰρ ἄξιοί εἰσιν.

B.   **English-to-Greek Sentences**

1.   Why am I being punished, master? Not understanding the laws, have I done a wrong of some sort?

2.   Having asked her how many books she wished to buy, they gave her as many as they had.

3.   Wherever that philosopher stood, he was able to destroy the enemy's triremes with clever contrivances.

4.   How many soldiers I see standing beside the wall and setting up their newly bought shields upon it!

5.   If you take care to learn the trade that I am teaching you, my son, you will give great joy to me.

C.   **READING**

THE PERFECT POLIS? — Part 1
(adapted from Book 5 of Plato's *Republic* 451d-452b)

About halfway through Plato's **Republic***, Socrates finishes his description of the ideal city and is about to go on to discuss governments that are less than ideal, when his enthusiastic young friends Glaucon, Polemarchus, and Adeimantus interrupt him. They ask him to elaborate on a comment that he made earlier, namely, that wives and children in the ideal city would all be held in common. The passage below comes from the ensuing dialogue between Socrates and Glaucon. Socrates speaks first.*

Ἐπεχειρήσαμεν δ' ὡς ἀγέλης φύλακας τοὺς ἄνδρας καθιστάναι τῷ λόγῳ.

Ναί.

Ἀκολουθῶμεν τοίνυν καὶ τὴν γένεσιν καὶ τροφὴν παραπλησίαν ἀποδιδόντες, καὶ σκοπῶμεν εἰ ἡμῖν πρέπει ἢ οὔ.

5   Πῶς; ἔφη.

Ὧδε. τὰς θηλείας τῶν φυλάκων κυνῶν συμφυλάττειν οἰόμεθα δεῖν ἃ οἱ ἄρρενες φυλάττωσι καὶ συνθηρεύειν καὶ τἄλλα κοινῇ πράττειν;

Κοινῇ, ἔφη, πάντα.

Οἷόν τ' οὖν, ἔφην ἐγώ, ἐπὶ τὰ αὐτὰ χρῆσθαί τινι ζῴῳ, ἂν μὴ τὴν αὐτὴν
10   τροφήν τε καὶ παιδείαν ἀποδιδῷς;

Οὐχ οἷόν τε.

Εἰ ἄρα ταῖς γυναιξὶν ἐπὶ ταὐτὰ χρησόμεθα καὶ τοῖς ἀνδράσι, ταὐτὰ καὶ διδακτέον αὐτάς.

Ναί.

15   Μουσικὴ μὴν ἐκείνοις γε καὶ γυμναστικὴ ἐδόθη.

Ναί.

Καὶ ταῖς γυναιξὶ ταύτας τὰς τέχνας καὶ τὰ περὶ τὸν πόλεμον ἀποδοτέον καὶ χρηστέον κατὰ ταῦτά. ἴσως δή, εἶπον, παρὰ τὸ ἔθος ὄντα, γελοῖα ἂν φαίνοιτο πολλὰ περὶ τὰ νῦν λεγόμενα, εἰ πράξεται ᾗ λέγεται.

20   Καὶ μάλα, ἔφη.

Τί, ἔφην ἐγώ, γελοιότατον αὐτῶν ὁρᾷς; ἢ δῆλα δὴ ὅτι γυμνὰς τὰς γυναῖκας ἐν ταῖς παλαίστραις γυμναζομένας μετὰ τῶν ἀνδρῶν;

Νὴ τὸν Δία, ἔφη· γελοῖον γὰρ ἄν, ὥς γ' ἐν τῷ παρεστῶτι, φανείη.

VOCABULARY

ἐπεχειρήσαμεν (line 1): from ἐπιχειρέω, ἐπιχειρήσω, ἐπεχείρησα, ἐπικεχείρηκα,
     ἐπικεχείρημαι, ἐπεχειρήθην (+ *infin.*): undertake, attempt
ὡς (line 1): here = "as"
ἀγέλης (line 1): from ἀγέλη, -ης, ἡ: herd
φύλακας (line 1): refers to the class of guardians who are to run Socrates' ideal
     city; in line 6 he equates them with guard-dogs
καθιστάναι (line 1): from καθίστημι: set down, establish
τῷ λόγῳ (line 1): here = "in our argument"
ναί (line 2): yes (*adv.*)
ἀκολουθῶμεν (line 3): from ἀκολουθέω, ἀκολουθήσω, ἠκολούθησα, ἠκολούθηκα,
     —, —: follow (*here* = "follow the thread of the argument")
γένεσιν (line 3): from γένεσις, -εως, ἡ: birth

τροφήν (line 3): from τροφή, -ῆς, ἡ: rearing, upbringing

παραπλησίᾱν (line 3): from παραπλήσιος, -ᾱ, -ον: close, resembling (here = "in keeping [with their role]")

ἀποδιδόντες (line 4): from ἀποδίδωμι: give back, assign

πρέπει (line 4): (impersonal + dat.) it is fitting (for), it suits

θηλείᾱς (line 6): from θῆλυς, -εια, -υ: female, feminine

κυνῶν (line 6): from κύων, κυνός, ὁ, ἡ: dog

συμφυλάττειν (line 6): from συμφυλάττω: guard together

οἰόμεθα (line 6): from οἴομαι (imperf. ᾤμην), οἰήσομαι, —, —, —, ᾠήθην (+ infin. in
indir. disc.): think, suppose

ἄρρενες (line 7): from ἄρρην, -εν: male, masculine

συνθηρεύειν (line 7): from συνθηρεύω, συνθηρεύσω, συνεθήρευσα, συντεθήρευκα,
συντεθήρευμαι, συνεθηρεύθην: hunt together

κοινῇ (line 7): = κοινῶς ("in common")

ἐπὶ τὰ αὐτά (line 9): i.e., for performance of the same tasks

παιδείᾱν (line 10): from παιδείᾱ, -ᾱς, ἡ: education

ἄρα (line 12): then, therefore (postpos. particle)

ταὐτὰ...αὐτᾱς (lines 12-13): both objects of διδακτέον ("teach them the same
things")

μουσική (line 15): from μουσική, -ῆς, ἡ (supply τέχνη): music, fine arts

γυμναστική (line 15): from γυμναστική, -ῆς, ἡ (supply τέχνη): athletics

χρηστέον κατὰ ταὐτά (line 18): i.e., the female guardians must be used for the same
tasks as the male guardians

ἔθος (line 18): from ἔθος, -ους, τό: custom

γελοῖα (line 18): from γελοῖος, -ᾱ, -ον: laughable, ridiculous

πολλὰ περὶ τὰ...λεγόμενα (line 19): many things related to what we're saying

πρᾱ́ξεται (line 19): future middle in form, but future passive in meaning

ᾗ (line 19): how, in which way (rel. adv.), i.e., in the way in which

καὶ μάλα (line 20): another way to say "yes"

ἢ δῆλα...ὅτι (line 21): or is it clear that the most ridiculous thing is seeing...?

γυμνᾱς (line 21): from γυμνός, -ή, -όν: naked

παλαίστραις (line 22): from παλαίστρᾱ, -ᾱς, ἡ: wrestling-school

γυμναζομένᾱς (line 22): from γυμνάζω, γυμνάσω, ἐγύμνασα, γεγύμνακα, γεγύμνασμαι,
ἐγυμνάσθην: train; (mid.) exercise (in the nude)

νή (line 23): yes, by... (affirmative particle + acc., used in oaths)

Δία (line 23): from Ζεύς, Διός, Διί, Δία, Ζεῦ, ὁ: Zeus, king of the gods

ὡς (line 23): here = "as far as"

παρεστῶτι (line 23): present circumstances (from παρίστημι: stand near)

LESSON 47

MI-VERBS (τίθημι, ἵημι)

ἐμὲ...μέθες ἱέναι ἐπὶ τὴν θήρην (Let me go hunting!)
—Atys, unaware that he is fated to be killed by a hunting-spear,
nags his dad, King Croesus, in Herodotus' *Histories* 1.37

273. Here are the paradigms of two more μι-verbs, **τίθημι** ("place"; basic stem = θε-/θη-) and **ἵημι** ("set in motion"; basic stem = ἑ-/ἡ-, originally σε–/ ση-). In the present and imperfect, the basic stem is **reduplicated** (with τι- or ἱ- in the present, with augmented ἐτι- or ἱ- in the imperfect). In the present active indicative, the **long** stem-vowel (η) appears in the **singular**, the **short** stem-vowel (ε) in the **plural**. There is usually **no thematic vowel** (ε or ο) between the stem and the ending, but a few exceptions occur.

Since τίθημι and ἵημι are similar to δίδωμι in their endings and contractions, the notes to the paradigms of δίδωμι in Lesson 46, §269 are applicable here as well. The paradigms below do not include regular ω-verb forms of τίθημι and ἵημι (e.g., θήσω, ἥσω). Words in parentheses are alternative forms less commonly used.

NOTE In the present tense of ἵημι, unaugmented ἱ- is long, even though it logically should not be! ἵημι is frequently compounded with a prefix such as ἀπο-, μετα-, παρα-. As a matter of fact, in tenses other than the present and imperfect, it is rare to find the verb without a prefix. See the vocabulary for more details.

τίθημι, θήσω, ἔθηκα, τέθηκα, τέθειμαι, ἐτέθην "place"		

INDICATIVE

Present Active	Imperfect Active	Aorist Active
Singular:		
τίθημι	ἐτίθην	ἔθηκα
τίθης	ἐτίθεις	ἔθηκας
τίθησι(ν)	ἐτίθει	ἔθηκε(ν)
Plural:		
τίθεμεν	ἐτίθεμεν	ἔθεμεν
τίθετε	ἐτίθετε	ἔθετε
τιθέᾱσι(ν)	ἐτίθεσαν	ἔθεσαν

INDICATIVE

Present Mid./Pass.	Imperfect Mid./Pass.	Aorist Middle
Singular:		
τίθεμαι	ἐτιθέμην	ἐθέμην
τίθεσαι	ἐτίθεσο	ἔθου
τίθεται	ἐτίθετο	ἔθετο
Plural:		
τιθέμεθα	ἐτιθέμεθα	ἐθέμεθα
τίθεσθε	ἐτίθεσθε	ἔθεσθε
τίθενται	ἐτίθεντο	ἔθεντο

SUBJUNCTIVE

Present Active	Aor. Active	Present Mid./Pass.	Aor. Mid.
Singular:			
τιθῶ	θῶ	τιθῶμαι	θῶμαι
τιθῇς	θῇς	τιθῇ	θῇ
τιθῇ	θῇ	τιθῆται	θῆται
Plural:			
τιθῶμεν	θῶμεν	τιθώμεθα	θώμεθα
τιθῆτε	θῆτε	τιθῆσθε	θῆσθε
τιθῶσι(ν)	θῶσι(ν)	τιθῶνται	θῶνται

OPTATIVE

Present Active		Aor. Active		Present Mid./Pass.		Aor. Mid.	
Singular:							
τιθείην		θείην		τιθείμην		θείμην	
τιθείης		θείης		τιθεῖο		θεῖο	
τιθείη		θείη		τιθεῖτο	(τιθοῖτο)	θεῖτο	(θοῖτο)
Plural:							
τιθεῖμεν	(τιθείημεν)	θεῖμεν	(θείημεν)	τιθείμεθα	(τιθοίμεθα)	θείμεθα	(θοίμεθα)
τιθεῖτε	(τιθείητε)	θεῖτε	(θείητε)	τιθεῖσθε	(τιθοῖσθε)	θεῖσθε	(θοῖσθε)
τιθεῖεν	(τιθείησαν)	θεῖεν	(θείησαν)	τιθεῖντο	(τιθοῖντο)	θεῖντο	(θοῖντο)

IMPERATIVE

Present Active	Aor. Active	Present Mid./Pass.	Aor. Mid.
Singular:			
τίθει	θές	τίθεσο	θοῦ
τιθέτω	θέτω	τιθέσθω	θέσθω
Plural:			
τίθετε	θέτε	τίθεσθε	θέσθε
τιθέντων	θέντων	τιθέσθων	θέσθων

Present Active Infinitive:
τιθέναι

Aorist Active Infinitive:
θεῖναι

Present Mid./Pass. Infinitive:
τίθεσθαι

Aorist Middle Infinitive:
θέσθαι

Present Active Participle:
τιθείς, τιθεῖσα, τιθέν (τιθέντος, τιθείσης, τιθέντος, etc.)

Present Mid./Pass. Participle:
τιθέμενος, -η, -ον

Aorist Active Participle:
θείς, θεῖσα, θέν (θέντος, θείσης, θέντος, etc)

Aorist Mid. Participle:
θέμενος, -η, -ον

ἵημι, ἥσω, ἧκα, εἷκα, εἷμαι, εἵθην "set in motion"

INDICATIVE

Present Active		Imperfect Active	Aorist Active
Singular:			
ἵημι		ἵην	ἧκα
ἵης	(ἱεῖς)	ἵεις	ἧκας
ἵησι(ν)		ἵει	ἧκε(ν)
Plural:			
ἵεμεν		ἵεμεν	εἷμεν
ἵετε		ἵετε	εἷτε
ἱᾶσι(ν)		ἵεσαν	εἷσαν

Present Mid./Pass.	Imperfect Mid./Pass.	Aorist Middle
Singular:		
ἵεμαι	ἱέμην	εἵμην
ἵεσαι	ἵεσο	εἷσο
ἵεται	ἵετο	εἷτο
Plural:		
ἱέμεθα	ἱέμεθα	εἵμεθα
ἵεσθε	ἵεσθε	εἷσθε
ἵενται	ἵεντο	εἷντο

SUBJUNCTIVE

Present Active	Aorist Active	Present Mid./Pass.	Aorist Mid.
Singular:			
ἱῶ	ὧ	ἱῶμαι	ὧμαι
ἱῇς	ἧς	ἱῇ	ᾗ
ἱῇ	ᾗ	ἱῆται	ἧται
Plural:			
ἱῶμεν	ὧμεν	ἱώμεθα	ὥμεθα
ἱῆτε	ἧτε	ἱῆσθε	ἧσθε
ἱῶσι(ν)	ὧσι(ν)	ἱῶνται	ὧνται

OPTATIVE

Present Active	Aorist Active	Present Mid./Pass.	Aorist Mid.
Singular:			
ἱείην	εἵην	ἱείμην	εἵμην
ἱείης	εἵης	ἱεῖο	εἷο
ἱείη	εἵη	ἱεῖτο	εἷτο
Plural:			
ἱεῖμεν (ἱείημεν)	εἷμεν (εἵημεν)	ἱείμεθα	εἵμεθα
ἱεῖτε (ἱείητε)	εἷτε (εἵητε)	ἱεῖσθε	εἷσθε
ἱεῖεν (ἱείησαν)	εἷεν (εἵησαν)	ἱεῖντο	εἷντο

IMPERATIVE

Present Active	Aorist Active	Present Mid./Pass.	Aorist Mid.
Singular:			
ἵει	ἕς	ἵεσο	οὗ
ἱέτω	ἕτω	ἱέσθω	ἕσθω
Plural:			
ἵετε	ἕτε	ἵεσθε	ἕσθε
ἱέντων	ἕντων	ἱέσθων	ἕσθων

Present Active Infin.:	Aorist Active Infin.:
ἱέναι	εἷναι

Present Mid./Pass. Infin.:	Aorist Mid. Infin.:
ἵεσθαι	ἕσθαι

Present Active Participle:
ἱείς, ἱεῖσα, ἱέν (ἱέντος, ἱείσης, ἱέντος, etc.)

Present Mid./Pass. Participle:
ἱέμενος, -η, -ον

Aorist Active Participle:
εἷς, εἷσα, ἕν (ἕντος, εἵσης, ἕντος, etc.)

Aorist Mid. Participle:
ἕμενος, -η, -ον

274.　　　The present and imperfect tenses of κεῖμαι, κείσομαι, —, —, —, —
("lie," "be situated"), a deponent μι-verb, are very much preferred to the
perfect and pluperfect passive of τίθημι (τέθειμαι "I have been placed
[and therefore am situated]"; ἐτεθείμην "I had been placed [and therefore
was situated]"). Here are the deponent forms of κεῖμαι (stem = κει-, before vowels κε-) that replace the passive forms of τίθημι:

Pres. Indic.	Imperfect	Pres. Subj.	Pres. Opt.	Pres. Imper.
Singular:				
κεῖμαι	ἐκείμην	κέωμαι	κεοίμην	
κεῖσαι	ἔκεισο	κέῃ	κέοιο	κεῖσο
κεῖται	ἔκειτο	κέηται	κέοιτο	κείσθω
Plural:				
κείμεθα	ἐκείμεθα	κεώμεθα	κεοίμεθα	
κεῖσθε	ἔκεισθε	κέησθε	κέοισθε	κεῖσθε
κεῖνται	ἔκειντο	κέωνται	κέοιντο	κείσθων

Present Infin.: κεῖσθαι　　**Present Participle:** κείμενος, -η, -ον

275.　　　**VOCABULARY**

δύναμαι, δυνήσομαι, —, —, δεδύνημαι, ἐδυνήθην
　　　　　　　　(*verbal adj.* δυνατός "powerful," "able,"
　　　　　　　　"possible") (+ *infin.*) be powerful
　　　　　　　　(enough to), be able (to), can

NOTE　　　In the present tense this deponent μι-verb has the same endings as
the present middle/passive of ἵστημι, but its subjunctives are accented as
if they were not contracted (e.g., ἱστῶμαι but δύνωμαι) and its optatives
have regular recessive accent (e.g., ἱσταῖτο but δύναιτο).

ἠμί (*3rd sg.* ἠσί(ν); *imperf. 1st sg.* ἦν, *3rd sg.* ἦ), —, —, —, —, —
　　　　　　　　(*occurs only in pres. & imperf. first- &
　　　　　　　　third-pers. sg.*) say

NOTE　　　ἠμί ("I say"), ἠσί ("he/she says"), and the idiomatic combinations ἦν
δ' ἐγώ ("I said"), ἦ δ' ὅς ("he said"), and ἦ δ' ἥ ("she said") are used only as

parenthetical expressions, inserted in the middle of a quoted sentence to show who is being quoted.

ἵημι, ἥσω, ἧκα, εἷκα, εἷμαι, εἵθην

> set in motion, let go, send, throw; (*mid.* + *infin.*) hasten (to), be eager (to)

NOTE   Common compounds of ἵημι are ἀφίημι ("throw away," "send away," "dismiss"), μεθίημι ("release," "relax," "permit"), and παρίημι ("let pass," "allow," "forgive"). The accent in the compound word usually occupies the same syllable as it would if the verb were not compounded (e.g., οὗ, ἀφοῦ; ἧκα, μεθῆκα; εἷς, παρείς), but in the aorist active second-pers. sg. and pl. imperative and the aorist middle second-pers. pl. imperative, the accent in the compound recedes to a different syllable (e.g., ἕς, ἄφες; ἕτε, μέθετε; ἕσθε, πάρεσθε).

κεῖμαι, κείσομαι, —, —, —, —

> lie, lie asleep, lie dead, be laid down, be placed, be situated

τίθημι, θήσω, ἔθηκα, τέθηκα, τέθειμαι, ἐτέθην

> place, put, set, lay down, establish, make [cf. *apothecary, epithet, thesis*]

γονεύς, -έως, ὁ   father, ancestor; (*pl.*) parents

δύναμις, -εως, ἡ   power, force, strength [cf. *dynamic, dynamite*]

κῦμα, -ατος, τό   wave, undulation [cf. *cyma, cyme, kymograph*]

ἄρα   (*postpositive particle*) then, therefore (*never elided*)

περ or -περ   (*enclitic particle, often attached to an adv., conj., or rel. pronoun; strengthens preceding word*) indeed, the very

NOTE   You already know καίπερ "even though"; other common combinations are εἴπερ, ἐάνπερ (ἥνπερ, ἄνπερ) "if indeed"; ὅσπερ, ἥπερ, ὅπερ "who indeed," "which indeed," "the very one who," "the very thing that"; ὥσπερ "as if," "as it were," "just as." All are accented as if -περ were a detached enclitic.

276. **EXERCISES**

A. Greek-to-English Sentences

1. κείσθω τὸ βοῶν παιδίον ἐν ταῖς χερσὶ τῆς μητρὸς ἥνπερ μάλιστα φιλεῖ.
2. ἱέμενος τιθέναι τὴν νέαν πόλιν, ὁ βασιλεὺς τοῖς πολίταις ἐδίδου πολλοὺς νόμους.
3. εἴπερ ἄρα ἵεσαι ἔχειν δύναμιν, ὦ μαθητά, πρῶτον εἶ παιδευτέος ἐμοί.
4. ἡ τριήρης ἵετο διὰ τῆς θαλάττης, ἐπὶ τῶν μεγάλων κῡμάτων φερομένη.
5. Θές, ἠσίν, ὦ φύλαξ, τὴν ἀσπίδα πρὸς τὸ τεῖχος καὶ παρ᾽ ἐμοὶ στῆθι.
6. εἴθε μεθεῖτέ με, ὦ γονῆς, ἱέναι εἰς τὴν ἀγορὰν καὶ πρίασθαι τὸν σῖτον.
7. τίς οἶδεν ὁπόσον θησαυρὸν ἔθεσαν ἐν τῇ τοῦ δυνατοῦ δεσπότου οἰκίᾳ;
8. τὸν ἀδελφὸν παρείς, οὐκέτι βουλεύομαι ὅπως λήψομαι δίκην παρ᾽ αὐτοῦ.
9. Δέδοικα γάρ, ἦ δ᾽ ὅς, μὴ οὐ δύνωμαι τὰς τῶν γονέων ψῡχὰς σῴζειν.
10. μεγάλην μὲν δύναμιν τῷ πρυτάνει οὖσαν ᾐσθόμεθα, ὀλίγην δὲ σοφίᾱν.

B. English-to-Greek Sentences

1. Our parents made (*use* τίθημι) a law for us, but we can (*use* δύναμαι) no longer, as if (we were) children, obey it.
2. "I am amazed at the force of the waves," she said, hastening (*use* ἵημι) into the sea.
3. Why are you lying down on the couch, young man? Throw the book away and stand up.
4. You (*pl.*) were not able to follow those ancestors of yours who indeed led a noble life.
5. "If indeed we wish to establish peace," I say, "let us release our passion and forgive our enemies."

C. READING

THE PERFECT POLIS? — Part 2
(adapted from Book 5 of Plato's *Republic* 457a-458b)

After further discussion Socrates and Glaucon agree that the women who are qualified by their nature to be guardians of the ideal city should be educated in the same way as the men who are qualified by their nature to be its guardians, for this will produce the best guardians and the best city. As we rejoin the conversation, Socrates is concluding that no better plan exists than to give identical education to the male and the female guardians.

Οὐ μόνον ἄρα δυνατὸν ἀλλὰ καὶ ἄριστον πόλει νόμον ἐτίθεμεν.

Οὕτως.

Τοῦτο τοίνυν ἓν ὥσπερ κῦμα φῶμεν διαφεύγειν τοῦ γυναικείου πέρι

νόμου λέγοντες, ὥστε μὴ πάντως κατακλυσθῆναι τιθέντες ὡς δεῖ κοινῇ πάντα ἐπιτηδεύειν
5   τούς τε φύλακας ἡμῖν καὶ τὰς φυλακίδας;

       Καὶ μάλα, ἔφη, οὐ μῑκρὸν κῦμα διαφεύγεις.

       Φήσεις γ᾽, ἦν δ᾽ ἐγώ, οὐ μέγα αὐτὸ εἶναι, ὅταν τὸ μετὰ τοῦτ᾽ ἴδῃς.

       Λέγε δή, ἴδω, ἔφη.

       Τούτῳ, ἦν δ᾽ ἐγώ, ἕπεται ὁ νόμος ὅδε.

10   Τίς;

       Τὰς γυναῖκας ταύτᾱς τῶν ἀνδρῶν τούτων πάντων πάσᾱς εἶναι κοινάς,
ἰδίᾳ δὲ μηδενὶ μηδεμίαν συνοικεῖν· καὶ τοὺς παῖδας αὖ κοινούς, καὶ μήτε
γονέᾱ ἔκγονον εἰδέναι τὸν αὐτοῦ μήτε παῖδα γονέᾱ.

       Πολύ, ἔφη, τοῦτ᾽ ἐκείνου μεῖζον πρὸς ἀπιστίᾱν καὶ τοῦ δυνατοῦ πέρι καὶ
15   τοῦ ὠφελίμου.

       Ἤδη οὖν καὶ αὐτὸς μαλθακίζομαι, καὶ ἐκεῖνα μὲν ἐπιθῡμῶ
ἀναβαλέσθαι καὶ ὕστερον σκέψασθαι ᾗ δυνατά, νῦν δ᾽ ὡς δυνατῶν ὄντων θεὶς
σκέψομαι, ἄν μοι παρῑῇς, πῶς διατάξουσιν αὐτὰ οἱ ἄρχοντες γιγνόμενα, καὶ ὅτι
πάντων συμφορώτατα ἂν εἴη πρᾱχθέντα τῇ τε πόλει καὶ τοῖς φύλαξιν. ταῦτα πειρᾱσομαι
20   σὺν σοὶ πρότερα σκοπεῖσθαι, ὕστερα δ᾽ ἐκεῖνα, εἴπερ παρῑεῖς.

       Ἀλλὰ παρῑημι, ἔφη, καὶ σκόπει.

VOCABULARY

ἐτίθεμεν (line 1): they have "established" it in their minds, not in real life
οὕτως (line 2): thus, i.e., yes
κῦμα (line 3): here = "wave of criticism"
φῶμεν (line 3): deliberative subjunctive
διαφεύγειν (line 3): from διαφεύγω: flee through, escape (*i.e., in the course of their
    discussion, they have overcome at least one imagined criticism, namely, the objec-
    tion that it would be neither possible nor good for the city to have female and male
    guardians sharing responsibilities*)
τοῦ γυναικείου πέρι νόμου (lines 3-4): = περὶ τοῦ γυναικείου νόμου (*when περί is put af-
    ter its object, its accent shifts to the penult—see line 14 too*)
γυναικείου (line 3): from γυναικεῖος, -ᾱ, -ον: having to do with women
κατακλυσθῆναι (line 4): from κατακλύζω, κατακλύσω, κατέκλυσα, κατακέκλυκα,
    κατακέκλυσμαι, κατεκλύσθην: inundate, flood, overwhelm
τιθέντες ὡς (line 4): begins indirect discourse ("making a claim that...")
ἐπιτηδεύειν (line 4): from ἐπιτηδεύω, ἐπιτηδεύσω, ἐπετήδευσα, ἐπιτετήδευκα,
    ἐπιτετήδευμαι, ἐπετηδεύθην: pursue, practice
φυλακίδας (line 5): from φυλακίς, -ίδος, ἡ: female guardian
καὶ μάλα (line 6): another way to say "yes"
ἴδω (line 8): hortatory subjunctive ("let me see [it]")

τὰς γυναῖκας...εἶναι κοινάς (line 11): object infinitive following an understood command ("[the law saying] that wives should be held in common")

ἰδίᾳ (line 12): from ἴδιος, -ᾱ, -ον: private (*dat. fem. sg. used as adverb*)

συνοικεῖν (line 12): from συνοικέω, συνοικήσω, συνῴκησα, συνῴκηκα, συνῴκημαι,
συνῳκήθην: live together

ἔκγονον (line 13): from ἔκγονος, -ου, ὁ: descendant, offspring

ἀπιστίᾱν (line 14): from ἀπιστίᾱ, -ᾱς, ἡ: disbelief, doubt

καὶ τοῦ...πέρι καὶ τοῦ... (lines 14-15): with regard to its being both...and...

ὠφελίμου (line 15): from ὠφέλιμος, -ον: helpful, useful

μαλθακίζομαι (line 16): from μαλθακίζω, μαλθακιῶ, ἐμαλθάκισα,
μεμαλθάκικα, μεμαλθάκισμαι, ἐμαλθακίσθην: soften; (*mid.*) become lazy

ἐπιθῡμῶ (line 16): from ἐπιθῡμέω, ἐπιθῡμήσω, ἐπεθῡμησα, ἐπιτεθῡμηκα, ἐπιτεθῡμημαι,
ἐπεθῡμήθην (+ *infin.*): desire (to)

ἀναβαλέσθαι (line 17): from ἀναβάλλω: put back; (*mid.*) postpone

ᾗ (line 17): how, in which way (*rel. adv.*) (ἐκεῖνα...ᾗ δυνατά = "those things how
they are possible," i.e., "the feasibility of those things")

ὡς δυνατῶν ὄντων θείς (line 17): making the assumption that they're possible

διατάξουσιν (line 18): from διατάττω, διατάξω, διέταξα, διατέταχα, διατέταγμαι,
διετάχθην or διετάγην: arrange

γιγνόμενα (line 18): as they happen

ὅτι (line 18): supply a verb like "I shall argue [that...]"

συμφορώτατα (line 19): from σύμφορος, -ον: advantageous, beneficial (*pred. adj. with*
εἴη πρᾱχθέντα, *but translate as if an adverb*)

ἂν εἴη πρᾱχθέντα (line 19): periphrastic equivalent of ἂν πρᾱχθείη (*potential
optative*); supply αὐτά as subject

πειρᾱσομαι (line 19): from πειράω, πειράσω, ἐπείρᾱσα, πεπείρᾱκα, πεπείρᾱμαι,
ἐπειρᾱθην (+ *infin.*) (*often in mid. voice*): try (to)

LESSON 48

MI-VERBS (δείκνῡμι); UNATTAINABLE WISHES

οἴμοι, μέγας θησαυρὸς ὡς ἀνοίγνυται / κακῶν
(Alas, what a great storehouse of evils lies open!)
—the chorus reacts to Creusa's song of woe in Euripides' *Ion* 923-924

277.   δίδωμι, ἵστημι, τίθημι, and ἵημι all belong to the **root** class of μι-verbs: personal endings are added directly to each verb's basic stem, i.e., to its root. There is only one other class of μι-verbs; it is made up entirely of **νῡμι-verbs**, which insert the letters **-νυ-** or **-νῡ-** between their basic stem and the personal endings.

νῡμι-verbs are less complicated than the other μι-verbs. They differ from ω-verbs only in the present and imperfect indicative, present imperative, present infinitive, and present participle. Their relationship to ω-verbs is so close that authors sometimes conjugate them as if they were regular ω-verbs (this happens mostly in the active, rarely in the middle/passive). You already know ἀνοίγνῡμι/ἀνοίγω ("open"), which may be inflected either as a μι-verb or as an ω-verb.

Below are paradigms of **δείκνῡμι** ("show"; basic stem = δεικ-). The upsilon in -νυ- is short except in the singular of the present and imperfect active indicative, in the second-person singular present active imperative, and in certain forms of the present active participle. **No thematic vowel** (ε or ο) is placed between -νυ-/-νῡ- and the personal endings.

339

δείκνῡμι, δείξω, ἔδειξα, δέδειχα, δέδειγμαι, ἐδείχθην "show"

INDICATIVE

Present Active	Imperfect Active
Singular:	
δείκνῡμι	ἐδείκνῡν
δείκνῡς	ἐδείκνῡς
δείκνῡσι(ν)	ἐδείκνῡ
Plural:	
δείκνυμεν	ἐδείκνυμεν
δείκνυτε	ἐδείκνυτε
δεικνύᾱσι(ν)	ἐδείκνυσαν

INDICATIVE

Present Middle/Passive	Imperfect Middle/Passive
Singular:	
δείκνυμαι	ἐδεικνύμην
δείκνυσαι	ἐδείκνυσο
δείκνυται	ἐδείκνυτο
Plural:	
δεικνύμεθα	ἐδεικνύμεθα
δείκνυσθε	ἐδείκνυσθε
δείκνυνται	ἐδείκνυντο

IMPERATIVE

Present Active	Present Middle/Passive
Singular:	
δείκνῡ	δείκνυσο
δεικνύτω	δεικνύσθω
Plural:	
δείκνυτε	δείκνυσθε
δεικνύντων	δεικνύσθων

Present Active Infinitive:	**Pres. Mid./Pass. Infinitive:**
δεικνύναι	δείκνυσθαι

Present Active Participle:	**Pres. Mid./Pass. Participle:**
δεικνύς, δεικνῦσα, δεικνύν	δεικνύμενος, -η, -ον
(*gen. sg.* δεικνύντος, -ύσης, -ύντος)	

Present **subjunctives** and **optatives** are regular, built on the stem δεικνυ-.

278. In Lesson 36 (§221) you learned that a **wish** may be expressed by a verb in the **optative**, with or without the introductory particles εἴθε or εἰ γάρ. Since the optative mood looks toward the future, the wish that it represents is hopeful and expects to be fulfilled (if it possibly can be) at a later date.

To express a wish that a situation were *not* the way it actually is, or a wish that a situation had *not* been the way it actually was, a different construction is needed. Because an **unattainable wish** desires things to be contrary to reality, it can be made to resemble the protasis of a contrary-to-fact condition:

εἴθε or εἰ γάρ + **imperfect indicative** = present contrary-to-fact wish
εἴθε or εἰ γάρ + **aorist indicative** = past contrary-to-fact wish

An unattainable wish of this sort *must* be introduced by εἴθε or εἰ γάρ. Since the wish takes the form of a protasis, its negative is always μή, not οὐ. Examples:

εἴθ᾽ εἶχες βελτίονα διδάσκαλον.
"Would that (If only) you had a better teacher [but you don't]!"

εἴθ᾽ ἔσχομεν βελτίονα διδάσκαλον.
"Would that (If only) we had had a better teacher [but we didn't]!"

An alternative way to express an unattainable wish is with a form of ὤφελον ("ought"), the second aorist of ὀφείλω, + the **present or aorist infinitive** (and μή if negative). The personal ending of ὤφελον shows who the subject is, while the tense of the infinitive marks the wish as present or past contrary-to-fact. εἴθε or εἰ γάρ *may* be placed before the form of ὤφελον, but need not be. Examples:

[εἴθ᾽/εἰ γὰρ] ὤφελες ἔχειν βελτίονα διδάσκαλον.
"Would that (if only) you had a better teacher [but you don't]!"
Literally: "You ought to have a better teacher."

[εἴθ᾽/εἰ γὰρ] ὠφέλομεν σχεῖν βελτίονα διδάσκαλον.
"Would that (if only) we had had a better teacher [but we didn't]!"
Literally: "We ought to have had a better teacher."

279.　　　　**Prolepsis** ("anticipation") is an important feature of Greek syntax. The nominative **subject of a dependent clause** (e.g., an indirect question) will often be placed *ahead* of its clause and transformed into the accusative (sometimes genitive or dative) **direct object of the main verb**. Examples:

ζητῶ **τὴν οἰκίᾱν** ὁποίᾱ ἐστίν.
" I am investigating the house, of what sort it is," i.e., "I am investigating what sort of house it is."

δήλου **τοὺς παῖδας** ὅπου ἔκειντο.
" Point out the children, where they were lying," i.e., "Point out where the children were lying."

On the basis of English we might think it more logical to write ζητῶ ὁποίᾱ ἡ οἰκίᾱ ἐστίν and δήλου ὅπου οἱ παῖδες ἔκειντο, but the proleptic style appealed to the Greeks.

280.　　　　　VOCABULARY

δείκνῡμι, δείξω, ἔδειξα, δέδειχα, δέδειγμαι, ἐδείχθην
　　　　　　　show, point out (*with indir. disc. + ptcple.*
　　　　　　　or ὅτι/ὡς) [cf. *apodictic, epideictic*]

NOTE　　　　The compound ἀποδείκνῡμι ("demonstrate," "prove") is common.

οἴομαι (*first-pers. sg. often contracts to* οἶμαι) (*imperf.* ᾤμην),
　　οἰήσομαι, —, —, —, ᾠήθην
　　　　　　　(*with indir. disc. + infin. or* ὅτι/ὡς) think,
　　　　　　　suppose
ὁμολογέω, ὁμολογήσω, ὡμολόγησα, ὡμολόγηκα, ὡμολόγημαι, ὡμολογήθην
　　　　　　　(+ *dat.*) agree (with); (*with complem. infin.*
　　　　　　　or indir. disc. + infin.) agree, confess,
　　　　　　　promise
ὀφείλω, ὀφειλήσω, ὠφείλησα or ὤφελον, ὠφείληκα, —, —
　　　　　　　owe, be in debt; (*second aor.*) ought
γένος, -ους, τό　　　　race, birth, class, type, kind [cf. *genocide*]
ἥλιος, -ου, ὁ　　　　sun; Ἥλιος = Sun (*personified as a god*)
　　　　　　　[cf. *heliacal, helium, perihelion*]
κύων, κυνός, ὁ, ἡ　　(*voc. sg.* = κύον) dog [cf. *cynic, cynosure*]

NOTE　　　　This noun is unusual only in its nominative singular (κύων) and
vocative singular (κύον). Its other forms are all built on the stem κυν- with
regular third-declension endings (ν drops out when the dative plural
ending is added: κυσί[ν]). In the genitive and dative singular and plural,
the accent shifts from κυ- to the ultima, as you would expect in a third-
declension noun with monosyllabic stem.

παράδειγμα, -ατος, τό　　model, example [cf. *paradigm*]
ὅμοιος, -ᾱ, -ον　　　　(+ *dat.*) similar (to), like [cf. *homeopathy*]
πάνυ　　　　　　(*adv.*) entirely, very; (*in positive answers*)
　　　　　　　by all means; (*in negative answers*)
　　　　　　　[not] at all
ἕνεκα　　　　　　(*postpositive prep. + gen.*) for the sake of,
　　　　　　　on account of [*similar to postpositive*
　　　　　　　χάριν + *gen.*]

281.　　　　　EXERCISES

A.　　Greek-to-English Sentences

　　1.　δεδιὼς μή τις τὰς ἁμαρτίᾱς δεικνύῃ, ἐγὼ τῆς ἐμῆς ψῡχῆς ἕνεκα ἔφυγον.

　　2.　ὁμολογῶμεν οὐδὲν πάνυ νέον ὑπὸ τῷ ἡλίῳ ποθ᾿ ὁρᾶσθαι δυνατὸν εἶναι.

　　3.　ἀπεδείκνῡ τοῖς πολίταις ὡς χρὴ τὸν γέροντα τῑμηθῆναι τῆς ἀρετῆς ἕνεκα.

4. ὤφελον οἱ διδάσκαλοι πολὺ βελτίω παραδείγματα διδόναι τοῖς μαθηταῖς.

5. Εἰ γάρ, ἦν δ᾽ ἐγώ, ᾤήθησαν πᾶσαι αἱ ἄλλαι γυναῖκες ὁμοίως ὑμῖν.

6. τῶν παίδων ἕνεκα τοὺς γονέᾱς δεῖ πάνυ ἀγαθὰ παραδείγματα γενέσθαι.

7. εἴθ᾽ ἐδύνασο πυθέσθαι τὴν κύνα ὅπως πάσχει ὑπὸ τοῦ πριαμένου αὐτήν.

8. μὴ ὤφελες εἰς τὸν ἥλιον ἰδεῖν μακρὰ ὥστε τοὺς ὀφθαλμοὺς ἔβλαψας.

9. οὐ πάνυ ὅμοιοι οἴδ᾽ οἱ κύνες εἰσί, καίπερ τοῦ αὐτοῦ γένους ὄντες.

10. ἆρ᾽ ἴσᾱσιν οἱ σοφώτατοι φιλόσοφοι τὸν ἥλιον πόσος καὶ ποῖός ἐστιν;

B. English-to-Greek Sentences

1. Will you (*sg.*) agree, for the sake of an example, that horses are very similar to dogs? Not at all, Socrates.

2. If only the Athenians had experienced better types of generals in the time of the war!

3. We wish to examine what sort of thing the sun is (*use prolepsis*). Would that it were visible in the sky!

4. Point out where your parents are standing (*use prolepsis*), child.

5. If only I did not owe her so much money and had not promised that I would give it to her today!

C.   READING

THE PERFECT POLIS? — Part 3
(adapted from Book 5 of Plato's *Republic* 472d-473e)

After describing marriage practices and child-rearing in the ideal city, Socrates guides Glaucon through a line of reasoning leading to the conclusion that communal ownership of wives and children would be of the greatest good. He then gets so carried away imagining what life would be like for the guardians that Glaucon feels compelled to interrupt and ask him to return to the question of whether this polis could ever really exist.

Socrates reminds Glaucon and the others that the goal of their present conversation is to determine the nature of justice and injustice. The dialogue continues as follows, with Socrates speaking.

Παραδείγματος ἄρα ἕνεκα, ἦν δ᾽ ἐγώ, ἐζητοῦμεν δικαιοσύνην θ᾽ ὁποῖά ἐστί, καὶ ἄνδρα τὸν τελέως δίκαιον εἰ γένοιτο καὶ ὁποῖος ἂν εἴη γενόμενος, καὶ ἀδικίᾱν αὖ καὶ τὸν ἀδικώτατον, ἵνα εἰς ἐκείνους ἀποβλέποντες, ἀναγκαζώμεθα καὶ περὶ ἡμῶν αὐτῶν ὁμολογεῖν, ὃς ἂν ἐκείνοις ὅτι ὁμοιότατος ᾖ, τὴν μοῖραν
5 ὁμοιοτάτην ἐκείνῃ ἕξειν, ἀλλ᾽ οὐ τούτου ἕνεκα, ἵν᾽ ἀποδείξωμεν ὡς δυνατὰ ταῦτα γίγνεσθαι.

Τοῦτο μέν, ἔφη, ἀληθὲς λέγεις.

Οἴει οὖν ἧττόν τι ἀγαθὸν ζωγράφον εἶναι ὃς ἄν, γράψας παράδειγμα οἷον

ἂν εἴη ὁ κάλλιστος ἄνθρωπος, μὴ ἔχῃ ἀποδεῖξαι ὡς καὶ δυνατὸν γενέσθαι

10 τοιοῦτον ἄνδρα;

Μὰ Δία, οὐκ ἔγωγ', ἔφη.

Τί οὖν; οὐ καὶ ἡμεῖς παράδειγμα ἐποιοῦμεν λόγῳ ἀγαθῆς πόλεως;

Πάνυ γε.

Ἧττόν τι οὖν οἴει ἡμᾶς εὖ λέγειν τούτου ἕνεκα, ἐὰν μὴ ἔχωμεν ἀποδεῖξαι

15 ὡς δυνατὸν οὕτω πόλιν οἰκῆσαι ὡς ἐλέγετο;

Οὐ πάνυ, ἔφη.

A few lines later, Socrates makes a radical suggestion:

Ἐὰν μή, ἦν δ' ἐγώ, ἢ οἱ φιλόσοφοι βασιλεύσωσιν ἐν ταῖς πόλεσιν ἢ οἱ

βασιλῆς νῦν λεγόμενοι φιλοσοφήσωσιν, οὐκ ἔστι κακῶν παῦλα, ὦ φίλε

Γλαύκων, ταῖς πόλεσι, δοκῶ δ' οὐδὲ τῷ ἀνθρωπίνῳ γένει, οὐδ' αὕτη ἡ

20 πολῑτείᾱ μήποτε πρότερον φύῃ τ' εἰς τὸ δυνατὸν καὶ φῶς ἡλίου ἴδῃ.

VOCABULARY

δικαιοσύνην θ' ὁποίᾱ ἐστί, καὶ ἄνδρα...εἰ γένοιτο καὶ ὁποῖος ἂν εἴη γενόμενος (lines 1-2): three indirect questions correlated by τε...καὶ...καί; the subject of ἐστί is δικαιοσύνη; the subject of γένοιτο and εἴη is ἀνήρ

δικαιοσύνην (line 1): from δικαιοσύνη, -ης, ἡ: justice

τελέως (line 2): from τέλεος, -ᾱ, -ον: complete, perfect

γένοιτο (line 2): in this passage all forms of γίγνομαι mean "exist"

γενόμενος (line 2): the participle has conditional force ("if...")

καὶ ἀδικίᾱν αὖ καὶ τὸν ἀδικώτατον (lines 2-3): parallel to δικαιοσύνην and ἄνδρα in the preceding clauses; the indirect questions from lines 1-2 are meant to be used over again with these two other substantives

ἀποβλέποντες (line 3): from ἀποβλέπω (*with* εἰς + *acc.*): gaze upon

ἀναγκαζώμεθα (line 3): from ἀναγκάζω, ἀναγκάσω, ἠνάγκασα, ἠνάγκακα, ἠνάγκασμαι, ἠναγκάσθην: force

ὃς ἂν ἐκείνοις ὅτι ὁμοιότατος ᾖ (line 4): this whole clause is the subject of the infinitive ἕξειν (*i.e., by reflecting on the fate of those hypothetical persons, we are made to realize that a fate very similar awaits whichever one of us is the closest possible match to those persons*)

τούτου ἕνεκα (line 5): for the sake of this, i.e., for the reason given in the following ἵνα clause

ὡς δυνατὰ ταῦτα γίγνεσθαι (lines 5-6): that these things are [*supply* ἐστί] able to exist (*indir. disc.—same construction in lines 9-10*)

ἧττόν τι (line 8): less in respect to anything, i.e., any less (*modifies* ἀγαθόν)

ἀγαθὸν ζωγράφον εἶναι ὃς ἄν...μὴ ἔχῃ ἀποδεῖξαι... (lines 8-9): present general condition in indirect discourse after οἴει; the relative conditional clause (ὃς ἄν...) is the protasis; εἶναι serves as the verb in the apodosis

ζωγράφον (line 8): from ζωγράφος, -ου, ὁ: painter

μά (line 11): no, by... (*negative particle + acc., used in oaths*)

Δία (line 11): from Ζεύς, Διός, Διί, Δία, Ζεῦ, ὁ: Zeus, king of the gods

ἧττόν τι (line 14): less in respect to anything, i.e., any less (*modifies* εὖ)

τούτου ἕνεκα (line 14): for the sake of this, i.e., under the condition set forth in the following ἐάν clause

οὕτω...ὡς (line 15): correlatives ("in such a way...as")

οἰκῆσαι (line 15): from οἰκέω, οἰκήσω, ᾤκησα, ᾤκηκα, ᾤκημαι, ᾠκήθην: be governed, i.e., function (*the phrase* πόλιν οἰκῆσαι *is linked to the predicate adj.* δυνατόν *by an understood* ἐστί)

βασιλεύσωσιν (line 17): βασιλεύω, βασιλεύσω, ἐβασίλευσα, βεβασίλευκα, βεβασίλευμαι, ἐβασιλεύθην: be king, rule

οἱ βασιλῆς νῦν λεγόμενοι (lines 17-18): those who are now called kings

φιλοσοφήσωσιν (line 18): from φιλοσοφέω, φιλοσοφήσω, ἐφιλοσόφησα, πεφιλοσόφηκα, πεφιλοσόφημαι, ἐφιλοσοφήθην: practice philosophy

παῦλα (line 18): from παῦλα, -ης, ἡ (+ *gen.*): pause (from), rest (from)

Γλαύκων (line 19): from Γλαύκων, -ωνος, ὁ: Glaucon

ἀνθρωπίνῳ (line 19): from ἀνθρώπινος, -η, -ον: human

οὐδ'...μήποτε...φύῃ (lines 19-20): double negative + subjunctive in strong denial ("nor will it ever grow")

πολῑτείᾱ (line 20): from πολῑτείᾱ, -ᾱς, ἡ: state, republic

πρότερον (line 20): i.e., before (unless) philosophers become kings, etc.

φύῃ (line 20): second aor. subjunctive from φύω, φύσω, ἔφῡσα or ἔφῡν, πέφῡκα, —, —: produce, bring forth; (*2nd aor. intrans. act.*) grew

εἰς τὸ δυνατόν (line 20): into a possibility

φῶς (line 20): from φῶς (*contracted from* φάος), φωτός, τό: light

LESSON 49

βαίνω, γιγνώσκω;
DIRECTIONAL SUFFIXES;
ACCUSATIVE OF RESPECT

τὰ δ' ἄλλα σῑγῶ· βοῦς ἐπὶ γλώσσῃ μέγας / βέβηκε
(About the rest, I'm silent—a great ox has stepped on my tongue.)
—the palace guard is afraid to say more in Aeschylus' *Agamemnon* 36-37

282.   In Lesson 46 you were introduced to ὠνέομαι, an ω-verb with an un-usual second aorist: ἐπριάμην lacks a thematic vowel (ο or ε) and thus re-sembles the second aorist of a μι-verb. Two other common ω-verbs are like ὠνέομαι in having an athematic second aorist: **βαίνω**, aor. **ἔβην** ("walk"; basic stem = βα-/βη-); **γιγνώσκω**, aor. **ἔγνων** ("recognize"; basic stem = γνο-/γνω-).

Here are all the second aorist intransitive active forms of βαίνω and γιγνώσκω; no second aorist middle forms exist.

βαίνω, βήσομαι, ἔβην, βέβηκα, —, — "walk"

Aorist Active Indicative	Aorist Active Subjunctive
Singular:	
ἔβην	βῶ
ἔβης	βῇς
ἔβη	βῇ
Plural:	
ἔβημεν	βῶμεν
ἔβητε	βῆτε
ἔβησαν	βῶσι(ν)

347

	Aorist Active Optative		**Aorist Active Imperative**

Singular:

βαίην

βαίης βῆθι

βαίη βήτω

Plural:

βαῖμεν (βαίημεν)

βαῖτε (βαίητε) βῆτε

βαῖεν (βαίησαν) βάντων

Aorist Active Infinitive:

βῆναι

Aorist Active Participle:

βάς, βᾶσα, βάν (βάντος, βάσης, βάντος, etc.)

γιγνώσκω, γνώσομαι, ἔγνων, ἔγνωκα, ἔγνωσμαι, ἐγνώσθην
"recognize"

Aorist Active Indicative	**Aorist Active Subjunctive**

Singular:

ἔγνων γνῶ

ἔγνως γνῷς

ἔγνω γνῷ

Plural:

ἔγνωμεν γνῶμεν

ἔγνωτε γνῶτε

ἔγνωσαν γνῶσι(ν)

	Aorist Active Optative		**Aorist Active Imperative**

Singular:

γνοίην

γνοίης γνῶθι

γνοίη γνώτω

Plural:

γνοῖμεν (γνοίημεν)

γνοῖτε (γνοίητε) γνῶτε

γνοῖεν (γνοίησαν) γνόντων

Aorist Active Infinitive:

γνῶναι

Aorist Active Participle:

γνούς, γνοῦσα, γνόν (γνόντος, γνούσης, γνόντος; declined like an -ων, -ουσα, -ον ptcple., but has -ους, not -ων, in nom. masc. sg.)

283. Greek has several suffixes that show **direction:**

-ι, -θι, -σι(ν)	=	place where
-θεν	=	place from which (or whence)
-δε, -ζε, -σε	=	place to which (or whither)

Place where may also be indicated by the genitive singular ending **-ου.** You have already seen -θεν in πόθεν ("from where?") and -ου in ποῦ ("where?").

Theoretically, directional suffixes could be added to almost any noun or substantive, but in practice they are rarely used except with **names of localities**, with **demonstratives**, and with certain other words that denote a particular place or reference point. You should learn all of the following directional adverbs:

[from ᾿Αθῆναι, -ων, αἱ, "Athens"]

᾿Αθήνησι(ν)	᾿Αθήνηθεν	᾿Αθήναζε
"in/at Athens"	"from Athens"	"to Athens"

[from οἶκος, -ου, ὁ, "house"]

οἴκοι	οἴκοθεν	οἴκαδε
"at home"	"from home"	"home(wards)"

[from ἄλλος, -η, -ο, "other"]

ἄλλοθι	ἄλλοθεν	ἄλλοσε
"in/at another place"	"from another place"	"to another place"

[from ὁμός, -ή, -όν, "same"]

ὁμοῦ	ὁμόθεν	ὁμόσε
"in/at the same place"	"from the same place"	"to the same place"

[related to ἐκεῖνος, -η, -ο, "that"]

ἐκεῖ	ἐκεῖθεν	ἐκεῖσε
"there"	"thence"	"thither"

[related to ὅδε, ἥδε, τόδε, "this" and οὗτος, αὕτη, τοῦτο, "this," "that"]

ἐνθάδε or ἐνταῦθα	ἐνθένδε or ἐντεῦθεν	δεῦρο
"here," "there"	"hence," "thence"	"hither," "thither"

NOTE If the context permits, these adverbs may show **time** rather than place (e.g., ἐκεῖθεν may mean "from that time on"; δεῦρο may mean "up to this time").

284. A noun in the accusative case may be used to make a general description more specific. For example, adding τὴν φύσιν to ἀγαθή ἐστι narrows the focus of the compliment ("she is virtuous" → "she is virtuous in respect to her nature"). This **accusative of respect** occurs mostly with adjectives and verbs that show qualities, attributes, or states of being. It may specify a part of the body (e.g., τυφλοὶ τοὺς ὀφθαλμούς "blind in their eyes").

The dative of manner is sometimes comparable to the accusative of respect, in which case it is called the **dative of respect** (e.g., ἡλικίᾳ νέος "young in age").

285.   **VOCABULARY**

βαίνω, βήσομαι, ἔβην, βέβηκα, —, —
> walk, step, go [cf. *acrobat, amphisbaena*]

γιγνώσκω, γνώσομαι, ἔγνων, ἔγνωκα, ἔγνωσμαι, ἐγνώσθην
> (*with indir. disc. + ptcple. or ὅτι/ὡς*) recognize, come to know, know; (+ *comp. infin.*) know how (to) [cf. *agnostic, diagnosis, prognosticate*]

NOTE   Whereas οἶδα means "know by reflecting" and ἐπίσταμαι means "know by being skilled in or familiar with," γιγνώσκω means "know by observing." An important compound of this verb is ἀναγιγνώσκω, meaning "read."

μιμνῄσκω, μνήσω, ἔμνησα, —, μέμνημαι, ἐμνήσθην (*fut. perf.* μεμνήσομαι)
> remind; (*mid., aor. pass., or fut. pass. + gen. or acc., complem. infin., or indir. disc. or ptcple. or ὅτι/ὡς*) recall, remember [cf. *amnesia, amnesty, mnemonic*]

NOTE   This verb is often compounded with a prefix like ἀνα-, ἐπι-, or ὑπο-. Present middle: "I am recalling"; imperfect middle: "I was recalling"; aorist passive (*with middle sense*): "I recalled"; future passive (*with middle sense*): "I shall recall"; perfect middle: "I remember"; pluperfect middle: "I remembered"; future perfect middle: "I shall remember."

πίπτω, πεσοῦμαι, ἔπεσον, πέπτωκα, —, —
> fall [cf. *peripeteia, ptomaine, symptom*]

Ἀθῆναι, -ῶν, αἱ
> Athens; Ἀθήνησι(ν) = in/at Athens; Ἀθήνηθεν = from Athens; Ἀθήναζε = to Athens

οἶκος, -ου, ὁ
> house, household, family; οἴκοι (*final -οι is long*) = at home; οἴκοθεν = from home; οἴκαδε = home, homewards [cf. *diocese, ecology, economy, parish*]

ἀλλήλων (*gen. pl.*), ἀλλήλοις/-αις (*dat. pl.*), ἀλλήλους/-ᾱς/-α (*acc. pl.*)
> (*reciprocal pron.*) one another [cf. *parallel*]

NOTE   This pronoun occurs only in the genitive, dative, and accusative plural. It is used with a first-, second- or third-person subject to show mutual action; e.g., ἀγαπητοί, ἀγαπῶμεν ἀλλήλους ("beloved, let us love one another," 1 John 4:7).

ἕκαστος, -η, -ον   each, every (*sg. often used with a plural verb*)

ἕτερος, -ᾱ, -ον   the one (*of two*), the other (*of two*), different [cf. *heterodoxy, heterogeneous*]

ὁμός, -ή, -όν   same; ὁμοῦ = in/at the same place; ὁμόθεν = from the same place; ὁμόσε = to the same place [cf. *homogeneous, homogenize*]

ἄλλοθι   (*adv.*) in/at another place; ἄλλοθεν = from another place; ἄλλοσε = to another place

ἐκεῖ   (*adv.*) in/at that place, there; ἐκεῖθεν = from there, thence; ἐκεῖσε = to there, thither

ἐνθάδε or ἐνταῦθα   (*adv.*) in/at this place, here, in/at that place, there; ἐνθένδε/ἐντεῦθεν = from here, hence, from there, thence; δεῦρο = to here, hither, to there, thither

NOTE   ἐνθάδε and ἐνταῦθα generally mean "here" or "there," but sometimes they show a destination and are better translated as "hither" or "thither." Both are derived from ἔνθα ("here," "there"), an adverb not much used in Attic prose.

εἶτα or ἔπειτα   (*adv.*) then, next

286.   **EXERCISES**

A.   **Greek-to-English Sentences**

1. ἀεὶ μεμνησόμεθα τῶν στρατιωτῶν οἳ ἐνθάδε κεῖνται πεπτωκότες ἐν μάχῃ.

2. γνοὺς τοίνυν σε δυνατὸν τὸ σῶμα ὄντα, οἶμαι χρῆναί σε ἐν τοῖς ἀγῶσιν ἀποδεικνύναι τὴν ἀρετήν.

3. Βῶμεν Ἀθήναζε, ἦ δ᾽ ὅς, οὗ ὀψόμεθα πολλά τε καὶ ἕτερα γένη πολιτῶν.

4. δεῦρο βέβηκεν ὁ φιλόσοφος ὡς δείξων ὑμῖν τὴν ὑμετέρᾱν πόλιν ἤδη πίπτουσαν εἰς κακοὺς τρόπους.

5. μὴ παρῇς τοὺς κήρῡκας ἀγγεῖλαι μηδὲν πρὶν ἂν ἀλλήλοις ὁμολογῶσιν.

6. ἔπειτα τὰ παιδία, οὐ ῥᾳδίως στάντα, ἔβη βραδέως ἐνθένδε εἰς τὰς χεῖρας τῶν χαιρόντων γονέων.

7. εἰ γὰρ ἐμιμνησκόμην ἐκείνην τὴν παλαιὰν ἀγορὰν ὅπου κεῖται.

8. ἔβησαν οἴκαδε ἕκαστος, οὐ γνόντες ὁπόταν πάλιν ἀλλήλους ἴδωσιν.

9. οἴκοι δὴ ἔπεσες κατὰ τῆς κλίμακος, εἶτα δ᾽ οὐκ ἐμνήσθης ἐκεῖ πεσών.

10. ὠφέλομεν γνῶναι ὅτι ὁ σῖτος οὐκέτι ὁμοῦ εἴη, ἀλλ᾽ ἄλλοσε ἐνεχθείη.

B.   **English-to-Greek Sentences**

1. I know that we are fond of walking home through the market, but today let us choose the other road.

2. (While) stepping from there to here, the child fell and began to cry, having been hurt in respect to his hand.

3. I remember that you were reading two books quite different in both type and nature, but I do not recall the names.

4. The wives each dismissed their maids to another place and stood in the same place, talking to one another.

5. Next you (*sg.*) must ride to Athens and must announce there that twenty soldiers have fallen in battle.

C.   **READING**

A PREVIEW OF WHAT'S TO COME — Part 1
(adapted from Book 10 of Plato's *Republic* 614d-619a)

The last book of Plato's **Republic** *contains an argument for the soul's immortality. Socrates concludes the discussion with a tale illustrating the rewards and punishments that await the soul after the death of the body.*

According to Socrates, there was once a brave soldier named Er who, after being killed in battle, suddenly came back to life on his funeral pyre and described what he had experienced while dead. His soul, he said, had traveled along with many others to a place where there were two openings leading down below the earth and two leading up into the heavens. Judges would weigh the merits of each soul and assign it to go either up or down. Every soul was required to travel for a thousand years, either along the pleasant path through the sky or via the torturous subterranean route. At the end of its thousand-year journey, the soul would be required to choose the life it wished to lead during its next incarnation.

Er was permitted to watch the souls as they left for their journeys (through one of the upper or lower openings) or returned from them (through the other upper or lower opening). The following excerpt begins with the encounter between Er and the judges of the souls. Since Socrates is reporting someone else's story, he uses ἔφη *("Er said that...") followed by infinitives in indirect discourse. If a sentence seems to lack a main verb, it is just that Socrates has not bothered to repeat* ἔφη, *assuming that you will supply it.*

ἑαυτοῦ δὲ προσελθόντος, τοὺς δικαστὰς εἰπεῖν ὅτι δέοι αὐτὸν ἄγγελον
ἀνθρώποις γενέσθαι τῶν ἐκεῖ καὶ ἀκούειν τε καὶ θεᾶσθαι πάντα τὰ ἐν τῷ τόπῳ.
ὁρᾶν δὴ τὰς ψῡχὰς ἐκ μὲν τοῦ χάσματος ἀνιέναι ἐκ τῆς γῆς μεστὰς αὐχμοῦ τε
καὶ κόνεως, ἐκ δὲ τοῦ ἑτέρου καταβαίνειν ἑτέρᾱς ἐκ τοῦ οὐρανοῦ καθαράς. καὶ
5 τὰς ἀφικνουμένᾱς ὥσπερ ἐκ πολλῆς πορείᾱς φαίνεσθαι ἥκειν, καὶ ἀσπάζεσθαί
τ' ἀλλήλᾱς καὶ πυνθάνεσθαι τάς τ' ἐκ τῆς γῆς ἠκούσᾱς παρὰ τῶν ἑτέρων τὰ

ἐκεῖ καὶ τὰς ἐκ τοῦ οὐρανοῦ τὰ παρ' ἐκείναις. διηγεῖσθαι δ' ἀλλήλαις τὰς μὲν κλαούσᾱς, μιμνησκομένᾱς ὅσα τε καὶ οἷα πάθοιεν καὶ ἴδοιεν ἐν τῇ ὑπὸ τῆς γῆς πορείᾳ, τὰς δ' αὖ ἐκ τοῦ οὐρανοῦ εὐπαθείᾱς διηγεῖσθαι καὶ θέᾱς θαυμαστὰς τὸ
10 κάλλος. *Later on, Er observed each returning soul choosing its next life:*

[τὸν προφήτην] ῥῖψαι ἐπὶ πάντας τοὺς κλήρους, τὸν δὲ παρ' αὐτὸν πεσόντα ἕκαστον ἀναιρεῖσθαι. μετὰ δὲ τοῦτ' αὖθις τὰ τῶν βίων παραδείγματα θεῖναι ἐπὶ τὴν γῆν. ἐνθάδε δή, ὦ φίλε Γλαύκων, ὁ πᾶς κίνδῡνος ἀνθρώπῳ, καὶ διὰ ταῦτα μάλιστα ἐπιμελητέον ὅπως ἕκαστος ἡμῶν μαθήσεται τὸν βελτίω ἐκ
15 τῶν δυνατῶν βίων ἀεὶ αἱρεῖσθαι. ἀδαμαντίνως δὴ δεῖ ταύτην τὴν δόξαν ἔχοντα εἰς Ἅιδου ἰέναι ἵνα ᾖ καὶ ἐκεῖ ἀνέκπληκτος ὑπὸ πλούτων τε καὶ τῶν τοιούτων κακῶν, καὶ μὴ ἐμπέσῃ εἰς τυραννίδας καὶ ἄλλᾱς τοιαύτᾱς πράξεις, ἀλλὰ γνῷ τὸν μέσον βίον αἱρεῖσθαι καὶ φεύγειν τὰ ὑπερβάλλοντα καὶ ἐν τῷδε τῷ βίῳ κατὰ τὸ δυνατὸν καὶ ἐν παντὶ τῷ ἔπειτα· οὕτω γὰρ εὐδαιμονέστατος γίγνεται ἄνθρωπος.

VOCABULARY

προσελθόντος (line 1): from προσέρχομαι: draw near, approach
δικαστάς (line 1): from δικαστής, -οῦ, ὁ: judge
τῶν ἐκεῖ (line 2): of the things there, i.e., of the things in the world beyond
θεᾶσθαι (line 2): from θεάομαι, θεάσομαι, ἐθεᾱσάμην, —, τεθέᾱμαι, —: behold
χάσματος (line 3): from χάσμα, -ατος, τό: opening, chasm
ἀνιέναι (line 3): from ἀνέρχομαι: go up
μεστάς (line 3): from μεστός, -ή, -όν (+ *gen.*): full (of)
αὐχμοῦ (line 3): from αὐχμός, -οῦ, ὁ: crud, dirt
κόνεως (line 4): from κόνις, -εως, ἡ: dust
καταβαίνειν (line 4): from καταβαίνω: go down
καθαράς (line 4): from καθαρός, -ά, -όν: clean, pure
πορείᾱς (line 5): from πορείᾱ, -ᾱς, ἡ: journey
ἥκειν (line 5): from ἥκω, ἥξω, —, —, —, —: have come (*pres. has perf. sense*)
ἀσπάζεσθαι (line 5): from ἀσπάζομαι, ἀσπάσομαι, ἠσπασάμην, —, —, —: greet
τάς...ἐκ τῆς γῆς ἡκούσᾱς (line 6): = subject of πυνθάνεσθαι "inquire about" (*the ptcple.*
    ἡκούσᾱς *comes from* ἥκω—*see note on* ἥκειν *in line 5*)
τὰς ἐκ τοῦ οὐρανοῦ [ἡκούσᾱς] (line 7): = second subject of πυνθάνεσθαι
τὰ παρ' ἐκείναις (line 7): the things with those, i.e., the others' experience
διηγεῖσθαι (line 7): from διηγέομαι, διηγήσομαι, διηγησάμην, —, διήγημαι, —:
    describe (*supply* τὰς ψῡχάς *as subject of* διηγεῖσθαι)
κλαούσᾱς (line 8): from κλάω, κλαήσω, ἔκλαυσα, —, —, —: weep
ὅσα...ἴδοιεν (line 8): this clause is the direct object of both διηγεῖσθαι and
    μιμνησκομένᾱς
εὐπαθείᾱς (line 9): from εὐπάθεια, -ᾱς, ἡ: good experience
θέᾱς (line 9): from θέᾱ, -ᾱς, ἡ: sight, spectacle
κάλλος (line 10): from κάλλος, -ους, τό: beauty (*here = acc. of respect*)

προφήτην (line 11): from προφήτης, -ου, ὁ: prophet, interpreter (*this spokesperson for the Fates supervised the distribution of lots*)

πάντας (line 11): supply τοὺς ἀνθρώπους (*the souls are thought of as persons*)

κλήρους (line 11): from κλῆρος, -ου, ὁ: lot (*showed the order of choosing*)

ἀναιρεῖσθαι (line 12): from ἀναιρέω: take up, pick up (*subject* = ἕκαστον)

θεῖναι (line 13): supply τὸν προφήτην as the subject

ἐνθάδε (line 13): here, i.e., at the moment of choosing a life (*Socrates interrupts his own recounting of Er's story to make a comment*)

Γλαύκων (line 13): from Γλαύκων, -ωνος, ὁ: Glaucon

ἀδαμαντίνως (line 15): from ἀδαμάντινος, -ον: firm, determined

ἔχοντα (line 16): modifies the understood subject (τινά "someone") of ἰέναι

Ἅιδου (line 16): from Ἅιδης, -ου, ὁ: Hades, god of the underworld (*gen. sg. is used to mean "[the house of] Hades"*)

ἀνέκπληκτος (line 16): from ἀνέκπληκτος, -ον: not dazzled, not awed

πλούτων (line 16); from πλοῦτος, -ου, ὁ: wealth; (*pl.*) riches

ἐμπέσῃ (line 17): from ἐμπίπτω: fall upon, stumble into

τυραννίδας (line 17): from τυραννίς, -ίδος, ἡ: tyranny, life of a tyrant

πρᾶξεις (line 17): from πρᾶξις, -εως, ἡ: activity, career

μέσον (line 18): from μέσος, -η, -ον: middle, moderate

ὑπερβάλλοντα (line 18): from ὑπερβάλλω: exceed, be in excess

κατὰ τὸ δυνατόν (line 19): according to possibility, i.e., as much as possible

ἐν παντὶ τῷ ἔπειτα (line 19): in all the [time] thereafter, i.e., forever

LESSON 50

REDUNDANT μή WITH VERBS OF HINDERING; USES OF μὴ οὐ AND οὐ μή; ATTRACTION OF RELATIVE PRONOUNS

ἔωσπερ ἂν ἐμπνέω καὶ οἷός τ' ὦ, οὐ μὴ παύσωμαι φιλοσοφῶν
(As long as I'm alive and fit, I just won't quit philosophizing.)
—Socrates in Plato's *Apology* 29d has no intention of retiring

287. After **verbs of hindering** (which include verbs of forbidding, preventing, guarding against, avoiding, denying, and refusing), an **infinitive** is often used (e.g., φυλάττομαί σε κλέπτειν τὰ χρήματα "I am on guard against your stealing the money" [literally, "against you to steal the money"]). Frequently the speaker will combine **μή** with the infinitive (e.g., φυλάττομαί σε **μὴ** κλέπτειν τὰ χρήματα "I am on guard against your stealing the money"). This **redundant μή** (also called **sympathetic μή**) reinforces, or sympathizes with, the negative notion inherent in the verb of hindering (i.e., the desire that something *not* happen—μή is almost equivalent to "lest" after a verb of fearing). Notice that the addition of a redundant μή to a sentence has no effect on the English translation.

If the verb of hindering itself has a negative combined with it, a redundant **μὴ οὐ** may be added—with no change in the translation—to the infinitive. Example: οὐ φυλάττομαί σε **μὴ οὐ** κλέπτειν τὰ χρήματα ("I am not on guard against your stealing the money").

NOTE Sometimes an **articular infinitive** in the **accusative** or **genitive** case is preferred to the simple infinitive (e.g., φυλάττομαί σε τὸ/τοῦ [μὴ] κλέπτειν τὰ χρήματα or οὐ φυλάττομαί σε τὸ/τοῦ [μὴ οὐ] κλέπτειν τὰ χρήματα).

288. **μὴ** and **μὴ οὐ** may be combined with a main verb in the **indicative** or **subjunctive** mood to indicate that the speaker is making an assertion or a denial but is not confident about it. A **cautious assertion with μή** de-

355

scribes what the speaker thinks is true (*indicative*) or may prove to be true (*subjunctive*). A **cautious denial with μὴ οὐ** describes what the speaker thinks is not true (*indicative*) or may prove not to be true (*subjunctive*). Translating cautious assertions and denials requires creativity on your part since a literal rendering is usually inadequate to convey the speaker's cautiousness. Examples:

μὴ τοῦτο δυνατόν ἐστιν.	"I am inclined to think this is possible."
μὴ τοῦτο δυνατὸν ᾖ.	"I suspect this may be possible."
μὴ οὐ τοῦτο δυνατόν ἐστιν.	"I have a feeling this is not possible."
μὴ οὐ τοῦτο δυνατὸν ᾖ.	"I am afraid this may not be not possible."

289.   οὐ **μή** may be combined with a main verb in the **subjunctive** or the **future indicative** to indicate an **emphatic denial** that something will happen (e.g., οὐ μὴ φύγητε or οὐ μὴ φεύξεσθε "you won't escape"—here the denial is actually a threat). The quotation at the beginning of this lesson is an emphatic denial; it implies that Socrates has confidence in the negative prediction he is making.

NOTE   Sometimes the combination of οὐ μή + subjunctive or future indicative indicates an **urgent prohibition** rather than an emphatic denial (e.g., in a different context, the emphatic denials οὐ μὴ φύγητε and οὐ μὴ φεύξεσθε could be urgent prohibitions and mean "don't flee!"). Another way to express an urgent prohibition is with a negative clause of effort (ὅπως μή + future indicative) minus its introductory verb (e.g., ὅπως μὴ φεύξεσθε "[see to it that you] don't flee!").

290.   The case of a relative pronoun, as you know, is normally determined by its function in the relative clause (subject = nominative; direct object = accusative, etc.). It is not uncommon, however, for the relative to be **attracted into the case of its antecedent**. This happens most often when the antecedent is in the genitive or dative and the relative pronoun should logically be in the accusative.

Examples (of a relative pronoun attracted into the case of its antecedent):
ἄξιοί εἰσι τῶν ὀνομάτων **ὧν** (*should logically be accusative* ἅ) ἔχουσιν.
"They are worthy of the names that they have."

οὐ βουλόμεθα ἕπεσθαι τῷ στρατηγῷ **ᾧ** (*should logically be* ὅν) εἵλεσθε.
"We do not wish to follow the general whom you chose."

In the above examples, both of the antecedents (ὀνομάτων, στρατηγῷ) are nouns. If the antecedent happens to be a **demonstrative pronoun**, that pronoun often drops out, leaving the relative pronoun to serve, essentially, as its own antecedent.

Examples (of an attracted relative replacing its demonstrative antecedent):

ἄξιοί εἰσιν ὧν (*should logically be* τούτων ἃ) ἔχουσιν.
"They are worthy of what they have."

οὐ βουλόμεθα ἕπεσθαι ᾧ (*should logically be* ἐκείνῳ ὃν) εἵλεσθε.
"We do not wish to follow whom you chose."

A **relative adverb** may also be attracted to a demonstrative antecedent and take its place. Example: ἄρξομαι τοῦ λόγου ἐκεῖθεν οὗ ἔλιπον → ἄρξομαι **ὅθεν** ἔλιπον ("I shall begin the argument from where [*from that place where*] I left it").

291.
Back in Lesson 23 you were told that the subordinating conjunction **ἕως** means "while" or "as long as" (i.e., *during* the time when); now you should know that it may also mean "**until**" (*up to* the time when). Whereas πρίν means "until" only when the main verb in the sentence is negative, ἕως may have that meaning in positive as well as negative sentences. Whether it means "while," "as long as," or "until," ἕως is always followed by a clause with a finite verb.

The moods and tenses used in ἕως clauses correspond to those used in **conditions**. Simply treat the ἕως clause as if it were a **protasis** (just the way you would treat a conditional relative clause; see Lesson 38). The context will help you decide whether to translate ἕως as "while," "as long as," or "until." Notice that the Socratic quotation beginning this lesson has ἕωσπερ with subjunctive + ἄν (the equivalent of the protasis of a future more vivid condition).

The subordinating conjunction **μέχρι** ("until") may be followed by the same moods and tenses as ἕως, in either positive or negative sentences (it always means "until," never "while" or "as long as"). Unlike πρίν and ἕως, μέχρι is also used as a **preposition** meaning "until" and taking an object in the **genitive**.

292.
Impersonal verbs and expressions are never used in genitive absolutes, but they regularly appear as **neuter singular** accusative participles in **accusative absolutes**, which function no differently from genitive absolutes. Examples: ἐξὸν φεύγειν, ἐβουλήθης μένειν ("it being possible to flee, you preferred to remain"); ὂν ἀναγκαῖον, παρὰ σοῦ δίκην λήψομαι ("it being necessary, I shall punish you").

293.
VOCABULARY

κωλύω, κωλύσω, ἐκώλυσα, κεκώλυκα, κεκώλυμαι, ἐκωλύθην
(+ *infin.*) hinder, prevent

λανθάνω, λήσω, ἔλαθον, λέληθα, —, —

> (+ *acc.*) escape the notice of; (+ *suppl.
> ptcple.*) escape the notice; (*mid. + gen.*)
> forget [cf. *lanthanum, lethargy, lethe*]

NOTE   When combined with a supplementary participle, λανθάνω does little more than show that the action expressed by the participle is/was/will be done without someone's being aware of it. The participle conveys the main idea. Examples: ἔλαθόν με γενόμενοι σοφοί ("they became wise without my knowing it" [literally, "in becoming wise, they escaped the notice of me"]); λανθάνουσι γιγνόμενοι σοφοί ("they are becoming wise without knowing it" [literally, "they escape their own notice that they are becoming wise"]). The compound ἐπιλανθάνομαι (+ *gen.*) "forget" is more common than the simple λανθάνομαι.

πίνω, πίομαι, ἔπιον (*imper.* πῖθι), πέπωκα, πέπομαι, ἐπόθην

> drink [cf. *symposium*]

τρέχω, δραμοῦμαι, ἔδραμον, δεδράμηκα, δεδράμημαι, —

> run [cf. *hippodrome, trochee*]

τυγχάνω, τεύξομαι, ἔτυχον, τετύχηκα, —, —

> (+ *dat.*) befall, happen (to); (+ *suppl.
> ptcple.*) happen; (+ *gen.*) hit (*a target*),
> chance upon, meet, obtain

NOTE   When combined with a supplementary participle, τυγχάνω does little more than show that the action expressed by the participle is/was/will be done by chance. The participle conveys the main idea. Example: ἔτυχον ὄντες σοφοί ("they by chance were wise" [literally, "they happened being wise"]).

νοῦς (*contracted from* νόος), νοῦ, ὁ

> mind [cf. *paranoia*]

ὄρος, -ους, τό   mountain, hill [cf. *oread, orogeny*]
πεδίον, -ου, τό   plain (*flat, open country*)
πούς, ποδός, ὁ   (*voc. sg.* = πούς) foot [cf. *octopus, pew,
                         podiatrist, podium*]

NOTE   πούς is unusual in its nom. sg. and voc. sg. Its other forms are all built on the stem ποδ- with regular third-declension endings (δ drops out in the dat. pl.: ποσί[ν]). In the gen. and dat. sg. and pl., the accent shifts from πο- to the ultima, as you would expect in a third-declension noun with monosyllabic stem.

τύχη, -ης, ἡ   chance, fortune, luck; Τύχη = Chance,
                         Fortune (*personified as a goddess*)
ὕδωρ, ὕδατος, τό   water [cf. *clepsydra, dropsy, hydraulic*]
χαλεπός, -ή, -όν   difficult, hard

ψευδής, -ές	lying, false, untrue; (*irreg. superl.*)
	ψευδίστατος, -η, -ον [cf. *pseudepigrapha, pseudonym*]
μέχρι	(*prep. + gen.*) until, up to; (*conj.*) until
ἕως	(*conj.*) until

294.   **EXERCISES**

A.   Greek-to-English Sentences

1. τοὺς μὲν πόδας τυγχάνει ὢν θάττων ἐμοῦ, τὸν δὲ νοῦν σωφρονέστερός εἰμι.

2. οὐ μὴ πάλιν λήσεις με κλέψᾱς τὴν ἐμοὶ φιλητὴν κύνα καὶ εὐθὺς φυγὼν διὰ τῶν ὀρῶν.

3. διὰ τί οὐ κεκωλύκᾱσι τοὺς παῖδας μὴ οὐ δραμεῖν οἷ κίνδῡνοί εἰσιν;

4. ἕως ἂν δῷ Τύχη ἡμῖν τὴν εἰρήνην, ὁ τῶν νεᾱνιῶν βίος ἔσται χαλεπώτατος.

5. οἱ θεοὶ κωλύουσί σε μήτε πιεῖν τὸ ἡδὺ ὕδωρ μήτε θεῖναι τὸν πόδα εἰς τὸν ποταμόν.

6. ἐν τούτῳ τῷ πεδίῳ μὴ τύχωμέν τινος ὕδατος οὗ οἱ ἐκεῖ ἡμῖν ἴσως δώσουσιν.

7. Ἐν ὕδατι, ἦν δ᾽ ἐγώ, δεῖ γράφειν τοὺς ψευδεῖς λόγους πᾱ́σης γυναικός.

8. οὐ μήποτ᾽ ἐπιλάθῃ, ὦ ἀδελφή, τῶν σαυτῆς γονέων ὧν ἀγαπᾷς.

9. ἐν τῷ σταδίῳ Ἀθήνησιν ἔτρεχεν ὁ γέρων καὶ μέχρι τοῦ θανάτου.

10. ἐξὸν εἰπεῖν τὰ ψευδῆ, ὦ ἀξίᾱ γύναι, οὐκ ἔλαθές με ἀληθῆ εἰποῦσα.

B.   English-to-Greek Sentences

1. You (*sg.*) must not hinder the dogs from running eagerly to where (*attraction*) their master is waiting.

2. It escaped my notice that Fortune rules all that (*attraction*) we see and is the very mind of the universe.

3. The strangers will not drink this water (*emphatic denial*) until they cease to say lying words to us.

4. Because I happen to be swift of foot, I may arrive at the plain beyond the mountains on the same day (*cautious assertion*).

5. It being difficult to chance upon that road (*acc. absolute*), what prevented you (*pl.*) from beginning to seek it immediately?

C. READING

A PREVIEW OF WHAT'S TO COME — Part 2
(adapted from Book 10 of Plato's *Republic* 620d-621d)

Er watched in amazement as each soul chose its next life. The choice seemed to depend upon the kind of life the soul had previously led; the soul of Agamemnon, for example, who had been murdered by his wife, wanted to avoid human beings and thus chose the life of an eagle. The soul of Odysseus, remembering all the sufferings it had endured in its former quest for fame, happily chose the inglorious life of a private citizen. When all of the selections had been made, it was time for the "processing" of the souls by the three Fates: Lachesis, Clotho, and Atropos.

What follows is the conclusion not only to Er's story (as told by Socrates), but also to the entire **Republic.** *Like the previous reading, this one begins in indirect discourse. If a sentence is missing its main verb, you should supply* ἔφη *("Er said that...").*

Ἐπειδὴ δ' οὖν πάσᾱς τὰς ψῡχὰς τοὺς βίους ᾑρῆσθαι, προσιέναι πρὸς τὴν Λάχεσιν· ἐκείνην δ' ἑκάστῳ ὃν εἵλετο τὸν δαίμονα, τοῦτον φύλακα συμπέμπειν τοῦ βίου. ὃν πρῶτον ἄγειν τὴν ψῡχὴν πρὸς τὴν Κλωθὼ ὑπὸ τὴν ἐκείνης χεῖρά τε καὶ τὸν ἄτρακτον· αὖθις δ' ἐπὶ τὴν Ἀτρόπου νῆσιν ἄγειν. ἐντεῦθεν δὲ
5 πορεύεσθαι πάντας εἰς πεδίον τι διὰ καύματός τε καὶ πνίγους δεινοῦ· καὶ γὰρ εἶναι αὐτὸ κενὸν δένδρων τε καὶ φυτῶν. σκηνᾶσθαι οὖν αὐτούς, ἤδη ἑσπέρᾱς γιγνομένης, παρὰ τὸν τῆς Λήθης ποταμόν. μέτρον μὲν οὖν τι τοῦ ὕδατος πᾶσιν ἀναγκαῖον εἶναι πιεῖν, τοὺς δὲ φρονήσει μὴ σῳζομένους πλέον πίνειν τοῦ μέτρου· τὸν δ' ἀεὶ πιόντα πάντων ἐπιλανθάνεσθαι. ἐπειδὴ δὲ καθεύδειν αὐτοὺς
10 τῆς νυκτός, βροντήν τε καὶ σεισμὸν γενέσθαι, καὶ ἐντεῦθεν ἐξαίφνης ἄλλον ἄλλῃ φέρεσθαι ἄνω εἰς τὴν γένεσιν, ὥσπερ ἀστέρας. αὐτὸς δὲ τοῦ μὲν ὕδατος κωλῡθῆναι πιεῖν· ὅπως μέντοι εἰς τὸ σῶμα ἀφίκοιτο, οὐκ εἰδέναι, ἀλλ' ἐξαίφνης ἀναβλέψᾱς ἰδεῖν ἕωθεν αὐτὸν κείμενον ἐπὶ τῇ πυρᾷ.

Καὶ οὕτως, ὦ Γλαύκων, μῦθος ἐσώθη, καὶ ἡμᾶς ἂν σώσειεν ἂν πειθώμεθα
15 αὐτῷ. ἀλλ' ἂν ἐμοὶ πειθώμεθα, νομίζοντες ἀθάνατον ψῡχήν, τῆς ἄνω ὁδοῦ ἀεὶ ἑξόμεθα καὶ δικαιοσύνην μετὰ φρονήσεως παντὶ τρόπῳ ἐπιτηδεύσομεν, ἵνα καὶ ἡμῖν αὐτοῖς φίλοι ὦμεν καὶ τοῖς θεοῖς, καὶ ἐπειδὰν τὰ ἆθλα δικαιοσύνης κομιζώμεθα, καὶ ἐνθάδε καὶ ἐν τῇ χῑλιέτει πορείᾳ, εὖ πράττωμεν.

VOCABULARY

ᾑρῆσθαι (line 1): a verb in a dependent clause may become an infinitive by attraction to the infinitive in the main clause of the indirect discourse
προσιέναι (line 1): from προσέρχομαι: go forward to, approach
Λάχεσιν (line 2): from Λάχεσις, -εως, ἡ: Lachesis, "Distributor of lots"

ἐκείνην...βίου (lines 2-3): English word order would be ἐκείνην συμπέμπειν ἑκάστῳ
    τοῦτον τὸν δαίμονα ὃν [ἕκαστος] εἵλετο φύλακα τοῦ βίου
ἑκάστῳ (line 2): masculine because Er thinks of the souls as persons
δαίμονα (line 2): each life had a guardian spirit associated with it
συμπέμπειν (line 2): from συμπέμπω (+ *dat.*): send along (with) (*as guardian*)
ὅν (line 3): whom, i.e., him (= τὸν δαίμονα), subject of ἄγειν
Κλωθώ (line 3): from Κλωθώ, -οῦς, ἡ: Clotho, "Spinner"
ἄτρακτον (line 4): ἄτρακτος, -ου, ὁ: spindle
Ἀτρόπου (line 4): Ἄτροπος, -ου, ἡ: Atropos, "Unturnable"
νῆσιν (line 4): from νῆσις, -εως, ἡ: spinning (*Clotho's spinning confirms the soul's cho-
    sen fate, while Atropos' spinning makes it irreversible*)
πορεύεσθαι (line 5): from πορεύω, πορεύσω, ἐπόρευσα, πεπόρευκα, πεπόρευμαι,
    ἐπορεύθην: make go, carry; (*mid./pass.*) go, journey
καύματος (line 5): from καῦμα, -ατος, τό: burning heat
πνίγους (line 5): from πνῖγος, -ους, τό: stifling heat
σκηνᾶσθαι (line 6): from σκηνάω, σκηνήσω, ἐσκήνησα, ἐσκήνηκα, ἐσκήνημαι, ἐσκηνήθην
    (*usually mid.*): encamp
Λήθης (line 7): from Λήθη, -ης, ἡ: Forgetfulness, river in the underworld
μέτρον (line 7): from μέτρον, -ου, τό: measure, i.e., a moderate portion
τοὺς...φρονήσει μὴ σῳζομένους (line 8): i.e., whichever souls were not wise enough
    to drink moderately and thus save part of their memory
φρονήσει (line 8): from φρόνησις, -εως, ἡ: good sense
βροντήν (line 10): from βροντή, -ῆς, ἡ: thunder
σεισμόν (line 10): from σεισμός, -οῦ, ὁ: earthquake
ἐξαίφνης (line 10): suddenly (*adv.*)
ἄλλον ἄλλη (lines 10-11): one to one place, another to another place (ἄλλη = *dat.*
    fem. sg. of ἄλλος *used as adv.:* "to another place")
γένεσιν (line 11): γένεσις, -εως, ἡ: birth
ἀστέρας (line 11): from ἀστήρ, -έρος, ὁ: star
τοῦ...ὕδατος (line 11): [any] of the water (*partitive genitive*)
ἀναβλέψᾱς (line 13): from ἀναβλέπω: look up
ἕωθεν (line 13): at dawn (*adv.*)
πυρᾷ (line 13): from πυρά, -ᾶς, ἡ: funeral pyre
Γλαύκων (line 14): from Γλαύκων, -ωνος, ὁ: Glaucon
μῦθος (line 14): from μῦθος, -ου, ὁ: story, tale (supply ὁ)
ἂν σώσειεν (line 14): subject = ὁ μῦθος (*potential optative*)
πειθώμεθα (lines 14, 15): here = "believe"
τῆς ἄνω ὁδοῦ (line 15): the upward path (*gen. with* ἐξόμεθα, "we'll keep to")
δικαιοσύνην (line 16): from δικαιοσύνη, -ης, ἡ: justice
ἐπιτηδεύσομεν (line 16): from ἐπιτηδεύω, ἐπιτηδεύσω, ἐπετήδευσα, ἐπιτετήδευκα,
    ἐπιτετήδευμαι, ἐπετηδεύθην: pursue
ἆθλα (line 17): from ἆθλον, -ου, τό: prize, reward
χῑλιέτει (line 18): from χῑλιέτης, -ες: lasting a thousand years
πορείᾳ (line 18): from πορείᾱ, -ᾱς, ἡ: journey

WORD LISTS

LESSON 3

γράφω
ἐθέλω
θύω
καί (καὶ...καί)
κλέπτω
μή
οὐ
παιδεύω
σπεύδω
φυλάττω

LESSON 4

ἀγορά
εἰς
ἐκ
ἐν
ἐπιστολή
ἡ
ἡσυχίᾱ
θεά
πέμπω
σκηνή
χώρᾱ
ὦ

LESSON 5

ἀκούω
βλάπτω
δέσποινα
ἐπεί
ἐπειδή
θάλαττα

θεράπαινα
κελεύω
κλίνη
μοῖρα (Μοῖρα)
ὥρᾱ

LESSON 5 READING

ἀγνοέω
ἀλεκτρυών
βούλευμα
ἔννυχος
ἴδιος
πονέω

LESSON 6

ἀλλά (ἀλλ᾽)
ἀλλάττω
διώκω
ἔτι
ἔχω
κόρη (Κόρη)
μέλλω
μηκέτι
οἰκίᾱ
οὐκέτι
πάλιν

LESSON 6 READING

Ἀφροδίτη
γαλῆ
γαμέω
εἶ
μῦς

νεᾱνίᾱς
πειράω
τρόπος

LESSON 7

ἀδελφή
ἀδελφός
ἄνθρωπος
ἀπό (ἀπ', ἀφ')
θεός
ἵππος
λίθος
λύπη
ὁ
ὁδός
ποταμός
χαίρω
χαρά

LESSON 7 READING

ἁλιεύς
βλέπω
ἕλκω
ἐμπειρίᾱ
ἐστί(ν)
ἰχθός
ὀρχέομαι
πολύς
σαγήνη

LESSON 8

ἀγαθός
ἄξιος
ἀπολείπω
βίος
δῶρον
ἔργον
εὑρίσκω
θησαυρός
καλός
λείπω
τέκνον
τό
φυτόν

LESSON 8 READING

ἄμπελος
γεωργός
δῆλος
πειράω
ποιέω
σκάπτω

LESSON 9

ἀθάνατος
ἀνάξιος
δεσπότης
δουλεύω
δούλη
δοῦλος
ἐλεύθερος
κακός
μαθητής
νεᾱνίᾱς
οἰκέτης
πρότερος

LESSON 9 READING

βυρσοδέψης
εὔχομαι
κεραμεύς
κηπουρός
ὄνος
ποθέω
πολύς

LESSON 10

ἀλήθεια
δέ (δ')
θάνατος (Θάνατος)
κίνδῡνος
λέγω
μέν
μὲν...δέ
ὁ μὲν...ὁ δέ
πράττω
φεύγω
φίλη
φίλος

LESSON 10 READING

ἄρκτος
δύο
ὀσφραίνομαι
οὖς
οὗτος
σωτηρίᾱ

LESSON 11

ἀλλάττομαι
ἅμαξα
γράφομαι
λίμνη
μακρός
μῑκρός
παιδεύομαι
πείθω
πόρρω
τόπος
τρέπω
τρόπος
ὑπό (ὑπ᾽, ὑφ᾽)
φυλάττομαι

LESSON 11 READING

βάτραχος
δύο
εἰμί
ἦσαν
ὕδωρ

LESSON 12

ἀρχή
γε (γ᾽)
διά (δι᾽)
εἰμί
εἰρήνη
ἐχθρός
λόγος
λύω
πολέμιος
πόλεμος

LESSON 12 READING

ἀποπέμπω
κύων
λύκος
πρόβατον

LESSON 13

βλέπω
γάρ
ἐκεῖνος
νῦν
ὅδε (ὅδ᾽)
οὗτος
σοφίᾱ
σοφός
τότε (τότ᾽, τόθ᾽)
φιλοσοφίᾱ
φιλόσοφος

LESSON 13 READING

γεωργός
δέσμη
θλάω
κατὰ μίαν
ὁμόνοια
πατήρ
ποιέω
ῥάβδος
ῥᾳδίως
στασιάζω

LESSON 14

αὐτός
βιβλίον
ἐγώ
ἐπί (ἐπ᾽, ἐφ᾽)
ἐπιπλήττω
ἡμεῖς
ἱμάτιον
πλήττω
σύ
ὑμεῖς
φέρω

LESSON 14 READING

γίγνομαι
δεῖ
μείζων
μήτηρ

LESSON 15

ἁρπάζω
βάλλω
γελάω
δῆλος
δηλόω
κομίζω
τῑμάω
τῑμή
φιλέω
ὠφελέω

LESSON 15 READING

δίκτυον
ἐσθίω
κυνηγέτης
λέων
μῦς
τρώγω

LESSON 16

ἀγών
ἀσπίς
ἤ (ἤ...ἤ)
κλώψ
λέων
ὄνομα
ποιέω
ῥήτωρ
φύλαξ
χάρις

LESSON 16 READING

γέρων
μένω
πυρετός
σκόλοψ

τοῖχος
φοβέω
χείρ

LESSON 17

αἰδώς
ἀληθής
γέρας
δαίμων
εὖ
εὐδαίμων
κακῶς
πρός
προσβάλλω
προσποιέω
Σωκράτης
τεῖχος
τριήρης

LESSON 17 READING

ἀλώπηξ
γῆρας
ἐσθίω
ζῷον
ἴχνος
οἴμοι
πολύς
σπήλαιον

LESSON 18

ἀγγέλλω
ἄγγελος
δραχμή
ἐρωτάω
μόνον
μόνος
ὀβολός
ὀλίγος
οὐ μόνον...ἀλλὰ καί
περί
πολλά (πόλλ')
πολύ
πολύς
πωλέω

LESSON 18 READING

ἄγαλμα
ἀγαλματοποιός
ἐργαστήριον
Ἑρμῆς
Ζεύς
Ἥρᾱ
κενόδοξος
πόσος

LESSON 19

αἰτίᾱ
αἴτιος
ἑαυτοῦ
ἐμαυτοῦ
λαμβάνω
μένω
μετά (μετ᾽, μεθ᾽)
σεαυτοῦ
συλλαμβάνω
σύν

LESSON 19 READING

ἄδειπνος
αἴλουρος
ἀλεκτρυών
ἐσθίω
κρᾱ́ζω
μήτηρ
νύξ
τίκτω
ὕπνος
φόβος
ᾠόν

LESSON 20

γῆ (Γῆ)
δένδρον
Ἑλλάς
Ἕλλην
Ἑλληνικός
ζητέω
κατά (κατ᾽, καθ᾽)

οὐρανός (Οὐρανός)
ῥίπτω
ὑπέρ

LESSON 20 READING

ἀλώπηξ
κόλαξ
κόραξ
κρᾱ́ζω
κρέας
πτερόν
φωνή

LESSON 21

ἀποθνῄσκω
ἀποκτείνω
ἐμός
ἡμέτερος
σός
τί (adv.)
τινὲς μὲν...τινὲς δέ
τίς/τις
ῡ̔μέτερος
φοβέω
φόβος

LESSON 21 READING

δράκων
κροκόδειλος
Νεῖλος
συγγενής
σωτηρίᾱ
ὕδωρ
φονεύς

LESSON 22

ἄγω
ἄλλος
ζῷον
νόμος
μηδέ (μηδὲ...μηδέ)
μήτε (μήτε...μήτε)
οὐδέ (οὐδὲ...οὐδέ)

οὔτε (οὔτε…οὔτε)
παρά (παρ')
τε (τ', θ')
τε…καί (τε…τε)
ψῡχή

LESSON 22 READING

ἀλώπηξ
βασιλεύς
κρέας
ὀρχέομαι
πάγη
πίθηκος
σύνοδος
φθονέω

LESSON 23

ἀμφί (ἀμφ')
ἀνά (ἀν')
ἔτος
ἕως
ἡμέρᾱ
νύξ
ὁράω
ὅς
πᾶς
τήμερον
χρόνος

LESSON 23 READING

αἴθυια
βᾰτος
ἐμπορικός
δανειστής
ναῦς
νυκτερίς
πάρειμι
πρότερον
χαλκός
χειμών

LESSON 24

ἄνευ
ἄτε
δεῖπνον
ἐλπίς
θύρᾱ
καίπερ
καλέω
ξενίᾱ
ξένος
ὡς (*particle + ptcple.*)

LESSON 24 READING

βαβαί
δειπνέω
κέρκος
κύων
μάγειρος
πῑνω
πῶς
σείω

LESSON 25

ἀεί
διδάσκαλος
διδάσκω
δόξα
μέγας
παιδίον
παῖς
παύω
πολλάκις
σῶμα

LESSON 25 READING

βάτραχος
δειλός
κρημνός
κτύπος
λαγωός

LESSON 26

ἆρα (ἆρ᾽)
εἰ (+ *indir. q′tion.*)
εἴτε…εἴτε
μῶν (μὴ οὖν)
ὁπόθεν (*interrog.*)
ὅποι (*interrog.*)
ὁπότε (*interrog.*)
ὅπου (*interrog.*)
ὅπως (*interrog.*)
ὅστις
οὐκοῦν
ὀφθαλμός
πόθεν/ποθέν
ποῖ/ποι
πότε/ποτέ (πότ᾽/ποτ᾽, πόθ᾽/ποθ᾽)
πότερον/πότερα…ἤ
ποῦ/που
πῶς/πως

LESSON 26 READING

ἁμαρτωλός
ἀνοίγω
Ἰησοῦς
νίζω
οἶδα
πηλός
προφήτης
σάββατον
σημεῖον
σχίσμα
τηρέω
τυφλός
Φαρισαῖοι
χρίω

LESSON 27

ἀνοίγω
ἀποκρίνω
ἄρτι
ἤδη
ἡλικίᾱ
κρίνω

νέος
πάλαι
παλαιός
τυφλός
υἱός

LESSON 27 READING

ἁμαρτωλός
γεννάω
γίγνομαι
γονεύς
Ἰησοῦς
οἶδα
Φαρισαῖοι

LESSON 28

ἁμαρτάνω
ἁμαρτίᾱ
γεννάω
κόσμος
κύριος
μήποτε
μήπω
οἶδα
ὅτι
οὔποτε
οὔπω
πιστεύω

LESSON 28 READING

αἰών
ἁμαρτωλός
γίγνομαι
ἐκβάλλω
ἔρχομαι
θαυμάζω
θεοσεβής
Ἰησοῦς
κρίμα
λοιδορέω
Μωϋσῆς
προσκυνέω

LESSON 29

ἄστυ
βασιλεύς
ἑσπέρᾱ
θόρυβος
θυγάτηρ
μήτηρ
πατήρ
πόλις
πρύτανις
στρατηγός

LESSON 29 READING

ἀναγκαῖος
βουλευτήριον
βουλή
δύναμις
ἐκκλησίᾱ
Ἐλάτεια
ἐξείργω
ἔρχομαι
εὐθύς
καταλαμβάνω
μεταπέμπω
ὅμως
πλήρης
σαλπιγκτής
συμβαίνω
ὑστεραῖος
Φίλιππος

LESSON 30

ἀνήρ
ἀφικνέομαι
βουλή
βούλομαι
εἷς
ἐκκλησίᾱ
κῆρυξ
κοινός
μηδείς
οὐδείς
πατρίς
φωνή

LESSON 30 READING

ἀγορεύω
ἀνίστημι
ἀπαγγέλλω
εὔνους
καιρός
νομίζω
ὀρθῶς
παρακολουθέω
πάρειμι
παρέρχομαι
πλούσιος
πρᾶγμα
προσαγγέλλω
συλλογίζομαι
σωτηρίᾱ
φαίνω
Φίλιππος

LESSON 31

αἰσχρός
ζάω
οὕτω(ς)
ῥᾴδιος
τοιόσδε
τοιοῦτος
τοσόσδε
τοσοῦτος
ὧδε
ὡς (exclam. adv.)
ὥστε

LESSON 31 READING

ἀγωνίζομαι
Ἀθηναῖος
ἁλίσκομαι
ἀναγκαῖος
ἀποδειλιάω
δοκέω
ἐκτίνω
ἐνδεής
Ἐπιγένης
ἐπιτίμιον
ἰδιώτης

ἰδιωτικός
καταφρονέω
καχεξίᾱ
μᾶλλον
Ὀλυμπίᾱ

LESSON 32

ἀλλὰ μήν
γίγνομαι
δεινός
ἤ (+ *comp.*)
καὶ μήν
καὶ τὰ λοιπά (κτλ.)
λοιπός
μάλιστα
μᾶλλον
μήν
ὅτι (+ *superl.*)
παλαίτατος
παλαίτερος
πρῶτος
σῴζω
τοῦ λοιποῦ
φίλτατος/φιλαίτατος
φίλτερος/φιλαίτερος
ὡς (+ *superl.*)

LESSON 32 READING

ἀφορμή
διανοέομαι
διαφέρω
διότι
εὐεξίᾱ
εὐσχήμων
ἰσχύω
καταλείπω
καταφρονέω
καχεξίᾱ
σφάλλω
ὑγιαίνω
ὑγιεινός
φαίνω
χρείᾱ
χρήσιμος

LESSON 33

αἴσχιστος
αἰσχίων
ἀμείνων
ἄριστος
βέλτιστος
βελτίων
ἐλάττων
ἐλάχιστος
ἔχθιστος
ἐχθίων
ἥδιστος
ἡδίων
ἡδύς
ἥκιστος
ἥττων
κάκιστος
κακίων
κάλλιστος
καλλίων
κράτιστος
κρείττων
μάλα
μέγιστος
μείζων
ὀλίγιστος
πλεῖστος
πλείων/πλέων
ῥᾷστος
ῥᾴων
χείριστος
χείρων

LESSON 33 READING

Ἀθήνηθεν
Ἀθήνησι(ν)
ἀμέλεια
ἀμελέω
ἀναπαύω
ἀριστάω
αὐτόματος
γηράσκω
δειπνέω
ἐκεῖσε

ἐκτείνων
ἕξ
ἐξορμάω
Ἐπιγένης
μέτριος
μηκΰνω
οἴκοι
Ὀλυμπίᾱ
ὁρμή
πέντε
περιπατέω
περίπατος
πορείᾱ
πορεύω
σχεδόν
ὑστερίζω

LESSON 34

ἅπαξ
ἀριθμός
δέκα
δέκατος
δεύτερος
δίς
δύο
δώδεκα
δωδέκατος
ἕβδομος
εἴκοσι(ν)
ἑκατόν
ἕκτος
ἔνατος
ἕνδεκα
ἑνδέκατος
ἐννέα
ἕξ
ἑπτά
μΰριοι
ὄγδοος
ὀκτώ
πέμπτος
πέντε
τέταρτος
τέτταρες

τρεῖς
τρίς
τρίτος
χίλιοι

LESSON 34 READING

Ἀθηναῖος
δαπάνη
δίδωμι
ἐκπλέω
ἐξαρτΰω
Ἐπίδαυρος
ἐπιφορά
εὐπρεπής
θρᾱνίτης
ἱππεύς
κενός
ναῦς
ναύτης
ὁπλῑταγωγός
ὁπλίτης
παρασκευάζω
παρασκευή
Περικλῆς
πολυτελής
σύμμαχος
συμπλέω
στόλος
τριήραρχος
ὑπηρεσίᾱ

LESSON 35

ἀργύριον
ἄργυρος
μάχη
μάχομαι
παρασκευάζω
παρασκευή
σύμμαχος
χρῆμα
χρῡσίον
χρῡσός
φαίνω
φανερός

LESSON 35 READING

᾽Αθηναῖος
ἀσφαλής
αὑτοῦ
δυνατός
θαρρέω
᾽Ιταλιώτης
Καρχηδόνιος
κῑνέω
Κόρινθος
κρύφα
Λακεδαίμων
πειράω
πλοῦς
πρέσβυς
Σικελίᾱ
Σικελός
συμμαχίᾱ
ταχύς
φιλίᾱ
χρήσιμος

LESSON 36

ἄν (+ potential optative)
εἰ γάρ
εἴθε (εἴθ᾽)
ἕτοιμος
ἱκανός
νίκη
στρατιά
στρατιώτης
στρατόπεδον
στρατός
χράομαι
χρήσιμος

LESSON 36 READING

ἄλλοτε
ἀμῡνω
ἀπορίᾱ
ἀσθενής
ἐπιστήμη
θάρρος
μιμνῄσκω

πανδημεί
παραίνεσις
παρέχω
πρόθῡμος
Σικελιώτης
τόλμη
ὑπερφρονέω
φίλιος

LESSON 37

ἀδικέω
ἀδικίᾱ
ἄδικος
᾽Αθηναῖος
ἄν (in conditions)
ἄν
διαφθείρω
δίκαιος
δίκη
ἐάν
εἰ (introducing conditions)
ἤν
ἴσος
νῑκάω
φύσις

LESSON 37 READING

ἆθλον
αὖ
γνώμη
δειλίᾱ
εὔλογος
θεραπεύω
παρέχω
πρόφασις
συγγενής
συμμαχίᾱ
συμμάχομαι

LESSON 38

ἄρχω
ἄρχων
ἐπάν
ἐπειδάν

ἐπήν
θῡμός
ὅθεν
οἶ
ὁπόθεν (*indef. rel. adv.*)
ὅποι (*indef. rel. adv.*)
ὁπόταν
ὁπότε (*indef. rel. adv.*)
ὅπου (*indef. rel. adv.*)
ὅπως (*indef. rel. adv.*)
ὅταν
ὅτε (ὅτ'/ὅθ')
οὗ
προθῡμίᾱ
πρόθῡμος
ὡς (*rel. adv.*)

LESSON 38 READING

ἄλογος
ἀνανέωσις
ἀνίημι
ἀντέχω
ἐκβάλλω
ἐπιβουλεύω
καιρός
μόριον
ναυτικός
συμμαχίᾱ
Σῡρᾱκόσιος
τύραννος
ὕποπτος

LESSON 39

ἄνω
βοάω
βοή
γαμέω
γάμος
γυνή
ἕπομαι
ἵνα (μή) (+ *purp. cl.*)
κάτω
κλῖμαξ
μή (+ *neg. purp. cl.*)

ὅπως (μή) (+ *purp. cl.*)
ὕστατος
ὕστερος
ὡς (μή) (+ *purp. cl.*)

LESSON 39 READING

ἀγρός
ἀπροσδόκητος
διαιτάω
διπλοῦς
δοκέω
ἐκφορᾱ́
ἔνδον
θηλάζω
καταβαίνω
κινδῡνεύω
οἰκίδιον
οἰκονόμος
ὑποπτεύω
φειδωλός

LESSON 40

αἱρέω
εἶμι
ἔνδον
ἔξω
ἐπιτήδειος
ἔρχομαι
εὐθύς
ὅτι (*conj. + indir. discourse*)
πάσχω
φράζω
ὡς (*conj. + indir. discourse*)
ὡς (*prep.*)

LESSON 40 READING

γυμνός
δᾷς
εἰσέρχομαι
ἐξέρχομαι
ἐπεγείρω
ἐπιδημέω
Ἐρατοσθένης
κατάκειμαι

μαστῑγόω
οἴκαδε
ὁπότερος
ὅτι (*quotation mark*)
σῑγή
συγγνώμη
τυγχάνω

LESSON 41

ἀγαπάω
ἀγάπη
βραδύς
ἑταίρᾱ
ἑταῖρος
μνᾶ
νομίζω
τάλαντον
ταχύς
φημί
φιλίᾱ

LESSON 41 READING

Ἀλέξανδρος
ἀπαγγέλλω
αὖθις
Δαρεῖος
δέομαι
ἐντός
Εὐφρᾱ́της
Παρμενίων
πρέσβυς
σύλλογος

LESSON 42

αἰσθάνομαι
αὖ
αὖθις
γέρων
γραῦς
μανθάνω
πρᾶγμα
πυνθάνομαι
σωφροσύνη

σώφρων
χείρ

LESSON 42 READING

Ἀλέξανδρος
ἀμελέω
ἀνατείνω
Ἀσίᾱ
Δαρεῖος
εὐνοῦχος
εὔχομαι
Ζεύς
θεραπείᾱ
κράτος
Μῆδος
νέμω
παραδίδωμι
Πέρσης
σωφρονέω
ὑβρίζω

LESSON 43

ἀναγκαῖος
ἀνάγκη
ἀρετή
δεῖ
δοκέω
ἔξεστι(ν)
πολίτης
πρίν
σχολή
χρή

LESSON 43 READING

ἀσχολέομαι
ἄσχολος
ἐνέργεια
εὐδαιμονίᾱ
θεωρέω
θεωρίᾱ
κάλλος
μέγεθος
νοῦς

περιποιέω
πολεμέω
πολεμικός
πολῑτεύω
πολῑτικός
πρᾱκτικός
πρᾶξις
προέχω
τέλειος

LESSON 44

αἰσχύνω
δή
ἐλαύνω
θαυμάζω
κενός
μέντοι
στάδιον
τοι
τοίνυν
χορός

LESSON 44 READING

ἀγοράζω
ἀντί
ἀπελαύνω
ἀτῑμίᾱ
γυμνάζω
ἐπίκλησις
ἐπονείδιστος
εὐδαιμονίᾱ
ᾖ
κάθημαι
κακοδαιμονίᾱ
κατεργάζομαι
Λακεδαίμων
Λυκοῦργος
μηχανάομαι
μῑμέομαι
πάλαισμα
παραλαμβάνω
παραλείπω
παραχωρέω
περιοράω

πληγή
συγγυμναστής
σύσκηνος

LESSON 45

βουλεύω
δέδοικα
ἐπιμελέομαι
ἐσθίω
καθεύδω
μή (οὐ) (+ *fear cl.*)
μηχανάομαι
μηχανή
ὅπως (μή) (+ *effort cl.*)
σῖτος
σκοπέω
ὕπνος
ὡς (μή) (+ *effort cl.*)

LESSON 45 READING

ἅμα
ἀναμάρτητος
ἀπεχθάνομαι
ἀπιστέω
ἀποβάλλω
δουλείᾱ
ἔνιοι
ἐπιτίθημι
ζημιόω
ζυγόν
καταπλήττω
Κῦρος
οἷος
παραδίδωμι
προαποθνήσκω
σωφρονίζω
ὑβρίζω
φόρημα
φυγάς

LESSON 46

δίδωμι
ἐπίσταμαι

ἐπιστήμη

ἵστημι

οἷος

οἷος τε

ὁποῖος

ὁπόσος

ὅσος

ποῖος

ποιός

πόσος

ποσός

τέχνη

ὠνέομαι

LESSON 46 READING

ἀγέλη

ἀκολουθέω

ἀποδίδωμι

ἄρα

ἄρρην

γελοῖος

γένεσις

γυμνάζω

γυμναστική

γυμνός

ἔθος

ἐπιχειρέω

Ζεύς

ἦ

θῆλυς

καθίστημι

καὶ μάλα

κύων

μουσική

ναί

νή

οἴομαι

παιδείᾱ

παλαίστρᾱ

παραπλήσιος

παρίστημι

πρέπει

συμφυλάττω

συνθηρεύω

τροφή

LESSON 47

ἄνπερ

ἄρα

ἀφίημι

γονεύς

δύναμαι

δύναμις

δυνατός

ἐάνπερ

εἴπερ

ἡμί

ἤνπερ

ἵημι

κεῖμαι

κῦμα

μεθίημι

ὅσπερ

παρίημι

περ/-περ

τίθημι

ὥσπερ

LESSON 47 READING

ἀναβάλλω

ἀπιστίᾱ

γυναικεῖος

διατάττω

διαφεύγω

ἔκγονος

ἐπιθῡμέω

ἐπιτηδεύω

ἦ

ἴδιος

κατακλύζω

μαλθακίζω

πειράω

σύμφορος

συνοικέω

φυλακίς

ὠφέλιμος

LESSON 48

ἀποδείκνῡμι
γένος
δείκνῡμι
ἕνεκα
ἥλιος (Ἥλιος)
κύων
οἴομαι
ὅμοιος
ὁμολογέω
ὀφείλω
πάνυ
παράδειγμα

LESSON 48 READING

ἀναγκάζω
ἀνθρώπινος
ἀποβλέπω
βασιλεύω
Γλαύκων
δικαιοσύνη
Ζεύς
ζωγράφος
μά
οἰκέω
παῦλα
πολῑτείᾱ
τέλεος
φιλοσοφέω
φύω
φῶς

LESSON 49

Ἀθῆναι
Ἀθήνησι(ν), Ἀθήνηθεν, Ἀθήναζε
ἀλλήλων
ἄλλοθι, ἄλλοθεν, ἄλλοσε
ἀναγιγνώσκω
βαίνω
γιγνώσκω
δεῦρο
ἕκαστος

ἐκεῖ, ἐκεῖθεν, ἐκεῖσε
ἔνθα
ἐνθάδε, ἐνθένδε
ἐνταῦθα, ἐντεῦθεν
ἕτερος
μιμνήσκω
οἴκοι, οἴκαδε, οἴκοθεν
οἶκος
ὁμός
ὁμοῦ, ὁμόθεν, ὁμόσε
πίπτω

LESSON 49 READING

ἀδαμάντινος
Ἅιδης
ἀναιρέω
ἀνέκπληκτος
ἀνέρχομαι
ἀσπάζομαι
αὐχμός
Γλαύκων
διηγέομαι
δικαστής
ἐμπίπτω
εὐπάθεια
ἥκω
θέᾱ
θεάομαι
καθαρός
κάλλος
καταβαίνω
κλῆρος
κόνις
μέσος
μεστός
πλοῦτος
πορείᾱ
πρᾶξις
προσέρχομαι
προφήτης
τυραννίς
ὑπερβάλλω
χάσμα

LESSON 50

ἐπιλανθάνομαι
ἕως
κωλύω
λανθάνω
μέχρι
νοῦς
ὄρος
πεδίον
πίνω
ποῦς
τρέχω
τυγχάνω
τύχη (Τύχη)
ὕδωρ
χαλεπός
ψευδής

LESSON 50 READING

ἆθλον
ἄλλη
ἀναβλέπω
ἀστήρ
ἄτρακτος
Ἄτροπος
βροντή
γένεσις
Γλαύκων
δικαιοσύνη
ἐξαίφνης
ἐπιτηδεύω
ἔωθεν
καῦμα
Κλωθώ
Λάχεσις
Λήθη
μέτρον
μῦθος
νῆσις
πνῖγος
πορείᾱ
πορεύω
προσέρχομαι
πυρά

σεισμός
σκηνάω
συμπέμπω
φρόνησις
χῑλιέτης

GREEK-TO-ENGLISH GLOSSARY

Lesson numbers appear in brackets; R means that the word is found in the reading rather than in the vocabulary.

ἀγαθός, -ή, -όν good (*at doing a thing*), brave, (*morally*) good, virtuous [8]

ἄγαλμα, -ατος, τό statue (*of a god*) [R18]

ἀγαλματοποιός, -οῦ, ὁ sculptor [R18]

ἀγαπάω, ἀγαπήσω, ἠγάπησα, ἠγάπηκα, ἠγάπημαι, ἠγαπήθην love; (+ *infin. or suppl. ptcple.*) be fond of (*doing*), be content (to) [41]

ἀγάπη, -ης, ἡ love [41]

ἀγγέλλω, ἀγγελῶ, ἤγγειλα, ἤγγελκα, ἤγγελμαι, ἠγγέλθην announce, report [18]

ἄγγελος, -ου, ὁ, ἡ messenger [18]

ἄγε (*imper. of* ἄγω–*strengthens another imperative*) come on now! [40]

ἀγέλη, -ης, ἡ herd [R46]

ἀγνοέω, ἀγνοήσω, ἠγνόησα, ἠγνόηκα, ἠγνόημαι, ἠγνοήθην not know, be ignorant of [R5]

ἀγορά, -ᾶς, ἡ marketplace, market [4]

ἀγοράζω, ἀγοράσω, ἠγόρασα, ἠγόρακα, ἠγόρασμαι, ἠγοράσθην be in the marketplace, shop [R44]

ἀγορεύω, ἀγορεύσω, ἠγόρευσα, ἠγόρευκα, ἠγόρευμαι, ἠγρορεύθην speak in the assembly [R30]

ἀγρός, -οῦ, ὁ countryside [R39]

ἄγω, ἄξω, ἤγαγον, ἦχα, ἦγμαι, ἤχθην lead [22]

ἀγών, -ῶνος, ὁ contest, competition, struggle; ἀγῶνα ἔχειν = hold a contest [16]

ἀγωνίζομαι, ἀγωνιοῦμαι, ἠγωνισάμην, —, ἠγώνισμαι, ἠγωνίσθην compete [R31]

ἀδαμάντινος, -ον firm, determined [R49]

ἄδειπνος, -ον unfed [R19]

ἀδελφή, -ῆς, ἡ sister [7]

ἀδελφός, -οῦ (*voc. sg.* ἄδελφε), ὁ brother [7]

ἀδικέω, ἀδικήσω, ἠδίκησα, ἠδίκηκα, ἠδίκημαι, ἠδικήθην be unjust, do wrong, injure [37]

ἀδικίᾱ, -ᾱς, ἡ injustice, wrong, injury [37]

ἄδικος, -ον unjust, wrong [37]

ἀεί (*adv.*) always, ever [25]

ἀθάνατος, -ον immortal, undying [9]

Ἀθήναζε (*adv.*) to Athens [49]

Ἀθῆναι, -ῶν, αἱ Athens [49]

Ἀθηναῖος, -ᾱ, -ον Athenian [R31, R34, R35, 37]

Ἀθήνηθεν (*adv.*) from Athens [R33, 49]

Ἀθήνησι(ν) (*adv.*) in Athens, at Athens [R33, 49]

ἆθλον, -ου, τό prize, reward [R37, R50]

Ἅιδης, -ου, ὁ Hades (*god of the underworld*) [R49]

αἰδώς, -οῦς, ἡ shame (*either good or bad sense*), modesty, respect [17]

αἴθυια, -ᾱς, ἡ seagull [R23]

αἴλουρος (= αἰόλος + οὐρά), -ου, ὁ, ἡ cat [R19]

αἱρέω, αἱρήσω, εἷλον (*stem* = ἑλ-), ᾕρηκα, ᾕρημαι, ᾑρέθην take; (*mid.*) choose [40]

αἰσθάνομαι, αἰσθήσομαι, ᾐσθόμην, —, ᾔσθημαι, — (+ *acc./gen. or ptcple., infin., or* ὅτι/ὡς *clause in indir. disc.*) perceive, sense [42]

αἴσχιστος, -η, -ον (*superl. of* αἰσχρός, -ά, -όν) most shameful, most disgraceful [33]

αἰσχίων, -ῑον (*comp. of* αἰσχρός, -ά, -όν) more shameful, more disgraceful [33]

αἰσχρός, -ά, -όν shameful, disgraceful [31]

αἰσχύνω, αἰσχυνῶ, ᾔσχῡνα, —, —, ᾐσχύνθην disgrace; (*mid.*) feel ashamed, be ashamed [44]

αἰτίᾱ, -ᾱς, ἡ blame, guilt, responsibility, accusation, charge, cause [19]

αἴτιος, -ᾱ, -ον blameworthy; (+ *gen.*) guilty (of), responsible (for) [19]

αἰών, -ῶνος, ὁ span of time, age [R28]

ἀκολουθέω, ἀκολουθήσω, ἠκολούθησα, ἠκολούθηκα, —, — (+ *dat.*) follow [R46]

ἀκούω, ἀκούσομαι, ἤκουσα, ἀκήκοα, —, ἠκούσθην (+ *gen. of person heard or acc. of thing heard*) hear, listen, listen to [5]

ἀλεκτρυών, -όνος, ὁ rooster [R5, R19]

Ἀλέξανδρος, -ου, ὁ Alexander the Great (*4th-century B.C. king of Macedonia, son of Philip II*) [R41, R42]

ἀλήθεια, -ᾱς, ἡ truth [10]

(τῇ) ἀληθείᾳ in truth, truly, really [10]

ἀληθής, -ές true, real, sincere [17]

ἁλιεύς, -έως, ὁ fisherman [R7]

ἁλίσκομαι, ἁλώσομαι, ἑάλων, ἑάλωκα, —, — be captured [R31]

ἀλλ᾽ see ἀλλά

ἀλλά (ἀλλ᾽) (*conj.*) but [6]

ἀλλὰ μήν but yet [32]

ἀλλάττω, ἀλλάξω, ἤλλαξα, ἤλλαχα, ἤλλαγμαι, ἠλλάχθην/ἠλλάγην change, alter [6]; (*mid.* + *acc., gen.*) take (*something*) in exchange for (*something*) [11]

ἄλλῃ (*adv.*) to another place (*dat. fem. sg. of* ἄλλος, -η, -ο) [R50]

ἀλλήλων, -οις/αις, -ους/ᾱς/α (*reciprocal pron.*) of one another, to one another, one another [49]

ἄλλοθεν (*adv.*) from another place [49]

ἄλλοθι (*adv.*) at another place, in another place [49]

(οἱ) ἄλλοι the others, the rest [22]

ἄλλος, -η, -ο other, another [22]

ἄλλοσε (*adv.*) to another place [49]

ἄλλοτε (*adv.*) at another time [R36]

ἄλογος, -ον illogical [R38]

ἀλώπηξ, -εκος, ἡ fox [R17, R20, R22]

ἅμα (*adv.*) at the same time [R45]

ἅμαξα, -ης, ἡ cart, wagon [11]

ἁμαρτάνω, ἁμαρτήσομαι, ἥμαρτον, ἡμάρτηκα, ἡμάρτημαι, ἡμαρτήθην make a mistake, fail, err, sin; (+ *gen.*) miss (a *target*), miss out on [28]

ἁμαρτίᾱ, -ᾱς, ἡ mistake, failure, error, sin [28]

ἁμαρτωλός, -όν sinful [R26, R27, R28]

ἀμείνων, -ον (*comp. of* ἀγαθός, -ή, -όν) better (*in ability or worth*) [33]

ἀμέλεια, -ᾱς, ἡ negligence [R33]

ἀμελέω, ἀμελήσω, ἠμέλησα, ἠμέληκα, ἠμέλημαι, ἠμελήθην be negligent, neglect, overlook [R33, R42]

ἄμπελος, -ου, ἡ vineyard, vine [R8]

ἀμύνω, ἀμυνῶ, ἤμῡνα, —, —, — ward off; (*mid.*) defend oneself [R36]

ἀμφ᾽ *see* ἀμφί

ἀμφί (ἀμφ᾽) (*prep. + gen.*) about, concerning; (*prep. + acc.*) around (*basic meaning of* ἀμφί = on both sides of); ἀμφ᾽ *before a vowel* [23]

ἄν particle used with subjunctive in protasis of present general or future more vivid condition, with indicative in apodosis of contrary-to-fact condition, with optative in apodosis of future less vivid condition, or with potential optative [36, 37]

ἄν contraction of εἰ ἄν [37]

ἀν᾽ *see* ἀνά

ἀνά (ἀν᾽) (*prep. + acc.*) up, up along, by (*in various idioms*); ἀν᾽ *before a vowel* [23]

ἀνὰ πᾶσαν ἡμέρᾱν day by day, daily [23]

ἀναβάλλω put back; (*mid.*) postpone (*see* βάλλω) [R47]

ἀναβλέπω look up [R50]

ἀναγιγνώσκω read (*see* γιγνώσκω) [49]

ἀναγκάζω, ἀναγκάσω, ἠνάγκασα, ἠνάγκακα, ἠνάγκασμαι, ἠναγκάσθην force [R48]

ἀναγκαῖος, -ᾱ, -ον necessary; (*as a neut. pl. substantive*) necessities [R31, 43]

ἀναγκαιότατος, -η, -ον (*superl. of* ἀναγκαῖος, -ᾱ, -ον) most necessary [R29]

ἀνάγκη, -ης, ἡ necessity; (+ ἐστί & *dat. or acc.* + *infin.*) there is need (to), it is necessary (to), one must [43]

ἀναιρέω take up, pick up (*see* αἱρέω) [R49]

ἀναμάρτητος, -ον having done no wrong [R45]

ἀνανέωσις, -εως, ἡ renewal [R38]

ἀνάξιος, -ον worthless; (+ *gen. or infin.*) unworthy (of, to), not deserving (of, to) [9]

ἀναπαύω stop, bring to a stop; (*mid.*) take a rest [R33]

ἀνατείνω, ἀνατενῶ, ἀνέτεινα, ἀνατέτακα, ἀνατέταμαι, ἀνετάθην lift up [R42]

ἄνδρες, -ῶν, οἱ gentlemen (*vocative used in addressing an audience*) [R40]

ἀνέκπληκτος, -ον not dazzled, not awed [R49]

ἀνέρχομαι go up (*see* ἔρχομαι) [R49]

ἄνευ (*prep. + gen.*) without [24]

ἀνήρ, ἀνδρός, ὁ man, husband [30]

ἀνθρώπινος, -η, -ον human [R48]

ἄνθρωπος, -ου, ὁ, ἡ (*masc.*) human being, person, man, mankind, humankind; (*fem.*) woman, womankind [7]

ἀνίημι, ἀνήσω, ἀνῆκα, ἀνεῖκα, ἀνεῖμαι, ἀνείθην let go, pass up [R38]

ἀνίστημι, ἀναστήσω, ἀνέστησα/(intrans.)
ἀνέστην, (intrans.) ἀνέστηκα,
ἀνέσταμαι, ἀνεστάθην (fut. perf.
intrans. ἀνεστήξω), make stand up;
(intrans. forms) stand up [R30]

ἀνοίγω/ἀνοίγνῡμι (imperf. ἀνέῳγον),
ἀνοίξω, ἀνέῳξα, ἀνέῳχα, ἀνέῳγμαι,
ἀνεῴχθην open, open up [R26, 27]

ἄνπερ if (ever) indeed [47]

ἀντέχω (+ dat.) hold out (against), resist
(see ἔχω) [R38]

ἀντί (prep. + gen.) in place of [R44]

ἄνω (adv.) up, upwards [39]; τὰ ἄνω the
upstairs [R39]

ἄξιος, -ᾱ, -ον worthy; (+ gen. or infin.)
worthy (of, to), deserving (of, to)
[8]

ἀπ' see ἀπό

ἀπαγγέλλω report back (see ἀγγέλλω)
[R30]

ἅπαξ (adv.) once [34]

ἀπελαύνω drive back [R44]

ἀπεχθάνομαι, ἀπεχθήσομαι, ἀπηχθόμην, —,
ἀπήχθημαι, — (+ dat.) become
hateful (to) [R45]

ἀπιστέω, ἀπιστήσω, ἠπίστησα, ἠπίστηκα,
ἠπίστημαι, ἠπιστήθην (+ dat.) distrust
[R45]

ἀπιστίᾱ, -ᾱς, ἡ disbelief, doubt [R47]

ἀπό (ἀπ', ἀφ') (prep. + gen.) away from; ἀπ'
before smooth breathing, ἀφ' before
rough breathing [7]

ἀποβάλλω cast aside, reject [R45]

ἀποβλέπω (with εἰς + acc.) gaze upon (see
βλέπω) [R48]

ἀποδείκνῡμι demonstrate, prove (see
δείκνῡμι) [48]

ἀποδειλιάω, ἀποδειλιάσω, —, —, —, — be
a coward [R31]

ἀποδίδωμι give back, assign (see δίδωμι)
[R46]

ἀποθνῄσκω, ἀποθανοῦμαι, ἀπέθανον,
τέθνηκα (fut. perf. τεθνήξω), —, —
die, be killed [21]

ἀποκρίνω separate, choose; (mid. + dat.)
answer, reply (see κρίνω) [27]

ἀποκτείνω, ἀποκτενῶ, ἀπέκτεινα, ἀπέκτονα,
—, — kill [21]

ἀπολείπω leave, leave behind, abandon
(see λείπω) [8]

ἀποπέμπω send away (see πέμπω) [R12]

ἀπορίᾱ, -ᾱς, ἡ difficulty, desperate
situation [R36]

ἀπροσδόκητος, -ον unexpected [R39]

ἆρ' see ἆρα

ἆρ' οὐ introduces a question expecting
the answer "yes" [26]

ἄρα (postpos. particle) therefore, then;
never elided [R46, 47]

ἆρα (ἆρ') (interrog. particle ἦ + inferential
particle ἄρα) introduces a question
not expecting a particular answer;
ἆρ' before a vowel [26]

ἆρα μή introduces a question expecting
the answer "no" [26]

ἀργύριον, -ου, τό piece of silver; (pl.)
money, cash [35]

ἄργυρος, -ου, ὁ silver [35]

ἀρετή, -ῆς, ἡ virtue, excellence [43]

ἀριθμός, -οῦ, ὁ number [34]

ἀριστάω, ἀριστήσω, ἠρίστησα, ἠρίστηκα,
ἠρίστημαι, ἠριστήθην eat lunch [R33]

ἄριστος, -η, -ον (superl. of ἀγαθός, -ή, -όν)
best (in ability or worth) [33]

ἄρκτος, -ου, ὁ, ἡ bear [R10]

ἁρπάζω, ἁρπάσω, ἥρπασα, ἥρπακα,
ἥρπασμαι, ἡρπάσθην seize, snatch,
plunder [15]

ἄρρην, -εν male, masculine [R46]

ἄρτι (*adv.*) just now [27]

ἀρχή, -ῆς, ἡ beginning, power, rule, political office [12]

ἄρχω, ἄρξω, ἦρξα, ἦρχα, ἦργμαι, ἤρχθην (+ *gen.*) rule; (+ *gen.*) make begin; (*mid. + gen., infin., or ptcple.*) begin [38]

ἄρχων, -οντος, ὁ archon (*one of the nine chief magistrates of Athens*) [38]

ἀσθενής, -ές weak [R36]

Ἀσίᾱ, -ᾱς, ἡ Asia [R42]

ἀσπάζομαι, ἀσπάσομαι, ἠσπασάμην, —, —, — greet [R49]

ἀσπίς, -ίδος, ἡ shield [16]

ἀστήρ, -έρος, ὁ star [R50]

ἄστυ, -εως, τό city [29]

ἀσφαλής, -ές safe [R35]

ἀσχολέομαι, ἀσχολήσομαι, ἠσχολησάμην, —, ἠσχόλημαι, ἠσχολήθην engage in business [R43]

ἄσχολος, -ον unleisured [R43]

ἄτε (*particle + ptcple.*) because [24]

ἀτῑμίᾱ, -ᾱς, ἡ dishonor [R44]

ἄτρακτος, -ου, ὁ spindle [R50]

Ἄτροπος, -ου, ἡ Atropos (*one of the three Fates*) [R50]

ἄττα (= τινά) *see* τις, τι

ἄττα (= ἄτινα) *see* ὅστις, ἥτις, ὅτι

αὖ (*adv.*) again, further, on the other hand, in turn [R37, 42]

αὖθις (*adv.*) again, further, on the other hand, in turn [R41, 42]

αὐτόματος, -η, -ον self-acting, automatic [R33]

αὐτός, -ή, -ό same; (*intens. adj.*) -self, the very; (*pers. pron.*) him, her, it, them [14]

αὐτοῦ (*adv.*) at the very place, here, there [R35]

αὑτοῦ, -ῆς, -οῦ *see* ἑαυτοῦ, -ῆς, -οῦ

αὕτως (*adv. of* αὐτός, -ή, -όν; *irreg. accent*) in this very way [31]

αὐχμός, -οῦ, ὁ crud, dirt [R49]

ἀφ᾽ *see* ἀπό

ἀφίημι throw away, send away, dismiss (*see* ἵημι) [47]

ἀφικνέομαι, ἀφίξομαι, ἀφῑκόμην, —, ἀφῖγμαι, — (*with* ἐπί *or* εἰς + *acc.*) arrive (at), come (to) [30]

ἀφορμή, -ῆς, ἡ starting-point, resource [R32]

Ἀφροδίτη, -ης, ἡ Aphrodite (*goddess of love*) [R6]

βαβαί (*exclamation of surprise or amazement*) wow! [R24]

βαίνω, βήσομαι, ἔβην, βέβηκα, —, — walk, step, go [49]

βάλλω, βαλῶ, ἔβαλον, βέβληκα, —, — throw, hit (*with a thrown weapon*), shoot [15]

βασιλεύς, -έως, ὁ king [R22, 29]

βασιλεύω, βασιλεύσω, ἐβασίλευσα, βεβασίλευκα, βεβασίλευμαι, ἐβασιλεύθην be king, rule [R48]

βάτος, -ου, ἡ bramble bush [R23]

βάτραχος, -ου, ὁ frog [R11, R25]

βέλτιστος, -η, -ον (*superl. of* ἀγαθός, -ή, -όν) best (*morally*), most virtuous [33]

βελτίων, -ιον (*comp. of* ἀγαθός, -ή, -όν) better (*morally*), more virtuous [33]

βιβλίον, -ου, τό book [14]

βίον ἄγειν lead a life [22]

βίος, -ου, ὁ life, lifetime, livelihood [8]

βλάπτω, βλάψω, ἔβλαψα, βέβλαφα, βέβλαμμαι, ἐβλάφθην/ἐβλάβην harm, hurt [5] βλέπω, βλέψομαι, ἔβλεψα, βέβλεφα, βέβλεμμαι, ἐβλέφθην see, behold; (*with* εἰς + *acc.*) look (at) [R7, R9, R10, 13]

βοάω, βοήσομαι, ἐβόησα, —, —, — cry, cry out, shout [39]

βοή, -ῆς, ἡ shout [39]

βούλευμα, -ατος, τό plan [R5]

βουλευτήριον, -ου, τό council-chamber [R29]

βουλεύω, βουλεύσω, ἐβούλευσα, βεβούλευκα, βεβούλευμαι, ἐβουλεύθην (+ *infin. or effort clause— often in middle voice*) take counsel (to), plan (to), decide (to), deliberate [45]

βουλή, -ῆς, ἡ plan, counsel, council (*a group of 500 citizens, 50 from each of the 10 tribes, chosen by lot to serve as Athens' senate for a year*) [R29, 30]

βούλομαι, βουλήσομαι, —, —, βεβούλημαι, ἐβουλήθην (+ *infin.*) wish (to), desire (to), prefer (to) [30]

βραδύς, -εῖα, -ύ slow [41]

βραδύτατος, -η, -ον (*superl. of* βραδύς, -εῖα, -ύ) slowest [41]

βραδύτερος, -ᾱ, -ον (*comp. of* βραδύς, -εῖα, -ύ) slower [41]

βροντή, -ῆς, ἡ thunder [R50]

βυρσοδέψης (= βύρσᾱ + δέψω), -ου, ὁ tanner [R9]

γ᾽ *see* γε

γαλῆ (= γαλέη), -ῆς, ἡ weasel [R6]

γαμέω, γαμῶ, ἔγημα, γεγάμηκα, γεγάμημαι, ἐγαμήθην take (*a woman*) as a wife, marry (*a woman*); (*mid.* + *dat.*) give oneself in marriage (*to a man*), marry (*a man*) [R6, 39]

γάμον ποιεῖν hold a wedding [39]

γάμος, -ου, ὁ marriage, wedding [39]

γάρ (*postpos. conj. introducing an explanation*) for, for indeed [13]

γε (γ᾽) (*enclitic particle*) at least, at any rate; γ᾽ *before a vowel* [12]

γελάω, γελάσομαι, ἐγέλασα, —, —, ἐγελάσθην laugh; (*with* ἐπί + *dat.*) laugh at, ridicule [15]

γελοῖος, -ᾱ, -ον laughable, ridiculous [R46]

γένεσις, -εως, ἡ birth [R46, R50]

γεννάω, γεννήσω, ἐγέννησα, γεγέννηκα, γεγέννημαι, ἐγεννήθην beget, give birth to, bear [R27, 28]

γένος, -ους, τό race, birth, class, type, kind [48]

γέρας, -ως, τό prize, privilege [17]

γέρων, -οντος, ὁ old man [R16, 42]

γεωργός (= γῆ + ἔργον), -οῦ, ὁ farmer [R8, R13]

γῆ (= γέᾱ), γῆς, γῇ, γῆν, ἡ (*rarely plural*) earth, ground, land; Γῆ = Earth (*personified as a goddess*) [20]

γῆρας, -ως, τό old age [R17]

γηράσκω, γηράσομαι, ἐγήρᾱσα, γεγήρᾱκα, —, — grow old [R33]

γίγνομαι, γενήσομαι, ἐγενόμην, γέγονα, γεγένημαι, — be born, become, happen [R14, R27, R28, 32]

γιγνώσκω, γνώσομαι, ἔγνων, ἔγνωκα, ἔγνωσμαι, ἐγνώσθην (*with indir. disc.* + *ptcple. or* ὅτι/ὡς) recognize, come to know, know (*by observing*); (+ *complem. infin.*) know how (to) [49]

Γλαύκων, -ωνος, ὁ Glaucon (*one of Socrates' friends*) [R48, R49, R50]

γνώμη, -ης, ἡ judgment, opinion [R37]

γονεύς, -έως, ὁ father, ancestor; (*pl.*) parents [R27, 47]

γράφω, γράψω, ἔγραψα, γέγραφα, γέγραμμαι, ἐγράφην write, draw [3]; (*mid.*) indict [11] γραῦς, γρᾱός, ἡ old woman [42]

γυμνάζω, γυμνάσω, ἐγύμνασα, γεγύμνακα, γεγύμνασμαι, ἐγυμνάσθην train; (*mid.*) exercise (*in the nude*) [R44, R46]

γυμναστική, -ῆς, ἡ (*supply* τέχνη) athletics [R46]

γυμνός, -ή, -όν naked [R40, R46]

γυναικεῖος, -ᾱ, -ον having to do with women [R47]

γυνή, γυναικός (*voc. sg.* γύναι), ἡ woman, wife [39]

δ᾽ *see* δέ

δαίμων, -ονος, ὁ, ἡ divine being, guardian spirit [17]

δανειστής, -οῦ, ὁ money-lender [R23]

δαπάνη, -ης, ἡ expense [R34]

Δαρεῖος, -ου, ὁ Darius (*4th-century B.C. king of Persia*) [R41, R42]

δᾷς (= δαίς), δᾳδός, ἡ torch [R40]

δέ (δ᾽) (*postpos. conj.*) and, but; δ᾽ *before a vowel* [10]

δέδοικα/δέδια (*pluperf.* ἐδεδοίκη/ἐδεδίη), —, ἔδεισα, —, —, — (+ *acc.*) fear, be afraid of; (+ *infin. or fear cl.*) fear (to), be afraid (to) [45]

δεῖ (*imperf.* ἔδει), δεήσει, ἐδέησε(ν), —, —, — (+ *gen.*) there is need (of); (+ *acc. & infin.*) it is necessary (to), one must [R14, 43]

δείκνῡμι, δείξω, ἔδειξα, δέδειχα, δέδειγμαι, ἐδείχθην show, point out [48]

δειλίᾱ, -ᾱς, ἡ cowardice [R37]

δειλός, -ή, -όν cowardly, miserable (*comp.* δειλότερος, -ᾱ, -ον more cowardly) [R25]

δεινός, -ή, -όν terrible, dreadful, marvelous, clever [32]

δειπνέω, δειπνήσω, ἐδείπνησα, δεδείπνηκα, δεδείπνημαι, ἐδειπνήθην dine, eat dinner [R24, R33]

δεῖπνον, -ου, τό meal, dinner [24]

δέκα (*indecl. numeral*) ten [34]

δέκατος, -η, -ον tenth [34]

δένδρον, -ου, τό tree [20]

δέομαι, δεήσομαι, —, —, δεδέημαι, ἐδεήθην need, have need of (+ *gen.*) [R41]

δέσμη, -ης, ἡ bundle [R13]

δέσποινα, -ης, ἡ mistress (*of the household*), lady, Lady (*title for goddess*) [5]

δεσπότης, -ου (*voc. sg.* δέσποτα), ὁ master (*of the household*), lord, despot [9]

δεῦρο (*adv.*) to here, hither, to there, thither [49]

δεύτερος, -ᾱ, -ον second [34]

δή (*postpositive particle*) certainly, quite, indeed (*emphasizes preceding word— can be ironic*) [44]

δῆλα (*neut. acc. pl. of* δῆλος, -η, -ον *used as adv.*) clearly [31]

δῆλον (*neut. acc. sg. of* δῆλος, -η, -ον *used as adv.*) clearly [31]

δῆλος, -η, -ον clear, visible, evident [R8, 15]

δηλόω, δηλώσω, ἐδήλωσα, δεδήλωκα, δεδήλωμαι, ἐδηλώθην make clear, show, explain [15]

δι᾽ *see* διά

διά (δι᾽) (*prep.* + *gen.*) through, throughout; (*prep.* + *acc.*) on account of; δι᾽ *before a vowel* [12]

διανοέομαι, διανοήσομαι, —, —, διανενόημαι, διενοήθην think [R32]

διαιτάω (*imperf.* διῄτων), διαιτήσω, διῄτησα, δεδιῄτηκα, δεδιῄτημαι, διῃτήθην sup-port; (*mid./pass.*) lead a life, live [R39]

διανοέομαι, διανοήσομαι, —, —, διανενόημαι, διενοήθην think [R32]

διατάττω, διατάξω, διέταξα, διατέταχα, διατέταγμαι, διετάχθην/διετάγην arrange [R47]

διαφέρω differ, make a difference (see φέρω) [R32]

διαφεύγω flee through, escape (see φεύγω) [R47]

διαφθείρω, διαφθερῶ, διέφθειρα, διέφθαρκα/διέφθορα, διέφθαρμαι, διεφθάρην corrupt, ruin [37]

διδάσκαλος, -ου, ὁ, ἡ teacher, dramatist [25]

διδάσκω, διδάξω, ἐδίδαξα, δεδίδαχα, δεδίδαγμαι, ἐδιδάχθην teach [25]

δίδωμι, δώσω, ἔδωκα, δέδωκα, δέδομαι, ἐδόθην give [R34, 46]

διηγέομαι, διηγήσομαι, διηγησάμην, —, διήγημαι, — describe [R49]

δίκαιος, -ᾱ, -ον just, right [37]

δικαιοσύνη, -ης, ἡ justice [R48, R50]

δικαστής, -οῦ, ὁ judge [R49]

δίκη, -ης, ἡ justice, right, penalty, punishment, lawsuit [37]

δίκην διδόναι be punished [46]

δίκην λαμβάνειν παρά τινος punish someone [37]

δίκτυον, -ου, τό net (for hunting) [R15]

διότι because (contraction of διὰ τοῦθ᾽ ὅτι) [R32, R36]

διπλοῦς (= -όος), -ῆ, -οῦν double [R39]

δίς (adv.) twice [34]

διώκω, διώξω, ἐδίωξα, δεδίωχα, δεδίωγμαι, ἐδιώχθην pursue, chase, hunt, drive away, banish [6]

δοκέω, δόξω, ἔδοξα, —, δέδογμαι, ἐδόχθην (+ infin. in indir. disc.) think; (+ complem. infin.) seem (to); (third-pers. sg. impersonal + subj. infin.) it seems (to), it seems good (to) [R31, R39, 43]

δόξα, -ης, ἡ opinion, reputation, fame, glory [25]

δουλείᾱ, -ᾱς, ἡ slavery [R37, R45]

δουλεύω, δουλεύσω, ἐδούλευσα, δεδούλευκα, δεδούλευμαι, ἐδουλεύθην (+ dat.) be a slave (to), serve [9]

δούλη, -ης, ἡ slave (female) [9]

δοῦλος, -η, -ον enslaved [9]

δοῦλος, -ου, ὁ slave (male) [9]

δράκων, -οντος, ὁ snake [R21]

δραχμή, -ῆς, ἡ drachma (unit of money and weight = 6 obols) [18]

δύναμαι, δυνήσομαι, —, —, δεδύνημαι, ἐδυνήθην (verbal adj. δυνατός) (+ infin.) be powerful (enough to), be able (to), can [47]

δύναμις, -εως, ἡ power, force, strength, military force, troops [R29, 47]

δυνατός, -ή, -όν (+ infin.) powerful (enough to), able (to), possible (to) [R35, 47]

δύο (nom., acc., voc.), δυοῖν (gen., dat.) two [R10, R11, 34]

δώδεκα (indecl. numeral) twelve [34]

δωδέκατος, -η, -ον twelfth [34]

δῶρον, -ου, τό gift [8]

ἐάν contraction of εἰ ἄν [37]

ἐάνπερ if (ever) indeed [47]

ἑαυτοῦ, -ῆς, -οῦ (αὑτοῦ, -ῆς, -οῦ) (reflex. pron.) himself, herself, itself, themselves [19]

ἕβδομος, -η, -ον seventh [34]

ἐγώ (*pers. pron.*) I, me [14]

ἐθέλω, ἐθελήσω, ἠθέλησα, ἠθέληκα, —, — (+ *infin.*) be willing (to), wish (to) [3]

ἔθος, -ους, τό custom [R46]

εἰ (*conj. introducing an indir. question*) whether [26]; (*conj. introducing protasis of a condition*) if [37]

εἶ you are (*second-pers. sg. pres. indic. of* εἰμί) [R6]

εἰ γάρ (*particles introducing a wish*) if only, would that [36]

εἰ μή (*conj. + neg. introducing protasis of a condition*) if not, unless [37]

εἴθ᾽ *see* εἴθε *or* εἴτε

εἴθε (εἴθ᾽) (*particle introducing a wish*) if only, would that; εἴθ᾽ *before a vowel* [36]

εἴκοσι(ν) (*indecl. numeral*) twenty [34]

εἰμί (*imperf.* ἦ/ἦν), ἔσομαι, —, —, —, — be, exist; (*third-pers. sg. with acc. + infin.*) it is possible (to) [R6, R7, R11, 12]

εἶμι, —, —, —, —, — (*verbal adj.* ἰτέος) go, come, travel [40]

εἴπερ if indeed [47]

εἰρήνη, -ης, ἡ peace [12]

εἰς (*prep. + acc.*) into, to [4]

εἷς, μία, ἕν one [30]

εἰσέρχομαι go into, come into (*see* ἔρχομαι) [R40]

εἴτ᾽ *see* εἴτε

εἶτα (*adv.*) then, next [49]

εἴτε (εἴτ᾽, εἴθ᾽)...εἴτε (εἴτ᾽, εἴθ᾽) (*correlatives introducing alternative indirect questions*) whether...or; εἴτ᾽ *before smooth breathing,* εἴθ᾽ *before rough breathing* [26]

ἐκ (*prep. + gen.*) out of; ἐξ *before a vowel* [4]

ἕκαστος, -η, -ον each, every (*sg. often used with a plural verb*) [49]

ἑκατόν (*indecl. numeral*) one hundred [34]

ἐκβάλλω throw out, reject (*see* βάλλω) [R28, R38]

ἔκγονος, -ου, ὁ descendant, offspring [R47]

ἐκεῖ (*adv.*) in that place, at that place, there [49]

ἐκεῖθεν (*adv.*) from there, thence [49]

ἐκεῖνος, -η, -ο (*dem. adj./pron.*) that, those, the well-known, the former [13]

ἐκεῖσε (*adv.*) to there, thither [R33, 49]

ἐκκλησία, -ᾶς, ἡ assembly (*from* ἐκκαλέω *because the citizens were "called forth" to assemble*) [R29, 30]

ἐκπλέω, ἐκπλεύσομαι/ἐκπλευσοῦμαι, ἐξέπλευσα, ἐκπέπλευκα, ἐκπέπλευσμαι, — (+ *gen.*) sail out (from) [R34]

ἐκτείνω, ἐκτενῶ, ἐξέτεινα, ἐκτέτακα, ἐκτέταμαι, ἐξετάθην stretch out [R33]

ἐκτίνω, ἐκτείσω, ἐξέτεισα, ἐκτέτεικα, ἐκτέτεισμαι, ἐξετείσθην pay out [R31]

ἕκτος, -η, -ον sixth [34]

ἐκφορά, -ᾶς, ἡ funeral [R39]

Ἐλάτεια, -ᾶς, ἡ Elatea (*town in central Greece*) [R29]

ἐλάττων, -ον (*comp. of* μῑκρός, -ά, -όν *or* ὀλίγος, -η, -ον) smaller, less, fewer [33]

ἐλαύνω, ἐλῶ (= ἐλάω), ἤλασα, ἐλήλακα, ἐλήλαμαι, ἠλάθην drive, ride, march, row, beat out (*metal*), forge [44]

ἐλάχιστος, -η, -ον (*superl. of* μῑκρός, -ά, -όν) smallest, least [33] ἐλεύθερος, -ᾱ, -ον free; (+ *gen.*) free of, free from [9]

ἕλκω, ἕλξω, εἵλκυσα, εἵλκυκα, εἵλκυσμαι, εἱλκύσθην drag, draw [R7]

Ἑλλάς, -άδος, ἡ Hellas, Greece [20]

Ἕλλην, -ηνος, ὁ, ἡ a Hellene, a Greek [20]

Ἑλληνικός, -ή, -όν Hellenic, Greek [20]

ἐλπίς, -ίδος, ἡ (+ *gen. or infin.*) hope [24]

ἐμαυτοῦ, -ῆς (*reflex. pron.*) myself [19]

ἐμός, -ή, -όν (*poss. adj.*) my, mine, my own [21]

ἐμπειρίᾱ, -ᾱς, ἡ experience [R7]

ἐμπίπτω fall upon, stumble into (*see* πίπτω) [R49]

ἐμπορικός, -ή, -όν having to do with trade [R23]

ἐν (*prep. + dat.*) in [4]

ἐν ἡλικίᾳ εἶναι be of age, be grown up [27]

ἔνατος, -η, -ον ninth [34]

ἐνδεής, -ές (+ *gen.*) lacking, in want of [R31]

ἕνδεκα (*indecl. numeral*) eleven [34]

ἐνδέκατος, -η, -ον eleventh [34]

ἔνδον (*adv.*) inside [R39, 40]

ἕνεκα (*postpos. prep. + gen.*) for the sake of, on account of [48]

ἐνέργεια, -ᾱς, ἡ activity, exercise [R43]

ἔνθα (*adv.*) here, there, hither, thither [49]

ἐνθάδε (*adv.*) at this place, in this place, here, at that place, in that place, there, hither, thither [49]

ἐνθένδε (*adv.*) from here, hence, from there, thence [49]

ἔνιοι, -αι, -α some [R45]

ἐννέα (*indecl. numeral*) nine [34]

ἔννυχος, -ον by night, at night; (*comp. adv.* ἐννυχέστερον more by night, i.e., earlier in the morning) [R5]

ἐνταῦθα (*adv.*) at this place, in this place, here, at that place, in that place, there, hither, thither [49]

ἐντεῦθεν (*adv.*) from here, hence, from there, thence [49]

ἐντός (*prep. + gen.*) within, on this side (of) [R41]

ἐξ *see* ἐκ

ἕξ (*indecl. numeral*) six [R33, 34]

ἐξαίφνης (*adv.*) suddenly [R50]

ἐξαρτύω, ἐξαρτύσω, ἐξήρτῡσα, ἐξήρτῡκα, ἐξήρτῡμαι, ἐξηρτύθην fit out, equip [R34]

ἐξείργω, ἐξείρξω, —, —, —, — drive out [R29]

ἐξέρχομαι go out, come out (*see* ἔρχομαι) [R40]

ἔξεστι(ν), ἐξέσται, —, —, —, — (+ *dat. & infin.*) it is possible (to) [43]

ἐξορμάω, ἐξορμήσω, ἐξώρμησα, ἐξώρμηκα, ἐξώρμημαι, ἐξωρμήθην start out [R33]

ἔξω (*adv.*) outside [40]

ἐπ᾽ *see* ἐπί

ἐπάν contraction of ἐπεί + ἄν [38]

ἐπεγείρω, ἐπεγερῶ, ἐπήγειρα, ἐπεγήγερκα, ἐπεγήγερμαι, ἐπηγέρθην awaken [R40]

ἐπεί (*conj.*) when, after, since, because [5]

ἐπειδάν contraction of ἐπειδή + ἄν [38]

ἐπειδή (*conj.*) when, after, since, because [5]

ἔπειτα (*adv.*) then, next [49]

ἐπήν contraction of ἐπεί + ἄν [38]

ἐπί (ἐπ᾽, ἐφ᾽) (*prep.* + *gen.*) upon, on (*the surface of*); in the time of; (*prep.* + *dat.*) on, at, by (*location*); (*prep.* + *acc.*) to, against (*basic meaning of* ἐπί = upon); ἐπ᾽ *before smooth breathing*, ἐφ᾽ *before rough breathing* [14]

ἐπιβουλεύω, ἐπιβουλεύσω, ἐπεβούλευσα, ἐπιβεβούλευκα, ἐπιβεβούλευμαι, ἐπεβουλεύθην (+ *dat.*) plot (against) [R38]

Ἐπιγένης, -ους, ὁ Epigenes [R31, R33]

ἐπίδειξις, -εως, ἡ display [R34]

ἐπιδημέω, ἐπιδημήσω, ἐπεδήμησα, ἐπιδεδήμηκα, —, — be at home [R40]

ἐπιθῡμέω, ἐπιθῡμήσω, ἐπεθύμησα, ἐπιτεθύμηκα, ἐπιτεθύμημαι, ἐπεθῡμήθην (+ *infin.*) desire (to) [R47]

ἐπίκλησις, -εως, ἡ bad name, reproach [R44]

ἐπιλανθάνομαι (+ *gen.*) forget (*see* λανθάνω) [50]

ἐπιμελέομαι, ἐπιμελήσομαι, —, —, ἐπιμεμέλημαι, ἐπεμελήθην (+ *gen.*) take care (of); (+ *infin. or effort cl.*) take care (to) [45]

ἐπιπλήττω, ἐπιπλήξω, ἐπέπληξα, ἐπιπέπληγα, ἐπιπέπληγμαι, ἐπεπλήχθην (+ *dat.*) strike at, rebuke (*see* πλήττω) [14]

ἐπίσταμαι, ἐπιστήσομαι, —, —, —, ἠπιστήθην (+ *ptcple in indir. disc.*) understand, know (*by being skilled in or familiar with*); (+ *infin.*) know how (to) [46]

ἐπιστήμη, -ης, ἡ understanding, knowledge, skill, science [R36, 46]

ἐπιστολή, -ῆς, ἡ letter, message [4]

ἐπιτήδειος, -ᾱ, -ον necessary; (*as a masc./ fem. substantive*) friend; (*as a neut. pl. substantive*) necessities, provisions [40]

ἐπιτηδεύω, ἐπιτηδεύσω, ἐπετήδευσα, ἐπιτετήδευκα, ἐπιτετήδευμαι, ἐπετηδεύθην pursue, practice [R47, R50]

ἐπιτίθημι, ἐπιθήσω, ἐπέθηκα, ἐπιτέθηκα, ἐπιτέθειμαι, ἐπετέθην place upon [R45]

ἐπιτίμιον, -ου, τό penalty [R31]

ἐπιφορά, -ᾶς, ἡ addition, bonus [R34]

ἐπιχειρέω, ἐπιχειρήσω, ἐπεχείρησα, ἐπικεχείρηκα, ἐπικεχείρημαι, ἐπεχειρήθην (+ *infin.*) undertake (to), attempt (to) [R46]

ἕπομαι (*imperf.* εἰπόμην), ἕψομαι, ἑσπόμην, —, —, — (+ *dat.*) follow [39]

ἐπονείδιστος, -ον ignominious [R44]

ἑπτά (*indecl. numeral*) seven [34]

Ἐρατοσθένης, -ους, ὁ Eratosthenes [R40]

ἐργαστήριον, -ου, τό workshop [R18]

ἔργον, -ου, τό work, task, occupation, deed [8]

Ἑρμῆς, -οῦ, ὁ Hermes (*one of the Olympian gods, famous as messenger and trickster*) [R18]

ἔρχομαι, ἐλεύσομαι, ἦλθον (*imper.* ἐλθέ, ἐλθέτε—irreg. accent), ἐλήλυθα, —, — go, come [R28, R29, 40]

ἐρωτάω, ἐρωτήσω, ἠρώτησα, ἠρώτηκα, ἠρώτημαι, ἠρωτήθην (+ *double acc.*) ask, question [18]

ἐσθίω, ἔδομαι, ἔφαγον, ἐδήδοκα, ἐδήδεσμαι, ἠδέσθην eat [R15, R17, R19, 45]

ἑσπέρᾱ, -ας, ἡ evening [29]

ἐστί(ν) he/she/it is (*third-pers. sg. pres. indic. of* εἰμί) [R7] ἑταίρᾱ, -ᾱς, ἡ comrade (*female*), companion (*female*), courtesan [41]

ἑταῖρος, -ου, ὁ comrade (*male*), companion (*male*) [41]

ἕτερος, -ᾱ, -ον the one (*of two*), the other (*of two*), different [49]

ἔτι (*adv.*) still, yet, longer [6]

ἕτοιμος, -η, -ον (+ *infin.*) ready (to) [36]

ἔτος, -ους, τό year [23]

εὖ (*adv.*) well, kindly [17]

εὖ ἔχειν fare well [17]

εὖ πάσχειν be treated well, fare well [40]

εὖ πράττειν fare well [17]

εὐδαιμονίᾱ, -ᾱς, ἡ happiness, prosperity [R43, R44]

εὐδαίμων, -ον happy, fortunate, prosperous [17]

εὐεξίᾱ, -ᾱς, ἡ good condition [R32]

εὐθύς (*adv.*) immediately [R29, 40]

εὔλογος, -ον well-reasoned [R37]

εὔνους (= εὔνοος), -ουν well-intentioned [R30]

εὐνοῦχος, -ου, ὁ eunuch [R42]

εὐπάθεια, -ᾱς, ἡ good experience [R49]

εὐπρεπής, -ές impressive-looking [R34]

εὑρίσκω (*imperf.* εὑρισκον/ηὑρισκον), εὑρήσω, εὗρον/ηὗρον, εὕρηκα/ηὕρηκα, εὕρημαι/ηὕρημαι, εὑρέθην/ηὑρέθην find, find out, discover [8]

εὐσχήμων, -ον dignified, respectable [R32]

Εὐφράτης, -ου, ὁ Euphrates (*river in Asia flowing into the Persian Gulf*) [R41]

εὔχομαι, εὔξομαι, ηὐξάμην, —, ηὖγμαι, — (+ *dat.*) pray (to) [R9, R42]

ἐφ’ *see* ἐπί

ἔχθιστος, -η, -ον (*superl. of* ἐχθρός, -ά, -όν) (+ *dat.*) most hateful (to), most hostile (to) [33]

ἐχθίων, -ῑον (*comp. of* ἐχθρός, -ά, -όν) (+ *dat.*) more hateful (to), more hostile (to) [33]

ἐχθρός, -ά, -όν (+ *dat.*) hateful (to), hostile (to); (*as a substantive*) enemy (*personal*) [12]

ἔχω (*imperf.* εἶχον), ἕξω/σχήσω, ἔσχον, ἔσχηκα, ἔσχημαι, ἐσχέθην (*verbal adj.* ἑκτέος *or* σχετέος) have, hold, possess; (+ *infin.*) be able (to), can [6]; fare [17]

ἔωθεν (*adv.*) at dawn [R50]

ἕως (*conj.*) while, as long as [23]; until [50]

ζάω, ζήσω, —, —, —, — live [31]

Ζεύς, Διός, ὁ Zeus (*king of the Olympian gods*) [R42, R46, R48]

ζημιόω, ζημιώσω, ἐζημίωσα, ἐζημίωκα, ἐζημίωμαι, ἐζημιώθην penalize, damage [R45]

ζητέω, ζητήσω, ἐζήτησα, ἐζήτηκα, ἐζήτημαι, ἐζητήθην seek, search for, investigate; (+ *infin.*) seek (to) [20]

ζυγόν, -οῦ, τό yoke [R45]

ζωγράφος, -ου, ὁ painter [R48]

ζῷον, -ου, τό animal [R17, 22]

ἤ (*conj.*) or [16]; (*conj. following a comparative*) than [32]

ἤ...ἤ (*correlatives*) either...or [16]

ἤδη (*adv.*) already [27]

ἥδιστος, -η, -ον (*superl. of* ἡδύς, -εῖα, -ύ) sweetest, most pleasant [33]

ἡδίων, ἥδῑον (*comp. of* ἡδύς, -εῖα, -ύ) sweeter, more pleasant [33]

ἡδύς, -εῖα, -ύ sweet, pleasant [33]

ᾗ (*rel. adv.*) how, in which way [R44, R46, R47]

ἥκιστα (*superl. adv. of* κακός, -ή, -όν) least of all [33]

ἥκιστος, -η, -ον (*superl. of* κακός, -ή, -όν) worst (*in might*), weakest, least [33]

ἥκω, ἥξω, —, —, —, — have come (*pres. has perf. sense*) [R49]

ἡλικίᾱ, -ᾱς, ἡ age, prime of life [27]

ἡλικίᾱν ἔχειν be of age, be grown up [27]

ἥλιος, -ου, ὁ sun; Ἥλιος = Sun (*personified as a god*) [48]

ἡμεῖς (*pers. pron.*) we, us [14]

ἡμέρᾱ, -ᾱς, ἡ day [23]

ἡμέτερος, -ᾱ, -ον (*poss. adj.*) our, ours, our own [21]

ἠμί (3rd sg. ἠσί(ν); imperf. 1st sg. ἦν, 3rd sg. ἦ), —, —, —, —, — (*occurs only in pres. & imperf. first- & third-pers. sg.*) say [47]

ἡμῶν αὐτῶν, -ῶν (*reflex. pron.*) ourselves [19]

ἤν contraction of εἰ ἄν [37]

ἤνπερ if (ever) indeed [47]

Ἥρᾱ, -ᾱς, ἡ Hera (*queen of the Olympian gods*) [R18]

ἦσαν they were (*third-pers. pl. imperf. act. indic. of* εἰμί) [R11]

ἡσυχίᾱ, -ᾱς, ἡ leisure, quiet, tranquillity [4]

ἥττων, -ον (*comp. of* κακός, -ή, -όν) worse (*in might*), weaker, less [33]

θ' *see* τε

θάλαττα, -ης, ἡ sea [5]

θάνατος, -ου, ὁ death; Θάνατος = Death (*personified as a god*) [10]

θαρρέω, θαρρήσω, ἐθάρρησα, τεθάρρηκα, τεθάρρημαι, ἐθαρρήθην take heart, be encouraged [R35]

θάρρος, -ους, τό boldness, courage [R36]

θάττων, θᾶττον (*comp. of* ταχύς, -εῖα, -ύ) faster, quicker, swifter [41]

θαυμάζω, θαυμάσομαι, ἐθαύμασα, τεθαύμακα, τεθαύμασμαι, ἐθαυμάσθην wonder (at), marvel (at), be amazed (at), be surprised (at), admire [R28, 44]

θεά, -ᾱς, ἡ goddess [4]

θέᾱ, -ᾱς, ἡ sight, spectacle [R49]

θεάομαι, θεάσομαι, ἐθεασάμην, —, τεθέαμαι, — behold [R49]

θεός, -οῦ (*voc. sg.* θεός *or* θεέ), ὁ, ἡ god, goddess [7]

θεοσεβής, -ές worshipping God, pious [R28]

θεράπαινα, -ης, ἡ servant (*female*), maid [5]

θεραπείᾱ, -ᾱς, ἡ service, treatment [R42]

θεραπεύω, θεραπεύσω, ἐθεράπευσα, τεθεράπευκα, τεθεράπευμαι, ἐθεραπεύθην serve [R37]

θεωρέω, θεωρήσω, ἐθεώρησα, τεθεώρηκα, τεθεώρημαι, ἐθεωρήθην contemplate [R43]

θεωρίᾱ, -ᾱς, ἡ contemplation [R43]

θηλάζω, θηλάσω, ἐθήλασα, τεθήλακα, τεθήλασμαι, ἐθηλάσθην nurse (*a baby*) [R39]

θῆλυς, -εια, -υ female, feminine [R46]

θησαυρός, -οῦ, ὁ treasure, treasury, storehouse [8]

θλάω, θλάσω, ἔθλασα, —, τέθλασμαι, ἐθλάσθην crush [R13]

θόρυβος, -ου, ὁ uproar, confusion [29]

θρᾱνίτης, -ου, ὁ thranite (*rower who sat in the top level of benches and guided the strokes of the two rowers beneath him*) [R34]

θυγάτηρ, -τρός, ἡ daughter [29]

θῡμός, -οῦ, ὁ spirit, soul, heart, passion (*usually courage or anger*) [38]

θύρᾱ, -ᾱς, ἡ door [24]

θύω, θύσω, ἔθῡσα, τέθυκα, τέθυμαι, ἐτύθην offer sacrifice, sacrifice, slay [3]

ἰδίᾳ (*dat. fem. sg. of* ἴδιος, -ᾱ, -ον *used as adverb*) privately [R47]

ἴδιος, -ᾱ, -ον private, one's own, personal [R5, R47]

ἰδιώτης, -ου, ὁ private citizen, a non-professional [R31]

ἰδιωτικός, -ή, -όν private [R31]

ἵημι, ἥσω, ἧκα, εἷκα, εἷμαι, εἵθην set in motion, let go, send, throw; (*mid. + infin.*) hasten (to), be eager (to) [47]

Ἰησοῦς, -οῦ, -οῦ, -οῦν, -οῦ, ὁ Jesus (*Hebrew name*) [R26, R27, R28]

ἴθι (*imper. of* εἶμι—*strengthens another imperative*) come on now! [40]

ἱκανός, -ή, -όν (+ *infin. or dat.*) sufficient (to, for), enough (to, for) [36]

ἱμάτιον, -ου, τό cloak; (*pl.*) clothes [14]

ἵνα (μή) (*conj. introducing purp. clause*) in order that (...not, lest) [39]

ἱππεύς, -έως, ὁ cavalryman [R34]

ἵππος, -ου, ὁ, ἡ horse, mare [7]

ἴσος, -η, -ον (+ *dat.*) equal (to); fair, impartial [37]

ἵστημι, στήσω, ἔστησα/ἔστην, ἕστηκα (*pluperf.* εἱστήκη), ἕσταμαι, ἐστάθην (*fut. perf.* ἑστήξω) make stand, set (up); (*perf. act.*) have stood (up), am standing; (*pluperf.*) had stood (up), was standing; (*second aor. act.*) stood (up); (*fut. perf. act.*) will be standing (ἵστημι *is the only* μι-*verb with a fut. perf.*) [46]

ἰσχύω, ἰσχύσω, ἴσχῡσα, ἴσχῡκα, —, — be strong [R32]

ἴσως (*adv. of* ἴσος, -η, -ον) fairly, perhaps, probably [37]

Ἰταλιώτης, -ου, ὁ Greek inhabitant of Italy [R35]

ἰχθύς, -ύος, ὁ fish [R7]

ἴχνος, -ους, τό footstep, track [R17]

καθ' *see* κατά

καθ' ἕνα one by one, singly [30]

καθ' ἡμέρᾱν day by day, daily [23]

καθαρός, -ά, -όν clean, pure [R49]

καθεύδω (*imperf.* ἐκάθευδον/καθηῦδον), καθευδήσω, —, —, —, — (*verbal adj.* καθευδητέος) sleep, be asleep [45]

κάθημαι (*perf. tense only*) sit [R44]

καθίστημι set down, establish (*see* ἵστημι) [R46]

καί (*conj.*) and; (*adv.*) also, even [3]

καί...καί (*correlatives*) both...and [3]

καὶ μάλα (*adv.*) yes [R46]

καὶ μήν and surely, and yet [32]

καὶ τὰ λοιπά (*abbreviated* κτλ.) etc. [32]

καίπερ (*particle + ptcple.*) although [24]

καιρός, -οῦ, ὁ critical moment, right time, opportunity [R30, R38]

κάκιστος, -η, -ον (*superl. of* κακός, -ή, -όν) worst (*morally*), most wicked [33]

κακίων, -ῑον (*comp. of* κακός, -ή, -όν) worse (*morally*), more wicked [33] κακοδαιμονίᾱ, -ᾱς, ἡ misfortune [R44]

κακός, -ή, -όν ugly, bad (*at doing a thing*), cowardly, (*morally*) bad, evil, wicked [9]

κακῶς (*adv.*) badly, wickedly [17]

κακῶς ἔχειν fare badly [17]

κακῶς πάσχειν be treated badly, fare badly [40]

κακῶς πράττειν fare badly [17]

καλέω, καλῶ, ἐκάλεσα, κέκληκα, κέκλημαι, ἐκλήθην call, summon, invite, name [24]

κάλλιστος, -η, -ον (*superl. of* καλός, -ή, -όν) most beautiful, finest [33]

καλλίων, -ῑον (*comp. of* καλός, -ή, -όν) more beautiful, finer [33]

κάλλος, -ους, τό beauty, nobility [R43, R49]

καλός, -ή, -όν beautiful, handsome, fair (*of appearance*), (*morally*) good, fine, noble [8]

Καρχηδόνιος, -ᾱ, -ον Carthaginian (*inhabitant of Carthage, a city on the North African coast opposite Sicily*) [R35]

κατ᾽ *see* κατά

κατά (κατ᾽, καθ᾽) (*prep. + gen.*) down from, against; (*prep. + acc.*) down, down along, in accordance with, according to, by (*in various idioms*); κατ᾽ *before smooth breathing,* καθ᾽ *before rough breathing* [20]

κατὰ γῆν by land [20]

κατὰ θάλατταν by sea [20]

κατὰ μίαν one by one [R13]

καταβαίνω go down (*see* βαίνω) [R39, R49]

κατάκειμαι, κατακείσομαι, —, —, —, — lie down, be lying down [R40]

κατακλύζω, κατακλύσω, κατέκλυσα, κατακέκλυκα, κατακέκλυσμαι, κατεκλύσθην inundate, flood, overwhelm [R47]

καταλαμβάνω seize (*see* λαμβάνω) [R29]

καταλείπω leave behind, bequeath (*see* λείπω) [R32]

καταπλήττω (*aor. pass.* κατεπλάγην) strike down, terrify [R45]

καταφρονέω, καταφρονήσω, κατεφρόνησα, καταπεφρόνηκα, καταπεφρόνημαι, κατεφρονήθην (*+ gen.*) think little of [R31, R32]

κατεργάζομαι, κατεργάσομαι, —, —, κατείργασμαι, κατειργάσθην (*+ obj. infin.*) accomplish, bring about [R44]

κάτω (*adv.*) down, downwards [39]; τὰ κάτω the downstairs [R39]

καῦμα, -ατος, τό burning heat [R50]

καχεξίᾱ, -ᾱς, ἡ bad condition [R31, R32]

κεῖμαι, κείσομαι, —, —, —, — lie, lie asleep, lie dead, be laid down, be placed, be situated [47]

κελεύω, κελεύσω, ἐκέλευσα, κεκέλευκα, κεκέλευσμαι, ἐκελεύσθην (*with acc. or dat. + infin.*) order (to), command (to), urge (to) [5]

κενόδοξος, -ον conceited [R18]

κενός, -ή, -όν (*+ gen.*) empty (of), devoid (of) [R34, 44]

κεραμεύς, -έως, ὁ potter [R9]

κέρκος, -ου, ἡ tail [R24]

κηπουρός (= κῆπος + οὖρος), -οῦ, ὁ gardener [R9]

κῆρυξ, -ῡκος, ὁ herald [30]

κινδῡνεύω, κινδῡνεύσω, ἐκινδῡνευσα κεκινδῡνευκα, κεκινδῡνευμαι, ἐκινδῡνεύθην run a risk, be in danger [R39] κίνδῡνος, -ου, ὁ danger, risk [10]

κῑνέω, κῑνήσω, ἐκίνησα, κεκίνηκα, κεκίνημαι, ἐκῑνήθην set in motion, stir up [R35]

κλάω, κλαήσω, ἔκλαυσα, —, —, — weep [R49]

κλέπτω, κλέψω, ἔκλεψα, κέκλοφα, κέκλεμμαι, ἐκλάπην (verbal adj. κλεπτέος) steal [3]

κλῆρος, -ου, ὁ lot [R49]

κλῖμαξ, -ακος, ἡ ladder, staircase [39]

κλίνη, -ης, ἡ couch, bed [5]

Κλωθώ, -οῦς, ἡ Clotho (one of the three Fates) [R50]

κλώψ, κλωπός, ὁ thief [16]

κοινός, -ή, -όν (+ dat. or gen.) common (to) [30]

κοινῶς (adv. of κοινός, -ή, -όν) commonly, in common [31]

κόλαξ, -ακος, ὁ flatterer [R20]

κομίζω, κομιῶ, ἐκόμισα, κεκόμικα, κεκόμισμαι, ἐκομίσθην care for, carry, escort; (mid.) acquire [15]

κόνις, -εως, ἡ dust [R49]

κόραξ, -ακος, ὁ crow [R20]

κόρη, -ης, ἡ maiden, girl, daughter; Κόρη = Maiden (another name for Persephone, daughter of the goddess Demeter) [6]

Κόρινθος, -ου, ἡ Corinth (city on the isthmus in Greece) [R35]

κόσμος, -ου, ὁ order, adornment, world, universe [28]

κράζω, κεκράξομαι, ἔκραξα/ἔκραγον, κέκρᾱγα, —, — caw, crow [R19, R20]

κράτιστος, -η, -ον (superl. of ἀγαθός, -ή, -όν) best (in might), strongest [33]

κράτος, -ους, τό power [R42]

κρέας, -ως, τό flesh, meat [R20, R22]

κρείττων, -ον (comp. of ἀγαθός, -ή, -όν) better (in might), stronger [33]

κρημνός, -οῦ, ὁ overhanging bank [R25]

κρῖμα, -ατος, τό judgment [R28]

κρίνω, κρινῶ, ἔκρῑνα, κέκρικα, κέκριμαι, ἐκρίθην separate, choose, judge, decide (a contest or dispute) [27]

κροκόδειλος, -ου, ὁ crocodile [R21]

κρύφα (adv.) secretly [R35]

κτλ. abbreviation of καὶ τὰ λοιπά [32]

κτύπος, -ου, ὁ loud noise [R25]

κῦμα, -ατος, τό wave, undulation [47]

κυνηγέτης, -ου, ὁ hunter [R15]

κύριος, -ᾱ, -ον having authority; (as a substantive) (masc.) lord, master, (fem.) lady, mistress [28]

Κῦρος, -ου, ὁ Cyrus (6th-century B.C. Persian king, conqueror of Babylon) [R45]

κύων, κυνός (voc. sg. κύον), ὁ, ἡ dog [R12, R24, R46, 48]

κωλύω, κωλύσω, ἐκώλῡσα, κεκώλῡκα, κεκώλῡμαι, ἐκωλύθην (+ infin.) hinder, prevent [50]

λαγωός, -οῦ, ὁ rabbit [R25]

Λακεδαίμων, -ονος, ἡ Lacedaemon, Sparta (city in southern Greece) [R35, R44]

λαμβάνω, λήψομαι, ἔλαβον, εἴληφα, εἴλημμαι, ἐλήφθην take, receive, grasp, understand [19]

λανθάνω, λήσω, ἔλαθον, λέληθα, —, — (+ acc.) escape the notice of; (+ suppl. ptcple.) escape the notice; (mid. + gen.) forget [50]

Λάχεσις, -εως, ἡ Lachesis (one of the three Fates) [R50]

λέγω, ἐρῶ/λέξω, εἶπον/ἔλεξα, εἴρηκα,
εἴρημαι/λέλεγμαι, ἐρρήθην/ἐλέχθην
say, speak, tell [10]

λείπω, λείψω, ἔλιπον, λέλοιπα, λέλειμμαι,
ἐλείφθην leave, leave behind [8]

λέων, -οντος, ὁ lion [R15, 16]

λήθη, -ης, ἡ forgetfulness; Λήθη =
Forgetfulness (a river in the
underworld) [R50]

λίθος, -ου, ὁ stone [7]

λίμνη, -ης, ἡ marsh, lake, pond [11]

λόγος, -ου, ὁ word, speech, story,
argument, reasoning [12]

λοιδορέω, λοιδορήσω, ἐλοιδόρησα,
λελοιδόρηκα, λελοιδόρημαι,
ἐλοιδορήθην reproach [R28]

λοιπόν (adv. of λοιπός, -ή, -όν) as for the
rest [32]

λοιπός, -ή, -όν remaining, rest; τοῦ λοιποῦ
(χρόνου) = in the future [32]

λύκος, -ου, ὁ wolf [R12]

Λυκοῦργος, -ου, ὁ Lycurgus (legendary
giver of laws to the Spartans) [R44]

λύπη, -ης, ἡ pain, grief [7]

λύω, λύσω, ἔλῡσα, λέλυκα, λέλυμαι, ἐλύθην
loosen, release, destroy [12]

μά (affirmative or negative particle + acc.,
used in oaths) yes, by...; no, by...
[R48]

μάγειρος, -ου, ὁ cook [R24]

μαθητής, -οῦ, ὁ student, disciple [9]

μακρά (neut. acc. pl. of μακρός, -ά, -όν used
as adv.) at length [31]

μακρόν (neut. acc. sg. of μακρός, -ά, -όν used
as adv.) at length [31]

μακρός, -ά, -όν long, long-lasting [11]

μάλα (adv.) very, much [33]

μαλθακίζω, μαλθακιῶ, ἐμαλθάκισα,
μεμαλθάκικα, μεμαλθάκισμαι,
ἐμαλθακίσθην soften; (mid.) become
lazy [R47]

μάλιστα (superl. of adv. μάλα) most [32]

μᾶλλον (comp. of adv. μάλα) more, rather
[R31, 32]

μανθάνω, μαθήσομαι, ἔμαθον, μεμάθηκα,
—, — (verbal adj. μαθητέος) (+ ptcple.
or ὅτι/ὡς clause in indir. disc.) learn
(by study); understand; (+ infin.)
learn how (to) [42]

μαστῑγόω, μαστῑγώσω, ἐμαστίγωσα,
μεμαστίγωκα, μεμαστίγωμαι,
ἐμαστῑγώθην whip [R40]

μάχη, -ης, ἡ battle, fight [35]

μάχομαι, μαχοῦμαι, ἐμαχεσάμην, —,
μεμάχημαι, — (verbal adj. μαχετέος)
(+ dat.) fight (against) [35]

μέγα (neut. acc. sg. of μέγας, μεγάλη, μέγα
used as adv.) greatly, much [25]

μεγάλα (neut. acc. pl. of μέγας, μεγάλη, μέγα
used as adv.) greatly, much [25]

μέγας, μεγάλη, μέγα (masc. voc. sg. μεγάλε/
μέγας) big, large, great, tall [R14,
25]

μέγεθος, -ους, τό size, grandeur [R43]

μέγιστος, -η, -ον (superl. of μέγας, μεγάλη,
μέγα) greatest, largest [33]

μεθ᾽ see μετά

μεθίημι release, relax, permit (see ἵημι)
[47]

μείζων, -ον greater, larger (comp. degree of
μέγας, μεγάλη, μέγα) [R14, 33]

μέλλω, μελλήσω, ἐμέλλησα, —, —, — (+
fut. infin. or pres. infin.) be about
(to), intend (to); (+ pres. infin.)
hesitate (to), delay (to) [6]

μέν (postpos. particle) indeed [10]

μὲν...δέ (*correlatives*) on the one hand...on the other hand [10]

μέντοι (*postpositive particle*) surely, however [44]

μένω, μενῶ, ἔμεινα, μεμένηκα, —, — (*verbal adj.* μενετέος) remain, stay; (+ *acc.*) wait for [R16, 19]

μέσος, -η, -ον middle, moderate [R49]

μεστός, -ή, -όν (+ *gen.*) full (of) [R49]

μετ᾽ *see* μετά

μετά (μετ᾽, μεθ᾽) (*prep. + gen.*) among, with, together with; (*prep. + acc.*) after; μετ᾽ *before smooth breathing*, μεθ᾽ *before rough breathing* [19]

μεταπέμπω (*usually mid.*) send after, summon (*see* πέμπω) [R29]

μέτριος, -ᾱ, -ον moderate, tolerable [R33]

μέτρον, -ου, τό measure [R50]

μέχρι (*prep. + gen.*) until, up to; (*conj.*) until [50]

μή (*adv.*) not (*used with subjunctives, imperatives, infinitives not in indirect discourse, optatives in wishes, and participles with conditional or general force*) [3]; introduces a question expecting the answer "no" [26]; (*introducing neg. purp. clause*) in order that...not, lest [39]; (*introducing fear clause*) that, lest [45]; introduces cautious assertion [50]

μὴ οὐ (*introducing neg. fear clause*) that...not, lest...not [45]; introduces cautious denial [50]

μηδ᾽ *see* μηδέ

μηδέ (μηδ᾽) (*conj.*) and not, nor; (*adv.*) not even; μηδ᾽ *before a vowel* [22]

μηδέ (μηδ᾽)...μηδέ (μηδ᾽) (*correlatives*) neither...nor [22]

μηδείς, μηδεμία, μηδέν none, no; (*as a substantive*) no one, nothing [30]

Μῆδος, -ου, ὁ a Mede [R42]

μήθ᾽ *see* μήτε

μηκέτι (*adv.*) no longer, no more [6]

μηκύνω, μηκυνῶ, ἐμήκῡνα, —, μεμήκυσμαι, ἐμηκύνθην lengthen [R33]

μήν (*postpositive particle*) surely, yet, however [32]

μήποθ᾽ *see* μήποτε

μήποτ᾽ *see* μήποτε

μήποτε (μήποτ᾽, μήποθ᾽) (*adv.*) never; μήποτ᾽ *before smooth breathing*, μήποθ᾽ *before rough breathing* [28]

μήπω (*adv.*) not yet [28]

μήτ᾽ *see* μήτε

μήτε (μήτ᾽, μήθ᾽) (*conj.*) and not, nor; μήτ᾽ *before smooth breathing*, μήθ᾽ *before rough breathing* [22]

μήτε (μήτ᾽, μήθ᾽)...μήτε (μήτ᾽, μήθ᾽) (*correlatives*) neither...nor [22]

μήτηρ, -τρός, ἡ mother [R14, R19, 29]

μηχανάομαι, μηχανήσομαι, ἐμηχανησάμην, —, μεμηχάνημαι, — (+ *infin. or effort cl.*) contrive (to), devise (to) [R44, 45]

μηχανή, -ῆς, ἡ machine, device, contrivance [45]

μῑκρά (*neut. acc. pl. of* μῑκρός, -ά, -όν *used as adv.*) a little, for a little while [R29, 31]

μῑκρόν (*neut. acc. sg. of* μῑκρός, -ά, -όν *used as adv.*) a little, for a little while [R29, 31]

μῑκρός, -ά, -όν small, little [11]

μῑμέομαι, μῑμήσομαι, ἐμῑμησάμην, —, μεμίμημαι, ἐμῑμήθην imitate [R44]

μιμνήσκω, μνήσω, ἔμνησα, —, μέμνημαι, ἐμνήσθην (*fut. perf.* μεμνήσομαι) remind; (*mid., aor. or fut. pass. + gen. or acc., complem. infin., or indir. disc. + ptcple. or ὅτι/ὡς*) recall, remember [R36, 49]

μνᾶ (= μνάα), -ᾶς, -ᾷ, -ᾶν; *pl.* -αῖ, -ῶν, -αῖς, -ᾶς, ἡ mina (*a weight or sum of money equal to 100 drachmas*) [41]

μοῖρα, -ᾶς, ἡ destiny, fate; Μοῖρα = Destiny, Fate (*personified as a goddess*) [5]

μόνον (*neut. acc. sg. of* μόνος, -η, -ον *used as adv.*) only [18]

μόνος, -η, -ον alone, only [18]

μόριον, -ου, τό small portion [R38]

μουσική, -ῆς, ἡ (*supply* τέχνη) music, fine arts [R46]

μῦθος, -ου, ὁ story, tale [R50]

μύριοι, -αι, -α ten thousand [34]

μῦς, μυός, ὁ mouse [R6, R15]

μῶν (= μή + *particle* οὖν) introduces a question expecting the answer "no" [26]

Μωϋσῆς, -έως, -εῖ, -ῆν, ὁ Moses (*Hebrew name*) [R28]

ναί (*adv.*) yes [R46]

ναῦς, νεώς, ἡ ship [R23, R34]

ναύτης, -ου, ὁ sailor [R34]

ναυτικός, -ή, -όν naval; (*as a neut. substantive*) navy [R38]

νεᾱνίᾱς, -ου, ὁ young man, youth [R6, 9]

Νεῖλος, -ου, ὁ Nile (*river in Egypt flowing into the Mediterranean Sea*) [R21]

νέμω, νεμῶ, ἔνειμα, νενέμηκα, νενέμημαι, ἐνεμήθην put in order, manage [R42]

νέον (*neut. acc. of* νέος, -ᾱ, -ον *used as adv.*) recently [31]

νέος, -ᾱ, -ον young, new [27]

νή (*affirmative particle + acc., used in oaths*) yes, by... [R46]

νῆσις, -εως, ἡ spinning [R50]

νίζω, νίψομαι, ἔνιψα, —, νένιμμαι, — wash [R26]

νῑκάω, νῑκήσω, ἐνίκησα, νενίκηκα, νενίκημαι, ἐνῑκήθην conquer, win [37]

νίκη, -ης, ἡ victory [36]

νομίζω, νομιῶ, ἐνόμισα, νενόμικα, νενόμισμαι, ἐνομίσθην think, consider, believe [R30, 41]

νόμος, -ου, ὁ law, custom [22]

νοῦς (= νόος), νοῦ, ὁ mind [R43]

νυκτερίς, -ίδος, ἡ bat (*animal*) [R23]

νῦν (*adv.*) now, at this time [13]

νύξ, νυκτός, ἡ night; νυκτός = at night [R19, 23]

ξενίᾱ, -ᾶς, ἡ hospitality, guest-friendship [24]

ξένος, -ου, ὁ stranger, guest, host [24]

ὁ, ἡ, τό (*def. article*) the [4, 7, 8]

ὁ μέν...ὁ δέ (*correlatives*) this one...that one; the one...the other; (*pl.*) some...others [10]

ὀβολός, -οῦ, ὁ obol (*small unit of money and weight*) [18]

ὄγδοος, -η, -ον eighth [34]

ὅδε, ἥδε, τόδε (ὅδ', ἥδ', τόδ') (*dem. adj./pron.*) this, these, the following; ὅδ', ἥδ', τόδ' *before a vowel* [13]

ὁδός, -οῦ, ἡ way, path, road, journey [7]

ὅθ' *see* ὅτε

ὅθεν (*rel. adv.*) from where [38]

οἷ (*rel. adv.*) to where [38]

οἶδα (*pluperf.* ᾔδη), εἴσομαι, —, —, —, — (*verbal adj.* ἰστέος) know (*by reflecting*); (+ *infin.*) know how (to) [R26, R27, 28]

οἴκαδε (*adv.*) home(wards) [R40, 49]

οἰκέτης, -ου, ὁ servant (*of the household*), family member [9] οἰκέω, οἰκήσω, ᾤκησα, ᾤκηκα, ᾤκημαι, ᾠκήθην inhabit, be settled, be governed [R48]

οἰκίᾱ, -ᾱς, ἡ house, household [6]

οἰκίδιον, -ου, τό little house (*diminutive of* οἰκίᾱ) [R39]

οἴκοθεν (*adv.*) from home [49]

οἴκοι (*adv.*) at home [R33, 49]

οἰκονόμος, -ου, ὁ, ἡ manager (*of the household*) [R39]

οἶκος, -ου, ὁ house, household, family [49]

οἶμαι *see* οἴομαι

οἴμοι (*exclamation of distress*) woe is me! [R17]

οἴομαι (*first-pers. sg. often contracts to* οἶμαι) (*imperf.* ᾤμην), οἰήσομαι, —, —, —, ᾠήθην (*with indir. disc. +* infin. *or* ὅτι/ὡς) think, suppose [R46, 48]

οἷος, -ᾱ, -ον (*rel. adj.*) of which sort, such as; (*exclam. adj.*) such a! [R45, 46]

οἷός, -ᾱ, -όν τε (+ *infin.*) able (to), possible (to) [46]

ὀκτώ (*indecl. numeral*) eight [34]

ὀλίγα (*neut. acc. pl. of* ὀλίγος, -η, -ον *used as adv.*) a little, for a little while [31]

ὀλίγιστος, -η, -ον (*superl. of* ὀλίγος, -η, -ον) least, fewest [33]

ὀλίγον (*neut. acc. of* ὀλίγος, -η, -ον *used as adv.*) a little, for a little while [31]

ὀλίγος, -η, -ον little, few [18]

Ὀλυμπίᾱ, -ᾱς, ἡ Olympia (*sanctuary of Zeus in southern Greece, site of the ancient Olympic Games*) [R31, R33]

ὁμόθεν (*adv.*) from the same place [49]

ὅμοιος, -ᾱ, -ον (+ *dat.*) similar (to), like [48]

ὁμολογέω, ὁμολογήσω, ὡμολόγησα, ὡμολόγηκα, ὡμολόγημαι, ὡμολογήθην (+ *dat.*) agree (with); (*with complem.* infin. *or indir. disc. +* infin.) agree, confess, promise [48]

ὁμόνοια, -ᾱς, ἡ concord [R13]

ὁμός, -ή, -όν same [49]

ὁμόσε (*adv.*) to the same place [49]

ὁμοῦ (*adv.*) in the same place, at the same place [49]

ὅμως (*particle*) nevertheless [R29]

ὄνομα, -ατος, τό name [16]

ὄνος, -ου, ὁ, ἡ donkey [R9]

ὁπλῑταγωγός, -όν carrying hoplites; ὁπλῑταγωγὸς ναῦς = transport ship [R34]

ὁπλίτης, -ου, ὁ hoplite (*heavy-armed foot-soldier*) [R34]

ὁπόθ' *see* ὁπότε

ὁπόθεν (*indir. interrog. adv.*) from where? whence? [26]; (*indef. rel. adv.*) from wherever [38]

ὅποι (*indir. interrog. adv.*) to where? whither? [26]; (*indef. rel. adv.*) to wherever [38]

ὁποῖος, -ᾱ, -ον (*indir. interrog. adj.*) of what sort? [46]; (*indef. rel. adj.*) of whichever sort [46]

ὁπόσος, -η, -ον (*indir. interrog. adj.*) how much? how many? [46]; (*indef. rel. adj.*) of whichever size, of whichever quantity [46]

ὁπότ' *see* ὁπότε

ὁπόταν contraction of ὁπότε + ἄν [38]

ὁπότε (ὁπότ', ὁπόθ') (*indir. interrog. adv.*) when? [26]; (*indef. rel. adv.*) whenever [38]; ὁπότ' *before smooth breathing,* ὁπόθ' *before rough breathing* ὁπότερος, -ᾱ, -ον which(ever) (*of two*) [R40]

ὅπου (*indir. interrog. adv.*) where? [26]; (*indef. rel. adv.*) wherever [38]

ὅπως (*indir. interrog. adv.*) how? [26]; (*indef. rel. adv.*) howsoever, as ever [38]

ὅπως (μή) (*conj. introducing purp. clause*) in order that (...not, lest) [39]; (*conj. introducing effort clause*) how (...not), that (...not) [45]

ὁράω (*imperf.* ἑώρων), ὄψομαι, εἶδον (*imper.* ἰδέ), ἑόρᾱκα/ἑώρᾱκα, ἑόρᾱμαι/ὦμμαι, ω″φθην see, behold, look (at); (*pass.*) be seen, appear [23]

ὀρθῶς (*adv.*) rightly [R30]

ὁρμή, -ῆς, ἡ a starting out [R33]

ὄρος, -ους, τό mountain, hill [50]

ὀρχέομαι, ὀρχήσομαι, ὠρχησάμην, —, —, ὠρχήσθην dance [R7, R22]

ὅς, ἥ, ὅ (*relative pron.*) who, which, that [23]

ὅσος, -η, -ον (*rel. adj.*) of which size, of which quantity, as much as, as many as [46]; (*exclam. adj.*) how great a! how many! [46]

ὅσπερ, ἥπερ, ὅπερ who indeed, which indeed, the very one who, the very thing that [47]

ὅστις, ἥτις, ὅ τι (*indir. interrog. adj./pron.*) (*adj.*) what? which?; (*pron.*) who? what? [26]; (*indef. rel. pron.*) whoever, whatever, whichever [38]

ὀσφραίνομαι, ὀσφρήσομαι, ὠσφρόμην, —, —, ὠσφράνθην sniff at [R10]

ὅτ᾽ *see* ὅτε

ὅταν contraction of ὅτε + ἄν [38]

ὅτε (*rel. adv.*) when; ὅτ᾽ *before smooth breathing,* ὅθ᾽ *before rough breathing* [38]

ὅτι (*conj.*) because, since; *never elided* [28]; (*particle preceding and strengthening a superlative*) as...as possible [32]; (*conj. introducing indir. discourse*) that [40]; equivalent of a quotation mark beginning a direct question [R40]

οὐ (οὔ, οὐκ, οὐχ) (*adv.*) not (*used with indicatives, optatives not in wishes, infinitives in indirect discourse, and participles without conditional or general force; proclitic except* οὔ *at end of a clause*); οὐκ *before smoooth breathing,* οὐχ *before rough breathing* [3]; introduces a question expecting the answer "yes" [26]

οὗ (*rel. adv.*) where [38]

οὐ μή introduces emphatic denial or urgent prohibition [50]

οὐ μόνον...ἀλλὰ καί (*correlatives*) not only...but also [18]

οὐδ᾽ *see* οὐδέ

οὐδέ (οὐδ᾽) (*conj.*) and not, nor; (*adv.*) not even; οὐδ᾽ *before a vowel* [22]

οὐδέ (οὐδ᾽)...οὐδέ (οὐδ᾽) (*correlatives*) neither...nor [22]

οὐδείς, οὐδεμία, οὐδέν none, no; (*as a substantive*) no one, nothing [30]

οὔθ᾽ *see* οὔτε

οὐκ *see* οὐ

οὐκέτι (*adv.*) no longer, no more [6]

οὐκοῦν (= οὐκ + *particle* οὖν) introduces a ques-tion expecting the answer "yes" [26]

οὖν (*postpos. particle*) therefore, then [10]

οὔποτε (οὔποτ᾽, οὔποθ᾽) (*adv.*) never; οὔποτ᾽ *before smooth breathing,* οὔποθ᾽ *before rough breathing* [28] οὔπω (*adv.*) not yet [28]

οὐρανός, -οῦ, ὁ sky, heaven; Οὐρανός = Sky
(*personified as a god*) [20]

οὖς, ὠτός, τό ear [R10]

οὔτ᾽ *see* οὔτε

οὔτε (οὔτ᾽, οὔθ᾽) (*conj.*) and not, nor; οὔτ᾽
before smooth breathing, οὔθ᾽ *before
rough breathing* [22]

οὔτε (οὔτ᾽, οὔθ᾽)...οὔτε (οὔτ᾽, οὔθ᾽)
(*correlatives*) neither...nor [22]

οὗτος, αὕτη, τοῦτο (*dem. adj./pron.*) this,
these, that, those, the aforesaid, the
well-known, the latter [R10, 13]

οὕτω(ς) (*adv.*) in this way, so, thus; οὕτως
before a vowel [31]

οὐχ *see* οὐ

ὀφείλω, ὀφειλήσω, ὠφείλησα/ω ὤφελον,
ὠφείληκα, —, — owe, be in debt;
(*second aor.*) ought [48]

ὀφθαλμός, -οῦ, ὁ eye [26]

πάγη, -ης, ἡ trap, snare [R22]

παιδείᾱ, -ᾱς, ἡ education [R46]

παιδεύω, παιδεύσω, ἐπαίδευσα, πεπαίδευκα,
πεπαίδευμαι, ἐπαιδεύθην teach,
educate; (*mid.*) have (*someone*)
taught [3]

παιδίον, -ου, τό young child, little child
(*diminutive of* παῖς) [25]

παῖς, παιδός (*gen. pl.* παίδων), ὁ, ἡ child,
son, daughter [25]

πάλαι (*adv.*) long ago [27]

παλαιός, -ά, -όν old, ancient [27]

πάλαισμα, -ατος, τό wrestling-bout [R44]

παλαίστρᾱ, -ᾱς, ἡ wrestling-school [R46]

παλαίτατος, -η, -ον (*superl. of* παλαιός, -ά,
-όν) oldest, most ancient [32]

παλαίτερος, -ᾱ, -ον (*comp. of* παλαιός, -ά, -
όν) older, more ancient [32]

πάλιν (*adv.*) back, backwards, again,
once more [6]

πανδημεί (*adv.*) in a mob, en masse [R36]

πάντως (*adv. of* πᾶς, πᾶσα, πᾶν) entirely, in
all respects [31]

πάνυ (*adv.*) entirely, very; (*in positive
answers*) by all means; (*in negative
answers*) [not] at all [48]

παρ᾽ *see* παρά

παρά (παρ᾽) (*prep. + gen.*) from, from the
side of; (*prep. + dat.*) at, at the side
of, beside, at the house of; (*prep. +
acc.*) to, to the side of, contrary to;
παρ᾽ *before a vowel* [22]

παράδειγμα, -ατος, τό model, example [48]

παραδίδωμι, παραδώσω, παρέδωκα,
παραδέδωκα, παραδέδομαι,
παρεδόθην hand over, transfer [R42,
R45]

παραίνεσις, -εως, ἡ exhortation [R36]

παρακολουθέω, παρακολουθήσω,
παρηκολούθησα, παρηκολούθηκα,
—, — follow closely [R30]

παραλαμβάνω associate with (*someone as
a...*) (*see* λαμβάνω) [R44]

παραλείπω pass over, neglect to mention
(*see* λείπω) [R44]

παραπλήσιος, -ᾱ, -ον close, resembling
[R46]

παρασκευάζω, παρασκευάσω,
παρεσκεύασα, παρεσκεύακα,
παρεσκεύασμαι, παρεσκευάσθην
prepare, provide, furnish [R34, 35]

παρασκευή, -ῆς, ἡ preparation, military
force [R34, 35]

παραχωρέω, παραχωρήσομαι, παρεχώρησα,
παρακεχώρηκα, παρακεχώρημαι,
παρεχωρήθην yield, step aside [R44]

πάρειμι (*imperf.* παρῄειν), —, —, —, —, —
pass by [R23]

πάρειμι (*imperf.* παρῆν), παρέσομαι, —, —,
—, — be present [R30]

παρέρχομαι, πάρειμι, παρῆλθον,
παρελήλυθα, —, — pass by, come
forward to speak [R30]

παρέχω offer, furnish, produce (*see* ἔχω)
[R36, R37]

παρίημι let pass, allow, forgive (*see* ἵημι)
[47]

παρίστημι stand near; τὸ παρεστός =
present circumstances (*see* ἵστημι)
[R46]

Παρμενίων, -ωνος, ὁ Parmenion
(*Macedonian noble and general,
Alexander's second-in-command*)
[R41]

πᾶς, πᾶσα, πᾶν all, every, whole, entire
[23]

πάσχω, πείσομαι, ἔπαθον, πέπονθα, —, —
suffer, experience, be treated, fare
[40]

πατήρ, -τρός, ὁ father [R13, 29]

πατρίς, -ίδος, ἡ fatherland, native country
[30]

παῦλα, -ης, ἡ (+ *gen.*) pause (from), rest
(from) [R48]

παύω, παύσω, ἔπαυσα, πέπαυκα, πέπαυμαι,
ἐπαύθην (*verbal adj.* παυστέος) stop,
bring to a stop; (*mid.*) stop oneself,
come to a stop, cease [25]

πεδίον, -ου, τό plain (*flat, open country*)
[50]

πείθω, πείσω, ἔπεισα, πέπεικα/πέποιθα,
πέπεισμαι, ἐπείσθην (*with acc. +
infin.*) persuade (to); (*mid. + dat.*)
obey [11]; πέποιθα (+ *dat.*) trust [20]

πειράω, πειράσω, ἐπείρᾱσα, πεπείρᾱκα,
πεπείρᾱμαι, ἐπειράθην (*often in mid.
voice*) (+ *gen.*) test, make trial of; (+
infin.) try (to) [R6, R8, R35, R47]

πέμπτος, -η, -ον fifth [34]

πέμπω, πέμψω, ἔπεμψα, πέπομφα, πέπεμμαι,
ἐπέμφθην send [4]

πέντε (*indecl. numeral*) five [R33, 34]

περ/-περ (*enclitic particle, often attached to
an adv., conj., or rel. pronoun;
strengthens preceding word*) indeed,
the very [47]

περί (*prep. + gen.*) concerning, about;
(*prep. + dat.*) around; (*prep. + acc.*)
around (*basic meaning of* περί =
around); *never elided* [18]

Περικλῆς, -έους, ὁ Pericles (*5th-century
B.C. Athenian leader*) [R34]

περιοράω overlook, put up with, endure
[R44]

περιπατέω, περιπατήσω, περιεπάτησα,
περιπεπάτηκα, περιπεπάτημαι,
περιεπατήθην walk around [R33]

περίπατος, -ου, ὁ a walking around, a
walk [R33]

περιποιέω aim at getting (*see* ποιέω) [R43]

Πέρσης, -ου, ὁ a Persian [R42]

πηλός, -οῦ, ὁ mud [R26]

πίθηκος, -ου, ὁ monkey [R22]

πίνω, πίομαι, ἔπιον (*imper.* πῖθι), πέπωκα,
πέπομαι, ἐπόθην drink [R24, 50]

πίπτω, πεσοῦμαι, ἔπεσον, πέπτωκα, —, —
fall [49]

πιστεύω, πιστεύσω, ἐπίστευσα, πεπίστευκα,
πεπίστευμαι, ἐπιστεύθην (+ *dat. or
with* εἰς + *acc.*) believe (in), trust
(in), have faith (in) [28]

πλεῖστος, -η, -ον (*superl. of* πολύς, πολλή,
πολύ) most [33]

πλείων/πλέων, -ον (*comp. of* πολύς, πολλή,
πολύ) more [33]

πληγή, -ῆς, ἡ blow, stroke [R44]

πλήρης, -ες (+ *gen.*) full (of) [R29]

πλήττω, πλήξω, ἔπληξα, πέπληγα,
πέπληγμαι, ἐπλήγην strike (*with a direct blow*) [14]

πλοῦς (= -όος), -οῦ, ὁ sailing-voyage [R35]

πλούσιος, -ᾱ, -ον wealthy [R30]

πλοῦτος, -ου, ὁ wealth; (*pl.*) riches [R49]

πνῖγος, -ους, τό stifling heat [R50]

πόθ' *see* πότε

ποθ' *see* ποτέ

πόθεν (*direct interrog. adv.*) from where?
whence? [26]

ποθέν (*enclitic adv.*) from somewhere [26]

ποθέω, ποθήσω, ἐπόθησα, —, —, — long
for, miss, regret [R9]

ποῖ (*direct interrog. adv.*) to where?
whither? [26]

ποι (*enclitic adv.*) to somewhere [26]

ποιέω, ποιήσω, ἐποίησα, πεποίηκα,
πεποίημαι, ἐποιήθην make, create, do
[R8, R13, 16]

ποῖος, -ᾱ, -ον (*direct interrog. adj.*) of what
sort? [46]

ποιός, -ᾱ́, -όν (*indef. enclitic adj.*) of some
sort [46]

πολεμέω, πολεμήσω, ἐπολέμησα,
πεπολέμηκα, πεπολέμημαι,
ἐπολεμήθην make war [R43]

πολεμικός, -ή, -όν military [R43]

πολέμιος, -ᾱ, -ον (+ *dat.*) at war (with),
hostile (to); (*as a substantive, usually
pl.*) enemy (*in war*) [12]

πόλεμος, -ου, ὁ war [12]

πόλις, -εως, ἡ city-state, city, state [29]

πολῑτείᾱ, -ᾱς, ἡ state, republic [R48]

πολῑτεύω, πολῑτεύσω, ἐπολῑτευσα,
πεπολίτευκα, πεπολίτευμαι,
ἐπολῑτεύθην be a citizen; (*mid.*)
participate in politics [R43]

πολίτης, -ου, ὁ citizen [43]

πολῑτικός, -ή, -όν political [R43]

πολλά (*neut. nom. pl. of* πολύς) many
[R17]; (*neut. acc. pl. of* πολύς *used as
adv.*) much [18]

πολλάκις (*adv.*) many times, often [25]

πολλᾱ́ς (*fem. acc. pl. of* πολύς) many [R9]

πολλούς (*acc. masc. sg. of* πολύς) many
[R7]

πολύ (*neut. acc. sg. of* πολύς *used as adv.*)
much [18]

πολύς, πολλή, πολύ much, many [R7, R9,
18]; οἱ πολλοί = the many, the
people [18]

πολυτελής, -ές expensive, extravagant
[R34]

πονέω, πονήσω, ἐπόνησα, πεπόνηκα,
πεπόνημαι, ἐπονήθην work, labor
[R5]

πορείᾱ, -ᾱς, ἡ journey [R33, R49, R50]

πορεύω, πορεύσω, ἐπόρευσα, πεπόρευκα,
πεπόρευμαι, ἐπορεύθην carry, make
go; (*mid./pass.*) go, journey [R33,
R50]

πόρρω (*adv.*) far, far off; (*prep. + gen.*) far
away from [11]

πόσος, -η, -ον (*direct interrog. adj.*) how
much? how many? [R18, 46]

ποσός, -ή, -όν (*indef. enclitic adj.*) of some
size, of some quantity [46]

πόσου (*from* πόσος, -η, -ον: how much?) at
what price? [R18]

πότ' *see* πότε

ποτ' *see* ποτέ

ποταμός, -οῦ, ὁ river [7]

πότε (πότ', πόθ') (*direct interrog. adv.*)
when?; πότ' *before smooth breathing,
πόθ' before rough breathing* [26]

ποτέ (ποτ', ποθ') (*enclitic adv.*) sometime, sometimes, ever, once; ποτ' *before smooth breathing,* ποθ' *before rough breathing* [26]

πότερον/πότερα...ἤ (*correlatives introducing alternative questions, direct or indirect*) either...or; whether...or [26]

ποῦ (*direct interrog. adv.*) where? [26]

που (*enclitic adv.*) somewhere [26]

πούς, ποδός (*voc. sg.* ποῦς), ὁ foot [50]

πρᾶγμα, -ατος, τό deed, affair, thing; (*pl.*) circumstances, matters of state, trouble [R30, 42]

πρᾱκτικός, -ή, -όν practical [R43]

πρᾶξις, -εως, ἡ action, pursuit, activity, career [R43, R49]

πράττω, πράξω, ἔπρᾱξα, πέπρᾱγα/πέπρᾱχα, πέπρᾱγμαι, ἐπράχθην do, act [10]; fare [17]

πρέπει, πρέψει, ἔπρεψε(ν), —, —, — it is fitting (to), it suits (+ *dat.*) [R46]

πρέσβυς, -εως, ὁ ambassador [R35, R41]

πρίν (*conj. + infin.*) before; (*conj. + subjunctive + ἄν or past tense of indicative*) until [43]

πρό (*adv.*) before [32]

προαποθνήσκω die early, commit suicide (*see* ἀποθνήσκω) [R45]

πρόβατον, -ου, τό sheep; (*pl.*) cattle [R12]

προέχω stand out (*see* ἔχω) [R43]

προθῡμίᾱ, -ᾱς, ἡ eagerness, goodwill [38]

πρόθῡμος, -ον (+ *gen. or infin.*) eager (for, to); (+ *dat. or* εἰς + *acc.*) well-disposed (toward) [R36, 38]

πρός (*prep. + gen.*) from, by (*in oaths*); (*prep. + dat.*) at, near; (*prep. + acc.*) to, toward, against (*basic meaning of* πρός = in the direction of, facing) [17]

προσαγγέλλω announce to (*see* ἀγγέλλω) [R30]

προσβάλλω (+ *dat.*) attack (*see* βάλλω) [17]

προσέρχομαι draw near, approach, go forward to (*see* ἔρχομαι) [R49, R50]

προσκυνέω, προσκυνήσω, προσεκύνησα, προσκεκύνηκα, προσκεκύνημαι, προσεκυνήθην (+ *dat.*) worship [R28]

προσποιέω add to; (*mid. + infin.*) pretend (to) (*see* ποιέω) [17]

πρότερον (*neut. acc. of* πρότερος, -ᾱ, -ον *used as adv.*) formerly, earlier [R23, 31]

πρότερος, -ᾱ, -ον (*comp.; pos. degree = adv.* πρό) former, earlier [9]

πρόφασις, -εως, ἡ excuse [R37]

προφήτης, -ου, ὁ prophet, interpreter (*of the gods' will*) [R26, R49]

πρύτανις, -εως, ὁ prytanis (*one of the fifty members of a tribe chosen by lot to run the administration of Athens for a month*) [29]

πρῶτα (*neut. acc. pl. of* πρῶτος, -η, -ον *used as adv.*) first, earliest [32]

πρῶτον (*neut. acc. sg. of* πρῶτος, -η, -ον *used as adv.*) first, earliest [32]

πρῶτος, -η, -ον (*superl. of* πρότερος, -ᾱ, -ον) first, earliest [32]

πτερόν, -οῦ, τό feather, wing [R20]

πυνθάνομαι, πεύσομαι, ἐπυθόμην, —, πέπυσμαι, — (*verbal adj.* πευστέος) (+ *gen.*) inquire (*of someone*); (+ *gen./ acc. or ptcple., infin., or* ὅτι/ὡς *clause in indir. disc.*) learn (*by inquiry*), learn (*by inquiry*) about, hear, hear about [42]

πυρά, -ᾱς, ἡ funeral pyre [R50]

πυρετός, -οῦ, ὁ fever [R16]

πωλέω, πωλήσω, ἐπώλησα, πεπώληκα, πεπώλημαι, ἐπωλήθην sell [18]

πῶς (direct interrog. adv.) how? [R24, 26]

πως (enclitic adv.) somehow [26]

ῥάβδος, -ου, ἡ stick [R13]

ῥᾴδιος, -ᾱ, -ον easy [31]

ῥᾳδίως (adv.) easily [R13]

ῥᾷστος, -η, -ον (superl. of ῥᾴδιος, -ᾱ, -ον) easiest [33]

ῥᾴων, -ον (comp. of ῥᾴδιος, -ᾱ, -ον) easier [33]

ῥήτωρ, -ορος, ὁ orator, speaker [16]

ῥίπτω, ῥίψω, ἔρρῑψα, ἔρρῑφα, ἔρρῑμμαι, ἐρρίφθην throw, hurl, cast aside [20]

σάββατον, -ου, τό sabbath, sabbath-day [R26]

σαγήνη, -ης, ἡ net (for fishing) [R7]

σαλπιγκτής, -οῦ, ὁ trumpeter [R29]

σαυτοῦ, -ῆς see σεαυτοῦ, -ῆς

σεαυτοῦ, -ῆς (σαυτοῦ, -ῆς) (reflex. pron.) yourself [19]

σεισμός, -οῦ, ὁ earthquake [R50]

σείω, σείσω, ἔσεισα, σέσεικα, σέσεισμαι, ἐσείσθην shake, wag [R24]

σημεῖον, -ου, τό sign, miracle [R26]

σῑγή, -ῆς, ἡ silence [R40]

Σικελίᾱ, -ᾱς, ἡ Sicily (large island just south of the Italian peninsula) [R35]

Σικελιώτης, -ου, ὁ Greek inhabitant of Sicily [R36]

Σικελός, -ή, -όν Sicilian [R35]

σῖτος, -ου (nom. pl. σῖτα), ὁ grain, food [45]

σκάπτω, σκάψω, ἔσκαψα, ἔσκαφα, ἔσκαμμαι, ἐσκάφην dig [R8]

σκέπτομαι see σκοπέω

σκηνάω, σκηνήσω, ἐσκήνησα, ἐσκήνηκα, ἐσκήνημαι, ἐσκηνήθην (usually mid.) encamp [R50]

σκηνή, -ῆς, ἡ tent [4]

σκόλοψ, -οπος, ὁ thorn [R16]

σκοπέω/σκέπτομαι (σκέπτομαι is not used in Attic), σκέψομαι, ἐσκεψάμην, —, ἔσκεμμαι, — (verbal adj. σκεπτέος) (+ fear or neg. effort cl.) look at, look into, examine [45]

σός, -ή, -όν (poss. adj.) your, yours, your own (one person's) [21]

σοφίᾱ, -ᾱς, ἡ wisdom [13]

σοφός, -ή, -όν wise [13]

σπεύδω, σπεύσω, ἔσπευσα, —, —, — (+ infin.) be eager (to), hasten (to), strive (to) [3]

σπήλαιον, -ου, τό cave [R17]

στάδιον, -ου (nom. pl. στάδια/στάδιοι), τό stade (distance equal to 600 Greek feet), racecourse, stadium [44]

στασιάζω, στασιάσω, ἐστασίασα, ἐστασίακα, ἐστασίασμαι, ἐστασιάσθην quarrel [R13]

στόλος, -ου, ὁ expedition [R34]

στρατηγός, -οῦ, ὁ general (one of the 10 officials elected annually to run Athens' army and navy) [29]

στρατιά, -ᾶς, ἡ army [36]

στρατιώτης, -ου, ὁ soldier [36]

στρατόπεδον, -ου, τό camp [36]

στρατός, -οῦ, ὁ army [36]

σύ (pers. pron.) you (sg.) [14]

συγγενής, -ές related (by birth), kin; (as a substantive) relative [R21, R37]

συγγνώμη, -ης, ἡ (+ gen.) pardon (for), forgiveness (of) [R40]

συγγυμναστής, -οῦ, ὁ exercise partner [R44]

συλλαμβάνω, συλλήψομαι, συνέλαβον, συνείληφα, συνείλημμαι, συνελήφθην gather together, collect, arrest [19]

συλλογίζομαι, συλλογίσομαι, συνελογισάμην, —, συλλελόγισμαι, — reckon together, infer [R30]

σύλλογος, -ου, ὁ gathering, meeting [R41]

συμβαίνω, συμβήσομαι, συνέβην, συμβέβηκα, συμβέβαμαι, συνεβάθην happen [R29]

συμμαχίᾱ, -ᾱς, ἡ alliance [R35, R37, R38]

συμμάχομαι fight together (see μάχομαι) [R37]

σύμμαχος, -ον (+ dat.) allied (to); (as a substantive) ally [R34, 35]

συμπέμπω (+ dat.) send along (with) (see πέμπω) [R50]

συμπλέω, συμπλεύσομαι/συμπλευσοῦμαι, συνέπλευσα, συμπέπλευκα, συμπέπλευσμαι, — sail together [R34]

σύμφορος, -ον advantageous, beneficial [R47]

συμφυλάττω guard together (see φυλάττω) [R46]

σύν (prep. + dat.) with, together with, with the help of [19]

συνθηρεύω, συνθηρεύσω, συνεθήρευσα, συντεθήρευκα, συντεθήρευμαι, συνεθηρεύθην hunt together [R46]

σύνοδος, -ου, ἡ meeting [R22]

συνοικέω, συνοικήσω, συνῴκησα, συνῴ κηκα, συνῴκημαι, συνῳκήθην live together [R47]

Συρᾱκόσιος, -ᾱ, -ον Syracusan [R38]

σύσκηνος, -ου, ὁ tentmate, messmate [R44]

σφάλλω, σφαλῶ, ἔσφηλα, ἔσφαλκα, ἔσφαλμαι, ἐσφάλην trip up (in wrestling), overthrow [R32]

σχεδόν (adv.) nearly [R33]

σχίσμα, -ατος, τό schism, division of opinion [R26]

σχολή, -ῆς, ἡ leisure, discussion, school [43]

σχολῇ in a leisurely way, at one's leisure [43]

σχολὴν ἄγειν have leisure [43]

σῴζω, σώσω, ἔσωσα, σέσωκα, σέσωσμαι/ σέσωμαι, ἐσώθην (verbal adj. σωστέος) save, bring safely (to) [32]

Σωκράτης, -ους, ὁ Socrates (famous 5th-century B.C. Athenian philosopher) [17]

σῶμα, -ατος, τό body [25]

σωτηρίᾱ, -ᾱς, ἡ safety [R10, R21, R30]

σωφρονέω, σωφρονήσω, ἐσωφρόνησα, σεσωφρόνηκα, σεσωφρόνημαι, ἐσωφρονήθην be self-controlled [R42]

σωφρονίζω, σωφρονιῶ, —, —, —, — teach discretion to, chastise [R45]

σωφροσύνη, -ης, ἡ prudence, discretion, temperance, self-control [42]

σώφρων, -ον prudent, discreet, temperate, self-controlled [42]

τ' see τε

τάλαντον, -ου, τό talent (a weight or sum of money equal to 60 minas) [41]

ταῦθ' see ταῦτα

ταῦτ' see ταῦτα

ταῦτα these (neut. pl. acc. of οὗτος) [13]

τάχιστος, -η, -ον (superl. of ταχύς, -εῖα, -ύ) fastest, quickest, swiftest [41]

ταχύς, -εῖα, -ύ fast, quick, swift [R35, 41]

τε (τ', θ') (enclitic conj.) and; τ' before smooth breathing, θ' before rough breathing [22] τε (τ᾽, θ᾽)...καί (*correlatives*) both...and [22]

τε (τ᾽, θ᾽)...τε (τ᾽, θ᾽) (*correlatives*) both...and [22]

τεῖχος, -ους, τό wall (*of a city*) [17]

τέκνον, -ου, τό child, offspring [8]

τέλειος/τέλεος, -α, -ον complete, perfect [R43, R48]

τέταρτος, -η, -ον fourth [34]

τέτταρες, τέτταρα four [34]

τέχνη, -ης, ἡ art, skill, craft, trade [46]

τήμερον (*adv.*) today [23]

τηρέω, τηρήσω, ἐτήρησα, τετήρηκα, τετήρημαι, ἐτηρήθην pay attention to, observe [R26]

τίθημι, θήσω, ἔθηκα, τέθηκα, τέθειμαι, ἐτέθην place, put, set, lay down, establish, make [47]

τίκτω, τέξω/τέξομαι, ἔτεκον, τέτοκα, τέτεγμαι, ἐτέχθην give birth to, lay (*eggs*) [R19]

τῑμάω, τῑμήσω, ἐτίμησα, τετίμηκα, τετίμημαι, ἐτῑμήθην honor, value [15]

τῑμή, -ῆς, ἡ honor, worth, price [15]

τίς, τί (*interrog. adj.*) what? which?; [21] (*interrog. pron.*) who? what? [21]; τί (*neut. sg. acc. used as adv.*) why? [21]

τις, τι (*indef. adj., enclitic*) a, an, a certain, some, any [21]; (*indef. pron., enclitic*) someone, something, anyone, anything, some, any [21]

τόθ᾽ *see* τότε

τοι (*enclitic postpositive particle*) you know, you see [44]

τοίνυν (*postpositive particle*) therefore, then [44]

τοιόσδε, τοιάδε, τοιόνδε of such a sort, such (*strengthened form of* τοῖος, -α, -ον) [31]

τοιοῦτος, τοιαύτη, τοιοῦτο(ν) of such a sort, such (*strengthened form of* τοῖος, -α, -ον; *Attic usually adds* -ν *to* τοιοῦτο) [31]

τοῖχος, -ου, ὁ wall (*of a house or enclosure*) [R16]

τόλμη, -ης, ἡ daring [R36]

τόπος, -ου, ὁ place, passage (*in a book*) [11]

τοσόσδε, τοσήδε, τοσόνδε so great, so much; (*pl.*) so many (*strengthened form of* τόσος, -η, -ον) [31]

τοσοῦτος, τοσαύτη, τοσοῦτο(ν) so great, so much; (*pl.*) so many (*strengthened form of* τόσος, -η, -ον; *Attic usually adds* -ν *to* τοσοῦτο) [31]

τότ᾽ *see* τότε

τότε (τότ᾽, τόθ᾽) (*adv.*) then, at that time; τότ᾽ *before smooth breathing,* τόθ᾽ *before rough breathing* [13]

τοῦθ᾽ *see* τοῦτο

τοῦτ᾽ *see* τοῦτο

τοῦτο this (*neut. sg. acc. of* οὗτος) [R10, 13]

τρεῖς, τρία three [34]

τρέπω, τρέψω, ἔτρεψα, τέτροφα, τέτραμμαι, ἐτρέφθην/ἐτράπην turn; (*mid. or pass.*) betake oneself, move [11]

τρέχω, δραμοῦμαι, ἔδραμον, δεδράμηκα, δεδράμημαι, — run [50]

τριήραρχος, -ου, ὁ trierarch (*rich Athenian citizen who paid for the outfitting of a trireme as his public service*) [R34]

τριήρης, -ους, ἡ trireme (*warship with three banks of oars*) [17]

τρίς (*adv.*) thrice [34]

τρίτος, -η, -ον third [34]

τρόπος, -ου, ὁ turn, way, manner, habit; (*pl.*) character [R6, 11]

τροφή, -ῆς, ἡ rearing, upbringing [R46]

τρώγω, τρώξομαι, ἔτρωξα/ἔτραγον, —, τέτρωγμαι, ἐτράγην gnaw [R15]

τυγχάνω, τεύξομαι, ἔτυχον, τετύχηκα, —, — (+ *dat.*) befall, happen (to); (+ *suppl. ptcple.*) happen; (+ *gen.*) hit (*a target*), chance upon, meet, obtain [R40, 50]

τυραννίς, -ίδος, ἡ tyranny, life of a tyrant [R49]

τύραννος, -ου, ὁ tyrant (*ruler who seizes power rather than inheriting it*) [R38]

τυφλός, -ή, -όν blind [R26, 27]

τύχη, -ης, ἡ chance, fortune, luck; Τύχη = Chance, Fortune (*personified as a goddess*) [50]

ὑβρίζω, ὑβριῶ, ὕβρισα, ὕβρικα, ὕβρισμαι, ὑβρίσθην act insolently, rebel; (*with* εἰς + *acc.*) commit an outrage (against) [R42, R45]

ὑγιαίνω, ὑγιανῶ, ὑγίᾱνα, —, —, — be healthy [R32]

ὑγιεινός, -ή, -όν healthy [R32]

ὕδωρ, ὕδατος, τό water [R11, R21, 50]

υἱός, -οῦ, ὁ son [27]

ὑμεῖς (*pers. pron.*) you (*pl.*) [14]

ὑμέτερος, -ᾱ, -ον (*poss. adj.*) your, yours, your own (*more than one person's*) [21]

ὑμῶν αὐτῶν, -ῶν (*reflex. pron.*) yourselves [19]

ὑπ' *see* ὑπό

ὑπέρ (*prep.* + *gen.*) over, above, on behalf of; (*prep.* + *acc.*) over, to a place over, beyond [20]

ὑπερβάλλω exceed, be in excess (*see* βάλλω) [R49]

ὑπερφρονέω, ὑπερφρονήσω, ὑπερεφρόνησα, ὑπερπεφρόνηκα, ὑπερπεφρόνημαι, ὑπερεφρονήθην look down at, scorn [R36]

ὑπηρεσίᾱ, -ᾱς, ἡ crew of rowers [R34]

ὕπνος, -ου, ὁ sleep [R19, 45]

ὑπό (ὑπ', ὑφ') (*prep.* + *gen.*) from under, by (*under the agency of*); (*prep.* + *dat.*) under; (*prep.* + *acc.*) under, to a place under; ὑπ' *before smooth breathing,* ὑφ' *before rough breathing* [11]

ὑποπτεύω, ὑποπτεύσω, ὑπώπτευσα, ὑπώπτευκα, ὑπώπτευμαι, ὑπωπτεύθην be suspicious, suspect [R39]

ὕποπτος, -ον suspicious; (*as a neut. substantive*) suspicion [R38]

ὕστατος, -η, -ον (*superl. of* ὕστερος, -ᾱ, -ον) latest, last [39]

ὑστεραῖος, -ᾱ, -ον following, next [R29]

ὑστερίζω, ὑστεριῶ, ὑστέρισα, —, —, — be late [R33]

ὕστερον (*neut. acc. of* ὕστερος, -ᾱ, -ον *used as adv.*) later [39]

ὕστερος, -ᾱ, -ον (*comp.; no positive degree exists*) later, next [39]

ὑφ' *see* ὑπό

φαίνω, φανῶ, ἔφηνα, πέφαγκα/(*intrans.*) πέφηνα, πέφασμαι, ἐφάνθην/ (*intrans.*) ἐφάνην make appear, show; (*mid. & intransitive forms*) appear [R30, R32, 35]

φανερός, -ά, -όν visible, evident, open [35]

Φαρισαῖοι, -ων, οἱ Pharisees (*a sect of Jews who believed in strict obedience to the law of Moses*) [R26, R27]

φειδωλός, -ή, -όν thrifty [R39]

φέρε (*imper. of* φέρω—*strengthens another imperative*) come on now! [40]

φέρω, οἴσω, ἤνεγκα/ἤνεγκον, ἐνήνοχα, ἐνήνεγμαι, ἠνέχθην (*verbal adj.* οἰστέος) bear, bring, carry [14]

φεύγω, φεύξομαι, ἔφυγον, πέφευγα, —, — (*verbal adj.* φευκτέος) flee, avoid, escape, be in exile [10]

φημί, φήσω, ἔφησα, —, —, — (*verbal adj.* φατέος) say, assert; οὔ φημι = deny [41]

φθονέω, φθονήσω, ἐφθόνησα, ἐφθόνηκα, ἐφθόνημαι, ἐφθονήθην (+ *dat.*) envy [R22]

φιλαίτατος, -η, -ον (*superl. of* φίλος, -η, -ον) (+ *dat.*) dearest (to) [32]

φιλαίτερος, -ᾱ, -ον (*comp. of* φίλος, -η, -ον) (+ *dat.*) dearer (to) [32]

φιλέω, φιλήσω, ἐφίλησα, πεφίληκα, πεφίλημαι, ἐφιλήθην love, kiss; (+ *infin.*) be fond of (*doing*), be accustomed (to) [15]

φίλη, -ης, ἡ friend (*female*) [10]

φιλίᾱ, -ᾱς, ἡ friendship [R35, 41]

φίλιος, -ᾱ, -ον friendly [R36]

Φίλιππος, -ου, ὁ Philip II (*4th-century B.C. king of Macedonia and father of Alexander the Great*) [R29]

φίλος, -η, -ον (+ *dat.*) dear (to) [10]

φίλος, -ου, ὁ friend (*male*) [10]

φιλοσοφέω, φιλοσοφήσω, ἐφιλοσόφησα, πεφιλοσόφηκα, πεφιλοσόφημαι, ἐφιλοσοφήθην practice philosophy [R48]

φιλοσοφίᾱ, -ᾱς, ἡ philosophy [13]

φιλόσοφος, -ον philosophical; (*as a substantive*) philosopher [13]

φίλτατος, -η, -ον (*superl. of* φίλος, -η, -ον) (+ *dat.*) dearest (to) [32]

φίλτερος, -ᾱ, -ον (*comp. of* φίλος, -η, -ον) (+ *dat.*) dearer (to) [32]

φοβέω, φοβήσω, ἐφόβησα, πεφόβηκα, πεφόβημαι, ἐφοβήθην frighten; (*mid./ pass.* + *acc.*) be frightened (of), be afraid (of), fear [R16, 21]

φόβος, -ου, ὁ fear, fright [R19, 21]

φονεύς, -έως, ὁ murderer [R21]

φόρημα, -ατος, τό burden [R45]

φράζω, φράσω, ἔφρασα, πέφρακα, πέφρασμαι, ἐφράσθην tell, declare, explain [40]

φρόνησις, -εως, ἡ good sense [R50]

φυγάς, -άδος, ὁ, ἡ exiled person, an exile [R45]

φυλακίς, -ίδος, ἡ guardian (*female*) [R47]

φύλαξ, -ακος, ὁ guard, guardian [16]

φυλάττω, φυλάξω, ἐφύλαξα, πεφύλαχα, πεφύλαγμαι, ἐφυλάχθην stand guard, guard, protect, preserve [3]; (*mid.*) be on guard against [11]

φύσις, -εως, ἡ nature [37]

φυτόν, -οῦ, τό plant, tree (*something that is grown in a garden or an orchard*) [8]

φύω, φύσω, ἔφῡσα/ἔφῡν, πέφῡκα, —, — produce, bring forth; (*second aor. intrans. act.*) grew [R48]

φωνή, -ῆς, ἡ voice, sound [R20, 30]

φῶς (= φάος), φωτός, τό light [R48]

χαίρω, χαιρήσω, ἐχαίρησα, κεχάρηκα, κεχάρημαι, ἐχάρην (+ *suppl. ptcple.*) be happy; (+ *dat.*) rejoice (in), take delight (in); χαῖρε, χαίρετε = hello! / farewell! [7]

χαλεπός, -ή, -όν difficult, hard [50]

χαλκός, -οῦ, ὁ copper, copper money [R23]

χαρά, -ᾶς, ἡ joy, delight [7]

χάριν (*acc. sg. of* χάρις, -ιτος, ἡ *used as postpos. prep.* + *gen.*) for the sake of [16] χάριν ἔχειν (+ *dat.*) be grateful (to) [16]

χάρις, -ιτος, ἡ grace, favor, gratitude [16]

χάσμα, -ατος, τό opening, chasm [R49]

χειμών, -ῶνος, ὁ storm [R23]

χείρ, χειρός (*dat. pl.* χερσί[ν]), ἡ hand [R16, 42]

χείριστος, -η, -ον (*superl. of* κακός, -ή, -όν) worst (*in ability or worth*) [33]

χείρων, -ον (*comp. of* κακός, -ή, -όν) worse (*in ability or worth*) [33]

χῑλιέτης, -ες lasting a thousand years [R50]

χίλιοι, -αι, -α one thousand [34]

χορός, -οῦ, ὁ dance, chorus (*of a Greek play*) [44]

χράομαι, χρήσομαι, ἐχρησάμην, —, κέχρημαι, ἐχρήσθην (+ *dat.*) use, be subject to, experience [36]

χρείᾱ, -ᾱς, ἡ use, function [R32]

χρή (*indecl.*) necessity; (+ ἐστί & *acc.* + *infin.*) there is need (to), it is necessary (to), one ought (to) (*imperf.* χρῆν/ἐχρῆν, *fut. indic.* χρῆσται, *pres. subj.* χρῇ, *pres. opt.* χρείη, *pres. infin.* χρῆναι, *indeclin. ptcple.* χρεών) [43]

χρῆμα, -ατος, τό thing; (*pl.*) goods, property, money [35]

χρήσιμος, -η, -ον useful, advantageous [R32, R35, 36]

χρῑω, χρῑσω, ἔχρῑσα, —, κέχρῑμαι, ἐχρῑσθην anoint [R26]

χρόνος, -ου, ὁ time [23]

χρόνῳ in time, eventually [R39]

χρῡσίον, -ου, τό piece of gold; (*pl.*) money, cash [35]

χρῡσός, -οῦ, ὁ gold [35]

χώρᾱ, -ᾱς, ἡ land, country, countryside, space, position [4]

ψευδής, -ές lying, false, untrue [50]

ψευδίστατος, -η, -ον (*superl. of* ψευδής, -ές) most lying, most false, most untrue [50]

ψῡχή, -ῆς, ἡ spirit, soul, life [22]

ὦ (*interj.* + *vocative*) O! [4]

ὧδε (*adv. of* ὅδε, ἥδε, τόδε) in this way, so, thus [31]

ὠνέομαι (*imperf.* ἐωνούμην), ὠνήσομαι, ἐπριάμην, —, ἐώνημαι, ἐωνήθην buy (*deponent in first three principal parts only*) [46]

ᾠόν, -οῦ, τό egg [R19]

ὥρᾱ, -ᾱς, ἡ season, hour; (*with acc. or dat.* + *infin.*) it is time (to) [5]

ὡς (*particle* + *ptcple.*) as if, with the avowed intention of, on the grounds of [24]; (*causal/temporal conj.*) as, since, because, after, when [24]; (*adv.* + *adv. or adj. in exclamation*) how! [31]; (*particle* + *superlative*) as...as possible [32]; (*rel. adv.*) how, as [38]; (*conj. introducing indir. discourse*) that, how [40]; (*prep.* + *acc.*; *only with persons as its object*) to [40]; (*conj. introducing effort clause*) how, that [45]

ὡς μή (*introducing neg. purp. clause*) in order that...not, lest [39]; (*introducing neg. effort clause*) how...not, that...not [45]

ὥσπερ as if, as it were, just as [47]

ὥστε (*conj.* + *infin.*) so as; (*conj.* + *finite verb in indic. mood*) so that [31]

ὠφελέω, ὠφελήσω, ὠφέλησα, ὠφέληκα, ὠφέλημαι, ὠφελήθην help, aid [15]

ὠφέλιμος, -ον helpful, useful [R47]

χάριν ἔχειν (+ *dat.*) be grateful (to) [16]

χάρις, -ιτος, ἡ grace, favor, gratitude [16]

χάσμα, -ατος, τό opening, chasm [R49]

χειμών, -ῶνος, ὁ storm [R23]

χείρ, χειρός (*dat. pl.* χερσί[ν]), ἡ hand [R16, 42]

χείριστος, -η, -ον (*superl. of* κακός, -ή, -όν) worst (*in ability or worth*) [33]

χείρων, -ον (*comp. of* κακός, -ή, -όν) worse (*in ability or worth*) [33]

χῑλιέτης, -ες lasting a thousand years [R50]

χίλιοι, -αι, -α one thousand [34]

χορός, -οῦ, ὁ dance, chorus (*of a Greek play*) [44]

χράομαι, χρήσομαι, ἐχρησάμην, —, κέχρημαι, ἐχρήσθην (+ *dat.*) use, be subject to, experience [36]

χρεία, -ᾱς, ἡ use, function [R32]

χρή (*indecl.*) necessity; (+ ἐστί & *acc.* + *infin.*) there is need (to), it is necessary (to), one ought (to) (*imperf.* χρῆν/ἐχρῆν, *fut. indic.* χρῆσται, *pres. subj.* χρῇ, *pres. opt.* χρείη, *pres. infin.* χρῆναι, *indeclin. ptcple.* χρεών) [43]

χρῆμα, -ατος, τό thing; (*pl.*) goods, property, money [35]

χρήσιμος, -η, -ον useful, advantageous [R32, R35, 36]

χρίω, χρίσω, ἔχρῑσα, —, κέχρῑμαι, ἐχρίσθην anoint [R26]

χρόνος, -ου, ὁ time [23]

χρόνῳ in time, eventually [R39]

χρῡσίον, -ου, τό piece of gold; (*pl.*) money, cash [35]

χρῡσός, -οῦ, ὁ gold [35]

χώρᾱ, -ᾱς, ἡ land, country, countryside, space, position [4]

ψευδής, -ές lying, false, untrue [50]

ψευδίστατος, -η, -ον (*superl. of* ψευδής, -ές) most lying, most false, most untrue [50]

ψῡχή, -ῆς, ἡ spirit, soul, life [22]

ENGLISH-TO-GREEK GLOSSARY

Lesson numbers appear in brackets; R means that the word is found in the reading rather than in the vocabulary.

a τις, τι [21]

abandon ἀπολείπω [8]

able (to) δυνατός, -ή, -όν + infin. [R35, 47] οἷός τε, οἵα τε, οἷόν τε + infin. [46]

about περί + gen. [18]; ἀμφί + gen. [23]

above ὑπέρ + gen. [20]

accomplish κατεργάζομαι + infin. [R45]

according to κατά + acc. [20]

accusation αἰτίᾱ, -ᾱς, ἡ [19]

acquire κομίζω (mid.) [15]

act πράττω [10]

act insolently ὑβρίζω [R45]

action πρᾶξις, -εως, ἡ [R43]

activity ἐνέργεια, -ᾱς, ἡ [R43]; πρᾶξις, -εως, ἡ [R49]

add to προσποιέω [17]

addition ἐπιφορά, -ᾶς, ἡ [R34]

admire θαυμάζω [44]

adornment κόσμος, -ου, ὁ [28]

advantageous χρήσιμος, -η, -ον [R32, R35, 36]; σύμφορος, -ον [R47]

affair πρᾶγμα, -ατος, τό [R30, 42]

(the) aforesaid οὗτος, αὕτη, τοῦτο [R10, 13]

after (conj.) ἐπεί [5]; ἐπειδή [5]; ὡς [24]

after (prep.) μετά + acc. [19]

again πάλιν [6]; αὖ [R37, 42]; αὖθις [R41, 42]

against ἐπί + acc. [14]; πρός + acc. [17]; κατά + gen. [20]

age (of a person) ἡλικίᾱ, -ᾱς, ἡ [27]

age (span of time) αἰών, -ῶνος, ὁ [R28]

agree (to) ὁμολογέω + infin. [48]

agree (with) ὁμολογέω + dat. [48]

aid ὠφελέω [15]

aim at getting περιποιέω [R43]

Alexander Ἀλέξανδρος, -ου, ὁ [R41, R42]

all πᾶς, πᾶσα, πᾶν [23]

alliance συμμαχίᾱ, -ᾱς, ἡ [R35, R37, R38]

413

allied (with) σύμμαχος, -ον + dat. [R34, 35]

allow παρίημι [47]

ally σύμμαχος, -ου, ὁ [R34, 35]

alone μόνος, -η, -ον [18]

already ἤδη [27]

also καί [3]

alter ἀλλάττω [6]

although καίπερ + ptcple. [24]

always ἀεί [25]

ambassador πρέσβυς, -εως, ὁ [R35, R41]

among μετά + gen. [19]

an τις, τι [21]

ancestor γονεύς, -έως, ὁ [47]

ancient παλαιός, -ά, -όν [27]; more ancient παλαίτερος, -ᾱ, -ον [32]; most ancient παλαίτατος, -η, -ον [32]

and καί [3]; δέ [10]; τε [22]

and not οὐδέ [22]; μηδέ [22]; οὔτε [22]; μήτε [22]

and yet καὶ μήν [32]

animal ζῷον, -ου, τό [R17, 22]

announce ἀγγέλλω [18]

announce to προσαγγέλλω [R30]

anoint χρίω [R26]

another ἄλλος, -η, -ο [22]

answer ἀποκρίνω (mid.) + dat. [27]

any τις, τι [21]

anyone τις [21]

anything τι [21]

Aphrodite Ἀφροδίτη, -ης, ἡ [R6]

appear ὁράω (pass.) [23]; φαίνω (mid. & intrans.) [R30, R32, 35]

approach προσέρχομαι [R49, R50]

archon ἄρχων, -οντος, ὁ [38]

argument λόγος, -ου, ὁ [12]

army στρατιά, -ᾶς, ἡ [36]; στρατός, -οῦ, ὁ [36]

around περί + dat. or acc. [18]; ἀμφί + acc. [23]

arrange διατάττω [R47]

arrest συλλαμβάνω [19]

arrive (at) ἀφικνέομαι with εἰς or ἐπί + acc. [30]

art τέχνη, -ης, ἡ [46]

as (conj.) ὡς [24]; (rel. adv.) ὡς [38]

as...as possible ὅτι + superl. [32]; ὡς + superl. [32]

as ever (indef. rel. adv.) ὅπως [38]

as far as regards ἕνεκα + gen. [48]

as for the rest λοιπόν [32]

as if (particle) ὡς + ptcple. [24]; (rel. adv.) ὥσπερ [47]

as it were ὥσπερ [47]

as long as ἕως [23]

as many as (rel. adj.) ὅσοι, -αι, -α [46]

as much as (rel. adj.) ὅσος, -η, -ον [46]

Asia Ἀσίᾱ, -ᾱς, ἡ [R42]

ask ἐρωτάω + double acc. [18]

assembly ἐκκλησίᾱ, -ᾱς, ἡ [R29, 30]

assert φημί [41]

assign ἀποδίδωμι [R46]

associate with παραλαμβάνω [R44]

at ἐπί + dat. [14]; πρός + dat. [17]; παρά + dat. [22]

at all πάνυ [48]

at another place ἄλλοθι [49]

at another time ἄλλοτε [R36]

at any rate γε [12]

at Athens Ἀθήνησι(ν) [R33, 49]

at home οἴκοι [R33, 49]

at least γε [12]

at length μακρόν [31]; μακρά [31]

at night ἔννυχος, -ον [R5]; νυκτός [R19, 23]

at one's leisure σχολῇ [43]

at that place ἐκεῖ [49]; ἔνθα [49]; ἐνθάδε [49]; ἐνταῦθα [49] at that time τότε [13]

at the house of παρά + dat. [22]

at the same place ὁμοῦ [49]; ἅμα [R45]

at the side of παρά + dat. [22]

at the very place αὐτοῦ [R35]

at this place ἔνθα [49]; ἐνθάδε [49];
 ἐνταῦθα [49]

at this time νῦν [13]

at war (with) πολέμιος, -ᾱ, -ον + dat. [12]

at what price? πόσου [R18]

Athenian Ἀθηναῖος, -ᾱ, -ον [R31, R34,
 R35, 37]

Athens Ἀθῆναι, -ῶν, αἱ [49]

athletics γυμναστική, -ῆς, ἡ (supply τέχνη)
 [R46]

Atropos Ἄτροπος, -ου, ἡ [R50]

attack προσβάλλω + dat. [17]

attempt (to) ἐπιχειρέω + infin. [R46]

automatic αὐτόματος, -η, -ον [R33]

avoid φεύγω [10]

awaken ἐπεγείρω [R40]

away from ἀπό + gen. [7]

back πάλιν [6]

backwards πάλιν [6]

bad (at doing a thing) κακός, -ή, -όν [9]

bad (morally) κακός, -ή, -όν [9]

bad condition καχεξίᾱ, -ᾱς, ἡ [R31, R32]

bad name ἐπίκλησις, -εως, ἡ [R44]

badly κακῶς [17]

banish διώκω [6]

bat (animal) νυκτερίς, -ίδος, ἡ [R23]

battle μάχη, -ης, ἡ [35]

be εἰμί [R6, R7, R11, 12]

be a citizen πολῑτεύω [R43]

be a coward ἀποδειλιάω [R31]

be a slave (to) δουλεύω + dat. [9]

be able (to) ἔχω + infin. [6]; δύναμαι +
 infin. [47]

be about (to) μέλλω + fut. infin. [6]

be accustomed (to) φιλέω + infin. [15]

be afraid (of) φοβέομαι + acc. [R16, 21];
 δέδοικα + acc. [45]

be afraid (to) φοβέομαι + infin. [R16, 21];
 δέδοικα + infin. [45]

be amazed (at) θαυμάζω [44]

be ashamed αἰσχύνω (mid.) [44]

be asleep καθεύδω [45]

be at home ἐπιδημέω [R40]

be born γίγνομαι [R14, R27, R28, 32]

be captured ἁλίσκομαι [R31]

be content (to) ἀγαπάω + infin. or suppl.
 ptcple. [41]

be eager (to) σπεύδω + infin. [3]; ἵημι
 (mid.) + infin. [47]

be encouraged θαρρέω [R35]

be fond of (doing) φιλέω + infin. [15];
 ἀγαπάω + infin. or suppl. ptcple. [41]

be governed οἰκέω [R48]

be grateful (to) χάριν ἔχειν + dat. [16]

be grown up ἡλικίᾱν ἔχειν [27]; ἐν ἡλικίᾳ
 εἶναι [27]

be happy χαίρω [7]

be healthy ὑγιαίνω [R32]

be ignorant of ἀγνοέω [R5]

be in danger κινδῡνεύω [R39]

be in debt ὀφείλω [48]

be in excess ὑπερβάλλω [R49]

be in exile φεύγω [10]

be in the marketplace ἀγοράζω [R44]

be killed ἀποθνῄσκω [21]

be king βασιλεύω [R48]

be laid down κεῖμαι [47]

be late ὑστερίζω [R33]

be lying down κατάκειμαι [R40]

be negligent ἀμελέω [R33]

be of age ἡλικίαν ἔχειν [27]; ἐν ἡλικίᾳ εἶναι [27]

be on guard against φυλάττω (*mid.*) [11]

be placed κεῖμαι [47]

be powerful enough (to) δύναμαι + infin. [47]

be present πάρειμι [R30]

be punished δίκην διδόναι [46]

be self-controlled σωφρονέω [R42]

be settled οἰκέω [R48]

be situated κεῖμαι [47]

be standing ἵστημι (*perf.*) [46]

be strong ἰσχύω [R32]

be subject to χράομαι + dat. [36]

be surprised θαυμάζω [R28]

be suspicious ὑποπτεύω [R39]

be treated badly κακῶς πάσχειν [40]

be treated well εὖ πάσχειν [40]

be unjust ἀδικέω [37]

be willing (to) ἐθέλω + infin. [3]

bear (*animal*) ἄρκτος, -ου, ὁ, ἡ [R10]

bear (*carry*) φέρω [14]; (*give birth to*) γεννάω [R27, 28]

beat out (*metal*) ἐλαύνω [44]

beautiful καλός, -ή, -όν [8]; more beautiful καλλίων, -ῑον [33]; most beautiful κάλλιστος, -η, -ον [33]

beauty κάλλος, -ους, τό [R43, R49]

because (*conj.*) ἐπεί [5]; ἐπειδή [5]; ὡς [24]; ὅτι [28]; διότι [R32, R36]; (*particle*) ἅτε + ptcple. [24]

become γίγνομαι [R14, R27, R28, 32]

become hateful (to) ἀπεχθάνομαι + dat. [R45]

become lazy μαλθακίζω (*mid.*) [R47]

bed κλίνη, -ης, ἡ [5]

befall τυγχάνω + dat. [50]

before (*adv.*) πρό [32]

before (*conj.*) πρίν + infin. [43]

beget γεννάω [R27, 28]

begin ἄρχω (*mid.*) + gen., infin., or ptcple. [38]

beginning ἀρχή, -ῆς, ἡ [12]

behind μετά + acc. [19]

behold βλέπω [R7, R9, R10, 13]; ὁράω [23]; θεάομαι [R49]

believe νομίζω [R30, 41]

believe (in) πιστεύω + dat. or εἰς + acc. [28]

beneficial σύμφορος, -ον [R47]

bequeath καταλείπω [R32]

beside παρά + dat. [22]

best (*in ability or worth*) ἄριστος, -η, -ον [33]

best (*in might*) κράτιστος, -η, -ον [33]

best (*morally*) βέλτιστος, -η, -ον [33]

betake oneself τρέπω (*mid.*) [11]

better (*in ability or worth*) ἀμείνων, -ον [33]

better (*in might*) κρείττων, -ον [33]

better (*morally*) βελτίων, -ῑον [33]

beyond ὑπέρ + acc. [20]

big μέγας, μεγάλη, μέγα [R14, 25]

birth γένεσις, -εως, ἡ [R46, R50]; γένος, -ους, τό [48]

blame αἰτίᾱ, -ᾱς, ἡ [19]

blameworthy αἴτιος, -ᾱ, -ον [19]

blind τυφλός, -ή, -όν [R26, 27]

blow πληγή, -ῆς, ἡ [R44]

body σῶμα, -ατος, τό [25]

boldness θάρρος, -ους, τό [R36]

bonus ἐπιφορά, -ᾶς, ἡ [R34]

book βιβλίον, -ου, τό [14]

both...and καὶ...καί [3]; τε...καί [22]; τε...τε [22]

bramble bush βάτος, -ου, ἡ [R23]

brave ἀγαθός, -ή, -όν [8]

bring φέρω [14]

bring about κατεργάζομαι + infin. [R44]

bring forth φύω [R48]

bring safely (to) σῴζω [32]

bring to a stop παύω [25]; ἀναπαύω [R33]

brother ἀδελφός, -οῦ, ὁ [7]

bundle δέσμη, -ης, ἡ [R13]

burden φόρημα, -ατος, τό [R45]

burning heat καῦμα, -ατος, τό [R50]

but ἀλλά [6]; δέ [10]

but yet ἀλλὰ μήν [32]

buy ὠνέομαι [46]

by (in oaths) πρός + gen. [17]

by (in various idioms) κατά + acc. [20]; ἀνά + acc. [23]

by (location) ἐπί + dat. [14]

by (under the agency of) ὑπό + gen. [11]

by all means πάνυ [48]

by land κατὰ γῆν [20]

by night ἔννυχος, -ον [R5]; νυκτός [R19, 23]

by sea κατὰ θάλατταν [20]

call καλέω [24]

camp στρατόπεδον, -ου, τό [36]

can ἔχω + infin. [6]; δύναμαι + infin. [47]

care for κομίζω [15]

career πρᾶξις, -εως, ἡ [R49]

carry φέρω [14]; κομίζω [15]; πορεύω [R33, R50]

carrying hoplites ὁπλῑταγωγός, -όν [R34]

cart ἅμαξα, -ης, ἡ [11]

Carthaginian Καρχηδόνιος, -ᾱ, -ον [R35]

cash ἀργύρια, -ων, τά [35]; χρῡσία, -ων, τά [35]

cast aside ῥίπτω [20]; ἀποβάλλω [R45]

cat αἴλουρος, -ου, ὁ, ἡ [R19]

cattle πρόβατα, -ων, τά [R12]

cause αἰτίᾱ, -ᾱς, ἡ [19]

cavalryman ἱππεύς, -έως, ὁ [R34]

cave σπήλαιον, -ου, τό [R17]

caw κράζω [R19, R20]

cease παύω (mid.) [25]

(a) certain τις, τι [21]

certainly δή [44]

chance τύχη, -ης, ἡ [50]

Chance (personified) Τύχη, -ης, ἡ [50]

chance upon τυγχάνω + gen. [R40, 50]

change ἀλλάττω [6]

character τρόποι, -ων, οἱ [R6, 11]

charge αἰτίᾱ, -ᾱς, ἡ [19]

chase διώκω [6]

chasm χάσμα, -ατος, τό [R49]

chastise σωφρονίζω [R45]

child τέκνον, -ου, τό [8]; παῖς, παιδός, ὁ, ἡ [25]

choose κρίνω [27]; ἀποκρίνω [27]; αἱρέω (mid.) [40]

chorus (of a Greek play) χορός, -οῦ, ὁ [44]

circumstances πράγματα, -ων, τά [42]

citizen πολίτης, -ου, ὁ [43]

city ἄστυ, -εως, τό [29]; πόλις, -εως, ἡ [29]

city-state πόλις, -εως, ἡ [29]

class γένος, -ους, τό [48]

clean καθαρός, -ά, -όν [R49]

clear δῆλος, -η, -ον [R8, 15]

clearly δῆλον [31]; δῆλα [31]

clever δεινός, -ή, -όν [32]

cloak ἱμάτιον, -ου, τό [14]

close παραπλήσιος, -ᾱ, -ον [R46]

clothes ἱμάτια, -ων, τά [14]

Clotho Κλωθώ, -οῦς, ἡ [R50]

collect συλλαμβάνω [19]

come ἔρχομαι [R28, R29, 40]; εἶμι [40]

come forward to speak παρέρχομαι [R30]

come into εἰσέρχομαι [R40]

come on now! ἄγε [40]; ἴθι [40]; φέρε [40]

come out ἐξέρχομαι [R40]

come (to) ἀφικνέομαι with ἐπί or εἰς + acc. [30]

come to know γιγνώσκω [49]

command (to) κελεύω + infin. [5]

commit an outrage (against) ὑβρίζω with εἰς + acc. [R42]

commit suicide προαποθνῄσκω [R45]

common (to) κοινός, -ή, -όν + dat. or gen. [30]

companion (*female*) ἑταίρᾱ, -ᾱς, ἡ [41]

companion (*male*) ἑταῖρος, -ου, ὁ [41]

compete ἀγωνίζομαι [R31]

competition ἀγών, -ῶνος, ὁ [15]

complete τέλειος/τέλεος, -ᾱ, -ον [R43, R48]

comrade (*female*) ἑταίρᾱ, -ᾱς, ἡ [41]

comrade (*male*) ἑταῖρος, -ου, ὁ [41]

conceited κενόδοξος, -ον [R18]

concerning περί + gen. [18]; ἀμφί + gen. [23]

concord ὁμόνοια, -ᾱς, ἡ [R13]

confess (to) ὁμολογέω + infin. [48]

confusion θόρυβος, -ου, ὁ [29]

conquer νῑκάω [37]

consider νομίζω [R30, 41]

contemplate θεωρέω [R43]

contemplation θεωρίᾱ, -ᾱς, ἡ [R43]

contest ἀγών, -ῶνος, ὁ [16]

contrary to παρά + acc. [22]

contrivance μηχανή, -ῆς, ἡ [45]

contrive (to) μηχανάομαι + infin. [R44, 45]

cook μάγειρος, -ου, ὁ [R24]

copper, copper money χαλκός, -οῦ, ὁ [R23]

Corinth Κόρινθος, -ου, ἡ [R35]

corrupt διαφθείρω [37]

couch κλίνη, -ης, ἡ [5]

council βουλή, -ῆς, ἡ [R29, 30]

council-chamber βουλευτήριον, -ου, τό [R29]

country χώρᾱ, -ᾱς, ἡ [4]

countryside ἀγρός, -οῦ, ὁ [R39]; χώρᾱ, -ᾱς, ἡ [4]

courage θάρρος, -ους, τό [R36]

courtesan ἑταίρᾱ, -ᾱς, ἡ [41]

cowardice δειλίᾱ, -ᾱς, ἡ [R37]

cowardly κακός, -ή, -όν [9]; δειλός, -ή, -όν [R25]

craft τέχνη, -ης, ἡ [46]

create ποιέω [R8, R13, 16]

crew of rowers ὑπηρεσίᾱ, -ᾱς, ἡ [R34]

critical moment καιρός, -οῦ, ὁ [R30]

crocodile κροκόδειλος, -ου, ὁ [R21]

crow (*noun*) κόραξ, -ακος, ὁ [R20]

crow (*verb*) κράζω [R19, R20]

crud αὐχμός, -οῦ, ὁ [R49]

crush θλάω [R13]

cry βοάω [39]

cry out βοάω [39]

custom νόμος, -ου, ὁ [22]; ἔθος, -ους, τό [R46]

Cyrus Κῦρος, -ου, ὁ [R45]

daily καθ' ἡμέρᾱν [23]; ἀνὰ πᾶσαν ἡμέρᾱν [23]

damage ζημιόω [R45]

dance (*noun*) χορός, -οῦ, ὁ [44]

dance (*verb*) ὀρχέομαι [R7, R22]

danger κίνδῡνος, -ου, ὁ [10]

daring τόλμη, -ης, ἡ [R36]

Darius Δαρεῖος, -ου, ὁ [R41, R42]

daughter κόρη, -ης, ἡ [6]; παῖς, παιδός, ἡ [25]; θυγάτηρ, -τρός, ἡ [29]

dawn ἕωθεν [R50]

day ἡμέρᾱ, -ᾱς, ἡ day [23]

day by day καθ' ἡμέρᾱν [23]; ἀνὰ πᾶσαν ἡμέρᾱν [23]

dear (to) φίλος, -η, -ον + dat. [10]

death θάνατος, -ου, ὁ [10]

Death (personified) Θάνατος, -ου, ὁ [10]

decide (a contest or dispute) κρίνω [27]

decide (to) βουλεύω + infin. [45]

declare φράζω [40]

deed ἔργον, -ου, τό [8]; πρᾶγμα, -ατος, τό [42]

defend oneself ἀμύνω (mid.) [R36]

delay (to) μέλλω + pres. infin. [6]

deliberate βουλεύω [45]

delight χαρά, -ᾶς, ἡ [7]

demonstrate ἀποδείκνῡμι [48]

deny οὔ φημι [41]

descendant ἔκγονος, -ου, ὁ [R47]

describe διηγέομαι [R49]

deserving (of, to) ἄξιος, -ᾱ, -ον + gen. or infin. [8]

desire (to) βούλομαι + infin. [30]; ἐπιθῡμέω + infin. [R47]

desperate situation ἀπορίᾱ, -ᾱς, ἡ [R36]

despot δεσπότης, -ου, ὁ [9]

destiny μοῖρα, -ᾱς, ἡ [5]

Destiny (personified) Μοῖρα, -ᾱς, ἡ [5]

destroy λύω [12]

determined ἀδαμάντινος, -ον [R49]

device μηχανή, -ῆς, ἡ [45]

devise μηχανάομαι [R44, 45]

devoid (of) κενός, -ή, -όν + gen. [44]

die ἀποθνήσκω [21]

die early προαποθνήσκω [R45]

differ διαφέρω [R32]

different ἕτερος, -ᾱ, -ον [49]

difficult χαλεπός, -ή, -όν [50]

difficulty ἀπορίᾱ, -ᾱς, ἡ [R36]

dig σκάπτω [R8]

dignified εὐσχήμων, -ον [R32]

dine δειπνέω [R24]

dinner δεῖπνον, -ου, τό [24]

dirt αὐχμός, -οῦ, ὁ [R49]

disbelief ἀπιστίᾱ, -ᾱς, ἡ [R47]

disciple μαθητής, -οῦ, ὁ [9]

discover εὑρίσκω [8]

discreet σώφρων, -ον [42]

discretion σωφροσύνη, -ης, ἡ [42]

discussion σχολή, -ῆς, ἡ [43]

disgrace αἰσχύνω [44]

disgraceful αἰσχρός, -ά, -όν [31]; more disgraceful αἰσχίων, -ῑον [33]; most disgraceful αἴσχιστος, -η, -ον [33]

dishonor ἀτῑμίᾱ, -ᾱς, ἡ [R44]

dismiss ἀφίημι [47]

display ἐπίδειξις, -εως, ἡ [R34]

distrust ἀπιστέω + dat. [R45]

divine being δαίμων, -ονος, ὁ [17]

division of opinion σχίσμα, -ατος, τό [R26]

do ποιέω [R8, R13, 16]; πράττω [10]

do wrong ἀδικέω [37]

dog κύων, κυνός, ὁ, ἡ [R12, R24, R46, 48]

donkey ὄνος, -ου, ὁ, ἡ [R9]

door θύρᾱ, -ᾱς, ἡ [24]

double διπλοῦς, -ῆ, -οῦν [R39]

doubt ἀπιστίᾱ, -ᾱς, ἡ [R47]

down (adv.) κάτω [39]

down (prep.) κατά + acc. [20]

down along κατά + acc. [20]

down from κατά + gen. [20]

(the) downstairs τὰ κάτω [R39]

downwards κάτω [39]

drachma δραχμή, -ῆς, ἡ [18]

drag ἕλκω [R7]

dramatist διδάσκαλος, -ου, ὁ, ἡ [25]

draw (drag) ἕλκω [R7]

draw (*write*) γράφω [3]

draw near προσέρχομαι [R49, R50]

dreadful δεινός, -ή, -όν [32]

drink πίνω [R24, 50]

drive ἐλαύνω [44]

drive away διώκω [6]

drive back ἀπελαύνω [R44]

drive out ἐξείργω [R29]

dust κόνις, -εως, ἡ [R49]

each ἕκαστος, -η, -ον [49]

eager (for, to) πρόθυμος, -ον + gen. or infin. [R36, 38]

eagerness προθυμίᾱ, -ᾱς, ἡ [38]

ear οὖς, ὠτός, τό [R10]

earlier (*adj.*) πρότερος, -ᾱ, -ον [9]

earlier (*adv.*) πρότερον [R23, 31]

earliest πρῶτος, -η, -ον [32]

earth γῆ, γῆς, ἡ [20]

Earth (*personified*) Γῆ, Γῆς, ἡ [20]

earthquake σεισμός, -οῦ, ὁ [R50]

easier ῥᾴων, -ον [33]

easiest ῥᾷστος, -η, -ον [33]

easily ῥᾳδίως [R13]

easy ῥᾴδιος, -ᾱ, -ον [31]

eat ἐσθίω [R15, R17, R19, 45]

eat dinner δειπνέω [R33]

eat lunch ἀριστάω [R33]

educate παιδεύω [3]

education παιδείᾱ, -ᾱς, ἡ [R46]

egg ᾠόν, -οῦ, τό [R19]

eight ὀκτώ [34]

eighth ὄγδοος, -η, -ον [34]

either…or ἤ…ἤ [16]; πότερον/πότερα…ἤ [26]

Elatea Ἐλάτεια, -ᾱς, ἡ [R29]

eleven ἕνδεκα [34]

eleventh ἑνδέκατος, -η, -ον [34]

empty (of) κενός, -ή, -όν + gen. [R34, 44]

en masse πανδημεί [R36]

encamp σκηνάω [R50]

endure περιοράω [R44]

enemy (*in war*) πολέμιος, -ου, ὁ [12]

enemy (*personal*) ἐχθρός, -οῦ, ὁ [12]

engage in business ἀσχολέομαι [R43]

enough (to, for) ἱκανός, -ή, -όν + infin. or dat. [36]

enslaved δοῦλος, -η, -ον [9]

entire πᾶς, πᾶσα, πᾶν [23]

entirely πάντως [31]; πάνυ [48]

envy φθονέω + dat. [R22]

Epigenes Ἐπιγένης, -ους, ὁ [R31]

equal (to) ἴσος, -η, -ον + dat. [37]

equip ἐξαρτύω [R34]

Eratosthenes Ἐρατοσθένης, -ους, ὁ [R40]

err ἁμαρτάνω [28]

error ἁμαρτίᾱ, -ᾱς, ἡ [28]

escape φεύγω [10]; διαφεύγω [R47]

escape the notice λανθάνω + suppl. ptcple. [50]

escape the notice of λανθάνω + acc. [50]

escort κομίζω [15]

establish καθίστημι [R46]; τίθημι [47]

etc. κτλ. [32]

eunuch εὐνοῦχος, -ου, ὁ [R42]

Euphrates (*river*) Εὐφράτης, -ου, ὁ [R41]

even καί [3]

evening ἑσπέρᾱ, -ᾱς, ἡ [29]

eventually χρόνῳ [R39]

ever ἀεί [25]; ποτέ [26]

every πᾶς, πᾶσα, πᾶν [23]; ἕκαστος, -η, -ον [49]

evident δῆλος, -η, -ον [R8, 15]; φανερός, -ά, -όν [35]

evil κακός, -ή, -όν [9]

examine σκοπέω [45]

example παράδειγμα, -ατος, τό [48]

exceed ὑπερβάλλω [R49]

excellence ἀρετή, -ῆς, ἡ [43]

excuse πρόφασις, -εως, ἡ [R37]

exercise (noun) ἐνέργεια, -ᾱς, ἡ [R43]

exercise (verb) γυμνάζω (mid.) [R44, R46]

exercise partner συγγυμναστής, -οῦ, ὁ [R44]

exhortation παραίνεσις, -εως, ἡ [R36]

exile (person) φυγάς, -άδος, ὁ, ἡ [R45]

exist εἰμί [12]

expedition στόλος, -ου, ὁ [R34]

expense δαπάνη, -ης, ἡ [R34]

expensive πολυτελής, -ές [R34]

experience (noun) ἐμπειρίᾱ, -ᾱς, ἡ [R7]

experience (verb) χράομαι + dat. [36]; πάσχω [40]

explain δηλόω [15]; φράζω [40]

extravagant πολυτελής, -ές [R34]

eye ὀφθαλμός, -οῦ, ὁ [26]

fail ἁμαρτάνω [28]

failure ἁμαρτίᾱ, -ᾱς, ἡ [28]

fair (impartial) ἴσος, -η, -ον [37]

fair (of appearance) καλός, -ή, -όν [8]

fairly ἴσως [37]

fall πίπτω [49]

fall upon ἐμπίπτω [R49]

false ψευδής, -ές [50]; most false ψευδίστατος, -η, -ον [50]

fame δόξα, -ης, ἡ [25]

family οἶκος, -ου, ὁ [49]

family member οἰκέτης, -ου, ὁ [9]

far πόρρω [11]

far away from πόρρω + gen. [11]

far off πόρρω [11]

fare badly κακῶς ἔχειν [17]; κακῶς πράττειν [17]; κακῶς πάσχειν [40]

fare well εὖ ἔχειν [17]; εὖ πράττειν [17]; εὖ πάσχειν [40]

farewell! χαῖρε/χαίρετε [7]

farmer γεωργός, -οῦ, ὁ [R8, R13]

fast ταχύς, -εῖα, -ύ [R35, 41]

faster θάττων, -ον [41]

fastest τάχιστος, -η, -ον [41]

fate μοῖρα, -ᾱς, ἡ [5]

Fate (personified) Μοῖρα, -ᾱς, ἡ [5]

father πατήρ, -τρός, ὁ [R13, 29]; γονεύς, -έως, ὁ [47]

fatherland πατρίς, -ίδος, ἡ [30]

favor χάρις, -ιτος, ἡ [16]

fear (noun) φόβος, -ου, ὁ [R19, 21]

fear (to) (verb) φοβέομαι + infin. [R16, 21]; δέδοικα + infin. [45]

feather πτερόν, -οῦ, τό [R20]

feel ashamed αἰσχύνω (mid.) [44]

female θῆλυς, -εια, -υ [R46]

feminine θῆλυς, -εια, -υ [R46]

fever πυρετός, -οῦ, ὁ [R16]

few ὀλίγοι, -αι, -α [18]

fewer ἐλάττων, -ον [33]

fewest ὀλίγιστος, -η, -ον [33]

fifth πέμπτος, -η, -ον [34]

fight μάχη, -ης, ἡ [35]

fight (against) μάχομαι + dat. [35]

fight together συμμάχομαι [R37]

find εὑρίσκω [8]

find out εὑρίσκω [8]

fine καλός, -ή, -όν [8]

fine arts μουσική, -ῆς, ἡ (supply τέχνη) [R46]

finer καλλίων, -ιον [33]

finest κάλλιστος, -η, -ον [33]

firm ἀδαμάντινος, -ον [R49]

first πρῶτος, -η, -ον [32]

fish ἰχθύς, -ύος, ὁ [R7]

fisherman ἁλιεύς, -έως, ὁ [R7]

fit out ἐξαρτύω [R34]

(it is) fitting (to) πρέπει + dat. [R46]

five πέντε [R33, 34]

flatterer κόλαξ, -ακος, ὁ [R20]

flee φεύγω [10]

flee through διαφεύγω [R47]

flesh κρέας, -ως, τό [R20, R22]

flood κατακλύζω [R47]

follow ἕπομαι + dat. [39]; ἀκολουθέω + dat. [R46]

follow closely παρακολουθέω [R30]

following ὑστεραῖος, -ᾱ, -ον [R29]

(the) following ὅδε, ἥδε, τόδε [13]

food σῖτος, -ου, ὁ [45]

foot πούς, ποδός, ὁ [50]

footstep ἴχνος, -ους, τό [R17]

for (conj.) γάρ [13]

for a little while μῑκρόν [R29, 31]; μῑκρά [R29, 31]; ὀλίγον [31]; ὀλίγα [31]

for indeed (conj.) γάρ [13]

for the sake of χάριν + gen. [16]; ἕνεκα + gen. [48]

force (noun) δύναμις, -εως, ἡ [R29, 47]

force (verb) ἀναγκάζω [R48]

forge ἐλαύνω [44]

forget λανθάνω (mid.) + gen. [50]; ἐπιλανθάνομαι + gen. [50]

forgetfulness λήθη, -ης, ἡ [R50]

Forgetfulness (river in the underworld) Λήθη, -ης, ἡ [R50]

forgive παρίημι [47]

forgiveness (of) συγγνώμη, -ης, ἡ + gen. [R40]

former πρότερος, -ᾱ, -ον [9]

(the) former ἐκεῖνος, -η, -ο [13]

formerly πρότερον [R23, 31]

fortunate εὐδαίμων, -ον [17]

fortune τύχη, -ης, ἡ [50]

Fortune (personified) Τύχη, -ης, ἡ [50]

four τέτταρες, τέτταρα [34]

fourth τέταρτος, -η, -ον [34]

fox ἀλώπηξ, -εκος, ἡ [R17, R20, R22]

free (of, from) ἐλεύθερος, -ᾱ, -ον + gen. [9]

friend (female) φίλη, -ης, ἡ [10]; ἐπιτηδείᾱ, -ᾱς, ἡ [40]

friend (male) φίλος, -ου, ὁ [10]; ἐπιτήδειος, -ου, ὁ [40]

friendly φίλιος, -ᾱ, -ον [R36]

friendship φιλίᾱ, -ᾱς, ἡ [R35, 41]

fright φόβος, -ου, ὁ [R19, 21]

frighten φοβέω [R16, 21]

frog βάτραχος, -ου, ὁ [R11, R25]

from πρός + gen. [17]; παρά + gen. [22]

from another place ἄλλοθεν [49]

from Athens Ἀθήνηθεν [R33, 49]

from here ἐνθένδε [49]; ἐντεῦθεν [49]

from home οἴκοθεν [49]

from somewhere ποθέν [26]

from the same place ὁμόθεν [49]

from the side of παρά + gen. [22]

from there ἐκεῖθεν [49]; ἐνθένδε [49]; ἐντεῦθεν [49]

from under ὑπό + gen. [11]

from where (rel. adv.) ὅθεν [38]

from where? πόθεν [26]; (indir.) ὁπόθεν [26]

from wherever (indef. rel. adv.) ὁπόθεν [38]

full (of) πλήρης + gen. [R29]; μεστός, -ή, -όν + gen. [R49]

function χρείᾱ, -ᾱς, ἡ [R32]

funeral ἐκφορά, -ᾱς, ἡ [R39]

funeral pyre πυρά, -ᾱς, ἡ [R50]

furnish παρασκευάζω [R34, 35]; παρέχω [R36, R37]

further (*adv.*) αὖ [42]; αὖθις [42]

gardener κηπουρός, -οῦ, ὁ [R9]

gather together συλλαμβάνω [19]

gathering σύλλογος, -ου, ὁ [R41]

gaze upon ἀποβλέπω with εἰς + acc. [R48]

general στρατηγός, -οῦ, ὁ [29]

gentlemen ἄνδρες, -ῶν, οἱ [40]

gift δῶρον, -ου, τό [8]

girl κόρη, -ης, ἡ [6]

give δίδωμι [R34]

give back ἀποδίδωμι [R46]

give birth to τίκτω [R19]; γεννάω [R27, 28]

give oneself in marriage (*to a man*) γαμέω (*mid.*) + dat. [39]

Glaucon Γλαύκων, -ωνος, ὁ [R48, R49, R50]

glory δόξα, -ης, ἡ [25]

gnaw τρώγω [R15]

go πορεύω (*mid./pass.*) [R33, R50]; ἔρχομαι [40]; εἶμι [40]; βαίνω [49]

go down καταβαίνω [R39, R49]

go forward to προσέρχομαι [R49, R50]

go into εἰσέρχομαι [R40]

go out ἐξέρχομαι [R40]

go up ἀνέρχομαι [R49]

god θεός, -οῦ, ὁ [7]

goddess θεά, -ᾶς, ἡ [4]; θεός, -οῦ, ἡ [7]

gold χρῡσός, -οῦ, ὁ [35]

good (*at doing a thing*) ἀγαθός, -ή, -όν [8]

good (*morally*) ἀγαθός, -ή, -όν [8]; καλός, -ή, -όν [8]

good condition εὐεξίᾱ, -ᾱς, ἡ [R32]

good experience εὐπάθεια, -ᾱς, ἡ [R49]

good sense φρόνησις, -εως, ἡ [R50]

goods χρήματα, -ων, τά [35]

goodwill προθῡμίᾱ, -ᾱς, ἡ [38]

grace χάρις, -ιτος, ἡ [16]

grain σῖτος, -ου, ὁ [45]

grandeur μέγεθος, -ους, τό [R43]

grasp λαμβάνω [19]

gratitude χάρις, -ιτος, ἡ [16]

great μέγας, μεγάλη, μέγα [R14, 25]

greater μείζων, -ον [R14, 33]

greatest μέγιστος, -η, -ον [33]

greatly μέγα [25]; μεγάλα [25]

Greece Ἑλλάς, -άδος, ἡ [20]

Greek Ἑλληνικός, -ή, -όν [20]

Greek (*person*) Ἕλλην, -ηνος, ὁ, ἡ [20]

Greek inhabitant of Italy Ἰταλιώτης, -ου, ὁ [R35]

Greek inhabitant of Sicily Σικελιώτης, -ου, ὁ [R36]

greet ἀσπάζομαι [R49]

grew φύω (*second aor. intrans. act.*) [R48]

grief λύπη, -ης, ἡ [7]

ground γῆ, γῆς, ἡ [20]

grow old γηράσκω [R33]

guard (*noun*) φύλαξ, -ακος, ὁ [16]

guard (*verb*) φυλάττω [3]

guard together συμφυλάττω [R46]

guardian (*male*) φύλαξ, -ακος, ὁ [16]; (*female*) φυλακίς, -ίδος, ἡ [R47]

guardian spirit δαίμων, -ονος, ὁ [17]

guest ξένος, -ου, ὁ [24]

guest-friendship ξενίᾱ, -ᾱς, ἡ [24]

guilt αἰτίᾱ, -ᾱς, ἡ [19]

guilty (of) αἴτιος, -ᾱ, -ον + gen. [19]

habit τρόπος, -ου, ὁ [R6, 11]

Hades Ἅιδης, -ου, ὁ [R49]

hand χείρ, χειρός, ἡ [R16, 42]

hand over παραδίδωμι [R42, R45]

handsome καλός, -ή, -όν [8]

happen γίγνομαι [R14, R27, R28, 32]; συμβαίνω [R29]; τυγχάνω + suppl. ptcple. [50]

happen (to) τυγχάνω + dat. [50]

happiness εὐδαιμονίᾱ, -ᾱς, ἡ [R43]

happy εὐδαίμων, -ον [17]

hard χαλεπός, -ή, -όν [50]

harm βλάπτω [5]

hasten (to) σπεύδω + infin. [3]; ἵημι (mid.) + infin. [47]

hateful (to) ἐχθρός, -ά, -όν + dat. [12]; more hateful (to) ἐχθίων, -ῑον + dat. [33]; most hateful (to) ἔχθιστος, -η, -ον + dat. [33]

have ἔχω [6]

have come ἥκω [R49]

have faith (in) πιστεύω + dat. or εἰς + acc. [28]

have leisure σχολὴν ἄγειν [43]

have need (of) δέομαι + gen. [R41]

have (someone) taught παιδεύω (mid.) [11]

having authority κύριος, -ᾱ, -ον [28]

having done no wrong ἀναμάρτητος, -ον [R45]

having to do with trade ἐμπορικός, -ή, -όν [R23]

having to do with women γυναικεῖος, -ᾱ, -ον [R47]

healthy ὑγιεινός, -ή, -όν [R32]

hear ἀκούω + gen. or acc. [5]; πυνθάνομαι + gen. or acc. [42]

hear about πυνθάνομαι + gen. or acc. [42]

heart θῡμός, -οῦ, ὁ [38]

heaven οὐρανός, -οῦ, ὁ [20]

Hellas Ἑλλάς, -άδος, ἡ [20]

Hellene (person) Ἕλλην, -ηνος, ὁ, ἡ [20]

Hellenic Ἑλληνικός, -ή, -όν [20]

hello! χαῖρε/χαίρετε [7]

help ὠφελέω [15]

helpful ὠφέλιμος, -ον [R47]

hence ἐνθένδε [49]; ἐντεῦθεν [49]

her αὐτῆς, αὐτῇ, αὐτήν [13]

Hera Ἥρᾱ, -ᾱς, ἡ [R18]

herald κῆρυξ, -ῡκος, ὁ [30]

herd ἀγέλη, -ης, ἡ [R46]

here αὐτοῦ [R35]; ἔνθα [49]; ἐνθάδε [49]; ἐνταῦθα [49]

Hermes Ἑρμῆς, -οῦ, ὁ [R18]

herself (reflex. pron.) ἑαυτῆς/αὑτῆς [19]

hesitate (to) μέλλω + pres. infin. [6]

hill ὄρος, -ους, τό [50]

him αὐτοῦ, αὐτῷ, αὐτόν [13]

himself (reflex. pron.) ἑαυτοῦ/αὑτοῦ [19]

hinder κωλύω + infin. [50]

hit (with a thrown weapon) βάλλω [15]; (a target) τυγχάνω + gen. [50]

hither δεῦρο [49]; ἔνθα [49]; ἐνθάδε [49]; ἐνταῦθα [49]

hold ἔχω [6]

hold a contest ἀγῶνα ἔχειν [16]

hold a wedding γάμον ποιεῖν [39]

hold out (against) ἀντέχω + dat. [R38]

home(wards) [R40, 49]

honor (noun) τῑμή, -ῆς, ἡ [15]

honor (verb) τῑμάω [15]

hope ἐλπίς, -ίδος, ἡ [24]

hoplite ὁπλίτης, -ου, ὁ [R34]

horse ἵππος, -ου, ὁ [7]

host ξένος, -ου, ὁ [24]

hostile (to) πολέμιος, -ᾱ, -ον + dat. [12]; ἐχθρός, -ά, -όν + dat. [12]; more hostile (to) ἐχθίων, -ῑον + dat. [33]; most hostile (to) ἔχθιστος, -η, -ον + dat. [33]

hour ὥρᾱ, -ᾱς, ἡ [5]

house οἰκίᾱ, -ᾱς, ἡ [6]; οἶκος, -ου, ὁ [49]

household οἰκίᾱ, -ᾱς, ἡ [6]; οἶκος, -ου, ὁ [49]

how (*rel. adv.*) ὡς [38]; ᾗ [R44, R46, R47]; (*conj. + indir. disc.*) ὡς [40]; (*conj. + effort clause*) ὅπως [45]; ὡς [45]

how? πῶς [R24, 26]; (*indir.*) ὅπως [26]

how! ὡς [31]

how great? πόσος, -η, -ον [46]; (*indir.*) ὁπόσος, -η, -ον [46]

how great a! ὅσος, -η, -ον [46]

how many? πόσοι, -αι, -α [46]; (*indir.*) ὁπόσοι, -αι, -α [46]

how many! ὅσοι, -αι, -α [46]

how much? πόσος, -η, -ον [R18, 46]; (*indir.*) ὁπόσος, -η, -ον [46]

how...not (*conj. + neg. effort clause*) ὅπως μή [45]; ὡς μή [45]

however μήν [32]; μέντοι [44]

howsoever (*indef. rel. adv.*) ὅπως [38]

human ἀνθρώπινος, -η, -ον [R48]

human being ἄνθρωπος, -ου, ὁ [7]

humankind ἄνθρωπος, -ου, ὁ [7]

hundred ἑκατόν [34]

hunt διώκω [6]

hunt together συνθηρεύω [R46]

hunter κυνηγέτης, -ου, ὁ [R15]

hurl ῥίπτω [20]

hurt βλάπτω [5]

husband ἀνήρ, ἀνδρός, ὁ [30]

I ἐγώ [14]

if εἰ [37]

if (ever) ἐάν [37]; ἤν [37]; ἄν [37]

if (ever) indeed ἐάνπερ [47]; ἤνπερ [47]; ἄνπερ [47]

if indeed εἴπερ [47]

if only εἰ γάρ [36]; εἴθε [36]

ignominious ἐπονείδιστος, -ον [R44]

illogical ἄλογος, -ον [R38]

imitate μῑμέομαι [R44]

immediately εὐθύς [R29, 40]

immortal ἀθάνατος, -ον [9]

impartial ἴσος, -η, -ον [37]

impressive-looking εὐπρεπής, -ές [R34]

in ἐν + dat. [4]

in a leisurely way σχολῇ [43]

in a mob πανδημεί [R36]

in accordance with κατά + acc. [20]

in all respects πάντως [31]

in another place ἄλλοθι [49]

in Athens Ἀθήνησι(ν) [49]

in common κοινῶς [31]

in order that ἵνα [39]; ὅπως [39]; ὡς [39]

in order that...not ἵνα μή [39]; ὅπως μή [39]; ὡς μή [39]; μή [39]

in place of ἀντί + gen. [R44]

in that place ἐκεῖ [49]; ἔνθα [49]; ἐνθάδε [49]; ἐνταῦθα [49]

in the future τοῦ λοιποῦ (χρόνου) [32]

in the same place ὁμοῦ [49]

in the time of ἐπί + gen. [14]

in this place ἔνθα [49]; ἐνθάδε [49]; ἐνταῦθα [49]

in this very way αὕτως [31]

in this way οὕτω(ς) [31]; ὧδε [31]

in time χρόνῳ [R39]

in truth (τῇ) ἀληθείᾳ [10]

in turn αὖ [42]; αὖθις [42]

in want (of) ἐνδεής, -ές + gen. [R31]

in which way (*rel. adv.*) ᾗ [R44, R46, R47]

indeed μέν [10]; δή [44]; περ/-περ [47]

indict γράφω (*mid.*) [11]

infer συλλογίζομαι [R30]

inhabit οἰκέω [R48]

injure ἀδικέω [37]

injury ἀδικίᾱ, -ᾱς, ἡ [37]

injustice ἀδικίᾱ, -ᾱς, ἡ [37]

inquire (of someone) πυνθάνομαι + gen. [42]

inside ἔνδον [R39, 40]

intend (to) μέλλω + fut. infin. [6]

interpreter προφήτης, -ου, ὁ [R49]

into εἰς + acc. [4]

inundate κατακλύζω [R47]

investigate ζητέω [20]

invite καλέω [24]

it αὐτοῦ, αὐτῷ, αὐτό [13]

itself (reflex. pron.) ἑαυτοῦ/αὑτοῦ [19]

Jesus Ἰησοῦς, -οῦ, -οῦ, -οῦν, -οῦ, ὁ [R26, R27, R28]

journey (noun) ὁδός, -οῦ, ἡ [7]; πορείᾱ, -ᾱς, ἡ [R33, R49, R50]

journey (verb) πορεύω (mid./pass.) [R33, R50]

joy χαρά, -ᾶς, ἡ [7]

judge (noun) δικαστής, -οῦ, ὁ [R49]

judge (verb) κρῑνω [27]

judgment κρῖμα, -ατος, τό [R28]; γνώμη, -ης, ἡ [R37]

just δίκαιος, -ᾱ, -ον [37]

just as ὥσπερ [47]

just now ἄρτι [27]

justice δίκη, -ης, ἡ [37]; δικαιοσύνη, -ης, ἡ [R48, R50]

kill ἀποκτείνω [21]

kin συγγενής, -ές [R37]

kind γένος, -ους, τό [48]

kindly (adv.) εὖ [17]

king βασιλεύς, -έως, ὁ [R22, 29]

kiss φιλέω [15]

know (by being skilled in or familiar with) ἐπίσταμαι [46]

know (by observing) γιγνώσκω [49]

know (by reflecting) οἶδα [R26, R27, 28]

know how (to) οἶδα + infin. [R26, R27, 28]; ἐπίσταμαι + infin. [46]; γιγνώσκω + infin. [49]

knowledge ἐπιστήμη, -ης, ἡ [R36, 46]

labor πονέω [R5]

Lacedaemon Λακεδαίμων, -ονος, ἡ [R44]

Lachesis Λάχεσις, -εως, ἡ [R50]

lacking ἐνδεής, -ές + gen. [R31]

ladder κλῖμαξ, -ακος, ἡ [39]

lady δέσποινα, -ης, ἡ [5]; κῡρίᾱ, -ᾱς, ἡ [28]

Lady (title of goddess) δέσποινα, -ης, ἡ [5]

lake λίμνη, -ης, ἡ [11]

land χώρᾱ, -ᾱς, ἡ [4]; γῆ, γῆς, ἡ [20]

large μέγας, μεγάλη, μέγα [R14, 25]

larger μείζων, -ον [R14, 33]

largest μέγιστος, -η, -ον [33]

last ὕστατος, -η, -ον [39]

lasting a thousand years χῑλιέτης, -ες [R50]

later (adj.) ὕστερος, -ᾱ, -ον [39]

later (adv.) ὕστερον [39]

latest ὕστατος, -η, -ον [39]

(the) latter οὗτος, αὕτη, τοῦτο [R10, 13]

laugh (at) γελάω with ἐπί + dat. [15]

laughable γελοῖος, -ᾱ, -ον [R46]

law νόμος, -ου, ὁ [22]

lawsuit δίκη, -ης, ἡ [37]

lay (eggs) τίκτω [R19]

lay down τίθημι [47]

lead ἄγω [22]

lead a life βίον ἄγω [22]; διαιτάω (mid./pass.) [R39]

learn (by inquiry) πυνθάνομαι + gen. or acc. [42]

learn (by inquiry) about πυνθάνομαι + gen. or acc. [42]

learn (*by study*) μανθάνω [42]

learn how (to) μανθάνω + infin. [42]

least ἥκιστος, -η, -ον [33]; ἐλάχιστος, -η, -ον [33]; ὀλίγιστος, -η, -ον [33]

least of all (*adv.*) ἥκιστα [33]

leave λείπω [8]; ἀπολείπω [8]; καταλείπω [R32]

leave behind λείπω [8]; ἀπολείπω [8]; καταλείπω [R32]

leisure ἡσυχίᾱ, -ᾱς, ἡ [4]; σχολή, -ῆς, ἡ [43]

lengthen μηκΰνω [R33]

less ἥττων, -ον [33]; ἐλάττων, -ον [33]

lest (*conj.* + *neg. purp. clause*) ἵνα μή [39]; ὅπως μή [39]; ὡς μή [39]; μή [39]; (*conj.* + *fear clause*) μή [45]

lest...not (*conj.* + *neg. fear clause*) μὴ οὐ [45]

let go ἀνΐημι [R38]; ἵημι [47]

let pass παρΐημι [47]

letter ἐπιστολή, -ῆς, ἡ [4]

lie κεῖμαι [47]

lie asleep κεῖμαι [47]

lie dead κεῖμαι [47]

lie down κατάκειμαι [R40]

life βίος, -ου, ὁ [8]; ψῡχή, -ῆς, ἡ [22]

life of a tyrant τυραννίς, -ίδος, ἡ [R49]

lifetime βίος, -ου, ὁ [8]

lift up ἀνατείνω [R42]

light φῶς, φωτός, τό [R48]

like ὅμοιος, -ᾱ, -ον + dat. [48]

lion λέων, -οντος, ὁ [R15, 16]

listen ἀκούω [5]

listen to ἀκούω + gen. or acc. [5]

little μῑκρός, -ά, -όν [11]; ὀλίγος, -η, -ον [18]

(a) little μῑκρόν [R29, 31]; μῑκρά [R29, 31]; ὀλίγον [31]; ὀλίγα [31]

little child παιδίον, -ου, τό [25]

little house οἰκίδιον, -ου, τό [R39]

live ζάω [31]; διαιτάω (*mid./pass.*) [R39]

live together συνοικέω [R47]

livelihood βίος, -ου, ὁ [8]

long μακρός, -ά, -όν [11]

long ago πάλαι [27]

long for ποθέω [R9]

longer (*adv.*) ἔτι [6]

long-lasting μακρός, -ά, -όν [11]

look (at) βλέπω with εἰς + acc. [R7, R9, R10, 13]; ὁράω [23]

look down at ὑπερφρονέω [R36]

look into σκοπέω [45]

look up ἀναβλέπω [R50]

loosen λύω [12]

lord δεσπότης, -ου, ὁ [9]; κύριος, -ου, ὁ [28]

lot κλῆρος, -ου, ὁ [R49]

loud noise κτύπος, -ου, ὁ [R25]

love (*noun*) ἀγάπη, -ης, ἡ [41]

love (*verb*) φιλέω [15]; ἀγαπάω [41]

luck τύχη, -ης, ἡ [50]

Lycurgus Λυκοῦργος, -ου, ὁ [R44]

lying ψευδής, -ές [50]; most lying ψευδίστατος, -η, -ον [50]

machine μηχανή, -ῆς, ἡ [45]

maid θεράπαινα, -ης, ἡ [5]

maiden κόρη, -ης, ἡ [6]

Maiden (*another name for Persephone*) Κόρη, -ης, ἡ [6]

make ποιέω [R8, R13, 16]; τίθημι [47]

make a difference διαφέρω [R32]

make a mistake ἁμαρτάνω [28]

make appear φαίνω [R30, R32, 35]

make begin ἄρχω + gen. [38]

make clear δηλόω [15]

make go πορεύω [R33, R50]

make stand ἵστημι [46]

make stand up ἀνίστημι [R30]

make trial of πειράω [R6, R8]

make war πολεμέω [R43]

male ἄρρην, -εν [R46]

man ἄνθρωπος, -ου, ὁ [7]; ἀνήρ, ἀνδρός, ὁ [30]

manage νέμω [R42]

manager (*of the household*) οἰκονόμος, -ου, ὁ, ἡ [R39]

mankind ἄνθρωπος, -ου, ὁ [7]

manner τρόπος, -ου, ὁ [R6, 11]

many πολύς, πολλή, πολύ [R7, R9, 18]

(the) many οἱ πολλοί [18]

many times πολλάκις [25]

march ἐλαύνω [44]

mare ἵππος, -ου, ἡ [7]

market ἀγορά, -ᾶς, ἡ [4]

marketplace ἀγορά, -ᾶς, ἡ [4]

marriage γάμος, -ου, ὁ [39]

marry (*a man*) γαμέω (*mid.*) + dat. [R6, 39]

marry (*a woman*) γαμέω (*act.*) [R6, 39]

marsh λίμνη, -ης, ἡ [11]

marvel (at) θαυμάζω [44]

marvelous δεινός, -ή, -όν [32]

masculine ἄρρην, -εν [R46]

master (*of the household*) δεσπότης, -ου, ὁ [9]; κύριος, -ου, ὁ [28]

matters of state πράγματα, -άτων, τά [R30]

me ἐμοῦ/μου, ἐμοί/μοι, ἐμέ/με [14]

meal δεῖπνον, -ου, τό [24]

measure μέτρον, -ου, τό [R50]

meat κρέας, -ως, τό [R20, R22]

Mede Μῆδος, -ου, ὁ [R42]

meet τυγχάνω + gen. [50]

meeting σύνοδος, -ου, ἡ [R22]; σύλλογος, -ου, ὁ [R41]

message ἐπιστολή, -ῆς, ἡ [4]

messenger ἄγγελος, -ου, ὁ, ἡ [18]

messmate σύσκηνος, -ου, ὁ [R44]

middle μέσος, -η, -ον [R49]

military πολεμικός, -ή, -όν [R43]

military force δύναμις, -εως, ἡ [R29]; παρασκευή, -ῆς, ἡ [R34, 35]

mina μνᾶ, -ᾶς, ἡ [41]

mind νοῦς, νοῦ, ὁ [R43, 50]

mine ἐμός, -ή, -όν [21]

miracle σημεῖον, -ου, τό [R26]

miserable δειλός, -ή, -όν [R25]

misfortune κακοδαιμονίᾱ, -ᾱς, ἡ [R44]

miss ποθέω [R9]

miss (a *target*) ἁμαρτάνω + gen. [28]

miss out on ἁμαρτάνω + gen. [28]

mistake ἁμαρτίᾱ, -ᾱς, ἡ [28]

mistress (*of the household*) δέσποινα, -ης, ἡ [5]; κῡρίᾱ, -ᾱς, ἡ [28]

model παράδειγμα, -ατος, τό [48]

moderate μέτριος, -ᾱ, -ον [R33]; μέσος, -η, -ον [R49]

modesty αἰδώς, -οῦς, ἡ [17]

money ἀργύρια, -ων, τά [35]; χρήματα, -ων, τά [35]; χρῡσία, -ων, τά [35]

money-lender δανειστής, -οῦ, ὁ [R23]

monkey πίθηκος, -ου, ὁ [R22]

more (*adj.*) πλείων/πλέων, -ον [33]

more (*adv.*) μᾶλλον [R31, 32]

Moses Μωϋσῆς, -έως, -εῖ, -ῆν, ὁ [R28]

most (*adj.*) πλεῖστος, -η, -ον [33]

most (*adv.*) μάλιστα [32]

mother μήτηρ, -τρός, ἡ [R14, R19, 29]

mountain ὄρος, -ους, τό [50]

mouse μῦς, μυός, ὁ [R6, R15]

move τρέπω (*mid.*) [11]

much (*adj.*) πολύς, πολλή, πολύ [R7, R9, 18]

much (*adv.*) πολύ [18]; πολλά [18]; μέγα [25]; μεγάλα [25]; μάλα [33]

mud πηλός, -οῦ, ὁ [R26]

murderer φονεύς, -έως, ὁ [R21]

music μουσική, -ῆς, ἡ (*supply* τέχνη) [R46]

must δεῖ + infin. [43]; ἀνάγκη with ἐστί(ν) + infin. [43]

my, my own ἐμός, -ή, -όν [21]

myself (*reflex. pron.*) ἐμαυτοῦ, -ῆς [19]

naked γυμνός, -ή, -όν [R40, R46]

name (*noun*) ὄνομα, -ατος, τό [16]

name (*verb*) καλέω [24]

native country πατρίς, -ίδος, ἡ [30]

nature φύσις, -εως, ἡ [37]

naval ναυτικός, -ή, -όν [R38]

navy ναυτικόν, -οῦ, τό [R38]

near πρός + dat. [17]

nearly σχεδόν [R33]

necessary ἀναγκαῖος, -ᾱ, -ον [R29, R31, 43]; ἐπιτήδειος, -ᾱ, -ον [40]

(it is) necessary (to) δεῖ + infin. [R14, 43]; ἀνάγκη with ἐστί(ν) + infin. [43]; χρή with ἐστί(ν) + infin. [43]

necessities ἀναγκαῖα, -ων, τά [R31]

necessity ἀνάγκη, -ης, ἡ [43]; χρή [43]

need δέομαι + gen. [R41]

(there is) need (of) δεῖ + gen. [43]

(there is) need (to) ἀνάγκη with ἐστί(ν) + infin. [43]; χρή with ἐστί(ν) + infin. [43]

neglect ἀμελέω [R42]

neglect to mention παραλείπω [R44]

negligence ἀμέλεια, -ᾱς, ἡ [R33]

neither...nor οὐδὲ...οὐδέ [22]; μηδὲ...μηδέ [22]; οὔτε...οὔτε [22]; μήτε...μήτε [22]

net (*for fishing*) σαγήνη, -ης, ἡ [R7]

net (*for hunting*) δίκτυον, -ου, τό [R15]

never οὔποτε [28]; μήποτε [28]

nevertheless ὅμως [R29]

new νέος, -ᾱ, -ον [27]

next (*adj.*) ὑστεραῖος, -ᾱ, -ον [R29]; ὕστερος, -ᾱ, -ον [39]

next (*adv.*) εἶτα [49]; ἔπειτα [49]

night νύξ, νυκτός, ἡ [R19, 23]

Nile (*river*) Νεῖλος, -ου, ὁ [R21]

nine ἐννέα [34]

ninth ἔνατος, -η, -ον [34]

no (*adj.*) οὐδείς, οὐδεμία, οὐδέν [30]; μηδείς, μηδεμία, μηδέν [30]

no, by...(*oath*) μά + acc. [R48]

no longer οὐκέτι [6]; μηκέτι [6]

no more οὐκέτι [6]; μηκέτι [6]

no one οὐδείς, οὐδεμία [30]; μηδείς, μηδεμία [30]

nobility κάλλος, -ους, τό [R43, R49]

noble καλός, -ή, -όν [8]

none οὐδείς, οὐδεμία, οὐδέν [30]; μηδείς, μηδεμία, μηδέν [30]

non-professional ἰδιώτης, -ου, ὁ [R31]

nor οὐδέ [22]; μηδέ [22]; οὔτε [22]; μήτε [22]

not οὐ [3]; μή [3]

not awed ἀνέκπληκτος, -ον [R49]

not dazzled ἀνέκπληκτος, -ον [R49]

not deserving (of, to) ἀνάξιος, -ον + gen. or infin. [9]

not even οὐδέ [22]; μηδέ [22]

not know ἀγνοέω [R5]

not only...but also οὐ μόνον...ἀλλὰ καί [18]

not yet οὔπω [28]; μήπω [28]

nothing οὐδέν [30]; μηδέν [30]

now νῦν [13]

number ἀριθμός, -οῦ, ὁ [34]

nurse (*a baby*) θηλάζω [R39]

O! ὦ [4]

obey πείθω (*mid.*) + dat. [11]

obol ὀβολός, -οῦ, ὁ [18]

observe τηρέω [R26]

obtain τυγχάνω + gen. [R40, 50]

occupation ἔργον, -ου, τό [8]

of some quantity ποσός, -ή, -όν [46]

of some size ποσός, -ή, -όν [46]

of some sort ποιός, -ά, -όν [46]

of such a sort τοιόσδε, τοιάδε, τοιόνδε [31]; τοιοῦτος, τοιαύτη, τοιοῦτο(ν) [31]

of what sort? ποῖος, -ᾱ, -ον [46]; (*indir.*) οἷος, -ᾱ, -ον [46]

of which quantity (*rel. adj.*) ὅσος, -η, -ον [46]

of which size (*rel. adj.*) ὅσος, -η, -ον [46]

of which sort (*rel. adj.*) οἷος, -ᾱ, -ον [R45, 46]

of whichever quantity (*indef. rel. adj.*) ὁπόσος, -η, -ον [46]

of whichever size (*indef. rel. adj.*) ὁπόσος, -η, -ον [46]

of whichever sort (*indef. rel. adj.*) ὁποῖος, -ᾱ, -ον [46]

offer παρέχω [R36]

offer sacrifice θύω [3]

offspring τέκνον, -ου, τό [8]; ἔκγονος, -ου, ὁ [R47]

often πολλάκις [25]

old παλαιός, -ά, -όν [27]

old age γῆρας, -ως, τό [R17]

old man γέρων, -οντος, ὁ [R16, 42]

old woman γραῦς, γρᾱός, ἡ [42]

older παλαίτερος, -ᾱ, -ον [32]

oldest παλαίτατος, -η, -ον [32]

Olympia Ὀλυμπίᾱ, -ᾱς, ἡ [R31, R33]

on (*location*) ἐπί + dat. [14]

on (*the surface of*) ἐπί + gen. [14]

on account of διά + acc. [12]; ἕνεκα + gen. [48]

on behalf of ὑπέρ + gen. [20]

on the grounds of ὡς + ptcple. [24]

on the one hand...on the other hand μέν...δέ [10]

on the other hand αὖ [R37, 42]; αὖθις [42]

on this side (of) ἐντός + gen. [R41]

once ποτέ [26]

once (*and for all*) ἅπαξ [34]

once more πάλιν [6]

one εἷς, μία, ἕν [30]

(the) one (*of two*) ἕτερος, -ᾱ, -ον [49]

one another ἀλλήλων, -οις/αις, -ους/-ᾱς/α [49]

one at a time καθ' ἕνα, κατὰ μίαν, καθ' ἕν [R13]

one by one καθ' ἕνα, κατὰ μίαν, καθ' ἕν [30]

one's own ἴδιος, -ᾱ, -ον [R5]

only (*adj.*) μόνος, -η, -ον [18]

only (*adv.*) μόνον [18]

open (*adj.*) φανερός, -ά, -όν [35]

open (*verb*) ἀνοίγω/ἀνοίγνῡμι [R26, 27]

open up ἀνοίγω/ἀνοίγνῡμι [R26, 27]

opening χάσμα, -ατος, τό [R49]

opinion δόξα, -ης, ἡ [25]; γνώμη, -ης, ἡ [R37]

opportunity καιρός, -οῦ, ὁ [R38]

or ἤ [16]

orator ῥήτωρ, -ορος, ὁ [16]

order (*noun*) κόσμος, -ου, ὁ [28]

order (to) (*verb*) κελεύω + infin. [5]

other ἄλλος, -η, -ο [22]

(the) other (*of two*) ἕτερος, -ᾱ, -ον [49]

ought (to) χρή with ἐστί(ν) + infin. [43]; ὤφελον + infin. [48]

our ἡμέτερος, -ᾱ, -ον [21]

our own ἡμέτερος, -ᾱ, -ον [21]

ours ἡμέτερος, -ᾱ, -ον [21]

ourselves (*reflex. pron.*) ἡμῶν αὐτῶν, -ῶν [19]

out of ἐκ + gen. [4]

outside ἔξω [40]

over ὑπέρ + gen. or acc. [20]

overhanging bank κρημνός, -οῦ, ὁ [R25]

overlook (*neglect*) ἀμελέω [R42]; (*put up with*) περιοράω [R44]

overthrow σφάλλω [R32]

overwhelm κατακλύζω [R47]

owe ὀφείλω [48]

pain λύπη, -ης, ἡ [7]

painter ζωγράφος, -ου, ὁ [R48]

pardon (for) συγγνώμη, -ης, ἡ + gen. [R40]

parents γονῆς, -έων, οἱ [R27, 47]

Parmenion Παρμενίων, -ωνος, ὁ [R41]

participate in politics πολῑτεύω (*mid.*) [R43]

particle with potential optative or in conditions ἄν [36, 37]

pass by πάρειμι [R23]; παρέρχομαι [R30]

pass over παραλείπω [R44]

pass up ἀνίημι [R38]

passage (*in a book*) τόπος, -ου, ὁ [11]

passion θῡμός, -οῦ, ὁ [38]

path ὁδός, -οῦ, ἡ [7]

pause (from) παῦλα, -ης, ἡ (+ *gen.*) [R48]

pay attention to τηρέω [R26]

pay out ἐκτίνω [R31]

peace εἰρήνη, -ης, ἡ [12]

penalize ζημιόω [R45]

penalty ἐπιτῑμιον, -ου, τό [R31]; δίκη, -ης, ἡ [37]

(the) people οἱ πολλοί [18]

perceive αἰσθάνομαι [42]

perfect τέλειος/τέλεος, -ᾱ, -ον [R43, R48]

perhaps ἴσως [37]

Pericles Περικλῆς, -έους, ὁ [R34]

permit μεθίημι [47]

Persian Πέρσης, -ου, ὁ [R42]

person ἄνθρωπος, -ου, ὁ [7]

personal ἴδιος, -ᾱ, -ον [R5]

persuade (to) πείθω + infin. [11]

Pharisees Φαρισαῖοι, -ων, οἱ [R26, R27]

Philip Φίλιππος, -ου, ὁ [R29]

philosopher φιλόσοφος, -ου, ὁ [13]

philosophical φιλόσοφος, -ον [13]

philosophy φιλοσοφίᾱ, -ᾱς, ἡ [13]

pick up ἀναιρέω [R49]

piece of gold χρῡσίον, -ου, τό [35]

piece of silver ἀργύριον, -ου, τό [35]

pious θεοσεβής, -ές [R28]

place (*noun*) τόπος, -ου, ὁ [11]

place (*verb*) τίθημι [47]

place upon ἐπιτίθημι [R45]

plain πεδίον, -ου, τό [50]

plan (*noun*) βούλευμα, -ατος, τό [R5]

plan (to) (*verb*) βουλεύω + infin. [45]

plant φυτόν, -οῦ, τό [8]

pleasant ἡδύς, -εῖα, -ύ [33]; more pleasant ἡδίων, -ῑον [33]; most pleasant ἥδιστος, -η, -ον [33]

plot (against) ἐπιβουλεύω + dat. [R38]

plunder ἁρπάζω [15]

point out δείκνῡμι [48]

political πολῑτικός, -ή, -όν [R43]

political office ἀρχή, -ῆς, ἡ [12]

pond λίμνη, -ης, ἡ [11]

position χώρᾱ, -ᾱς, ἡ [4]

possess ἔχω [6]

possible (to) οἷόν τε + infin. [46]; δυνατόν + infin. [47]

(it is) possible (to) ἔστι(ν) + infin. [12]; ἔξεστι(ν) + infin. [43]

postpone ἀναβάλλω (*mid.*) [R47]

potter κεραμεύς, -έως, ὁ [R9]

power ἀρχή, -ῆς, ἡ [12]; κράτος, -ους, τό [R42]; δύναμις, -εως, ἡ [47]

powerful (enough to) δυνατός, -ή, -όν + infin. [R35, 47]

practical πρᾱκτικός, -ή, -όν [R43]

practice ἐπιτηδεύω [R47, R50]

practice philosophy φιλοσοφέω [R48]

pray (to) εὔχομαι + dat. [R9, R42]

prefer (to) βούλομαι + infin. [30]

preparation παρασκευή, -ῆς, ἡ [R34, 35]

prepare παρασκευάζω [R34, 35]

present circumstances παρεστός, -ῶτος, τό [R46]

preserve φυλάττω [3]

pretend προσποιέω (mid.) [17]

prevent κωλύω + infin. [50]

price τῑμή, -ῆς, ἡ [15]

prime of life ἡλικίᾱ, -ᾱς, ἡ [27]

private ἰδιωτικός, -ή, -όν [R31]; ἴδιος, -ᾱ, -ον [R47]

private citizen ἰδιώτης, -ου, ὁ [R31]

privately ἰδίᾳ [R47]

privilege γέρας, -ως, τό [17]

prize γέρας, -ως, τό [17]; ἆθλον, -ου, τό [R37, R50]

probably ἴσως [37]

produce παρέχω [R36]; φύω [R48]

promise (to) ὁμολογέω + infin. [48]

property χρῆμα, -ατος, τό [35]

prophet προφήτης, -ου, ὁ [R26]

prosperity εὐδαιμονίᾱ, -ᾱς, ἡ [R44]

prosperous εὐδαίμων, -ον [17]

protect φυλάττω [3]

prove ἀποδείκνῡμι [48]

provide παρασκευάζω [R34, 35]

provisions ἐπιτήδεια, -ων, τά [40]

prudence σωφροσύνη, -ης, ἡ [42]

prudent σώφρων, -ον [42]

prytanis πρύτανις, -εως, ὁ [29]

punish δίκην λαμβάνειν [37]

punishment δίκη, -ης, ἡ [37]

pure καθαρός, -ά, -όν [R49]

pursue διώκω [6]; ἐπιτηδεύω [R47, R50]

pursuit πρᾶξις, -εως, ἡ [R43]

put τίθημι [47]

put back ἀναβάλλω [R47]

put in order νέμω [R42]

put up with περιοράω [R44]

quarrel στασιάζω [R13]

question ἐρωτάω [18]

question expecting the answer "no" ἆρα μή [26]; μῶν [26]; μή [26]

question expecting the answer "yes" ἆρ' οὐ [26]; οὐκοῦν [26]; οὐ [26]

question not expecting a particular answer ἆρα [26]

quick τᾱχύς, -εῖα, -ύ [R35, 41]

quicker θάττων, -ον [41]

quickest τάχιστος, -η, -ον [41]

quiet ἡσυχίᾱ, -ᾱς, ἡ [4]

quite δή [44]

quotation mark equivalent ὅτι [R40]

rabbit λαγωός, -οῦ, ὁ [R25]

race γένος, -ους, τό [48]

racecourse στάδιον, -ου, τό [44]

rather μᾶλλον [R31, 32]

read ἀναγιγνώσκω [49]

ready (to) ἕτοιμος, -η, -ον + infin. [36]

real ἀληθής, -ές [17]

really (τῇ) ἀληθείᾳ [10]

rearing τροφή, -ῆς, ἡ [R46]

reasoning λόγος, -ου, ὁ [12]

rebel ὑβρίζω [R45]

rebuke ἐπιπλήττω + dat. [14]

recall μιμνῄσκω (*mid., aor. pass., or fut. pass.*) + gen. or acc. [49]

receive λαμβάνω [19]

recently νέον [31]

reckon together συλλογίζομαι [R30]

recognize γιγνώσκω [49]

regret ποθέω [R9]

reject ἐκβάλλω [R38]; ἀποβάλλω [R45]

rejoice (in) χαίρω + dat. [7]

related συγγενής, -ές [R21, R37]

relative συγγενής, -οῦς, ὁ, ἡ [R21]

relax μεθίημι [47]

release λύω [12]; μεθίημι [47]

remain μένω [R16, 19]

remaining λοιπός, -ή, -όν [32]

remember μιμνῄσκω (*mid., aor. pass., or fut. pass.*) + gen. or acc. [R36, 49]

remind μιμνῄσκω [R36, 49]

renewal ἀνανέωσις, -εως, ἡ [R38]

reply ἀποκρίνω (*mid.*) + dat. [27]

report ἀγγέλλω [18]

report back ἀπαγγέλλω [R30, 41]

reproach λοιδορέω [R28]; ἐπίκλησις, -εως, ἡ [R44]

republic πολῑτείᾱ, -ᾱς, ἡ [R48]

reputation δόξα, -ης, ἡ [25]

resembling παραπλήσιος, -ᾱ, -ον [R46]

resist ἀντέχω + dat. [R38]

resource ἀφορμή, -ῆς, ἡ [R32]

respect αἰδώς, -οῦς, ἡ [17]

respectable εὐσχήμων, -ον [R32]

responsibility αἰτίᾱ, -ᾱς, ἡ [19]

responsible (for) αἴτιος, -ᾱ, -ον + gen. [19]

rest (adj.) λοιπός, -ή, -όν [32]

(the) rest οἱ ἄλλοι [22]

rest (from) παῦλα, -ης, ἡ + gen. [R48]

reward ἆθλον, -ου, τό [R50]

riches πλοῦτοι, -ων, οἱ [R49]

ride ἐλαύνω [44]

ridicule γελάω with ἐπί + dat. [15]

ridiculous γελοῖος, -ᾱ, -ον [R46]

right (adj.) δίκαιος, -ᾱ, -ον [37]

right (noun) δίκη, -ης, ἡ [37]

right time καιρός, -οῦ, ὁ [R38]

rightly ὀρθῶς [R30]

risk κίνδῡνος, -ου, ὁ [10]

river ποταμός, -οῦ, ὁ [7]

road ὁδός, -οῦ, ἡ [7]

rooster ἀλεκτρυών, -όνος, ὁ [R5, R19]

row ἐλαύνω [44]

ruin διαφθείρω [37]

rule (noun) ἀρχή, -ῆς, ἡ [12]

rule (verb) ἄρχω + gen. [38]; βασιλεύω [R48]

run τρέχω [50]

run a risk κινδῡνεύω [R39]

sabbath σάββατον, -ου, τό [R26]

sabbath-day σάββατον, -ου, τό [R26]

sacrifice θύω [3]

safe ἀσφαλής, -ές [R35]

safety σωτηρίᾱ, -ᾱς, ἡ [R10, R21, R30]

sail out (from) ἐκπλέω + gen. [R34]

sail together συμπλέω [R34]

sailing-voyage πλοῦς, -οῦ, ὁ [R35]

sailor ναύτης, -ου, ὁ [R34]

same αὐτός, -ή, -ό [14]; ὁμός, -ή, -όν [49]

save σῴζω [32]

say λέγω [10]; φημί [41]; ἠμί [47]

schism σχίσμα, -ατος, τό [R26]

school σχολή, -ῆς, ἡ [43]

science ἐπιστήμη, -ης, ἡ [46]

scold ἐπιπλήττω [14]

scorn ὑπερφρονέω [R36]

sculptor ἀγαλματοποιός, -οῦ, ὁ [R18]

sea θάλαττα, -ης, ἡ [5]

seagull αἴθυια, -ᾱς, ἡ [R23]

search for ζητέω [20]

season ὥρᾱ, -ᾱς, ἡ [5]

second δεύτερος, -ᾱ, -ον [34]

secretly κρύφα [R35]

see βλέπω [R7, R9, R10, 13]; ὁράω [23]

seek (to) ζητέω + infin. [20]

seem (to) δοκέω + infin. [R31, 43]

(it) seems good (to) δοκεῖ + infin. [R39, 43]

(it) seems (to) δοκεῖ + infin. [43]

seize ἁρπάζω [15]; καταλαμβάνω [R29]

-self (intens. adj.) αὐτός, -ή, -ό [14]

self-acting αὐτόματος, -η, -ον [R33]

self-control σωφροσύνη, -ης, ἡ [42]

self-controlled σώφρων, -ον [42]

sell πωλέω [18]

send πέμπω [4]; ἵημι [47]

send along (with) συμπέμπω + dat. [R50]

send away ἀποπέμπω [R12]; ἀφίημι [47]

sense αἰσθάνομαι [42]

separate κρίνω [27]; ἀποκρίνω [27]

servant (female) θεράπαινα, -ης, ἡ [5]

servant (of the household) οἰκέτης, -ου, ὁ [9]

serve δουλεύω + dat. [9]; θεραπεύω [R37]

service θεραπείᾱ, -ᾱς, ἡ [R42]

set τίθημι [47]

set down καθίστημι [R46]

set in motion κῑνέω [R35]; ἵημι [47]

set (up) ἵστημι [46]

seven ἑπτά [34]

seventh ἕβδομος, -η, -ον [34]

shake σείω [R24]

shame αἰδώς, -οῦς, ἡ [17]

shameful αἰσχρός, -ά, -όν [31]; more shameful αἰσχίων, -ῑον [33]; most shameful αἴσχιστος, -η, -ον [33]

sheep πρόβατον -ου, τό [R12]

shield ἀσπίς, -ίδος, ἡ [16]

ship ναῦς, νεώς, ἡ [R23, R34]

shop ἀγοράζω [R44]

shoot βάλλω [15]

shout (noun) βοή, -ῆς, ἡ [39]

shout (verb) βοάω [39]

show δηλόω [15]; φαίνω [R30, R32, 35]; δείκνῡμι [48]

Sicilian Σικελός, -ή, -όν [R35]

Sicily Σικελίᾱ, -ᾱς, ἡ [R35]

sight θέᾱ, -ᾱς, ἡ [R49]

sign σημεῖον, -ου, τό [R26]

silence σῑγή, -ῆς, ἡ [R40]

silver ἄργυρος, -ου, ὁ [35]

similar (to) ὅμοιος, -ᾱ, -ον + dat. [48]

sin (noun) ἁμαρτίᾱ, -ᾱς, ἡ [28]

sin (verb) ἁμαρτάνω [28]

since ἐπεί [5]; ἐπειδή [5]; ὡς [24]; ὅτι [28]

sincere ἀληθής, -ές [17]

sinful ἁμαρτωλός, -όν [R26, R27, R28]

singly καθ' ἕνα, κατὰ μίαν, καθ' ἕν [30]

sister ἀδελφή, -ῆς, ἡ [7]

sit κάθημαι [R44]

six ἕξ [R33, 34]

sixth ἕκτος, -η, -ον [34]

size μέγεθος, -ους, τό [R43]

skill ἐπιστήμη, -ης, ἡ [R36]; τέχνη, -ης, ἡ [46]

sky οὐρανός, -οῦ, ὁ [20]

Sky (personified) Οὐρανός, -οῦ, ὁ [20]

slave (female) δούλη, -ης, ἡ [9]

slave (male) δοῦλος, -ου, ὁ [9]

slavery δουλείᾱ, -ᾱς, ἡ [R37]

slay θύω [3]

sleep (noun) ὕπνος, -ου, ὁ [R19]

sleep (verb) καθεύδω [45]

slow βραδύς, -εῖα, -ύ [41]

slower βραδύτερος, -ᾱ, -ον [41]

slowest βραδύτατος, -η, -ον [41]

small μῑκρός, -ά, -όν [11]

small portion μόριον, -ου, τό [R38]

smaller ἐλάττων, -ον [33]

smallest ἐλάχιστος, -η, -ον [33]

snake δράκων, -οντος, ὁ [R21]

snare πάγη, -ης, ἡ [R22]

snatch ἁρπάζω [15]

sniff at ὀσφραίνομαι [R10]

so οὕτω(ς) [31]; ὧδε [31]

so as ὥστε [31]

so great τοσόσδε, τοσήδε, τοσόνδε [31];
  τοσοῦτος, τοσαύτη, τοσοῦτο(ν) [31]

so many τοσοίδε, τοσαίδε, τοσάδε [31];
  τοσοῦτοι, τοσαῦται, τοσαῦτα [31]

so much τοσόσδε, τοσήδε, τοσόνδε [31];
  τοσοῦτος, τοσαύτη, τοσοῦτο(ν) [31]

so that ὥστε [31]

Socrates Σωκράτης, -ους, ὁ [17]

soften μαλθακίζω [R47]

soldier στρατιώτης, -ου, ὁ [36]

some τις, τι [21]; ἔνιοι, -αι, α [R45]

somehow πως [26]

someone τις [21]

something τι [21]

sometime ποτέ [26]

sometimes ποτέ [26]

somewhere που [26]

son παῖς, παιδός, ὁ [25]; υἱός, -οῦ, ὁ [27]

soul ψῡχή, -ῆς, ἡ [22]; θῡμός, -οῦ, ὁ [38]

sound φωνή, -ῆς, ἡ [30]

space χώρᾱ, -ᾱς, ἡ [4]

span of time αἰών, -ῶνος, ὁ [R28]

Sparta Λακεδαίμων, -ονος, ἡ [R35, R44]

speak λέγω [10]

speak in the assembly ἀγορεύω [R30]

speaker ῥήτωρ, -ορος, ὁ [16]

spectacle θέᾱ, -ᾱς, ἡ [R49]

speech λόγος, -ου, ὁ [12]

spindle ἄτρακτος, -ου, ὁ [R50]

spinning νῆσις, -εως, ἡ [R50]

spirit ψῡχή, -ῆς, ἡ [22]; θῡμός, -οῦ, ὁ [38]

stade στάδιον, -ου, τό [44]

stadium στάδιον, -ου, τό [44]

staircase κλῖμαξ, -ακος, ἡ [39]

stand ἵστημι (perf.) [46]

stand guard φυλάττω [3]

stand near παρίστημι [R46]

stand out προέχω [R43]

stand up ἀνίστημι (mid. or second aor. act.)
  [R30]; ἵστημι (mid. or second aor. act.)
  [46]

star ἀστήρ, -έρος, ὁ [R50]

start out ἐξορμάω [R33]

(a) starting out ὁρμή, -ῆς, ἡ [R33]

starting-point ἀφορμή, -ῆς, ἡ [R32]

state πόλις, -εως, ἡ [29]; πολῑτείᾱ, -ᾱς, ἡ [R48]

statue (of a god) ἄγαλμα, -ατος, τό [R18]

stay μένω [R16, 19]

steal κλέπτω [3]

step βαίνω [49]

step aside παραχωρέω [R44]

stick ῥάβδος, -ου, ἡ [R13]

stifling heat πνῖγος, -ους, τό [R50]

still (adv.) ἔτι [6]

stir up κῑνέω [R35]

stone λίθος, -ου, ὁ [7]

stop (*bring to a stop*) παύω [25]; ἀναπαύω [R33]

stop (*come to a stop*) παύω (*mid.*) [25]

storehouse θησαυρός, -οῦ, ὁ [8]

storm χειμών, -ῶνος, ὁ [R23]

story λόγος, -ου, ὁ [12]; μῦθος, -ου, ὁ [R50]

stranger ξένος, -ου, ὁ [24]

strength δύναμις, -εως, ἡ [47]

stretch out ἐκτείνω [R33]

strike (*with direct blow*) πλήττω [14]

strike at ἐπιπλήττω + dat. or acc. [14]

strike down καταπλήττω [R45]

strive (to) σπεύδω + infin. [3]

stroke πληγή, -ῆς, ἡ [R44]

stronger κρείττων, -ον [33]

strongest κράτιστος, -η, -ον [33]

struggle ἀγών, -ῶνος, ὁ [15]

student μαθητής, -οῦ, ὁ [9]

stumble into ἐμπίπτω [R49]

such τοιόσδε, τοιάδε, τοιόνδε [31]; τοιοῦτος, τοιαύτη, τοιοῦτο(ν) [31]

such a! οἷος, -ᾱ, -ον [46]

such as (*rel. adj.*) οἷος, -ᾱ, -ον [46]

suddenly ἐξαίφνης [R50]

suffer πάσχω [40]

sufficient (to, for) ἱκανός, -ή, -όν + infin. or dat. [36]

(it) suits πρέπει + dat. [R46]

summon καλέω [24]; μεταπέμπω [R29]

sun ἥλιος, -ου, ὁ [48]

Sun (*personified*) Ἥλιος, -ου, ὁ [48]

support διαιτάω [R39]

suppose οἴομαι/οἶμαι [R46, 48]

surely μήν [32]; τοι [44]; μέντοι [44]

suspect ὑποπτεύω [R39]

suspicion ὕποπτον, -ου, τό [R38]

suspicious ὕποπτος, -ον [R38]

sweet ἡδύς, -εῖα, -ύ [33]

sweeter ἡδίων, -ῑον [33]

sweetest ἥδιστος, -η, -ον [33]

swift ταχύς, -εῖα, -ύ [R35, 41]

swifter θάττων, -ον [41]

swiftest τάχιστος, -η, -ον [41]

Syracusan Σῡρᾱκόσιος, -ᾱ, -ον [R38]

tail κέρκος, -ου, ἡ tail [R24]

take λαμβάνω [19]; αἱρέω [40]

take a rest ἀναπαύω (*mid.*) [R33]

take as a wife γαμέω (*act.*) [R6, 39]

take care (of) ἐπιμελέομαι + gen. [45]

take care (to) ἐπιμελέομαι + infin. [45]

take counsel (to) βουλεύω + infin. or effort cl. [45]

take delight (in) χαίρω + dat. [7]

take heart θαρρέω [R35]

take in exchange for ἀλλάττω (*mid. + acc. & gen.*) [11]

take up ἀναιρέω [R49]

tale μῦθος, -ου, ὁ [R50]

talent τάλαντον, -ου, τό [41]

tall μέγας, μεγάλη, μέγα [R14, 25]

tanner βυρσοδέψης, -ου, ὁ [R9]

task ἔργον, -ου, τό [8]

teach παιδεύω [3]; διδάσκω [25]

teach discretion to σωφρονίζω [R45]

teacher διδάσκαλος, -ου, ὁ, ἡ [25]

tell λέγω [10]; φράζω [40]

temperance σωφροσύνη, -ης, ἡ [42]

temperate σώφρων, -ον [42]

ten δέκα [34]

ten thousand μύριοι, -αι, -α [34]

tent σκηνή, -ῆς, ἡ [4]

tenth δέκατος, -η, -ον [34]

tentmate σύσκηνος, -ου, ὁ [R44]

terrible δεινός, -ή, -όν [32]

terrify καταπλήττω [R45]

test πειράω [R6, R8]

than ἤ + comp. [32]

that (conj. + indir. disc.) ὅτι [40]; ὡς [40]; (conj. + effort clause) ὅπως [45]; ὡς [45]; (conj. + fear clause) μή [45]

that (dem. adj./pron.) οὗτος, αὕτη, τοῦτο [R10, 13]; ἐκεῖνος, -η, -ο [13]

that (rel. pron.) ὅς, ἥ, ὅ [23]

that...not (conj. + neg. effort clause) ὅπως μή [45]; ὡς μή [45]; (conj. + neg. fear clause) μὴ οὐ [45]

the ὁ, ἡ, τό [4, 7, 8]

them αὐτῶν, αὐτοῖς, αὐταῖς, αὐτούς, αὐτάς, αὐτά [13]

themselves (reflex. pron.) ἑαυτῶν/αὑτῶν, -ῶν/-ῶν, -ῶν/-ῶν [19]

then (at that time) τότε [13]

then (drawing a conclusion) οὖν [10]; τοίνυν [44]; ἄρα [R46, 47]

then (next) εἶτα [49]; ἔπειτα [49]

thence ἐκεῖθεν [49]; ἐνθένδε [49]; ἐντεῦθεν [49]

there αὐτοῦ [R35]; ἐκεῖ [49]; ἔνθα [49]; ἐνθάδε [49]; ἐνταῦθα [49]

therefore οὖν [10]; τοίνυν [44]; ἄρα [R46, 47]

these οὗτοι, αὗται, ταῦτα [R10, 13]; οἵδε, αἵδε, τάδε [13]

thief κλώψ, κλωπός, ὁ thief [16]

thing πρᾶγμα, -ατος, τό [R30, 42]; χρῆμα, -ατος, τό [35]

think νομίζω [R30, 41]; διανοέομαι [R32]; δοκέω [43]; οἴομαι/οἶμαι [R46, 48]

think little (of) καταφρονέω + gen. [R31, R32]

third τρίτος, -η, -ον [34]

this οὗτος, αὕτη, τοῦτο [R10, 13]; ὅδε, ἥδε, τόδε [13]

thither ἐκεῖσε [49]; δεῦρο [49]; ἔνθα [49]; ἐνθάδε [49]; ἐνταῦθα [49]

thorn σκόλοψ, -οπος, ὁ [R16]

those οὗτοι, αὗται, ταῦτα [R10, 13]; ἐκεῖνοι, -αι, -α [13]

thousand χίλιοι, -αι, -α [34]

thranite θρᾱνίτης, -ου, ὁ [R34]

three τρεῖς, τρία [34]

thrice τρίς [34]

thrifty φειδωλός, -ή, -όν [R39]

through διά + gen. [12]

throughout διά + gen. [12]

throw βάλλω [15]; ῥίπτω [20]; ἵημι [47]

throw away ἀφίημι [47]

throw out ἐκβάλλω [R28, R38]

thunder βροντή, -ῆς, ἡ [R50]

thus οὕτω(ς) [31]; ὧδε [31]

time χρόνος, -ου, ὁ [23]

(it is) time (to) ὥρᾱ, -ᾱς, ἡ + infin. [5]

to εἰς + acc. [4]; ἐπί + acc. [14]; πρός + acc. [17]; παρά + acc. [22]; ὡς + acc. (person) [40]

to a place over ὑπέρ + acc. [20]

to a place under ὑπό + acc. [11]

to another place ἄλλοσε [49]; ἄλλη [R50]

to Athens Ἀθήναζε [49]

to here δεῦρο [49]; ἔνθα [49]; ἐνθάδε [49]; ἐνταῦθα [49]

to somewhere ποι [26]

to the same place ὁμόσε [49]

to the side of παρά + acc. [22]

to there ἐκεῖσε [R33, 49]; δεῦρο [49]; ἔνθα [49]; ἐνθάδε [49]; ἐνταῦθα [49]

to where (rel. adv.) οἷ [38]

to where? ποῖ [26]; (indir.) ὅποι [26]

to wherever (*indef. rel. adv.*) ὅποι [38]

today τήμερον [23]

together with σύν + dat. [19]; μετά + gen. [19]

tolerable μέτριος, -ᾱ, -ον [R33]

torch δᾱς, δᾳδός, ἡ [R40]

toward πρός + acc. [17]

track ἴχνος, -ους, τό [R17]

trade τέχνη, -ης, ἡ [46]

train γυμνάζω [R44, R46]

tranquillity ἡσυχίᾱ, -ᾱς, ἡ [4]

transfer παραδίδωμι [R42, R45]

transport ship ὁπλῑταγωγὸς ναῦς [R34]

trap πάγη, -ης, ἡ [R22]

treasure θησαυρός, -οῦ, ὁ [8]

treasury θησαυρός, -οῦ, ὁ [8]

treatment θεραπείᾱ, -ᾱς, ἡ [R42]

tree φυτόν, -οῦ, τό [8]; δένδρον, -ου, τό [20]

trierarch τριήραρχος, -ου, ὁ [R34]

trip up σφάλλω [R32]

trireme τριήρης, -ους, ἡ [17]

troops δύναμις, -εως, ἡ [R29]

trouble πρᾱ́γματα, -ων, τά [42]

true ἀληθής, -ές [17]

truly (τῇ) ἀληθείᾳ [10]

trumpeter σαλπιγκτής, -οῦ, ὁ [R29]

trust (in) πέποιθα + dat. [20]; πιστεύω + dat. or εἰς + acc. [28]

truth ἀλήθεια, -ᾱς, ἡ [10]

try (to) πειράω + infin. [R35, R47]

turn (*noun*) τρόπος, -ου, ὁ [R6, 11]

turn (*verb*) τρέπω [11]

twelfth δωδέκατος, -η, -ον [34]

twelve δώδεκα [34]

twenty εἴκοσι(ν) [34]

twice δίς [34]

two δύο, δυοῖν, δυοῖν, δύο [R10, R11, 34]

type γένος, -ους, τό [48]

tyranny τυραννίς, -ίδος, ἡ [R49]

tyrant τύραννος, -ου, ὁ [R38]

ugly κακός, -ή, -όν [9]

under ὑπό + dat. or acc. [11]

understand λαμβάνω [19]; μανθάνω [42]; ἐπίσταμαι [46]

understanding ἐπιστήμη, -ης, ἡ [46]

undertake (to) ἐπιχειρέω + infin. [R46]

undulation κῦμα, -ατος, τό [47]

undying ἀθάνατος, -ον [9]

unexpected ἀπροσδόκητος, -ον [R39]

unfed ἄδειπνος, -ον [R19]

universe κόσμος, -ου, ὁ [28]

unjust ἄδικος, -ον [37]

unleisured ἄσχολος, -ον [R43]

unless εἰ μή [37]

until (*conj.*) πρίν [43]; ἕως [50]; μέχρι [50]

until (*prep.*) μέχρι + gen. [50]

untrue ψευδής, -ές [50]; most untrue ψευδίστατος, -η, -ον [50]

unworthy (of, to) ἀνάξιος, -ον + gen. or infin. [9]

up (*adv.*) ἄνω [39]

up (*prep.*) ἀνά + acc. [23]

up along ἀνά + acc. [23]

up to μέχρι + gen. [50]

upbringing τροφή, -ῆς, ἡ [R46]

upon ἐπί + gen. [14]

uproar θόρυβος, -ου, ὁ [29]

(the) upstairs τὰ ἄνω [R39]

upwards ἄνω [39]

urge (to) κελεύω + infin. [5]

us ἡμῶν, ἡμῖν, ἡμᾶς [14]

use (*noun*) χρείᾱ, -ᾱς, ἡ [R32]

use (*verb*) χράομαι + dat. [36]

useful χρήσιμος, -η, -ον [R32, R35, 36];
ὠφέλιμος, -ον [R47]

value τῑμάω [15]

very (*adv.*) μάλα [33], πάνυ [48]

(the) very (*intens. adj.*) αὐτός, -ή, -ό [14];
(*intens. particle*) περ/-περ [47]

(the) very one who ὅσπερ, ἥπερ [47]

(the) very thing that ὅπερ [47]

victory νίκη, -ης, ἡ [36]

vine ἄμπελος, -ου, ἡ [R8]

vineyard ἄμπελος, -ου, ἡ [R8]

virtue ἀρετή, -ῆς, ἡ [43]

virtuous ἀγαθός, -ή, -όν [8]; more virtuous
βελτῑων, -ῑον [33]; most virtuous
βέλτιστος, -η, -ον [33]

visible φανερός, -ά, -όν [35]

voice φωνή, -ῆς, ἡ [R20, 30]

wag σείω [R24]

wagon ἄμαξα, -ης, ἡ [11]

wait for μένω + acc. [R16, 19]

walk (*noun*) περίπατος, -ου, ὁ [R33]

walk (*verb*) περιπατέω [R33]; βαίνω [49]

walk around περιπατέω [R33]

(a) walking around περίπατος, -ου, ὁ [R33]

wall (*of a city*) τεῖχος, -ους, τό [17]

wall (*of a house or enclosure*) τοῖχος, -ου, ὁ
[R16]

war πόλεμος, -ου, ὁ [12]

ward off ἀμύνω [R36]

wash νίζω [R26]

water ὕδωρ, ὕδατος, τό [R11, R21, 50]

wave κῦμα, -ατος, τό [47]

way ὁδός, -οῦ, ἡ [7]; τρόπος, -ου, ὁ [R6, 11]

we ἡμεῖς [14]

weak ἀσθενής, -ές [R36]

weaker ἥττων, -ον [33]

weakest ἥκιστος, -η, -ον [33]

wealth πλοῦτος, -ου, ὁ [R49]

wealthy πλούσιος, -ᾱ, -ον [R30]

weasel γαλῆ, -ῆς, ἡ [R6]

wedding γάμος, -ου, ὁ [39]

weep κλάω [R49]

well εὖ [17]

well-disposed (toward) πρόθῡμος, -ον +
dat. or εἰς + acc. [38]

well-intentioned εὔνους, -ουν [R30]

(the) well-known οὗτος, αὕτη, τοῦτο [R10,
13]; ἐκεῖνος, -η, -ο [13]

well-reasoned εὔλογος, -ον [R37]

what? (*adj./pron.*) τί [21]; (*indir.*) ὅ τι [26]

whatever (*indef. rel. pron.*) ὅ τι [38]

when ἐπεί [5]; ἐπειδή [5]; ὡς [24]; (*rel. adv.*)
ὅτε [38]

when? πότε [26]; (*indir.*) ὁπότε [26]

whence (*rel. adv.*) ὅθεν [38]

whence? πόθεν [26]; (*indir.*) ὁπόθεν [26]

whencesoever (*indef. rel. adv.*) ὁπόθεν [38]

whenever (*indef. rel. adv.*) ὁπότε [38]

where (*rel. adv.*) οὗ [38]

where? ποῦ [26]; (*indir.*) ὅπου [26]

wherever (*indef. rel. adv.*) ὅπου [38]

whether εἰ [26]

whether...or? εἴτε...εἴτε [26]; πότερον/
πότερα...ἤ [26]

which (*rel. pron.*) ὅ [23]

which? τί [21]; (*indir.*) ὅ τι [26]

which indeed ὅπερ [47]

whichever (*indef. rel. pron.*) ὅ τι [38]

which(ever) (*of two*) ὁπότερος, -ᾱ, -ον [R40]

while ἕως [23]

whip μαστῑγόω [R40]

whither (*rel. adv.*) ὅθεν [38]

whither? ποῖ [26]; (*indir.*) ὅποι [26]

whithersoever (*indef. rel. adv.*) ὁπόθεν [38]

who (*rel. pron.*) ὅς, ἥ [23]

who? τίς [21]; (*indir.*) ὅστις, ἥτις [26]

who indeed (*rel. pron.*) ὅσπερ, ἥπερ [47]

whoever (*indef. rel. pron.*) ὅστις, ἥτις [38]

whole πᾶς, πᾶσα, πᾶν [23]

why? τί [21]

wicked κακός, -ή, -όν [9]; more wicked
    κακίων, -ῑον [33]; most wicked
    κάκιστος, -η, -ον [33]

wickedly κακῶς [17]

wife γυνή, γυναικός, ἡ [39]

win νῑκάω [37]

wing πτερόν, -οῦ, τό [R20]

wisdom σοφίᾱ, -ᾱς, ἡ [13]

wise σοφός, -ή, -όν [13]

wish (to) ἐθέλω + infin. [3]; βούλομαι +
    infin. [30]

with σύν + dat. [19]; μετά + gen. [19]

with the avowed intention of ὡς + ptcple. [24]

with the help of σύν + dat. [19]

within ἐντός + gen. [R41]

without ἄνευ + gen. [24]

woe is me! οἴμοι [R17]

wolf λύκος, -ου, ὁ [R12]

woman ἄνθρωπος, -ου, ἡ [7]; γυνή, γυναικός,
    ἡ [39]

womankind ἄνθρωπος, -ου, ἡ [7]

wonder (at) θαυμάζω [44]

word λόγος, -ου, ὁ [12]

work (*noun*) ἔργον, -ου, τό [8]

work (*verb*) πονέω [R5]

workshop ἐργαστήριον, -ου, τό [R18]

world κόσμος, -ου, ὁ [28]

worse (*in ability or worth*) χείρων, -ον [33]

worse (*in might*) ἥττων, -ον [33]

worse (*morally*) κακίων, -ῑον [33]

worship προσκυνέω + dat. [R28]

worshipping God θεοσεβής, -ές [R28]

worst (*in ability or worth*) χείριστος, -η, -ον [33]

worst (*in might*) ἥκιστος, -η, -ον [33]

worst (*morally*) κάκιστος, -η, -ον [33]

worth τῑμή, -ῆς, ἡ [15]

worthless ἀνάξιος, -ον [9]

worthy (*of, to*) ἄξιος, -ᾱ, -ον + gen. or infin.
    [8]

would that εἰ γάρ [36]; εἴθε [36]

wow! βαβαί [R24]

wrestling-bout πάλαισμα, -ατος, τό [R44]

wrestling-school παλαίστρᾱ, -ᾱς, ἡ [R46]

write γράφω [3]

wrong (*adj.*) ἄδικος, -ον [37]

wrong (*noun*) ἀδικίᾱ, -ᾱς, ἡ [37]

year ἔτος, -ους, τό [23]

yes καὶ μάλα [R46]; ναί [R46]

yes, by... (*oath*) νή + acc. [R46]

yet ἔτι [6]; μήν [32]

yield παραχωρέω [R44]

yoke ζυγόν, -οῦ, τό [R45]

you (*pl.*) ὑμεῖς, ὑμῶν, ὑμῖν, ὑμᾶς [14]

you (*sg.*) σύ, σοῦ/σου, σοί/σοι, σέ/σε [14]

you know τοι [44]

you see τοι [44]

young νέος, -ᾱ, -ον [27]

young child παιδίον, -ου, τό [25]

young man νεᾱνίᾱς, -ου, ὁ [R6, 9]

your (*more than one person's*) ὑμέτερος, -ᾱ,
    -ον [21]

your (*one person's*) σός, -ή, -όν [21]

your own (*more than one person's*) ὑμέτερος,
    -ᾱ, -ον [21]

your own (*one person's*) σός, -ή, -όν [21]

yours (*more than one person's*) ὑμέτερος,
   -α, -ον [21]

yours (*one person's*) σός, -ή, -όν [21]

yourself (*reflex. pron.*) σεαυτοῦ/σαυτοῦ,
   σεαυτῆς/σαυτῆς [19]

yourselves (*reflex. pron.*) ὑμῶν αὐτῶν, -ῶν [19]

youth νεανίας, -ου, ὁ [R6, 9]

Zeus Ζεύς, Διός, ὁ [R18, R42, R48]

APPENDIX

NOUNS

First Declension - Feminines
Stems ending in -ᾱ/-ᾱς or -η/-ης:

	("goddess")	("leisure")	("place")	("tent")
Singular:				
Nom.	θεά	ἡσυχίᾱ	χώρᾱ	σκηνή
Gen.	θεᾶς	ἡσυχίᾱς	χώρᾱς	σκηνῆς
Dat.	θεᾷ	ἡσυχίᾳ	χώρᾳ	σκηνῇ
Acc.	θεάν	ἡσυχίᾱν	χώρᾱν	σκηνήν
Voc.	θεά	ἡσυχίᾱ	χώρᾱ	σκηνή
Dual:				
N./A./V.	θεά	ἡσυχίᾱ	χώρᾱ	σκηνά
G./D.	θεαῖν	ἡσυχίαιν	χώραιν	σκηναῖν
Plural:				
Nom.	θεαί	ἡσυχίαι	χῶραι	σκηναί
Gen.	θεῶν	ἡσυχιῶν	χωρῶν	σκηνῶν
Dat.	θεαῖς	ἡσυχίαις	χώραις	σκηναῖς
Acc.	θεάς	ἡσυχίᾱς	χώρᾱς	σκηνάς
Voc.	θεαί	ἡσυχίαι	χῶραι	σκηναί

Stems ending in -α/-ᾱς or -α/-ης:

	("fate")	("sea")
Singular:		
Nom.	μοῖρα	θάλαττα
Gen.	μοίρᾱς	θαλάττης
Dat.	μοίρᾳ	θαλάττῃ
Acc.	μοῖραν	θάλατταν
Voc.	μοῖρα	θάλαττα
Dual:		
N./A./V.	μοίρᾱ	θαλάττᾱ
G./D.	μοίραιν	θαλάτταιν

Plural:

Nom.	μοῖραι	θάλατται
Gen.	μοιρῶν	θαλαττῶν
Dat.	μοίραις	θαλάτταις
Acc.	μοίρᾱς	θαλάττᾱς
Voc.	μοῖραι	θάλατται

First Declension - Masculines

	("student")	("youth")

Singular:

Nom.	μαθητής	νεᾱνίᾱς
Gen.	μαθητοῦ	νεᾱνίου
Dat.	μαθητῇ	νεᾱνίᾳ
Acc.	μαθητήν	νεᾱνίᾱν
Voc.	μαθητά[1]	νεᾱνίᾱ

Dual:

N./A./V.	μαθητά	νεᾱνίᾱ
G./D.	μαθηταῖν	νεᾱνίαιν

Plural:

Nom.	μαθηταί	νεᾱνίαι
Gen.	μαθητῶν	νεᾱνιῶν
Dat.	μαθηταῖς	νεᾱνίαις
Acc.	μαθητάς	νεᾱνίᾱς
Voc.	μαθηταί	νεᾱνίαι

Second Declension - Masculines[2]

	("human being")	("river")

Singular:

Nom.	ἄνθρωπος	ποταμός
Gen.	ἀνθρώπου	ποταμοῦ
Dat.	ἀνθρώπῳ	ποταμῷ
Acc.	ἄνθρωπον	ποταμόν
Voc.	ἄνθρωπε	ποταμέ

Dual:

N./A./V.	ἀνθρώπω	ποταμώ
G./D.	ἀνθρώποιν	ποταμοῖν

---

[1] The vocative singular ends in -α if the nominative singular ends in -της or if the word is a compound or the name of a nationality; otherwise the voc. sg. ends in -η.

[2] Most nouns of this type are masculine, but those denoting persons or animals may be either masculine or feminine, depending on whether the person or animal being denoted is male or female (e.g., ὁ ἵππος "horse"; ἡ ἵππος "mare"). A few second-declension nouns are always feminine (e.g., ὁδός, -οῦ, ἡ "road").

Plural:

Nom.	ἄνθρωποι	ποταμοί
Gen.	ἀνθρώπων	ποταμῶν
Dat.	ἀνθρώποις	ποταμοῖς
Acc.	ἀνθρώπους	ποταμούς
Voc.	ἄνθρωποι	ποταμοί

Second Declension - Neuters

	("gift")	("plant")
Singular:		
Nom.	δῶρον	φυτόν
Gen.	δώρου	φυτοῦ
Dat.	δώρῳ	φυτῷ
Acc.	δῶρον	φυτόν
Voc.	δῶρον	φυτόν
Dual:		
N./A./V.	δώρω	φυτώ
G./D.	δώροιν	φυτοῖν
Plural:		
Nom.	δῶρα	φυτά
Gen.	δώρων	φυτῶν
Dat.	δώροις	φυτοῖς
Acc.	δῶρα	φυτά
Voc.	δῶρα	φυτά

Third Declension - Stems ending in a stop:

	ἀσπίς, -ίδος, ἡ (stem = ἀσπιδ-) ("shield")	χάρις, -ιτος ἡ (stem = χαριτ-) ("grace")	λέων, -οντος, ὁ (stem = λεοντ-) ("lion")	ὄνομα, -ατος, τό (stem = ὀνοματ-) ("name")	κλώψ, κλωπός, ὁ (stem = κλωπ-) ("thief")	φύλαξ, -ακος, ὁ (stem = φυλακ-) ("guard")
Singular:						
Nom.	ἀσπίς	χάρις	λέων	ὄνομα	κλώψ	φύλαξ
Gen.	ἀσπίδος	χάριτος	λέοντος	ὀνόματος	κλωπός	φύλακος
Dat.	ἀσπίδι	χάριτι	λέοντι	ὀνόματι	κλωπί	φύλακι
Acc.	ἀσπίδα	χάριν	λέοντα	ὄνομα	κλῶπα	φύλακα
Voc.	ἀσπί	χάρι	λέον	ὄνομα	κλώψ	φύλαξ
Dual:						
N./A./V.	ἀσπίδε	χάριτε	λέοντε	ὀνόματε	κλῶπε	φύλακε
G./D.	ἀσπίδοιν	χαρίτοιν	λεόντοιν	ὀνομάτοιν	κλώποιν	φυλάκοιν
Plural:						
Nom.	ἀσπίδες	χάριτες	λέοντες	ὀνόματα	κλῶπες	φύλακες
Gen.	ἀσπίδων	χαρίτων	λεόντων	ὀνομάτων	κλωπῶν	φυλάκων
Dat.	ἀσπίσι(ν)	χάρισι(ν)	λέουσι(ν)	ὀνόμασι(ν)	κλωψί(ν)	φύλαξι(ν)
Acc.	ἀσπίδας	χάριτας	λέοντας	ὀνόματα	κλῶπας	φύλακας
Voc.	ἀσπίδες	χάριτες	λέοντες	ὀνόματα	κλῶπες	φύλακες

Third Declension - Stems ending in a liquid or a nasal:

		ῥήτωρ, -ορος, ὁ (stem = ῥητορ-) ("orator")	ἀγών, -ῶνος, ὁ (stem = ἀγων-) ("contest")
Singular:	Nom.	ῥήτωρ	ἀγών
	Gen.	ῥήτορος	ἀγῶνος
	Dat.	ῥήτορι	ἀγῶνι
	Acc.	ῥήτορα	ἀγῶνα
	Voc.	ῥῆτορ	ἀγών
Dual:	N./A./V.	ῥήτορε	ἀγῶνε
	G./D.	ῥητόροιν	ἀγώνοιν
Plural:	Nom.	ῥήτορες	ἀγῶνες
	Gen.	ῥητόρων	ἀγώνων
	Dat.	ῥήτορσι(ν)	ἀγῶσι(ν)
	Acc.	ῥήτορας	ἀγῶνας
	Voc.	ῥήτορες	ἀγῶνες

Third Declension - Stems ending in a vowel or a diphthong:

		πόλις, -εως, ἡ (stem = πολι/ε/η-) ("city-state")	ἄστυ, -εως, τό (stem = ἀστυ/ε/η-) ("city")	βασιλεύς, -έως, ὁ (stem = βασιλευ/ηυ/ηϝ-) ("king")
Singular:	Nom.	πόλις	ἄστυ	βασιλεύς
	Gen.	πόλεως	ἄστεως	βασιλέως
	Dat.	πόλει	ἄστει	βασιλεῖ
	Acc.	πόλιν	ἄστυ	βασιλέᾱ
	Voc.	πόλι	ἄστυ	βασιλεῦ
Dual:	N./A./V.	πόλει	ἄστει	βασιλῆ
	G./D.	πολέοιν	ἀστέοιν	βασιλέοιν
Plural:	Nom.	πόλεις	ἄστη	βασιλῆς or -εῖς
	Gen.	πόλεων	ἄστεων	βασιλέων
	Dat.	πόλεσι(ν)	ἄστεσι(ν)	βασιλεῦσι(ν)
	Acc.	πόλεις	ἄστη	βασιλέᾱς
	Voc.	πόλεις	ἄστη	βασιλῆς or -εῖς

Third Declension - Contracted - Stems ending in a sigma:

	Σωκράτης, -ους, ὁ (stem = Σωκρατεσ-) ("Socrates")	τριήρης, -ους, ἡ (stem = τριηρεσ-) ("trireme")	τεῖχος, -ους, τό (stem = τειχεσ-) ("wall")	γέρας, -ως, τό (stem = γερασ-) ("reward")	αἰδώς, -οῦς, ἡ (stem = αἰδοσ-) ("shame")
Singular:					
Nom.	Σωκράτης	τριήρης	τεῖχος	γέρας	αἰδώς
Gen.	Σωκράτους	τριήρους	τείχους	γέρως	αἰδοῦς
Dat.	Σωκράτει	τριήρει	τείχει	γέραι/-ᾳ[1]	αἰδοῖ
Acc.	Σωκράτη	τριήρη	τεῖχος	γέρας	αἰδῶ
Voc.	Σώκρατες	τριῆρες	τεῖχος	γέρας	αἰδώς
Dual:					
N./A./V.	no dual	τριήρει	τείχει	γέρᾱ	no dual
G./D.		τριήροιν	τειχοῖν	γερῷν	
Plural:					
Nom.	no plural	τριήρεις	τείχη	γέρᾱ	no plural
Gen.		τριήρων[2]	τειχῶν	γερῶν	
Dat.		τριήρεσι(ν)	τείχεσι(ν)	γέρασι(ν)	
Acc.		τριήρεις	τείχη	γέρᾱ	
Voc.		τριήρεις	τείχη	γέρᾱ	

Third Declension - Syncopated - Stems ending in -ερ/-ηρ/-ρ:

	πατήρ, -τρός, ὁ (stem = πατερ-) ("father")	μήτηρ, -τρός, ἡ (stem = μητερ-) ("mother")	θυγάτηρ, -τρός, ἡ (stem = θυγατερ-) ("daughter")	ἀνήρ, ἀνδρός, ὁ (stem = ἀνερ-) ("man")
Singular:				
Nom.	πατήρ	μήτηρ	θυγάηρ	ἀνήρ
Gen.	πατρός	μητρός	θυγατρός	ἀνδρός
Dat.	πατρί	μητρί	θυγατρί	ἀνδρί
Acc.	πατέρα	μητέρα	θυγατέρα	ἄνδρα
Voc.	πάτερ	μῆτερ	θύγατερ	ἄνερ
Dual:				
N./A./V.	πατέρε	μητέρε	θυγατέρε	ἄνδρε
G./D.	πατέροιν	μητέροιν	θυγατέροιν	ἀνδροῖν
Plural:				
Nom.	πατέρες	μητέρες	θυγατέρες	ἄνδρες
Gen.	πατέρων	μητέρων	θυγατέρων	ἀνδρῶν
Dat.	πατράσι(ν)	μητράσι(ν)	θυγατράσι(ν)	ἀνδράσι(ν)
Acc.	πατέρας	μητέρας	θυγατέρας	ἄνδρας
Voc.	πατέρες	μητέρες	θυγατέρες	ἄνδρες

---

[1]The ending -ᾳ is illogical (α should be short); nevertheless it is often used.
[2]The accent should be τριηρῶν (from τριηρέων); nevertheless τριήρων is preferred.

DEFINITE ARTICLE ("the")

Singular:				Plural:			
	Masc.	Fem.	Neut.		Masc.	Fem.	Neut.
Nom.	ὁ	ἡ	τό		οἱ	αἱ	τά
Gen.	τοῦ	τῆς	τοῦ		τῶν	τῶν	τῶν
Dat.	τῷ	τῇ	τῷ		τοῖς	ταῖς	τοῖς
Acc.	τόν	τήν	τό		τούς	τάς	τά

Dual:			
N./A.	τώ	τώ	τώ
G./D.	τοῖν	τοῖν	τοῖν

PRONOUNS

Relative Pronouns ("who," "whom," "that," "which")

Singular:				Plural:			
	Masc.	Fem.	Neut.		Masc.	Fem.	Neut.
Nom.	ὅς	ἥ	ὅ		οἵ	αἵ	ἅ
Gen.	οὗ	ἧς	οὗ		ὧν	ὧν	ὧν
Dat.	ᾧ	ᾗ	ᾧ		οἷς	αἷς	οἷς
Acc.	ὅν	ἥν	ὅ		οὕς	ἅς	ἅ

Dual:			
N./A.	ὥ	ὥ	ὥ
G./D.	οἷν	οἷν	οἷν

Demonstrative Pronouns

ὅδε, ἥδε, τόδε ("this" / "these") - final ε may be elided before a vowel

Singular:				Plural:			
	Masc.	Fem.	Neut.		Masc.	Fem.	Neut.
Nom.	ὅδε	ἥδε	τόδε		οἵδε	αἵδε	τάδε
Gen.	τοῦδε	τῆσδε	τοῦδε		τῶνδε	τῶνδε	τῶνδε
Dat.	τῷδε	τῇδε	τῷδε		τοῖσδε	ταῖσδε	τοῖσδε
Acc.	τόνδε	τήνδε	τόδε		τούσδε	τάσδε	τάδε

Dual:			
N./A.	τώδε	τώδε	τώδε
G./D.	τοῖνδε	τοῖνδε	τοῖνδε

οὗτος, αὕτη, τοῦτο ("this" / "these" or "that" / "those")

Singular:

	Masc.	Fem.	Neut.	
Nom.	οὗτος	αὕτη	τοῦτο	(τοῦτ')
Gen.	τούτου	ταύτης	τούτου	
Dat.	τούτῳ	ταύτῃ	τούτῳ	
Acc.	τοῦτον	ταύτην	τοῦτο	(τοῦτ')

Plural:

	Masc.	Fem.	Neut.	
Nom.	οὗτοι	αὗται	ταῦτα	(ταῦτ')
Gen.	τούτων	τούτων	τούτων	
Dat.	τούτοις	ταύταις	τούτοις	
Acc.	τούτους	ταύτᾱς	ταῦτα	(ταῦτ')

Dual:

	Masc.	Fem.	Neut.
N./A.	τούτω	τούτω	τούτω
G./D.	τούτοιν	τούτοιν	τούτοιν

ἐκεῖνος, ἐκείνη, ἐκεῖνο ("that" / "those")

Singular:

	Masc.	Fem.	Neut.
Nom.	ἐκεῖνος	ἐκείνη	ἐκεῖνο
Gen.	ἐκείνου	ἐκείνης	ἐκείνου
Dat.	ἐκείνῳ	ἐκείνῃ	ἐκείνῳ
Acc.	ἐκεῖνον	ἐκείνην	ἐκεῖνο

Plural:

	Masc.	Fem.	Neut.
Nom.	ἐκεῖνοι	ἐκεῖναι	ἐκεῖνα
Gen.	ἐκείνων	ἐκείνων	ἐκείνων
Dat.	ἐκείνοις	ἐκείναις	ἐκείνοις
Acc.	ἐκείνους	ἐκείνᾱς	ἐκεῖνα

Dual:

	Masc.	Fem.	Neut.
N./A.	ἐκείνω	ἐκείνω	ἐκείνω
G./D.	ἐκείνοιν	ἐκείνοιν	ἐκείνοιν

Reciprocal Pronoun

ἀλλήλων, -οις/-αις, -ους/-ᾱς/-α ("one another")

Interrogative Adjective or Pronoun τίς
("who?" "what?" "which?")

	Masc./Fem.		Neut.	
Singular:				
Nom.	τίς		τί	
Gen.	τίνος	(τοῦ)	τίνος	(τοῦ)
Dat.	τίνι	(τῷ)	τίνι	(τῷ)
Acc.	τίνα	(τίν')	τί	
Dual:				
N./A.	τίνε		τίνε	
G./D.	τίνοιν		τίνοιν	
Plural:				
Nom.	τίνες		τίνα	(τίν')
Gen.	τίνων		τίνων	
Dat.	τίσι(ν)		τίσι(ν)	
Acc.	τίνας		τίνα	(τίν')

Indefinite Adjective or Pronoun τις
("a," "a certain," "some," "someone," "something")

	Masc./Fem.		Neut.	
Singular:				
Nom.	τις		τι	
Gen.	τινός	(του)	τινός	(του)
Dat.	τινί	(τῳ)	τινί	(τῳ)
Acc.	τινά	(τιν')	τι	
Dual:				
N./A.	τινέ		τινέ	
G./D.	τινοῖν		τινοῖν	
Plural:				
Nom.	τινές		τινά	(τιν') or ἄττα
Gen.	τινῶν		τινῶν	
Dat.	τισί(ν)		τισί(ν)	
Acc.	τινάς		τινά	(τιν') or ἄττα

Indirect Interrogative Adjective or Pronoun or
Indefinite Relative Pronoun
ὅστις, ἥτις, ὅ τι (*indir. interrog. adj.*) "what?" "which?";
(*indir. interrog. pron.*) "who?" "what?"; (*indef. rel. pron.*)
"whoever," "whatever," "whichever"

	Masc.		Fem.	Neut.	
Singular:					
Nom.	ὅστις		ἥτις	ὅ τι	
Gen.	οὗτινος	(ὅτου)	ἧστινος	οὗτινος	(ὅτου)
Dat.	ᾧτινι	(ὅτῳ)	ᾗτινι	ᾧτινι	(ὅτῳ)
Acc.	ὅντινα	(ὅντιν')	ἥντινα	ὅ τι	
Dual:					
N./A.	ὥτινε		ὥτινε	ὥτινε	
G./D.	οἷντινουν		οἷντινουν	οἷντινουν	
Plural:					
Nom.	οἵτινες		αἵτινες	ἅτινα	(ἅτιν') or ἄττα
Gen.	ὧντινων	(ὅτων)	ὧντινων	ὧντινων	(ὅτων)
Dat.	οἷστισι(ν)	(ὅτοις)	αἷστισι(ν)	οἷστισι(ν)	(ὅτοις)
Acc.	οὕστινας		ἅστινας	ἅτινα	(ἅτιν') or ἄττα

Personal Pronouns

First-Person Singular ("I"):   First-Person Plural ("we"):

Nom.	ἐγώ	ἡμεῖς
Gen.	ἐμοῦ[1]	or μου	ἡμῶν
Dat.	ἐμοί[1]	or μοι	ἡμῖν
Acc.	ἐμέ[1]	or με	ἡμᾶς

First-Person Dual ("we two"):

N./A.	νώ
G./D.	νῷν

Second-Person Singular ("you"):   Second-Person Plural ("you"):

Nom.	σύ	ὑμεῖς
Gen.	σοῦ[1]	or σου	ὑμῶν
Dat.	σοί[1]	or σοι	ὑμῖν
Acc.	σέ[1]	or σε	ὑμᾶς

Second-Person Dual ("you two"):

N./A.	σφώ
G./D.	σφῷν

Third-Person Singular & Plural ("he," "she," "it," "they"):

Singular:

	Masc.	**Fem.**	**Neut.**
Nom.[2]	ὅδε, οὗτος, ἐκεῖνος	ἥδε, αὕτη, ἐκείνη	τόδε, τοῦτο, ἐκεῖνο
Gen.	αὐτοῦ	αὐτῆς	αὐτοῦ
Dat.	αὐτῷ	αὐτῇ	αὐτῷ
Acc.	αὐτόν	αὐτήν	αὐτό

Plural:

	Masc.	**Fem.**	**Neut.**
Nom.[2]	οἵδε, οὗτοι, ἐκεῖνοι	αἵδε, αὗται, ἐκεῖναι	τάδε, ταῦτα, ἐκεῖνα
Gen.	αὐτῶν	αὐτῶν	αὐτῶν
Dat.	αὐτοῖς	αὐταῖς	αὐτοῖς
Acc.	αὐτούς	αὐτάς	αὐτά

---

[1] The emphatic, non-enclitic forms are preferred for the objects of prepositions.

[2] In the nominative (predicate position) αὐτός, -ή, -όν is an intensive meaning "himself," "herself," "itself," or "themselves." To say "he," "she," "it," or "they" (nominative case), one of the demonstrative pronouns must be used.

Reflexive Pronouns

First-Person Singular
("myself"):

	Masc.	Fem.
Gen.	ἐμαυτοῦ	ἐμαυτῆς
Dat.	ἐμαυτῷ	ἐμαυτῇ
Acc.	ἐμαυτόν	ἐμαυτήν

First-Person Plural
("ourselves"):

	Masc.	Fem.
Gen.	ἡμῶν αὐτῶν	ἡμῶν αὐτῶν
Dat.	ἡμῖν αὐτοῖς	ἡμῖν αὐταῖς
Acc.	ἡμᾶς αὐτούς	ἡμᾶς αὐτάς

Second-Person Singular
("yourself"):

	Masc.		Fem.	
Gen.	σεαυτοῦ	(σαυτοῦ)	σεαυτῆς	(σαυτῆς)
Dat.	σεαυτῷ	(σαυτῷ)	σεαυτῇ	(σαυτῇ)
Acc.	σεαυτόν	(σαυτόν)	σεαυτήν	(σαυτήν)

Second-Person Plural
("yourselves"):

	Masc.	Fem.
Gen.	ὑμῶν αὐτῶν	ὑμῶν αὐτῶν
Dat.	ὑμῖν αὐτοῖς	ὑμῖν αὐταῖς
Acc.	ὑμᾶς αὐτούς	ὑμᾶς αὐτάς

Third-Person Singular ("himself," "herself," "itself"):

	Masc.		Fem.		Neut.	
Gen.	ἑαυτοῦ	(αὐτοῦ)	ἑαυτῆς	(αὐτῆς)	ἑαυτοῦ	(αὐτοῦ)
Dat.	ἑαυτῷ	(αὐτῷ)	ἑαυτῇ	(αὐτῇ)	ἑαυτῷ	(αὐτῷ)
Acc.	ἑαυτόν	(αὐτόν)	ἑαυτήν	(αὐτήν)	ἑαυτό	(αὐτό)

or[1] **Masc./Fem./Neut.**

Gen.	οὗ	(emphatic)	or οὑ	(unemphatic enclitic)
Dat.	οἷ	(emphatic)	or οἱ	(unemphatic enclitic)
Acc.	ἕ	(emphatic)	or ἑ	(unemphatic enclitic)

Third-Person Plural ("themselves"):

	Masc.		Fem.		Neut.	
Gen.	ἑαυτῶν	(αὐτῶν)	ἑαυτῶν	(αὐτῶν)	ἑαυτῶν	(αὐτῶν)
Dat.	ἑαυτοῖς	(αὐτοῖς)	ἑαυταῖς	(αὐταῖς)	ἑαυτοῖς	(αὐτοῖς)
Acc.	ἑαυτούς	(αὐτούς)	ἑαυτάς	(αὐτάς)	ἑαυτά	(αὐτά)

or[1] **Masc./Fem./Neut.**

Nom.	σφεῖς
Gen.	σφῶν
Dat.	σφίσι(ν)
Acc.	σφᾶς

NOTE

In the first- and second-person plural, if the reflexive is showing possession (e.g., "our own book," "your own book"), the pronouns ἡμῶν and ὑμῶν are usually replaced by the adjectives ἡμέτερος, -ᾱ, -ον and ὑμέτερος, -ᾱ, -ον (e.g., τὸ ἡμέτερον βιβλίον αὐτῶν, τὸ ὑμέτερον βιβλίον αὐτῶν). Similarly, σφέτερος, -ᾱ, -ον αὐτῶν is preferred to σφῶν αὐτῶν when possession is being indicated ("their own").

---

[1] In Attic prose these alternative forms are relatively rare and always function as **indirect** reflexives (i.e., they look back not to the subject of the subordinate clause in which they appear, but to the subject of the main clause in the sentence).

Correlative Adjectives/Pronouns

Demonstratives:

τόσος, -η, -ον "so much/many"	τοσοῦτος, τοσαύτη, τοσοῦτο(ν) "so much/many"	τοσόσδε, τοσήδε, τοσόνδε "so much/many"
τοῖος, -ᾱ, -ον "of such a sort"	τοιοῦτος, τοιαύτη, τοιοῦτο(ν) "of such a sort"	τοιόσδε, τοιάδε, τοιόνδε "of such a sort"

Dir. Interrog.:	Indefinite (enclitic):	Relative:	Indirect Interrogative/ Indefinite Relative:
πόσος, -η, -ον "how much/ many?"	ποσός, -ή, -όν "of some size/ quantity"	ὅσος, -η, -ον "of which size" or "as much/ many as"	ὁπόσος, -η, -ον "how much/many?" or "of whichever size/quantity"
ποῖος, -ᾱ, -ον "of what sort?"	ποιός, -ά, -όν "of some sort"	οἷος, -ᾱ, -ον "of which sort" or "such as"	ὁποῖος, -ᾱ, -ον "of what sort?" or "of whichever sort"

ADJECTIVES

Adjectives - First/Second Declension

Stems ending in -ε, -ι, or -ρ (ἄξιος, -ᾱ, -ον "worthy"):

	Singular: Masc.	Fem.	Neut.	Plural: Masc.	Fem.	Neut.
Nom.	ἄξιος	ἀξίᾱ	ἄξιον	ἄξιοι	ἄξιαι	ἄξια
Gen.	ἀξίου	ἀξίᾱς	ἀξίου	ἀξίων	ἀξίων	ἀξίων
Dat.	ἀξίῳ	ἀξίᾳ	ἀξίῳ	ἀξίοις	ἀξίαις	ἀξίοις
Acc.	ἄξιον	ἀξίᾱν	ἄξιον	ἀξίους	ἀξίᾱς	ἄξια
Voc.	ἄξιε	ἀξίᾱ	ἄξιον	ἄξιοι	ἄξιαι	ἄξια

	Dual: Masc.	Fem.	Neut.
N./A./V.	ἀξίω	ἀξίᾱ	ἀξίω
G./D.	ἀξίοιν	ἀξίαιν	ἀξίοιν

Adjectives - First/Second Declension

Stems not ending in -ε, -ι, or -ρ (ἀγαθός, -ή, -όν "good"):

	Singular: Masc.	Fem.	Neut.	Plural: Masc.	Fem.	Neut
Nom.	ἀγαθός	ἀγαθή	ἀγαθόν	ἀγαθοί	ἀγαθαί	ἀγαθά
Gen.	ἀγαθοῦ	ἀγαθῆς	ἀγαθοῦ	ἀγαθῶν	ἀγαθῶν	ἀγαθῶν
Dat.	ἀγαθῷ	ἀγαθῇ	ἀγαθῷ	ἀγαθοῖς	ἀγαθαῖς	ἀγαθοῖς
Acc.	ἀγαθόν	ἀγαθήν	ἀγαθόν	ἀγαθούς	ἀγαθάς	ἀγαθά
Voc.	ἀγαθέ	ἀγαθή	ἀγαθόν	ἀγαθοί	ἀγαθαί	ἀγαθά

Dual:

	Masc.	Fem.	Neut.
N./A./V.	ἀγαθώ	ἀγαθά	ἀγαθώ
G./D.	ἀγαθοῖν	ἀγαθαῖν	ἀγαθοῖν

NOTE   Two-ending adjectives like ἄδικος, -ον, ἀθάνατος, -ον, ἀνάξιος, -ον, πρόθῡμος, -ον, and φιλόσοφος, -ον use masculine endings to signify either masculine or feminine. They do not use the normal set of feminine endings.

Adjectives - Third Declension

Stems ending in a nasal (εὐδαίμων, -ον "happy"):

Singular:

	Masc./Fem.	Neut.
Nom.	εὐδαίμων	εὔδαιμον
Gen.	εὐδαίμονος	εὐδαίμονος
Dat.	εὐδαίμονι	εὐδαίμονι
Acc.	εὐδαίμονα	εὔδαιμον
Voc.	εὔδαιμον	εὔδαιμον

Dual:

	Masc./Fem.	Neut.
N./A./V.	εὐδαίμονε	εὐδαίμονε
G./D.	εὐδαιμόνοιν	εὐδαιμόνοιν

Plural:

	Masc./Fem.	Neut.
Nom.	εὐδαίμονες	εὐδαίμονα
Gen.	εὐδαιμόνων	εὐδαιμόνων
Dat.	εὐδαίμοσι(ν)	εὐδαίμοσι(ν)
Acc.	εὐδαίμονας	εὐδαίμονα
Voc.	εὐδαίμονες	εὐδαίμονα

Stems ending in a sigma (contracted) (ἀληθής, -ές "true"):

Singular:

	Masc./Fem.	Neut.
Nom.	ἀληθής	ἀληθές
Gen.	ἀληθοῦς	ἀληθοῦς
Dat.	ἀληθεῖ	ἀληθεῖ
Acc.	ἀληθῆ	ἀληθές
Voc.	ἀληθές	ἀληθές

Dual:

	Masc./Fem.	Neut.
N./A./V.	ἀληθεῖ	ἀληθεῖ
G./D.	ἀληθοῖν	ἀληθοῖν

Plural:

	Masc./Fem.	Neut.
Nom.	ἀληθεῖς	ἀληθῆ
Gen.	ἀληθῶν	ἀληθῶν
Dat.	ἀληθέσι(ν)	ἀληθέσι(ν)
Acc.	ἀληθεῖς	ἀληθῆ
Voc.	ἀληθεῖς	ἀληθῆ

Adjectives - Mixed Declension (πᾶς, πᾶσα, πᾶν "all")

	Singular:			Plural:		
	Masc.	Fem.	Neut.	Masc.	Fem.	Neut.
N./V.	πᾶς	πᾶσα	πᾶν	πάντες	πᾶσαι	πάντα
Gen.	παντός	πάσης	παντός	πάντων	πᾱσῶν	πάντων
Dat.	παντί	πάσῃ	παντί	πᾶσι(ν)	πάσαις	πᾶσι(ν)
Acc.	πάντα	πᾶσαν	πᾶν	πάντας	πάσᾱς	πάντα
Dual:	none					

Adjectives - Mixed Declension (ἡδύς, -εῖα, -ύ "sweet")

	Singular:			Plural:		
	Masc.	Fem.	Neut.	Masc.	Fem.	Neut.
Nom.	ἡδύς	ἡδεῖα	ἡδύ	ἡδεῖς	ἡδεῖαι	ἡδέα
Gen.	ἡδέος	ἡδείᾱς	ἡδέος	ἡδέων	ἡδειῶν	ἡδέων
Dat.	ἡδεῖ	ἡδείᾳ	ἡδεῖ	ἡδέσι(ν)	ἡδείαις	ἡδέσι(ν)
Acc.	ἡδύν	ἡδεῖαν	ἡδύ	ἡδεῖς	ἡδείᾱς	ἡδέα
Voc.	ἡδύ	ἡδεῖα	ἡδύ	ἡδεῖς	ἡδεῖαι	ἡδέα
	Dual:					
N./A./V.	ἡδέε	ἡδείᾱ	ἡδέε			
G./D.	ἡδέοιν	ἡδείαιν	ἡδέοιν			

Adjectives - Irregular (πολύς, πολλή, πολύ "much," "many")

	Singular:			Plural:		
	Masc.	Fem.	Neut.	Masc.	Fem.	Neut.
Nom.	πολύς	πολλή	πολύ	πολλοί	πολλαί	πολλά
Gen.	πολλοῦ	πολλῆς	πολλοῦ	πολλῶν	πολλῶν	πολλῶν
Dat.	πολλῷ	πολλῇ	πολλῷ	πολλοῖς	πολλαῖς	πολλοῖς
Acc.	πολύν	πολλήν	πολύ	πολλούς	πολλάς	πολλά
Voc.	none	none	none	πολλοί	πολλαί	πολλά
Dual:	none					

Adjectives - Irregular (μέγας, μεγάλη, μέγα "big")

	Singular:			Plural:		
	Masc.	Fem.	Neut.	Masc.	Fem.	Neut.
Nom.	μέγας	μεγάλη	μέγα	μεγάλοι	μεγάλαι	μεγάλα
Gen.	μεγάλου	μεγάλης	μεγάλου	μεγάλων	μεγάλων	μεγάλων
Dat.	μεγάλῳ	μεγάλῃ	μεγάλῳ	μεγάλοις	μεγάλαις	μεγάλοις
Acc.	μέγαν	μεγάλην	μέγα	μεγάλους	μεγάλᾱς	μεγάλα
Voc.	μεγάλε or μέγας	μεγάλη	μέγα	μεγάλοι	μεγάλαι	μεγάλα
Dual:						
N./A./V.	μεγάλω	μεγάλᾱ	μεγάλω			
G./D.	μεγάλοιν	μεγάλαιν	μεγάλοιν			

Comparison of Adjectives
Adjectives with Regular Comparison
(-τερος, -ᾱ, -ον & -τατος, -η, -ον)

δῆλος, -η, -ον	δηλότερος, -ᾱ, -ον	δηλότατος, -η -ον
κοινός, -ή, -όν	κοινότερος, -ᾱ, -ον	κοινότατος, -η, -ον
μακρός, -ά, -όν	μακρότερος, -ᾱ, -ον	μακρότατος, -η, -ον
σοφός, -ή, -όν	σοφώτερος, -ᾱ, -ον	σοφώτατος, -η, -ον
ἀληθής, -ές	ἀληθέστερος, -ᾱ, -ον	ἀληθέστατος, -η, -ον
εὐδαίμων, -ον	εὐδαιμονέστερος, -ᾱ, -ον	εὐδαιμονέστατος, -η, -ον

Exceptions to regular comparison of adjectives:

παλαιός, -ά, -όν	παλαίτερος, -ᾱ, -ον	παλαίτατος, -η, -ον
φίλος, -η, -ον	φίλτερος, -ᾱ, -ον	φίλτατος, -η, -ον
	or φιλαίτερος, -ᾱ, -ον	or φιλαίτατος, -η, -ον
[πρό]	πρότερος, -ᾱ, -ον	πρῶτος, -η, -ον

Adjectives with Irregular Comparison
(-[ῑ]ων, -[ῑ]ον & -ιστος, -η, -ον)

Adjectives with positive degree ending in -ρος, -ᾱ, -ον:

αἰσχρός, -ά, -όν	αἰσχῑ́ων, -ῑον	αἴσχιστος, -η, -ον
ἐχθρός, -ά, -όν	ἐχθῑ́ων, -ῑον	ἔχθιστος, -η, -ον
μῑκρός, -ά, -όν	μῑκρότερος, -ᾱ, -ον	μῑκρότατος, -η, -ον
	or ἐλάττων, -ον	or ἐλάχιστος, -η, -ον

Other adjectives with irregular comparison:

ἀγαθός, -ή, -όν	βελτῑ́ων, -ῑον	βέλτιστος, -η, -ον
	or ἀμείνων, -ον	or ἄριστος, -η, -ον
	or κρείττων, -ον	or κράτιστος, -η, -ον
κακός, -ή, -όν	κακῑ́ων, -ῑον	κάκιστος, -η, -ον
	or χείρων, -ον	or χείριστος, -η, -ον
	or ἥττων, -ον	or ἥκιστος, -η, -ον
καλός, -ή, -όν	καλλῑ́ων, -ῑον	κάλλιστος, -η, -ον
μέγας, μεγάλη, μέγα	μείζων, -ον	μέγιστος, -η, -ον
ὀλίγος, -η, -ον	ἐλάττων, -ον	ὀλίγιστος, -η, -ον
πολύς, πολλή, πολύ	πλείων/πλέων, -ον	πλεῖστος, -η, -ον
ῥᾴδιος, -ᾱ, -ον	ῥᾴων, -ον	ῥᾷστος, -η, -ον

Declension of Irregular Comparatives

Singular:

	Masc./Fem.		Neut.
Nom.	βελτίων		βέλτῑον
Gen.	βελτίονος		βελτίονος
Dat.	βελτίονι		βελτίονι
Acc.	βελτίονα	(βελτίω)	βέλτῑον
Voc.	βέλτῑον		βέλτῑον

Dual:

	Masc./Fem.		Neut.	
N./A.	βελτίονε		βελτίονε	
G./D.	βελτῑόνοιν		βελτῑόνοιν	

Plural:

	Masc./Fem.		Neut.	
Nom.	βελτίονες	(βελτίους)	βελτίονα	(βελτίω)
Gen.	βελτῑόνων		βελτῑόνων	
Dat.	βελτίοσι(ν)		βελτίοσι(ν)	
Acc.	βελτίονας	(βελτίους)	βελτίονα	(βελτίω)

NUMERALS

"one"

Singular:

	Masc.	Fem.	Neut.
Nom.	εἷς	μία	ἕν
Gen.	ἑνός	μιᾶς	ἑνός
Dat.	ἑνί	μιᾷ	ἑνί
Acc.	ἕνα (ἕν᾽)	μίαν	ἕν

"none," "no," "no one," "nothing"

Singular:[1]

	Masc.		Fem.		Neut.	
Nom.	οὐδείς	(μηδείς)	οὐδεμία	(μηδεμία)	οὐδέν	(μηδέν)
Gen.	οὐδενός	(μηδενός)	οὐδεμιᾶς	(μηδεμιᾶς)	οὐδενός	(μηδενός)
Dat.	οὐδενί	(μηδενί)	οὐδεμιᾷ	(μηδεμιᾷ)	οὐδενί	(μηδενί)
Acc.	οὐδένα[2]	(μηδένα[2])	οὐδεμίαν	(μηδεμίαν)	οὐδέν	(μηδέν)

"two"   "three"

	Masc./Fem./Neut.	Masc./Fem.	Neut.
Nom.	δύο	τρεῖς	τρία
Gen.	δυοῖν	τριῶν	τριῶν
Dat.	δυοῖν	τρισί(ν)	τρισί(ν)
Acc.	δύο	τρεῖς	τρία

"four"

	Masc./Fem.	Neut.
Nom.	τέτταρες	τέτταρα
Gen.	τεττάρων	τεττάρων
Dat.	τέτταρσι(ν)	τέτταρσι(ν)
Acc.	τέτταρας	τέτταρα

---

[1] οὐδείς and μηδείς are sometimes found in the plural (e.g., οὐδένες and μηδένες), meaning "no people" or "nobodies."

[2] elided as οὐδέν᾽ (μηδέν᾽).

	Cardinals:	Ordinals:	Numerical Adverbs:
1.	εἷς, μία, ἕν	πρῶτος, -η, -ον	ἅπαξ
2.	δύο	δεύτερος, -α, -ον	δίς
3.	τρεῖς, τρία	τρίτος, -η, -ον	τρίς
4.	τέτταρες, τέτταρα	τέταρτος, -η, -ον	τετράκις
5.	πέντε	πέμπτος, -η, -ον	πεντάκις
6.	ἕξ	ἕκτος, -η, -ον	ἑξάκις
7.	ἑπτά	ἕβδομος, -η, -ον	ἑπτάκις
8.	ὀκτώ	ὄγδοος, -η, -ον	ὀκτάκις
9.	ἐννέα	ἔνατος, -η, -ον	ἐνάκις
10.	δέκα	δέκατος, -η, -ον	δεκάκις
11.	ἕνδεκα	ἑνδέκατος, -η, -ον	ἑνδεκάκις
12.	δώδεκα	δωδέκατος, -η, -ον	δωδεκάκις
13.	τρεῖς/τρία καὶ δέκα	τρίτος καὶ δέκατος	τρεισκαιδεκάκις
14.	τέτταρες/-α καὶ δέκα	τέταρτος καὶ δέκατος	τετταρεσκαιδεκάκις
15.	πεντεκαίδεκα	πέμπτος καὶ δέκατος	πεντεκαιδεκάκις
16.	ἑκκαίδεκα	ἕκτος καὶ δέκατος	ἑκκαιδεκάκις
17.	ἑπτακαίδεκα	ἕβδομος καὶ δέκατος	ἑπτακαιδεκάκις
18.	ὀκτωκαίδεκα	ὄγδοος καὶ δέκατος	ὀκτωκαιδεκάκις
19.	ἐννεακαίδεκα	ἔνατος καὶ δέκατος	ἐννεακαιδεκάκις
20.	εἴκοσι(ν)	εἰκοστός, -ή, -όν	εἰκοσάκις
21.	εἷς/μία/ἕν καὶ εἴκοσι(ν) or εἴκοσι (καὶ) εἷς/μία/ἕν	πρῶτος καὶ εἰκοστός	εἰκοσάκις ἅπαξ
30.	τριάκοντα	τριᾱκοστός, -ή, -όν	τριᾱκοντάκις
40.	τετταράκοντα	τετταρακοστός, -ή, -όν	τετταρακοντάκις
50.	πεντήκοντα	πεντηκοστός, -ή, -όν	πεντηκοντάκις
60.	ἑξήκοντα	ἑξηκοστός, -ή, -όν	ἑξηκοντάκις
70.	ἑβδομήκοντα	ἑβδομηκοστός, -ή, -όν	ἑβδομηκοντάκις
80.	ὀγδοήκοντα	ὀγδοηκοστός, -ή, -όν	ὀγδοηκοντάκις
90.	ἐνενήκοντα	ἐνενηκοστός, -ή, -όν	ἐνενηκοντάκις
100.	ἑκατόν	ἑκατοστός, -ή, -όν	ἑκατοντάκις
200.	διᾱκόσιοι, -αι, -α	διᾱκοσιοστός, -ή, -όν	διᾱκοσιάκις
300.	τριᾱκόσιοι, -αι, -α	τριᾱκοσιοστός, -ή, -όν	τριᾱκοσιάκις
400.	τετρακόσιοι, -αι, -α	τετρακοσιοστός, -ή, -όν	τετρακοσιάκις
500.	πεντακόσιοι, -αι, -α	πεντακοσιοστός, -ή, -όν	πεντακοσιάκις
600.	ἑξακόσιοι, -αι, -α	ἑξακοσιοστός, -ή, -όν	ἑξακοσιάκις
700.	ἑπτακόσιοι, -αι, -α	ἑπτακοσιοστός, -ή, -όν	ἑπτακοσιάκις
800.	ὀκτακόσιοι, -αι, -α	ὀκτακοσιοστός, -ή, -όν	ὀκτακοσιάκις
900.	ἐνακόσιοι, -αι, -α	ἐνακοσιοστός, -ή, -όν	ἐνακοσιάκις
1000.	χίλιοι, -αι, -α	χιλιοστός, -ή, -όν	χῑλιάκις
2000.	δισχίλιοι, -αι, -α	δισχῑλιοστός, -ή, -όν	δισχῑλιάκις
3000.	τρισχίλιοι, -αι, -α	τρισχῑλιοστός, -ή, -όν	τρισχῑλιάκις
10,000.	μύριοι, -αι, -α	μῡριοστός, -ή, -όν	μῡριάκις
11,000.	μύριοι καὶ χίλιοι	μῡριοστὸς καὶ χῑλιοστός	μῡριάκις καὶ χῑλιάκις
20,000.	δισμύριοι, -αι, -α	δισμῡριοστός, -ή, -όν	δισμῡριάκις
100,000.	δεκακισμύριοι, -αι, -α	δεκακισμῡριοστός, -ή, -όν	δεκακισμῡριάκις

ADVERBS

Regular formation of adverbs from adjectives (gen. pl. + ς):

ἐλεύθερος, -ᾱ, -ον	→	ἐλευθέρως
σοφός, -ή, -όν	→	σοφῶς
ἀληθής, -ές	→	ἀληθῶς
εὐδαίμων, -ον	→	εὐδαιμόνως
ἡδύς, -εῖα, -ύ	→	ἡδέως
πᾶς, πᾶσα, πᾶν	→	πάντως

Adverbs formed from adjectives in an unpredictable way:

αὐτός, -ή, -όν	→	αὕτως	
ὅδε, ἥδε, τόδε	→	ὧδε	
πρότερος, -ᾱ, -ον	→	πρότερον	
ἀγαθός, -ή, -όν	→	εὖ	(or ἀγαθῶς)
δῆλος, -η, -ον	→	δῆλον	(or δῆλα, δήλως)
μακρός, -ά, -όν	→	μακρόν	(or μακρά, μακρῶς)
μέγας, μεγάλη, μέγα	→	μέγα	(or μεγάλα, μεγάλως)
μῑκρός, -ά, -όν	→	μῑκρόν	(or μῑκρά, μῑκρῶς)
μόνος, -η, -ον	→	μόνον	(or μόνως)
νέος, -ᾱ, -ον	→	νέον	(or νέως)
ὀλίγος, -η, -ον	→	ὀλίγον	(or ὀλίγα, ὀλίγως)
πολύς, πολλά, πολύ	→	πολύ	(or πολλά)

Comparison of Adverbs

σοφῶς	σοφώτερον	σοφώτατα
καλῶς	κάλλῑον	κάλλιστα
μάλα	μᾶλλον	μάλιστα

Correlative Adverbs

Direct Interrogative Adverbs:		Indefinite Adverbs:	
πόθεν	from where? whence?	ποθέν	from somewhere
ποῖ	to where? whither?	ποι	to somewhere
ποῦ	where?	που	somewhere
πότε	when?	ποτέ	sometime, ever, once
πῶς	how?	πως	somehow

Indirect Interrog. Adverbs =		Indef. Rel. Adverbs:	Relative Adverbs:	
ὁπόθεν	from where? whence?	from wherever	ὅθεν	from where
ὅποι	to where? whither?	to wherever	οἷ	to where
ὅπου	where?	wherever	οὗ	where
ὁπότε	when?	whenever	ὅτε	when
ὅπως	how?	howsoever	ὡς	how, as

NOTE — -ι, -θι, -σι(ν), or the genitive ending -ου may show place where; -θεν may show place from which; -δε, -ζε, or -σε may show place to which (e.g., Ἀθήνησι(ν), Ἀθήνηθεν, Ἀθήναζε; οἴκοι, οἴκοθεν, οἴκαδε; ἄλλοθι, ἄλλοθεν, ἄλλοσε; ὁμοῦ, ὁμόθεν, ὁμόσε; ἐκεῖ, ἐκεῖθεν, ἐκεῖσε; ἐνθάδε/ἐνταῦθα, ἐνθένδε/ἐντεῦθεν, δεῦρο).

VERBS

(Second- and third-person duals are included; there is no first-person dual.)
Active Voice - Indicative Mood

	Present Active:		**Imperfect Active:**
Singular:	παιδεύω	**Singular:**	ἐπαίδευον
	παιδεύεις		ἐπαίδευες
	παιδεύει		ἐπαίδευε(ν)
Dual:	παιδεύετον	**Dual:**	ἐπαιδεύετον
	παιδεύετον		ἐπαιδευέτην
Plural:	παιδεύομεν	**Plural:**	ἐπαιδεύομεν
	παιδεύετε		ἐπαιδεύετε
	παιδεύουσι(ν)		ἐπαίδευον

Future Active:

Singular:	παιδεύσω
	παιδεύσεις
	παιδεύσει
Dual:	παιδεύσετον
	παιδεύσετον
Plural:	παιδεύσομεν
	παιδεύσετε
	παιδεύσουσι(ν)

	First Aorist Active:		**Second Aorist Active:**
Singular:	ἐπαίδευσα	**Singular:**	ἔβαλον
	ἐπαίδευσας		ἔβαλες
	ἐπαίδευσε(ν)		ἔβαλε(ν)
Dual:	ἐπαιδεύσατον	**Dual:**	ἐβάλετον
	ἐπαιδευσάτην		ἐβαλέτην
Plural:	ἐπαιδεύσαμεν	**Plural:**	ἐβάλομεν
	ἐπαιδεύσατε		ἐβάλετε
	ἐπαίδευσαν		ἔβαλον

	First Perfect Active:[1]		**First Pluperfect Active:[1]**
Singular:	πεπαίδευκα	**Singular:**	ἐπεπαιδεύκη
	πεπαίδευκας		ἐπεπαιδεύκης
	πεπαίδευκε(ν)		ἐπεπαιδεύκει(ν)
Dual:	πεπαιδεύκατον	**Dual:**	ἐπεπαιδεύκετον
	πεπαιδεύκατον		ἐπεπαιδευκέτην

[1]Second perfects and second pluperfects lack the κ characteristic of first perfects and first pluperfects (e.g., γέγραφα, ἐγεγράφη).

Plural:	πεπαιδεύκαμεν	Plural:	ἐπεπαιδεύκεμεν
	πεπαιδεύκατε		ἐπεπαιδεύκετε
	πεπαιδεύκᾱσι(ν)[1]		ἐπεπαιδεύκεσαν[2]

Future Perfect Active:

Singular:	τεθνήξω
	τεθνήξεις
	τεθνήξει
Dual:	τεθνήξετον
	τεθνήξετον
Plural:	τεθνήξομεν
	τεθνήξετε
	τεθνήξουσι(ν)

NOTE ἀποθνήσκω and ἵστημι (fut. perf. = ἑστήξω) are the only Greek verbs that form their future perfect active in the above way. Otherwise this periphrasis is used:

Singular:	πεπαιδευκώς, -υῖα, -ὸς ἔσομαι
	πεπαιδευκώς, -υῖα, -ὸς ἔσῃ (-ει)
	πεπαιδευκώς, -υῖα, -ὸς ἔσται
Dual:	πεπαιδευκότε, -υίᾱ, -ότε ἔσεσθον
	πεπαιδευκότε, -υίᾱ, -ότε ἔσεσθον
Plural:	πεπαιδευκότες, -υῖαι, -ότα ἐσόμεθα
	πεπαιδευκότες, -υῖαι, -ότα ἔσεσθε
	πεπαιδευκότες, -υῖαι, -ότα ἔσονται

Active Voice - Subjunctive Mood

	Present Active:	First Aorist Active:	Second Aorist Active:
Singular:	παιδεύω	παιδεύσω	βάλω
	παιδεύῃς	παιδεύσῃς	βάλῃς
	παιδεύῃ	παιδεύσῃ	βάλῃ
Dual:	παιδεύητον	παιδεύσητον	βάλητον
	παιδεύητον	παιδεύσητον	βάλητον
Plural:	παιδεύωμεν	παιδεύσωμεν	βάλωμεν
	παιδεύητε	παιδεύσητε	βάλητε
	παιδεύωσι(ν)	παιδεύσωσι(ν)	βάλωσι(ν)

---

[1] In later Greek the third-person plural perfect active indicative sometimes ends in -αν (e.g., πεπαίδευκαν) instead of -ᾱσι(ν).

[2] In later Greek the pluperfect active indicative has a different set of endings: ἐπεπαιδεύκειν, -κεις, -κει, -κειτον, -κείτην, -κειμεν, -κειτε, -κεισαν.

Perfect Active:

Singular:	πεπαιδευκώς, -υῖα, -ὸς ὦ	(πεπαιδεύκω)
	πεπαιδευκώς, -υῖα, -ὸς ᾖς	(πεπαιδεύκῃς)
	πεπαιδευκώς, -υῖα, -ὸς ᾖ	(πεπαιδεύκῃ)
Dual:	πεπαιδευκότε, -υῖα, -ότε ἦτον	(πεπαιδεύκητον)
	πεπαιδευκότε, -υῖα, -ότε ἦτον	(πεπαιδεύκητον)
Plural:	πεπαιδευκότες, -υῖαι, -ότα ὦμεν	(πεπαιδεύκωμεν
	πεπαιδευκότες, -υῖαι, -ότα ἦτε	(πεπαιδεύκητε)
	πεπαιδευκότες, -υῖαι, -ότα ὦσι(ν)	(πεπαιδεύκωσι(ν))

Active Voice - Optative Mood

	Present Active:	Future Active:	First Aorist Active:	
Singular:	παιδεύοιμι	παιδεύσοιμι	παιδεύσαιμι	
	παιδεύοις	παιδεύσοις	παιδεύσειας	(παιδεύσαις)
	παιδεύοι	παιδεύσοι	παιδεύσειε(ν)	(παιδεύσαι)
Dual:	παιδεύοιτον	παιδεύσοιτον	παιδεύσαιτον	
	παιδευοίτην	παιδευσοίτην	παιδευσαίτην	
Plural:	παιδεύοιμεν	παιδεύσοιμεν	παιδεύσαιμεν	
	παιδεύοιτε	παιδεύσοιτε	παιδεύσαιτε	
	παιδεύοιεν	παιδεύσοιεν	παιδεύσειαν	(παιδεύσαιεν)

Second Aorist Active:

Singular:	βάλοιμι
	βάλοις
	βάλοι
Dual:	βάλοιτον
	βαλοίτην
Plural:	βάλοιμεν
	βάλοιτε
	βάλοιεν

Perfect Active:

Singular:	πεπαιδευκώς, -υῖα, -ὸς εἴην	(πεπαιδεύκοιμι)
	πεπαιδευκώς, -υῖα, -ὸς εἴης	(πεπαιδεύκοις)
	πεπαιδευκώς, -υῖα, -ὸς εἴη	(πεπαιδεύκοι)
Dual:	πεπαιδευκότε, -υῖα, -ότε εἴητον	(πεπαιδεύκοιτον)
	πεπαιδευκότε, -υῖα, -ότε εἰήτην	(πεπαιδευκοίτην)
Plural:	πεπαιδευκότες, -υῖαι, -ότα εἴημεν	(πεπαιδεύκοιμεν)
	πεπαιδευκότες, -υῖαι, -ότα εἴητε	(πεπαιδεύκοιτε)
	πεπαιδευκότες, -υῖαι, -ότα εἴησαν	(πεπαιδεύκοιεν)

Active Voice - Imperative Mood

	Present Active:	First Aorist Active:	Second Aorist Active:
Singular:	παίδευε	παίδευσον	βάλε
	παιδευέτω	παιδευσάτω	βαλέτω
Dual:	παιδεύετον	παιδεύσατον	βάλετον
	παιδευέτων	παιδευσάτων	βαλέτων
Plural:	παιδεύετε	παιδεύσατε	βάλετε
	παιδευόντων[1]	παιδευσάντων[1]	βαλόντων[1]

Perfect Active:

Singular:	πεπαιδευκώς, -υῖα, -ὸς ἴσθι	(πεπαίδευκε)
	πεπαιδευκώς, -υῖα, -ὸς ἔστω	(πεπαιδευκέτω)
Dual:	πεπαιδευκότε, -υίᾱ, -ότε ἔστον	(πεπαιδεύκετον)
	πεπαιδευκότε, -υίᾱ, -ότε ἔστων	(πεπαιδευκέτων
Plural:	πεπαιδευκότες, -υῖαι, -ότα ἔστε	(πεπαιδεύκετε)
	πεπαιδευκότες, -υῖαι, -ότα ὄντων	

Active Voice - Infinitives

Present Active:	παιδεύειν
Future Active:	παιδεύσειν
First Aorist Active:	παιδεῦσαι
Second Aorist Active:	βαλεῖν
First Perfect Active[2]:	πεπαιδευκέναι
Future Perfect Active:	πεπαιδεύσειν

Middle/Passive Voice - Indicative Mood

	Present Mid./Pass.:		Imperfect Mid./Pass.:
Singular:	παιδεύομαι	Singular:	ἐπαιδευόμην
	παιδεύῃ (-ει)		ἐπαιδεύου
	παιδεύεται		ἐπαιδεύετο
Dual:	παιδεύεσθον	Dual:	ἐπαιδεύεσθον
	παιδεύεσθον		ἐπαιδευέσθην
Plural:	παιδευόμεθα	Plural:	ἐπαιδευόμεθα
	παιδεύεσθε		ἐπαιδεύεσθε
	παιδεύονται		ἐπαιδεύοντο

---

[1]In later Greek the present active imperative and the second aorist active imperative in the third-person plural end in -ετωσαν (e.g., παιδευέτωσαν, βαλέτωσαν) instead of -οντων, and the first aorist active imperative in the third-person plural ends in -σατωσαν (e.g. παιδευσάτωσαν) instead of -σαντων.

[2]Second perfect active infinitives lack the κ characteristic of first perfect infinitives (e.g., γεγραφέναι).

	Future Middle:		**Future Passive[1]:**
Singular:	παιδεύσομαι	**Singular:**	παιδευθήσομαι
	παιδεύσῃ (-ει)		παιδευθήσει (-ῃ)
	παιδεύσεται		παιδευθήσεται
Dual:	παιδεύσεσθον	**Dual:**	παιδευθήσεσθον
	παιδεύσεσθον		παιδευθήσεσθον
Plural:	παιδευσόμεθα	**Plural:**	παιδευθησόμεθα
	παιδεύσεσθε		παιδευθήσεσθε
	παίδεύσονται		παιδευθήσονται

	First Aorist Mid.:	**Second Aorist Mid.:**	**First Aorist Pass.[2]:**
Singular:	ἐπαιδευσάμην	ἐβαλόμην	ἐπαιδεύθην
	ἐπαιδεύσω	ἐβάλου	ἐπαιδεύθης
	ἐπαιδεύσατο	ἐβάλετο	ἐπαιδεύθη
Dual:	ἐπαιδεύσασθον	ἐβάλεσθον	ἐπαιδεύθητον
	ἐπαιδευσάσθην	ἐβαλέσθην	ἐπαιδευθήτην
Plural:	ἐπαιδευσάμεθα	ἐβαλόμεθα	ἐπαιδεύθημεν
	ἐπαιδεύσασθε	ἐβάλεσθε	ἐπαιδεύθητε
	ἐπαιδεύσαντο	ἐβάλοντο	ἐπαιδεύθησαν

	Perfect Middle/Passive:
Singular:	πεπαίδευμαι
	πεπαίδευσαι
	πεπαίδευται
Dual:	πεπαίδευσθον
	πεπαίδευσθον
Plural:	πεπαιδεύμεθα
	πεπαίδευσθε
	πεπαίδευνται

	Labial Stem: λείπω (λειπ-)	**Palatal Stem:** διώκω (διωκ-)	**Dental Stem:** ἁρπάζω (ἁρπαζ-)	**Liquid Stem:** ἀγγέλλω (ἀγγελ-)
Singular:	λέλειμμαι	δεδίωγμαι	ἥρπασμαι	ἤγγελμαι
	λέλειψαι	δεδίωξαι	ἥρπασαι	ἤγγελσαι
	λέλειπται	δεδίωκται	ἥρπασται	ἤγγελται
Dual:	λέλειφθον	δεδίωχθον	ἥρπασθον	ἤγγελθον
	λέλειφθον	δεδίωχθον	ἥρπασθον	ἤγγελθον
Plural:	λελείμμεθα	δεδιώγμεθα	ἡρπάσμεθα	ἠγγέλμεθα
	λέλειφθε	δεδίωχθε	ἥρπασθε	ἤγγελθε
	λελειμμένοι,	δεδιωγμένοι,	ἡρπασμένοι,	ἠγγελμένοι,
	-αι, -α εἰσί(ν)	-αι, -α εἰσί(ν)	-αι, -α εἰσί(ν)	-αι, -α εἰσί(ν)

---

[1]Verbs with a second aorist passive indicative form their future passive indicative with -η- rather than -θη- (e.g., γραφήσομαι).

[2]Verbs with a second aorist passive indicative lack the θ characteristic of a first aorist passive indicative (e.g., ἐγράφην).

Pluperfect Middle/Passive:

Singular:	ἐπεπαιδεύμην
	ἐπεπαίδευσο
	ἐπεπαίδευτο
Dual:	ἐπεπαίδευσθον
	ἐπεπαιδεύσθην
Plural:	ἐπεπαιδεύμεθα
	ἐπεπαίδευσθε
	ἐπεπαίδευντο

	Labial Stem:	Palatal Stem:	Dental Stem:	Liquid Stem:
Singular:	ἐλελείμμην	ἐδεδιώγμην	ἡρπάσμην	ἠγγέλμην
	ἐλέλειψο	ἐδεδίωξο	ἥρπασο	ἤγγελσο
	ἐλέλειπτο	ἐδεδίωκτο	ἥρπαστο	ἤγγελτο
Dual:	ἐλέλειφθον	ἐδεδίωχθον	ἥρπασθον	ἤγγελθον
	ἐλελείφθην	ἐδεδιώχθην	ἡρπάσθην	ἠγγέλθην
Plural:	ἐλελείμμεθα	ἐδεδιώγμεθα	ἡρπάσμεθα	ἠγγέλμεθα
	ἐλέλειφθε	ἐδεδίωχθε	ἥρπασθε	ἤγγελθε
	λελειμμένοι,	δεδιωγμένοι,	ἡρπασμένοι,	ἠγγελμένοι,
	-αι, -α ἦσαν	-αι, -α ἦσαν	-αι, -α ἦσαν	-αι, -α ἦσαν

Future Perfect Middle/Passive:

Singular:	πεπαιδεύσομαι	or	πεπαιδευμένος, -η, -ον ἔσομαι
	πεπαιδεύσῃ (-ει)	or	πεπαιδευμένος, -η, -ον ἔσῃ (-ει)
	πεπαιδεύσεται	or	πεπαιδευμένος, -η, -ον ἔσται
Dual:	πεπαιδεύσεσθον	or	πεπαιδευμένω, -ᾱ, -ω ἔσεσθον
	πεπαιδεύσεσθον	or	πεπαιδευμένω, -ᾱ, -ω ἔσεσθον
Plural:	πεπαιδευσόμεθα	or	πεπαιδευμένοι, -αι, -α ἐσόμεθα
	πεπαιδεύσεσθε	or	πεπαιδευμένοι, -αι, -α ἔσεσθε
	πεπαιδεύσονται	or	πεπαιδευμένοι, -αι, -α ἔσονται

Middle/Passive Voice - Subjunctive Mood

	Present Mid./Pass.:	First Aorist Mid.:	Second Aorist Mid.:
Singular:	παιδεύωμαι	παιδεύσωμαι	βάλωμαι
	παιδεύῃ	παιδεύσῃ	βάλῃ
	παιδεύηται	παιδεύσηται	βάληται
Dual:	παιδεύησθον	παιδεύσησθον	βάλησθον
	παιδεύησθον	παιδεύσησθον	βάλησθον
Plural:	παιδευώμεθα	παιδευσώμεθα	βαλώμεθα
	παιδεύησθε	παιδεύσησθε	βάλησθε
	παιδεύωνται	παιδεύσωνται	βάλωνται

	First Aorist Passive[1]:	Perfect Middle/Passive:
Singular:	παιδευθῶ	πεπαιδευμένος, -η, -ον ὦ
	παιδευθῇς	πεπαιδευμένος, -η, -ον ᾖς
	παιδευθῇ	πεπαιδευμένος, -η, -ον ᾖ
Dual:	παιδευθῆτον	πεπαιδευμένω, -ᾱ, -ω ἦτον
	παιδευθῆτον	πεπαιδευμένω, -ᾱ, -ω ἦτον
Plural:	παιδευθῶμεν	πεπαιδευμένοι, -αι, -α ὦμεν
	παιδευθῆτε	πεπαιδευμένοι, -αι, -α ἦτε
	παιδευθῶσι(ν)	πεπαιδευμένοι, -αι, -α ὦσι(ν)

Middle/Passive Voice - Optative Mood

	Present Mid./Pass.:	Future Mid.:	Future Pass.[2]:
Singular:	παιδευοίμην	παιδευσοίμην	παιδευθησοίμην
	παιδεύοιο	παιδεύσοιο	παιδευθήσοιο
	παιδεύοιτο	παιδεύσοιτο	παιδευθήσοιτο
Dual:	παιδεύοισθον	παιδεύσοισθον	παιδευθήσοισθον
	παιδευοίσθην	παιδευσοίσθην	παιδευθησοίσθην
Plural:	παιδευοίμεθα	παιδευσοίμεθα	παιδευθησοίμεθα
	παιδεύοισθε	παιδεύσοισθε	παιδευθήσοισθε
	παιδεύοιντο	παιδεύσοιντο	παιδευθήσοιντο

	First Aorist Middle:	First Aorist Passive[3]:	
Singular:	παιδευσαίμην	παιδευθείην	
	παιδεύσαιο	παιδευθείης	
	παιδεύσαιτο	παιδευθείη	
Dual:	παιδεύσαισθον	παιδευθείητον	(παιδευθεῖτον)
	παιδευσαίσθην	παιδευθειήτην	(παιδευθείτην)
Plural:	παιδευσαίμεθα	παιδευθείημεν	(παιδευθεῖμεν)
	παιδεύσαισθε	παιδευθείητε	(παιδευθεῖτε)
	παιδεύσαιντο	παιδευθείησαν	(παιδευθεῖεν)

Second Aorist Middle:

Singular:	βαλοίμην
	βάλοιο
	βάλοιτο
Dual:	βάλοισθον
	βαλοίσθην
Plural:	βαλοίμεθα
	βάλοισθε
	βάλοιντο

---

[1]Verbs with a second aorist passive subjunctive lack the θ characteristic of a first aorist passive subjunctive (e.g., γραφῶ).

[2]Verbs with a second aorist passive optative form their future passive optative with -η- rather than -θη- (e.g., γραφησοίμην).

[3]Verbs with a second aorist passive optative lack the θ characteristic of a first aorist passive optative (e.g., γραφείην).

Perfect Middle/Passive:

Singular:	πεπαιδευμένος, -η, -ον εἴην	
	πεπαιδευμένος, -η, -ον εἴης	
	πεπαιδευμένος, -η, -ον εἴη	
Dual:	πεπαιδευμένω, -ᾱ, -ω εἴητον	(εἶτον)
	πεπαιδευμένω, -ᾱ, -ω εἰήτην	(εἴτην)
Plural:	πεπαιδευμένοι, -αι, -α εἴημεν	(εἶμεν)
	πεπαιδευμένοι, -αι, -α εἴητε	(εἶτε)
	πεπαιδευμένοι, -αι, -α εἴησαν	(εἶεν)

Middle/Passive - Imperative Mood

	Present M./P.:	First Aorist Mid.:	Second Aorist Mid.:
Singular:	παιδεύου	παίδευσαι	βαλοῦ
	παιδευέσθω	παιδευσάσθω	βαλέσθω
Dual:	παιδεύεσθον	παιδεύσασθον	βάλεσθον
	παιδευέσθων	παιδευσάσθων	βαλέσθων
Plural:	παιδεύεσθε	παιδεύσασθε	βάλεσθε
	παιδευέσθων[1]	παιδευσάσθων[1]	βαλέσθων[1]

First Aorist Pass.[2] :

Singular:	παιδεύθητι
	παιδευθήτω
Dual:	παιδεύθητον
	παιδευθήτων
Plural:	παιδεύθητε
	παιδευθέντων[3]

Perfect Middle/Passive:

Singular:	πεπαίδευσο	(πεπαιδευμένος, -η, -ον ἴσθι)
	πεπαιδεύσθω	(πεπαιδευμένος, -η, -ον ἔστω)
Dual:	πεπαίδευσθον	(πεπαιδευμένω, -ᾱ, -ω ἔστον)
	πεπαιδεύσθων	(πεπαιδευμένω, -ᾱ, -ω ἔστων)
Plural:	πεπαίδευσθε	(πεπαιδευμένοι, -αι, -α ἔστε)
	πεπαιδεύσθων	(πεπαιδευμένοι, -αι, -α ὄντων)

---

[1]In later Greek the present middle imperative and the second aorist middle imperative in the third-person plural end in -εσθωσαν (e.g., παιδευέσθωσαν, βαλέσθωσαν) instead of -εσθων, and the first aorist middle imperative in the third-person plural ends in -σασθωσαν (e.g., παιδευσάσθωσαν) instead of -σασθων.

[2]Second aorist passive imperatives lack the θ characteristic of δ first aorist passive imperatives (e.g., κλαπήτω); in the second-person singular they use the original ending -ηθι instead of -θητι (e.g., κλάπηθι).

[3]In later Greek the third-person plural aorist passive imperative ends in -θήτωσαν (e.g., παιδευθήτωσαν, κλαπήτωσαν) instead of -θεντων.

Middle/Passive Voice - Infinitives

Present Middle/Passive:	παιδεύεσθαι
Future Middle:	παιδεύσεσθαι
Future Passive[1]:	παιδευθήσεσθαι
First Aorist Middle:	παιδεύσασθαι
Second Aorist Middle:	βαλέσθαι
First Aorist Passive[2]:	παιδευθῆναι
Perfect Middle/Passive:	πεπαιδεῦσθαι

Examples of consonant-stem perfect middle/passive infinitives:

Labial Stem:	**Palatal Stem:**	**Dental Stem:**	**Liquid Stem:**
λελεῖφθαι	δεδιῶχθαι	ἡρπάσθαι	ἠγγέλθαι

Future Perf. Mid./Pass.: πεπαιδεύσεσθαι

Contract Verbs
-άω (τῑμάω)
Indicative Mood

	Present Act.:	**Present M./P.:**	**Imperf. Act.:**	**Imperf. M./P.:**
Singular:	τῑμῶ	τῑμῶμαι	ἐτίμων	ἐτῑμώμην
	τῑμᾷς	τῑμᾷ	ἐτίμᾱς	ἐτῑμῶ
	τῑμᾷ	τῑμᾶται	ἐτίμᾱ	ἐτῑμᾶτο
Dual:	τῑμᾶτον	τῑμᾶσθον	ἐτῑμᾶτον	ἐτῑμᾶσθον
	τῑμᾶτον	τῑμᾶσθον	ἐτῑμάτην	ἐτῑμάσθην
Plural:	τῑμῶμεν	τῑμώμεθα	ἐτῑμῶμεν	ἐτῑμώμεθα
	τῑμᾶτε	τῑμᾶσθε	ἐτῑμᾶτε	ἐτῑμᾶσθε
	τῑμῶσι(ν)	τῑμῶνται	ἐτίμων	ἐτῑμῶντο

	Present Active Subjunctive:	**Present M./P. Subjunctive:**
Singular:	τῑμῶ	τῑμῶμαι
	τῑμᾷς	τῑμᾷ
	τῑμᾷ	τῑμᾶται
Dual:	τῑμᾶτον	τῑμᾶσθον
	τῑμᾶτον	τῑμᾶσθον
Plural:	τῑμῶμεν	τῑμώμεθα
	τῑμᾶτε	τῑμᾶσθε
	τῑμῶσι(ν)	τῑμῶνται

---

[1] Verbs with a second aorist passive infinitive form their future passive infinitive with -η- rather than -θη- (e.g. γραφήσεσθαι).

[2] A second aorist passive infinitive lacks the θ characteristic of a first aorist passive infinitive (e.g., γραφῆναι).

	Present Active Optative:		Present M./P. Optative:
Singular:	τῑμῴην	(τῑμῷμι)	τῑμῴμην
	τῑμῴης	(τῑμῷς)	τῑμῷο
	τῑμῴη	(τῑμῷ)	τῑμῷτο
Dual:	τῑμῷτον	(τῑμῴητον)	τῑμῷσθον
	τῑμῴτην	(τῑμῳήτην)	τῑμῴσθην
Plural:	τῑμῷμεν	(τῑμῴημεν)	τῑμῴμεθα
	τῑμῷτε	(τῑμῴητε)	τῑμῷσθε
	τῑμῷεν	(τῑμῴησαν)	τῑμῶντο

	Present Active Imperative:	Present M./P. Imperative:
Singular:	τίμᾱ	τῑμῶ
	τῑμάτω	τῑμάσθω
Dual:	τῑμᾶτον	τῑμᾶσθον
	τῑμάτων	τῑμάσθων
Plural:	τῑμᾶτε	τῑμᾶσθε
	τῑμώντων	τῑμάσθων

Present Active Infin.: τῑμᾶν   **Present M./P. Infin.:** τῑμᾶσθαι

Contract Verbs
-έω (φιλέω)

Indicative Mood

	Present Act.:	Present M./P.:	Imperfect Act.:	Imperfect M./P.:
Singular:	φιλῶ	φιλοῦμαι	ἐφίλουν	ἐφιλούμην
	φιλεῖς	φιλῇ (-εῖ)	ἐφίλεις	ἐφιλοῦ
	φιλεῖ	φιλεῖται	ἐφίλει	ἐφιλεῖτο
Dual:	φιλεῖτον	φιλεῖσθον	ἐφιλεῖτον	ἐφιλεῖσθον
	φιλεῖτον	φιλεῖσθον	ἐφιλείτην	ἐφιλείσθην
Plural:	φιλοῦμεν	φιλούμεθα	ἐφιλοῦμεν	ἐφιλούμεθα
	φιλεῖτε	φιλεῖσθε	ἐφιλεῖτε	ἐφιλεῖσθε
	φιλοῦσι(ν)	φιλοῦνται	ἐφίλουν	ἐφιλοῦντο

	Present Active Subjunctive:	Present M./P. Subjunctive:
Singular:	φιλῶ	φιλῶμαι
	φιλῇς	φιλῇ
	φιλῇ	φιλῆται
Dual:	φιλῆτον	φιλῆσθον
	φιλῆτον	φιλῆσθον
Plural:	φιλῶμεν	φιλώμεθα
	φιλῆτε	φιλῆσθε
	φιλῶσι(ν)	φιλῶνται

	Present Active Optative:		**Present M./P. Optative:**
Singular:	φιλοίην	(φιλοῖμι)	φιλοίμην
	φιλοίης	(φιλοῖς)	φιλοῖο
	φιλοίη	(φιλοῖ)	φιλοῖτο
Dual:	φιλοῖτον	(φιλοίητον)	φιλοῖσθον
	φιλοίτην	(φιλοιήτην)	φιλοίσθην
Plural:	φιλοῖμεν	(φιλοίημεν)	φιλοίμεθα
	φιλοῖτε	(φιλοίητε)	φιλοῖσθε
	φιλοῖεν	(φιλοίησαν)	φιλοῖντο

	Present Active Imperative:	**Present M./P. Imperative:**
Singular:	φίλει	φιλοῦ
	φιλείτω	φιλείσθω
Dual:	φιλεῖτον	φιλεῖσθον
	φιλείτων	φιλείσθων
Plural:	φιλεῖτε	φιλεῖσθε
	φιλούντων	φιλείσθων

Present Active Infin.: φιλεῖν   Present M./P. Infin.: φιλεῖσθαι

Contract Verbs
-όω (δηλόω)

Indicative Mood

	Present Act.:	**Present M./P.:**	**Imperfect Act.:**	**Imperfect M./P.:**
Singular:	δηλῶ	δηλοῦμαι	ἐδήλουν	ἐδηλούμην
	δηλοῖς	δηλοῖ	ἐδήλους	ἐδηλοῦ
	δηλοῖ	δηλοῦται	ἐδήλου	ἐδηλοῦτο
Dual:	δηλοῦτον	δηλοῦσθον	ἐδηλοῦτον	ἐδηλοῦσθον
	δηλοῦτον	δηλοῦσθον	ἐδηλούτην	ἐδηλούσθην
Plural:	δηλοῦμεν	δηλούμεθα	ἐδηλοῦμεν	ἐδηλούμεθα
	δηλοῦτε	δηλοῦσθε	ἐδηλοῦτε	ἐδηλοῦσθε
	δηλοῦσι(ν)	δηλοῦνται	ἐδήλουν	ἐδηλοῦντο

	Present Active Subjunctive:	**Present M./P. Subjunctive:**
Singular:	δηλῶ	δηλῶμαι
	δηλοῖς	δηλοῖ
	δηλοῖ	δηλῶται
Dual:	δηλῶτον	δηλῶσθον
	δηλῶτον	δηλῶσθον
Plural:	δηλῶμεν	δηλώμεθα
	δηλῶτε	δηλῶσθε
	δηλῶσι(ν)	δηλῶνται

	Present Active Optative:		**Present M./P. Optative:**
Singular:	δηλοίην	(δηλοῖμι)	δηλοίμην
	δηλοίης	(δηλοῖς)	δηλοῖο
	δηλοίη	(δηλοῖ)	δηλοῖτο
Dual:	δηλοῖτον	(δηλοίητον)	δηλοῖσθον
	δηλοίτην	(δηλοιήτην)	δηλοίσθην
Plural:	δηλοῖμεν	(δηλοίημεν)	δηλοίμεθα
	δηλοῖτε	(δηλοίητε)	δηλοῖσθε
	δηλοῖεν	(δηλοίησαν)	δηλοῖντο

	Present Active Imperative:	**Present M./P. Imperative:**
Singular:	δήλου	δηλοῦ
	δηλούτω	δηλούσθω
Dual:	δηλοῦτον	δηλοῦσθον
	δηλούτων	δηλούσθων
Plural:	δηλοῦτε	δηλοῦσθε
	δηλούντων	δηλούσθων

Present Active Infin.: δηλοῦν   **Present M./P. Infin.:**   δηλοῦσθαι

Verbs with Contracted Futures
(stem ends in a liquid, a nasal, or -ζ)

Indicative Mood

	Present Act.:	**Future Act.:**	**Present M./P.:**	**Future Mid.:**
Singular:	βάλλω	βαλῶ	βάλλομαι	βαλοῦμαι
	βάλλεις	βαλεῖς	βάλλῃ (-ει)	βαλῇ (-εῖ)
	βάλλει	βαλεῖ	βάλλεται	βαλεῖται
Dual:	βάλλετον	βαλεῖτον	βάλλεσθον	βαλεῖσθον
	βάλλετον	βαλεῖτον	βάλλεσθον	βαλεῖσθον
Plural:	βάλλομεν	βαλοῦμεν	βαλλόμεθα	βαλούμεθα
	βάλλετε	βαλεῖτε	βάλλεσθε	βαλεῖσθε
	βάλλουσι(ν)	βαλοῦσι(ν)	βάλλονται	βαλοῦνται

	Future Active Optative:	**Future M./P. Optative:**
Singular:	βαλοίην	βαλοίμην
	βαλοίης	βαλοῖο
	βαλοίη	βαλοῖτο
Dual:	βαλοῖτον	βαλοῖσθον
	βαλοίτην	βαλοίσθην
Plural:	βάλοιμεν	βαλοίμεθα
	βάλοιτε	βαλοῖσθε
	βάλοιεν	βαλοῖντο

Present Active Infin.:   βάλλειν   Present M./P. Infin.: βάλλεσθαι
Future Active Infin.:   βαλεῖν   Future Mid. Infin.:   βαλεῖσθαι

Present Active Participle: βάλλων, -ουσα, -ον
Future Active Participle: βαλῶν, -οῦσα, -οῦν

Present Middle/Passive Participle: βαλλόμενος, -η, -ον
Future Middle Participle: βαλούμενος, -η, -ον

First Aorist of Liquid and Nasal Verbs
(stem ends in -λ, -μ, -ν, or -ρ)

	Aor. Act. Indic.:	Aor. Mid. Indic.:	Aor. Act. Subj.:
Singular:	ἤγγειλα	ἠγγειλάμην	ἀγγείλω
	ἤγγειλας	ἠγγείλω	ἀγγείλῃς
	ἤγγειλε(ν)	ἠγγείλατο	ἀγγείλῃ
Dual:	ἠγγείλατον	ἠγγείλασθον	ἀγγείλητον
	ἠγγειλάτην	ἠγγειλάσθην	ἀγγείλητον
Plural:	ἠγγείλαμεν	ἠγγειλάμεθα	ἀγγείλωμεν
	ἠγγείλατε	ἠγγείλασθε	ἀγγείλητε
	ἤγγειλαν	ἠγγείλαντο	ἀγγείλωσι(ν)

	Aorist Mid. Subj.:	Aorist Act. Opt.:		Aorist Mid. Opt.:
Singular:	ἀγγείλωμαι	ἀγγείλαιμι		ἀγγειλαίμην
	ἀγγείλῃ	ἀγγείλειας	(-αις)	ἀγγείλαιο
	ἀγγείληται	ἀγγείλειε(ν)	(-αι)	ἀγγείλαιτο
Dual:	ἀγγείλησθον	ἀγγείλαιτον		ἀγγείλαισθον
	ἀγγειλήσθην	ἀγγειλαίτην		ἀγγειλαίσθην
Plural:	ἀγγειλώμεθα	ἀγγείλαιμεν		ἀγγειλαίμεθα
	ἀγγείλησθε	ἀγγείλαιτε		ἀγγείλαισθε
	ἀγγείλωνται	ἀγγείλειαν	(-αιεν)	ἀγγείλαιντο

	Aorist Active Imperative:	Aorist Middle Imperative:
Singular:	ἄγγειλον	ἄγγειλαι
	ἀγγειλάτω	ἀγγειλάσθω
Dual:	ἀγγείλατον	ἀγγείλασθον
	ἀγγειλάτων	ἀγγειλάσθων
Plural:	ἀγγείλατε	ἀγγείλασθε
	ἀγγειλάντων	ἀγγειλάσθων

Aorist Active Infinitive: ἀγγεῖλαι
Aorist Mid. Infinitive: ἀγγείλασθαι

Aorist Active Participle: ἀγγείλᾱς, -ᾱσα, -αν
Aorist Mid. Participle: ἀγγειλάμενος, -η, -ον

PARTICIPLES

Present Active Participle

Singular:	Masc.	Fem.	Neut.
Nom./Voc.	παιδεύων	παιδεύουσα	παιδεῦον
Gen.	παιδεύοντος	παιδευούσης	παιδεύοντος
Dat.	παιδεύοντι	παιδευούσῃ	παιδεύοντι
Acc.	παιδεύοντα	παιδεύουσαν	παιδεῦον
Dual:			
N./A./V.	παιδεύοντε	παιδευούσᾱ	παιδεύοντε
G./D.	παιδευόντοιν	παιδευούσαιν	παιδευόντοιν
Plural:			
Nom./Voc.	παιδεύοντες	παιδεύουσαι	παιδεύοντα
Gen.	παιδευόντων	παιδευουσῶν	παιδευόντων
Dat.	παιδεύουσι(ν)	παιδευούσαις	παιδεύουσι(ν)
Acc.	παιδεύοντας	παιδευούσᾱς	παιδεύοντα

Future Active Participle

Singular:	Masc.	Fem.	Neut.
Nom./Voc.	παιδεύσων	παιδεύσουσα	παιδεῦσον
Gen.	παιδεύσοντος	παιδευσούσης	παιδεύσοντος
Dat.	παιδεύσοντι	παιδευσούσῃ	παιδεύσοντι
Acc.	παιδεύσοντα	παιδεύσουσαν	παιδεῦσον
Dual:			
N./A./V.	παιδεύσοντε	παιδευσούσᾱ	παιδεύσοντε
G./D.	παιδευσόντοιν	παιδευσούσαιν	παιδευσόντοιν
Plural:			
Nom./Voc.	παιδεύσοντες	παιδεύσουσαι	παιδεύσοντα
Gen.	παιδευσόντων	παιδευσουσῶν	παιδευσόντων
Dat.	παιδεύσουσι(ν)	παιδευσούσαις	παιδεύσουσι(ν)
Acc.	παιδεύσοντας	παιδευσούσᾱς	παιδεύσοντα

First Aorist Active Participle

Singular:	Masc.	Fem.	Neut.
Nom./Voc.	παιδεύσᾱς	παιδεύσᾱσα	παιδεῦσαν
Gen.	παιδεύσαντος	παιδευσάσης	παιδεύσαντος
Dat.	παιδεύσαντι	παιδευσάσῃ	παιδεύσαντι
Acc.	παιδεύσαντα	παιδεύσᾱσαν	παιδεῦσαν
Dual:			
N./A./V.	παιδεύσαντε	παιδευσάσᾱ	παιδεύσαντε
G./D.	παιδευσάντοιν	παιδευσάσαιν	παιδευσάντοιν

Plural:

	Masc.	Fem.	Neut.
Nom./Voc.	παιδεύσαντες	παιδεύσᾱσαι	παιδεύσαντα
Gen.	παιδευσάντων	παιδευσᾱσῶν	παιδευσάντων
Dat.	παιδεύσᾱσι(ν)	παιδευσάσαις	παιδεύσᾱσι(ν)
Acc.	παιδεύσαντας	παιδευσάσᾱς	παιδεύσαντα

Second Aorist Active Participle

Singular:	Masc.	Fem.	Neut.
Nom./Voc.	βαλών	βαλοῦσα	βαλόν
Gen.	βαλόντος	βαλούσης	βαλόντος
Dat.	βαλόντι	βαλούσῃ	βαλόντι
Acc.	βαλόντα	βαλοῦσαν	βαλόν

Dual:			
N./A./V.	βαλόντε	βαλούσᾱ	βαλόντε
G./D.	βαλόντοιν	βαλούσαιν	βαλόντοιν

Plural:			
Nom./Voc.	βαλόντες	βαλοῦσαι	βαλόντα
Gen.	βαλόντων	βαλουσῶν	βαλόντων
Dat.	βαλοῦσι(ν)	βαλούσαις	βαλοῦσι(ν)
Acc.	βαλόντας	βαλούσᾱς	βαλόντα

Perfect Active Participle[1]

Singular:	Masc.	Fem.	Neut.
Nom./Voc.	πεπαιδευκώς	πεπαιδευκυῖα	πεπαιδευκός
Gen.	πεπαιδευκότος	πεπαιδευκυίᾱς	πεπαιδευκότος
Dat.	πεπαιδευκότι	πεπαιδευκυίᾳ	πεπαιδευκότι
Acc.	πεπαιδευκότα	πεπαιδευκυῖαν	πεπαιδευκός

Dual:			
N./A./V.	πεπαιδευκότε	πεπαιδευκυίᾱ	πεπαιδευκότε
G./D.	πεπαιδευκότοιν	πεπαιδευκυίαιν	πεπαιδευκότοιν

Plural:			
Nom./Voc.	πεπαιδευκότες	πεπαιδευκυῖαι	πεπαιδευκότα
Gen.	πεπαιδευκότων	πεπαιδευκυιῶν	πεπαιδευκότων
Dat.	πεπαιδευκόσι(ν)	πεπαιδευκυίαις	πεπαιδευκόσι(ν)
Acc.	πεπαιδευκότας	πεπαιδευκυίᾱς	πεπαιδευκότα

Future Perfect Active Participle
πεπαιδεύσων, -ουσα, -ον

---

[1] Stems of second perfect active participles end in a letter other than κ, (e.g. γεγραφώς).

Present Middle/Passive Participle

Singular:	Masc.	Fem.	Neut.
Nom.	παιδευόμενος	παιδευομένη	παιδευόμενον
Gen.	παιδευομένου	παιδευομένης	παιδευομένου
Dat.	παιδευομένῳ	παιδευομένη	παιδευομένῳ
Acc.	παιδευόμενον	παιδευομένην	παιδευόμενον
Voc.	παιδευόμενε	παιδευομένη	παιδευόμενον
Dual:			
N./A./V.	παιδευομένω	παιδευομένᾱ	παιδευομένω
G./D.	παιδευομένοιν	παιδευομέναιν	παιδευομένοιν
Plural:			
Nom./Voc.	παιδευόμενοι	παιδευόμεναι	παιδευόμενα
Gen.	παιδευομένων	παιδευομένων	παιδευομένων
Dat.	παιδευομένοις	παιδευομέναις	παιδευομένοις
Acc.	παιδευομένους	παιδευομένᾱς	παιδευόμενα

Future Middle Participle

Singular:	Masc.	Fem.	Neut.
Nom.	παιδευσόμενος	παιδευσομένη	παιδευσόμενον
Gen.	παιδευσομένου	παιδευσομένης	παιδευσομένου
Dat.	παιδευσομένῳ	παιδευσομένη	παιδευσομένῳ
Acc.	παιδευσόμενον	παιδευσομένην	παιδευσόμενον
Voc.	παιδευσόμενε	παιδευσομένη	παιδευσόμενον
Dual:			
N./A./V.	παιδευσομένω	παιδευσομένᾱ	παιδευσομένω
G./D.	παιδευσομένοιν	παιδευσομέναιν	παιδευσομένοιν
Plural:			
Nom./Voc.	παιδευσόμενοι	παιδευσόμεναι	παιδευσόμενα
Gen.	παιδευσομένων	παιδευσομένων	παιδευσομένων
Dat.	παιδευσομένοις	παιδευσομέναις	παιδευσομένοις
Acc.	παιδευσομένους	παιδευσομένᾱς	παιδευσόμενα

Future Passive Participle[1]

Singular:	Masc.	Fem.	Neut.
Nom.	παιδευθησόμενος	παιδευθησομένη	παιδευθησόμενον
Gen.	παιδευθησομένου	παιδευθησομένης	παιδευθησομένου
Dat.	παιδευθησομένῳ	παιδευθησομένη	παιδευθησομένῳ
Acc.	παιδευθησόμενον	παιδευθησομένην	παιδευθησόμενο
Voc.	παιδευθησόμενε	παιδευθησομένη	παιδευθησόμενο
Dual:			
N./A./V.	παιδευθησομένω	παιδευθησομένᾱ	παιδευθησομένω
G./D.	παιδευθησομένοιν	παιδευθησομέναιν	παιδευθησομένοιν

---

[1] Verbs with a second aorist passive participle form their future passive participle with -η-, rather than -θη- (e.g., γραφησόμενος).

Plural:

N./V.	παιδευθησόμενοι	παιδευθησόμεναι	παιδευθησόμενα
Gen.	παιδευθησομένων	παιδευθησομένων	παιδευθησομένων
Dat.	παιδευθησομένοις	παιδευθησομέναις	παιδευθησομένοις
Acc.	παιδευθησομένους	παιδευθησομένᾱς	παιδευθησόμενα

First Aorist Middle Participle

Singular:	Masc.	Fem.	Neut.
Nom.	παιδευσάμενος	παιδευσαμένη	παιδευσάμενον
Gen.	παιδευσαμένου	παιδευσαμένης	παιδευσαμένου
Dat.	παιδευσαμένῳ	παιδευσαμένῃ	παιδευσαμένῳ
Acc.	παιδευσάμενον	παιδευσαμένην	παιδευσάμενον
Voc.	παιδευσάμενε	παιδευσαμένη	παιδευσάμενον

Dual:			
N./A./V.	παιδευσαμένω	παιδευσαμένᾱ	παιδευσαμένω
G./D.	παιδευσαμένοιν	παιδευσαμέναιν	παιδευσαμένοιν

Plural:			
Nom./Voc.	παιδευσάμενοι	παιδευσάμεναι	παιδευσάμενα
Gen.	παιδευσαμένων	παιδευσαμένων	παιδευσαμένων
Dat.	παιδευσαμένοις	παιδευσαμέναις	παιδευσαμένοις
Acc.	παιδευσαμένους	παιδευσαμένᾱς	παιδευσάμενα

Second Aorist Middle Participle

Singular:	Masc.	Fem.	Neut.
Nom.	βαλόμενος	βαλομένη	βαλόμενον
Gen.	βαλομένου	βαλομένης	βαλομένου
Dat.	βαλομένῳ	βαλομένῃ	βαλομένῳ
Acc.	βαλόμενον	βαλομένην	βαλόμενον
Voc.	βαλόμενε	βαλομένη	βαλόμενον

Dual:			
N./A./V.	βαλομένω	βαλομένᾱ	βαλομένω
G./D.	βαλομένοιν	βαλομέναιν	βαλομένοιν

Plural:			
Nom./Voc.	βαλόμενοι	βαλόμεναι	βαλόμενα
Gen.	βαλομένων	βαλομένων	βαλομένων
Dat.	βαλομένοις	βαλομέναις	βαλομένοις
Acc.	βαλομένους	βαλομένᾱς	βαλόμενα

First Aorist Passive Participle[1]

Singular:	Masc.	Fem.	Neut.
Nom./Voc.	παιδευθείς	παιδευθεῖσα	παιδευθέν
Gen.	παιδευθέντος	παιδευθείσης	παιδευθέντος
Dat.	παιδευθέντι	παιδευθείσῃ	παιδευθέντι
Acc.	παιδευθέντα	παιδευθεῖσαν	παιδευθέν

[1]The second aorist passive participle lacks the θ characteristic of the first aorist passive participle (e.g. γραφείς).

Dual:

N./A./V.	παιδευθέντε	παιδευθείσα	παιδευθέντε
G./D.	παιδευθέντοιν	παιδευθείσαιν	παιδευθέντοιν

Plural:

Nom./Voc.	παιδευθέντες	παιδευθεῖσαι	παιδευθέντα
Gen.	παιδευθέντων	παιδευθεισῶν	παιδευθέντων
Dat.	παιδευθεῖσι(ν)	παιδευθείσαις	παιδευθεῖσι(ν)
Acc.	παιδευθέντας	παιδευθείσᾱς	παιδευθέντα

Perfect Middle/Passive Participle[1]

Singular:	Masc.	Fem.	Neut.
Nom.	πεπαιδευμένος	πεπαιδευμένη	πεπαιδευμένον
Gen.	πεπαιδευμένου	πεπαιδευμένης	πεπαιδευμένου
Dat.	πεπαιδευμένῳ	πεπαιδευμένῃ	πεπαιδευμένῳ
Acc.	πεπαιδευμένον	πεπαιδευμένην	πεπαιδευμένον
Voc.	πεπαιδευμένε	πεπαιδευμένη	πεπαιδευμένον

Dual:

N./A./V.	πεπαιδευμένω	πεπαιδευμένᾱ	πεπαιδευμένω
G./D.	πεπαιδευμένοιν	πεπαιδευμέναιν	πεπαιδευμένοιν

Plural:

Nom./Voc.	πεπαιδευμένοι	πεπαιδευμέναι	πεπαιδευμένα
Gen.	πεπαιδευμένων	πεπαιδευμένων	πεπαιδευμένων
Dat.	πεπαιδευμένοις	πεπαιδευμέναις	πεπαιδευμένοις
Acc.	πεπαιδευμένους	πεπαιδευμένᾱς	πεπαιδευμένα

Future Perfect Middle/Passive Participle
πεπαιδευσόμενος, -η, -ον

Present Active Participles of Contract Verbs
-άω

Singular:	Masc.	Fem.	Neut.
Nom./Voc.	τῑμῶν	τῑμῶσα	τῑμῶν
Gen.	τῑμῶντος	τῑμώσης	τῑμῶντος
Dat.	τῑμῶντι	τῑμώσῃ	τῑμῶντι
Acc.	τῑμῶντα	τῑμῶσαν	τῑμῶν

Dual:

N./A./V.	τῑμῶντε	τῑμώσᾱ	τῑμῶντε
G./D.	τῑμῶντοιν	τῑμώσαιν	τῑμῶντοιν

Plural:

Nom./Voc.	τῑμῶντες	τῑμῶσαι	τῑμῶντα
Gen.	τῑμώντων	τῑμωσῶν	τῑμώντων
Dat.	τῑμῶσι(ν)	τῑμώσαις	τῑμῶσι(ν)
Acc.	τῑμῶντας	τῑμώσᾱς	τῑμῶντα

---

[1] A consonant at the end of the stem may undergo change before -μεν-: labial + μ = μμ; palatal + μ = γμ; dental or ν + μ = σμ; λ + μ = λμ; ρ + μ = ρμ.

-έω

Singular:	Masc.	Fem.	Neut.
Nom./Voc.	φιλῶν	φιλοῦσα	φιλοῦν
Gen.	φιλοῦντος	φιλούσης	φιλοῦντος
Dat.	φιλοῦντι	φιλούσῃ	φιλοῦντι
Acc.	φιλοῦντα	φιλοῦσαν	φιλοῦν
Dual:			
N./A./V.	φιλοῦντε	φιλούσᾱ	φιλοῦντε
G./D.	φιλούντοιν	φιλούσαιν	φιλούντοιν
Plural:			
Nom./Voc.	φιλοῦντες	φιλοῦσαι	φιλοῦντα
Gen.	φιλούντων	φιλουσῶν	φιλούντων
Dat.	φιλοῦσι(ν)	φιλούσαις	φιλοῦσι(ν)
Acc.	φιλοῦντας	φιλούσᾱς	φιλοῦντα

-όω

Singular:	Masc.	Fem.	Neut.
Nom./Voc.	δηλῶν	δηλοῦσα	δηλοῦν
Gen.	δηλοῦντος	δηλούσης	δηλοῦντος
Dat.	δηλοῦντι	δηλούσῃ	δηλοῦντι
Acc.	δηλοῦντα	δηλοῦσαν	δηλοῦν
Dual:			
N./A./V.	δηλοῦντε	δηλούσᾱ	δηλοῦντε
G./D.	δηλούντοιν	δηλούσαιν	δηλούντοιν
Plural:			
Nom./Voc.	δηλοῦντες	δηλοῦσαι	δηλοῦντα
Gen.	δηλούντων	δηλουσῶν	δηλούντων
Dat.	δηλοῦσι(ν)	δηλούσαις	δηλοῦσι(ν)
Acc.	δηλοῦντας	δηλούσᾱς	δηλοῦντα

Present Middle/Passive Participles of Contract Verbs

-άω	τῑμώμενος, -η, -ον
-έω	φιλούμενος, -η, -ον
-όω	δηλούμενος, -η, -ον

εἰμί ("be")

Indicative Mood

	Present Active:	Future Middle (deponent):	Imperfect Active:	
Singular:				
	εἰμί	ἔσομαι	ἦ	(ἦν)
	εἶ	ἔσῃ (ἔσει)	ἦσθα	
	ἐστί(ν)	ἔσται	ἦν	
Dual:				
	ἐστόν	ἔσεσθον	ἦστον	
	ἐστόν	ἔσεσθον	ἤστην	
Plural:				
	ἐσμέν	ἐσόμεθα	ἦμεν	
	ἐστέ	ἔσεσθε	ἦτε (ἦστε)	
	εἰσί(ν)	ἔσονται	ἦσαν	

	Pres. Act. Subj.:	Pres. Act. Opt.:		Fut. Mid. (dep.) Opt.:
Singular:				
	ὦ	εἴην		ἐσοίμην
	ᾖς	εἴης		ἔσοιο
	ᾖ	εἴη		ἔσοιτο
Dual:				
	ἦτον	εἶτον	(εἴητον)	ἔσοισθον
	ἦτον	εἴτην	(εἰήτην)	ἐσοίσθην
Plural:				
	ὦμεν	εἶμεν	(εἴημεν)	ἐσοίμεθα
	ἦτε	εἶτε	(εἴητε)	ἔσοισθε
	ὦσι(ν)	εἶεν	(εἴησαν)	ἔσοιντο

Present Active Imperative:

Singular:

ἴσθι
ἔστω

Dual:

ἔστον
ἔστων

Plural:

ἔστε
ἔστων

Present Active Infinitive:	εἶναι
Future Middle (deponent) Infinitive:	ἔσεσθαι

Present Active Participle:

Singular:	Masc.	Fem.	Neut.
Nom./Voc.	ὤν	ὄν	
Gen.	ὄντος	οὔσης	ὄντος
Dat.	ὄντι	οὔσῃ	ὄντι
Acc.	ὄντα	οὖσαν	ὄν
Dual:			
N./A./V.	ὄντε	οὔσᾱ	ὄντε
Gen./Dat.	ὄντοιν	οὔσαιν	ὄντοιν
Plural:			
Nom./Voc.	ὄντες	οὖσαι	ὄντα
Gen.	ὄντων	οὐσῶν	ὄντων
Dat.	οὖσι(ν)	οὔσαις	οὖσι(ν)
Acc.	ὄντας	οὔσᾱς	ὄντα

Future Middle (deponent) Participle: ἐσόμενος, -η, -ον

εἶμι ("go")

	Present Active Indic.:	Imperfect Active Indic.:	
Singular:			
	εἶμι	ᾖα	(ᾔειν)
	εἶ	ᾔεισθα	(ᾔεις)
	εἶσι(ν)	ᾔειν (ᾔει)	
Dual:			
	ἴτον	ᾖτον	
	ἴτον	ᾔτην	
Plural:			
	ἴμεν	ᾖμεν	
	ἴτε	ᾖτε	
	ἴᾱσι(ν)	ᾖσαν	(ᾔεσαν)

	Present Active Subj.:	Present Active Optative:	
Singular:			
	ἴω	ἴοιμι	(ἰοίην)
	ἴῃς	ἴοις	
	ἴῃ	ἴοι	
Dual:			
	ἴητον	ἴοιτον	
	ἴητον	ἰοίτην	
Plural:			
	ἴωμεν	ἴοιμεν	
	ἴητε	ἴοιτε	
	ἴωσι(ν)	ἴοιεν	

Present Active Imperative:
Singular:

ἴθι
ἴτω

Dual:

ἴτον
ἴτων

Plural:

ἴτε
ἰόντων

Present Active Infinitive:　ἰέναι

Present Active Participle:

Singular:	Masc.	Fem.	Neut.
Nom./Voc.	ἰών	ἰοῦσα	ἰόν
Gen.	ἰόντος	ἰούσης	ἰόντος
Dat.	ἰόντι	ἰούσῃ	ἰόντι
Acc.	ἰόντα	ἰοῦσαν	ἰόν
Dual:			
N./A./V.	ἰόντε	ἰούσᾱ	ἰόντε
Gen./Dat.	ἰόντοιν	ἰούσαιν	ἰόντοιν
Plural:			
Nom./Voc.	ἰόντες	ἰοῦσαι	ἰόντα
Gen.	ἰόντων	ἰουσῶν	ἰόντων
Dat.	ἰοῦσι(ν)	ἰούσαις	ἰοῦσι(ν)
Acc.	ἰόντας	ἰούσᾱς	ἰόντα

φημί ("say")

	Present Active Indicative:	Imperfect Active Indicative:	
Singular:			
	φημί	ἔφην	
	φῄς	ἔφησθα	(ἔφης)
	φησί(ν)	ἔφη	
Dual:			
	φατόν	ἔφατον	
	φατόν	ἐφάτην	
Plural:			
	φαμέν	ἔφαμεν	
	φατέ	ἔφατε	
	φᾱσί(ν)	ἔφασαν	

Present Active Subj.:	Present Active Optative:	
Singular:		
φῶ	φαίην	
φῇς	φαίης	
φῇ	φαίη	
Dual:		
φῆτον	none	
φῆτον	none	
Plural:		
φῶμεν	φαῖμεν	(φαίημεν)
φῆτε	φαῖτε	(φαίητε)
φῶσι(ν)	φαῖεν	(φαίησαν)

Present Active Imperative:

Singular:		
	φαθί	(φάθι)
	φάτω	
Dual:		
	φάτον	
	φάτων	
Plural:		
	φάτε	
	φάντων	

Present Active Infinitive:	φάναι
Present Active Participle:	φάσκων, -ουσα, -ον (φάς, φᾶσα, φάν)

οἶδα ("know")

Indicative Mood

	Perfect Active:	Pluperfect Active:
Singular:		
	οἶδα	ᾔδη
	οἶσθα	ᾔδησθα
	οἶδε(ν)	ᾔδει(ν)
Dual:		
	ἴστον	ᾖστον
	ἴστον	ᾖστην
Plural:		
	ἴσμεν	ᾖσμεν
	ἴστε	ᾖστε
	ἴσᾱσι(ν)	ᾖσαν

	Fut. Perf. Mid. (dep.):	Perf. Active Subjunctive:
Singular:	εἴσομαι	εἰδῶ
	εἴσῃ (-ει)	εἰδῇς
	εἴσεται	εἰδῇ
Dual:	εἴσεσθον	εἰδῆτον
	εἴσεσθον	εἰδῆτον
Plural:	εἰσόμεθα	εἰδῶμεν
	εἴσεσθε	εἰδῆτε
	εἴσονται	εἰδῶσι(ν)

Perfect Active Optative:

Singular:	εἰδείην	
	εἰδείης	
	εἰδείη	
Dual:	εἰδείητον	(εἰδεῖτον)
	εἰδειήτην	(εἰδείτην)
Plural:	εἰδείημεν	(εἰδεῖμεν)
	εἰδείητε	(εἰδεῖτε)
	εἰδείησαν	(εἰδεῖεν)

Perfect Active Imperative:

Singular:	ἴσθι
	ἴστω
Dual:	ἴστον
	ἴστων
Plural:	ἴστε
	ἴστων

Perfect Active Infinitive: εἰδέναι

Perfect Active Participle: εἰδώς, εἰδυῖα, εἰδός

δέδοικα ("fear")

	Perfect Active Indicative:		Pluperf. Active Indicative	
Singular:	δέδοικα	(δέδια)	ἐδεδοίκη	(ἐδεδίη)
	δέδοικας	(δέδιας)	ἐδεδοίκης	(ἐδεδίης)
	δέδοικε(ν)	(δέδιε(ν))	ἐδεδοίκει(ν)	(ἐδεδίει(ν))
Dual:	δέδιτον		ἐδέδιτον	
	δέδιτον		ἐδεδίτην	
Plural:	δέδιμεν	(δεδοίκαμεν)	ἐδέδιμεν	(ἐδεδοίκεμεν)
	δέδιτε	(δεδοίκατε)	ἐδέδιτε	(ἐδεδοίκετε)
	δεδίασι(ν)	(δεδοίκᾱσι(ν))	ἐδέδισαν	(ἐδεδοίκεσαν)
Perf. Active Infinitive:	δεδιέναι	(δεδοικέναι)		
Perf. Active Participle:	δεδιώς, -υῖα, -ός	(δεδοικώς, -υῖα, -ός)		

NOTE   The perfect active subjunctive δεδίω, the perfect active optative δεδιείην, and the perfect active second-person singular imperative δέδιθι are used only rarely.

μι-VERBS

δίδωμι ("give")

Indicative Mood

	Present Active:	Imperfect Active:	Aorist Active:
Singular:	δίδωμι	ἐδίδουν	ἔδωκα
	δίδως	ἐδίδους	ἔδωκας
	δίδωσι(ν)	ἐδίδου	ἔδωκε(ν)
Dual:	δίδοτον	ἐδίδοτον	ἔδοτον
	δίδοτον	ἐδιδότην	ἐδότην
Plural:	δίδομεν	ἐδίδομεν	ἔδομεν
	δίδοτε	ἐδίδοτε	ἔδοτε
	διδόᾱσι(ν)	ἐδίδοσαν	ἔδοσαν

	Present M./P.:	Imperfect M./P.:	Aorist Mid.:
Singular:	δίδομαι	ἐδιδόμην	ἐδόμην
	δίδοσαι	ἐδίδοσο	ἔδου
	δίδοται	ἐδίδοτο	ἔδοτο
Dual:	δίδοσθον	ἐδίδοσθον	ἔδοσθον
	δίδοσθον	ἐδιδόσθην	ἐδόσθην
Plural:	διδόμεθα	ἐδιδόμεθα	ἐδόμεθα
	δίδοσθε	ἐδίδοσθε	ἔδοσθε
	δίδονται	ἐδίδοντο	ἔδοντο

	Pres. Act. Subj.:	Aor. Act. Subj.:	Pres. Act. Imper.:
Singular:	διδῶ	δῶ	
	διδῷς	δῷς	δίδου
	διδῷ	δῷ	διδότω
Dual:	διδῶτον	δῶτον	δίδοτον
	διδῶτον	δῶτον	διδότων
Plural:	διδῶμεν	δῶμεν	
	διδῶτε	δῶτε	δίδοτε
	διδῶσι(ν)	δῶσι(ν)	διδόντων

	Pres. M./P. Subj.:	Aor. Mid. Subj.:	Pres. M./P. Imper.:
Singular:	διδῶμαι	δῶμαι	
	διδῷ	δῷ	δίδοσο
	διδῶται	δῶται	διδόσθω
Dual:	διδῶσθον	δῶσθον	δίδοσθον
	διδῶσθον	δῶσθον	διδόσθων
Plural:	διδώμεθα	δώμεθα	
	διδῶσθε	δῶσθε	δίδοσθε
	διδῶνται	δῶνται	διδόσθων

	Pres. Act. Opt.:		Aor. Act. Opt.:		Aor. Act. Imper.:
Singular:	διδοίην		δοίην		
	διδοίης		δοίης		δός
	διδοίη		δοίη		δότω
Dual:	διδοῖτον		δοῖτον		δότον
	διδοίτην		δοίτην		δότων
Plural:	διδοῖμεν	(διδοίημεν)	δοῖμεν	(δοίημεν)	
	διδοῖτε	(διδοίητε)	δοῖτε	(δοίητε)	δότε
	διδοῖεν	(διδοίησαν)	δοῖεν	(δοίησαν)	δόντων

	Present M./P. Opt.:	Aorist Mid. Opt.:	Aorist Mid. Imper.:
Singular:	διδοίμην	δοίμην	
	διδοῖο	δοῖο	δοῦ
	διδοῖτο	δοῖτο	δόσθω
Dual:	διδοῖσθον	δοῖσθον	δόσθον
	διδοίσθην	δοίσθην	δόσθων
Plural:	διδοίμεθα	δοίμεθα	
	διδοῖσθε	δοῖσθε	δόσθε
	διδοῖντο	δοῖντο	δόσθων

Present Active Infin.:	διδόναι	**Aorist Active Infin.:**	δοῦναι
Present M./P. Infin.:	δίδοσθαι	**Aorist Mid. Infin.:**	δόσθαι

Present Active Ptcple.: διδούς, διδοῦσα, διδόν
Present M./P. Ptcple.: διδόμενος, -η, -ον
Aorist Active Ptcple.: δούς, δοῦσα, δόν
Aorist Mid. Ptcple.: δόμενος, -η, -ον

ἵστημι ("make stand")

Indicative Mood

	Present Active:	Imperfect Active:	Second Aorist Active:
Singular:	ἵστημι	ἵστην	ἔστην
	ἵστης	ἵστης	ἔστης
	ἵστησι(ν)	ἵστη	ἔστη
Dual:	ἵστατον	ἵστατον	ἔστητον
	ἵστατον	ἱστάτην	ἐστήτην
Plural:	ἵσταμεν	ἵσταμεν	ἔστημεν
	ἵστατε	ἵστατε	ἔστητε
	ἱστᾶσι(ν)	ἵστασαν	ἔστησαν

	Present M./P.:	Imperfect M./P.:	Second Aorist Mid.:
Singular:	ἵσταμαι	ἱστάμην	[ἐπριάμην]
	ἵστασαι	ἵστασο	[ἐπρίω]
	ἵσταται	ἵστατο	[ἐπρίατο]
Dual:	ἵστασθον	ἵστασθον	[ἐπρίασθον]
	ἵστασθον	ἱστάσθην	[ἐπριάσθην]
Plural:	ἱστάμεθα	ἱστάμεθα	[ἐπριάμεθα]
	ἵστασθε	ἵστασθε	[ἐπρίασθε]
	ἵστανται	ἵσταντο	[ἐπρίαντο]

	Perfect Active:		Pluperfect Active:
Singular:	ἕστηκα		εἱστήκη
	ἕστηκας		εἱστήκης
	ἕστηκε(ν)		εἱστήκει(ν)
Dual:	ἕστατον		ἕστατον
	ἕστατον		ἑστάτην
Plural:	ἕσταμεν		ἕσταμεν
	ἕστατε		ἕστατε
	ἑστᾶσι(ν)		ἕστασαν

	Pres. Act. Subj.:	Second Aor. Act. Subj.:	Perf. Act. Subj.:
Singular:	ἱστῶ	στῶ	ἑστῶ
	ἱστῇς	στῇς	ἑστῇς
	ἱστῇ	στῇ	ἑστῇ
Dual:	ἱστῆτον	στῆτον	ἑστῆτον
	ἱστῆτον	στῆτον	ἑστῆτον
Plural:	ἱστῶμεν	στῶμεν	ἑστῶμεν
	ἱστῆτε	στῆτε	ἑστῆτε
	ἱστῶσι(ν)	στῶσι(ν)	ἑστῶσι(ν)

	Pres. M./P. Subjunctive:	Second Aorist Mid. Subj.:
Singular:	ἱστῶμαι	[πρίωμαι]
	ἱστῇ	[πρίῃ]
	ἱστῆται	[πρίηται]
Dual:	ἱστῆσθον	[πρίησθον]
	ἱστῆσθον	[πρίησθον]
Plural:	ἱστώμεθα	[πριώμεθα]
	ἱστῆσθε	[πρίησθε]
	ἱστῶνται	[πρίωνται]

	Pres. Act. Optative:		Second Aor. Act. Opt.:		Perf. Active Opt.:	
Singular:						
	ἱσταίην		σταίην		ἑσταίην	
	ἱσταίης		σταίης		ἑσταίης	
	ἱσταίη		σταίη		ἑσταίη	
Dual:						
	ἱσταῖτον	(ἱσταίητον)	σταῖτον	(σταίητον)	ἑσταῖτον	(ἑσταίητον)
	ἱσταίτην	(ἱσταιήτην)	σταίτην	(σταιήτην)	ἑσταίτην	(ἑσταιήτην)
Plural:						
	ἱσταῖμεν	(ἱσταίημεν)	σταῖμεν	(σταίημεν)	ἑσταῖμεν	(ἑσταίημεν)
	ἱσταῖτε	(ἱσταίητε)	σταῖτε	(σταίητε)	ἑσταῖτε	(ἑσταίητε)
	ἱσταῖεν	(ἱσταίησαν)	σταῖεν	(σταίησαν)	ἑσταῖεν	(ἑσταίησαν)

	Present M./P. Optative:	Second Aorist Mid. Optative:
Singular:	ἱσταίμην	[πριαίμην]
	ἱσταῖο	[πρίαιο]
	ἱσταῖτο	[πρίαιτο]
Dual:	ἱσταῖσθον	[πρίαισθον]
	ἱσταίσθην	[πριαίσθην]
Plural:	ἱσταίμεθα	[πριαίμεθα]
	ἱσταῖσθε	[πρίαισθε]
	ἱσταῖντο	[πρίαιντο]

Imperative Mood

	Present Active:	Second Aorist Active:	Perfect Active:
Singular:	ἵστη	στῆθι	ἔσταθι
	ἱστάτω	στήτω	ἑστάτω
Dual:	ἵστατον	στῆτον	ἔστατον
	ἱστάτων	στήτων	ἑστάτων
Plural:	ἵστατε	στῆτε	ἔστατε
	ἱστάντων	στάντων	ἑστάντων

	Present M./P.:	Second Aorist Middle:
Singular:	ἵστασο	[πρίω]
	ἱστάσθω	[πριάσθω]
Dual:	ἵστασθον	[πρίασθον]
	ἱστάσθων	[πριάσθων]
Plural:	ἵστασθε	[πρίασθε]
	ἱστάσθων	[πριάσθων]

Present Active Infin.: ἱστάναι   **Second Aorist Active Inf.:**   στῆναι

Present M./P. Infin.:   ἵστασθαι   **Second Aorist Mid. Inf.:**   [πρίασθαι]

Perfect Active Infin.: ἑστάναι

Present Active Ptcple.:   ἱστάς, ἱστᾶσα, ἱστάν

Present M./P. Ptcple.:   ἱστάμενος, -η, -ον

Second Aorist Active Ptcple.: στάς, στᾶσα, στάν

Second Aorist Mid. Ptcple.: [πριάμενος, -η, -ον]

Perfect Active Ptcple.:   ἑστώς, ἑστῶσα, ἑστός (ἑστῶτος, ἑστώσης,
                                ἑστῶτος, etc.)

τίθημι ("place")

Indicative Mood

	Present Active:	Imperfect Active:	Aorist Active:
Singular:	τίθημι	ἐτίθην	ἔθηκα
	τίθης	ἐτίθεις	ἔθηκας
	τίθησι(ν)	ἐτίθει	ἔθηκε(ν)
Dual:	τίθετον	ἐτίθετον	ἔθετον
	τίθετον	ἐτιθέτην	ἐθέτην
Plural:	τίθεμεν	ἐτίθεμεν	ἔθεμεν
	τίθετε	ἐτίθετε	ἔθετε
	τιθέᾱσι(ν)	ἐτίθεσαν	ἔθεσαν

	Present M./P.:	Imperfect M./P.:	Aorist Mid.:
Singular:	τίθεμαι	ἐτιθέμην	ἐθέμην
	τίθεσαι	ἐτίθεσο	ἔθου
	τίθεται	ἐτίθετο	ἔθετο
Dual:	τίθεσθον	ἐτίθεσθον	ἔθεσθον
	τίθεσθον	ἐτιθέσθην	ἐθέσθην
Plural:	τιθέμεθα	ἐτιθέμεθα	ἐθέμεθα
	τίθεσθε	ἐτίθεσθε	ἔθεσθε
	τίθενται	ἐτίθεντο	ἔθεντο

	Pres. Act. Subj.:	Aor. Act. Subj.:	Pres. Act. Imper.:
Singular:	τιθῶ	θῶ	
	τιθῇς	θῇς	τίθει
	τιθῇ	θῇ	τιθέτω
Dual:	τιθῆτον	θῆτον	τίθετον
	τιθῆτον	θῆτον	τιθέτων
Plural:	τιθῶμεν	θῶμεν	
	τιθῆτε	θῆτε	τίθετε
	τιθῶσι(ν)	θῶσι(ν)	τιθέντων

	Pres. M./P. Subj.:	Aor. Mid. Subj.:	Pres. M./P. Imper.:
Singular:	τιθῶμαι	θῶμαι	
	τιθῇ	θῇ	τίθεσο
	τιθῆται	θῆται	τιθέσθω
Dual:	τιθῆσθον	θῆσθον	τίθεσθον
	τιθῆσθον	θῆσθον	τιθέσθων
Plural:	τιθώμεθα	θώμεθα	
	τιθῆσθε	θῆσθε	τίθεσθε
	τιθῶνται	θῶνται	τιθέσθων

	Pres. Act. Opt.:	Aor. Act. Opt.:		Aor. Act. Imper.:
Singular:	τιθείην	θείην		
	τιθείης	θείης		θές
	τιθείη	θείη		θέτω
Dual:	τιθεῖτον	θεῖτον	(θείητον)	θέτον
	τιθείτην	θείτην	(θειήτην)	θέτων
Plural:	τιθεῖμεν (τιθείημεν)	θεῖμεν	(θείημεν)	
	τιθεῖτε (τιθείητε)	θεῖτε	(θείητε)	θέτε
	τιθεῖεν (τιθείησαν)	θεῖεν	(θείησαν)	θέντων

	Pres. M./P. Opt.:		**Aor. Mid. Opt.:**		**Aor. Mid. Imper.:**
Singular:	τιθείμην		θείμην		
	τιθεῖο		θεῖο		θοῦ
	τιθεῖτο	(τιθοῖτο)	θεῖτο	(θοῖτο)	θέσθω
Dual:	τιθεῖσθον		θεῖσθον		θέσθον
	τιθείσθην		θείσθην		θέσθων
Plural:	τιθείμεθα	(τιθοίμεθα)	θείμεθα	(θοίμεθα)	
	τιθεῖσθε	(τιθοῖσθε)	θεῖσθε	(θοῖσθε)	θέσθε
	τιθεῖντο	(τιθοῖντο)	θεῖντο	(θοῖντο)	θέσθων

Present Active Infin.: τιθέναι   **Aorist Active Infin.:** θεῖναι

Present M./P. Infin.: τίθεσθαι   **Aorist Mid. Infin.:** θέσθαι

Present Act. Ptcple.: τιθείς, τιθεῖσα, τιθέν (τιθέντος, τιθείσης, τιθέντος, etc.)

Present M./P. Ptcple.: τιθέμενος, -η, -ον

Aorist Active Ptcple.: θείς, θεῖσα, θέν (θέντος, θείσης, θέντος, etc.)

Aorist Mid. Ptcple.: θέμενος, -η, -ον

ἵημι ("set in motion")

Indicative Mood

	Present Active:		**Imperfect Active:**	**Aorist Active:**
Singular:	ἵημι		ἵην	ἧκα
	ἵης	(ἱεῖς)	ἵεις	ἧκας
	ἵησι(ν)		ἵει	ἧκε(ν)
Dual:	ἵετον		ἵετον	εἷτον
	ἵετον		ἱέτην	εἵτην
Plural:	ἵεμεν		ἵεμεν	εἷμεν
	ἵετε		ἵετε	εἷτε
	ἱᾶσι(ν)		ἵεσαν	εἷσαν

	Present M./P.:	**Imperfect M./P.:**	**Aorist Mid.:**
Singular:	ἵεμαι	ἱέμην	εἵμην
	ἵεσαι	ἵεσο	εἷσο
	ἵεται	ἵετο	εἷτο
Dual:	ἵεσθον	ἵεσθον	εἷσθον
	ἵεσθον	ἱέσθην	εἵσθην
Plural:	ἱέμεθα	ἱέμεθα	εἵμεθα
	ἵεσθε	ἵεσθε	εἷσθε
	ἵενται	ἵεντο	εἷντο

	Pres. Act. Subj.:	Aorist Act. Subj.:	Pres. Act. Imper.:
Singular:	ἱῶ	ὦ	
	ἱῇς	ᾗς	ἵει
	ἱῇ	ᾗ	ἱέτω
Dual:	ἱῆτον	ἦτον	ἵετον
	ἱῆτον	ἦτον	ἱέτων
Plural:	ἱῶμεν	ὦμεν	
	ἱῆτε	ἦτε	ἵετε
	ἱῶσι(ν)	ὦσι(ν)	ἱέντων

	Present M./P. Subj.:	Aorist Mid. Subj.:	Pres. M./P. Imper.:
Singular:	ἱῶμαι	ὦμαι	
	ἱῇ	ᾗ	ἵεσο
	ἱῆται	ἦται	ἱέσθω
Dual:	ἱῆσθον	ἦσθον	ἵεσθον
	ἱῆσθον	ἦσθον	ἱέσθων
Plural:	ἱώμεθα	ὤμεθα	
	ἱῆσθε	ἦσθε	ἵεσθε
	ἱῶνται	ὦνται	ἱέσθων

	Present Active Opt.:		Aorist Active Opt.:		Aorist Act. Imper.:
Singular:	ἱείην		εἵην		
	ἱείης		εἵης		ἕς
	ἱείη		εἵη		ἕτω
Dual:	ἱεῖτον	(ἱείητον)	εἷτον	(εἵητον)	ἕτον
	ἱείτην	(ἱειήτην)	εἵτην	(εἱήτην)	ἕτων
Plural:	ἱεῖμεν	(ἱείημεν)	εἷμεν	(εἵημεν)	
	ἱεῖτε	(ἱείητε)	εἷτε	(εἵητε)	ἕτε
	ἱεῖεν	(ἱείησαν)	εἷεν	(εἵησαν)	ἕντων

	Present M./P. Opt.:	Aorist Mid. Opt.:	Aorist Mid. Imper.:
Singular:	ἱείμην	εἵμην	
	ἱεῖο	εἷο	οὗ
	ἱεῖτο	εἷτο	ἕσθω
Dual:	ἱεῖσθον	εἷσθον	ἕσθον
	ἱείσθην	εἵσθην	ἕσθων
Plural:	ἱείμεθα	εἵμεθα	
	ἱεῖσθε	εἷσθε	ἕσθε
	ἱεῖντο	εἷντο	ἕσθων

Present Active Infin.: ἱέναι   **Aorist Active Infin.:** εἷναι

Present M./P. Infin.: ἵεσθαι   **Aorist Mid. Infin.:** ἕσθαι

Present Active Ptcple.: ἱείς, ἱεῖσα, ἱέν (ἱέντος, ἱείσης, ἱέντος, etc.)
Present M./P. Ptcple.: ἱέμενος, -η, -ον
Aorist Active Ptcple.: εἵς, εἵσα, ἕν (ἕντος, εἵσης, ἕντος, etc.)
Aorist Mid. Ptcple.: ἕμενος, -η, -ον

κεῖμαι ("lie")

	Pres. Indic.:	**Pres. Subj.:**	**Pres. Opt.:**	**Pres. Imper.:**
Singular:	κεῖμαι	κέωμαι	κεοίμην	
	κεῖσαι	κέῃ	κέοιο	κεῖσο
	κεῖται	κέηται	κέοιτο	κείσθω
Dual:	κεῖσθον	κέησθον	κέοισθον	κεῖσθον
	κεῖσθον	κέησθον	κεοίσθην	κείσθων
Plural:	κείμεθα	κεώμεθα	κεοίμεθα	
	κεῖσθε	κέησθε	κέοισθε	κεῖσθε
	κεῖνται	κέωνται	κέοιντο	κείσθων

	Imperfect Indic.:		**Present Infin.:** κεῖσθαι
Singular:	ἐκείμην		**Present Ptcple.:** εἱμενος, -η, -ον
	ἔκεισο		
	ἔκειτο		
Dual:	ἔκεισθον		
	ἐκείσθην		
Plural:	ἐκείμεθα		
	ἔκεισθε		
	ἔκειντο		

δείκνῡμι ("show")

	Present Active Indicative:	**Imperfect Active Indicative:**
Singular:	δείκνῡμι	ἐδείκνῡν
	δείκνῡς	ἐδείκνῡς
	δείκνῡσι(ν)	ἐδείκνῡ
Dual:	δείκνυτον	ἐδείκνυτον
	δείκνυτον	ἐδεικνύτην
Plural:	δείκνυμεν	ἐδείκνυμεν
	δείκνυτε	ἐδείκνυτε
	δεικνύᾱσι(ν)	ἐδείκνυσαν

	Present M./P. Indicative:	**Imperfect M./P. Indicative:**
Singular:	δείκνυμαι	ἐδεικνύμην
	δείκνυσαι	ἐδείκνυσο
	δείκνυται	ἐδείκνυτο
Dual:	δείκνυσθον	ἐδείκνυσθον
	δείκνυσθον	ἐδεικνύσθην

Plural:	δεικνύμεθα	ἐδεικνύμεθα
	δείκνυσθε	ἐδείκνυσθε
	δείκνυνται	ἐδείκνυντο

	Present Active Imperative:	Present M./P. Imperative:
Singular:	δείκνῡ	δείκνυσο
	δεικνύτω	δεικνύσθω
Dual:	δείκνυτον	δείκνυσθον
	δεικνύτων	δεικνύσθων
Plural:	δείκνυτε	δείκνυσθε
	δεικνύντων	δεικνύσθων

Present Active Infin.: δεικνύναι   **Present M./P. Infin.:** δείκνυσθαι

Present Active Ptcple.: δεικνύς, δεικνῦσα, δεικνύν (δεικνύντος, -ύσης, -ύντος, etc.)
Present M./P. Ptcple.: δεικνύμενος, -η, -ον

Present Active Subj.: δεικνύω, -ύῃς, -ύῃ, etc.
Present M./P. Subj.: δεικνύωμαι, -ύῃ, -ύηται, etc.

Present Active Opt.: δεικνύοιμι, -ύοις, -ύοι, etc.
Present M./P. Opt.: δεικνυοίμην, -ύοιο, -ύοιτο, etc.

<h3 style="text-align:center;">βαίνω ("walk")</h3>

	Aorist Active Indicative:	Aorist Active Subjunctive:
Singular:	ἔβην	βῶ
	ἔβης	βῇς
	ἔβη	βῇ
Dual:	ἔβητον	βῆτον
	ἐβήτην	βῆτον
Plural:	ἔβημεν	βῶμεν
	ἔβητε	βῆτε
	ἔβησαν	βῶσι(ν)

	Aorist Active Optative:		Aorist Active Imperative:
Singular:	βαίην		
	βαίης		βῆθι
	βαίη		βήτω
Dual:	βαῖτον	(βαίητον)	βῆτον
	βαίτην	(βαιήτην)	βήτων
Plural:	βαῖμεν	(βαίημεν)	
	βαῖτε	(βαίητε)	βῆτε
	βαῖεν	(βαίησαν)	βάντων

Aorist Active Infinitive: βῆναι
Aorist Active Participle: βάς, βᾶσα, βάν (βάντος, βάσης, βάντος, etc.)

γιγνώσκω ("recognize")

	Aorist Active Indicative:	**Aorist Active Subjunctive:**
Singular:	ἔγνων	γνῶ
	ἔγνως	γνῷς
	ἔγνω	γνῷ
Dual:	ἔγνωτον	γνῶτον
	ἐγνώτην	γνῶτον
Plural.	ἔγνωμεν	γνῶμεν
	ἔγνωτε	γνῶτε
	ἔγνωσαν	γνῶσι(ν)

	Aorist Active Optative:		**Aorist Active Imperative:**
Singular:	γνοίην		
	γνοίης		γνῶθι
	γνοίη		γνώτω
Dual:	γνοῖτον	(γνοίητον)	γνῶτον
	γνοίτην	(γνοιήτην)	γνώτων
Plural:	γνοῖμεν	(γνοίημεν)	
	γνοῖτε	(γνοίητε)	γνῶτε
	γνοῖεν	(γνοίησαν)	γνόντων

Aorist Active Infinitive: γνῶναι

Aorist Active Participle: γνούς, γνοῦσα, γνόν (γνόντος, γνούσης, γνόντος, etc.)

INDEX

Unless preceded by p. or pp., numerals refer to sections, not pages; superscript numerals designate footnotes.

A

Absolute, *see* Accusative case, Genitive case

Abstract nouns, use of definite article with, 30

Accenting, general principles of, 15; recessive, 20; of finite verb forms, 20; of proclitics, 24; persistent, 29; of first-declension nouns, 29, 34, 58; of second-declension nouns, 43, 49; of first/second-declension adjectives, 52; of enclitics, 80; of ἔστι (after οὐκ, μή, καί, ἀλλ', τοῦτ', ὡς, εἰ), 81, 84, 152; of demonstratives, 84; of contract verbs, 92; of third-declension stop-stem, liquid/nasal-stem nouns, 99.7; of third-declension monosyllabic-stem nouns, 99.7; of third-declension sigma-stem nouns, 104.6; of third-declension adjectives, 105; of first aorist active infinitive, 109; of second aorist active and middle infinitives, second-person singular middle imperative, 115[1]; of perfect active infinitive, 122; of interrogatives, 126, 163, 165; of indefinites, 127, 163; of perfect middle/passive infinitive, 133; of participles, 147-148, 156, 170, 175; of aorist passive infinitive, 170; of future passive infinitive, 175; of third-declension vowel-stem nouns, 180; of third-declension syncopated-stem nouns, 181.3; of comparatives and superlatives, 196; of irregular comparatives, 204; of subjunctives, 215; of optatives (-αι, -οι long), 220

Accents, pitch, 11; marks (acute, grave, circumflex), 12; placement of, 12-14

Accompaniment, *see* Dative case, Genitive case

Accusative case, overview, 28; uses: direct object, 18, 28; subject of infinitive, 36, 192, 244, 252-253, 287; double accusative, 112; extent of time, 142; cognate accusative, 227; extent of space, 259; accusative of respect, 284; accu-sative absolute (with impersonal verbs), 292; *see* Prepositions

Active, *see* Voice

Acute accent, defined, 12

Adjectives, paradigms: first/second declension (three-ending), 52, p. 453; first/second declension (two-ending), 59; demonstrative, 84, pp. 448-449; intensive, 87.2, p. 451[2]; third declension nasal-stem, 105, p. 454; third declension sigma-stem (contracted), 105, p. 454; irregular (πολύς), 112, p. 455; interrogative, 126, p. 449; indefinite, 127, p. 450; mixed declension (πᾶς), 141, p. 455; participles, 146, pp. 474-479; irregular (μέγας), 161, p. 455; mixed declension (εἷς, δύο, τρεῖς, τέτταρες), 186, 210, p. 458; correlative demonstrative, 193, p. 453; regular comparative and superlative, 197, p. 456; irregular comparative and superlative, 203-204, pp. 456-457; mixed declension (ἡδύς), 205, p. 455; correlative direct and indirect interrogative, correlative indefinite, correlative definite and indefinite relative, 270, p. 453; defined, 52; agreement with nouns, 53; position of, predicate and attributive, 54; used as substantives, 60; positive, comparative, superlative degrees, defined, 195; comparison using μᾶλλον/μάλιστα, 196; regular comparison of, 196; comparative/superlative with ἤ or genitive of comparison, 198; comparative/superlative with partitive genitive, 199; superlative with ὡς/ὅτι, 200; irregular comparison of, 203-204; comparative with adverb or dative of degree of difference, 206; comparison of verbal adjectives in -τός, 258

Adscript, *see* Iota

Adverbs, paradigms: positive degree, 190, p. 460; comparative and superlative degrees, 196, p. 460; correlative direct and indirect interrogative, 163, 165.5, p. 460; correlative indefinite, 163, p. 460; correlative relative and